Ḥakirah

The Flatbush Journal of Jewish Law and Thought

Volume 31 / Winter 2022

A publication of
Hakirah, Inc.
www.Hakirah.org

Ḥakirah
The Flatbush Journal of Jewish Law and Thought

Volume 31 / Winter 2022

HISTORY OF HALAKHAH

TORAH AND MEDICINE

MINHAG

Introduction

This volume of *Ḥakirah* begins with the final installment of Rav Yosef Dov Soloveitchik, *zz"l*'s, "Lectures on Genesis." Here, the Rav explains that the concept of *yemot ha-Mashiaḥ* consists of the merger of the natural scientific order with the moral order. In delving into the connection between *aggadah* and *halakhah* he clarifies the Kabbalistic concept of the three Sabbath meals. The second essay in the *Jewish Thought* section, titled "A Light unto the Nation: R. Meir Simḥah of Dvinsk's Approach to Nationhood and Zionism in *Meshekh Ḥokhmah*," sheds light on the views of a *gadol* from the previous generation who had much in common with the Rav in the depth and breadth of his religious thought and in some of the positions he took with regard to confronting the modern world. The third essay in the section, "Ignoring the Writing on the Wall: Semiology vs. Metaphysics," discusses the issue of creation and science from a unique perspective, incorporating the thought of a scholar who lived both in the world of the *beit midrash* and the university.

Our *Talmud Torah* section features two articles disputing claims made by Orthodox academic scholars that challenge fundamentals of our faith. In "Of Dogma & Dissimulation: Marc Shapiro's Analysis of Maimonides' Thirteen Principles Reappraised," the author refutes the suggestion that Rambam was insincere in stating three of the *ikkarei emunah*. In "The Exodus and Historical Truth: A Critique of *Ani Maamin* by Joshua Berman and the Late Date Exodus Theory," the author rejects the claim that the traditional dating of Israel's Exodus cannot be reconciled with historic data. Other articles in this section feature acute textual analyses of traditional sources. "Emotion and Intent in Prayer" studies Rambam's exact choice of words in *Mishneh Torah* when defining the religious experience of prayer as well as other *mitzvot*. "Untangling the Mystery of Women's Hair Covering in Talmudic Passages" analyzes the individual Talmudic passages in Bavli and Yerushalmi to detect differing views regarding women covering their hair.

In the *History of Halakhah* section, the authors reveal facts known by few Talmudic scholars. "Yom Tov Sheini: Reasons and Relevance" shows that the *geonim* felt that *Yom Tov Sheini* was not an accommodation to those who did not know when *Rosh Ḥodesh* was, but rather an early—or perhaps even Torah—law, to strengthen Judaism in the *galut*. The essay "The Origin and Evolution of '*Masorat ha-Shas*'" reveals the real originator of an important tool in Talmud study and traces the story of its misattribution. Another article in this section, "Let Him Bray: The Stormy Correspondence Between Samuel David Luzzatto and Elia Benamozegh," tells the little-known story of two outstanding nineteenth-century Jewish religious figures who took "polar opposite positions with regard to the value of the mystical teachings of the *Kabbalah*."

In our *Torah and Medicine* section, two essays deal with the history of Jews in the modern western medical world. In "The Mystery of the Medical Training of the Many Isaac Wallichs: Amsterdam (1675), Leiden (1675), Padua (1683), Halle (1703)," the author solves a riddle with regard to the identity of an early Jewish university-trained medical student, and in so doing gives us a glimpse into the beginning of Jews entering the medical profession in Western Europe. And in "What Does It Mean to Be a Jewish Hospital in America Today?" the author gives us the history of Jewish hospitals in North America, beginning with a wave of them c. 1850.

The two Hebrew articles deal with issues related to death. One essay disputes a claim made in an earlier *Ḥakirah* article that halakhah allows a parent to excuse a child from *avelut.* The other article deals with the issue of whether communities should make up for the lost reading of the weekly *parashah* when communal services were disrupted by causes such as the Covid pandemic. In contrast, in our *Minhag* section the origin and meaning of the Jewish toast/blessing of *L-Ḥayyim* are traced.

With sadness, we note the recent passing of two exceptional people whose articles appeared in the previous volume of *Ḥakirah.*

Rabbi Dr. Moshe Dovid Tendler *ztz"l* was an icon of Torah *u-madda* who had a long and distinguished career in the field of both Torah and biology and who worked on the synthesis of the two. We are honored that the last of the many articles he co-authored during his lifetime, "Halakhic Issues Related to Synthetic Biology" appeared in *Ḥakirah* volume 30.

Marshall M Joffe, MD, PhD was a leading light in the field of Biostatistics and Epidemiology, who in his last work "Danger in Sabbath Law: A Novel Perspective Using Causality and Statistics," applied his mathematical and medical knowledge to the field of Torah for the first time. His premature death at the age of 59 deprives the Torah world of a voice that would have given added insight into the intersection of science and Torah.

Along with their families, we take some comfort in knowing that the work and the words of these special men will continue to live on.

Special thanks to all those who worked hard to make this volume of *Ḥakirah* a reality, including Nina Ackerman Indig, copy-editing; Tuvia Ganz, cover design and production; and Chaim Lam, design and maintenance of our Web page, www.Hakirah.org.

It is our continuing hope that the articles in this journal will stimulate thought, study, and discussion, and inspire other members of the public to contribute their own insights. The articles we print thus reflect a wide range of opinion and do not necessarily represent the views of our editorial board. ꟹ

Instructions for Contributors

Ḥakirah, The Flatbush Journal of Jewish Law and Thought, publishes original, interesting, well-researched and well-organized manuscripts that provide new or profound insights into areas of Jewish *halakhah* and *hashkafah.*

Manuscripts should be in Microsoft Word format and sent as an email attachment to HakirahFlatbush@msn.com. Short references—for example, to a Biblical verse or to a page within the Talmud—should be embedded directly into the text of the manuscript. Insert longer references as footnotes, rather than endnotes.

The author's name should not appear on the manuscript, as it is the Journal's policy to forward the articles for evaluation without disclosing the author's identity. On a separate cover sheet, include your name, a short bio, an abstract of your article, your telephone number, fax number, and e-mail address.

After reviewing and accepting your manuscript, we are likely to request clarification of certain points. A revised electronic copy of your manuscript will then be required.

To encourage a wide variety of contributors, the Journal accepts articles employing the Hebrew transliteration style of either *Encyclopedia Judaica* or *ArtScroll.* If you have no preference, we suggest you follow the pronunciation rules used by the *Encyclopedia Judaica.* Words in languages other than English should always be italicized, unless the foreign words have become part of the English language.

For more information about writing an article for *Ḥakirah* see <www.Hakirah.org\HakirahGuideToWriting.pdf>.

Letters to the Editor

The Code of Esther

A CLOSE LOOK AT "The Code of Esther: A Counter-Investigation," by Dr. Emmanuel Bloch (*Ḥakirah,* vol. 28, 2020) shows that his investigation contains gaps, contradictions and inaccuracies and in fact does not address the evidence. [1] Here are just a few:

1. The article fails to mention the first and most significant detail: that unlike the rest of the *Megillah*, which is written in regular format, the names of Haman's sons are written in two columns—one for the names, and the other for the word *v-et.*
   This raises three questions:
   - Why would such an insignificant detail of the story have such a significant formatting change?
   - Why, in the list of names, are they connected with *v-et*? That is not the usual way names are written (cf. *Megillah* 1:10, 1:14).
   - Why are the names not simply connected with *v'*? Why the extra *et*?

One answer is that we come across a similar format when songs appear in the Torah: *Ha'azinu*; *Shirat Ha-Yam*. In fact, the Talmud calls the list of names a song. Many commentaries on these songs show how they are prophecies of future events.

2. Next, Bloch tells us that the Talmud speaks about the large *vav* but not about the small letters. He then shows an image of the *Leningrad Codex* to demonstrate that there are no small letters. However:
   a) The *Codex* itself does not show the large *vav* from the Talmud either!
   b) The *Codex* has vowels. This shows that it is not meant to be an accurate text of the *Megillah.*
   c) The *Codex*, as Bloch tells us, does have a masoretic note about the small letters.

Later, Bloch says that the *Leningrad Codex* and others like it do not follow tradition so it is not a valid source for defining our tradition. Why bring a source that he himself renders invalid?

3. He says that there are no ancient texts which speak of small letters. He then goes on to say that:
   - *Midrash D-Rabbi Akiva*, "an ancient text," contains the first mention of small letters.
   - The *Leningrad Codex*, an ancient text from 1008

- C.E., has a masoretic note of the small letters.
- The Northern Europeans received their customs of small letters from "ancient Babylonian traditions."

Having said there are no ancient texts with small letters, he then shows two examples of ancient texts with small letters and one ancient tradition of small letters.

4. He does not address why there are small letters if they are not mentioned in the Talmud.

5. He mentions that there are at least seven different traditions of small letters which appear in the names of Haman's sons. He says "for whatever reason" the correct one was standardized out of the seven possibilities. What is that reason? In fact, it is the least likely one to be chosen seeing as it was the most recent, and therefore the least likely to be accurate.

6. The statistical probability of the three small letters, out of all the possible combinations of the 22 letters of the Hebrew alphabet, matching the year of the hanging of the Nazis, is 1 in 10,648. That is not even taking into account that there could have been more or fewer small letters—vastly increasing the statistical improbability.

7. He completely fails to address why the letters appear specifically in this, the relevant part of the text. They could have appeared anywhere. They could have been spread out: one at the beginning, one in the middle, one at the end; but no, they all appear in the names of Haman's sons "for whatever reason" …

8. Dating systems are mentioned, saying a millennia designation was seldom used. That means it was used, albeit seldom, and is a valid way of counting. By the 10th century, it was widely used, 1000 years before Nuremberg. It is very simple. There are 6 millennia, the *vav* is 6, the Nuremberg trials happened in that millennium.

9. There were only two letters out of the 22 letters of the Hebrew alphabet that would have worked—the *vav*—6th millennium, or the *hay,* 5, for the year 5707. That makes a 1 in 11 chance that the big letter would fit the picture.

10. He says it is not strange that she asked that they be hanged once they were dead as there are precedents to that in Tanakh. Notwithstanding this, it is still a strange request, as she could have asked for anything: to return to Israel, that Jews never be taxed …
    More importantly, he does not even mention that she used the word *maḥar,* tomorrow. Why specify? Our Sages teach us that

maḥar can mean "in the future."

11. He says that the parallel is not amazing as 24 Nazis were on trial, not 10. That makes it EVEN MORE amazing: that even though 24 were on trial, and 12 were sentenced, only 10 were actually hanged. That makes it a 1 in 24 chance of getting the right number.

12. He is confused about Hoshana Rabbah. Rosh Hashanah is when the sentences are passed for wicked nations, but the carrying out of the sentences is not until Hoshana Rabbah. [2]

13. He says Hitler committed suicide a year earlier whereas Haman was hanged just before his sons. That is just not true. Haman was hanged almost a year before his sons.

14. He says that it is not surprising Streicher shouted "Purim Fest"—he knew about Purim and the revenge of the Jews. Nonetheless, it is still remarkable that a Nazi shouted those words while being led to his death, as if admitting defeat.

Overall, apart from the inconsistencies, errors and omissions, Bloch has missed the whole point of the argument. Even if each individual fact has an explanation (which it does not), the statistical probability of all those facts coming together and working as they do is zero.

He has failed to explain:

- Why the formatting change for the names, which are insignificant?
- Why *v-et* between the names?
- Why she asked that they be hanged instead of something more meaningful?
- Why she said *maḥar*?
- Why only 10 out of 24 Nazis were hanged?
- Why there are small letters at all in the *Megillah?*
- How they all appear in the relevant place?
- How and why out of at least 10,648 possibilities of three small letters combinations and out of the seven traditions passed down, the one that was eventually standardized over 600 years ago was the one with the exact right letters in the exact right order. The statistical probability of such a thing is staggeringly, astronomically tiny—basically 0.
- How this whole story took place in the 6th millennium and the names have a big *vav.*

Bloch's proposition is that "for some reason" small letters have appeared in the *Megillah* since at least the 11th century. That those small letters "for some reason/by chance" appear all together, for some reason/by chance in exactly the relevant part of the text. For "whatever reason" the accepted version just happened to include only three small letters, out of the tens of thousands of possible letter combinations of the 22 letters of the Hebrew alphabet, which got there "by error" and "by chance" in the right order that, coincidentally, happens to be the exact year. That exactly the same number of people (only 10 out of the 24 on trial were actually hanged) were punished in exactly the same way for exactly the same reason.

That is like saying that someone by chance rolled more than seven double sixes in a row.

One can look at events and try to say it is all just a coincidence (against the facts and statistics) or one can see the guiding hand of G-d making everything "for some reason" work out exactly to plan.

Dov Ber Cohen
Jerusalem, Israel

I WANT TO POINT OUT an error in "The Code of Esther: A Counter-Investigation" by Dr. Emmanuel Bloch (*Ḥakirah,* vol. 28, 2020). He claims that 10 sons of Haman were killed soon after their father. That is not accurate. Haman was killed in Nissan and his children almost a year later.

Michael Rosen

Emmanuel Bloch responds:

I would like to thank both Rabbi Dov Ber Cohen and Michael Rosen for reading my 2020 *Ḥakirah* article.

While I cannot agree with any of Rabbi Cohen's criticisms, as will become apparent in the following paragraphs, I am sincerely grateful for his interest, as well as for the opportunity to re-open the fascinating discussion on the small letters ("Code of Esther") in *Megillat Esther.*[3]

Ḥazal famously remarked that Torah scholars, just like iron, sharpen one another.[4] While I cannot claim to be a *talmid ḥakham*, I believe that such correspondence in the open-ended pursuit of truth leaves us enriched with a deeper appreciation of the vastness of Torah.

I answer Rabbi Cohen's points in the same order he raised them, with the exception of the statistical arguments which are tackled as a group at the end of this response.

1. Rabbi Cohen argues that I should have discussed the unusual format (in two columns) of the names of Haman's sons (point 1).

I find this point rather puzzling, as this textual oddity is already abundantly discussed in Bavli,[5] in Yerushalmi[6] and in tractate *Soferim.*[7] All these sources answer the first question raised by Rabbi Cohen ("*Why the formatting change?*"): The names of the *b'nei* Haman are written in the form of "*a half-brick over a half-brick and a brick over a brick*" (אריח ע"ג אריח ולבינה ע"ג לבינה) to signal that these individuals will never rise from their downfall.

Rabbi Cohen's other questions are equally perplexing. It is in fact quite usual, and entirely grammatically correct, for the Torah to list different names by repeating the word "וְאֶת". For illustrations, see the groups of names in *Bereishit* 10:13–14; 22:20–24, and 25:1–3. This list is clearly not exhaustive.

Finally, I fail to see any connection to the topic at hand, viz. the "Code of Esther."

2. Rabbi Cohen argues that the *Leningrad Codex* cannot be a valid *Megillah* because it has vowels (point 2).

This argument misunderstands the nature and functions of a codex. Very succinctly, the codex is the historical ancestor of the modern book (the main difference being that codices were made with sheets of vellum or papyrus, whereas modern books are made with sheets of paper). Because of its many advantages, the codex quickly replaced the scroll, in both non-Jewish and Jewish societies, as a medium for literature.[8]

No Jewish codex was *ever* meant to be used in the synagogue as a *Megillah* or *Sefer Torah;* a codex was a repository of knowledge, not a ritual object. To put this idea in somewhat simplistic terms, the *Leningrad Codex* was the medieval equivalent of the computer software used to check the accuracy of our modern Torah scrolls.

In this role, there is little doubt that the *Leningrad Codex* was "valid." In fact, its remarkable accurateness was stressed by all the specialists in the field (Mordekhai Breuer, Menaḥem Cohen...). I am unaware of any scholar who disagrees with this conclusion.

Interested readers can also consult the *Aleppo Codex*, which similarly has the vowels and masoretic notes in the margins.[9] No one ever claimed that this codex was therefore somehow worthless. On the contrary, according to almost all scholars, this was the codex consulted by Rambam to codify the *Hilkhot Sefer Torah* in the *Yad ha-Ḥazakah.*

(Rabbi Cohen's remark on the absence of a long *vav* in the *Leningrad Codex* is answered in the original article, p. 139, note 37.)

3. Rabbi Cohen believes that the *Midrash of Rabbi Akiva on small and large letters*, which I discuss in the original article (pp. 133–134), contradicts my claim that no "ancient" text speaks of small letters (point 3).

I certainly could have been more precise when using the word "ancient" in the original article. But the argument is still straightforward: in the entire ספרות חז"ל, there is not one single source that discusses the small letters in the names of *b'nei* Haman. This includes Bavli, Yerushalmi, Tractate *Soferim*, the midrashic literature, and so forth.

The *Midrash of Rabbi Akiva* is a pseudonymous medieval text; it was not written by the famous Tanna Rabbi Akiva, but several centuries later by an unknown author. It belongs to a body of semi-obscure writings that left almost no traces in the classical corpuses, only to be rediscovered several centuries later in the Cairo Genizah and eventually published.

Scholars have variously estimated the date of composition of this late midrash. Yet they agree, at any rate, that it was written several centuries after the closing of the Talmud. That is still "ancient," but in no way refutes my claim that the small letters represent a later addition in the *Megillah*.

The other sources, viz. the masoretic notes and the texts from Northern European communities, similarly support my previous conclusions, as they all date from the 11th to the 14th centuries.

4. Rabbi Cohen claims that I fail to discuss why there are small letters in our current *Megillah* when the Talmud ignored their existence (point 4).

I must respectfully disagree: this point is addressed—as much as possible, at least—in the original article (pp. 134–135). Professor Menaḥem Cohen, arguably the greatest scholar alive on all questions pertaining to the accuracy of the Biblical text, has noted that the phenomenon is much wider than the three letters of the "Code of Esther": the small and large letters noted by the Masorah are never reflected in the texts of the oldest manuscripts in our possession.[10]

Global challenges require global solutions: according to Cohen, the first lists of small and big letters appeared toward the very end of the masoretes' period of activity. Yet, in the eyes of the medieval scribes, these lists remained unauthoritative, and it took several additional centuries for the unusually sized letters to worm their way into the Biblical text.

This insight dovetails quite precisely with our textual observations regarding *Esther*, chapter 9: It took approximately three centuries for the small letters reflected in the masoretic notes to be reflected in the medieval manuscripts of the *Megillah*.[11]

5. Rabbi Cohen then suggests that I failed to explain the standardization of the "Code of Esther" (point 5).

Here I would like to respectfully suggest that my contradictor read again pp. 137–138 in the original article. In my efforts to understand how the early fourteenth-century version of the *Orḥot Ḥayyim* became predominant, I have distinguished between two stages.

First stage: the publication of the second edition of the *Mikraot Gedolot* in 1524–1526. In this context, I used the words "*for whatever reason*" to imply two points: 1) we do not know why Jacob ben Ḥayyim chose the version of the *Orḥot Ḥayyim* as the basis for the Biblical text. It would be a fascinating topic for further research: when encountering disagreements between older authorities, did he always prioritize the same source(s)? I am unaware of any published scholarship on this question. But this is hardly significant for our purposes, because 2) Jacob ben Ḥayyim made sure to carefully note the existence of other versions in the critical apparatus printed in the margins. In other words, it is quite possible that all versions were equally valid in his eyes, yet practical necessities dictated that one version be printed at the center—for whatever reason, indeed.

Second stage: later printed editions of the Tanakh simply omitted the critical apparatus printed in the margins of Jacob ben Ḥayyim's original edition, thus sanctifying the *Orḥot Ḥayyim*'s version over its competitors.

This represents the best way to account for our textual findings; in the final analysis, the remaining area of uncertainty is rather modest.

6. Rabbi Cohen asserts that it is "very simple" that the *vav* refers to the sixth millennium (point 8).

This is simply erroneous. As noted on p. 140 of the original article, whenever a reference to the current millennium is needed, it is *always* the *heh* that is used, and never the *vav*. I have provided several examples from various sources, and additional illustrations are relatively easy to find.[12] On the flipside, I do not know of a single case where the *vav* represents the sixth millennium.

Is it possible to find explanations *ex post facto*? Certainly, but these explanations are not worth much. Think about it. If we had a long *tsady* (צ) in *Megillat Esther*, the defenders of the Code could claim that its numerical value in the Atbash system is worth 5, which is arguably a reference to the years 5,001–6,000. If we had a long *peh* (פ), they could claim that its numerical value in the Atbash system is worth 6, which is (again) a reference to the sixth millennium. And so forth. Such explanations לאחר המעשה are easy enough. Given sufficient time and ingenuity, one can always come up with something.

The only criterion that makes sense consists in the hallowed practice of rabbinic authorities and laypeople across the ages; and, as far as I know, there is no Jewish way to measure the time that ever used the *vav* in the fashion suggested by Rabbi Cohen.

7. Rabbi Cohen believes that the request to hang the sons of Haman "tomorrow" is strange (point 10).

I sincerely apologize but do not understand this point. As I have demonstrated at length (pp. 140–142), the public display of corpses made perfect sense in the sociocultural context of the time. Esther's request is therefore easily understandable: she was asking the king to perform an act of deterrence that would act as a signal to the enemies of the Jews.

Yes, *Ḥazal* teach us that the word מחר can mean "in the future." But they also teach us that the plain meaning of a verse can never be nullified (אין מקרא יוצא מידי פשוטו).[13] In this instance, I do believe that we must interpret Esther's request according to the *pshat* and simply forgo the more convoluted and less convincing explanations.

8. Rabbi Cohen thinks that the parallelism between the ten Nazi dignitaries and the ten sons of Haman is still remarkable—perhaps even more so (points 11 and 13).

However, to reach this conclusion, Rabbi Cohen was forced to adopt a double standard: he focused heavily on the similarities between the Nuremberg trials and the story of Purim while completely ignoring their dissimilarities.[14]

Let me present the full information in a synoptic table and perhaps my esteemed contradictor will come to share my perspective.

Names of the Nazi leaders	**Sentence and Fate**	**Parallels in the Story of Purim?**
Hans Fritzsche, Franz von Papen, Hjalmar Schacht	Acquitted	No parallel
Gustav Krupp, Robert Ley	No decision	No parallel
Karl Dönitz, Walther Funk, Rudolf Hess, Konstantin von Neurath, Erich Raeder, Baldur von Schirach, Albert Speer	Prison	No parallel
Martin Bormann	Death (*in absentia*) Unclear if he committed suicide or was killed while trying to flee Berlin	No parallel
Hermann Göring	Sentenced to death by hanging but committed suicide	No parallel in the verses of the *Megillah*. Somewhat reminiscent of the aggadic story of Haman's daughter (Bavli *Megillah* 16a). But important differences exist in terms of gender (male/female); scenario (Göring never disparaged Hitler, Haman's daughter was never sentenced); timing (Göring died after Hitler, the daughter before Haman); and, generally speaking, the wording of the Gemara seems to indicate that Haman's daughter died by accident and not by suicide.
Hans Frank, Wilhelm Frick, Alfred Jodl, Ernst Kaltenbrunner, Wilhelm Keitel, Joachim von Ribentropp,	Death by hanging	Reminiscent of the hanging of the ten sons of Haman. But the sons of Haman died by the sword (*Esther* 9:5) and were

Names of the Nazi leaders	Sentence and Fate	Parallels in the Story of Purim?
Alfred Rosenberg, Fritz Sauckel, Arthur Seyss-Inquart, Julius Streicher		exposed publicly one day later; the Nazis, on the other hand were killed by hanging, then incinerated on the same day.
Adolf Hitler	Committed suicide / shot himself	No parallel. (Haman did not commit suicide but was hanged.)

Moreover, according to the Talmud,[15] Haman had a much larger progeniture: 30 sons according to Rav (10 who died in childhood, 10 who were hanged and 10 who became beggars); 90 sons according to Rabanan; and 208 sons according to Rami bar Abba. Clearly, reconciling these large numbers of children with the historical account of the Nuremberg trials is an impossible task.

Now, I do not insist that such aggadic statements be taken as historical truths; but intellectual honesty certainly requires our approach toward Aggadah to be consistent. Either it "counts" or it does not. If aggadic concepts are not considered, then Haman had no daughter, the word מחר means "tomorrow," etc. If they are, then Haman had significantly more than 10 sons. Either way, in my humble opinion, the dissimilarities largely outweigh the similarities.

As can be seen, the parallelism between the story of Purim and the Nuremberg trials is only an illusory artifact that does not withstand critical scrutiny.

9. Rabbi Cohen claims that I am confused about Hoshana Rabbah (point 12).

For once, I must agree: Hoshana Rabbah is a mysterious day. In fact, there is so much material that a separate essay would be needed to do justice to the complexities raised by Hoshana Rabbah as a day of judgment.

Given the space limitations, I will keep the argumentation relatively simple. There exists a basic distinction between *nigleh* and *nistar*. In non-Kabbalistic sources, I was not able to find anywhere the concept that the divine sentences are not carried out until the last day of Sukkot. As noted by the Gemara, the *ẓadikim gemurim* as well as the *resha'im gemurim* are judged and sealed immediately (לאלתר) on Rosh Hashanah.[16] That is all. There is no indication that Hoshana Rabbah plays a role in these yearly dynamics of judgment and retribution.[17]

The situation is much more complex in Kabbalistic sources. Already in the *Zohar*, one finds that Hoshana Rabbah is considered a day of judgment[18]: on the seventh day of Sukkot (viz. Hoshanah Rabbah), the verdict is sealed with an additional seal, and the paper (*pitka*) containing the verdict is given over to the messengers who will carry it out. However, in all the later mystical sources I have consulted, the divine messengers cannot execute the judgment on Hoshana Rabbah. On the contrary, they must wait until Shemini Atzeret to carry it out.[19]

This execution on Shemini Atzeret does not help Rabbi Cohen, since the Nazi leaders were killed on Hoshana Rabbah itself. I am unaware of any text that supports R. Cohen's thesis.

10. Rabbi Cohen continues to believe Streicher's last words are surprising (point 14).

Another scholar, Rabbi Dr. Zvi Ron, has recently critically examined this claim and confirmed that references to Purim were a common trope in Nazi propaganda.[20] Furthermore, according to this author, Streicher's last words can be understood as a reference to the famous 1944 radio broadcast speech in which Hitler identified himself with the villains of *Megillat Esther* and stated that, if the Nazis were defeated, the Jews "*could celebrate the destruction of Europe in a second triumphant Purim festival.*"

Again, fantastic claims apart, it seems a relatively easy task to understand Streicher's last words in their sociocultural context.

11. I have kept the discussion on R. Cohen's statistical arguments (points 6, 9, 11 and concluding paragraphs) for the end of this rejoinder.

The only honest answer is that neither R. Cohen nor myself are qualified to discuss the calculations of probabilities. Probability Theory is a complex field that requires years of dedicated study before it can be mastered. In an ideal world, such questions would be presented to an expert in the field, like CalTech Professor of Mathematics Barry Simon (who also happens to be an observant Jew).[21]

Nevertheless, as our Sages teach: פטור בלא כלום אי אפשר. But I will limit myself to note some obvious mistakes made by R. Cohen.

First, it is incorrect to note that "*two letters out of the 22 letters of the Hebrew alphabet … would have worked*" (point 9). As explained above, Jews (rabbis and laymen alike) have always used the *heh* to refer to the years 5,001–6,000. The (supposed) relevance of the *vav* is merely a *post facto* rationalization.

Second, it makes no sense to focus exclusively on the number of hangings (point 11) when the dissimilarities between the story of Purim and the Nuremberg trials are so overwhelming.

Third, it is not exact that the statistical probability of three small letters matching the year of the hanging of the Nazis is 1 in 10,648 (point 6). There exist six different combinations of three letters that add up to the value of 707 (תשז, תזש, שזת, שתז, זשת, זתש), which brings us to 6/10,648 or roughly 1 in 1,775. However, the same number could be obtained with many combinations of 4 or more letters (ששקדג, תרקז), which singularly complicates the calculation of a probability. And a real calculation should also take into account the basic reality that certain letters are more frequent than others in Hebrew (or in the *Megillah*), which signifies that the probability of each individual letter cannot simply be understood to be 1/22. Etc.

Fourth, and from a wider perspective, there is simply no agreement between my contradictor and myself on the phenomenon to be measured. Most of the observations that R. Cohen considers to be significant, I strongly believe, are entirely trivial or easily explained (the formatting change for the names, the word "וְאֵת" between the names, the word *maḥar*, and much more). Do we really need to calculate the probability that the sun shines in the middle of the day?

Fifth, probabilities are not supposed to be calculated *a posteriori*, but rather *a priori*. An anecdote will best illustrate this point. It is reported that Einstein would teach his students: "*Life is finite. Time is infinite. The probability that I am alive today is zero. In spite of this, I am now alive. Now how is that?*" Typically, none of the students would have an answer. After a pause, Einstein would say, "*Well, after the fact, one should not ask for probabilities.*"[22]

In conclusion of this point, I believe Rabbi Cohen's probabilities are computed by methods contrary to the accepted laws of probability and used in situations where it is essentially impossible to assign meaningful probabilities. Moreover, I strongly believe that this argument should be submitted to the judgment of those professionals whose job it is to evaluate mathematical arguments.

At the conclusion of this response, let us recapitulate. How many of the claims advanced in our original article has Rabbi Cohen successfully refuted?

1. The original *Ḥakirah* article has noted that the first sources that *discuss* small letters date from the 10th–11th centuries, even though we find systematic discussions of Biblical textual oddities in much older sources (Talmud). Rabbi Cohen has not found one single text challenging this point.
2. The original *Ḥakirah* article has advanced that the first *Megillah* manuscript that *evidences* small letters dates from year 1312 (even though we have much older manuscripts of the *Megillah*). Rabbi Cohen has not indicated a single older manuscript challenging this point.
3. As a result, the conclusion that "*the Megillat Esther was written for many centuries with no difference between the size of the letters in the names of B'nei Haman and the rest of the text*" remains entirely valid.
4. The original *Ḥakirah* article has observed that no Jew has ever measured the passage of time by referring to the sixth millennium with the letter *vav*. Rabbi Cohen has not produced a single source disputing this claim.
5. The original *Ḥakirah* article has demonstrated that the public

display of dead enemies was entirely understandable in the context of the times. Rabbi Cohen has indicated that this is "*still a strange request*" but has failed to demonstrate why.

6. The original *Ḥakirah* article has shown that Purim was regularly quoted in Nazi propaganda as an example of the violence exerted by the Jews against the nations who welcome them. Here too this point remains entirely unchallenged.

Not only did Rabbi Cohen fail, contrary to his claim, to evidence any "inconsistency, error or omission," but many of the points he views as significant are in fact entirely trivial. What is so surprising in finding the word "וְאֵת" in between names? Why is *Ḥazal*'s explanation of the formatting change insufficient? Why do we need to interpret the word מחר independently of its literal meaning? These, and many other questions, remain without satisfying demonstration in Rabbi Cohen's letter.

Mark Twain once said: "*The glory which is built upon a lie soon becomes a most unpleasant incumbrance … How easy it is to make people believe a lie, and how hard it is to undo that work again!*"[23] As people say, the amount of energy needed to refute falsehoods is at least an order of magnitude larger than is needed to produce them. And yet, it is my sincerest hope that my esteemed contradictor will use the opportunity of this exchange to give a new, fresh look at the *Code of Esther* and notice the innumerable difficulties that beset it.

And if, as I truly hope, this correspondence leaves us with a keener appreciation of the complexities of Jewish tradition as it unfolded over time, then perhaps this may also be considered as a form of השגחה פרטית, G-d's guiding hand as it manifested itself in the vicissitudes of history.

Thank you, Michael Rosen, for your remark. If one follows the chronology presented in the midrash[24] then Mr. Rosen's point is absolutely well-founded. I am very grateful for this clarification. I should have specified, on p. 144 in the original *Ḥakirah* article, that my approach follows the *pshat* of the verses.

However, this is a minor point that does not affect the conclusions of our inquiry in any way. This aggadic source brings the story of Purim slightly closer to the Nuremberg trial,[25] but the dissimilarities between the two events, as noted in the original article and in my response to Rabbi Cohen, remain overwhelming.

Again, I would like to caution against the selective use of aggadic texts. In the midrash, one also finds that Haman had many more than 10 sons, that the corpses remained hanged on the tree for several months, and many other details that have no counterpart whatsoever in the historical account of the Nuremberg trials.

The Origin of the Molad

I WAS UNABLE TO REPRODUCE Eng. J. Jean Ajdler's *molad* calculations in his "A Short History of the Jewish Fixed Calendar: The Origin of the *Molad*" (*Ḥakirah,* vol. 20, 2015).

On investigation, I discovered that in his *Appendix A* at the top of p. 177 in the above-mentioned article he gives a formula for calculation of the *molad* moment. As written, it would be subject to rounding errors using ordinary floating point arithmetic, albeit not too badly for the ancient and historical *moladot* that he focused on, but aside from that, he gave the number of *ḥalakim* in the *molad* interval as 765443, **which is 10 *ḥalakim* in excess of the correct value**. If he did employ this incorrect value in his *molad* calculations that could explain many of the strange results that he obtained.

The correct total number of parts per *molad* interval = 1080 parts per hour × (29 days × 24 hours per day + 12 hours) + 793 parts = 765433 parts, which is easy to remember because it can be written as the descending sequence 765432+1.

The incorrect coefficient appears 5 times in the article's appendix and 5 times in the supplementary appendix, suggesting that it is not a typing error, whereas the correct coefficient never appears.

Dr. Irv Bromberg
University of Toronto, Canada

Eng. J. Jean Ajdler responds:

Professor Bromberg notes a misprint which occurs 5 times in my paper "A Short History of the Fixed Jewish Calendar" (*Ḥakirah,* Vol. 20, 2015).

The length of the Jewish lunation is 29 days, 12 hours and 793 *ḥalakim* (1 hour is 1080 *ḥalakim*). When we convert this span of time into *ḥalakim* we have: 29 * 24 * 1080 + 12 * 1080 + 793 = 765,433 *ḥalakim.*

On p. 177, lines 1, 4 and 5, and on p. 178, lines 11 and 22, this number was misprinted as 765443 instead of 765433.

This misprint had no consequence on the various calculations.

I thank Professor Bromberg for his remarks and take responsibility for this misprint.

May Parents Waive the Requirements of Avelut?

I RECENTLY HAD THE GREAT pleasure and privilege to read Rabbi Shlomo Brody's "May Parents Waive the Requirements of Avelut?" (*Ḥakirah,* vol. 29, 2021). In it, Rabbi Brody writes, "within Talmudic and post-halakhic literature, there is a discussion about whether the deceased can exempt his relatives to mourn for him, and that furthermore these relatives may be obligated to fulfill this request. The discussion begins with questions of burial and eulogies but extends to *shiv'ah*, *shloshim*, and particularly the extended 12-month period ("*yud-bet ḥodesh*") observed while mourning for parents," and, "What about the extended 12-month period which exclusively marks the passing of one's mother or father? In this circumstance, Rabbi Weil, in the same passage noted above, asserts that parents may waive this requirement since the extended period of mourning is only done out of a sense of honor for them (*kibbud av va-em*). Accordingly, they may waive this honorary rite… This position is affirmed in *Shakh YD* 344:917 and from there by all subsequent *poskim*…"

I believe that the original responsa that introduced this sweeping leniency are still subject to dispute, and that at the very least Maimonides' understanding of the sources does not allow for such a dispensation. The entirety of my argument is presented in the Hebrew section of this volume.

Avi Grossman
Kokhav Ya'akov, Israel

Shlomo Brody responds:

I thank Rabbi Avi Grossman for taking the time to write his response.

Rabbi Grossman wants to argue, based on sources in Rambam, that mourning for 12 months is a bona fide decree. It is therefore not subject to question of whether this practice was instituted to honor the deceased. As such, it cannot be waived like other matters of *kibbud av va-em* or other burial rituals like eulogies.

Unfortunately, none of the citations from Rambam that he cites make this case. Rambam does not speak too much about *yud-bet ḥodesh* and so it is hard to know exactly how he understood this practice. But as Rabbi Grossman notes and I discuss in footnote 12 of my article, there are several *aḥronim* who think that Rambam believes that all *avelut* (including *shiv'ah* and *shloshim*) are for the honor of the deceased and therefore may be waived. As such, it is far from clear that Rambam thinks this is a bona fide law that cannot be waived.

In terms of the Rama: It is true that Rama does not explicitly state in the *Mapah* that a person may waive *yud-bet ḥodesh*, as does the Mahari Weil. Instead, he only mentions that one cannot waive *shiv'ah* or *shloshim*. However, Rama does cite the Mahari Weil in full in his *Darkei Moshe*, indicating that he agrees with his full position. This is certainly the conclusion of Shakh, who understands Rama to follow the Mahari Weil and himself rules accordingly.

(Occasionally, Rama will cite a position in *Darkei Moshe* but not in the *Mapah*, just as R. Yosef Karo will sometimes cite a position in the *Bet Yosef* but not record it in the *Shulḥan Arukh*. There are no set rules in such cases to determine whether R. Karo or R. Isserles changed their minds. For relevant sources, see R. Yitzḥak Yosef, *Ein Yitzḥak* Vol 3, p. 544–546 and p. 608.).

As I document in my article, the Mahari Weil and Shakh's opinion is universally affirmed by *poskim* throughout the subsequent generations, *halakhah le-ma'aseh*. In fact, it is so accepted that it has even been utilized by some prominent *gedolim* to allow *avelim* to participate in various *smachot* even when their parent did not explicitly waive *avelut*. As such, it is hard to argue that this is anything but a *halakhah pesukah*.

I do agree with Rabbi Grossman that it would have been helpful had other earlier *rishonim* clarified that *yud-bet ḥodesh* is a matter of *kibud av va-em* and that it may be waived. It is an interesting question why the issue was not raised earlier. But the Mahari Weil and Shakh filled in this lacuna and this is the established halakhah.

Again, thank you to Rabbi Grossman for his thoughtful letter.

NOTES

[1] This piece is to show the flaws in the "counter-investigation" and is by no means, G-d forbid, a personal attack on Emmanuel Bloch. I am sure he is a wonderful, kind, well-educated man and I wish him all the best.

[2] *Zohar* (*Vayikra* 31b), "On the 7th day of Sukkot the judgment of the nations of the world is finalized… Judgments are aroused and carried out that day."

[3] This correspondence also gives me the chance to repair a prior omission: I should have noted that my original French article has greatly benefited from the help of Dr. Gabriel Wasserman, who was most generous with his time and wide-ranging knowledge in all fields of Torah study. My thanks also go to Mr. Zvi Erenyi, librarian at the Gottesman Library of Yeshiva University, for scanning and sending me many sources which are inaccessible to me due to Covid restrictions.

[4] *Ta'anit* 7a.

[5] *Megillah* 16b.

[6] *Megillah* 3:7.

[7] Chapter 13:3–4.

[8] To my knowledge, the best book on the topic is still Colin H. Roberts and T. C. Skeat, *The Birth of the Codex*, Oxford University Press, 1987. A briefer (but still useful) introduction can be found in Michelle P. Brown, *Understanding Illuminated Manuscripts: A Guide to Technical Terms*, Getty Publications 2018, p. 30.

[9] Online copies can be accessed on several websites. For instance, see this link: https://people.brandeis.edu/~brettler/online-texts.html .

[10] See his introduction to the Keter edition of the *Mikraot Gedolot*, pp. *47–*49.

[11] See p. 135 footnote 18 in the original article: to the best of my knowledge, the first recorded instance dates from the year 1312.

[12] For instance, one can check the front pages of the *sefarim* published on HebrewBooks.

[13] See for instance Bavli *Shabbat* 63a, and many other places.

[14] As noted in the article, p. 144–145, this is a normal cognitive bias that evolution has bequeathed to all human beings.

[15] Bavli *Megillah* 15b, commenting on *Esther* 5:11.

[16] Bavli *Rosh Hashanah* 16b.

[17] This absence is so complete that it raises interesting questions. Thus, if Hoshana Rabbah is a *Yom ha-Din*, how can we explain that the *Hallel* is recited on this day? For a possible answer, see R. Yitzḥak Weiss, *Shu"t Siaḥ Yitzḥak*, *siman* 315 (reference found in an online article by R. Eliezer Brodt).

[18] *Zohar* 1:220a and other sources cited in original article footnote 56.

[19] See *Kaf ha-Ḥayyim* 664:18; Ben Ish Ḥay, Halakhot 1st year, *Ve-Zot ha-Berakhah*, chapter 2; *Shenei Luḥot ha-Brit*, *Aseret ha-Diberot*, *Sukkah*, *Torah Ohr*.

[20] Zvi Ron, "The Nuremberg Trial in *Megillat Esther*," *Modern Judaism*, volume 41, Issue 1 (February 2021), pp. 31–46, esp. pp. 34–35.

[21] http://www.math.caltech.edu/simon/simon.html

[22] Cf. Andrew Szanton, *The Recollections of Eugene P. Wigner*, Basic Books, 2003.

[23] Quote found on this webpage: https://www.snopes.com/fact-check/did-mark-

twain-say-its-easier-to-fool-people-than-to-convince-them-that-they-have-been-fooled/. Check also the rhetorical device known as "Gish Gallop."

24 *Esther Rabbah* 10:4.

25 11 months between Haman's death and the hanging of his sons vs. 18 months between Hitler's death and the hanging of the Nazi leaders.

Rabbi Joseph B. Soloveitchik's Lectures on Genesis, X through XIII

Based upon Rabbi Robert Blau's notes taken at Bernard Revel Graduate School in the late 1940s. This is the third of a three-part series covering thirteen lectures.

Edited and Annotated by: MEIR TRIEBITZ

Introduction to Lecture X

In this lecture, the Rav discusses the Jewish understanding of eschatology, the culmination of history. For the *Kabbalah*, this is described by the historical and metaphysical merger of the two concepts of God: *Deus Persona*, the personal God, and *Deus Mundus*, the God of creation. According to the Rav, this represents the merger of the natural scientific order with the moral order, thereby uniting ontology and ethics.

Lecture X

1) *Keter, Ḥokhmah, Binah*—intellectual
2) *Gevurah-Gedulah*—ethical
3) *Tiferet, Netzaḥ, Hod*—Esthetical Affective *Deus Persona*
4) *Yesod*—synthesis of 2–3
5) *Malkhut*—natural order of the cosmos or *Deus Mundus*[1]

---

1 In Lecture IX (*Ḥakirah* vol. 29, pp. 48–57), the Rav says that *Keter* is God's "will to reveal Himself"; *Ḥokhmah* is the "emergence of wisdom" which begins with "God's self-knowledge"; and *Binah* (p. 28) is "instinctive knowledge." There he says that "aesthetical affective persona" refers to "feeling, love, grace, etc." Here, he says that *Gevurah-Gedulah*, which are called *Gevurah* and *Ḥessed* in Lecture IX, refer to ethical relationship between God and man, whereas *Tiferet, Netzaḥ*, and *Hod* refer to the Aesthetical relationship between man and God which comprise feeling, love, and grace. The above nine *sefirot* are part of God's personal relationship with man which the Rav calls *Deus Persona*. The tenth *sefirah*, *Malkhut*,

---

Meir Triebitz studied at Yeshiva Beit Yosef in Borough Park where he received *semikhah* from Ha-Rav Yaakov Yaffen, *ztz"l*. He is currently a Rosh Kollel and lecturer at Mekhon Shlomo in Har Nof, and has published articles in various Torah journals. Audio recordings of his *shiurim* are available at HashkafaCircle.com.

Both Saadiah and Maimonides explained all anthropomorphic terms as being allegorical. To the *Zohar*, however, these anthropomorphic terms are revelations of God's personality.[2]

The synonym of *Malkhut* is *Shekhinah,* from the word *shekhen,* to dwell, because God's will is imprisoned in nature.[3] There are other synonyms, all being feminine because the concrete order is dependent on the transcendental order. Femininity in *Kabbalah* is always passive, being dependent on something.[4]

Revelation for the *Zohar* is what medieval philosophers called *"processio Dei ad extra,"* the procession of God toward externalization. For Maimonides there were two types of revelation[5]:

---

refers to God's relationship with man through the objective order of creation. The Rav refers to these relationships as *Deus Persona* and *Deus Mundus.*

2 This is based upon the distinction drawn by the Rav in Lecture VIII between medieval philosophy, which views God's creation as creation of the natural world, and *Kabbalah*, which views creation as revelation. As a result, anthropomorphism of God, for Saadiah and Rambam, is paganistic, for by viewing the world as possessed of spiritual content, it attributes physical dimensions to God. Therefore, to the rationalists, anthropomorphism must be understood allegorically. On the other hand, the Kabbalistic understanding of creation as revelation allows anthropomorphism to exist in "spiritual realms" alone, thereby avoiding paganism. The spiritual realm is referred to by the Arizal as אצילות. This realm eschews any concept of physicality. For a detailed discussion, see לשם שבו ואחלמה ספר הדעה דרוש עולם התוהו חלק א' דרוש ה' סימן ו' אות ד'.

3 It is not to be understood that God dwells in nature, but rather that His will, or ethic, is hidden within nature.

4 The basic idea expressed by the Rav here is that the physical world is viewed by *Kabbalah* as a type of receptacle which contains the spiritual. This idea, which is called *Malkhut* or *Shekhinah*, lends itself naturally to a male-female metaphor, in which the physical world is likened to a female who acts as a receptacle for the male who emerges from the transcendental. This relationship is characterized by the Rav as "dependent," for the entire *raison d'être* of the physical receptacle is to receive its transcendental content, which emerges from higher spiritual worlds in order to dwell within it.

5 According to the Rav, Maimonidean rationalism and *Kabbalah* share the concept of revelation in which God emerges through a process of externalization. The difference between Maimonides and Kabbalistic thought is that for Maimonides, physical creation and prophetic revelation are two separate processes of revelation, whereas, in Kabbalistic thought, the physical and prophetic are part of one continuum.

1) Through the cosmos, *Deus Mundus.*
2) The prophetic,[6] or *Deus Persona.*

The Jewish mystics and the medieval philosophical rationalists both reached the same conclusions in explaining Genesis. How two movements so diametrically opposed reached the same conclusions is a paradox of the history of culture.[7]

From this point of view of Jewish mysticism we may now come to the idea of a Jewish eschatology in regard to Shabbat.[8] It would appear that an eschatology is a purely human hope. For God has no need for the end of time, since He already abides in eternity. However [despite the fact that eschatology is a "purely human hope"], in Jewish philosophy, man has little to do with an eschatology and it is, rather, a Divine affair.

> ועלו מושיעים בהר ציון לשפוט את הר עשיו והיתה לה' המלוכה. והיה ה' למלך על כל הארץ. ביום ההוא יהיה ה' אחד ושמו אחד. (עובדיה א: כ"א)
> The saviors will ascend Mount Zion to judge Esau's mountain, and the kingdom will be God's. Then God will be King over all the world. On that day, God will be one and His name will be one. (Obadiah 1: 21)[9]

True, man is also concerned, but he is only secondary. It is a parenthetical motive, the prime motive being Divine. That man is secondary,

---

6 The use of the term "prophetic" in relation to *Deus Persona* indicates that God relates to man in a personal manner through the act of prophecy. In *Kabbalah* this is expressed by the concept of *Partzufim* (פרצופים) in *Atzilut* (אצילות).

7 That is to say, both systems come up with the idea of two aspects of God: *Deus Mundus* and *Deus Persona.* It seems that the Rav is drawing an important parallel between the Kabbalistic notion of revelation and Maimonidean revelation as expressed either through the physical world (the "cosmos") or "prophecy." The Rav is basing himself on a passage in Chapter 12 of Section II in the *Guide*, in which Rambam discusses the thoughts of God as a series of intellects emanating outward and culminating in the active intellect, which serves as the basis of the creation of the intellectual celestial sphere, and, afterwards, of the physical world. In that very same chapter, Rambam describes the prophetic process in much the same way: the prophet senses God's emanating intellects by means of his rational and imaginative faculty, and uses them to express his prophecy. These, however, are two distinct processes, as opposed to the Kabbalistic notion of one process of revelation, where the emergence of the Divine begins with the spiritual and proceeds to the physical in one continuum.

8 By eschatology, the Rav means the conclusion of history.

9 The Rav invokes the verse to show that the end of history is primarily for God, and not for man; namely, that God and His Name will be one.

however, is not important. The point is [that a question remains:] what can God expect to attain in eschatology, since He is already in eternity.

Some explain the passage of ביום ההוא וגו' as meaning when all idols will disappear.

והאלילים כרות יכרתון.

And false gods will be utterly cut off.[10]

However, this interpretation for us is insufficient, since *Avodah Zarah* today is only limited, most religions being monotheistic. Secondly, idolatry is not a cosmic evil, but a social evil. As the Midrash says, "If God didn't want man to worship the stars, why did He not destroy them? So they answered, for a few human fools, should God destroy the cosmos?" So we see that idolatry is a social affair.[11]

This the medieval philosophers did not answer.[12] But the period of classical mysticism answered it. They say that at the end of time, the twofold modus [of] revelation, the *Deus Persona* and *Deus Mundus*, will merge. The disjunction of subject-object will disappear. Personality and concreteness will merge into one great order. *Malka Kadisha* and *Shekhinah* will unite. The prime objective of the universal purpose is this merger. In short, the vision of *kol ha-yamim,* כל הימים (not *aḥarit hayamim,* אחרית הימים, which will take place in the historical time), anticipates the ascent of a mechanical, insensate, automatic, scientific cosmos imprisoned in natural laws to a free intelligible order of Being.[13]

In science, all that is done is [the forming of relationships between] natural phenomena: A in relation to B. A cannot be seen but only in relation to B. What A or B is, science does not know. Terms philosophers of science employ [such as] force, matter, substance, electricity, are metaphors. A exists not by the virtue of itself, but of B. B exists because of C,

---

10 From the liturgy of the Jewish prayer *Aleinu.*

11 The Rav is referring to a passage in עבודה זרה נ"ד ע"ב. What the Rav means by "social affair" is that idolatry is not a serious theology but the phenomenon of foolish human behavior.

12 That is, the medieval thinkers did not answer why the end of days is so important for God.

13 The Rav's point is that on the Sabbath, the metaphysical worlds undergo a process and transformation which is similar to that which the entire world will experience at the end of history. Although God in and of Himself "has no need for the end of time," God reveals to man a metaphysical process which culminates every Sabbath in the union of the Personal God with the God of nature. As such, the eschatology of world history plays itself out every week, thereby giving cosmic significance to man's observance of the Sabbath.

and so on. This all implies necessity. When the *Deus Mundus* emerges with the *Deus Persona*, this is what *Kabbalah* called a free intellectual order of Being—from necessity to freedom.[14]

Man has two types of experience. One, for example: I see the table as a separate faction, as dead matter, as a mathematical formula, as the physicist would see it, or as a bundle of sensations to me. I can see it, touch it, bang it, and produce a sound. Two, for example, I can see another person. Here the experience is looking at someone like me. However, merely seeing him through the senses is only seeing his external and not his real self. His physical features are only a disguise. When I see the physical world there is no disguise. The world is revealed and open. No mysteriousness. I and the table exist in two different orders. I cannot love or hate the table in a personal sense. To summarize, there are two types of experience:

1) Knowability.
2) Feelings of strangeness or otherness. The table and I can never merge.[15]

Now my feeling of a person is first a feeling of homogeneity. We belong; we are related. Number two, the feeling of disguise: I know that my sensations do not reveal to me the real essence which is inaccessible to my perception. When the *Zohar* says that there is no answer to *mi* in regard to God, the same may be applied to man. As Kant said,

---

14 In other words, science is limited to a deterministic theory of the world, and so the meaning of a scientific term or concept reduces to either the effect it has on something else, or how it is itself affected. In the merger of the personal and natural God which, according to the *Kabbalah*, takes place every Sabbath, the world ceases to be deterministic and is instead possessed of free will. As a result the entire cosmos takes on a more human nature, as will be described in the following lines.

15 The Rav is asserting a fundamental epistemological distinction between the objective world and another person. The objective world can be completely known through sensation and other types of information. Another person, save for his external features, is inaccessible. This inaccessibility, however, allows for the possibility of what the Rav calls "merger" and "a feeling of homogeneity." In his eulogy for Rav Chaim Heller, published in the collection *In Aloneness, in Togetherness*, the Rav expands on this idea to describe man's relationship to God. There are themes in common between the Rav's thought and the philosophy of Emanuel Levinas who also asserted the absolute unknowability of the "Other" in his work *Totality and Infinity*. Levinas, however, used this idea in order to develop a philosophy of ethics and responsibility. The Rav, rooted in traditional Jewish sources, is elaborating a philosophy of man's relationship to God within the framework of the halakhah, in this case, the Shabbat.

When I investigate something which is perceptible to my senses I can then form abstractions, but since the personality cannot be seen through the senses I can never know the personality.[16] Modern psychology investigates the personality in defeat, claiming that there is no personality, rather than admit defeat.

Man possesses a *tzelem Elokim,* which cannot be investigated. When I speak of God as a *mi,* I mean God is inaccessible, but, nevertheless related. Man as a spiritual personality feels related to others though they are unknowable. The same experience is applied to the finite thou as is applied to the infinite thou.

However, when you investigate God through the cosmos, God addressing Himself through matter, it is an objective experience. There is no relation between myself and the spiral nebulae or the table. There is a feeling of strangeness. Loneliness means man is surrounded by strangeness. I feel the world is hostile, or at least neutral to me. This is metaphysical strangeness. When I'm in a subway at rush hour, crowded together with the rest of humanity, this is accidental strangeness. When a person has an enemy he does not feel strange, since he lives in a relation. Loneliness is only when I exist alone without any relations. God, therefore, seen through the cosmos is knowable, but strange. God as seen through this [is] *mi.* The *Deus Persona* is friendly, but unknowable. This is the experience of *Malka Kadisha* on the one hand, and the *Shekhinah* on the other.[17]

Now let us see what is the eschatological idea: to discover that the cosmic order is not one ruled by necessity, but a free order. The trouble is that we see only an infinitesimal part of the universe, never seeing the

---

16 In *Critique of Pure Reason*, Book 1, Section 3 titled "On the Relation of the Understanding to Objects in General, and the Possibility of Knowing Them a priori" (p. 109 in F. Max Muller translation), Kant describes the relationship of our understanding of the world with the world itself. Through perception of a phenomenon, we accumulate sense data with which the mind constructs a representation through which it understands the world. The Rav is asserting that this process, being dependent on the mind of the observer, cannot apply to the mind of another person. See previous note for the comparison to the French Jewish philosopher Emanuel Levinas.

17 The term "*Malka Kadisha*" appears in the *Zohar.* The Ari interprets it as the *Partzuf* of *Zeir Anpin* which spans what the Rav described above, in this lecture, as the ethical-aesthetic *sefirot* of *Gevurah, Gedulah, Tiferet, Netzaḥ, Hod.* The relationship of God with man through ethics and aesthetics is what the Rav calls *Deus Persona.* God's relationship with man through the cosmos, *Deus Mundus*, corresponds to the *sefirah* of *Malkhut*, which is also referred to as the *Shekhinah.* The merger (*zivug*) of *Malka Kadisha* and *Malkhut* is the theme of the Shabbat and the culmination of human history.

whole, and this microcosmic part is not typical of the macrocosmic universe. That is why the world appears to be impersonal and mechanistic. But the macro cosmos as a whole is a great personality.[18] Just as if I saw only the finger of a man I would look upon it as an object and not as part of [a] whole, expressing or revealing a personality, since every movement of the body reveals some part of the personality.

When the Torah says,

השמים מספרים כבוד א-ל וגו'. (תהילים י"ט: ב)

When the heavens sings God's praise. (Psalms 19: 2)

true, it is only a metaphor, since the heavens are dead and cannot sing. But the ocean as part of a great cosmic anthropos possesses a personality.

For Christianity, when they wait for the coming of Christ it is just dependent on the whim of Christ, when he decides to come. Man has no part in bringing it about. However, in Judaism, man can bring about this eschatology when man will attain a knowledge or experience of the universe as a whole. When man will encompass the whole order of creation, man will realize the *Deus Mundus* as the *Deus Persona*-God imprisoned in the concrete order of things, the same as if a man be imprisoned in the cell of a prison. My investigating the prison yard or walk does not reveal to me the prisoner locked away in the cell. The same is true of man investigating the cosmos. The *Kabbalah* says that if man should conquer the universe through knowledge, he would then realize that the cosmos is just a disguise. How it should be done, the *Kabbalah* did not tell us, i.e., as to the final merger but the approach [is] through the logos.[19]

---

18 The Rav appears to be saying here that knowledge of the entire universe reveals the personal God. By knowledge he appears to mean scientific knowledge, as is implied at the end of this lecture when he says, "man can bring about this eschatology when man will attain a knowledge or experience of the universe as a whole." Although Kabbalistic sources speak of bringing about of the Messiah and the messianic age through studying the secrets of the Torah, they clearly refer to metaphysical, not [just] scientific, knowledge. The Rav is claiming that science, which he describes as "the approach through the logos, " is also alluded to in the *Kabbalah*.

Rav Tzadok Ha-Cohen makes a similar point in *Tzidkut Ha-Tzadik* (section 30) where he claims, based upon a *Zohar*, that there is a correspondence between Torah knowledge and "secular" knowledge; and that, as Torah (apparently Kabbalistic knowledge) progresses, "secular" knowledge advances accordingly. The same idea is expressed by Rav Kook in *Orot Ha-Kodesh*, II, Fifth discourse pp. 537–551, ההתפתחות המתעלה.

19 The Rav is claiming that through the advance of scientific knowledge, the merger between *Deus Persona* and *Deus Mundus* will take place. The Kabbalistic claim

השמים מספרים כבוד א-ל וגו'

The union of God's will and *Shekhinah*: The *Deus Persona* addressing me through the natural law is the I and the Thou, addressing me through the ethical law.[20] Of course, the idea[21] is a philosophical one, but *Kabbalah* used images which they called *yesod ha-zivug*, where the I and Thou merge.

Introduction to Lecture XI

It is useful to summarize some of the ideas mentioned in previous lectures in order to understand the way they apply to this lecture. In Lecture X, the Rav divided up the *sefirot* into two general groups: the upper nine (*Keter, Ḥokhmah, Binah, Gevurah, Gedulah, Tiferet, Netzaḥ and Hod*), which constitute the revelation of the personal God, *Deus Persona*; and the tenth *sefirah* (*Malkhut*), which reveals the creator God, *Deus Mundus*. The natural order which man beholds in the cosmos, *Malkhut*, is the feminine, which passively receives, and therefore hides, the other *sefirot*; i.e., the personal God. The *Zohar* quoted in Lecture IX, which questions, "Who created these?" (מי ברא אלה) identified the term "these" (*eleh*, which refers to *ma*) with the revealed *Deus Mundus*, and the hidden, personal God, *Deus Persona*, with the term "who" (*mi*). The only question that man can ask, and of which he can achieve some degree of understanding, is "what" (*ma*), about the revealed universe. The hidden God, "who" (*mi*), can never be proven, and one who asks about Him is left with an unanswerable question.

---

of this merger at the end of history is that it will take place when man's exploration of the nature of the universe, *Malkhut*, will be completed. At this point, there will be nothing else to achieve except for its merger with the personal God.

20 The Rav is claiming that ultimately, natural law and ethical law merge. This corresponds to the merger of *Deus Mundus* and *Deus Persona*. The Rav's point here is that the personal relationship between God and man, *Deus Persona*, is one of mutual God-man responsibility, which the Rav refers to as ethics. Much as man is required to respect his fellow man, man is required to respect the will of God and thereby merit God's blessings and reward. This relationship is referred to by the Rav as an I-Thou relationship.
A source for the idea that the personal relationship with God is an ethical relationship with parallels to human ethical relationships, is the passage in *Shabbat* 33a in which a potential proselyte comes to Hillel and requests that he teach him the entire Torah while standing on one foot. Hillel responds, "That which you would not want your friend to do to you, you shall not do to him." Rashi, in his commentary, writes that "friend" can refer both to man and to God. It follows that the fulfillment of the commandments of the Torah, which constitute Jewish ethics, are an expression of man's ethical relationship with God.

21 I.e., the merger of ontology and ethics.

In this lecture, the Rav makes use of these ideas in explaining the Kabbalistic understanding of the three meals of Shabbat. Tur writes:

> The reason [the Men of the Great Assembly] established three different types of prayers on the Sabbath: 1) אתה קדשת, You have sanctified; 2) ישמח משה, Moshe will rejoice; and 3) אתה אחד, You are One, as opposed to festivals when only one form of prayer, אתה בחרתנו, was established, is because these three prayers correspond to three Sabbaths: 1) אתה קדשת corresponds to the Sabbath of Creation, as is clear from the liturgy; 2) ישמח משה corresponds to the Sabbath on which the Torah was given, for all opinions (in the Talmud) concur that the Torah was given on the Sabbath; and 3) אתה אחד corresponds to the Sabbath of the future. (*Oraḥ Ḥayyim* 292)

This passage makes evident that the liturgy of the Sabbath spans the entire history of the world and of the Jewish people, beginning with creation and culminating in the final Sabbath, which heralds the "end" of the world. Hence, the idea of the Sabbath is bound up with Jewish eschatology, and it is on this basis that the Rav proceeds in this lecture and the next.

Lecture XI

Let us now examine the Sabbath idea. In Exodus 20:8 it states, "זכור את יום השבת לקדשו", "Remember the day of Shabbat to keep it holy," while in Deuteronomy 5:12 it states "שמור את יום השבת לקדשו", "Observe the day of Shabbat to keep it holy." Ramban on *Yitro* (Exodus 20:8) asks:

> ואני תמה אם נאמר זכור ושמור מפי הגבורה, למה לא נכתב בלוחות הראשונות. ויתכן שהיה בלוחות הראשונות ובשניות כתוב זכור, ומשה פירש לישראל כי שמור נאמר עמו. וזו כוונתם באמת:
>
> ובמדרשו של רבי נחוניא בן הקנה (ספר הבהיר, אות קפב) הזכירו עוד סוד גדול בזכור ושמור, ועל הכלל תהיה הזכירה ביום והשמירה בלילה, וזהו מאמר החכמים (ב"ק לב ב) שאומרים בערב שבת באי כלה באי כלה, באו ונצא לקראת שבת מלכה כלה, ויקראו לברכת היום קדושא רבא (פסחים קו א) שהוא הקדוש הגדול, ותבין זה. ואמת הוא ג"כ כי מדת זכור רמזו במצות עשה, והוא היוצא ממדת האהבה והוא למדת הרחמים, כי העושה מצות אדוניו אהוב לו ואדוניו מרחם עליו, ומדת שמור במצות לא תעשה, והוא למדת הדין ויוצא ממדת היראה, כי הנשמר מעשות דבר הרע בעיני אדוניו ירא אותו, ולכן מצות עשה גדולה ממצות לא תעשה, כמו שהאהבה גדולה מהיראה, כי המקיים ועושה בגופו ובממונו רצון אדוניו הוא גדול מהנשמר מעשות הרע בעיניו, ולכך אמרו דאתי עשה ודחי לא תעשה, ומפני זה יהיה העונש במצות לא תעשה גדול ועושין בו דין כגון מלקות ומיתה, ואין עושין בו דין במצות עשה כלל

אלא במורדין, כמו לולב וציצית איני עושה, סוכה איני עושה, שסנהדרין היו מכין אותו עד שיקבל עליו לעשות או עד שתצא נפשו:

I ask, if both *Zakhor* and *Shamor* were heard from the mouth of the Mighty One, why were they not both written in the first set of tablets? The answer seems to be that only *Zakhor* was written on both the first and second tablets, but Moshe explained to the people that *Shamor* was also said at the same time. This seems to be the true explanation.

In the Midrash of R' Neḥuniah ben Ha-Kanah they mention another great secret of *Zakhor* and *Shamor*. The principle is that *zekhirah* must be in the daytime and *shemirah* at night. This is the meaning of the statement of the Sages (*Bava Kamma* 32b) that in the evening we say "Welcome bride, welcome bride, let us go outside and welcome the Shabbat queen bride." And the blessings of the day are called "*Kiddush Rabba,*" the great sanctification (*Pesaḥim* 106a) because it is the greater holiness. Understand this. The truth is also that the concept of *Zakhor* refers to the positive *mitzvot*, which comes out of love and this is the attribute of mercy. For someone who does the command of his master loves him, and his master will have mercy on him. And *Shamor* refers to the negative commandments, which is the attribute of judgment which comes from the attribute of fear. Someone who is careful not to do something that is bad in the eyes of his master, fears him. Therefore, the positive commandments are greater than the negative commandments, just as love is greater than fear. Someone who keeps and fulfils the will of his master with his body and his money is greater than someone who refrains from doing something bad in his eyes. Therefore, the [Sages] said that a positive commandment overrides a negative commandment. Because of this, the punishment of a negative commandment is greater and he is punished with [such things as] lashes or death. But there is no punishment for someone who transgresses a positive commandment unless they are rebellious. For example [if they declare] "I will not do [the *mitzvot* of] *lulav* or *tzitzit,*" "I will not do [the *mitzvah* of] *succah.*" In such a case, the Sanhedrin gives him lashes until he accepts upon himself to do them, or until his soul departs his body.

זכור refers to the day of Shabbat. שמור refers to the night of Shabbat. Because שמור is feminine, we say, בואי כלה בואי כלה; זכור is masculine and so it is referred to as קדושא רבא.[22] לילה, although masculine, has a feminine

[22] According to Ramban (*Shemot* 20:8), *shamor* is called feminine because it refers to the negative commandments, and *zakhor* is called masculine because it refers

ending, and so the *Kabbalah* always used it in the feminine form. We have here the correlate of the masculine and feminine principle.

Ramban wanted to prove this halakhically and so he said (ibid.): זכור is the זכרו בקידוש and שמור is the לאו of *melakhah*.[23]

In *Bereishit* (chapters 2, 3) on ויברך, ויקדש Ramban [interprets] מֶעֶין הברכות as מַעַיָן הברכות although in halakhah it means מֵעֵין.[24]

---

to the positive commandments. Negative commandments are associated with the *middah* of *din*, which is seen by the *Kabbalah* as possessing feminine qualities; positive commandments are associated with the *middah* of *ḥessed* and therefore possess masculine qualities.

23 Ramban, according to the Rav, is drawing a similarity between the Kabbalistic distinction between זכור and שמור and the halakhic distinction. According to the *Kabbalah*, זכור refers to the upper 9 *sefirot* which represent the personal God, *Deus Persona*, and שמור refers to the *sefirah* of *Malkhut*, which represents the God of creation, *Deus Mundus*. Just as the *sefirah* of *Malkhut* "receives" and thereby hides the upper 9 *sefirot*, so does the God of creation "hide" the personal God. Correspondingly, זכור, which refers to the positive commandments, express man's service to God out of love, and שמור refers to the negative commandments which express man's service to God out of fear. The halakhic distinction between service from love and service from fear corresponds to the distinction between *Deus Persona* and *Deus Mundus*. A halakhic consequence of this distinction is the halakhic concept that a positive commandment can suspend (push away) a negative one.

24 The expression מעין הברכות appears in the blessing said after *Ma'ariv* on Shabbat evening where the Gemara in *Shabbat* 24b discusses שליח צבור היורד לפני התיבה. There Rashi describes it as ברכה מעין שבע meaning that it is an abridged version of the seven *berakhot* said in the *tefillah* of Shabbat night. The halakhic meaning of מעין is "abridged." Ramban in his commentary is using the word מעין with altered vowels to indicate that it refers to a wellspring of *berakhah*.

The *Zohar* says in *Va-Yakhel*[25] our faith is completely integrated with the different phases of [our relationship to God].[26] Shabbat consists of three phases:[27]

1) Transcendental.[28]
2) Day as an idea.[29]

---

25 The *Zohar* to which the Rav is referring is in *Yitro* 88a. בעי בר נש לאתענגא תלת זימנין אלין דהא בהא תליא מהימנותא דלעילא בעתיקא קדישא ובזעיר אמפין ובחקלא דתפוחין. The three relationships to God are: עתיקא קדישא is the *Partzuf* corresponding to the *sefirah* of *Keter,* which represents God's will; זעיר אנפין is the *Partzuf* of the *sefirot* of *Ḥessed, Gevurah, Tiferet, Netzaḥ, Hod, Yesod* which represents God's ethical and aesthetical relationship with man; and חקלא דתפוחין refers to the *sefirah* of *Malkhut* which represents God's relationship with man through the physical creation.

26 The Rav refers to the three Kabbalistic notions of God and His relationship to man and the cosmos, as represented by the three Shabbat meals.

27 The Rav does not list these phases in order. In reality, the night meal comes first, the second meal is transcendence, and the third meal is an "idea" of the day. In the Ari, the evening meal corresponds to the *sefirah* of *Malkhut* and is therefore referred to as the meal of חקל תפוחין. This is expressed in the song he composed to be sung at that meal, אזמר בשבחין, למיעאל גו פתחין, דבחקל תפוחין, דאינון קדישין, נזמין לה השתא. The second meal, on Shabbat morning, corresponds to the *Partzuf* of עתיקא קדישא. This is expressed in the song he composed to be sung in the second meal, אסדר לסעודתא, בצפרא דשבתא, ואזמין בה השתא, עתיקא קדישא. The third meal, towards the end of Shabbat, corresponds to עתיק יומין which, like עתיקא קדישא, is the *Partzuf* of the *sefirah* of *Keter* which is God's will. This, like the first two, is expressed in the song he composed to be sung at the third meal, והא אזמין עתיק יומין, למנחה עדי יהון חלפין.
The difference between the second meal and the third meal, explains the Ari, is that in the third meal, זעיר ענפין ascends to עתיק and unites with it whereas in the morning meal it ascends but does not unite.
The Rav describes what takes place in the second meal as "transcendental" whereas he describes what takes place in the third as "an idea" which will not be fully reached until the final stage of history. For this reason, he uses the term *Atika* to refer to the second meal and *Zeir Anpin* to refer to the third.

28 The Rav uses the term "transcendental" to describe the second meal during which the *Partzuf* of עתיקא קדישא reveals the personal God, *Deus Persona,* which transcends the physical world. In truth, this *Partzuf* transcends all aspects of God, for it is the *Partzuf* corresponding to the *sefirah* which, representing the will of God, transcends all of the other *sefirot.* In the Rav's language, עתיקא קדישא has a "rendezvous" with *Malkhut* during this meal, but the ultimate merger will take place only in the future.

29 The Rav's expression "Day as an Idea" refers to the third meal, the meal of זעיר אנפין, wherein the ultimate merger of *Deus Mundus* and *Deus Persona* remains a

3) Night.[30]

All these unite into one whole called "Shabbat," and each aspect when it prevails invites the other to accompany him. With the night of Shabbat comes the idea of *Shabbat Ha-Malkah*, who invites the *Shabbat De-Yemama*[31] to her palace for a rendezvous. Then, when the transcendental idea of Shabbat comes, the two merge.[32] The *Zohar* in *Shemot* (*Yitro* 88a) says:

> יהודה אמר: בעי לאתענגא בהאי יומא ולמיכל תלת סעודתי בשבתא בגין דישתכח שבעיו ועינוגא בהאי יומא דעלמא. זהר שמות פ"ח ע"א...
>
> R' Yehudah says: One is obligated to take pleasure on this day [Shabbat] and to eat three meals in order that this day bring spiritual sustenance to the other days of the week.
>
> R' Abba says: One must [set the table and take pleasure in the meals] in order to connect with the supernal days (meaning *sefirot*) which receive their blessing from this day (meaning *Binah*). From this day (the *sefirah Binah*) the head of the "Little Face" (*Zeir Anpin*) is filled with dew (spiritual flow), which falls from the "Holy Ancient One" (the *Partzuf Arich*), and brings spiritual flow to the "Holy Field of Apples" (*Malkhut*), so that all of the worlds may be blessed at once. Therefore, one is obligated to take pleasure three times (three meals), for these three worlds (*Atika*, *Zeir Anpin* and *Malchut*) produce the spiritual flow and therefore one is required to take delight and to

---

vision of the future, which presently is not yet realized. The reason the meal is called זעיר אנפין and not עתיקא קדישא, as the second meal is called, is because it is not realized and therefore does not directly involve *Malkhut*. The Ari writes:

> ולכן צריך לומר בקול רם דא היא סעודתא דזער אנפין כי המלכות איננה עולה עמו רק הוא לבדו (שער בכוונות ע"ה ע"ד).
>
> Therefore one must declare loudly, "This is the meal of *Zeir Anpin*," because the *Malkhut* does not ascend (to *Atika Kadisha*), only *Zeir Anpin*.

This is interpreted by the Rav that the merger does not actually occur; it is a vision of the future.

The Rav's distinction between the second meal which he describes as a "rendezvous" of *Deus Mundus* and *Deus Persona* and the third meal which expresses a future merger has its source in the Ari:

> והנה בסעודת שחרית עולה זעיר עד אריך אפין הנקרא כתר ולכן אמרו בתפילת מוסף כתר יתנו לך וכו' ולפיכך הסעודה הזו נק' סעודתא דעתיקא ר"ל שעולה עד עתיקא ואינה סעודת עתירא עצמו (שער הכוונות סעודת שחרית של שבת ע"ד ע"ג).

30 This refers to the first meal of Shabbat, which expresses the concept of God as creator, *Deus Mundus*, as represented by the *sefirah* of *Malkhut*, which yearns to be united with the personal hidden God, *Deus Persona*.

31 Shabbat day.

32 The Rav is saying *Deus Mundus* and *Deus Persona,* meet, but do not yet merge.

> rejoice in them. But one who detracts from these meals acts as if these worlds are blemished and will be punished.
> R' Shimon says: For He who completes the three meals on Shabbat, a voice comes out and announces, "Then you shall delight with God,"[33] (meaning *Arich*). This verse refers to the meal which one receives from *Atika Kadisha De-Kol Kadishin* "The Ancient Holy One, of all which is holy."
> "I will cause you to ride upon the high places."[34] This refers to (סעודתא תנינא) the second meal which man eats from the "Holy Field of Apples" (*Ḥakal Tapuḥin*).
> "And I will feed you from your inheritance of Yaakov your father."[35] This is the final of the three meals which is completed with "the Little Face" (*Zeir Anpin*).[36]

Each *avodah* is assigned to a different aspect.

The evening meal symbolizes the *ḥakal tapuḥin*, and is also the meal of the *Matronita*.

> R. Elazar asked his father R. Shimon in what order the three meals corresponded to the three divine grades. R. Shimon replied: Concerning the meal of Sabbath night (i.e., Friday night) it is written: "I will cause thee to ride upon the high places of the earth."[37] והרכבתיך על במתי ארץ.

In this night the *Holy Matronita* (*Shekhinah*) is greatly blessed and the whole "Field of Apples" (*ḥakal tapuḥin*) also, and the man's table is blessed, who partakes of his meal daily and with joy, and a new soul is added unto him. This signifies the rejoicing of the *Shekhinah*.

---

33 Isaiah 58:14.

34 Ibid.

35 Ibid.

36 In the above statement, R' Shimon is not listing the meals in order, but is describing them in the order of the clauses of the verse in Isaiah 58 (*Matok Mi-Dvash*). Therefore, according to R' Shimon we have the following correspondence:
First meal—"Then you shall delight with God"—*Malkhut, Ḥakal Tapuḥin Kadishin.*
Second meal—"I will cause you to ride upon the high places"—*Arich, Atika Kadisha.*
Third meal—"And I will feed you from your inheritance from Yaakov your father"—*Zeir Anpin.*

37 *Zohar* 88b.

The evening meal symbolizes the *ḥakal tapuḥin*, the "Field of Apples," and is also the meal of the *Matronita*, the *Holy Matrona*. *Matronita* is synonymous with *Shekhinah, Malkhut*, and *ḥakal tapuḥin*. This refers to God as a *Deus Mundus* in the cosmos; the unalterable sequence of necessity. *Malkhut* expresses necessity, the natural law, a certain order: determinability in scientific terms, the reverse of freedom.

Malkhut also expresses femininity, *Shekhinah-Deus* abiding in the cosmic drama; a metaphysical term. This expresses the presence of Deity in the cosmos, or, as *Kabbalah* expressed it, "The King imprisoned in the cosmos." *Matronita* expresses the feminine aspect of revelation, of passivity, or dependability.[38] It [suppresses] (expresses)[39] the revelation of *Deus Persona*—a metaphysical principle, the experience which is hidden behind the guise of the objective experience, a personalistic order beyond the cosmic order.

The *Kabbalah* and Naḥmanides always pictured nature as a bride waiting for her Lover to free her from the bonds of nature. God, Who is mute and silent in His self-imposed imprisonment, is the *Shekhinah*. Divinity in exile, homeless and lonely, is longing for redemption and elevation to transcendental order of personalistic experience.[40]

The world suffers because God suffers. There is tragedy in the world because the whole act of creation was a tragic act upon God: Divine suffering, which is eo-ipso cosmic suffering reflected in every individual.[41]

---

38 In other words, *Malkhut* has two meanings. On one hand, *Malkhut* designates the physical universe as viewed objectively and scientifically; on the other hand *Malkhut* is Femininity, which means it exists as the repository for something other. Taken together, these meanings of *Malkhut* express the concept that the objective physical world is a repository for a Divine spirituality. The physical world, identified with God as creator, *Deus Mundus*, encloses and houses the metaphysical worlds, identified with the personal God, *Deus Persona*.

39 The original appears to be a mistake in the text. It means, "It contains and hides the revelation."

40 In other words, God as *Deus Mundus* is "trapped" within the physical world, and is compared to a bride who longs to be united with her "groom," God as *Deus Persona*, who will redeem and elevate her through reestablishing a personal-ethical relationship. The Rav understands this as the merger of ontology and ethics.

41 The root of all human suffering is that the physical world creates a barrier between man and God. This is only possible because God Himself is imprisoned within the physical world. As a result, God Himself experiences suffering. The idea of God's suffering as a result of human suffering is understood by R' Ḥayyim Volozhiner in his work *Nefesh Ha-Ḥayyim* as the basis of prayer, the purpose of which is to alleviate Divine suffering (*sha'ar* 2, chapter 11).

God, *keviyokhol*, is the helpless prisoner, and man is the omnipotent *moshiakh* who will break down the barrier of objectivity [nature?] and free the *Shekhinah* and bring her to her Lover.

> בשם יחוד קודשא בריך הוא ושכינתיה בדחילו ורחימו ליחד י"ה בו"ה ביחודא שלם בשם כל ישראל:
>
> In the name of the union of the Holy One, Blessed be He and the *Shekhinah*, with awe and love, to unite the two letters [of the Tetragramaton] *Yud-Heh* with *Vav-Heh* in a complete unison in the name of all of Israel.[42]

To unite the *Shekhinah* with her Lover, the motif of Shabbat is the uniting of *kallah* (bride) with *ḥatan* (bridegroom); Shabbat [as] the bride chained to mechanical activity and awaiting freedom. *Shekhinah, ḥakal tapuḥin,* is dependent on rain, *tal.* This is symbolized by the Sabbath night representing loneliness; man surrounded by thinghood is lonely. *Shamor* means to wait. The night waits for the day to come. Man waiting for the answer to *mi* (who), not *eleh*. This is man's anticipation of the *ketz hayamim*, where not only the question of *eleh* will be solved but also the unanswerable question of *mi*.

> נפשי לה', משמרים לבקר שמרים לבקר. (תהילים ק"ל: ו)
>
> My soul waits for Hashem more than they who watch for the morning: more than watchmen for the morning.

The *Zohar* interprets (it as) *nafshi le-Hashem*—man surrounded by the strange universe awaits for the *Deus Persona* to whom he feel close to and related. The entire world awaits the Great Day of eschatology.

There is another[43] symbol infused in Shabbat. *Zeir Anpin*, the "Little Face"—the *Deus Persona*—God as living master of the universe as experienced by the apocalyptic vision of the moral law, of the *ve-amor* of the

---

42 The *Yud-Heh* of the Tetragramaton refer to the *sefirot* of *Ḥokhmah* and *Binah*, or in terms of *Partzufim*, *Abba* and *Imma*. The letters *Vav-Heh* refer to the *sefirot* of the *Partzuf* of *Zeir Anpin* (*Ḥessed, Gevurah, Tiferet, Netzaḥ, Hod, Yesod*) and *Malkhut*. The full Tetragramaton thus refers to the full union of all *Partzufim* which includes the complete merger of *Deus Mundus* and *Deus Persona*. This statement of intentionality recited before the performance of each *mitzvah* expresses the metaphysical teleology of the commandments and, thereby, man's service to God.

43 As mentioned in the introduction to Lecture X, the three prayers of Sabbath correspond to the three Sabbaths: the Sabbath of creation, the Sabbath of the *Matan Torah*, and the great "*Sabbath*" of the future. In the following section, the Rav understands the personal God, Kabbalistically referred to as *Zeir Anpin*, the "Little Face," in terms of the moral law which God reveals to man. This was the

actus.[44] This is *yoma de-Shabbat*, the Day of the Sabbath, or זכור (*zakhor*), masculine and independent. *Deus* as root of ethos, not natural law which is *Deus Mundus*, but God, who addresses himself through the world, not phenomena which is *midat ha-din*, [with] no exception, no changing of rules, [where] man feels insignificant—no deviation or *rahamim*. Man experiences misery, wretchedness and helplessness in the face of the cosmic order.

God then addresses Himself through the *Deus Persona* or the world, the moral law. Here man is the center of creation, which is subordinate to him. There is a mutual relationship of man to God, of sympathy and friendliness. Their address can be the apocalyptic level through prophetic revelation and also through the inner revelation or natural revelation of man.[45]

Existence, if seen from the personalistic level, gains meaning: *Tiferet*, the unity of all objective matter evolving through the moral law. God at Sinai addressed Himself at the coming of dawn. Man alone[46] can give meaning to existence, as the agnostics have done. For man is driven to unity by the mere fact that he exists. This personalistic revelation lends meaning to existence.[47]

---

law that was revealed by the giving of the Torah at Sinai and corresponds to the prayer of Sabbath morning. This moral law, the Torah, creates a "personal relationship" of man to God as opposed to the "impersonal relationship" which defines man's relationship to the created cosmos. As explained above in Lecture IX, the "personal" relationship is one of warmth and friendliness, as opposed to the "impersonal" one which is described by the Rav in this paragraph as full of "misery, wretchedness and helplessness."

44 The phrase "the *ve-amor* of the *actus*" is not clear. What the Rav may mean is that Man experiences God's moral law in his act of cognition in a similar way to God's act of cognition as discussed by Maimonides in chapter 68 of volume 1 of the *Guide*. This is translated as "intellect in *actu*" (see Pines 165).

45 In other words, the moral law is discovered by man in one of two ways, either through revelation, such as we experienced at Sinai, or through man's own "inner natural" sense. The Rav already mentioned these two sources of morality in lecture III. While most of the Torah laws can only be known through revelation, there is a class of general moral habits which man can discern through reason and nature.

46 That is, without the prophetic revelation at Sinai, man can give meaning to existence by discovering ethics within the creation. See *Eiruvin* 100b where the Sages assert that had the Torah not been given, one could derive ethics from nature. The Rav elaborates on this theme in *The Emergence of Ethical Man*.

47 The Tur writes in Section 292 that the second *tefillah* on the Shabbat corresponds to the Shabbat of the giving of the Torah at Sinai. The Rav is asserting that at the revelation at Sinai, God revealed the "unity of all objective matters evolving

Suddenly, the great mystery of union meets in Shabbat.[48] The bride meets the groom, who is God Himself. For creation and God's revelation are united to Himself. God and world are one. This is eschatology.

Shabbat shows this duality of God and unites the *Kallah* with the *Zeir Anpin*. Two *modi* relationships merged into one. Of course, the duality is only as man sees it. For God, nothing exists and this merger is עתיקא קדישא סתימא דכל סתימין,[49] the complete unity of God. Man finds his home in this world because he finds friendship between himself and the world which expresses the *Deus Persona.*

The word "Shabbat" grammatically in the *Ḥumash* is read (*kri*) as feminine היא. The *ketiv,* however, is הוא, masculine. It is interesting that the *kri* is feminine because we cannot yet pronounce the masculine, which represents the *Deus Persona.* The *ketiv* tells what the true Being is and the *kri* as man experiences it.[50] In *ketz ha-yamim* (the end of days) only the *ketiv* will be read.[51] This is exactly what *Ḥazal* have said:

---

through the moral law." The second meal, similarly, represents the ascension of the objective world to the ethics of God. The discovery of the ethics embedded in nature can be achieved, however, without the Sinaitic revelation. As a consequence, all men are privy to natural ethics and, therefore, obligated to it. Divine ethics, however, can only come through the revelation at Sinai, and therefore obligates the Jewish nation. The uniqueness of the Shabbat is that the Divinely revealed law at Sinai merges with the natural world. This is what the Rav refers to below as the "great mystery of union" which takes place on the Shabbat.

48 While in terms of the Sabbath prayers, it is the third prayer, at the *Minḥah* service, which refers to the "Great Sabbath" of the future, the eschatological Sabbath, as the Rav calls it, nonetheless, it is the second and not the third meal which is the meal of *Atika Kadisha* (עתיקא קדישא), "The Holy Ancient One," which is the highest world of absolute unity not recognizing any dualism, so that God is united unto Himself. The Rav is therefore referring here to what happens at the second meal. The third meal, of *Zeir Anpin* ("The Little Face"), closes the Shabbat by reminding us that the great unity has yet to be achieved.

49 "The Holy Ancient One, Hidden of all Hiddenness." The phrase עתיקא קדישא refers to the *Partzuf* of עתיק, which has no distinction between male and female, זכר ונקבה. See *Eitz Ḥayyim* שער עתיק שער י"ב פרק ב.

50 The Rav is referring to the fact that while the word Shabbat itself is feminine, nevertheless, the Torah also refers to it in the masculine gender. In fact, the Shabbat is referred to in three ways: feminine, masculine, and plural. These three usages appear in each of the three prayers of Shabbat. On Shabbat night, Shabbat is referred to in the feminine (*Malkhut, Deus Mundus*); in the morning, in the masculine (*Malka Kadisha, Deus Persona*), and in the evening, in the plural; which reflects the fact that the two never merge.

51 See *Pesaḥim* 50a.

מזמור שיר ליום השבת: יום שכולו שבת ומנוחה לחיי העולמים. (מסכת תמיד ז:)

A psalm and song for the Shabbat: for the day which is entirely Shabbat and rest for He Who is the life of all of the worlds. [52]

These main motifs were already in the Midrash.

Let us analyze the three meals. What happens *lele de-Shabbta*, on the night of the Sabbath? The world on the night of Shabbat is lonely and in a state of expectancy. The S*hekhinah* arises from the depths of thinghood to an upward path endowed with grace and friendliness. Haunted by loneliness and frightened by the muteness of mechanistic existence to the bright light of a personalistic existence, the meal expresses the feeling of a community of existence. The *Shekhinah* takes the upward path toward merger and we join in. The day belongs to *Malka Kadisha*, belonging to the *Deus Persona.* While in the weekdays there is passivity to (muteness) [indifference], on Shabbat, there is revolt. The *Deus Persona* then descends from the finite recesses to meet the *Shekhinah* or Himself.

This is the *Zeir Anpin*, the Little Face, which is the third meal. It should have been second[53] but it was placed as third because they never meet. It is in the twilight of the day [in] which [it] is done. The last meal is of joy and of parting because it is never realized; only a dream in the distant future. There is then eternal vigilance for the next encounter during the following week and so the cycle goes on.

The Sabbath morning meal is symbolic of self-awareness and self-consciousness. The world is experiencing its selfhood and experiencing God Himself. This *seudah* is related to the "great end" and is placed in the middle to show that the "great end" is never reached—splitting [Shabbos] by the second [meal], which is the meeting of the eschatological realization described above.

Introduction to Lectures XII and XIII

In the first lecture, the Rav declares that in the "analysis of the metaphysics of Genesis," his audience will explore the issues of the "dichotomy between Jewish and Christian hermeneutics," as well as the "dichotomy between modern science and the Bible." In these lectures, the two issues are discussed in relationship to each other. This is because the two opposing methods of interpretation of Judaism and Christianity result in two

---

52 That is, the Midrash itself refers to *Ketz Ha-Yamim* (eschatology) by the term "a day which is entirely Shabbat." On that day, the *Kallah* and *Zeir Anpin* unite forever, and man will directly experience the personal God.

53 Because the second stage would be yearning to meet but not meeting yet.

entirely different anthropologies. This, in turn, results in two opposing theological responses to the modern scientific concept of man. Christian Biblical interpreters have always exclusively emphasized man's "transcendental being," thus isolating the description of the creation of man in Genesis from the rest of the account of creation. The Talmudic Sages, however, recognize man as a natural being occupying a place among the rest of creation. Man's transcendental component, the "image of God," instead of excluding his natural aspects, complements them. This concept is the basis of the Jewish halakhah, which emphasizes the significance of man as a physical being in his natural environment. In the following two lectures, the Rav draws upon a variety of sources from verse and liturgy, which express man's natural aspects.

Lecture XII

Should we ask an educated Christian what he understands by the word "man," by sheer force of association he will refer to:

1) Biblical interpretation of man[54]
2) Greek
3) Scientific

To further elucidate he would say that 1) and 2) contrast man to the animal kingdom and plant. The only difference is that the Bible explains man as a unique, divine image possessing two opposing forces, man's obedience to and his [Satanic] revolt against his Creator.[55]

---

54 It seems that there is a mistake in the notes as it read "Biological." In *The Emergence of Ethical Man* (p. 3) the Rav writes:

> Should we inquire of a modern historian of philosophy or of any educated person well acquainted with the history of ideas what he understands by the word "man," he would immediately advise us about a basic controversy concerning the destiny or essence of this being. By the sheer force of associative thinking, he would at once refer to three disparate anthropological-philosophical viewpoints: the Biblical (referred to by many as the Judeo-Christian view), the classical Greek, and the modern empirico-scientific. Pressed further, he would probably say that the discrepancy between the concepts of man dating back to antiquity—the Biblical and the classical Greek—is by far not as wide as the gap separating those two from the empirico-scientific one. As a matter of fact, he would say we may speak of some degree of affinity, of commensurability between the Biblical and classical anthropologies. Both are united in opposition to the scientific approach to man: they set man apart from other forms of organic life.

55 In *The Emergence of Ethical Man* (p. 8) the Rav writes:

The Greeks also believed man to be different from the animal and plant kingdom as one who is endowed with the logos, with reason. He has the capacity of grasping the essence of things, of raising himself from a sensuous being to an abstract order of being.

The modern scientific theory in contrast to Biblical spurns the idea of human autonomy and denies that there is an ontic discrepancy between man and plant. There is one continuity of man, animal and plant. The difference concerns just the degree of diversity and complexity of life processes. Life as such is a common grant to all exponents of nature and they share it alike. Man arose later in nature and even his psychosomatic faculty is part of the natural scheme.[56]

The conflict of the mechanists and vitalists is indifferent to our problem. Whether life is the end of a chemical or physical process or is a unique endowment of matter and directed by finality, not by accidents, does not matter in the controversy between Biblical and scientific theories. For if you accept vitalistic theory then it applies to plants too, and the problem is not changed.[57]

> The New Testament, drawing on the idea of individual *het* ("sin") which found its full formulation in Ezekiel, shifted man to a different plane and portrayed him in a different light. Man is not any longer the pendulum, that swings between birth and decay but the being who is torn by satanic revolt, sin and obedience, between living and falling from his God-Father. Both sin and submission are traits related to man as a spiritual-transcendental being.

56 In *The Emergence of Ethical Man* (p. 4) the Rav writes:

> In contradistinction, the modern scientific viewpoint spurns the idea of human autonomy as mythical and unfounded and denies the ontic discrepancy between man and animal-plant. The unity and continuity of organic life is looked upon as an indispensable postulate of all chemical sciences. Man, animal and plant are all placed in the realm of matter, organized in living structures and patterns. The differences between the vegetative-animal and human life concern just the degree of diversity, complexity and organization of life-processes. Life as such is a common grant from nature to all three forms of organic matter, and they share it alike. As a matter of fact, the contemporary scientific view insists that man emerged very late in the process of organic evolution and thus differs very little from his non-human ancestors as far as his biological existence is concerned. He is an integral part of nature. Even his so-called spiritual activities cannot lay claim to autonomy and singularity. There is no unique grant of spirituality in man. The alleged spirit is nothing but a mere illusion, an appearance, the sum total of transformed natural drives and sense experiences. Spirit, or soul, is reduced to psyche, and the latter—to a function of the biological occurrence.

57 In *The Emergence of Ethical Man* (p. 4 note 1) the Rav writes:

Indeed, one of the most annoying scientific facts which religious man encounters is the problem of evolution and creation. However, this is not the real problem. What actually is irreconcilable is the concept of man as the bearer of a divine image and the idea of man as an intelligent animal in science. Evolution and creation can be reconciled merely by saying that six days is not absolutely so, but is indefinite and may be longer.[58] Maimonides spoke of Creation in terms of phases[59] and the *Kabbalah* in terms of *sefirot*, the time of which may be indefinite.[60] Our conflict, however, is man as a unique being and man as a friend of the animal. Science can never explain how being came into being, for it is out of the realm of science, while the Bible is concerned with the problem of *ex nihilo.* Aristotle could not accept evolution because he believed in the eternity of forms.[61]

> The controversy between mechanists and vitalists is impertinent to our problem. Whether life be considered as an accidental end-result of physical and chemical processes similar to those appearing elsewhere, or is a unique endowment of matter whose unfolding is determined by finality, not by accidence, does not alter the implications of the controversy between the scientific and Biblical-classical formulae. Even the staunchest vitalist would accept the scientific thesis concerning the unity and continuity of organic matter. The simplest organism and man are determined by a specific bio-causality.

58 See *The Emergence of Ethical Man* (pp. 4–5):

> Indeed, one of the most annoying scientific facts which the modern homo religiosus encounters and tries vainly to harmonize with his belief is the so-called theory of evolution. In our daily jargon, we call this antinomy "evolution versus creation." The phrase does not exactly reflect the crux of the controversy for the question does not revolve around divine creation and mechanistic evolution as such. We could find a solution of some kind to this controversy. What in fact is theoretically irreconcilable is the concept of man as the bearer of the divine image with the equaling of man and animal-plant existences. In other words, the ontic autonomy or heteronomy of man is the problem. The Bible and Greek philosophical thought separated man from the flora and the fauna; science brought him back to his organic co-beings.

59 See *Moreh Nevukhim* chapter 30 of part II. See also Abarbanel, *Commentary on Bereishit, Introduction.*

60 See Ramban, *Commentary on Bereishit* 1: 1. See also Leshem, *Sefer Ha-De'ah* II 74–75 (חלק ב' דרוש ג' ענף כ"א).

61 See Lecture I, footnote 12.

Is man autonomous or one of the organic forms of existence? This is our problem. All we know of man in the Bible through Christian channels [is] that he is a separate being.[62]

Whether an idea is typically Jewish can best be judged by the halakhah, not by Aggadah.

(To understand any work as the authority meant to convey it you must have lived in the same social environment and cultural forces as the author. Mankind is changeable in his cognitive adventures, and to say that I understand Aristotle means in the tradition of Aristotle, which, of course, has been subject to change. In halakhah there is a *masoret*, a tradition as to method, but if I give an interpretation to Maimonides, it does not necessarily mean that Maimonides meant just that. If measured by halakhic standards it is correct; that suffices. As to Aggadah, however, there is no tradition, nor in philosophy do we have a tradition. In halakhah there is a certain *kabbalah* without any missing links,[63] while in Aggadah and certainly philosophy there are many such missing links. True, there are certain episodes and revelations, but they are isolated incidents without any correction. As to halakhah, it would be ridiculous to say that the Vilna Gaon and Rabbi Akiva Eiger were not as great as some of the *Geonim*. Anyone can apply his own interpretation to a *Gemara*, even against Rashi or Tosafot. However, as to practical application as a halachic decision, there is a certain reverence paid to authority in legislation.[64])

---

62 In *The Emergence of Ethical Man* (p. 9) the Rav writes:

> Man's haughtiness becomes for Christianity the metaphysical pride of an allegedly unconditioned existence. Jewish Biblical pride signifies only overemphasis upon man's abilities and power. In view of all that, the New Testament stresses man's alien status in the world of nature and his radical uniqueness. To be sure, all these ideas are not only Christian but Jewish as well. Christianity did not add much to the Biblical-philosophical anthropology. We come across a dual concept of man in the Bible. His element of transcendence was well-known to the Biblical Jew. Yet transcendence was always seen against the background of naturalness. The canvas was man's immanence; transcendence was just projected on it as a display of colors. It was more a modifying than a basic attribute of man. At any rate, both ideas were considered inseparable by the Bible; Christianity succeeded in isolating them and reducing the element of naturalness to a state of corruption and encountering the transcendent being with an alternative: death or life, while death means transcendental forms of existence and non-existence.

63 In his book *The Halachic Mind*, p. 101, the Rav writes that "there is only a single source from which a Jewish philosophical Weltanschauung could emerge; the objective order—the Halakhah."

64 See the Rav "שני מיני מסורת" in שיעורים לזכר אבא מארי.

To return to our subject, there is only one criterion by which to judge whether something is genuinely Jewish, and that is the Halakhah. The Halakhah is a well-organized, codified system, while the Aggadah is a jungle land without any definite path.

We often wonder whether the Psalmist did not have an insight into the affinity of man to nature (Psalms 8: 4–6)

ד כִּי-אֶרְאֶה שָׁמֶיךָ, מַעֲשֵׂה אֶצְבְּעֹתֶיךָ—
יָרֵחַ וְכוֹכָבִים, אֲשֶׁר כּוֹנָנְתָּה.
מָה-אֱנוֹשׁ כִּי-תִזְכְּרֶנּוּ; וּבֶן-אָדָם, כִּי תִפְקְדֶנּוּ.

When I behold Thy heavens, the work of Thy fingers,
the moon and the stars, which Thou has established;
What is man that Thou art mindful of him?
And the son of man that Thou thinks of him?"

What troubled the Psalmist? Man is a natural being seen as a low level of natural things. Then he says:

וַתְּחַסְּרֵהוּ מְּעַט, מֵאֱלֹהִים; וְכָבוֹד וְהָדָר תְּעַטְּרֵהוּ. (תהילים ח: ד'–ו')

Yet You have made him but little lower than the angels. And You crowned him with glory and honor.

Man is also a unique, glorious, almost divine being.

זְרַמְתָּם, שֵׁנָה יִהְיוּ;

You carry them away as with a flood; they are as asleep.

Man, carried by a forceful stream of existence that drifts away on a tide like a nightmare, represents the natural process of birth, life and death.

בַּבֹּקֶר, כֶּחָצִיר יַחֲלֹף.
בַּבֹּקֶר, יָצִיץ וְחָלָף;
לָעֶרֶב, יְמוֹלֵל וְיָבֵשׁ. (תהילים צ': ה')

In the morning, they are like grass, which grows up.
In the morning, it flourishes and grows up.
In the evening, it is cut down and withers. (Psalms 90: 5)[65]

---

65 See *The Emergence of Ethical Man* (p. 6, note 3):

The Psalmist already came across the miracle called man and defined in no uncertain terms his paradoxality and the discrepancy. Sometimes we wonder whether the Psalmist did have an insight into man's affinity with nature. "What is man, that You art mindful of him? And the son of man, that You visit him" (Ps. 8:5). Ben Adam should be interpreted in the sense of "the son of the earth" and in the very moment he deprecates man to a low degree in the natural frame of things, he exclaims in rapture, "Yet You have made

Man as a natural being was known to [men] of the Bible and the antinomy and discrepancy of man was known to them. Man as a natural being is a weak being, even in comparison to other forms of organic nature. On the other hand, man in certain respects is unique. This discrepancy, however, troubled more the minds of the Christians than the Jews, because the Jewish scholar was more concerned with the practical problem of what man should do than with the metaphysics. The naturalistic formula of man was common knowledge among *Ḥazal*. But the Christians, beginning with St. Augustine, down to today are still struggling with this problem.

The discrepancy lies between the Old and New Testaments. Man as a natural being, put into contrast with the eternity of God, was a popular theme of the Prophets. This led to the emphasis of the ethical norm. Whereas to the Christians, if man is a natural being, why should he be ethical?[66] But man is a transcendental being, a spiritual being, and therefore ethical. If he were a natural being, there would be no reason for him to be ethical.

---

him a little lower than the angels, and You dost crown him with glory and honor" (Ps. 8:6). Man's autonomy and uniqueness find glorious expression in other psalms: "You turn man back to dust; and say, return, you children of men" (90:3); "You engulf them, they are like sleepers, they are like the short-lived grass in the morning. In the morning it flourishes, and fades; by evening it is withered and dried" (90:5–6). There is no naturalist who could describe [the] nature of man in more effective and beautiful words. In the metaphor "You engulf them," man is carried by a forceful stream of existence, constituting just a particle of an all-powerful process; the human individual being likened to a flower of the field that blossoms and withers is a most striking presentation.

66 In *The Emergence of Ethical Man* (p. 6–7) the Rav writes:

Surveying the history of the problem of man's autonomy or heteronomy (which came to the fore long before Darwin, when people were ignorant of evolution), we notice that this problem troubled Christian theologians more than Jewish scholars. The naturalistic formula of man was to a certain extent common knowledge among *Ḥazal*, who did not resent it, while Christian theologians, beginning with Augustine of Hippo and ending with the neo-scholastics, are still struggling with the secularization of human existence by scientific research. The reason lies in the discrepancy between the Jewish Bible and the Christian gospels, the "Old" and "New" Testaments. The Hebrew Bible is cognizant of man as a natural being found on the same plane as the animal and the plant. Indeed, such an idea is a motivating force in Jewish ethics and metaphysics. The nihility, instability, helplessness and vulnerability of man—human life and death—are popular themes of prophets who contrast him with the eternity, unchangeability, everlasting

מה אנחנו, מה חיינו, מה חסדינו, מה צדקינו, מה כחינו, מה גבורתינו... ומותר האדם מן הבהמה אין כי הכל הבל.[67]

What are we? What is our life? What is our piety? What is our righteousness? What is our helplessness? What is our strength? What is our might? And the pre-eminence of man over the beast is nought; for all is vanity.

Man is a natural being coexisting with plant and animal. Nevertheless, following this we say: אתה הבדלת אנוש מראש, "You distinguished man from the very beginning." But the Christians could not understand. If man were a natural being, why should he be ethical? He should revolt and adopt an Epicurean philosophy.

Death in Hebrew, *mavet*, applies equally to man and animal. כי ימות מן הבהמה, "and if any beast. . . die."[68]

Man is presented by the Prophets under the aspect of temporality, who tries to transform into glory and magnificence. And so the Prophets say to him, "Man, as the plant of the field, why are you proud?" In all this, man and nature come into intimacy.[69]

Now the New Testament draws the idea of *ḥet*, sin, from Ezekiel, while Isaiah represented to them the prediction of a redeemer because Isaiah is the prophet of the Messiah. Their theology, therefore, was not influenced by the optimistic Isaiah, but, rather, by the pessimistic Ezekiel, the prophet of Jewish calamity in exile and in whose writings the idea of *ḥet*, sin, comes to the fore with tremendous force.[70]

---

life and omnipotence of the Creator. All those negative traits suggest the naturalness and immanence of man rather than his spirituality and transcendence.

67 From the liturgy of the Jewish daily prayer.

68 Leviticus 11:39.

69 See *The Emergence of Ethical Man* (p. 8):

"Death," in Hebrew, *mavet*, applies equally to man and animal—"and if any beast. . . die" (Leviticus 11:39)—and bespeaks the end of the organic process. Man is presented by the prophet under the aspect of temporality which he tries to convert to eternity, of weakness that in his pride man disguised as glory and magnificence. In all this the intimacy and immediacy of man with the physis comes to expression.

70 In *The Emergence of Ethical Man* (p. 8) the Rav writes:

The New Testament, drawing on the idea of individual *ḥet* ("sin") which found its full formulation in Ezekiel, shifted man to a different plane and portrayed him in a different light. Man is not any longer the pendulum, that swings between birth and decay but the being who is torn by satanic revolt, sin and obedience, between living and falling from his God-Father. Both

The New Testament did not see man as the pendulum that swings between life and death, but as a man who is torn by two drives, the Satanic and the Divine, a man who swings toward God and away from Him; between the devil and the Divine Being. Man-animal can neither sin nor humble himself before God. But the spirit revolts or the spirit submits himself, and reaches out to regions of absoluteness. The source of all evil for Christianity is metaphysical pride, when man wants to become unconditioned and independent. Man is an alien in the world of nature and his uniqueness is totally different.

The Psalmist believed in the unity of man, who is at the same time transcendental and natural. But he couldn't understand why man is sometimes weak and helpless and sometimes so strong and powerful. But for Christianity the body and spirit are at an eternal struggle and in order to save man, defeat of the body is necessary. Christianity reduced the element of the natural being to a state of corruption and [man] has two alternatives; damnation or salvation. Death and life in the Bible to Christians is either damnation or salvation, and not natural life or death.[71]

The Bible was aware of the duality of man and the emphasis on the natural being of man. The influence was an ethical one and man has a certain unity, whereas in Christianity man is on the one hand a Divine being and on the other flesh, corrupt, evil, and the most mortal enemy of his spirit. To resolve it he must overcome the flesh—mortification of the flesh. This often leads to suicide. This, however, is prohibited because God should redeem the spirit, but in life, man should overcome the body and suppress it.

Somehow many Jewish scholars were influenced by this, but put it in terms of modification. In the fourteenth century, the *Ḥassidic* movement in Germany, Rokeaḥ, fell under the impact of medieval spirit which was full of disgust and despair, and the Inquisition led to this type of mentality.

> sin and submission are traits related to man as a spiritual-transcendental being. Man-animal can never sin nor humble himself. It is the spirit that revolts, the spirit that submits itself. Man as a biological being is incapable of either. "The spirit is in an eternal quest for self-transcendence, to exceed its own relativity and conditionality and reaches out beyond itself toward regions of absoluteness and indeterminacy."

71 In *The Emergence of Ethical Man* (p. 9) the Rav writes:

> Christianity succeeded in isolating them and reducing the element of naturalness to a state of corruption and encountering the transcendent being with an alternative: death or life, while death means transcendental forms of existence and non-existence.

Asceticism is a sign of decadence and sophistication when one becomes weary of simplicity.

Yissurim for *Ḥazal* was not self-infliction of physical punishment, but disappointment: E.g., if a man asks the waiter for a glass of hot tea and receives a glass of cold tea; or being short of change for the subway.

If there were any ascetic tendencies in Maimonides, it would be found in the *Moreh Nevukhim*, not in the *Mishneh Torah*. Asceticism is an inclination, not a philosophy, and was influenced not by Jewish thought but by a certain Arab sect of Sufism. Whatever these Jewish philosophers found acceptable in another philosophy, they assumed that it was taken from Judaism. And no doubt some of this is true, as with Plato. There is also an ascetic movement in the school of the Ari, though due to a different reason.

Lecture XIII

The Christian theologians never tried to relate the story of man with the first five days of Creation or to the wholeness of Creation. But they confined it to the story of man on the sixth day as a transcendental being and so detached him from his environment.

For Judaism, however, the story of Creation is the story of nature unrelated to any transcendental world. The *ḥakhmei ha-Kabbalah* tried to lend a mystical interpretation to Creation, but in the Pentateuch, in its simple terms this transcendentalism is not emphasized. God Who created the world is *Elokim*, a powerful king Who is in contact with His creation. The medieval philosophers and *Ḥazal* interpreted *Elokim* as being the owner behind Creation, the source of the world related to it, not only as the artisan but the source of the dynamics of Creation.[72]

---

72 The Rav writes *in The Emergence of Ethical Man* (pp. 9–10):

> The story of creation is the biography of nature. The story is not related to any transcendental world or any supernatural phenomena. On the contrary, the Creator is depicted not as transcendent God, who creates a world with which He will never come in contact (what would be a contradictio in adjecto), but as E-lokim, as the powerful being who dominates all, and who is not at an infinite distance from His creatures. There is no doubt that E-lokim bespeaks the dynamics of the world whose source is the Creator. Creation of the earth, light, water, darkness, vegetation, planets, atmosphere (sky), the sun, animals, constitute the main phases of the story. Even the elements with which the Torah begins its story are concrete natural phenomena.

True, Rambam interpreted *shamayim* as being the spiritual transcendental world, but he also admitted that in its simplest terms it was sky of the world.[73] In a word, there is no mention of a transcendental realm.

Secondly, the story expresses the idea of unity and regular systematic emergence of the world; some logical and dynamic sequence by which the world emerged. First, *shamayim ve-aretz*, the frame of the universe. Then light, the earth, vegetation, animal kingdom and, last, man. There is a clear-cut, stable order. One phase leading into the other. The first two days—inorganic matter. The third, organic, the appearance of life. Beginning with the

תַּדְשֵׁא הָאָרֶץ דֶּשֶׁא עֵשֶׂב מַזְרִיעַ זֶרַע. (בראשית א: י"א)

Let the earth bring forth grass, herbs yielding seed. (Genesis 1: 11)

The fourth—heavenly bodies
The fifth—the aquarium life and birds.
The sixth—animal, and finally man.[74]

All three reports of creation of plant, animal and man all seem identical as to the emergence of each. All have the common origin of life, viz. the earth. Moreover, man's name *Adam* bespeaks his arising while (animal) [woman] is identified by the fact of life, *ḥayah*. Man, however, is *adam me-ha-adamah*. The curse of man being condemned to death is a return to his origin.[75]

It is obvious that man as a Divine being cannot be identified with the soil that nourishes him. The Torah, however, emphasized man as an

---

73 See *Moreh Nevukhim* 2:30.

74 The Rav writes in *The Emergence of Ethical Man* (pp. 10–11):

> Secondly, the story bespeaks the idea of the unity of the created universe. The emergence of the world by the word of God is presented to us according to a certain principle of order, of a logical dynamic sequence. First Heaven and earth—the frame of the universe—then light, the emergence of the earth-globe, the coming forth of vegetative life, animal, and finally man. The Torah pursues a meaningful pattern of succession; there is no heterogeneity of a disorderly creation. Of utmost importance is the description of the creation of life.

75 The Rav writes in *The Emergence of Ethical Man* (p. 11-12):

> All three reports about creation then, of plant, animal and man are almost identical. All three, for example, take account of the common origin of life, namely the earth. All three exponents of living matter emerged out of Mother Earth. Moreover, the fact that man is named Adam bespeaks his origin. The curse of death which was imposed on man after his first sin is founded on the affinity of man with his "Mother" Earth: " . . . for dust you are, and to dust shall you return" (Gen. 3:19).

earthly creature. Primordial man, *adam ha-kadmon*, of the Bible, is a natural man.

וַיֹּאמֶר in regard to plant is used in terms of a command. In man וַיֹּאמֶר אֱלֹהִים, נַעֲשֶׂה אָדָם בְּצַלְמֵנוּ כִּדְמוּתֵנוּ (א': כ"ו), is in the sense of deliberation, but this should not disturb us (in the time being). The term ויעש is also used in other phases of creation (וַיַּעַשׂ אֱלֹהִים אֶת-חַיַּת הָאָרֶץ לְמִינָהּ (א': כ"ה although it is used in regard to animals:

The uniqueness of man is thus not in regard to terminology but only in regard to the *tzelem Elokim*.[76]

All in all man in the story of creation does not occupy a unique, ontic position but is a particle that falls into the scheme of the concrete order. Man is only the last of three stages of living matter. Science and evolution interpret man only as part of the emergence of organic matter. Christianity splits the story into two and explained man without taking into consideration animal and plant and misinterpreted Biblical philosophical anthropology.[77]

---

76 The Rav writes in *The Emergence of Ethical Man* (p. 12):

> It is obvious that man as a divine being, endowed with a transcendental image, is not one with the soil that nourishes him. Adam—man as an earthly creature—is the first man in the Bible. But man is not only identical with the universal source of life, the earth. He is also enmeshed within the entire physical environment. Let us not forget that *ruaḥ* in the Bible means "wind, breath," related to the atmosphere surrounding man. While the Bible's first chapter speaks of *tzelem E-lokim*, "image of God," the second chapter mentions "and breathed into his nostrils the breath (*ruaḥ*) of life" (v. 7). The fact that in regard to vegetative and animal the Bible uses the term *va-yomer* ("said" or "spoke") as the direct command of becoming and in regard to man the *va-yomer* is used in the sense of deliberation should not disturb us much. The same verbs (e. g., *va-ya'as, va-yivra*) are applied to plant and animal in the same manner as in reference to man.

77 The Rav writes in *The Emergence of Ethical Man* (p. 12):

> Man in the story of creation does not occupy a unique ontic position. He is, rather, a drop of the cosmos that fits into the schemata of naturalness and concreteness. The Torah presents to us a successive order of life-emergence and divides it into three phases; the last of those living structures is man. The viewpoint is very much akin to modern science. Christianity split the story of creation in two, and analyzed the story of man without taking cognizance of that of animal and plant. That is why it arrived at half-truths and misinterpreted the Biblical anthropology.

Ḥakhmei Yisrael interpreted death as part of a natural phenomenon. Maimonides says that death is not due to the "Original Sin." The Christians say that death is the direct result of the "Original Sin." However, Maimonides said that if man is biological then he must die.[78]

"For on the day that thou eat thereof thou shalt surely die." This passage should not be interpreted as a curse, but it could mean, rather, that "you are worthy of death," as with the transgression of any other halakhah that is punishable by death. ☙

78 The Rav writes in *The Emergence of Ethical Man* (p. 13):

> The relationships of Jewish scholars and Christian theologians to death will serve as a very conspicuous illustration. Jewish scholars are inclined to accept death as a natural phenomenon that is a part of the biological process (Maimonides, *Guide to the Perplexed* III:10; Ibn Ezra on Genesis 3:6; Naḥmanides, Genesis 2:17 and many statements of *Ḥazal*), while Christian theologians consider death a punishment for what they term the original sin.

A Light Unto Our Nation: R. Meir Simḥah of Dvinsk's Approach to Nationhood and Zionism in Meshekh Ḥokhmah[1]

By: JONAH STEINMETZ

I. Introduction

Biblical Commentary: A Forum for Defense and Expression of Traditional Values

Classically, biblical commentaries focus on simple understanding, homiletics, halakhah, and philosophy. A commentator may have additional goals and views of and responses to contemporary issues interwoven into the fabric of his elucidation. The interpretations and expositions may relate to the zeitgeist of the contemporary society as well as address significant issues relevant to the current social and political movements. For example, 19th century traditionalist commentators often incorporated responses to the Haskalah and Reform movements' modernization and modification of Jewish law and theology.[2] As Jay M. Harris explains, biblical exegesis has long been the "means through which rabbis established the authority of the extrabiblical laws and practices they inherited... and it was the tool they used to resolve more far-reaching problems, such as

1 Many thanks to my teacher, Dr. Joshua Karlip, and my dear friend, Rabbi Dovid Bashevkin, who both reviewed and commented on an earlier version of this article. Mrs. Leslie Newman's patient, rigorous editing helped shorten and sharpen this piece, as well. Her time and effort are very much appreciated.

2 This was a particularly popular forum, as the *maskilim* and Reformers attempted to sever "any connection between Jewish law and theology, on the one hand, and Jewish exegesis, whether halakhic or aggadic, on the other." See Jay M. Harris, *How Do We Know This? Midrash and the Fragmentation of Modern Judaism* (NY: SUNY, 1994), p. 138. In context, Harris describes the second of two strategies Israel ben Moshe Zamosc (a teacher of Moses Mendelssohn) promoted. Although Zamosc's role in the historical context of our discussion is not entirely direct or apparent, the words above seem reflective of the general trend he influenced.

Rabbi Jonah Steinmetz is a fellow in the Wexner Kollel Elyon at Yeshiva University and the director of Asicha Seminars, a learning program for post-seminary women.

contradictions within the Torah, or between the Torah and other biblical books."[3]

R. Yehuda Cooperman asserts, however, that R. Meir Simḥah ha-Kohen of Dvinsk's biblical commentary, *Meshekh Ḥokhmah*, differed from those of earlier traditionalist advocates.[4] R. Cooperman contends that the context in which R. Meir Simḥah lived did not demand his engagement in polemic against ideological oppositions.[5] His composition, *Meshekh Ḥokhmah*, in no way served as an attack against or response to contemporary issues. Rather, he dealt exclusively with interpretation and explanation of the verses themselves.

It is my contention, however, that *Meshekh Ḥokhmah* was R. Meir Simḥah's platform to—not *only*, but *also*—consider, critique, and combat what he perceived as anti-Torah values permeating his historical and geographical context. R. Meir Simḥah utilized his biblical commentary as the forum for dissemination of ideals and ideologies countering the opposing views of his surrounding society.[6] There are many examples that establish this fact.[7]

The goal of this essay is to note and investigate examples of R. Meir Simḥah's conception of Eretz Yisrael and his responses to Nationalism, Zionism, and anti-Zionism in the period in which he wrote. A clear sense of R. Meir Simḥah's ideological and political positions in relation to these movements is gleaned from an analysis of *derashot* in *Meshekh Ḥokhmah*. Comparing and contrasting his responses with the ideologies and policies of other leading figures in his geographic and intellectual circle yields a fuller picture of R. Meir Simḥah's approach to Eretz Yisrael as a land and

---

3 Ibid., p. 3. Both Harris and R. Yehuda Cooperman list R. Jacob Zvi Meklenburg and R. Meir Leibush Malbim, among others, as leading traditionalist figures who fought the Haskalah and Reform through their biblical commentaries. See Harris, pp. 211-223 and R. Yehuda Cooperman, *Pirkei Mavo le-Feirush "Meshekh Ḥokhmah" la-Torah*, p. 1. Other noteworthy leaders, R. Samson Raphael Hirsch and R. David Zvi Hoffman, are equally significant, but beyond the scope of this essay. Harris treats these two figures, among still others, in his chapter titled "Midrash and Orthodoxy."

4 See R. Cooperman, *Pirkei Mavo le-Feirush Meshekh Ḥokhmah*, p. 1. Cooperman associates this style with the "school of thought of the Gaon, R. Elijah of Vilna."

5 R. Cooperman, ibid. See also Yaakov Elman, "The Rebirth of Omnisignificant Biblical Exegesis in the Nineteenth and Twentieth Centuries," *JSIJ* 2 (2003) 199-249, p. 219, for a clear, concise summary of R. Cooperman's thesis.

6 Elman (p. 222) makes a similar argument against R. Cooperman's thesis as well.

7 A closer analysis of this statement will, please God, be published by this author in the future. However, space constraints exclude that analysis here.

as a value. Ultimately, scrutinizing these passages in *Meshekh Ḥokhmah* allows for a better understanding of R. Meir Simḥah's loyalty to, but lack of affiliation with, political parties such as Agudath Israel and Mizraḥi.

II. The Time and Place of *Meshekh Ḥokhmah*

Analyzing the thematic responses to contemporary issues found in *Meshekh Ḥokhmah* demands a note on the time and place in which it was composed. Actually, "the times and places in which it was composed" is a more accurate formulation. A brief biographical timeline provides for contextualization of *Meshekh Ḥokhmah*'s composition.

R. Meir Simḥah was born in 1843 (5603)[8] in Butrimonys (Baltrimantz, in Yiddish), a small town in southern Lithuania. A child prodigy, he spent his first decade learning with his father and mastering vast amounts of biblical and talmudic literature.[9] In 1856, his father brought him to Eishishok, a city bordering Belorussia in southeastern Lithuania, famous for its dense Jewish population. There, R. Meir Simḥah studied in the *Kollel Perushim* for three years under the guidance of a distinguished older student, R. Moshe Denishevsky. In 1859, he married Ḥaya Makovski and moved to her hometown of Bialystok, Poland.[10] Ḥaya operated a business, assuming the family's financial responsibility while her husband studied in the local *beit midrash* for twenty-six years.[11] R. Meir Simḥah arrived in

---

8 Although there are contradictory records as to the exact year, this seems to be the most accurate report. See Yaakov M. Rapoport, *The Light from Dvinsk: Rav Meir Simcha, The Ohr Somayach* (Southfield: Targum Press, 1990), p. 18; R. Zev Aryeh Rabiner, *Maran Rabeinu Meir Simḥah ha-Kohen* (Hebrew), pp. 22 and 232; R. Noson Kamenetsky, *Making of a Godol: A Study of Episodes in the Lives of Great Torah Personalities* (Jerusalem: Hamesorah Publishers, 2002), p. 420, note *n*.

9 R. Meir Simḥah periodically quotes his father in his work. See *Meshekh Ḥokhmah*, *Shemot* 3:15-17; *Va-Yikra* 18:27.

10 The date and age of marriage are recorded by Rapoport, p. 27 and corroborated by the Bialystok ledger (*pinkas*), referenced in Rabiner, p. 22, footnote.

11 There are conflicting reports on this. See Rabiner, p. 22 (footnote), quoting the Bialystok ledger (p. 283). See also Rapoport, p. 29. In studying his responsa, one notices that R. Meir Simḥah was still writing from Bialystok as late as 1886-7 (5647) and began writing from Dvinsk in 1887-8 (the year he assumed his rabbinic post there). We have no record of R. Meir Simḥah taking a professional position during his time in Bialystok, thus it is safe to assume that he spent all twenty-six years learning in the *beit midrash*.

Dvinsk (then Dunaburg, currently Daugavpils), a large city in southeastern Latvia with a significant Jewish population[12] in the spring of 1888 (5648). There, he assumed the rabbinical post which he would hold for the next four decades. R. Meir Simḥah died on the fourth of Elul, 1926 (5686).

It is well known that R. Meir Simḥah composed the manuscript for *Meshekh Ḥokhmah* before engaging in concrete work on his *Ohr Sameaḥ*.[13] Based on anecdotal evidence, the majority—if not all—of *Meshekh Ḥokhmah* was composed by R. Meir Simḥah during his early years in Bialystok. But if R. Meir Simḥah spent his days and nights in the *beit midrash* studying Torah, it is hard to imagine he had any political awareness or involvement in those years. A lack of cognizance of and connection to socio-political surroundings makes it challenging to write a book responding to contemporary issues. Research, however, shows he was, in fact, keenly aware of and involved in the world outside of the *beit midrash*, even during his time in Bialystok.

Some of R. Meir Simḥah's published responsa were composed while he resided in Bialystok. Although only a small number of published responsa are from this period, the fact that he was consulted and the severity of the issues about which he was consulted are both noteworthy.[14] Alt-

---

12 The 1897 census reported that 757,038 Jews resided in the greater Lithuanian territories. Dvinsk had a total population of 69,675, including a Jewish population of 32,400 (44 percent). See Mordechai Zalkin, "Daugavpils," *YIVO Encyclopedia of Jews in Eastern Europe*. See also Joshua D. Zimmerman, *Poles, Jews, and the Politics of Nationality* (University of Wisconsin Press, 2004), p. 16, table 1.7.

13 Rabiner (p. 66) quotes R. Meir Simḥah's testimony to this. Rabiner (ibid., p. 65) and Rapoport (p. 117) report that R. Meir Simḥah held off so long on publishing *Meshekh Ḥokhmah* because his grandfather, R. Ḥananyah ha-Kohen of Vawkavysk (Yiddish: Volkovisk) warned him to first publish novellae on topics in halakhah or Talmud, lest he forever be remembered as a *darshan* (preacher) and not a *lamdan* (Talmudist).

14 Only four such responsa exist in R. Meir Simḥah ha-Kohen, *She'eilot u'Teshuvot Ohr Sameaḥ*, ed. R. Avrohom Ausband and R. Zvi Yehoshua Leitner (Jerusalem: Machon Yerushalayim, 5758/1980). See Vol. 1, No. 1; Vol. 1, No. 7; Vol. 1, No. 8; Vol. 3, No. 26. Although this is a small sampling, only a fraction of R. Meir Simḥah's written responsa have been located and published. (See "Editors' Introduction," Ausband in *She'eilot u-Teshuvot Ohr Sameaḥ* [p. 13] and "Editors' Introduction," Leitner [ibid., p. 15] regarding the discovery and publishing of the manuscripts. See also Rapoport, p. 130.) Additionally, the use of this sampling of responsa relies not on quantity, but on content. The fact that major rabbinic

hough he had never assumed any professional position, the rabbis of Europe still turned to him for guidance and halakhic decisions.[15] In this sampling of cases, he was consulted on major issues in the *Even ha-Ezer* section of *Shulḥan Arukh*, which comprises the laws of marriage and divorce, often regarded as the most severe.[16] R. Meir Simḥah responded to a question about an adulterous woman and the potential dissolution of marriage based on a husband's unbacked testimony as to his wife's infidelity.[17] He also addressed the permissibility of remarriage during a generally forbidden time period due to the life-threatening situation in which a woman and her infant child were living.[18] He fielded inquiries regarding the legitimacy of *gittin* (writs of divorce) containing nicknames, as opposed to the preferred full name of the husband.[19] In one case, R. Meir Simḥah references what he perceives as the lack of halakhic observance characterizing much of European Jewry, discarding a leniency so as not to exacerbate the problem.[20] Significantly, these responsa are addressed to rabbinic figures more active and experienced than he. In one case, R. Meir Simḥah responded to a query from R. Isaac Shur, the head of the *beit din* (rabbinical court) in Bucharest.[21] Further, during R. Meir Simḥah's time in Bialystok, the town rabbi, R. Yom Tov Lippman Halperin, passed away.[22] The large, prominent community turned to R. Meir Simḥah, unsuccessfully requesting he assume the position.[23]

The reliance of major rabbinic figures on R. Meir Simḥah for *psak halakhah* in these stringent cases is telling not only of his erudition, but of his ability to assess situations and controversies beyond the four walls of

---

figures relied on R. Meir Simḥah for guidance on major halakhic issues is itself telling.

15 In almost every responsum, it is clear R. Meir Simḥah is responding to rabbinic figures, not laypeople.

16 *Poskim*—from medieval to contemporary—consistently describe their nervousness to decide on matters related to marriage and divorce as being due to "*ḥumra d-eishet ish*" (the severity of [the status of] a married woman).

17 *She'eilot u-Teshuvot*, Vol. 1, No. 1.

18 Ibid., Vol. 1, No. 7.

19 Ibid., Vol. 1, No. 8.

20 Vol. 1, No. 7.

21 Bucharest, the capital of Romania, had a significant Jewish population. In addition to leading the rabbinical court, R. Shur authored more than a dozen books on halakhah and other topics.

22 Halperin is most famous for his work *She'eilot u-Teshuvot Oneg Yom Tov*, which has a unique style consisting of a combination of halakhah and *pilpul*. He died in 1879.

23 Rapoport, p. 50.

the study hall. It is also difficult to imagine such a distinguished rabbinical post being offered to a socially ignorant recluse. R. Meir Simḥah clearly had exposure to society, making him a significant source of guidance on halakhic matters and a suitable candidate for a prestigious rabbinic post.

Further evidence of R. Meir Simḥah's societal awareness and activity surfaces in the record of his involvement in a famous political episode involving R. Yehoshua Leib Diskin, the rabbi of Brisk. In 1876, Russian authorities arrested R. Diskin, threatening him with a lengthy prison sentence and potential exile to Siberia.[24] R. Yosef Dov Soloveitchik took charge of a major rabbinical effort to obtain a reprieve for R. Diskin. He raised large sums of money for lawyers and bribes and formed a committee of rabbis and political activists devoted to freeing R. Diskin. R. Soloveitchik called upon a young R. Meir Simḥah—still quietly studying in Bialystok—to join the coalition, travel to Grodno, and partake in the rescue efforts.[25] R. Meir Simḥah acquiesced, joining an impressive group of older, established rabbis, including Rabbis Soloveitchik, Eliyahu Ḥayyim Meizel of Lodz, Abraham Shmuel of Plonsk, Yitzḥak Yeruḥum Diskin, and others. R. Diskin was ultimately released as a direct result of this organized rabbinic effort. The fact that R. Soloveitchik requested R. Meir Simḥah's assistance in these efforts shows that the latter was considered a capable, effective force. A certain social and political aptness is undoubtedly one of the requisite qualifications of an activist in such a mission. Given this diverse evidence of his social and political awareness, it is no surprise that R. Meir Simḥah's *Meshekh Ḥokhmah* contains reference to and commentary on contemporary issues.[26]

Although it has been noted that *Meshekh Ḥokhmah* was composed during his younger years in Bialystok, it seems that the author either continued to add to his earlier composition, or at least returned to consult and edit it until well into his second project, *Ohr Sameaḥ*. First, it has been

---

24 For the full story, see Rapoport (pp. 33-38); see also Shalom Meir ben Mordekhai Valakh, *Ha-Seraf mi-Brisk: Toldot Ḥayav u-Fo'olo Shel ha-Gaon* etc. (Bnei Brak: Hotsa'at Tevunah, 1998 or 1999), pp. 216-252 (or the English version: Wallach, *Seraph of Brisk*, pp. 328-464); see also R. Ḥayyim Karlinsky, *Rishon l'Shoshelet Brisk* (Jerusalem: Machon Yerushalayim, 5764), pp. 267-275.

25 During this episode, R. Meir Simḥah and R. Soloveitchik developed a close relationship, ultimately contributing to the former's attainment of the rabbinic post in Dvinsk. (See Rapoport, pp. 48-9.)

26 See, for example, *Meshekh Ḥokhmah, Shemot* 12:1; 12:27; 14:24; *Va-Yikra* 19:18; 19:32; *Devarim* 10:20; *Devarim* 30:20; *Megillat Esther* 9:24.

noted that R. Meir Simḥah would frequently reference his biblical commentary during his sermons in Dvinsk.[27] Further, *Meshekh Ḥokhmah* contains many explicit references to *Ohr Sameaḥ*, including the exact location of specific passages.[28] In one place, R. Meir Simḥah references events which occurred in the year 5677 (1917/1918), the last decade of his life.[29] It is clear, then, that R. Meir Simḥah consulted and edited the manuscript of *Meshekh Ḥokhmah* regularly during the many years until its posthumous publication. This point is significant, because if one knows that *Meshekh Ḥokhmah* was composed and edited during two different times and in two different places, one can analyze its messages as responses to both settings' respective zeitgeists. As such, any given piece in *Meshekh Ḥokhmah* may have been written in either Bialystok or Dvinsk and is thus viewed considering the socio-political contexts of each.[30]

27 Rabiner, p. 66.

28 See, for example: *Meshekh Ḥokhmah, Shemot* 4:19; ibid., 19:17; ibid., 20:13; ibid., 21:14; ibid., 21:19; ibid., 22:16; ibid., 29:42; ibid., *Haftarat Parshat Tetzaveh*; *Va-Yikra* 2:14; ibid., 6:20; ibid., 15:13; ibid., 18:10; ibid., 19:16; ibid., 20:12; *Be-Midbar* 6:9; ibid., 9:7; ibid., 38:28; *Devarim* 16:5; ibid., 17:1; ibid., 17:5; ibid., 22:2; ibid., 25:14.

29 See *Meshekh Ḥokhmah, Haftarat Shabbat ha-Gadol* 3:17.

30 It is unnecessary to prove that R. Meir Simḥah was aware of and involved in socio-political issues as rabbi of Dvinsk. There are, however, many specific examples of R. Meir Simḥah's involvement in such issues. He participated in the early stages of Agudath Israel, taking strong stances on issues like the propriety of rabbis learning the Russian language at the convention in St. Petersburg. The majority of his responsa are from his time as rabbi of Dvinsk. He was approached for advice on many sensitive decisions including the possibility of moving the Slabodka Yeshiva to Palestine (see Kamenetsky, *Godol*, p. 418; see also Shlomo Tikochinski, *Lamdanut, Mussar, v-Elitism: Yeshivat Slabodka m-Lita l-Eretz Yisrael* [Jerusalem: Shazar, 2016], p. 215) and dealing with controversial statements of R. Abraham Isaac ha-Kohen Kook (see Shlomo Zalman Sonnenfeld, *Ha-Ish al ha-Ḥomah* [Heb.], Vol. 3, p. 408). Reportedly, he also took a stance against the *Mussar* movement, in a conversation with R. Simḥah Zissel Ziv (see R. Shmuel David Wolkin, *Kitvei Aba Mori*, ed. Moshe Yoel Wolkin [Brooklyn: Moriah, 1982], p. 265). Some claim that R. Meir Simḥah was consulted regarding whether to close the Volozhin Yeshiva (see Shulamith Soloveitchik Meiselman, *The Soloveitchik Heritage: A Daughter's Memoir* [Hoboken: KTAV, 1995], p. 72; see also R. Hershel Schachter, *Divrei ha-Rav* [NY: OU Press, 2010], p. 215). As confirmed by Dr. Shaul Stampfer (in an email correspondence), there is no historical proof to this claim, and it is likely being confused with the convention in St. Petersburg (see also Schachter, ibid., note 33). Each of these episodes requires its own study.

III. Nationalism and Zionism in Bialystok and Dvinsk

If 19th century Eastern Europe, characterized by political instability and constant cultural fluctuation, was like a turbulent ocean, then Eastern European Jewry was like a ship in stormy seas. Virulent anti-Semitism was rampant, contributing to both the volatility of the current Jewish situation as well as the danger to its future. Jonathan Frankel suggests that it was these main factors combined with "population explosion, chronic underemployment (and unemployment), poverty... and governmental harassment" that created the "crisis of Russian Jewry in the period of 1881-1917."[31] The strongest organized Jewish political reaction to this crisis was a sharp turn to nationalism and socialism.[32] Nationalist trends were sweeping through Eastern Europe in this period, and many prominent figures, particularly from the Russian-Jewish intelligentsia, were swept away by them.

> The sudden and drastic reversal in attitudes that marked the emergence of the new ethos was summed up brilliantly by Lev Pinsker in 1882 with his slogan, "self-emancipation." Contained in this term was the conviction that the Jewish question could not—and would not—be solved by the grant of equal rights from above nor by a return to the status quo ante of traditional Judaism, but had to be won by total change, collective action, political planning, and organization. With liberalism and individualism pronounced a failure, the radical and collectivist ideologies—nationalism and socialism—naturally came into their own.[33]

The general nationalist ideologies to which so many secular Jews suddenly subscribed had certain widely accepted features, but also broke off into multiple subgroups.[34]

---

31 Jonathan Frankel, *Prophecy and Politics: Socialism, Nationalism, and the Russian Jews, 1862-1917* (Cambridge University Press, 1981), p. 1.

32 According to Ehud Luz, the crisis of Russian Jewry was but a catalyst. It was "the crisis of Jewish identity" which "was the decisive factor in the birth of modern Jewish nationalism." Ehud Luz, *Parallels Meet: Religion and Nationalism in the Early Zionist Movement, 1882-1904* (JPS, 1988), p. 23.

33 Frankel, ibid., p. 2.

34 It is beyond the scope of this essay to carefully analyze the defining characteristics of the various factions of Jewish nationalism. For excellent research devoted to this end, see Simon Rabinovitch, *Jewish Rights, National Rites: National Autonomy in Late Imperial and Revolutionary Russia* (Stanford University Press, 2014) p. 50. See also Joshua M. Karlip, *The Tragedy of a Generation: The Rise and Fall of Jewish Nationalism in Eastern Europe* (Harvard University Press, 2013), pp. 5-6.

Although "the relationship of Zionism to Diaspora nationalism has proven far more complicated than once imagined,"[35] it is abundantly clear that there is a deep connection between the two movements.[36] This is evidenced by the fact that Leon Pinsker, an original nationalist, was selected as the first head of the Ḥovevei Ẓion movement in 1884. Zionism itself splits into multiple subgroups, most of which are subsumed under the branches of secular Zionism and religious Zionism, but the general Zionist ideology draws heavily from nationalist philosophies and motivations.

From the earliest years of nationalism and Zionism, Latgalia—one of three major Russian provinces making up the region of Latvia[37]—was a hotbed of pre-Zionist and Zionist activity. Within that area, "the most prominent activity of pre-Zionists was in Dinaburg-Dvinsk (now Daugavpils), which was considered to be one of the movement centers in Russia."[38] Critical nationalist-Zionist organizations, including Ḥovevei Zion, had been founded in Dvinsk in the 1880s.[39] During this time, the committees in Dvinsk organized lectures on history and philosophy which, in large part, included discussions of nationalist and Zionist ideologies. "Lecturers tried to arouse in the audience love [of] the national culture, religion, and language of the forefathers."[40] In his 1948 book, *Years of Life*, writer and Dvinsk native Aleksander Isbakh (pseudonym of Isaak Bakhrakh) reports that the "Zionist organization was very influential among the Jews of our town."[41] Of course, Zionism is but one example of nationalist movements that swept through Eastern Europe in these years.

Bialystok was no stranger to nationalist and Zionist movements. Aside from containing its fair share of Jewish socialists and Bundists, Bialystok served as the center for the young Ḥibbat Ẓion movement. In fact,

---

35 Karlip, p. 8.

36 See, for example, Yosef Salmon, "The Historical Imagination of Jacob Katz: On the Origins of Jewish Nationalism," *Jewish Social Studies, New Series*, Vol. 5, No. 3 (Spring-Summer, 1999), p. 161.

37 See Dov Levin, "Latvia," *YIVO Encyclopedia of Jews in Eastern Europe,* 26 August 2010.

38 Boris Volkovich, "Zionist Movement in Latgale (till 1917)," *Comparative Studies Vol. II (1): Latgale as a Culture Borderzone* (Daugavpils: Daugavpils University Academic Press "Saule," 2009), p. 55.

39 Ibid., p. 56.

40 Ibid., p. 57.

41 Ibid., p. 63. See also Benjamin Pinkus, *The Soviet Government and the Jews: A Documented Study* (Cambridge University Press, 1984), p. 176.

the chief rabbi of Bialystok, R. Samuel Mohilever (1824-1898) was especially active in founding the Ḥibbat Ẓion movement, eventually becoming a central leader of the organization.[42]

Given the strong nationalist and Zionist trends in late 19th and early 20th centuries Dvinsk and Bialystok, it is no surprise that R. Meir Simḥah was intimately familiar with the ideologies, arguments, and plans of these movements.[43] His brilliance and societal awareness combined with his being deeply steeped in all Jewish literature made him eminently capable of developing and expressing his nuanced approach to the questions of Jewish nationhood and Zionism.

IV. R. Meir Simḥah's Approach to Jewish Nationhood and Nationalism

Nationhood and nationalism are not inherently secular concepts. The concept of a nation is Jewish—in some ways it is uniquely Jewish—and it is a topic of discussion amongst many religious Jewish thinkers.[44] The popular nationalistic ideology that permeated secular Jewish culture during this period, however, was inherently unorthodox. Nationalism was a natural transition from the Haskalah movement.[45] Jewish nationalism went even further, however, in disregarding the premier place of Torah observance in Judaism. The famed maskilic intellectual journalist Perets Smolenskin argued that "national feeling, more than religious institutions, constitutes the most important force for preserving the unity of the Jewish people."[46] Smolenskin stated further that "the national covenant is the main thing, and religion can only strengthen this covenant."[47] Smolenskin, along with many Eastern European Jewish nationalists, viewed religion as a means to the end of preserving Jewish nationhood. It would follow that if religious observance should ever pose a threat or even an inconvenience

---

42 See Luz, *Parallels*, p. 14. See also Yosef Salmon, "*Ha-Rav Shmuel Mohilever: Rabam Shel Ḥovevei Zion,*" *Zion* (Historical Society of Israel, 1991) (Heb.), pp. 47-78.

43 In fact, we see a record of his personal interaction with R. Mohilever in Elyakim Getsel, *Ramat Shemuel* (Vilna: 1899), p. 22.

44 In many cases, these thinkers discuss and debate foundational concepts of nationhood, including when and how the Jewish nation came into being. See, for example, R. Hershel Schachter, *Eretz ha-Zvi* (Brooklyn: Flatbush Beth Hamedrosh, 1992), ch. 17 for a collection of halakhic and philosophic literature on this topic.

45 See Immanuel Etkes, "Haskalah," *YIVO Encyclopedia of Jews in Eastern Europe*, 27 October 2010.

46 See Luz, *Parallels*, p. 21.

47 Ibid.

to the realization and maintenance of national unity, religion should be sacrificed for the ultimate goal of nationalism.

The concepts of nationhood and national unity are constant and consistent themes in *Meshekh Ḥokhmah*. R. Meir Simḥah regularly refers to the Jewish nation as singular and separate from the other nations of the world.[48] R. Meir Simḥah also repeatedly stresses the centrality of nationhood and national unity. R. Meir Simḥah is clear in holding nationhood as a necessary means to the goal of unification of God's name in the world.[49] In fact, he claims that most commandments found in the Torah are aimed at the goal of national unity. In explaining the reason for the tribes of Israel being represented on the Priest's breastplate, R. Meir Simḥah writes,

> But on the heart, the source of all feelings, the nation of Israel is inscribed, to teach that one's feelings should be directed towards the commandments, of which the majority are [a means to] the unification of the nation; like the [building of the] Temple, ascension to Jerusalem during the holidays...tithes...because this is [all for] unification of the nation...[50]

R. Meir Simḥah regularly describes the unity of the Jewish people as a single organism made up of various limbs and organs that are the individual members of the nation.[51]

The assertion of secular nationalists that this significant aspect of Judaism reigns supreme, however, is disputed aggressively by R. Meir Simḥah. The thought that preservation of national unity would trump the observance of God's commandments is ludicrous to any Orthodox rabbi,[52] and R. Meir Simḥah argues that the Torah and its observance are the very source of Jewish nationhood.

> There is no [true] concept of community for gentiles, because each gentile is independent. And the connection of the Jewish people is

---

48 *Meshekh Ḥokhmah, Bereishit* 33:18; *Shemot* 6:6; *Haftarat Parshat Be-Midbar; Shemot* 6:6.

49 *Meshekh Ḥokhmah, Va-Yikra* 18:4-5.

50 Ibid., *Shemot* 12:21. This is a theme that repeats itself in *Meshekh Ḥokhmah.* I hope to produce a study on this in the future.

51 See, for example, *Meshekh Ḥokhmah, Shemot* 19:8; *Haftarat Parshat Devarim*; *Devarim* 4:29; ibid., 14:3; ibid., 29:9; ibid., 34:8.

52 See R. Dr. Leo Levi, *Facing Current Challenges: Essays on Judaism* (Brooklyn: Hemed Books, 1998), p. 7, where this is explained in a succinct yet poignant manner. Levi is writing at the end of the 20th century; the context is quite different, but the sentiment is the same.

> their birth and their unification to [the ends of] believing in one Lord and their collective guarantee and their bond one to the other within Torah and its commandments, as each one [of them] is completed by his friend through Torah.[53]
> Indeed, [in the case of] all other nations, their connection to one another is a civil, nationalistic matter which stems from their birth into the nation, their dwelling in the same land, and their shared ideologies. Not so is the potion of Jacob [i.e., the Jewish nation]. The national connection is so great because the Torah was given to the nation, and according to the decisions of its sages and great [leaders], so are the ways of God and His providence continued.[54]

The very bond of the Jewish people exists only within the context of Torah commandments. Jewish nationhood, says R. Meir Simḥah, is not a form of pragmatic unification of individuals with common ideologies and ancestries and a shared concept of society and ethics. It is not simply a genetic or geographic coincidence that the Jewish nation exists. Jewish nationhood is founded solely upon Torah values, as per the divine will.[55] In one place, R. Meir Simḥah even suggests that if the Jewish people "forget the covenant of their forefathers and do not walk in their ways" they will have essentially dismissed their status as an ancient nation, dissolving their nationhood and forfeiting the benefit of the divine presence resting upon them.[56]

While R. Meir Simḥah stresses the significance of the concept of Jewish nationhood and national unity, he repeatedly clarifies that such ideologies are meaningless when divorced from Torah observance. The notion of Jewish nationhood is a product of God's Torah, and its preservation is predicated on unflagging commitment to its commandments.

V. R. Meir Simḥah's Approach to Eretz Yisrael and Zionism

Love of Eretz Yisrael

The fact that R. Meir Simḥah opposed secular Zionism need not be proven. His feelings about the Land of Israel notwithstanding, no movement divorced of commitment to Torah could elicit any respect or approval from him.[57] This section will analyze R. Meir Simḥah's approach

53 Ibid., *Be-Midbar* 15:13-14.

54 Ibid., *Va-Yikra* 23:21.

55 See also ibid., *Shemot* 12:14 and *Va-Yikra* 18:4-5.

56 *Bereishit* 46:2.

57 Although, in contrast to many other Orthodox rabbis of his time, R. Meir Simḥah did not lash out against secular Zionists. In fact, he was described as

to Zionism overall, with specific focus on his reaction to religious Zionism and the Mizraḥi movement.

R. Meir Simḥah's feelings towards Zionism have long been clouded in ambiguity. This ambiguity is perhaps best summarized by R. Isaac Nissenbaum in recording his visit to Dvinsk. R. Nissenbaum writes,

> I asked the Zionists how the rabbis of Dvinsk relate to Zionism. Are they with us or against us? I heard the following answer: "R. Meir Simḥah quibbles about this from time to time, but we cannot discern his true opinion. Anyway, he certainly does not oppose [us]."[58]

R. Meir Simḥah was not shy about his love and longing for the Land of Israel. He was always eager to hear reports from those who travelled to Palestine and were witnesses to or participants in its settlement.[59] On more than one occasion, he expressed his deep yearning for the land in writing. Rabiner notes that R. Meir Simḥah would regularly sign his letters with poetic pining for redemption and return to the Land of Israel.[60] When R. Yisrael Abba Citron eulogized his teacher, R. Meir Simḥah, he described him as a "*ḥovev Ẓion amiti*" ("true lover of Zion").[61]

In 1917, the Balfour Declaration was passed, stating Great Britain's support of "the establishment in Palestine of a national home for the Jewish people." The reactions to this proclamation varied based on political and religious affiliation.[62] In Dvinsk, the Jews celebrated, gathering in a local synagogue for special ceremonies. They invited R. Meir Simḥah to attend the events, but many were uncertain that he would. When he received the invitation, R. Meir Simḥah replied that he would attend "without any hesitation or doubt whatsoever." He continued to say that he did not care in the least bit that "some people will not be pleased with this

---

"tolerant" of them (see note below). See also Rabiner (p. 161 and p. 165). See also Rapoport (pp. 106-7). For an example of the contrasting approach of Orthodox rabbis, see Luz, *Parallels*, pp. 48-9, 51, 214.; see also Shimon Yosef Meller, *Uvdot v'Hanhagot l'Beit Brisk*, Vol. 4, pp. 187-211.

58 R. Isaac Nissenbaum, *Alei Ḥeldi* (Jerusalem, 1968), Ch. 17. See also *Ḥidushei R. Citron* where, in his eulogy for R. Meir Simḥah, R. Citron says, "Even though [R. Meir Simḥah] was concerned that Zionism should not turn into messianism, he was satisfied to simply stand apart from, but not fight against it."

59 Rabiner, p. 161.

60 P. 165.

61 *Ḥidushei R. Citron*, p. 572.

62 See Yitzhak Krauss, "*Ha-Tigboret ha-Teologit al Hazharat Balfour,*" Bar Ilan, Vol. 28-9 (5761), pp. 81-104; and Isaiah Friedman, "The Response to the Balfour Declaration," *Jewish Social Studies*, Vol. 35, No. 2 (Apr., 1973), pp. 105-124.

[decision]."[63] In 1921, Menahem Mendel Finkelman, an emissary of the World Zionist Organization, visited Dvinsk. Finkelman requested that R. Meir Simḥah publish an official letter encouraging Jews of Latvia to donate to Keren ha-Yesod, the main organization involved in the settlement of Palestine.[64] R. Meir Simḥah agreed to write a letter, penning what would become his famous published remarks about the Balfour Declaration and his attitude towards settlement of Palestine.[65]

> ... From the day our holy Torah was given, prophecy has never ceased to command us to settle the land [of Israel]. There is no section in the Torah which bears no mention of the Land of Israel... From the day that Zion and Jerusalem were singled out, David in his praises [i.e., Psalms], Isaiah in his visions, Jeremiah in his rebukes, and Ezekiel in his parables never ceased to stress the commandment of settling the land... So too in the Grace after Meals, we pray for the land and Jerusalem... Indeed, in this century, rays of light have shone through the efforts of activists... but many rabbis have opposed it... However, providence has intervened, and at a conference... it was decreed that the Land of Israel will be [given] to the nation of Israel... [And so,] the command to settle the Land of Israel which is as weighty as all the Torah commandments [combined] has returned to its place. It is [therefore] incumbent upon each person to support, to the extent that he can, the fulfillment of this command.
>
> The words of the one who awaits seeing the salvation of Israel,
> Meir Simḥah Kohen[66]

In another letter, R. Meir Simḥah notes that it is "simply superfluous" to express the significance of the command to settle the Land of Israel.

---

63 Rabiner (p. 160); Rapoport (pp. 105-6).

64 See Rabiner (p. 162) and Rapoport (pp. 101-2).

65 Although the letter was written in the context of an appeal on behalf of Keren ha-Yesod, R. Meir Simḥah's letter deals exclusively with feelings towards and support of settling Palestine, without any explicit mention of Keren ha-Yesod or any Zionist organization. This important observation was also made by Eitam Henkin (see Eitam Henkin, "*Yaḥaso shel ha-Ray"h Kook l-Keren ha-Yesod*," *Ha-Maayan*, Vol. 51, No. 4 (2011), pp. 75-90 (Heb.).

66 This letter was first published in *Ha-Tor*, Vol. 3 (1922). It has subsequently been published in Rabiner, pp. 163-5; R. Menahem Mendel Kasher, *Ha-Tekufah ha-Gedolah* (Jerusalem, 5629), Vol. 1, pp. 206-7 (see also ibid., Vol. 2, pp. 729-30); Abraham Jacob Slucki, *Shivat Zion* (Warsaw, 5652) (in the republished edition: Jerusalem, 5745); Rapoport, pp. 102-4.

> [W]hat Jewish person would doubt this?... All the details of the Torah fit with the promise of the land [of Israel] and its settlement... And so too, our Torah is filled with praise for the Land of Israel...[67]

R. Meir Simḥah stresses the imperative to settle and dwell in the Land of Israel in various places in his *Meshekh Ḥokhmah* as well.[68]

In fact, it is this yearning for the land and its settlement that contributed to the difficulty of a major decision in his life. Over the course of his four decades in Dvinsk, R. Meir Simḥah received many requests from large Jewish communities to become their rabbinic leader.[69] Perhaps most notable is the invitation to become the Chief Rabbi of Jerusalem, which R. Meir Simḥah received in 1906. He was invited to come to Jerusalem, at R. Ḥayyim Ozer Grodzenski's suggestion.[70] R. Meir Simḥah refused this offer, but not without a heavy internal struggle. His deep, abiding love for the Land of Israel and the city of Jerusalem was no small factor in the challenge of this decision.[71]

---

67 This letter appears in R. Asher Bergman's *Ha-Ohr Sameaḥ* and was republished at the end of the R. Cooperman edition of *Meshekh Ḥokhmah*, Vol. 3. In 1889, religious Zionists—particularly the Nes Ẓiyyonah society—commenced an initiative to gather approbations for religious Zionism from Orthodox rabbis. A.J. Slucki volunteered to collect and edit an anthology of these approbations. In 1892, he published this anthology under the title, *Shivat Ẓion*. See Luz, pp. 111-13. For a complete, detailed recounting of the background to this publication, see Yosef Salmon's introduction to the 1998 Dinur Center edition of *Shivat Ẓion*. R. Meir Simḥah was asked to contribute to this volume. He wrote a significant and detailed letter to Slucki, outlining the imperative to settle the Land of Israel and registering his complaints against certain movements. Slucki, however, did not publish this letter. R. Cooperman suggests that he did so because he feared "revelation of the bitter truth about the Ḥovevei Ẓion movement." The letter was later discovered and printed in *Dos Vort* (Vilna, 14 Ḥeshvan 5687) and *Kol Yisrael* (Vol. 9, 5687).

68 For example, see *Meshekh Ḥokhmah*, *Bereishit* 12:5; *Devarim* 11:31. Interestingly, in *Meshekh Ḥokhmah*, *Bereishit* 12:5, R. Meir Simḥah argues that this biblical command applied to Abraham as well, even though he well predated the giving of the Torah. This is characteristic of R. Meir Simḥah's style, as discussed by R. Cooperman in his *Pirkei Mavo*.

69 See Rabiner, p. 49 (footnote).

70 See Rabiner, p. 50. See also *Uvdot v'Hanhagot* (ibid.). See also Shlomo Zalman Sonnenfeld, *Ha-Ish al ha-Ḥomah* (Heb.), Vol. 1, p. 251, for a partial list of other rabbis who were approached at the time, including R. Isaac Blazer and R. Eliezer Gordon.

71 See Rabiner (p. 49). The community of Dvinsk was extremely opposed to losing their beloved leader. On 22 Adar, 1906, the community wrote a letter to the

The clear, public affection R. Meir Simḥah displayed for the Land of Israel and its settlement sets him apart from the camp of traditionalist anti-Zionists. Aside from his reaction to Zionism being significantly more muted than that of his contemporary religious leaders, R. Meir Simḥah rejected one of their prime arguments against Zionism and settlement of Israel. Traditionalist anti-Zionist activists, like those affiliated with Agudath Israel, relied heavily upon a literal read of an aggadic statement in the Talmud.[72] The sages delineate three oaths that are binding among Jews and gentiles, one of which is an oath that the Jewish people will not ascend to reconquer the Land of Israel by force. R. Meir Simḥah accepted this literal understanding of the Talmud. He even used his characteristic creativity to locate a scriptural reference to these oaths.[73] However, in his letter relating to the Balfour Declaration, R. Meir Simḥah proclaimed that the nations of the world now agree to our right to settle the Land of Israel, thus it is no longer a violation of the oath to do so.[74] This proclamation, along with the aforementioned textual and anecdotal evidence, shows that R. Meir Simḥah did not fit neatly into the camp of Agudath Israel's leading rabbis.

Based on this and other anecdotal evidence, some have claimed that R. Meir Simḥah embraced and supported the Mizraḥi movement wholeheartedly.[75] It is critical, however, that the distinction between love of Israel and Zionism be clarified.[76] R. Meir Simḥah's deep affection and yearning for Eretz Yisrael, concern and respect for its settlers, and excitement regarding the Balfour Declaration in no way make him a Zionist. In

---

rabbis of Jerusalem begging them to cease and desist. See Rabiner (p. 50) and Rapoport (p. 65). Rabiner claims that this is the reason that R. Meir Simḥah ultimately decided to remain in Dvinsk. See, however, *Ḥidushei ha-Rav Citron*, p. 572 (referenced in Rabiner, pp. 232-3) where R. Citron contends that he refused the Jerusalem offer due to family reasons.

72 Bavli, *Masechet Ketubot* 111a.

73 See *Meshekh Ḥokhmah, Bereishit* 50:24.

74 Compare to R. Abraham Borenstein's approach (*She'eilot u-Teshuvot Avnei Nezer, Yoreh Deah* 454:56).

75 See Rabiner (p. 158) for R. Samuel Jacob Rabinowitz's remarks to this effect.

76 For more examples of the articulation of this distinction, see Levi, *Facing Current Challenges*, p. 14; see also R. Dr. Joseph Ber Soloveitchik, *Hamesh Derashot* (Jerusalem: Mahon Tal Orot, 5734), pp. 24-5; see also R. Soloveitchik, "*Mah Dodech mi-Dod*" in *Divrei Hagut v-Haaracha* (Jerusalem: World Zionist Organization), pp. 91-2 about R. Yitzhak Zev Soloveitchik; see also R. Meir Halperin, *Ha-Gadol mi-Minsk: R. Yeruḥum Yehuda Leib Perlman, Toldotav v-Korotav* (Feldheim, 5673, 5751, 5754, republished: 1993), p. 184.

one letter, he explicitly criticizes the Ḥovevei Zion movement.[77] Along with fourteen other leading religious rabbis, he signed a strongly worded letter that opposed the establishment of *Vaad ha-Leumi*.[78] R. Meir Simḥah notably never joined the Mizraḥi movement; nor did he ever publicize his unofficial loyalty to them. As Citron described,

> He was a true lover of Zion, and [he was] tolerant of the freethinkers... [H]e felt satisfied standing apart [from Zionism] but did not fight against it.[79]

In fact, on more than one occasion, R. Meir Simḥah expressed hesitation about Zionism and doubts about the motives and actions of Zionist movements. In a eulogy delivered in honor of R. Meir Simḥah, R. Ḥayyim Zev Harash reported that

> the *Gaon* [i.e., R. Meir Simḥah] was beloved in the eyes of all. Everyone claimed him as their own. Agudath Israel says he was theirs, the Ḥasidim say he was theirs, and the "Zionists" say he was theirs. And this is the truth, because he would find positive aspects in every group. And so, he once said to me in conversation... that in every group and in every organization, there are found good aspects and evil aspects… [A] person who stands on the side, a neutral person, is able to truly know and understand the good aspects found even in the lowliest of the groups; and to find the evil aspect which exists even in the finest of the groups.[80]

His failure to officially associate with the Mizraḥi or other Zionist movements, then, cannot be viewed as a technicality. Rather, R. Meir Simḥah intentionally avoided any Zionist affiliation.

Although he never officially joined Agudath Israel either, he never objected to his selection as a member of its *Moetzet Gedolei ha-Torah* (Council of Torah Masters) and was highly apologetic about his absence at the first conference of the organization, saying

> Alas, with all the desire of my heart I chose to be a comrade to [you] God-fearing [men]... and to be counted among [those present] at the time of the gathering of the righteous. But my poor health and other

---

77 See his letter to Slucki, referenced above.

78 See R. Ḥayyim Ozer Grodzenski, *Iggerot R. Ḥayyim Ozer*, vol. 1, pp. 311-12 (no. 289).

79 *Ḥidushei R. Citron*, ibid.

80 Ḥayyim Zev Harash, *Simḥat Ḥayyim,* pp. 170-1. See also Rabiner, p. 28, where this is quoted, but the explicit references to Agudath Israel, Ḥasidism, and Zionism are omitted.

> reasons prevented me from realizing this desire... God should help you to benefit our holy religion and to promulgate knowledge of God and His Torah amongst [the people of] Israel.[81]

Given Agudath Israel's harsh stance against Mizraḥi and Zionism,[82] it is hard to imagine that a man could pledge allegiance to both.

It is as confusing as it is fascinating that both Zionist and anti-Zionist movements claimed R. Meir Simḥah as their own while fully aware of his association with the rival camp.[83] What is unmistakable, however, is that R. Meir Simḥah never wholeheartedly embraced any religious-Zionist movement. Given his unique passion for settlement of Palestine and his more liberal stance towards irreligious settlers, one wonders why he avoided such affiliation. A closer look at excerpts from *Meshekh Ḥokhmah* and other writings allows for a fuller understanding of R. Meir Simḥah's approach to Eretz Yisrael and his abstention from Zionist and religious-Zionist movements.

R. Samuel Mohilever and Ḥovevei Zion

Pre-state religious Zionism posed many theological threats to religious Judaism leaving leading rabbinic figures skeptical about the tolerability of such a movement.[84] Not the least disconcerting of the many features of Zionism and religious Zionism were their messianic undertones.[85]

---

81 Moshe Shonfeld, et. al., *Mi-Kattovitz ad Yerushalayim* (Tel Aviv: Hotzaat Netzah, 1953/4), p. 37.

82 See, for example, Gershon Bacon, "Agudas Yisroel," *YIVO Encyclopedia of Jews in Eastern Europe* (19 August 2010); see also Gershon Bacon, "Imitation, Rejection, Cooperation: Agudat Yisrael and the Zionist Movement in Interwar Poland," *The Emergence of Modern Jewish Politics: Bundism and Zionism in Eastern Europe* (University of Pittsburgh Press, 2003), pp. 85-94.

83 See, for example, Rabiner (pp. 158-9). This was not the case with other religious-Zionist figures such as R. Isaac Jacob Reines who were categorically rejected by Agudath Israel. (See Geula Bat-Yehuda, *Ish ha-Meorot* [Jerusalem: Mosad ha-Rav Kook, 1985], pp. 128-9; see also Luz, p. 229.)

84 See, for example, Aviezer Ravitzky, *Messianism, Zionism, and Jewish Religious Radicalism* (translated by Michael Swirsky and Jonathan Chipman) (Chicago: Chicago Press, 1996), p. 10.

85 A discussion of the theological issues within messianic ideology is beyond the scope of this essay. For a brief introduction, see Eli Lederhendler's contribution to Jonathan Frankel and Universitah ha-'Ivrit bi-Yerushalayim, *Studies in Contemporary Jewry: Volume VII: Jews and Messianism in the Modern Era: Metaphor and Meaning* (Institute of Contemporary Jewry, Hebrew University of Jerusalem, 1991), p. 14.

Whereas the foundational messianic idea was always linked to a passionate but passive pining for Heavenly redemption, "[r]eligious Zionism did, indeed, introduce an activist element to the idea of national redemption."[86] The best known "forerunners of Zionism," Rabbis Zvi Hirsh Kalischer and Judah Ḥai Alkalai, certainly incorporated messianic ideas.[87]

R. Samuel Mohilever, representative of many leading thinkers of the Ḥibbat Zion societies, continued this trend by utilizing messianic ideology and imagery to convey his religious-Zionist message, albeit less radically than his predecessors.[88] When the first Ḥovevei Zion societies were founded across *fin de siècle* Russia, a diverse crowd of assimilated, semi-assimilated, moderate, and observant Jews joined forces to achieve nationalist-Zionist goals. This new relationship which spanned the gamut of Judaism was emphasized by leaders like Pinsker.[89] R. Mohilever was among the many leaders who viewed this reconciliation as one of the main achievements of the fledgling movement.[90] An extreme stress on national unity can be doubly problematic for the traditional religious thinker. One of the issues in focusing heavily on national unity is that it conjures messianic images of utopian redemption. In fact, R. Mohilever drew this connection himself. Ehud Luz notes that

> Rabbi Mohilever, for example, saw in it a sign of "the beginning of the redemption" (*atḥalta d'geulah*) and thought that if Ḥibbat Zion had come into existence only for that end, it had served its purpose.[91]

In referring to the national unity engendered by Ḥibbat Zion as the "*atḥalta d'geulah*," R. Mohilever explicated the link between Zionism and Messianism.[92] Elsewhere, R. Mohilever is quoted to have said,

---

86 Eliezer Don-Yehiya, "Messianism and Politics: The Ideological Transformation of Religious Zionism," *Israel Studies*, Vol. 19, No. 2, p. 241.

87 Ibid., pp. 241-2. See also Ravitzky, *Messianism*, pp. 26-32.

88 Ravitzky (p. 32) notes these overtones in R. Mohilever's thought and writing as well but claims that this approach was waning.

89 See Luz, *Parallels*, p. 31.

90 See Luz, Chapter 2 note 54, quoting M.L. Lilienblum as reporting that R. Mohilever once told him that his endeavors for Zion were "not only because of the sanctity of Eretz Yisrael," but "for the sake of national survival."

91 Ibid., p. 47.

92 This is not to say that the term "*atḥalta d'geulah*" is inherently irreligious or even radically messianic. Major leaders of the traditional Orthodox school of thought have entertained or even accepted such a notion. For an example of the former, see Ravitzky's (pp. 1-3) discussion of R. Moses Soffer. For an example of the latter, see Ravitzky's (Chapter 1, note 68) quotation from R. Naftali Zvi Yehuda Berlin.

> It is self-understood that men who have devoted all their lives to Torah and worship and know nothing beyond the walls of the House of Study, are incapable of bringing about our redemption through natural means."[93]

Aside from being a seemingly disparaging remark about his opposition and an insinuated disregard for the place of halakhists, this statement yet again refers to the religious-Zionist movement as one aimed at "bringing about our redemption through natural means."

R. Meir Simḥah explicitly and emphatically rejects the messianic philosophy which he associates with the Ḥovevei Zion movement.

> You asked me... to express my opinion regarding the new movement which came to be in our times... by the name of "Ḥovevei Zion" are they called... [F]or one who looks at the history of the Jewish people in exile with open eyes sees that at some times crazy, imaginative people arise from among our nation... and place their trust [in the idea] that the redemption is close in coming. And being that their words are [destructive] and all their acts are [ensnaring], many from the nation of God left the religion and the nation and denied the hope of the future… Behold! How terrifying is the sight of the enthusiastic [people] who go out saying: "This is the way which leads to the ultimate redemption!"[94]

R. Meir Simḥah rejects Ḥovevei Zion's messianic tone and argues that its effects can be disastrous to the Jewish people and their faith.[95] This is corroborated by Citron's report that his teacher's main concern was that "Zionism should not turn into messianism."[96] R. Meir Simḥah continues in his letter by comparing the messianic underpinnings of Ḥovevei Zion to the 17th century Sabbateanism that wreaked havoc within Judaism.[97]

As mentioned, R. Mohilever's focus on national unity as an end is doubly problematic. Aside from the messianic implications of this approach, such a philosophy implies a nationalism theoretically divorced of

---

93 See *Sefer Shemuel*, p. 154, translated by Luz in *Parallels*, Chapter 1, note 48.

94 From R. Meir Simḥah's letter to Slucki.

95 See Maimonides's "Epistle to Yemen" for a similar argument as to the destructive effects of attempting to determine the time of Messiah's arrival.

96 *Ḥidushei R. Citron*, ibid.

97 R. Meir Simḥah is not the only one to compare Zionist movements to Sabbateanism. R. Yosef Dov Soloveitchik denounced Ḥibbat Zion as a "new sect like that of Shabbetai Zvi, may the name of the wicked rot, which it is a [positive commandment] to annihilate!" See Luz, p. 116 and Ravitzky, p. 13.

religious observance. Even if unintended, such a focus opens the way to assuming national unity can trump observance.[98] According to R. Mohilever, the restoration of Jewish national unity had "decisive" weight.[99] R. Mohilever wrote,

> It is better to live in the Land of Israel, in a city whose majority are non-Jews, even though this may lead one to throw off the yoke of the Torah and commandments, than to live outside of the land in a city whose majority are Jews, even if he observes the commandments.[100]

In *Meshekh Ḥokhmah*, R. Meir Simḥah almost explicitly disputes R. Mohilever's assertion that a life in Israel devoid of Torah observance is valuable.

> ...[You] should not say that you inherited the land [of Israel] because of your righteousness and that if you sin like all other nations there will still be no more righteous nation than you; and [that God will say] "What shall I do? [Would I] switch my faithful nation with an idolatrous nation?!" This is not so!... [Rather,] if you become evil, the land will spew you out just as it spewed out the nations which preceded you.[101]

Here, R. Meir Simḥah stresses that God will only allow for Jewish inhabitance of the Land of Israel if they adhere strictly to the commandments of His Torah. Elsewhere, R. Meir Simḥah states that the miraculous blessings that the Land of Israel is to give its Jewish inhabitants will not be realized unless they are fully committed to the observance of Torah. With this, he explains a difficult sentence structure. The verse (Deuteronomy 6:3) states: "You shall hearken, O Israel, and beware to perform, so that it will be good for you... as *Hashem*, the God of your forefathers, spoke for you—a land flowing with milk and honey."[102]

> According to the rules of Hebrew language, it should have said, "in the land flowing etc." [i.e., "so that it will be good for you... in the land flowing milk and honey," as opposed to "so that it will be good for you...a land flowing with milk and honey"]. However, it is hinting that the blessing of the Land of Israel is dependent upon the choice of its children [i.e., its Jewish inhabitants]. If they listen to the voice of God, then the land will flow with milk and honey... This is what

---

98 See Luz, *Parallels*, p. 47.

99 Ibid.

100 See R. Mohilever's letter in Slucki, *Shivat Zion*. The translation above is taken from Luz, Chapter 2, note 54.

101 *Meshekh Ḥokhmah, Shemot* 3:8.

102 Translation: Artscroll's *Chamishah Chumshei Torah*, Stone Edition.

> is meant [by the words]: "to perform, so that it should be good for you..." and the land will be "as *Hashem*, the God of your forefathers, spoke for you—a land flowing with milk and honey." For if you do not listen to His voice, then the land will not flow with milk and honey.[103]

To live in the land without observing the Torah is not better than living outside the land with Torah observance. In fact, according to R. Meir Simḥah, quite the opposite is true.[104]

R. Mohilever and Ḥibbat Zion's emphasis on national unity as an end was intolerable to R. Meir Simḥah. True, R. Mohilever accepted Torah observance as generally significant, but any compromise on halakhah for the sake of nation or state is inarguably out of bounds in the thought of R. Meir Simḥah. The idea of religious nationalism as an end is rejected within the very same passages in *Meshekh Ḥokhmah* which reject secular nationalism.

R. Isaac Jacob Reines and Mizraḥi

Though prevalent in early stages of religious Zionism, the doctrine of redemption made very little impact and gained very little support among the majority of religious Jewry and its rabbinic leadership. Even the subsequent leaders of movements tied to R. Mohilever and Ḥovevei Zion steered clear of messianism, stressing motives such as Jewish unity and sanctity of the Land of Israel, while repressing any redemptive inuendo.[105] R. Isaac Jacob Reines was no stranger to messianic Zionism and the Ḥibbat Zion movement. He worked closely with Kalischer in the 1860s and

---

103 *Meshekh Ḥokhmah, Devarim* 6:3.

104 See also *Meshekh Ḥokhmah, Shemot* 15:16.

105 Ravitzky, p. 32. In fact, this departure from messianism from the mid-1880s and on was a conscious one. See Ravitzky, pp. 35-6. A more comprehensive investigation would certainly consider the writings of R. Isaac Nissenbaum. Nissenbaum served as R. Mohilever's assistant in the Ḥibbat Zion movement in the late 1800s. He was exceedingly active within the general Zionist movement throughout his lifetime, eventually emerging as one of the most talented and prolific promulgators of religious Zionism. Nissenbaum's writings are religious in nature and content and, in many ways, they correlate with those of R. Meir Simḥah. However, messianic imagery and messages are represented in his works. Many examples of this can be found in Nissenbaum's "*Ha-Yahadut ha-Leumit*" and still more are collected by Gershon C. Bacon in his "Birth Pangs of the Messiah: The Reflections of Two Polish Rabbis on their Era," in Frankel, *Studies in Contemporary Jewry*: Volume VII, pp. 86-99.

was a supporter of Ḥibbat Zion from its inception.[106] In 1902, he founded the Mizraḥi movement and became its first spiritual head. His previous intimate exposure notwithstanding, R. Reines emerged as one of the strongest critics of messianic Zionism.[107]

Scholars commonly describe R. Reines's Zionist motives and goals as pragmatic. It was the outburst of costly pogroms in 1881-1882 and the rise of European anti-Semitism that inspired R. Reines and likeminded activists to pursue radical solutions. They claimed that the only way to attain and maintain Jewish safety and continuity as a nation was to establish a Jewish-controlled state.[108] This ideology, marked by pragmatism and politicism, eventually became known as "political Zionism."[109]

The pragmatic approach of political Zionism allows for the severing of ties between religion and Zionism. Undoubtedly, R. Reines was observant and he was religiously motivated in his Zionist activism. Furthermore, he clearly conceived of a Zionism soundly set on the bedrock of religion.[110] However, about the connection between religion and Zionism, R. Reines would say, "this is my personal opinion, which I have not imposed on Mizraḥi."

R. Reines's hesitance to impose his religious views on the party left its religious nature and affiliation hazy. Due to goals decided upon at the initial conference, Mizraḥi did not officially call itself a religious-Zionist party. The bylaws highlighted a "spirit of Orthodoxy" and sympathy to the comfort of observant members, but Mizraḥi welcomed all members and decidedly left any activities unrelated to Zionism off the agenda.[111] The Mizraḥi movement was essentially neutral regarding the question of the interplay between religion and Zionism.[112] Luz notes the constant vacillation between Zionism and religion that accompanied Mizraḥi from its inception. Their failure to formulate a positive religious alternative to anti-Zionist Orthodoxy left them with the "paradoxical position that 'Zionism

---

106 Luz, p. 228.

107 Ravitzky, p. 33 and Luz, p. 236.

108 See Don-Yehiya, "Messianism and Politics," p. 242; see also Ravitzky, p. 33.

109 Don-Yehiya, p. 242 and Luz, pp. 234-5, 238.

110 See Luz, p. 247.

111 Luz, p. 230.

112 Luz (p. 239) notes that this neutrality even drew criticism from R. Abraham Isaac ha-Kohen Kook who was known to be a more tolerant religious Zionist.

has nothing to do with religion.'"[113] Mizraḥi, perhaps led by R. Reines's vagueness or passivity, had thus presented Zionism as its own dogma, essentially detaching it from religion.[114]

The separation of religion and Torah observance from Zionism—even if only theoretical—is impossible in the thought of R. Meir Simḥah. Throughout his discussions of the Land of Israel and its significance, he repeatedly proclaims that settling the land is a positive commandment.[115] This emphasis stresses the inherent connection between settling the Land of Israel and religion and frames it in the context of the will of God. The import of a Jewish nation in a Jewish land is not simply pragmatic. It is a divine imperative that motivates us to settle and build our land. The concepts of Jewish nationhood and a Jewish homeland are inextricably linked with every detail of religion.

> And the idea is that the Torah and faith are the foundation of the nation of Israel. And all things holy, including the Land of Israel, Jerusalem, etc., are [but] details and branches of Torah, and they are sanctified with the sanctity of Torah.[116]

R. Meir Simḥah dispels the notion of a pragmatic approach to Jewish nationhood and a Jewish homeland again, in a letter. A Jew's love for the Land of Israel is "unlike a Frenchman" who "loves his homeland and its capital, Paris." The latter's love is based on "a feeling of nationalism and a love of his birthplace, which is the product of humanness and manners." Jewish love of Israel, however, "shall not be founded upon nationalist feelings. Rather it is founded upon holy mountains."[117] Love of Zion is a holy love, based not on nationalist sentiment or pragmatic concern, but on total commitment to fulfillment of the will of God. A Mizraḥi which could allow for the separation of Zionism and religion was a Mizraḥi with which R. Meir Simḥah could not affiliate.

---

113 Luz, p. 235-6. See also Luz, p. 293. For more discussion regarding the tension between modernity and tradition which plagued the religious-Zionist movement, see Yosef Salmon, "Tradition and Modernity in Early Religious-Zionist Thought," *Tradition*, Vol. 18, No. 1 (Summer, 1979), pp. 79-98.

114 See Dov Schwartz, *Faith at the Crossroads: A Theological Profile of Religious Zionism* (translated by Batya Stein) (Boston: Brill, 2002), p. 22, for a source in Nissenbaum's writing to this effect. Schwartz compares this approach to R. Reines's.

115 See above, note 101.

116 *Meshekh Ḥokhmah, Shemot* 32:19. R. Meir Simḥah repeatedly stresses this point that there is no concept of inherent holiness. The holiness of every item and place is fully dependent on the fulfillment of commands linked to the item or place. See *Meshekh Ḥokhmah, Shemot* 19:13.

117 Letter to Slucki.

R. Reines's conception is problematic to R. Meir Simḥah in another aspect as well. A pragmatic Zionism essentially believes in the founding of a national homeland as a practical solution to a threat to Jewish continuity. Although Zionists certainly did set their sights on Israel as the ideal haven, the realization of their goals was not limited to that destination. Perhaps the most confusing episode in the history of Zionism was the Uganda controversy. Theodore Herzl's novel proposal to consider Jewish settlement in East Africa was presented at the Sixth Zionist Congress in 1903, commencing a bitter dispute within the general Zionist movement.[118]

One would think that a religious Zionist could never support such a proposal. Is the Land of Israel not the official Jewish homeland designated by God in His Torah? If Zionism "should be based on religion," then is not the religious imperative to settle Eretz Yisrael nonnegotiable? R. Reines's approach to this issue, therefore, is perplexing. On the one hand, we find his unequivocal affirmation of the significance of the Land of Israel as the Jewish land.

> A fundamental basis of faith is to believe in the return of the people of Israel to their land. We cannot construe a unique people that will forever be dispersed and scattered among the nations, without a land of their own.[119]

At the same time, however, R. Reines and contemporary leaders of Mizraḥi supported the Uganda plan.[120] Mizraḥi's abandonment of the concept of Eretz Yisrael as the only option for the Jewish people is surprising only if we conceive of their party as a Zionist movement based firmly in religious values. If R. Reines and Mizraḥi submit to a Zionism defined as "a pragmatic solution for the sufferings of the Jews in exile," however, it becomes understandable that they would grab the first practical opportunity to emigrate from Europe to another safe country.[121] To R. Reines, Eretz Yisrael was of value, but it was not of exclusive value.[122]

---

118 See Chapter 10 of Luz's book for more information on this controversy.

119 R. Reines, *Ohr Ḥadash al Zion Ta'ir* (translation from Schwartz, *Faith at the Crossroads*, p. 8).

120 See Yehiya-Don, p. 242; see also Luz, pp. 258-9.

121 Yehiya-Don, ibid.

122 Of course, saving Jewish lives is one of the highest Torah values. In this sense, the Uganda plan certainly had the merit of an attempt at salvation, if not a strictly Zionistic one. Herzl's opposition pegged him as a "covert Territorialist," obsessed only with the attainment of an autonomous Jewish homeland (see Luz,

R. Meir Simḥah could never align himself with an organization that could set its sights on any land other than Eretz Yisrael. He describes a longing for the land which is natural to every Jew.

> And with this, was set in the soul of his [i.e., Jacob's] sons a natural connection to desire the land of their forefathers and to consider themselves strangers [in any other land].[123]

Furthermore, abandoning the plan to settle Israel because of practical concerns constitutes a serious lack of faith, according to R. Meir Simḥah. God made it clear to Abraham that nothing would impede Jewish settlement of their land in the right time. No matter the obstacle, God promises that He will conquer the land for His nation.[124] The theoretical possibility of supporting the settlement of another land not only denies this inner yearning but downplays the intrinsic spiritual significance of Eretz Yisrael and its supremacy over all other lands. R. Meir Simḥah claims that the supreme quality of this land is as old as time itself, assuming that the entire world was created "from the holy land," and that, in this way, it is "the center of the world."[125] While he assumes that holiness does not inhere in the land, as its holiness is dependent upon faith and Torah observance,[126] R. Meir Simḥah does hold that the Land of Israel is innately primed for holiness. He describes the land as being "designated for [divine] service" already from the times of Abraham.[127] R. Meir Simḥah attributes a spike in Abraham's level of prophecy to the purging power of dwelling in the Land of Israel.[128] He maintains that the sanctity and power

p. 257). However, his motives and the motives of his supporters were understandably nuanced and complex. This article neither attempts to defend nor support the plan, only to contrast it with the outlook of R. Meir Simḥah.

123 *Meshekh Ḥokhmah*, *Va-Yikra* 26:44. See also *Meshekh Ḥokhmah*, *Devarim* 30:1. See also *Meshekh Ḥokhmah*, *Devarim* 28:4, where R. Meir Simḥah clarifies that this natural "yearning" is not for physical luxuries. Rather, it seems to be a spiritual yearning. It is anything but pragmatic.

124 *Meshekh Ḥokhmah, Bereishit* 15:1.

125 *Meshekh Ḥokhmah, Bereishit* 13:14-15.

126 *Meshekh Ḥokhmah*, *Shemot* 12:21. This is one way in which R. Meir Simḥah's conception of *kedushat ha-aretz* differs from earlier commentators. As Avinoam Rosenak notes, medieval thinkers attribute inherent holiness to the Land of Israel which, among other things, obligates a higher level of observance. See Avinoam Rosenak, *Ha-Halakhah ha-Nevuit* (*Hotza'at sefarim*: Jerusalem, 2007), pp. 150-3. I hope to elaborate on this in the future.

127 *Meshekh Ḥokhmah, Bereishit* 12:1.

128 Ibid., 12:7.

of the land exist even when it is controlled by foreign forces.[129] In many places, R. Meir Simḥah asserts that there is a significantly higher level of divine providence extant in the chosen land as well.

> Jerusalem is the place of personal [divine] providence. And that is the meaning of the verse: "God is there" (Ezekiel 48:34). He is there, and His eyes are watching it constantly. For even regarding the [entire] Land of Israel, the verse says: "[the land] which God, your Lord, seeks out constantly" (*Devarim* 11:12). Certainly [it is so, regarding] Jerusalem.[130]

Elsewhere, R. Meir Simḥah clarifies that Israel and Jerusalem are especially guided by personal providence, as opposed to all other lands which are subject to a less direct influence from God.

> And that which He will bring them to another land and does not allow them redemption in the land of Egypt; nor does He kill the Egyptians and allow them to inherit the land in their stead... So too, the Nation of Israel is worthy of meriting the treasure [that is] the place of [their source], the place in which they were conceived, and [the place which] is suited for their souls. [It is a place] which is under the providence of God alone...[131]

In fact, R. Meir Simḥah argues that the true "body" of the land is entirely spiritual. The land itself is but a physical embodiment of a sanctified, spiritual entity. With this, he explains how Abraham could acquire the land by simply gazing at it.

> "For the land which you see, to you I will give it..." Perhaps [we can explain as follows]. The act of gazing [at an object] effects an acquisition [of that object], since the object is not owned by anyone else. And the ownership [of Israel] which the Canaanites, etc., had was only an ownership of the produce [i.e., rights of usage], as Rashi explained in the beginning of *Bereishit.* The spiritual body—the holy land—was never acquired by any person. Therefore, God said that this man [i.e., Abraham] will acquire it by gazing alone...[132]

R. Meir Simḥah is unequivocal in his claims that the Land of Israel bears metaphysical significance.[133] It is inherently primed for sanctity from time immemorial and it offers opportunities for growth to otherwise

---

129 Ibid., 13:14.

130 *Meshekh Ḥokhmah, Shemot* 3:16.

131 Ibid., *Shemot* 4:3.

132 Ibid., 13:15.

133 See also *Meshekh Ḥokhmah, Devarim* 28:8.

unattainable spiritual heights. Furthermore, Eretz Yisrael and Jerusalem are subject to a uniquely personal divine providence. All these factors make the land exclusively suited for the Jewish nation.

In what serves as almost a direct rebuttal of the Uganda proposal, R. Meir Simḥah writes,

> And, if a prophet will tell them to ascend to a different land (i.e., other than the Land of Israel), then he is a false prophet. [He shall be believed] only if he prophesies that they should ascend "to the land which was promised to our forefathers," as it was with Moses our master.[134]

Escaping the Diaspora to settle the Land of Israel is not a matter of pragmatism for R. Meir Simḥah. It is a biblical imperative to be viewed in the framework of the greater body of the Torah's laws and ethics, and any compromise on this theological clause is unacceptable.

R. Reines and his conception of Zionism may have been religious, but his philosophies and actions allowed for and resulted in an abandonment of the Land of Israel. R. Meir Simḥah conceives of the Land of Israel as a spiritual, sanctified entity to which the Jewish nation belongs and for which it yearns. Thus, he could never have affiliated with Mizraḥi.

VI. Conclusion and Further Research

R. Meir Simḥah's political associations have long been ambiguous. Traditionalists and Zionists each claimed him as their own. And both did so with good reason. R. Meir Simḥah embodied many of the values fundamental to these organizations without ever officially joining either.

Here, I utilized relevant pieces in *Meshekh Ḥokhmah* in systematically noting and analyzing the various reasons that R. Meir Simḥah could not and would not affiliate with any Zionist or anti-Zionist organization. Given his nuanced and uncompromising approach to the issues at hand, association with any given party would have been tantamount to concession of his theological convictions.

Many points foundational to a comprehensive, holistic presentation of R. Meir Simḥah's approach to the Land of Israel were noted. It is my hope that the door has been opened to even broader research that yields a more pointed, complete analysis. Questions that should be answered by this research include, but are not limited to: Is there any religious-Zionist

---

134 *Meshekh Ḥokhmah, Bereishit* 50:24.

party with which R. Meir Simḥah could have affiliated? Are there any major traditionalist thinkers—before, after, or contemporaneous with R. Meir Simḥah—who shared significant common ground with him on these issues?[135] How would R. Meir Simḥah approach the contemporary world of Israeli politics with his nuanced religious and political worldview? One who attempts such research will certainly uncover significant and fascinating understandings of Israel and Zionism's place in religion as well as a deeper understanding of the uniquely captivating personality that is R. Meir Simḥah ha-Kohen of Dvinsk.

135 A comparison to the thought of R. Dr. Joseph B. Soloveitchik would be of interest. Although R. Soloveitchik eventually joined with Mizraḥi, it was not without much deliberation and inner turmoil, and it was only after being a longtime member of Agudath Israel. Furthermore, it was not the same Mizraḥi that R. Meir Simḥah avoided. One wonders where these two giants in Jewish law and philosophy agreed and disagreed.

Ignoring the Writing on the Wall: Semiology vs. Metaphysics

By: ABE HALEVY FAUR

Astronomical Miscellanea

An amateur astronomer sitting atop a Sedona, Arizona canyon aims his telescope into the moonless night sky, perusing different celestial objects, while reviewing a detailed star map. He comes across an asteroid-like object, one which had not previously been identified on NASA's asteroid list. Intrigued by this discovery, our young astronomer contacts NASA, and while they confirm that this is indeed a newly discovered object, careful calculations put the Earth directly in its trajectory, with an impact date of only a couple of weeks away. The day of impact arrives. Concern about where it will land is replaced with awe, as the object methodically slows down upon entering the atmosphere, eventually coming to a gentle landing on the Great Lawn of New York's Central Park. Scientists become increasingly intrigued when they find a pentagonal object lined with various orthographic markings on the outside, and a hollow inside. Investigations proceed immediately as to the physical and chemical composition of this object, leading to the discovery of new metallic alloys and opening the gates for advance studies in the quantum properties of these new metallic alloys. Scientists the world over are beside themselves in glee as the Periodic Table is expanded to include newly discovered elements, while universities worldwide open new courses based upon the scientific discoveries deriving from this object. Long thin probes prod its hollow inte-

---

- This article is dedicated to the loving memory of my father, Rabbi, Dr. José Faur, *zz"l*, who taught me Torah all of my life, who continues to teach me Torah after his passing through the numerous articles, books and private notes he left behind, and whose timeless wisdom allowed me to conceptualize this article.

Abe Halevy Faur, son of Rabbi Dr. José Faur, *zz"l*, is the Rabbi of Congregation Ohel David & Shelomo in Brooklyn, NY. He spends his time studying and teaching Torah in accordance with the Andalusian traditions of learning, of which Maimonides was the most prominent. His YouTube channel "Torat Andalus" contains hundreds of classes on Halakhah, Talmud, Parashah and Jewish Philosophy.

rior, revealing geometrical markings, patterns and symbols, as well as calligraphic ambigrammatic designs, all quickly explained away as the effects of corrosive forces from the long journey. Eventually, this stone, now affectionately called the "Philosopher's Stone," is placed down the block on display in the Hayden Planetarium of the NY Museum of Natural History. And so ends the attempt of an advanced alien species to communicate with the human race. The purposes of this communication, and the messages contained in the Philosopher's Stone will never be known, because 99% of all scientists derisively criticized anyone who dared suggest that the symbols were meant to be read, branding them as modern-day heretics for their unscientific thinking. The only thing that is important is that scientists determined that the markings and letters covering the exterior and interior of the Philosopher's Stone were unimportant in comparison to the far more important task of studying the material from which the stone is made. To ensure that this narrative dominates public discourse and interest, as a public service, and with a view to promote democratic ideals, Twitter, Facebook and Google all agree to shut down the accounts of dissenting voices, eventually waging a monopolistic attack on other media that dare violate democratic conventions by giving a voice to nonconventional opinions.

To Be or Not to Be—Is It Really the Question?

Metaphysics, which is the branch of philosophy that studies the essence and reality of things, seeks to answer questions about how the world is. To quote William Shakespeare in *Hamlet*, "to be or not to be, that is the question." For the Greek mind, "the world is eternal. It can have no goal; it can only be."[1] This ontological perspective focuses on the existence of things, especially (but not only) on objects and their properties. Accordingly, classical Greek philosophers (and to a great extent, today's modern scientific community) are often concerned with the nature of reality, what is really real, the composition of things, physical properties, and those universal principles that define fundamental beingness.

This metaphysical outlook is related to a particular mythological outlook, on the one hand, and an anti-text / anti-semiology perspective, on the other hand. Mythologically, the Greeks conceived of gods who had fantastic powers: the thunderbolts of Zeus, the great bow and arrows of Artemis, and the speed of Hermes. These gods all exist in the realm of

1 Kostas Papaioannou, "Nature and History in the Greek Conception of the Cosmos," *Diogenes* 25 (1959): 9, quoted in José Faur, *Golden Doves and Silver Dots: Semiotics and Textuality in Rabbinic Tradition* (Bloomington: Indiana University Press, 1986), xxii.

nature and beingness; they share a common sphere of existence with humans while, admittedly, they perform impressive feats that mere mortals cannot. Notwithstanding their powers, as pointed out by Ḥakham José Faur, "None of them, however, could either write or read: the Greek gods were illiterate. Indeed, the Muses could inspire the poets, but neither they nor the poets they inspired could express their thoughts in writing."[2] Such debility was not due to a lack of teachers or a poor education. Rather, it was intentional, and is related to the attitudes of the Greeks towards writing and reading. Specifically, for the Greeks, oral communication was the best way to deliver a message clearly and precisely, while the written text was considered to be a falsified version of the spoken word, distorting meaning. "It is *logos* and not writing that exists at the heart of democratic Athens's self-definition and the good speaker—not the writer—who keeps popular government on course."[3] Good citizens of Athens recognized "the alien character of writing, its necessary exclusion from the lives of right-minded citizens."[4] To be sure, at the political level, there was a certain ambivalence in the Greek attitude towards writing, in that equality under the law required a written legal code that was visible to the public. Thus, while writing was viewed as a tool that served democratic political objectives, a necessary evil of sorts, necessary for the publication of laws essential to establish an egalitarian society, the Greeks also recognized

> the association between writing, totalitarianism and imperialistic aggression…whereby a dominant power asserts its rights of ownership over the man and land it would possess, both at home and abroad.[5]

Hence, writing enabled totalitarianism, since despots would write laws, which were used to abuse its citizenry and suck away its wealth.

At the philosophical level, the disdain for the written text is best expressed by Socrates, who says to Phaedrus,

> even the best of writings are but a reminiscence of what we know, and that only in principles of justice and goodness and nobility taught and communicated orally… is there clearness and perfection.[6]

---

2 Faur, José. "God As a Writer: Omnipresence and the Art of Dissimulation." *Religion and Intellectual Life,* vol. 6 (1989), p. 31.

3 Steiner, Deborah Tarn. *The Tyrant's Writ* (Princeton University Press, 1994), p. 7.

4 Ibid.

5 Ibid, pp. 8–9.

6 Jowett, Benjamin. *The Dialogues of Plato in Five Volumes.* (Oxford University Press, 1982). Vol. 1, p. 278.

Ominously, Socrates warns that writing is but a reminiscence through which

> you give your disciples not truth, but only the semblance of truth; they will be hearers of many things and will have learned nothing; they will appear to be omniscient and will generally know nothing; they will be tiresome company, having the show of wisdom without the reality.[7]

As pointed out by Jorge Louis Borges (1899–1986), because of the hostile attitudes towards the written text, "Pythagoras did not leave a single written line."[8] As expressed by Plato, "books are like statues: they may seem alive, but when you ask them something, they do not reply."[9]

The Greek disdain towards the written text, being as it were an imperfect replication of truth, is an extension of their attitude towards the ontological world, searching always for *the* real objective truth, which as discussed below, is obscured by the opaque written word.

Let us understand this more deeply. In metaphysical realism, "whatever exists does so, and has the properties and relations it does, independently of deriving its existence or nature from being thought of or experienced."[10] Hence, for truths to exist, you do not need thinkers to experience them. Plato's introduction of abstract objects or ideal forms leads from metaphysical realism to mathematical realism. This further developed into ethical realism,[11] which posits an existent morality out there, existing firmly and independently of any human mind or written text.[12] Accordingly, metaphysical reality could best be apprehended by the mind, uncluttered by the lifeless words of a written composition, which stubbornly stay on the page and refuse to leave. Once the metaphysical truth is apprehended, the words serve no further purpose, and they should then disappear. Since this is only possible in speech, writing is an impediment to knowledge.

Greek antipathy towards the written word requires one to accept that the ultimate meaning of a text is grounded on authorial intent. If this is the case, once the author's intent is known, those stubborn written words serve no further purpose and actually obfuscate matters. In contrast to a

---

7 Ibid, p. 275.

8 Borges, Jorge Luis. *Seven Nights* (New York: A New Directions Book, 1984), p. 96.

9 Quoted ibid.

10 Laird Addis, Greg Jesson, Erwin Tegtmeier (eds.), *Ontology and Analysis: Essays and Recollections about Gustav Bergmann* (Walter de Gruyter, 2007), p. 107.

11 Cf. https://en.wikipedia.org/wiki/Philosophical_realism#cite_note-10.

12 Perhaps in a future study, I will examine the influence of Greek ethical realism on Jewish scholarship.

written text, oral communication is composed of words that conveniently exist just long enough for the hearer to get the message. Spoken words carry the thought of the speaker, reach the listener, thusly penetrating his mind, then quickly disappearing, they leave behind only the speaker's ideas, which have now been deposited into the mind of the listener.

The Torah View of Text as the Source of Knowledge

In contrast to the Greek philosophers and modern-day scientists, who perceive of the Universe in metaphysical terms, and who, at least in the case of the Greeks, viewed the written text as some sort of counterfeit impeding true knowledge, for the Hebrews, "meaning, signification, etc., are inseparable from text. Judaism does not recognize an a-textual problem: meaning is a function of text."[13] When the rabbis would discuss even the most abstract philosophical concepts, they would point to how such concepts derive from the text of the bible. Hence, Maimonides (1138–1204) sets forth the intellectual axioms of Judaism by relating them to specific verses in the bible. When describing the supreme level of God's existence,[14] Maimonides brings the verse, "God, our Lord is veritable!"[15] When describing God's dominion over His creations,[16] Maimonides brings the verse, "I am God your Lord!"[17] When rejecting anthropomorphism,[18] Maimonides brings numerous verses, mixed with textual analysis, to support this axiom.[19] Part I of Maimonides's *Guide to the Perplexed* contains an analysis of the semantic and lexical fields of numerous words and of corresponding verses,[20] thusly setting the groundwork for related deep philosophical discussions, indicating that even the most abstract and esoteric ideas are grounded in the written text of the bible.

Similarly, rabbinic thought is set forth in the midrash literature, in which the biblical text is an essential aspect of the various ideas under discussion. Indeed, it is usually the text that generates the ideas and not the other way around. This is because for "Judaism, writing borders on

---

13 *Golden Doves and Silver Dots*, p. xxvii.

14 *Mishneh Torah, Yesodei ha-Torah*, I, 2.

15 Jer. 10:10.

16 *Yesodei ha-Torah*, I, 3.

17 Ex 20:2.

18 *Yesodei ha-Torah*, I, 6.

19 See ibid.

20 Maimonides, R. Moses, *Dalalat al-Ha'irin.* Ed. Issachar Joel and Solomon Munk (Jerusalem, 1931). Hebrew translation: *Moreh ha-Nebukhim*, ed. and trans. R. Joseph Qafiḥ (Jerusalem: Mossad Harav Kook, 1973).

the realm of the sacred. It is not merely an instrument for memorization, it generates meaning."[21] In describing the idea of the Pentateuch being a sacred text, Borges states:

> "The idea is this: The Pentateuch, the Torah, is a sacred book. An infinite intelligence has condescended to the human task of producing a book…. In that book, nothing can be accidental. (In human writing there is always something accidental.)"[22]

Therefore, every word contains meaning, every letter must be examined for purpose, and even the crowns of the letters can insinuate numerous *halakhot*, which in turn can regulate human conduct and behavior. R. 'Akiba would "on every single crown, hang batches and batches of law." For the Western mind, the idea of any text being analyzed and scrutinized in this way, to generate new meanings—some of which then attain the status of law—appears bizarre.

It would not be an exaggeration to say that rabbinic knowledge, whether legal, political, esoteric, or historical, is almost always expressed in and through the biblical text. In fact, the Talmud and the various *Midrash Halakhah* compendia on the *Ḥumash* present detailed analyses of thousands of verses and the meanings as well as laws that are learnt from these verses. A few examples are in order. In the field of history, a Talmudic analysis of the years leading up to and following the destruction of the first commonwealth[23] provides a detailed explanation of two verses, one in Jeremiah[24] and the second in Daniel,[25] as a basis for the historical conclusions presented by the Talmudic text. In the field of political science, the Talmud alludes to the political structures and hierarchies of the nations,[26] reporting an incident between Bar Sheshakh, a Persian government minister, and Raba (c. 280–352 CE), one of the great Talmudic authorities. The discussion concludes by bringing various verses[27] that illustrate the political science lessons learnt from the reported incident. Similarly, in the field of esoterica and Jewish philosophy, Tractate *Ḥagigah* is

---

21 "God As a Writer: Omnipresence and the Art of Dissimulation," p. 34.

22 *Seven Nights*, p. 98.

23 *Megillah* 11b.

24 29:10.

25 9:2.

26 The story of Bar Sheshakh, the Persian government official, is reported in *Avodah Zarah* 65a. Cf. the outstanding political analysis of this Talmudic story in José Faur, "Of Cultural Intimidation and Other Miscellanea: Bar-Sheshakh vs. Raba," in *Review of Rabbinic Judaism*, vol 5 (2002), pp. 34–50.

27 Ps. 45:10 and Is. 64:3.

filled with the textual analysis of verses contained in the biblical text, while abstract philosophy is almost entirely absent from any such discussions.[28] In the field of Jewish law, expressing halakhah through verses is ubiquitous and is one of the primary functions of certain kinds of rabbinic literature.[29]

Based upon the above, we may conclude that while Greek ontological truths are out there ready to be discerned by the Greek philosopher, Hebrew textual truths are available to be read by any literate Jew. While the Greeks emphasize the abstract idea, the Jews emphasize the written text. The preceding is significant insomuch as it results in diametrically opposed world views: the Greek focus on ideas that need to be apprehended in a metaphysical sense, in opposition to the Hebrew study of texts that need to be interpreted, in a semiological sense.

The Ultimate Grounds of Truth

The divergent attitudes of Hebrews and Greeks towards ontology and text reflect divergent attitudes towards what is the ultimate ground of truth. For the Greeks, truth is already out there, waiting to be discovered by a logical thinking mind. The Greek word used to express truth or disclosure is *aletheia*. Let us consider this word more closely. It literally means the state of not being hidden, or of being self-evident. The semantic connotation of this word is factuality or reality. This suggests that factual reality is self-evident, and merely needs to be discovered, or revealed. Such reality exists ontologically and independently of the observer. Heidegger relates but does not equate *aletheia* with truth: "*Aletheia*, disclosure regarded as the opening of presence, is not yet truth. Is *aletheia* then less than truth? Or is it more…"?[30] For Heidegger, the presence of the truth is arguably greater than the truth being perceived. This means that truth, existing ontic-ontologically, may be superior to an ontological truth being observed and understood by an observer. Similarly, "To raise the question of *aletheia*, of disclosure as such, is not the same as raising the question of truth. For this reason, it was inadequate and misleading to call *aletheia*, in the sense of opening, truth."[31] For Heidegger, truth is much like Snow

---

28 See, especially, the Talmudic discussions contained in the second chapter of tractate *Hagigah*.

29 For example, *cf.* the *Mekhilta,* the *Sifra* and the *Sifre.*

30 Martin Heidegger, *On Time and Being* (New York: Harper and Row, 1972), p. 69, translation amended. Cited in Nikolas Kompridis, *Critique and Disclosure: Critical Theory Between Past and Future* (Boston: MIT Press, 2006), p. 189.

31 Ibid., p. 188.

White after biting the witch's poisoned apple, existing as she then does in a static state of unchanging beauty, possibly (but not necessarily) waiting for true love's kiss to awaken her.

In Talmudic thinking, the truth cannot be discovered or un-covered. Rather, it begins with a text and a text requires a reader to decode and interpret it. Hence, the reader is not a passive participant but rather "the reader acts as a writer and becomes finally the text itself: it is a creative and dynamic process."[32] The reader becomes "the text itself" in the sense that meaning is generated by the conjunction of text and reader. As the Talmud states, "At the beginning [the Torah] is called on the name of the Lord, but at the end it will be called on his [the student's] name."[33] Initially, the text of the Torah is superior to the reader/student, and for this reason, the Talmud states that those who stand up in honor of scholars who study Torah, "how much more should they stand up for the actual Torah scroll!"[34] Subsequently, after the reader/student has read the text of the Torah and generated an interpretation of the text, he then becomes greater than the Torah scroll. "How ignorant are those that stand up in honor of the Torah scroll but do not stand up for a great individual."[35] It follows, then, that for the Hebrews, truth does not exist outside the context of text. Moreover, the truth is not hidden somewhere under the words, but rather it is generated by the reader, who interprets the words by combining them together, forming new oppositions and relationships resulting in new interpretations and insights.

Impotent Reading

Aletheia and Greek metaphysics are analogous to the literary theory that says that reading a literary work based on authorial intent can result in an objective understanding of the text. What is important is that the author had a specific thing in his mind, and it is this specific thing which is transformed into words that are then laid down in a textual format. The goal of reading this text is to use its words to reach this specific thing. Hence, the words are tools used to reach the mind of the author. By uncovering the text from the intended thing, the words become marginal as one now has direct access to the author's mind. Emphasis on authorial intent implies that the author stands in a privileged position to interpret his work, since the author best knows what the intended thing is.

---

32 "God As a Writer: Omnipresence and the Art of Dissimulation," p. 34.

33 *Avodah Zarah* 19a.

34 *Kiddushin* 33b.

35 *Makkot* 22b. The source for this idea is contained in "God As a Writer: Omnipresence and the Art of Dissimulation," p. 35.

A good reader, then, would be one who tries to understand the author, precedes to read the text from the author's perspective, and thusly reveals the objective truth intended by the author. It would be instructive to consider how using authorial intent to understand a literary piece would play out: to *really* understand a literary piece, it would be helpful to learn the author's biography, language, culture, particular beliefs, etc.—in short, to get into the mind of the author—and then read the piece through the mind of the author. Only by reading the text through the mind of the author can the truth that was in the mind of the author be fully revealed. This is precisely what happens in Borges's "Pierre Menard, Author of *Don Quixote.*" The protagonist of the story, one Pierre Menard, embarks on a literary project, the goal of which is for Menard to write Cervantes's *Don Quixote* all over again. Menard's initial goal is not to merely copy *Don Quixote* but rather to write the original *Don Quixote*, by becoming Cervantes, by learning seventeenth-century Spanish, by learning what Cervantes may have learnt, all in the hope of being able to create *Don Quixote ab initio.* The project meets with limited success, in that Menard actually succeeds in writing two and a half chapters of *Don Quixote* (which are identical in every detail to Cervantes' version). However, Menard's preoccupation with authorial intent results in an impotent type of knowledge so that there can be no progress. Therefore, twentieth-century Menard ultimately succeeds in recreating the original *Don Quixote* (at least partially)—a feat accomplished more fully by Cervantes centuries earlier.

New criticism (from the Post-World War I era) argued that authorial intent is irrelevant to understanding a work of literature and was opposed to the critical practice of bringing historical or biographical data to bear on the interpretation of a literary work. Wimsatt (1907–1975) and Beardsley (1915–1985) wrote that "the design or intention of the author is neither available nor desirable as a standard for judging the success of a work of literary art."[36] Hence, the author of a literary piece cannot be reconstructed from it, and therefore, details of the author's "mind" or intent are extraneous.

Similarly, the rabbis taught that the Torah can be interpreted in a multiplicity of ways. On the verse, "seventy shekels of the shekel used in the *kodesh*,"[37] the Midrash says: "Why [seventy]? Just like the sum of wine is

---

[36] Wimsatt, William K. and Monroe C. Beardsley. "The Intentional Fallacy." *Sewanee Review*, vol. 54 (1946): 468–488. Revised and republished in *The Verbal Icon: Studies in the Meaning of Poetry* (University Press of Kentucky, 1954), 3–18.

[37] Numbers 7:13.

seventy,[38] so also the Torah has seventy faces." By comparing the Torah to wine, the rabbis meant to indicate that the same way wine ages and obtains new and subtle flavors, so also the Torah, with time, obtains new meanings and interpretations.[39] Authorial intent cannot be the correct measure of interpretation since the original wine is never as rich or developed as the aged wine. Hence, with every serious reader, the Torah becomes richer and more beautiful. *The Golden Doves*[40] quotes the following teaching of the rabbis, which bears upon the polysemic nature of the Torah:

> A single verse may unfold into many senses, but a single sense may not unfold from two verses. [Someone] from the school of R. Ismael transmitted: "[Is not my word like fire, said the Lord] and like a hammer that shatters the rock?" (Jer. 23:29). Just as each blow of a hammer strikes forth many sparks, so a single verse unfolds into many senses.[41]

For the rabbis, every Jewish reader of the Torah, acting within the perimeters of the Oral Law and the Covenant entered into at Sinai, has a right to read and interpret the verses of the Torah, in new and hitherto unforeseen ways. This suggests an infinite (but emphatically not a total) variety of readings. In the words of Ḥakham Faur:

> The *derashah* serves to express these variations. To begin with, the *derashah* implies a denial of a supreme reading, of a supreme synthesis capable of concentrating all shades of emotion and meaning.[42]

Hence, like wine properly aged in French oak barrels, the verses of the Torah become richer and more appealing with the passage of time, as the reading public generates new and ever deeper meanings from the text.

The Divine Wisdom

King Solomon describes wisdom as follows: "Wisdoms [*sic*] built her home and has hewn her seven pillars."[43] Wisdom "built her home," means that wisdom itself is the ultimate context of wisdom. In other words, wisdom is an independent system, not relying on anything else, as there is nothing above wisdom that conditions or affects it. Significantly, the divine wisdom is seminal, so that this home becomes a place where new wisdom grows, in the language of King Solomon, it "has hewn her seven

---

38 The Hebrew word for wine is יין, which has a *gematria* of seventy.

39 *Midrash Rabbah* 13:16.

40 P. xiii.

41 *Sanhedrin* 34a.

42 *Golden Doves and Silver Dots*, p. xviii.

43 Pr. 9:1.

pillars." Hence, wisdom is self-contained and self-generating. Like a tree, it produces fruits spontaneously, but unlike a tree, it does not require a particular context to thrive. Consider an orchard that contains rows of nicely lined fruit trees, growing at the proper spacing from each other, and producing beautiful fruits. The orchard is alive, and self-generating, but it is not self-contained, since it requires external circumstances to thrive such as proper irrigation, particular weather conditions, rich soil, and the presence of bees or other pollinating insects. In contrast to this orchard, King Solomon views divine wisdom as creating its own context, wisdom "built *her* [emphasis added] home." Like the orchard, wisdom's home is fruitful, as it "has hewn her seven pillars," which are the foundations of further intellectual systems and disciplines, such as mathematics, physics, music, etc. As noted, however, unlike the orchard, wisdom creates the context for its dynamic existence. This is so because wisdom preceded and existed prior to the Universe. Hence, its existence is completely independent and does not require a particular context. "God fashioned me at the beginning of His ways," declares wisdom, "prior to any of His early actions!"[44] Before there was a cosmos, the divine wisdom existed within itself, so that the Universe became a feature of the divine wisdom and not the other way around. "I was created in the eternal past, before the beginnings of the world. Prior to the existence of space, I was shaped, before the great torrents of water."[45] Hence, wisdom predates the very existence of space and time itself. It is worth emphasizing the following point: it is not the Universe that is the context for wisdom, but rather, it is wisdom that is the context for the Universe.

There is an amazing passage that helps us understand what King Solomon meant by wisdom's home. In discussing Jacob's vision of the angels ascending and descending the ladder, which is crowned with the "House of God,"[46] Philo penned the following:

> Who, then, can that House be, save the Word (*Logos*) who is antecedent to all that has come into existence? The Word (*Logos*), which the Helmsman of the Universe grasps as a rudder to guide all things on their course? Even as, when He was fashioning the World, He employed it as His instrument, that the fabric of His handiwork might be without reproach.[47]

---

44 Pr. 8:22.

45 Ibid., 23–24.

46 Gen. 28:17.

47 Quoted in *Golden Doves and Silver Dots,* p. 24. Philo, *The Migration of Abraham,* I, 6 (Loeb Classical Library), vol 4, p. 135.

Hence, the *amon* is not only the first creation, but it is the catalyst for the scientific and mathematical constructs that form the very fabric of the cosmos. To be sure, the Universe in the form created by God could only exist within these scientific and mathematical constructs.

In contrast to the divine wisdom, the Greek *logos* exists within and is subsumed by an eternal universe. "In Platonic thought *logos* is metaphysical; it 'gathers,' it synthesizes and organizes according to a pre-established order."[48] From this perspective, the *logos* represents the nature of the Universe, or as some would put it, the soul of the Universe. Ultimately, the Greek *logos* is subservient to and somehow located within this eternal Universe.

To understand this matter more fully, the Aramaic word for *logos* is *memra.* In discussing *memra,* Ḥakham Faur writes:

> Similarly, the Targumic *Memra "Word"* is a semiological, rather than a metaphysical, entity. *Memra* does not function according to some pre-established order: it *establishes* the order. More precisely, it is the actual manifestation of God… *Memra* expresses speech as a dynamic, active force manifesting God's activities in the realm of both spiritual and natural phenomena.[49]

Hence, the divine wisdom not only stands supremely above the cosmos, always governing it, establishing vectors and outcomes, it also has a semiological function; it is speech at its most fundamental level. However, it is not the oral speech of the Greeks, which disappears after having served its merely communicative role. The speech of God, the *memra* of the Targum, is actually a kind of writing or mega-text, permanently and dynamically presenting itself, always ready to be read and interpreted by new readers, who are invited to criticize the writer and seek revisions to the story. To highlight the interaction between Writer and reader, the Torah relates that when God was angered at the sin of the Golden Calf, he asks Moses's consent to "destroy them [i.e., the Jewish nation], and make you into a great nation!"[50] Recognizing that the Universe is God's great book (thus highlighting the semiological essence of the *logos*) Moses disapprovingly demands that God change the story; otherwise, says Moses, "erase me, please, from the book that You have written!"[51] This is remarkable. The semiological view of the Universe not only places God as an author, but as an author seeking His reader's approval, even willing to re-write the plot line to satisfy their preferences!

---

48 *Golden Doves and Silver Dots*, p. 24.

49 Ibid.

50 Ex. 32:10.

51 Ex. 32:32.

A Deeper Understanding of the Divine Wisdom

Significantly, King Solomon not only describes the relationship between the Universe and the divine wisdom, with the latter being the context for the former, he also describes the relationship between God and the divine wisdom. In King Solomon's words, wisdom declares: "I was His [i.e., God's] *amon* [i.e., apprentice], and I was His daily merriment, playing before Him at all times."[52] The divine wisdom is God's apprentice, created before Creation, for God's merriment. King Solomon's brilliant allegory comparing the *logos*/speech of God to an apprentice that gives his mentor joy insinuates a fundamental principle. Creation *ex nihilo* commenced with the *amon* solely for His joy or merriment. This means that there is nothing about God that requires either the *amon*/divine wisdom, or the subsequent development of the Universe. It was done for the sake of enjoyment.

The verse continues with the *amon* declaring that, "I was a source of daily delight." The Hebrew word used for delight is *sha'ashou'im*. The word *sha'ashou'im* refers to the special delight that a father attains when he interacts playfully with his young boy, as in the verse, "What a precious son Ephra'im was to Me. Nay! He was a child of *sha'ashou'im*!"[53] R. David Qimhi (1160–1235) explains *sha'ashou'im* to refer to the special pleasure that a father attains from interacting playfully with his beloved son. Thus, God's joy in creating and interacting with the *amon* is not a necessity for God. It is for pure joy.

To be precise, the Universe exists solely because of God's speech/*amon*. "With the words of God, the heavens were created," says the Psalmist.[54] However, this is a one-way road. The Universe only exists and only could exist because God wrote the Universe into existence. On the other hand, God's existence does not require the Universe and is not affected by its presence. To quote Maimonides (1135–1204),

> all of the existences in the heavens, earth and in between, exist only by virtue of His lofty existence. If one were to speculate that He does not exist, then nothing else could exist. If one were to speculate that none of the existences (other than Him) exist, then He alone will exist, and He will not be annulled with their annulment. This is because all of the existences depend on Him, and He, blessed He be, does not depend on them or on any of them.[55]

---

52 Ibid., 8:30.

53 Jer. 31:20.

54 Ps. 33:6.

55 *Mishneh Torah, H. Yesodei ha-Torah* 1:1–2.

"With the words of God, the heavens were created,"[56] also highlights the semiological function of the *amon*. The relationship between God and the *amon* is parallel to the relationship between a writer and his writing. To appreciate this, consider a craftsman. For example, a watchmaker can fashion a physical watch with his hands using delicate tools, while a carpenter can craft a wooden armoire with his hands using a different set of tools. In both cases, there is an ontological and causal relationship between the craftsman, the tools used, and the products created. In contrast, the author of a written text exists independently of the written word. Shakespeare was well aware of what was happening in *Hamlet*, but Shakespeare's existence was separate from and independent of *Hamlet*'s existence. There is no ontological relationship between the words written by an author and the author, since the author exists in a realm that is independent of the text. Similarly, there is no ontological relationship between God and His speech/*logos*/*amon* or the Universe that develops with this speech. Because we humans are created within this cosmos, all we can know clearly are those words, which are visible in the creations we discern. Just like an author remains hidden from the characters created in his story, God, *ad intra*, is eternally hidden from His creations. Thus, when Moses asks to "behold God's glory,"[57] God replies that no "human can behold me and live!"[58]

Because of this, the *amon* acts independently of God, mirthfully following it owns internal mechanisms while God merrily beholds the *amon*'s machinations. God's merriment is essential: this means that the *amon* acts independently of God, so that surprising outcomes of the *amon*'s mirth, as in any whimsical story, are viewed with joyful merriment.

Finding the Creator

As discussed above, from the rabbinic perspective, the world out there, the cosmos, from the great superclusters of galaxies to the infinitesimally small quarks and muons, are all but passages in a great book written by the Creator. Unlike the Greek gods who were illiterate, the God of Abraham, Isaac and Jacob is a Writer. As a corollary, for the Hebrews, the ultimate truth is not a static ontic-ontological reality, but rather a mega-

---

56 Ps. 33:6.

57 Ex. 33:19.

58 Ibid., 20.

text, generating meaning with every new interaction of the observer/reader and the observed/text.[59] The Universe without an observer to interact with it is a like a blank mirror with no looking back. The presence of the observer not only brings the mirror into the consciousness of the observer, but actually changes the mirror in a way that reflects the observer looking back at it.

For many years, modern rabbis and scientists have been debating whether the world is created or came into being by some accident. I do not discount the importance of such debates. Indeed, the "fine-tuning" of the Universe discovered over the last few decades offers highly compelling evidence observable to all that the Universe is indeed created.[60]

Still, I think that the arguments offered regarding the origin of the Universe, the respective proofs, and counterproofs, miss an important point. How can progress be made? We must start with a shift of perspective and emphasize new horizons. Specifically, how do we wish to view the Universe? The debates between modern rabbis and scientists invariable assume a Greek concept of the Universe. It exists; and it is out there ready to be observed. With the ontological Universe as the starting point, explanations are then offered and debated for how it came into "being." That is after all the question, is it not?[61] Scientists posit some sort of accidental "big bang" while modern rabbis argue for a planned Creation. Both start with metaphysical beingness.

Starting with metaphysical beingness is problematic, as the existence of an ontological Universe out there is, even from a scientific perspective, of dubious validity. Studies in Quantum Mechanics firmly indicate that actually, to a certain extent, the observer acts upon and changes the reality he observes.[62] Thus, there is no bare beingness out there. What to do? The classical rabbinic starting point is to view the Universe as a semiological unit, expressing language and meaning. If this is the starting point, the debate of Creation or evolution becomes mute. A book requires an author as a painting requires a painter. The discussion then turns to a far more meaningful arena: What is He trying to tell us? What can we learn from this mega-text? This shift in perspective is both long overdue and rich with possibilities.

---

59 For a discussion of the interaction between the human observer of the Universe, and the "reality" of the Universe, please see my "A Rabbinic Perspective on the Double Slit Experiment," *The Review of Rabbinic Judaism,* vol. 21 (2018), pp. 257–267.

60 *Cf.* Martin J. Fees, *Just Six Numbers: The Deep Forces That Share the Universe* (Great Britain: Weidenfeld & Nicolson, 1999).

61 See *Hamlet*, quoted above, p. 2.

62 *Cf.* Fn. 59 above, and especially the description of the double slit experiment, pp. 263–266.

To be sure, yes, the Universe may be viewed ontologically and Shakespeare's view of what the "question" is can be a starting point. Like the scientists in the story that was related at the beginning of this study, the Philosopher's Stone may be viewed as a lifeless object expressing no meaning. With that as their starting point, scientists then proceeded to study the Philosopher's Stone, making amazing discoveries along the way. That is all wonderful, of course. But at what cost? Viewing the Philosopher's Stone as dead, obfuscates a far more wonderful discovery: messages from an advanced civilization and all that this implies. Similarly, scientists may (and actually do) choose to view the Universe as a dead stone, and in so doing, have made amazing discoveries regarding what the Universe is. This author appreciates these discoveries and would not wish that they were not made. The contrary is true. These discoveries are truly wonderful. However, every choice has its consequences. The choice was to ignore the semiological dimensions of the Universe. In so doing, scientists chose not to read the messages that the Universe expresses. By refusing to read the writing on the wall, worst yet they obfuscate the very existence of the Writer. The rabbi's choice (a far more reasonable choice in my estimation) to view the Universe semiologically, turns the world from a dead stone to a beautiful work of literature, with living stories and beautiful visions. The positive implications for humanity, the knowledge that there is a meaning to all of this, are too many and too profound to summarize in the context of a short article. Suffice it to say that it is precisely this shift from an ontological view of the Universe to a semiological view that will usher in the messianic era,[63] and with it the salvation of all humanity.

I want to end with the words of my father, the late Ḥakham José Faur, whose words, set forth below, inspired this study:

> Ultimately, the whole issue as to whether there is a Creator or whether the universe simply *is* revolves on whether one wishes to regard this world in the Greek or the Hebrew fashion. Were one to consider this world as an ontological entity pointing to nothing except itself, the whole notion of a Maker is useless. On the other hand, one cannot possibly begin to decode a mark unless one presupposes that it is *significant*, that it was *intentional*: There cannot be "writing" without a "writer." The search for "meaning" and "sense," the notion that things and events have an explanation, the quest for cryptographic and hermeneutic methods that will unlock the "mysteries" of the universe—all these presuppose a cosmic book and communicative Author.[64]

63 This may be the subject of a future study by this author.

64 "God As a Writer: Omnipresence and the Art of Dissimulation," p. 36.

Ultimately, the greatest author cannot compel the reader to open the front cover of a great masterpiece. Humanity may choose to leave the book closed and ignore its pages. But only for so long. The semiological view introduced by the Jewish people emphatically calls upon humanity to open the book, to enjoy its stories and paintings, and begin communicating with the Author. ☙

Of Dogma & Dissimulation: Marc Shapiro's Analysis of Maimonides' Thirteen Principles Reappraised

By: BETZALEL SOCHACZEWSKI

"...אלא שדרכי תמיד בכל מקום שיש איזה רמז בעניני
אמונה אבאר משהו, כי חשוב אצלי להסביר יסוד
מהיסודות יותר מכל דבר אחר שאני מלמד." – רמב"ם[1]

Dr. Marc Shapiro is renowned within the world of Jewish academic scholarship for his important contributions to the field of Jewish intellectual history. His meticulous and indefatigable research, shared in his celebrated books and widely followed online classes and postings, regularly yields fascinating discoveries from obscure corners of Torah literature and Jewish history. Significantly, his work has captured the interest of those beyond the walls of academia, popularizing awareness of nuance and development within Judaism that often goes unnoticed.

One of his earlier works, *The Limits of Orthodox Theology: Maimonides' Thirteen Principles Reappraised*,[2] sought to demonstrate that the Thirteen Principles of Jewish faith composed by Maimonides—traditionally viewed as the basic creed of Judaism—do not represent the universal consensus of Jewish scholarship. One by one, Shapiro examines the Principles and documents numerous sources in which traditional scholars, from the famous to the obscure and from the authoritative to the mediocre,

---

The author expresses his profound gratitude to Professor Haym Soloveitchik for reviewing the section on *Iggeret ha-Shemad* and for sharing his expertise; to Professor Shnayer Leiman for reviewing the essay and his encouragement; to Rabbis N. Daniel Korobkin, Jeffrey Saks, and Yitzhak Grossman, and Dr. Michael Shmidman for reviewing the essay and providing helpful observations; to Rabbi Eliyahu Krakowski and Uriel Hinberg for their meticulous editorial review of the manuscript and keen insights. Above all, to my wife Chana—for sharing me with this project and for so much more.

1 *Commentary on the Mishnah*, ed. Kafiḥ (Jerusalem: Mossad ha-Rav Kook, 1963), vol. 1, p. 53.

2 Marc B. Shapiro, *The Limits of Orthodox Theology: Maimonides' Thirteen Principles Reappraised* (Portland: Littman Library, 2004).

Betzalel Sochaczewski received *semikhah* from Beth Medrash Govoha. He currently serves as a research fellow, translator and editor of *sifrei kodesh* and Torah periodicals, and is pursuing a Master's degree in Jewish Studies at Touro College.

express views on theology that are either openly, seemingly, or purportedly inconsistent with Maimonides' standard. Understandably, the work touched a raw nerve within the observant community, as it tampered with what has long been the untouchable bedrock of Orthodox theology, prompting much discussion over the nature of dogma within Judaism. Since then, the book has become one of the primary academic sources on the topic and is consistently referenced in the literature.

Yet despite this, while Shapiro's general thesis and methodology have been critiqued and a few errors identified,[3] his research has, surprisingly, never been subjected to thorough critical examination. This essay attempts to fill some of that void.[4]

While Shapiro's treatment of each of the Thirteen Principles deserves its own analysis, this essay will focus on one of the book's secondary theses. Shapiro contends that there are a number of dogmas articulated by Maimonides that he could not have truly believed in. Shapiro therefore

---

3 See Yitzchak Blau, "Flexibility With a Firm Foundation: On Maintaining Jewish Dogma," *The Torah u-Madda Journal* 12 (2004), pp. 179-191; Gil Student, "Crossroads: Where Theology Meets Halakhah," *Modern Judaism* 24:3 (2004), pp. 272-295; Gidon Rothstein, "Review," *AJS Review* 29:1 (April 2005), pp. 169-171; Zev Leff, "The Thirteen Principles of Rambam," *Jewish Action* (Summer 2007), pp. 76-79; Shmuel Phillips, *Judaism Reclaimed* (n.p., Mosaica Press, 2019), pp. 85-89. For an endorsement of Shapiro's work, including the thesis critiqued in this essay, see Menachem Kellner, *Science in the Bet Midrash: Studies in Maimonides* (Brighton, MA: Academic Studies Press, 2009), ch. 10.

4 As this essay was nearing completion, two reviews of such nature surprisingly materialized: Phillips, *Judaism*, pp. 67-84, and Herschel Grossman, "The Limits of Academic Criticism," *Dialogue* 8 (Fall 2019), pp. 35-83. The former focuses on the third chapter of *Limits*, which is not the subject of the current essay. The latter critiques various points throughout the book. Rabbi Grossman makes several important observations about particular items in Shapiro's research, and I second his call for greater appreciation of the traditional assumptions and attitudes regarding dogma. However, at times he seems to display ignorance of the subject matters (e.g., see further in this essay, fn. 49, 50) and fails to appreciate the very real problems Shapiro addresses (such as the implications of *Guide* 2:25; see later in this essay). On occasion, Grossman appears to completely misread Shapiro (e.g., Grossman, p. 54, where it's clear that Shapiro is adducing evidence from the philosopher quoted by Rivash, and not from Rivash himself). Furthermore, Grossman adopts the approach of extreme harmonization, in which the positions of all Torah authorities are axiomatically presumed consistent with one another, even when sound judgment dictates otherwise. For example, Shapiro's observations about later authorities departing from Maimonides' positions and these authorities' unfamiliarity with medieval philosophy—which is obvious to any educated reader—are described by Grossman (p. 37) as making a mockery of them.

proposes that Maimonides presented these ideas as fundamental aspects of Judaism, despite his full awareness that they are not, for the purpose of maintaining the religious standards of the masses. According to Shapiro, while Maimonides subscribed to most of the content of the Principles, "certain other elements are not true but only 'necessary'… for the masses to believe… all these beliefs have in common the fact that, through them, people are kept from straying from the proper path" (pp. 119-120). This idea serves almost as a subplot to the book's primary theme: Not only are Maimonides' Principles not representative of the consensus of Jewish scholarship throughout the ages, they aren't necessarily representative of Maimonides' personal views, either.

Shapiro uses this theory to explain: discrepancies in Maimonides' attitude towards the dogma of *creation ex nihilo* (pp. 74-77); how Maimonides seemingly attested to the unimpeachable integrity of the scriptural text despite its clear variations (pp. 118-121); and his confidence in the eternally binding nature of the *mitzvot* despite evidence to the contrary (pp. 122-124). Taken together with certain statements made in the *Guide of the Perplexed*, Shapiro asserts that this body of evidence compellingly establishes that Maimonides' presentation to the public of certain core beliefs of Jewish faith was a façade.[5]

Without question, such a proposition touches on sensitive matters. Judaism, like all religions, is based on certain theological foundations, and tampering with Judaism's theology risks undermining its very essence. Moreover, dogma has significant ramifications in practical halakhah, as heretics are given a distinct status that drastically alters their relationship with their peers and the community, and their capacity to perform halakhic rituals.[6] If Maimonides did indeed invent mandatory beliefs, he would have consigned individual Jews otherwise in good standing to the status of heretics, with all of its attendant halakhic consequences. More fundamentally, considering the important role the *Rishonim*, the great medieval rabbinic authorities, played in the elucidation and transmission of Jewish theology, a claim such as this deserves cautious analysis. For, as with their role in the preservation of all areas of the Oral Law, the execution of this responsibility depends squarely upon the public trust in their

---

5 Shapiro revisited this topic in his more recent Hebrew-language essay "*Emunot Hekhreḥiot be-Mishnat ha-Rambam*," *Mesorah le-Yosef* 9 (Netanya: Makhon Mishnat ha-Rambam, 2016), pp. 353-376, which recasts many of his earlier arguments in a more traditional tone (presumably due to the change of audience) and with much supplementary material.

6 See Student, "Crossroads," p. 277ff., for examples.

integrity and competence. If Maimonides did, indeed, engage in disingenuousness in this crucial matter, the integrity of all his teachings risks being undermined.

Of course, one cannot know with certainty the true intentions of any individual—Maimonides included. It is therefore impossible to prove that he did not secretly disavow that which he publicly espoused, and this article will make no attempt to prove this. However, the presumption generally applied to all expressed views (barring those of individuals with a reputation for dishonesty) is that they reflect the convictions of those who endorse them, unless compelling evidence to the contrary is provided. Moreover, the perception of Maimonides within the collective memory of the Jewish people as a faithful transmitter of the received tradition as he understood it, in the same mold as the giants of Jewry who preceded and succeeded him, strengthens that presumption.[7] To be sure, com-

7 Shapiro would argue that this historical image is itself incorrect. In his more recent work, *Changing the Immutable: How Orthodox Judaism Rewrites Its History* (Portland: Littman Library, 2015), pp. 25-26, Maimonides' alleged contrivances are woven into a broader tapestry of not infrequent misrepresentation by Torah scholars throughout the ages for a variety of goals. While an analysis of that work is beyond the scope of this essay, for the moment, I would note the following: All the examples cited by Shapiro relating to misrepresentation of Torah (which isn't the subject of the majority of the book) can be included in one or more of the following categories: a) the claim of misrepresentation is ambiguous, as Shapiro's source can plausibly be understood in an alternative fashion; b) the perpetrator isn't one of the *gedolei ha-dor*, rather a mediocre scholar or layman; c) the misrepresentation has no practical bearing on the subject; d) the agent is of the view that the item he is suppressing or misrepresenting is incorrect or does not reflect the final halakhah and thus deserves to be suppressed or misrepresented; e) the misrepresentation was made temporarily for some constructive purpose and was thereafter corrected; f) it was directed to an individual, a group, or even the unlearned masses to accomplish specific halakhically-mandated goals, while the authentic teachings were accurately preserved for posterity within the academy and accessible to any serious student. The upshot of all this is that Shapiro's research does not seem to yield a single unambiguous instance of the following significant category: *willful* distortion *for posterity* of the *historical body* of Jewish tradition at the hands of one of its custodians, the *gedolei ha-dorot*. By contrast, this is exactly what Shapiro attributes to Maimonides.

Shapiro (ibid., p. 243) also cites a body of halakhic sources which "permit misrepresentation and outright falsification of the halakhah if a good purpose were served by doing so." Once again, there are important distinctions between what those sources sanctioned and what is being pegged onto Maimonides: a) the misrepresentation was to particular parties involved in a specific situation and did not tamper with the formal body of halakhah (*Mishpetei Shmuel*, *Ateret Ḥakhamim*, *Torah li-Shemah*, *Niv Sefatayim*); b) the misrepresentation was a temporary

monly held beliefs are not necessarily accurate ones,[8] yet there is certainly good reason not to dismiss them without persuasive reasoning. What follows, then, is a careful consideration as to whether Shapiro's arguments are indeed credible enough to cast doubts upon Maimonides' intentions.

Some of what will be presented here will be elementary to the reader familiar with Maimonidean studies and the general history of medieval Jewish philosophy; I include it to provide the context necessary to evaluate some of Shapiro's arguments. This is particularly pertinent considering the popularity that *The Limits of Orthodox Theology* enjoys even with those who are not personally familiar with the classic works of medieval Jewish thought and its academic analysis. That said, much of what follows is, to my mind, groundbreaking treatment of a number of sources, which I hope will be of interest even to the learned readership.

Methodological Misrepresentation

Shapiro sets the stage for his theory by portraying Maimonides as one experienced in cutting corners with the truth. Quoting the contemporary Maimonidean scholar Alfred Ivry, Shapiro states (p. 118) that Maimonides adopted in the *Guide* "the daring method of admitting right off to misspoken utterances… and to half-truths… His endorsement of these views is necessary for obvious political reasons, reasons which he obviously cannot divulge." To this Shapiro adds the observation of the medieval Rabbis Balbo and Ashkenazi that "even in the *Mishneh torah* Maimonides said things which did not reflect his true view, but were 'formulated according to the conventional manner of speaking, in order to ease the

---

measure to facilitate the proliferation of a rabbinic edict and set to lapse upon the edict's acceptance (*Shut ha-Rashba*); c) *migdar milta*, which is the prerogative of the posek; since the act in question is now in any event prohibited the reason provided is of no practical value and may be distorted if deemed necessary (*Benei Tzion* as understood by R. Ovadiah Yosef and R. Zinner; *Benei Banim*); d) the *Keli Yakar* is completely irrelevant as he discusses *hora'at sha'ah*, i.e., the Sanhedrin openly legislating the temporary contravening of the halakhah (to which he proposes that even the particular "transgression" demands a pseudo-halakhic rationalization). As noted above, Shapiro's theory has Maimonides inventing a new, permanent category of heresy with vast practical consequences, none of which could be justified through *migdar milta*.

8 A good example is the aforementioned myth of the static biblical text, whose impossibility is demonstrated by Shapiro in chapter seven of the work in question. Yet, a perusal of contemporary books and lectures on Jewish thought from even the most erudite *talmidei ḥakhamim* reveals just how entrenched it has become in the Jewish consciousness.

way for beginners' who were not yet able to grasp metaphysical concepts." Expanding on these impressions, Shapiro contends that "the same tendency is apparent in Maimonides' Principles. Here, however, we do not simply find Maimonides putting forth 'misspoken utterances', but rather stating them as dogma." That is, if Maimonides did indeed make regular use of untruths, it is not much of a stretch to suggest that he also fabricated theology.

I would argue that although Ivry views Maimonides' admission of adopting these inaccuracies as "daring," Maimonides himself did not see it that way. The "admission" in question appears in the preface to the *Guide*,[9] where Maimonides lists seven causes that "account for the contradictory or contrary statements to be found *in any book or compilation*." Any internal contradictions in the *Guide* itself, states Maimonides, are to be attributed to one of two of these causes:[10] educational purposes, i.e., to explain something simplistically—and thus inaccurately—to facilitate understanding of a point at hand, or, to conceal aspects of "exceedingly deep" matters (i.e., metaphysical concepts) from the unprepared reader. The casual, unapologetic tone of this preface indicates that Maimonides viewed these literary tools as routine and accepted didactic conventions. Indeed, he states that the first of the causes relevant to the *Guide* accounts for all contradictions found in works of Greek philosophy, while the second can be found in the Aggadah and perhaps even in the Prophets. This innocent, self-explanatory preface to the *Guide* is dismissively characterized by Ivry as an "elaborate defense of artifice," "devious[ly]" constructed to "cloak his true reasons in excuses and rationales that have in themselves a certain methodological and pedagogical plausibility" in order to "assure the traditional reader of Maimonides' orthodoxy." The very presence of the preface is "prima facie evidence for the non-orthodox nature of Maimonides' beliefs… [through which he] is telling the reader who is ready to hear it not to believe him when he seems to be endorsing traditional views." Ivry states this without offering any hard evidence whatsoever, and his views can therefore be regarded as baseless speculation.[11]

---

9 R. Yosef Kafiḥ (trans.), *Moreh ha-Nevukhim* (Jerusalem: Mossad ha-Rav Kook, 1977), pp. 13-14; translation from Shlomo Pines (trans.), *The Guide of the Perplexed* (Chicago: University of Chicago Press, 1963), p. 17, with emphasis added.

10 The Fifth and Seventh Causes, respectively.

11 To fully appreciate the grossly speculative nature of Ivry's comments, a description of his broader thesis is in order. In his "Islamic and Greek Influences on Maimonides' Philosophy" in Pines & Yovel (eds.), *Maimonides & Philosophy* (Dordrecht: Matinus Nijhoff, 1986) (from which the above quotations are taken, pp. 141-142) Ivry vividly portrays Maimonides as nothing less than a professional

It is without question that a long tradition of esoteric interpretation of the *Guide*, from as early as Samuel ibn Tibbon, laid the groundwork for Ivry's approach. Commentators such as Falaquera, Zeraḥiah Ḥen, Ibn Kaspi, Narbonne, Efodi, and Shem Tov took license from the Seventh Cause and other comments of Maimonides in his preface[12] to comb the *Guide* for allusions to endorsement of Aristotelian beliefs and for parallel contradictions intended to distract the unworthy reader from these philosophical truths. Significantly, though, they viewed this not as political subterfuge with the intention of undermining the Torah, as Ivry contends, but as Maimonides himself describes it: the explication of the *Ma'aseh Bereishit* and *Ma'aseh Merkavah* passages in the manner legislated by the

---

conniver. His *Guide* is a masterpiece of deception, written specifically with a methodology of "confusing and misleading the uninitiated and unwary" so as to pass off his radical philosophical views without the notice of his rabbinic opponents. He had developed this approach during his earlier experience with the Resurrection controversy, for which he composed his famous letter which gave the appearance of conforming to the majority opinion whilst secretly maintaining his unorthodox interpretation. Ivry's rendering of Maimonides comes complete with a psychoanalytical sketch of the man: Maimonides learned the art of subterfuge during his formative years spent, according to Ivry, pretending to be a Muslim. This experience so well trained him in deception "that it became second nature for him" (p. 140), and, thanks to his exposure to the methodological dissimulation found in Shi'i Islamic literature, he subsequently elevated this would-be vice "[in]to a virtue" (p. 141).

It should also be noted that the notion that Maimonides' entire oeuvre deserves a default suspicion of pretense, even in the absence of cryptic language or contradictory sources, effectively pulls the floor out from under the very institution of Maimonidean scholarship.

(Ivry's approach is, of course, a product of the influence of the towering Maimonidean scholar of the twentieth century Leo Strauss, whose esoteric reading of Maimonides went so far as to intimate that he was a closet atheist. For an extensive review and a refreshingly blunt rejection of the Straussian analysis of the *Guide*, see Herbert Davidson, *Moses Maimonides: The Man and His Works* [New York: Oxford University, 2005], pp. 393-402. For a sense of just how far adrift Straussianism renders any attempt to understand the *Guide*, see Warren Z. Harvey, "How Strauss Paralyzed the Study of the Guide of the Perplexed in the 20th Century," *Iyyun* 50 [2001]; see also Kenneth Seeskin, *Searching for a Distant God: The Legacy of Maimonides* [New York: Oxford University, 2000], p. 187 and the literature cited there, n. 23.)

I assume that even Shapiro would disagree with Ivry's radical portrayal of Maimonides; he therefore limits his quotation of him to a brief sentence. However, the mindset which produced this view is pertinent to assessing its soundness.

12 Ed. Kafiḥ, p. 6; Ed. Pines, pp. 6-7.

Sages, i.e., by making them comprehensible only to the deserving.[13] Thus, these commentators would take Maimonides at his word that this was done in a manner in which his true opinion would be discernable to the proficient student,[14] that this was an accepted educational practice with much precedent, and, most importantly, that Maimonides explicitly forewarned the reader of his intention to do so.[15] By the same token, there is nothing novel in the quotation from R. Balbo and Ashkenazi other than the contention that Maimonides' philosophical formulations in the *Mishneh Torah* were expressed in accordance with his self-stated Fifth Cause of

13 Ibid.

14 "אך המאמרים המסתתרים הנאמרים בזולתו מן הענינים ... יסתור קצתם לקצתם ... אך כולם בענין שיוכל המעיין בהם להכיר מה שיתחייב שיוכר ויתקיים מהם, והם אשר נאמרו על האמת" (Ibn Tibbon, cited in Aviezer Ravitzky, "The Secrets of the 'Guide of the Perplexed': Between the Thirteenth and the Twentieth Centuries," in *Jerusalem Studies in Jewish Thought,* vol. 5 [Jerusalem: 1986], p. 26.)

15 This is in contrast to the modern method of esoteric analysis developed by Strauss; see Ravitzky, "Secrets," pp. 42-45. Broadly speaking, the esoteric approach to the *Guide* has been the subject of criticism in recent years. Marvin Fox, *Interpreting Maimonides* (Chicago: University of Chicago, 1990), chapter four, first challenged the assumption that in the aforementioned introduction to the *Guide* Maimonides was referring to deliberate concealment of his opinions. Herbert Davidson (ibid., p. 391) has since suggested that even if Maimonides had intended to utilize the Seventh Cause in the *Guide*, there is no clear evidence that he actually did so. Most notably, Yair Lorberbaum, "On Contradictions, Rationality, Dialectics, and Esotericism in Maimonides' 'Guide of the Perplexed,'" *The Review of Metaphysics* 55, No. 4, pp. 711-750, has compellingly argued on the basis of textual analysis that the Seventh Cause has nothing to do with hiding controversial views. Rather, the nature of metaphysical discussion demands usage of contradictory premises, which need to be masked to avoid unsettling the inexperienced reader. This would seem to be the implication of the "deep matters" that Maimonides refers to in that introductory passage. If this is correct, the entire enterprise of esoterically expounding the *Guide* would consequently evaporate, and would relieve its students of the nagging question as to why Maimonides would compose a work whose true meaning could seemingly never be clarified with any degree of certainty. R. Shlomo Aviner, in his commentary to the *Guide* (Jerusalem: Hava Books, 2016), vol. 1, pp. 73-74, adopts this understanding. For a similar approach, see Seeskin, *Searching*, pp. 177-188. For an examination of this trend, see Ravitzky, "Maimonides: Esotericism & Philosophical Education," *Da'at* 53 (Winter 2004), pp. 60-62.

the *Guide*, simplification for the sake of education,[16] and there is no indication that they considered such an approach underhanded.[17]

This is rather different than the form of artifice Shapiro attributes to Maimonides. In all his writings, never once does Maimonides mention the concept of misguiding the public for the purpose of maintaining religious conformity (see following section). Furthermore, the text of the Thirteen Principles contains no disclaimer that warns the reader of incorrect information embedded within it and seemingly no hints directing him or her as to how to decode its true intentions. It therefore seems questionable to argue that Maimonides' use of these conventional inaccuracies supports the contention that he was predisposed to presenting wholly false ideas with the goal of indoctrinating his readership.

True and Necessary Beliefs

To buttress his theory, Shapiro quotes a passage in the *Guide* (3:28) in which Maimonides distinguishes between different "beliefs" legislated by the Torah.

> ואבאר שכל אלו וכיוצא בהן בהחלט יש להן מבוא באחד משלשת הענינים, או לתקון דעה, או תקון מצבי המדינה שהם נעשים בשני דברים בסלוק העול ובקניית מדה נעלה. והבן מה שאמרנוהו בדעות, לפי שיש שתהא המצוה מתן דעה נכונה היא המטרה לא יותר, כגון הדעה ביחוד, וקדמות האלוה, ושאינו גוף. ויש שתהא אותה הדעה הכרחית בסלוק עול או הקנית מדה נעלה, כגון הדעה שהוא יתעלה יחרה אפו על עושה עול, כמו שאמר וחרה אפי והרגתי וגו', וכגון הדעה שהוא יתעלה עונה לצעקת העשוק או המתאנה מיד, והיה כי יצעק אלי ושמעתי כי חנון אני.[18]
>
> I shall explain that all these [commandments] and others of the same kind are indubitably related to one of the three notions referred to [earlier]—either to the welfare of a belief or to the welfare of the conditions of the city, which is achieved through two things: abolition of reciprocal wrongdoing and acquisition of excellent characters. Sum up what we have said concerning beliefs as follows: In some cases a *commandment* communicates a correct belief, which is the one and only thing aimed at—as, for instance, the belief in the unity and eternity of the deity and in His not being a body. In other

---

16 Cf. Aviezer Ravitsky, *History and Faith* (Amsterdam: J.C. Gieben, 1996), p. 130, n. 63 and 71. This work is an English-language adaptation of *Al Da'at ha-Makom*, referenced by Shapiro in n. 182.

17 See ibid., n. 65 for an additional quotation from R. Balbo in which Maimonides' above practice is grouped together with similar contradictory teachings in Scripture and rabbinic writings.

18 Ed. Kafiḥ, p. 339.

> cases the belief is necessary for the abolition of reciprocal wrongdoing or for the acquisition of a noble moral quality—as, for instance, the belief that He, may He be exalted, has a violent anger against those who do injustice, according to what is said: *And My wrath shall wax hot, and I will kill, and so on*, and as the belief that He, may He be exalted, responds instantaneously to the prayer of someone wronged or deceived: *And it shall come to pass, when he crieth unto Me, that I will hear; for I am gracious.*[19]

To Shapiro's mind, Maimonides understands that the Torah itself employs untruths as vehicles for social regulation. In Shapiro's words:

> 'True beliefs' are those which teach, in a literal fashion, some truth about God, such as his existence, unity, eternity, and omnipotence. Their purpose is to enable one to attain intellectual perfection. 'Necessary beliefs', which are based on tradition rather than philosophy, are expressed in a figurative manner and fulfil a political function in that, by instilling obedience to the Torah, they regulate the social relations of human beings. In addition, they enable people to acquire noble qualities. For example, the Torah teaches that God is angry with those who disobey him. Although in truth God does not possess the characteristic of anger, the Torah found it advantageous to use this concept for the effect it would have. It is 'necessary' for the masses to believe that God is angry if they disobey him in order for them to control their behaviour. In addition, it is 'necessary' for the masses to believe that God responds instantly to the prayer of someone wronged or deceived; for them to believe otherwise would be damaging to their faith.[20]

In other words, God in fact does not anger and does not respond instantly to the prayers of the wronged; the Torah says that He does so in order to condition us into adopting certain behaviors.[21] If indeed Maimonides had such a conception of the Torah's pragmatic approach to untruths, suggests Shapiro, it is not a stretch to claim that he himself followed suit in his own presentation of dogma. Hence, Maimonides fabricated concepts of Jewish theology and branded their denial heresy for practical reasons that will be described below.

A careful reading of the *Guide*'s language and context, however, demonstrates that Maimonides meant nothing of the sort. In this section

---

19 Ed. Pines, pp. 513-514.

20 P. 119.

21 As noted by Shapiro, "Emunot," p. 354, this understanding was adopted by Shem Tov in another context, as well as Rav Kook (ibid., p. 353) and, seemingly, Abarbanel (ibid., p. 355).

of the *Guide*, Maimonides discusses the functions of the *mitzvot*, i.e., what they are meant to accomplish for their practitioners. Some *mitzvot* instill certain beliefs, some ennoble one's character, and some regulate proper social behavior. In this vein, Maimonides distinguishes between the *functions* of the different beliefs that we are commanded to hold. Some are השקפות נכונות, "correct beliefs," i.e., their *function* (or better yet, their *value*) lies simply in their being true conceptions of God. This is in line with Maimonides' understanding, which he mentions at the opening of the chapter in question, that the ultimate human perfection (השלמות הסופית) is achieved by acquiring cognition of God. Other beliefs, however, are השקפות הכרחיות, "necessary beliefs," i.e., beliefs whose *function* lies not in awareness of them, but in the behavior they promote. For example, the knowledge of how God interacts with mankind, such as the fact that He punishes sin or that He defends the wronged, does not, in Maimonides' view, confer any inherent perfection, because it is not philosophical knowledge of God Himself. However, this does not detract from the authenticity of this knowledge. Just as one who knows, for example, that the capital of Russia is Moscow is aware of an accurate piece of information that inherently does nothing to better him, so it is with one who has true knowledge of God's *behavior*. Thus, the only *value* there is in our awareness of these beliefs is the personal qualities and proper social behaviors they generate, for these qualities and behaviors are "necessary" to create an environment conducive to acquiring intellectual perfection. None of this has any bearing on the veracity of either of these types of beliefs and Maimonides makes no such distinction. Both types of beliefs are true; they only differ in that one's value is its very truthfulness and the other's is in the behavior it prompts.

The correctness of this interpretation is evident from a careful reading of the middle of the chapter:[22]

> המסקנה מכל מה שהקדמנו עתה בענין זה, היא שכל מצוה בין שהיתה צווי או אזהרה, תהיה מטרתה סלוק עול, או זירוז על מדה נעלה המביאה ליחסים טובים בין בני אדם, *או מתן השקפה נכונה שצריך להיות בה בדעה אם כפי הצווי עצמו או בהיותו הכרחי לסלוק עול או הקנית מדה נעלה*, הרי אותה המצוה טעמה ברור ותועלתה גלויה וכו'.
>
> What results from what we have now stated as a premise regarding this subject is that whenever a commandment, be it a prescription or a prohibition, requires abolishing reciprocal wrongdoing, or urging

22 Kafiḥ, pp. 338-9 and Pines, p. 513, with emphasis added. Editions Ibn Tibbon (Jerusalem, 1960), sec. 3, p. 41b, Friedlander (New York: Dover, 1956), p. 314, and Schwartz (Tel Aviv: Tel Aviv University, 2002), p. 519 all yield the same understanding.

to a noble moral quality leading to a good social relationship, *or communicating a correct opinion that ought to be believed either on account of itself or because it is necessary for the abolition of reciprocal wrongdoing or for the acquisition of a noble moral quality*, such a commandment has a clear cause and is of a manifest utility.

It is clear from the highlighted section that השקפות נכונות/true beliefs ("correct opinions" as Pines translates it) contain two varieties: those of intrinsic value and those of necessary value. Maimonides describes both as "true," and there is no indication to the contrary in the rest of the chapter.[23] The reader is encouraged to read chapters 27 and 28 in their entirety, and I trust that the correct sense of Maimonides' intention, as described above, will be apparent.[24]

---

23 See also the opening of the same chapter: "כי ההשקפות הנכונות אשר בהן תושג השלימות הסופית [...] והוא מציאות השם ית' ויחודו [...] וכן גם קראה התורה להיות בדעה בדברים אשר סבירתן הכרחית בתקינות המצבים המדיניים, כגון זה שאנו בדעה שהוא ית' יחרה אפו על מי שמרד בו [...] אבל שאר ההשקפות הנכונות בכל המציאות הזו אשר אלה הם כל המדעים העיוניים לכל ריבוי מיניהם וכו'". Even-Shmuel (see next note) rejects Ephodi's interpretation of the emphasized words.

24 The core of this reading is also asserted by Even-Shmuel (ed.), *Moreh ha-Nevukhim* (Jerusalem: Mossad ha-Rav Kook, 2001), intro. p. 68, n. 110, as well as by Hannah Kasher, "Meetos 'ha-El ha-ko'es' ba-*Moreh Nevukhim*," *Eshel Be'er Sheva* 4 (1995), p. 96. (I am indebted to Dr. Charles Manekin for referring me to and sending me a copy of the latter source.) See also Fox, *Interpreting*, pp. 319-321. (Subsequent to this writing, there appeared in print the third volume of the Mif'al Mishneh Torah edition of the *Guide* [Kedumim, 2021], which also utilizes the argument advanced above, among other reasons, to reject the reading adopted by Shapiro [p. 204].)
Shapiro's basic understanding of this passage of the *Guide* is shared by Ephodi and Shem Tov in their comments there. They affirm that Maimonides' distinction between "true" and "necessary" beliefs indicates that there is something "untrue" about the latter. However, aside from the above evidence that this is incorrect, there is a vast difference between Ephodi and Shem Tov's understanding and Shapiro's. In their view, the "untruths" refer to the use of anthropomorphisms. Anyone familiar with the first section of the *Guide* knows that Maimonides did not consider scriptural references to God's anger, compassion for the cheated, or similar attributes "false" in the sense of complete fiction. Rather, they describe real divine activity in a literary fashion that can be appreciated by finite human beings. And, as Shem Tov adds, the Torah expects that the intelligent reader will realize that the language is true in the figurative sense yet untrue in the literal sense. This is also clearly the intent of both Albo (referenced by Shapiro, n. 184) and Arthur Hyman, from whom Shapiro borrowed the "dialectical" characterization of the "necessary beliefs" (p. 119). To quote the latter:

Further evidence that Shapiro's reading of this passage is incorrect is furnished by Shapiro himself. In his later *Mesorah le-Yosef* (p. 354, n. 3) he notes the extreme difficulty presented by Maimonides' (supposed) assertion that the Torah intended for the masses to believe that God is literally susceptible to anger. As Falaquera already observed, this seems impossible to square with Maimonides' insistence (*Guide* 1:35) that the same masses be educated in God's absolute disconnect from emotion. And as R. Chaim Rapoport has pointed out (*Mesorah le-Yosef*, p. 356, n. 9), it's also betrayed by Maimonides' explicit codification of God's emotionlessness in his *Mishneh Torah*, a work intended for all strata of society.[25] Shapiro does not even suggest an approach to resolve these difficulties; according to our reading, they simply do not exist.[26]

> That the "necessary beliefs" are dialectical rather than sophistic becomes clear once they are considered in the light of other aspects of Maimonides' philosophy. In discussing anthropopathic terms applied to God—God's anger being one of his examples—Maimonides shows that propositions containing such terms are not completely false. "The Torah uses the language of ordinary men." Though it is false to ascribe passions to God, it is correct to state that God produces actions similar to those resulting from man's anger. This correct interpretation of the proposition yields its truth. Thus, Maimonides' "necessary beliefs" are seen to be dialectical propositions which attain their "correctness" from the cognitive content they possess. It is their cognitive content which makes them superior to other propositions which may be useful for instilling obedience. ("Spinoza's Dogmas of Universal Faith," A. Altmann [ed.] *Biblical and Other Studies* [Cambridge: Brandeis, 1963], pp. 189-190.)

While Shapiro incorporates this point into his comments, his expansion of the idea, that the Principles are "dialectical" in that they are generally accurate with some fictitious details thrown in, is unwarranted. There is a world of difference between the literary tool of anthropomorphism and making theological statements that have no basis whatsoever in reality. If Maimonides knew, to use an example we will discuss, that the scriptural text is imperfect and that the Torah does not legislate a belief in its perfection, a statement to the contrary is false—period. It is not softened by including it among other, factually true elements in the broader Eighth Principle. In his later *Mesorah le-Yosef* (p. 355), Shapiro acknowledges this distinction.

25 See also *Mesorah le-Yosef*, p. 359, n. 16.

26 There are many other difficult items in Maimonides' writings that are presented in *Mesorah le-Yosef* as evidence of "necessary beliefs." However, it is not hard to imagine how many of them could be resolved with a more nuanced understanding of Maimonides' views on the more "local" issues of biblical interpretation and the like. For example, Shapiro notes Maimonides' codification of the literal rendering of the narrative of Reuben and Bilhah in the presence of the *sotah* despite the Talmud's (*Shabbat* 55b) reinterpretation and that *Kessef Mishneh* seems

The *Iggeret ha-Shemad*

One particular piece of evidence of Maimonides' "disingenuousness" adduced by Shapiro (p. 86), in this case regarding a halakhic matter, is from Maimonides' *Iggeret ha-Shemad.* In this epistle, he addresses Moroccan Jewry, who were coerced by the ruling Almohads to declare acceptance of Islam and thus conduct themselves outwardly as Muslims. Maimonides presents an overview of the parameters of *mesirat nefesh*, as well as *kiddush* and *ḥillul ha-Shem* and applies them to this community's circumstances, while affirming their good standing as Jews and the continued value of their *mitzvah* performance. The crux of this sympathetic approach is Maimonides' ruling that one who is confronted with the choice between coerced conversion to Islam and death should indeed convert to save his or her own life—a ruling which, undoubtedly, helped to ameliorate the guilt of the Moroccan apostates. Shapiro cites Prof. Haym Soloveitchik's thorough analysis of this epistle,[27] in which Soloveitchik details various difficulties with Maimonides' halakhic reasoning and therefore argues that the epistle was intended to serve not as an authentic legal exposition, but as a work of rhetoric designed to rescue its audience from spiritual demise resulting from the shame of apostasy. It was in this spirit, contends Soloveitchik, that Maimonides handed down his lenient ruling—despite his conviction that martyrdom in the face of Islamic conversion is indeed obligatory.[28] Shapiro, in turn, posits that this interpretation supports the case that Maimonides' public stance, even in the realm of halakhah, was

---

to view this as an imposition of a "necessary belief." However, as Shapiro also notes (quoting R. Rapoport), many authorities—and even tannaitic opinions within the *Shabbat* passage—*did* accept the literal reading of the Reuben and Bilhah incident, and it is plausible that Maimonides was of the same mind. (One could add the possibility that they understood the non-literal rendering as an additional interpretative layer of *derash.* See the sources referenced in Shapiro, *Changing*, p. 5, n. 19, regarding the similar issue of David and Bathsheba.)
The explanations of R. Leon Modena, R. Chaim Elazar Shapiro, R. Yosef Mazuz, *et al.*, while demonstrating a rabbinic precedent for "necessary beliefs" and thus making for interesting intellectual history, do not necessarily reflect on Maimonides' views (and, as Shapiro notes, are sometimes inconsistent with them). Other items found in Maimonides' correspondence which are cited in *Mesorah le-Yosef*, if indeed not reflective of his true views, are of a private nature and are subjective to the correspondent and therefore categorically different from his official and public teachings (see above n. 7).

27 Reprinted in his *Collected Essays* II (London: Littman, 2014), pp. 288-328.

28 In agreement is Moshe Halbertal, *Maimonides: Life and Thought* (Princeton: Princeton University Press, 2014), p. 31.

at times tailored to the public need and did "not necessarily represent Maimonides' true view."[29]

I would note that while Prof. Soloveitchik's thesis is a landmark contribution to the study of the *Iggeret*, it is by no means conclusive and alternative resolutions—which uphold the work's halakhic integrity—have been proposed.[30] Yet assuming that his reading is indeed correct and that Maimonides countenanced an inaccurate portrayal of the halakhah in this instance, an important distinction between a work such as the *Iggeret ha-Shemad* and Maimonides' formal writings must be noted. Like much of responsa literature, the former was addressed to a specific community dealing with specific circumstances and it needed to address those particulars in the most effective manner possible. In this instance, the issue was the specter of the dissolution of an entire community and Maimonides' message was designed to deal with that concern head on. If misrepresentation of a particular halakhah was necessary to achieve the outcome which was more halakhically viable in the bigger picture, Maimonides' prerogative as a halakhic authority allowed for (and perhaps demanded) that option. However, we have no indication that Maimonides intended for this letter to be viewed by other communities who did not face this challenge or that it should be preserved for posterity. It was not included in any compendium, unlike published works of responsa, and is not referenced in any of Maimonides' later writings. In fact, citations of the *Iggeret* only begin to appear some two centuries after Maimonides' death, leading some to argue that its authorship is misattributed.[31] In any event, this is

---

29 In *Limits*, Shapiro merely notes that this approach precludes the need to resolve any contradictions between Maimonides' formal writings, which are presumed to be sincere reflections of his thought, and his popular works such as the *Iggeret*, which are not. In *Mesorah le-Yosef* (p. 367), however, he cites this as evidence to the artfulness he asserts exists in both categories of Maimonides' oeuvre.

30 See Hillel Novetsky, "Halakhah, Polemikah, ve-Retorikah be-Iggeret ha-Shemad shel ha-Rambam," available at <www.haym-soloveitchik.org>. Prof. Soloveitchik's response appears in *Collected Essays*, pp. 352-364. See most recently David Henshke, "Iggeret ha-Shemad: le-Tiv Tokhnah ha-Hilkhati u-le-Yiḥusah la-Rambam," *Dinei Yisrael* 33 (2020), pp. 109-146, for a survey of the literature, a critique of Prof. Soloveitchik's thesis, and an alternative approach.

31 See Davidson, *Moses Maimonides*, pp. 501-509, who also raises difficulties with the *Iggeret*. I would note that his observation from *Hil. Teshuvah* (p. 506) misunderstands the term "said" used in that context. Evidence against his position can be brought from Novetsky's (p. 11) observation that *Mishneh Torah*'s inclusion of *ye-hareig ve-al ya'avor* in a private setting under the rubric of the positive act of *kiddush ha-Shem*, which is a novel opinion among the *Rishonim*, is found in the *Iggeret* as well. See Henshke, "Iggeret," pp. 109-118.

categorically different from a work such as the *Commentary on the Mishnah* which was intended to present Torah in its ideal form and for a national audience—both contemporary and of generations yet to be born. For Maimonides to have legislated for posterity anything less than the absolute truth of Torah as he conceived it would seem to be a dereliction of his responsibility as a transmitter of the *Mesorah*.[32] The instance of the *Iggeret ha-Shemad*, therefore, cannot serve as more than weak evidence that Maimonides would have taken such a significant leap.

Shapiro believes that the specious dogmatization of the specific beliefs at hand was necessitated by the theological challenges which threatened Maimonides' contemporaries—seemingly in a spirit similar to the one which prompted the *Iggeret ha-Shemad*. Regarding the textual infallibility of the Torah, Shapiro notes that "[i]n [Maimonides'] time, Muslims were challenging the Jews, claiming that they had altered the text of the Torah.... In the face of such an assault, it is not hard to see why Maimonides felt it was important for the masses to believe that their text was the exact equivalent of Moses' text. The masses then (and today) could not be expected to understand the problems relating to the biblical text. Exposing them to some of this knowledge could have undermined their unquestioned faith, especially in the face of Islamic polemics" (p. 120). Similarly, regarding the eternity of the *mitzvot*, "Maimonides was formulating a 'necessary belief', directed towards the masses and designed to help them deal with ideological assaults from the Islamic world" (p. 131). Shapiro indicates that a similar concern existed with regard to creation *ex nihilo* (p. 120).[33] Despite this, I would contend that a work such as the *Commentary*, which had the potential—if abused—to permanently alter the content of the Torah beyond the time and place in which these concerns

---

32 See above n. 7.

33 Shapiro suggests no particular motive for dogmatizing the rejection of the Platonic position. As Maimonides himself explains in the *Guide*, the theory does not interfere with the other tenets of Judaism and could be easily reconciled with the biblical account of creation, assuming that it could be demonstrated to be philosophically harmonious with the concept of divine unity. One must, therefore, assume that Shapiro would adopt the approach of other scholars who attribute to Maimonides an unorthodox position on creation—that Maimonides hid his view to protect himself from the ire of his traditionalist peers. Shapiro's thesis would thus demand an additional concession: that Maimonides took liberties with the truth not only for the benefit of communal stability, but for his own personal welfare, as well.

existed, would be the wrong medium for Maimonides to utilize in addressing them.[34]

Further on this point, Shapiro[35] also notes that Prof. Soloveitchik's take on the *Iggeret* was anticipated by R. Shimon b. Ẓemaḥ Duran (Rashbaẓ)—thus providing a significant medieval source for Maimonides' supposed disingenuousness, in halakhic matters at the least. I assume that Shapiro was aware that the two interpretations are diametrically opposed: Duran proposes that Maimonides was *stricter* than the ideal halakhah in his condemnation of those who fail to flee from apostasy when able, while Prof. Soloveitchik claims that Maimonides was more *lenient*, in his allowance of professing conversion to save one's life; the common denominator is that Maimonides' words were measured to elicit a response from his audience. What bears mentioning is that when taken in context, Duran's words would seem to offer no support for Shapiro's position.

Duran argues that a coerced apostate who failed to use an opportunity to escape to a hospitable environment could not face sanctions at the hands of the Jewish community. Being that we could never be completely certain that there were no practical or psychological obstacles to such a move, the individual's presumed status (*ḥazakah*) of innocence should demand an assumption of his being coerced. Maimonides' ruling in the *Mishneh Torah*[36] to the contrary is interpreted by Duran as referring to heavenly judgment, for God is aware of all the personal circumstances and can gauge the individual's culpability. In other words: theoretically, such a scenario condemns the apostate even in interpersonal halakhah; practically speaking, we are incapable of recognizing it. It is in this vein that Duran suggests that Maimonides' inclusion of this harsh pronouncement in his

---

34 Shapiro's personal difficulty with the *Iggeret* for which he invokes Prof. Soloveitchik—its citation of the midrash which attributes wrongdoing to the angels despite Maimonides' denial of their capacity for such—would seem to have a simple resolution. Maimonides cites the midrash because it reflects the sentiment he is discussing—that God does not take well to criticism of the Jewish people; his rejection of other elements of the midrash's narrative is irrelevant in this context. See R. Moshe Maimon, *Peirush ha-Torah le-Rabbeinu Avraham ben ha-Rambam* (Monsey: *Makhon le-Heker Torat ha-Kadmonim*, 2019), *Bereishit* p. 248, n. 63, who assumes this as well.

35 *Mesorah le-Yosef*, p. 367. This was noted as well in his earlier *Studies in Maimonides and His Interpreters* (Scranton: University of Scranton Press, 2008), p. 85.

36 "אבל אם יכול למלט נפשו ולברוח מתחת יד המלך הרשע ואינו עושה הנה הוא ככלב שב על קיאו והוא נקרא עובד עבודה זרה במזיד, והוא נטרד מן העוה"ב ויורד למדרגה התחתונה של גיהנום" (הל' יסוה"ת פ"ה ה"ד). The evidence of this passage's inauthenticity is irrelevant to our discussion as this is the version of the text utilized by Duran.

Iggeret,[37] despite its lack of practical application to any individual, was designed to stir his readership to greater efforts in escaping their pitiful circumstances. This statement is not a misrepresentation as Shapiro would have it, since it is indeed true in principle, as Maimonides himself states in the *Mishneh Torah*, according to Duran's understanding. Therefore, there would seem to be no evidence that Duran would attribute knowingly untrue statements to Maimonides.

The Fourth Principle: Creation *Ex Nihilo*

We now turn to the specific dogma that Maimonides allegedly contrived. As mentioned, the first item relevant to this discussion is Maimonides' position on creation *ex nihilo*. In the standard version of his *Commentary on the Mishnah*, Maimonides' Fourth Principle posits the belief in God's priority to all other beings. Because this could be construed as referring to ontological priority—that is, that God and the universe have eternally coexisted in a cause-and-effect relationship—Maimonides clarified,[38] in a note added to a later edition and published in all modern editions, that all beings were created after absolute non-existence, thus rejecting the Aristotelian concept of the eternal universe as well as the Platonic concept of the eternal prime matter.

> והיסוד הרביעי הקדמות. והוא, שזה האחד המתואר הוא הקדמון בהחלט, וכל נמצא זולתו הוא בלתי קדמון ביחס אליו, והראיות לזה בספרים הרבה. וזה היסוד הרביעי הוא שמורה עליו מה שנ' מענה אלקי קדם. *ודע כי היסוד הגדול של תורת משה רבינו הוא היות העולם מחודש, יצרו ה' ובראו אחר ההעדר המוחלט, וזה*

---

37 Which Duran did not personally read, as made clear from: "ולפי שהוגד לי כי הרמב"ם ז"ל ביאר דעתו במאמר קידוש השם וכו'."

38 As per the majority view that Maimonides had intended as such in his original formulation; see Menachem Kellner, *Dogma in Medieval Jewish Thought* (Oxford: Littman, 2004), p. 57 (cited by Student, *Crossroads*, n. 72). Kellner's arguments to the contrary (pp. 54-57) aren't compelling: a) He ascribes to the mortal Maimonides the inability to fall short in his written expression; in the event that Maimonides' words did require clarification, Kellner feels confident in determining, without basis, at what point in Maimonides' life he ought to have made this realization; b) Maimonides' refraining from clarifying the controversial Thirteenth Principle is no better understood according to Kellner's preferred approach. For even if his amendment to the Fourth Principle wasn't an elucidation, what was to stop him from elucidating the Thirteenth Principle? Apparently, he felt that his language was clear enough; c) Nuriel's observation is taken up later in this essay, n. 50(d); d) the language of *Hilkhot Teshuvah* is addressed shortly below in the text. Shapiro (p. 71, n. 3) rejects Kellner's understanding for another reason.

שתראה שאני סובב סביב ענין קדמות העולם לפי דעת הפילוסופים הוא כדי שיהא המופת מוחלט על מציאותו יתעלה כמו שביארתי ובררתי במורה.

And the Fourth Principle is that of priority. That is to say, that the aforementioned Unity [i.e., God] was—in the absolute sense—the first of all existents; all other beings are, in comparison to Him, of later origin. There is much evidence to this adduced in the [philosophical] literature. This Fourth Principle is indicated by the [scriptural] reference to *a dwelling for the first God. Be aware that the great foundation of Mosaic Law is the concept of creation, that God created it after absolute non-existence. That which you may observe that in my philosophical discussions I presume the eternity of the Universe, that is only so that my demonstrations of God's existence will be absolute [i.e., acceptable even to opponents of Creationism], as I have explained and clarified in the* Guide.[39]

Shapiro points out that while Maimonides seems to be consistent in his rejection of Aristotelian eternalism throughout his writings, his attitude towards the Platonic approach appears far more tolerant, having left the door open for its possible legitimacy should it be philosophically proven.[40] For "[i]n contrast to the Aristotelian view that the world is eternal, which according to Maimonides would destroy the Torah, he claims that there is no religious reason to reject the Platonic view" (p. 76). Shapiro therefore argues that "there is simply no way one can take seriously his contention that someone who even doubts this Principle is a heretic" (ibid.), and proposes that Maimonides, indeed, did not subscribe to such a position, while his statement to the contrary was stated only for purposes of social manipulation (p. 120).

The first source in Maimonides that Shapiro (p. 74) cites as evidence is *Hilkhot Teshuvah* (3:7). Among those deemed heretics we find listed:[41]

וכן האומר שאינו לבדו ראשון וצור לכל.

Likewise one who says that He alone is not the "*Rishon*" and "*Ẓur*" of all.

Shapiro finds significant the absence of an explicit reference to creation *ex nihilo*, which, he argues, allows for the interpretation that Maimonides was only insisting on belief in God as the eternal cause or source of all beings in the Platonic sense. Without presenting the reader with the Hebrew text, Shapiro takes the liberty of translating the term ראשון as

39 Hebrew from ed. Kafiḥ, p. 142; free translation. Emphasis added to indicate the later addition.

40 *Guide* 2:25.

41 Translation adapted from <www.sefaria.org>.

"First Cause." It would seem, however, more reasonable to translate it as "First Existent," considering that the word is used more commonly in a temporal sense than in a causative one.[42] This would also resolve the redundancy of the phrase צור לכל, which clearly refers to God as the Source, or Cause, of existence.[43] This is also the more accurate formulation of the principle of creation *ex nihilo*. The theological rejection of Platonism does not stem from an objection to the existence of eternal matter qua eternal matter; rather, a corollary of God's definition as the מוכרח המציאות, the only truly real Existent, precludes the existence of any being except by His Will. Thus, Maimonides, in his uniquely precise language, framed the concept of creation *ex nihilo* from God's perspective.[44] This also correlates with his language in the original version of the Fourth Principle— "שזה האחד המתואר הוא הקדמון בהחלט וכל נמצא זולתו הוא בלתי קדמון ביחס אליו"— which, as Shapiro states (p. 71, n. 3), was understood by the overwhelming majority of scholars as implying creation *ex nihilo*. Interestingly, Shapiro rejects Menachem Kellner's attempt to interpret this as ontological priority, which is precisely how Shapiro reads *Hilkhot Teshuvah* despite the clearly parallel language.[45]

Shapiro's second source for Maimonides' tolerance of the Platonic view of creation is a passage in the *Guide* (2:25). There, Maimonides declares that his rejection of the Platonic view is not because of its incompatibility with Scripture or theology, but rather because of its shaky phil-

---

42 This is how Maimonides explains the term in *Guide* 2:30.

43 *Guide* 1:16. *Kessef Mishneh*, *Lehem Mishneh*, and *Ikkarim* 1:12 all take the basic position that the passage in *Hilkhot Teshuvah* is precluding the Platonist position. This also seems to be Rabad's understanding, as he illustrates the heresy referenced with the words שאינו לבדו ראשון with one who posits creation from prime matter. (R. Dovid Aramah may have understood Maimonides as sidestepping the issue.) See *Mirkevet ha-Mishneh*, *Avodat ha-Melekh*, and Rav Kafiḥ ad loc., who also take Maimonides as denying the Platonic position.

44 See *Ḥovot ha-Levovot*, ed. Kafiḥ (Nanuet: Feldheim, 2004), p. 43. This would also resolve Shapiro's observation (p. 74) of the omission of creation *ex nihilo* from the beginning of *Hilkhot Yesodei ha-Torah*. Maimonides did indeed include it with the words שיש שם מצוי ראשון, as observed by the marginal note in the Frankel edition, ad loc.

45 Shapiro cites Halbertal that Maimonides' Provencal detractors indeed assumed Shapiro's reading of *Hilkhot Teshuvah* and therefore accused Maimonides of denying creation *ex nihilo*, lending credence to this interpretation. It should be noted, however, that Halbertal's source is R. Meir b. Shimon ha-Me'ili's *Meishiv Nefesh* (which has since been printed, *Yeshurun* 27 [2012], p. 60), who disproves his anonymous contemporaries' understanding on textual grounds and from the extensive contradictory evidence in the *Guide*, some of which is quoted below.

osophical basis. Should this view be demonstrated in a compelling fashion, Maimonides concedes that Scripture could be interpreted to be consistent with this idea. Quoting Marvin Fox, Shapiro summarizes: "[I]t seems evident that, even though he does not consider the Platonic view to be the preferred or the exclusively correct view, Maimonides does admit it, alongside the theory of creation out of nothing, as a legitimate and acceptable opinion on both philosophical and religious grounds. It can be shown to accord with one acceptable reading of Scripture and with the teachings of numerous canonical midrashim. From this evidence, we seemingly must conclude that Maimonides accepts the Platonic position as consistent with prophetic teaching.... If someone finds it persuasive, there is no reason to object, since it does not contradict any principle of the Torah or of philosophy" (p. 76). Shapiro emphasizes that this portrayal of Maimonides' opinion is a completely straightforward one; there is no claim of an esoteric reading of his position. Thus, Maimonides' unqualified equation of the Platonic view with heresy in the Thirteen Principles is necessarily an untruth directed to the masses. Shapiro presumably feels that while Maimonides shared his true view in the *Guide*, which was accessible only to scholars with a background in philosophy, he used his popular *Commentary on the Mishnah* to indoctrinate the less educated proletariat.

The difficulty with this evidence is that while the above is an accurate depiction of the passage in *Guide* 2:25, one cannot have a complete picture of Maimonides' view as expressed even in the *Guide* without being aware of his comments in 2:13 there. While Shapiro felt that this source could be relegated to a brief footnote with an assurance that it has been sufficiently dealt with by Fox and other authors,[46] I suggest that to appreciate the contradiction between these sources—arguably one of the most vexing difficulties with the *Guide*—Maimonides' complete remarks ought to be cited.

> ההשקפה הראשונה והיא השקפת כל המאמין בתורת משה רבנו ע"ה, היא, שהעולם בכללותו כלומר כל נמצא פרט לה' יתעלה, ה' המציאו אחר ההעדר המוחלט והגמור, ושה' יתעלה לבדו היה מצוי, ואין מאומה זולתו לא מלאך ולא גלגל ולא מה שבתוך הגלגל, והמציא כל הנמצאים הללו כפי שהם בחפצו ורצונו מן האין, וגם הזמן עצמו מכלל הנבראים [...] והתבונן נא מאד בענין זה, כדי שלא יחייבוך התשובות אשר אין מפלט מהן למי שלא ידע את זה, כי כאשר תקיים זמן לפני העולם נתחייבת לסבור את הקדמות, כי הזמן מקרה והכרחי שיהא לו נושא, אם כן חיובי שימצא דבר לפני מציאות העולם הזה המצוי עתה, ומזה היא הבריחה. זוהי אחת ההשקפות, והיא יסוד תורת משה רבינו ע"ה בלי ספק, והיא שניה ליסוד היחוד, ואל יעלה בלבך זולת זה. ואברהם אבינו ע"ה החל בפרסום השקפה זו אשר הביאו אליה העיון [...] ואין הבדל אצלינו בין מי שסובר שהשמים הוה

46 Grossman (*Limits*, p. 63) missed Shapiro's reference.

מדבר בהחלט ונפסדת אל דבר, או דעת ארסטו הסובר שהיא לא הוה ולא נפסדת. כי מטרת כל הולך בתורת משה ואברהם אבינו, או מי שהלך בדרכם אינו אלא הדעה שאין שום דבר קדמון כלל עם ה', ושהמצאת המצוי מן ההעדר כלפי ה' אינו מסוג הנמנע וגו'.[47]

The first opinion, which is the opinion of all who believe in the Law of Moses our Master, is that the world as a whole—I mean to say, every existent other than God—was brought into existence by God after having been purely and absolutely nonexistent, and that God had existed alone, and nothing else—neither an angel nor a sphere nor what subsists within the sphere. Afterwards, through His will and His volition, He brought into existence out of nothing all the beings as they are, time itself being one of the created things.... [Maimonides proceeds to argue at length for the nonessential nature of time.] Consider this matter thoroughly. For thus you will not be necessarily attached to objections from which there is no escape for him who does not know it. For if you affirm as true the existence of time prior to the world, you are necessarily bound to believe in the eternity [of the world]. For time is an accident which necessarily must have a substratum. Accordingly it follows necessarily that there existed some thing prior to the existence of this world existing now. [This "thing" could be satisfied with the Platonic prime mass; even it must be avoided at all costs.] But this notion must be avoided. This is one of the opinions. And it is undoubtedly a basis of the Law of Moses our Master. And it is second to the basis that is the belief in the unity [of God]. Nothing other than this should come to your mind. It was Abraham our Father, who began to proclaim in public this opinion to which speculation had led him.... [Maimonides continues to describe the respective opinions of Plato and Aristotle.] ... and there is, in our opinion, no difference between those who believe that heaven must of necessity be generated from a thing and pass away into a thing [i.e., the Platonic view] or the belief of Aristotle who believed that it is not subject to generation and corruption. For the purpose of every follower of the Law of Moses and Abraham our Father or of those who go the way of these two is to believe that there is nothing eternal in any way at all existing simultaneously with God; to believe also that the bringing into existence of a being out of nonexistence is for the deity not an impossibility...[48]

As is evident from this passage, Maimonides passionately believed that creation *ex nihilo* is Judaism's sole conception of the "origins" of the world. What we have before us, then, is not a discrepancy between the

---

47 Kafiḥ, pp. 189-193.

48 Pines, pp. 281-285. Honorifics have been omitted to allow for greater readability.

"elitist" *Guide* and the "popular" *Commentary*, but a conflict between two passages, mere chapters apart, in the *Guide*, one of which perfectly reflects Maimonides' statement in the *Commentary*.

Resolving the conflict requires one of two approaches.[49] One possibility would be to discount the passage in 2:13 of the *Guide*—with all its zeal—as mere political posturing. This is indeed the position taken by the many scholars, medieval and modern, enumerated by Shapiro (p. 77), and is in line with their general advocacy for reading the *Guide* esoterically. As touched upon earlier, this approach is rather suppositious and is possibly completely foreign to Maimonides' thinking.[50] It also expands the target

---

49 Marvin Fox's proposed solution to this problem is no solution at all. After a lengthy exposition within which Fox soundly affirms taking Maimonides' statements at face value, he digresses to discuss Maimonides' general model of the natural world, which harmonizes particular positive aspects of the Aristotelian and Kalam conceptions. Within this polychromatic backdrop, claims Fox, we can resolve the conflicting statements at hand as born from different worldviews holistically spun together. Furthermore, the Platonic view of Creation in particular, although potentially compatible with Judaism and science, "suffers from a serious methodological defect," namely that it is born of the conviction that creation *ex nihilo* is beyond God's capability. So while the conclusion can't be rejected, its method is unsound.

This does nothing to resolve the issue at hand. The aspects of Aristotelianism and the Kalam which Fox harmonizes for us are general ones, are evidently compatible to any reader of the *Guide*, and have no relevance to Maimonides' statements about the religious legitimacy of the Platonic view. Fox's second point also completely avoids the heart of the matter: If Platonism merely suffers from a methodological problem, how does that translate into a full-throated theological rejection?

Student (*Crossroads*, p. 283) proposes that the resolution of the conflict between the passage in the *Commentary* and *Guide* 2:25 lies in a shift in Maimonides' assessment of the theological significance of creation *ex nihilo*. This approach is untenable as it ignores *Guide* 2:13, in which Maimonides held of his position from the *Commentary* even as he composed the *Guide*.

Grossman (*Limits*, pp. 63-64) asserts that Maimonides' disclaimer in the revision of the Fourth Principle—"וזה שתראה שאני סובב וכו'"—precludes attaching any significance to 2:25. It should be obvious that Maimonides' disclaimer refers to his demonstrations in 2:15-17 ("כדי שיהא המופת מוחלט על מציאותו יתעלה"), as noted by Kafiḥ, and has no relevance to 2:25.

50 To touch briefly upon each of these sources:

a) Ibn Tibbon. Shapiro asserts that Ibn Tibbon's esoteric reading of Maimonides "must be taken very seriously" because Maimonides recognized that Ibn Tibbon "completely understood the secrets of the *Guide*." This would seem to be negated by Shapiro's observation (in a footnote) that this comment of Maimonides does not appear in any of the manuscripts of its alleged source, R. Abraham

Maimoni's *Milḥamot ha-Shem* (Jerusalem: Mossad ha-Rav Kook, n.d.). See also R. Reuven Margolies' remarks (ibid., p. 7, unreferenced by Shapiro) where he opines that the passage in question is distinctly uncharacteristic of R. Abraham and is one of a number of strange interpolations in the printed edition. In other words: Maimonides never said such a thing.

b) Ibn Kaspi. He contends that *Guide* 2:26 understood Lamentations 5:19, which says that God's throne ("*kisei*") will last for all generations (כסאך לדור ודור), as stating the eternity of the heavens. This is clearly incorrect because (a) in the following chapter Maimonides is explicit that by "eternity" he meant its future perpetuation despite its having been created (as observed by Duran, *Tashbeẓ* 3:53); and (b) Maimonides there is trying to understand the outlying opinion of R. Eliezer, which Maimonides dismisses as baffling, in contrast to the mainstream rabbinic consensus which ascribed creation to the כסא הכבוד (see ibid.). This source, then, does not reflect Maimonides' personal view. (c) It is clear that in this passage the *kisei* is not identified as the heavens. For even R. Eliezer, whom Maimonides suspects of asserting the existence of a prime mass, is quoted here as teaching that the heavens were created from the light of God's garment, while the earth emerged from the snow under His throne. As Duran explains, the *kisei* refers to the כסא הכבוד, and Maimonides is rejecting the possibility that it could be eternal unless it refers to God's inseparable Glory, as explained in *Guide* 1:9. (R. Profiat Duran and Ibn Shem Tov are clearly following Ibn Kaspi's lead.) In his commentary to 2:13, Ibn Kaspi offers no evidence for his reading of the *Guide* other than explaining how its statements supporting creationism could, in his opinion, be *potentially* read in a manner that does not contradict eternalism, and Ibn Kaspi expresses his satisfaction that Maimonides' words can be interpreted in accordance with the prevailing philosophic opinion (see following note). Grossman (*Limits*, p. 63) attacks Shapiro's citation of Ibn Kaspi as evidence for his position, claiming that Ibn Kaspi openly accepts creation *ex nihilo* in that very passage. Unfortunately, Grossman seems to have read no further than the second sentence of the two relevant pages. Immediately thereafter, Ibn Kaspi argues at length that not only is Scripture ambiguous on the matter, but that even Maimonides' passionate assertion of creationism can be twisted into conformity with eternalism.

c) Moses of Narbonne. It is worth pointing out that in his introduction (p. 28) Shapiro himself had declared Narboni and Albalag and "a host of other radical medieval philosophers" (which undoubtedly includes Nissim b. Moses, who is also included in the list at hand) as beyond the pale for the purposes of his work. In any event, to appreciate the motivations of Narboni and other Aristotelian commentators of the *Guide*, it is worth quoting Davidson at length (*Moses Maimonides*, pp. 391-392):

> Soon after Maimonides' death, his contemporary Averroes was hailed in Jewish philosophic circles as the authoritative interpreter of Aristotle, and a small number of commentators on the *Guide* undertook to bring Maimonides into as close a harmony as possible with Averroes and his version of Aristotelian philosophy. A rationale is articulated by Moses Narboni, who read Aristotle through the filter of Averroes' commentaries and was the

> most accomplished Jewish philosopher of the Averroist school. Narboni determined that Maimonides had represented Aristotle's position incorrectly on a matter bearing on the crucial question of the creation or eternity of the world. After giving "close consideration to what Maimonides wrote," Narboni decided that Maimonides "did not fail to understand Aristotle's position as thoroughly as might appear, his efforts at hiding secrets lead him to express himself in this problematic manner, and his words are amendable to an interpretation bringing them into harmony with the [philosophic] truth. Commentators have the obligation to interpret Maimonides in a fashion that harmonizes with the truth, as long as Maimonides' words permit. Particularly in instances where something he wrote does contain statements in harmony with the truth, the commentator must construe, combine, and integrate the words until they are… completely in harmony with the truth, which is reflected in the [occasional] statements." In short, it is a pious duty to mold Maimonides' words so that they agree with Averroes' version of Aristotle's philosophy, especially when something Maimonides wrote lends itself to such an interpretation.

Charles Manekin, in a lengthy critique of the esoteric approach to Maimonides' creationism, contends that this attitude of Narboni prevails with the modern advocates of the esoteric approach: "…to put Moses of Narbonne's principle more crudely: if some passages of the *Guide* assume Aristotle's position and others don't, reinterpret the latter to conform to the former. Narboni's hermeneutical principle informs creationism-denial to this day" (*Jewish Philosophy: Perspectives and Retrospectives*, ed. Jospe & Schwartz, Boston: Academic Studies, p. 218); "…creationism-denial not only reads Maimonides incorrectly; it *goes about* reading Maimonides incorrectly because it brackets vast amounts of text in the pursuit of an (sic) preconceived, idealized Maimonides, using exegetical methods [described] as 'midrashic'" (ibid., p. 232).

While the esoteric strand of Maimonidean interpretation makes for important study of intellectual history, if we are indeed serious about determining Maimonides' true intentions, the admitted biases of its proponents must be forefront in our minds.

d) Nuriel. Nuriel's thesis, that the term בורא is used in the *Guide* to allude to God as the cause of an *uncreated* world, hinges on Maimonides' observation in the *Guide* 3:10 that בריאה is associated with העדר (absence), as seen from the first verse of the Torah. Nuriel misunderstood this to be mean that God did not actively create the world but rather serves "passively" ("absent" from activity) as its cause. The correct understanding (as pointed out by Kafiḥ and Schwartz) is apparent from the end of 2:30: since the world was created *after* (or, to use the popular, yet imprecise, formulation: *from*) absolute non-existence (העדר) the term בריאה is appropriate. This, of course, yields the exact opposite of Nuriel's reading. See Yisrael Ravitzky, *"The Question of a Primordial or Created World in the Philosophy of Maimonides," Tarbiz* 35, p. 347 who dismisses Nuriel's reading as incoherent. Ravitzky's article (pp. 333-348) is dedicated to rejecting the methodological basis of Nuriel's thesis and to demonstrating the speciousness of the allusions he "uncovers" throughout the *Guide.*

of Maimonides' disingenuousness to include the sophisticated readership of the *Guide.*

The other option is to accept both passages and to harmonize them by developing a new understanding of Maimonides' position on the issues at hand. Considering that the theological rejection of the Platonic view in 2:13 (as well as in many other sources within the *Guide* and other works of Maimonides[51]) is starkly unambiguous, while its acceptance in 2:25 is merely a logical extension of his comments there, it would seem reasonable to modify our understanding of 2:25. Perhaps, as some have argued, Maimonides was of the opinion that although a Platonic reading of Genesis 1 is *potentially* legitimate should the theory be compellingly demonstrated, so long as that hasn't happened, the straightforward reading is by

---

e) Herbert Davidson. Shapiro accurately references Davidson as merely "adduc[ing] evidence that Maimonides held the Platonic view." This evidence consists of the contradiction dealt with in the text and similar contradictions. Davidson acknowledges that these contradictions may be nothing more than imprecise wording (a point he reiterates in his *Moses Maimonides*, p. 369) and, as mentioned earlier, that there may be no esoteric belief at all (ibid., p. 391). The point of Davidson's essay was to demonstrate that even if one were to assume that Maimonides had an esoteric belief in this area, the argument that that belief is Aristotelian eternalism is without basis.

51 See Davidson, *Moses Maimonides*, p. 400.

default the legitimate one and determines normative belief.[52, 53]

The Eighth Principle: The Integrity of the Scriptural Text

As mentioned at the outset, the second major piece of evidence for Shapiro's proposition involves the integrity of the biblical text. Shapiro's discussion of Maimonides' Eighth Principle begins with the observation that one of the ideas seemingly expressed within it—that the Torah in the possession of the Jewish people today is identical to the one given to Moses at Sinai—simply cannot be true. Shapiro clearly demonstrates this by way of dozens of talmudic and rabbinic sources that openly refer to the existence of variant texts of Scripture from as early as the days of Ezra, as well as the reality of conflicting textual traditions among different communities until this very day. Without question, the popular liturgical formula of this principle, the eighth of the "*Ani Ma'amins,*" which certainly reflects this notion, is incorrect.

However, Shapiro further submits that Maimonides intended to convey this very idea to the readership of his Thirteen Principles. Indeed, this

---

52 See <http://blog.dovidgottlieb.com/2018/06/guide-following-is-myformulation-of.html>. This seems to me to be the understanding of *Tashbez* (cited in n. 50(b), emphasis added):

> ואם יאמין [...] שהוא קדמון, אם כן אינו על דעת תורתנו, ויהיה על דעת אפלטון [...] אף על פי שאינה על דרך אריסטוטאליס, מכל מקום אינה גם כן על דעת <u>הנגלה</u> מתורתנו, <u>ואין לנו כח להוציאו מנגלהו</u> כמו שפירש הרב ז"ל בפרקים הקודמים לו.

In this responsum, Duran is explaining the *Guide*'s (2:26) treatment of R. Eliezer's cryptic statements about the origins of heaven and earth (which were discussed earlier in this essay in reference to Ibn Kaspi). He takes Maimonides as saying that if, indeed, R. Eliezer posited the eternalism position, even if not in the Aristotelian version (which is anathema to Maimonides), it would still run counter to normative Judaism because of its inconsistency with the *apparent* reading of the Genesis narrative. While accommodation is, at times, valid in scriptural interpretation, Maimonides felt that in this instance the evidence for eternalism does not justify such an accommodation. Consequently, the apparent reading of Scripture remains the only valid one, and deviation from the takeaway of that reading—the doctrine of creationism—is heretical. This understanding of Maimonides by Duran is particularly striking in light of Duran's assertion (cited by Shapiro, n. 40) that, if necessary, he could reinterpret Genesis 1 even in accordance with the Aristotelian view.

53 Shapiro (once again, in a footnote, *Mesorah le-Yosef*, p. 371, n. 58) later acknowledges that although *Guide* 2:25 is widely cited, intellectual honesty demands noting the contradiction with 2:13. His suggested solution is to invoke the *Guide*'s Seventh Cause for contradictions and to reference Davidson, *Maimonides' Secret Position*; both of these propositions have been addressed above.

seems to be indicated by a plain reading of the text.[54] This, of course, leads to the question of why Maimonides would write something that is plainly false. Shapiro (pp. 120-121) proposes that Maimonides intentionally created this bit of dogma because he deemed it necessary to help anchor the masses in their confidence in the Torah's authenticity. Jews in Arab lands were confronted with the Islamic accusation of *taḥrif*, i.e., that their ancestors had edited out significant details from what was originally an Islamo-oriented Scripture. The Eighth Principle would reassure them that this was a non-issue: the scriptural text had been preserved with such assiduity that it was faithful to the original Mosaic version down to the letter and thus beyond reproach.[55]

A noticeable difficulty with Shapiro's theory is that it seems to violate the most important rule about successful lying: do not tell a lie that is clearly a lie.[56] How could Maimonides try to pass off the idea that the scriptural text is flawless if, as Shapiro details at length, there is abundant proof to the contrary? In Shapiro's words (p. 121): "[Maimonides] is denying a fact which was obvious to anyone with even a perfunctory knowledge of the Pentateuch, namely, that there were differences in texts." Why, then, was he not concerned about this fabrication being exposed and possibly destroying his reputation? Shapiro (p. 120) contends that "[t]he masses then (and today) could not be expected to understand the problems relating to the biblical text." In other words, Maimonides' ruse was directed at the unlearned masses and not at the scholars who would not have been taken in by it. This seems difficult to square with Maimonides' inclusion of his Thirteen Principles as part of his *Commentary on the Mishnah*, which would have been used not by the ignorant masses but by the learned, or, at the least, by the intellectually curious. And regardless of his primary target audience, did Maimonides expect that this work, and particularly its groundbreaking essay on the theological underpinnings of Judaism—arguably its most prominent section—would go unread by his rabbinic peers?[57] Similarly, with regard to the supposed inclusion of this idea in the *Iggeret Teiman* (which will be discussed shortly),

54 See further for a full citation of the relevant passage of Maimonides.

55 See earlier, p. 122, for the relevant citations from Shapiro.

56 As per the popular adage: הרוצה לשקר ירחיק עדיו. See *Kitvei Ramban*, ed. Chavel (Jerusalem: Mossad ha-Rav Kook, 1963), vol. 1, p. 310; R. Asher b. Yeḥiel, T.B. *Shevuot* (6:13).

57 Abarbanel's suggestion (*Rosh Amanah*, chs. 6, 9, and 23, quoted by Shapiro, p. 7) that the Principles, as well as the entirety of the *Commentary on the Mishnah*, were written for the "masses," does not contradict this point. As indicated in the pas-

while it is reasonable to assume that Maimonides' chief concern was to preserve the faith of the simple Yemenite masses, the epistle was addressed to the *ḥakham* Rabbi Yaakov, whom Maimonides addresses as a scholar, and Maimonides waxes eloquent about the scholarship found in the Yemenite community.[58] Assuming that Maimonides was not engaging in mere social niceties, he seems to have been aware of, or presumed, a minimal degree of sophistication at the receiving end of his letter.[59]

It bears noting that whereas today the masses (and many of the learned) would accept a teaching of Maimonides on his authority, he did not enjoy such influence in his own lifetime. His writings were not beyond critique, and his contemporaries did not shy away from polemicizing over what they saw as his theological errors, whether real or imagined. This is particularly relevant with regard to his *Commentary on the Mishnah*, which he completed at the age of thirty, when he did not have the religious and social authority he would command later in life. It thus seems difficult to imagine that Maimonides deluded himself into thinking that the educated public would swallow his writings whole, contrivances included.

As mentioned, the plain reading of Maimonides' language does indeed convey the popular notion that the contemporary text of the Torah is identical to that of Sinai. This language is found in two sources: the Eighth Principle, included in the *Commentary on the Mishnah* (*Sanhedrin* 10:1, Kafiḥ vol. 2, p. 143) and the *Iggeret Teiman* (*Letter to Yemen*) (*Igrot ha-Rambam,* ed. Sheilat, pp. 131-132). In his analysis of the *Commentary on the Mishnah* passage, Shapiro (pp. 115-116) at first suggests that Maimonides never intended to say that Scripture isn't susceptible to mistakes creeping into it over time; his point, rather, is that Moses did not tamper with the Torah communicated from God and presented it faithfully to the Jewish people.[60] Shapiro (p. 120) subsequently abandons this approach because of

---

sage Shapiro quotes, and more so in Abarbanel's full language, Abarbanel's intention is not to the hopelessly naïve but to those insufficiently sophisticated to distill a systematic set of dogma from the Torah.

58 "לכבוד גדולת קדושת מרנא ורבנא יעקב החכם הנחמד היקר הנכבד [...] ולכלל כל אחינו אלופינו, כל תלמידי הקהילות אשר בתימן [...]. וכל היום הוגים בתורת משה, הולכים בדרך הורה רב אשי [...]. וכאשר הגיע אלינו כתבך [...] והוא העיד בפנינו עליך כי [...] ומרודפי התורה ואהבי דתותיה השוקדים על דלתותיה וכו'" (*Igrot ha-Rambam*, ed. Sheilat [Ma'aleh Adumim: Sheilat, 1995], pp. 113-115).

59 See Abraham Halkin (ed.), *Iggeret Teiman* (New York: American Academy for Jewish Research, 1952), p. vii.

60 As Shapiro notes, this approach was advanced by R. Chaim Hirschensohn, *Malki ba-Kodesh* (St. Louis: Moinester, 1921), vol. 2, pp. 234-235 and by R. Dovid Cohen, *Mas'at Kapai* (New York: Mesorah, 1984), vol. 1, p. 92. Shapiro (p. 91, n.

other problems emerging from this passage: Shapiro (p. 106) takes Maimonides as positing that the entirety of the Torah, including its final eight verses, are indisputably part of the Mosaic revelation, despite the talmudic opinion that the final eight verses were written by Joshua.[61] Shapiro also finds it impossible to accept that Maimonides would consider Ibn Migash and Ibn Ezra—who denied the Mosaic authorship of the final eight verses (and, in the latter instance, of other sections of Scripture)—heretics. Shapiro therefore adopts the position that Maimonides was putting up a front when presenting this idea as a required belief. Once that concept is in play with regard to this principle, Shapiro finds it reasonable to assume that the "textual infallibility concept" is disingenuous as well.

I would contend that Shapiro's discarded approach is the more reasonable one.[62] It is evident that the thrust of Maimonides' assertion throughout the entire passage is that one must believe that the Torah transmitted *by Moses beginning at Sinai and concluding at the end of his life* was identical to that which God had communicated to him and that its entire content is holy and valuable. As the communication of virtually the entire Torah was not received by the Jews directly from God rather through the medium of an individual human being, there existed the concern that the communication may have been compromised, thus casting doubt on Judaism's claim that the Torah reflects authentic revelation. It was, therefore, critical to establish Moses' unimpeachable integrity, and God did indeed do so through the circumstances surrounding Moses' prophecy.[63]

---

3) observes that they were working with the deficient standard edition of the *Commentary*, in which the crucial words הנמצאת בידינו היום הזה are absent. It should be noted that even that edition contains the latter relevant section from the *Commentary* passage (highlighted below) and yet this did not prevent R. Hirschenson and R. Cohen from advancing this proposition. In his more recent *ha-Emunah ha-Ne'emanah* (New York: Mesorah, 2012), p. 95, R. Cohen maintains the argument despite his usage of the more accurate Kafiḥ edition.

Another source quoted by Shapiro is R. Yaakov Weinberg as recorded in *Fundamentals & Faith* (Southfield: Targum, 1991), pp. 90-91; *Even She'tiyah*, ed. Y. Bechhopfer (Jerusalem: Makhon Even She'tiyah, 2010), p. 80-81, and this despite R. Weinberg's use of the Kafiḥ edition.

61 R. Judah or R. Nehemiah, T.B. *Bava Batra* 15a and *Menaḥot* 30a.

62 See Aharon Wexler, "Reflections on Maimonides' Eighth Principle of Faith: Its Implications for Orthodox Bible Students," *Jewish Bible Quarterly* (January-March 2013) who advances this approach as well. His synthesizing of Halivni's "Ḥat'u Yisrael" theology with this approach, while of a similar motif, is unnecessary for resolving Maimonides' position.

63 According to *Hilkhot Yesodei ha-Torah* 8:1, this was the Jews' prophetic viewing of God communicating with Moses at Sinai. As to why a different basis is given

Accordingly, Maimonides, in this principle, asserts that adherence to Jewish belief hinges on the recognition of this reliability of Moses' personal transmission. It is this concept that Maimonides fleshes out with numerous examples and which he anchors in scriptural and rabbinic sources.

In contrast, the idea that the Mosaic revelation was perfectly maintained by subsequent generations until our day is indicated only in the brief phrase הנמצאת בידינו היום הזה at the beginning of the passage and the words וזה שאנו עושים היום [...] היא עצמה הצורה שאמר ה' למשה ואמר לנו near the end. In both instances, the idea is mentioned in passing, with the conclusive point being the aforementioned reliability of Moses himself. Regarding the notion of an eternally infallible transmission, Maimonides does not elaborate upon it, provide illustrations for it, or cite its source. Critically, when he distills the principle at hand in the language of the Talmud, he pointedly says that its denier posits *Moses'* manipulation of the Torah. It is therefore reasonable to assume that Maimonides did not mention כל התורה הזו הנמצאת בידינו היום הזה with dogmatic intent, but out of a sense of confidence in the general reliability of the tradition's preservation as a whole.[64]

---

in the Eighth Principle, see Cohen, *ha-Emunah ha-Ne'emanah*, pp. 103-104. Some add that Moses' free will was suspended, thus removing his capacity to tamper with his prophecies, see R. Meir Simchah of Dvinsk, *Meshekh Ḥokhmah*, introduction to *Shemot*; Weinberg, *Fundamentals & Faith*, pp. 91-92.

64 The phenomenon of inexactitude in Maimonides' writings, including its acknowledgment by traditionalist scholars, is documented at length by Shapiro, *Studies in Maimonides* (pp. 1-68); see p. 9 regarding the *Commentary* in particular. The language of the *Commentary*, with emphasis added, is reproduced at length so that the reader can see for himself how the above understanding rings true (English translation adapted from Kellner, *Dogma*, pp. 14-15 quoting trans. D. Blumenthal, with emphasis added).

והיסוד השמיני הוא תורה מן השמים. והוא, שנאמין שכל התורה הזו הנמצאת בידינו היום הזה היא התורה שניתנה למשה, ושהיא כולה מפי הגבורה, כלומר שהגיעה אליו כולה מאת ה' הגעה שקורים אותה על דרך ההשאלה דבור, ואין יודע איכות אותה ההגעה אלא הוא עליו השלום אשר הגיעה אליו, ושהוא במעלת לבלר שקורין לפניו והוא כותב כולה תאריכיה וספוריה ומצותיה, וכך נקרא מחוקק. ואין הבדל בין ובני חם כוש ומצרים ופוט וכנען, ושם אשתו מהיטבאל בת מטרד, או אנכי ה', ושמע ישראל ה' אלקינו ה' אחד, הכל מפי הגבורה והכל תורת ה' תמימה טהורה קדושה אמת. ולא נעשה מנשה אצלם כופר ופוקר יותר מכל כופר אחר אלא לפי שחשב שיש בתורה תוך וקליפה, ושאלו התאריכים והסיפורים אין תועלת בהם, ומשה מדעתו אמרם, *וזהו ענין אין תורה מן השמים*, *אמרו שהוא האומר שכל התורה כולה מפי הקב"ה חוץ מפסוק אחד שלא אמרו הקב"ה אלא משה מפי עצמו וזה הוא כי דבר ה' בזה* - יתעלה ה' ממה שאומרים הכופרים - אלא כל אות שבה יש בה חכמות ונפלאות למי שהבינו ה', ולא תושג תכלית חכמתה, ארוכה מארץ מדה ורחבה מני ים. ואין לאדם אלא להתפלל כמו דוד משיח אלקי יעקב שהתפלל גל עיני ואביטה נפלאות מתורתיך. וכן פירושה המקובל גם הוא מפי הגבורה, וזה שאנו עושים היום צורת הסוכה והלולב והשופר והציצית והתפילים וזולתם היא עצמה

Further support for this reading can be found in Maimonides' formulation in his *Mishneh Torah*.[65] As noted by Shapiro himself (p. 115), there the heresy is unambiguously limited to denying divine authorship of what was transmitted at Sinai.

> שלשה הן הכופרים בתורה. האומר שאין התורה מעם ה', אפילו פסוק אחד אפילו תיבה אחת <u>אם אמר משה אמרו מפי עצמו</u> הרי זה כופר בתורה.
> There are three types of "deniers of the Torah:" (a) One who believes that the Torah isn't divine—even regarding one verse or even

---

הצורה שאמר ה' למשה ואמר לנו, והוא רק מוביל שליחות נאמן במה שהביא, *והדבור המורה על היסוד הזה השמיני הוא אמרו בזאת תדעון כי ה' שלחני וכו' כי לא מלבי.*

The Eighth Foundation is that the Torah is from heaven; to wit, it (must) be believed that the whole of this Torah which is in our hand today is the Torah that was brought down to Moses, our teacher; that all of it is from God (by) the transmission which is called 'speech'; that no one knows the quality of that transmission except he to whom it was transmitted, peace be upon him; and, that it was dictated to him while he was the rank of a scribe; and, that he wrote down all of its dates, its narratives, and its laws—and, for this, he is called a legislator. There is no difference between *the sons of Ham were Kush, Mizrayim, Fut, and Canaan* and *the name of his wife was Mehetabel, the daughter of Matred* on the one hand, and *I am the Lord your God* and *Hear, O Israel, the Lord, our God, the Lord is One* on the other hand. Everything is from the mouth of the Mighty One; everything is the Torah of God: whole, pure, holy [and] true. Indeed, Menasseh became, in the eyes of the Sages, the person strongest in heresy and hypocrisy for he thought that the Torah was composed of kernels and husks and that these dates and these narratives had no value and that they were composed by Moses. *This is the issue of 'the Torah is not from heaven.' And the Sages have said that he who believes that 'the Torah is entirely from the mouth of the Almighty except for this (i.e., any given) verse which was not said by the Holy One, blessed be He, <u>but Moses said it on his own authority</u>,' is one to whom the following verse applies,* He disdains the word of God. May God be exalted above that which the heretics say! Rather, every letter of the Torah contains wisdom and wonders for him whom God has given to understand it. Its ultimate wisdom cannot be perceived as it is said, *Its measure is greater than the earth and broader than the sea.* A man can only follow in the steps of David, the anointed of the God of Jacob, the most pleasant singer of the hymns of Israel, who prayed singing, *Unmask my eyes that I may see wonders from Your Torah.* Similarly, its interpretation as it has been handed down is also 'From the mouth of the Almighty.' That which we observe today, such as the form of the Sukkah, the Lulav, the Shofar, the Ẓiẓit, the Tefillin, and other such forms are the actual forms which God told to Moses and which he told to us. He is the transmitter of the Message, faithful in its transmission. *The verse on the basis of which this eighth foundation is attested is his [i.e., Moses'] saying,* By this shall you know that the Lord has sent me to do all these things.

65 *Hilkhot Teshuvah* 3:8, with this author's translation and emphasis added.

one word—*if he believes that Moses himself devised it,* he is a denier of the Torah.

Shapiro fails to explain why this passage—which was also intended for the masses—was not written in a manner reflecting Maimonides' supposed agenda.[66]

Regarding Shapiro's concerns over Maimonides' supposed attitude towards Ibn Migash and Ibn Ezra, the following should be noted. We have no evidence that Maimonides had high regard for, or was even familiar with, the writings of Ibn Ezra. His name appears only once in all of Maimonides' writings, in an offhand reference within a letter to Ibn Tibbon.[67] And with regard to Ibn Migash, whom Maimonides certainly revered, there is no evidence that he adopted the non-Mosaic origin of the final eight verses. The source cited by Shapiro (p. 105, n. 88), Ibn Migash's commentary to T.B. *Bava Batra* 15a, is merely an explanation of the opinion cited in the Talmud. If the fragment preserved in the standard edition is at first glance misleading, the newly-published edition from manuscript[68] plainly shows that it is only a section of an explication of the entire talmudic passage.

That said, the primary question of how Maimonides viewed R. Judah's attribution of the Torah's concluding eight verses to Joshua is indeed a serious one. A possible resolution lies in the approach of R. Wolf Boskowitz (d. 1818).[69] He posits that all agree that the final eight verses were

66 As to the possibility that Maimonides abandoned this approach before composing the *Mishneh Torah*, it should be noted that *Hilkhot Teshuvah* was seemingly written during the seven years which elapsed between the completion of the *Commentary on the Mishnah* and the writing of the *Iggeret Teiman*, which, according to Shapiro, also reflected this stratagem; see Sheilat, *Igrot*, pp. 78-79.

67 *Igrot ha-Rambam*, ed. Sheilat, p. 530. The ethical will attributed to Maimonides in which he adulates Ibn Ezra's writings is widely considered a fabrication. See Sheilat, *Igrot*, p. 697; Isadore Twersky, *Did Ibn Ezra Influence Maimonides?* in *Rabbi Abraham Ibn Ezra: Studies in the Writings of a Twelfth-Century Jewish Polymath* (Cambridge: Harvard University, 1993), pp. 23-24 (Heb. section). Twersky's general conclusion concurs that there is no substantial evidence of influence. This was also the view of the esteemed bibliographer R. Shmuel Ashkenazi, *Igrot Shmuel* (Jerusalem, 2021), vol. 2, p. 1092. Shapiro himself took note of this consensus, <https://www.torahinmotion.org/podcast/the-making-of-my-most-recent-book-a-thirty-year-story-part-42> (at 12:50). See also Maimon, *Peirush ha-Torah, Bereishit,* p. 236, n. 26.

68 Ed. Politensky & DeHan, n.p. 2015.

69 *Seder Mishneh* (Jerusalem, 1966), vol. 1, pp. 128-130. He was the son of the famed author of the *Maḥaẓit ha-Shekel* and one of the outstanding *geonim* of his generation.

communicated by God to Moses. R. Judah and R. Simon disagree whether Moses then relayed these verses to Joshua, who recorded them in the scriptural text, or whether Moses recorded these verses himself. For Maimonides' purposes, both opinions are theologically valid, for so long as the entire Torah's provenance is the Mosaic revelation, the identity of who set quill to parchment is irrelevant. Consistent with this, the sources in Maimonides' writings in which he dogmatically insists on the entire Torah's Mosaic origin could be read to refer to communication and not publication.[70]

The second source relevant to Shapiro's position is the *Iggeret Teiman*, or *Letter to Yemen*, in which Maimonides directly addresses the Islamic claim of *taḥrif.* His response is that the universal uniformity of the scriptural text, despite its proliferation over the vast geography of the Jewish world, renders the possibility of coordinated tampering highly unlikely. It would have been virtually impossible to orchestrate the editing of every Torah scroll in every far-flung community, especially considering the meticulousness with which Jews everywhere copied and maintained them, as evidenced by their consistency.

Shapiro (p. 120) reads this passage literally, taking Maimonides to mean that absolutely no discrepancies whatsoever exist amongst Torah scrolls. In the same vein, Shapiro notes that Ibn Daud[71] and Albo[72] simi-

---

70 *Igrot ha-Rambam*, ed. Sheilat, p. 127, 410; Introduction to *Mishneh Torah.* R. Boskowitz was attempting to resolve the question (cited by Shapiro, p. 118, n. 180, in the name of contemporary sources) as to why Maimonides (*Hil. Tefillah* 13:6) ruled like R. Simon (שמונה פסוקים שבסוף התורה [...] ומשה מפי הגבורה אמרם) over R. Judah despite the general rule to the contrary. His proposition was that Maimonides had indeed ruled like R. Judah that Joshua wrote the final verses; Maimonides' intent there was that they were revealed to Moses by God. This approach is difficult, for, as referenced by Shapiro, Maimonides states clearly in the introduction to his *Commentary on the Mishnah* that Moses wrote thirteen complete Torah scrolls just before his death. For our purposes, however, this is irrelevant, for while Maimonides assumed for historical purposes in accordance with R. Simon's opinion, nowhere does he state that it is a matter of dogma that Moses *transcribed* every word of his revelation of the Torah.

71 ואנו מוצאים התורה מפורסמת בנוסח אחד אין חילוף בו בין קהילות ישראל אשר מארצות הודו, עד קצה ספרד והמערב באורך היישוב, ומקצות גבולי אפריקא, והאגט וכוש, ותימן בדרום, עד קצה ערי אל מוגוס אשר על הים המקיף הצפוני, ולא חלק חולק, Daud, *ha-Emunah ha-Ramah* (n.p.: Makhon Hagut ve-Da'at Yisrael, 2019), p. 297.

72 וזה לאות כי היא שמורה בידם כמו שנתנה למשה בלי שנוי. והראיה , שהיא נמצאת היום ביד כל ישראל המפוזרים בכל העולם מקצה מזרח עד סוף המערב על נוסח אחד בלי שנוי, Albo, *Sefer ha-Ikkarim* (Jerusalem: Horeb, 1995), vol. 2, p. 375.

larly made this argument to buttress the reliability of the biblical text. Being that they could not have truly believed in such a patently false idea, Shapiro contends that these three great thinkers—polemically enmeshed as they were—allowed themselves to bend the truth for the sake of the greater good.

It is, however, plausible that their intention was not to the consistency of the text of Scripture, but its meaning. After all, the charge being deflected is that someone or some group (in Ibn Daud and Albo's case: Ezra) deliberately altered the text to suit their purposes.[73] What would that party have changed—the spelling of a word from מלא (plene) to חסר (deficient), or from פצוע דכה to פצוע דכא, or some other inconsequential minutia? Of course not. Rather, such a person would have added to or detracted from the significant *content*. To this, Ibn Daud, Maimonides, and Albo could confidently point to the uniformity of Scripture's *content*, which is virtually perfect down to the word, as precluding such a possibility.[74] The fact that insignificant variations invariably crept into the text does not contradict this point, and these authorities likely considered this obvious enough that it need not be mentioned. It would therefore seem a reasonable alternative to not read their words in a literal fashion, thus obviating the need to conclude that they were denying an obvious fact.

Such an understanding reads well with the thrust of the passages of Ibn Daud and Albo. Maimonides' language, though, demands more concerted attention.

> ועוד בהיותה קבלה רבים מרבים במזרח הארץ ובמערבה, ולא נמצא בכלם חלוף כלל, ואפילו בנקדה ובמקומה לא נמצא חלוף, ואף כי בענין.[75]
> Secondly, there is a uniform tradition as to the text of the Bible both in the East and the West, with the result that no differences in the text exist at all, not even in the vocalization, for they are all correct. Nor do any differences effecting the meaning exist.[76]

---

73 אכן החולקים עלינו אמרו [...] וכאשר הגיעו לבבל, קם בהם איש, שמו עזרא, ונזכר ממקצת התורה ושכח קצתה, והפך פסוקים מה היה זכור מהם אל מה שהיה מסכים לסברתו, וכתב להם זאת התורה הנמצאת עתה בידם וכו', Daud, p. 294. ואחר שנשארו שם כל הגדולים ויודעי התורה לא היה רשאי לשנות דבר בתורה, כי לא תהיה תורתו מסכמת עם תורת כל הנשארים בבבל והנמצאים בערי שומרון ובארץ אשור ובמקומות אחרים שלא הסכימו לעלות עמו, Albo, ibid.

74 The solitary known textual discrepancy which affects the meaning of a word occurs in Genesis 9:29, where a letter *vav* is in question; even there, the general sense of the verse is unaffected. See Cassel, *ha-Olam ha-Mufla shel Nusaḥ ha-Torah* (Jerusalem: Carmel, 2019), pp. 187-190.

75 *Igrot ha-Rambam*, ed. Sheilat, pp. 131-132, which utilizes Ibn Tibbon's translation.

76 Translation by Boaz Cohen in Halkin, *Iggeret*, English section p. viii.

This does seem to plainly state that no differences exist even in a single "point" (נקודה) or iota. Upon critical examination, however, the nature of this sentence becomes rather less straightforward.

The manuscripts of the *Iggeret Teiman* have come down to us in four formats: the Arabic original and the Hebrew translations of Samuel ibn Tibbon, Nahum ha-Ma'aravi,[77] and Abraham ibn Ḥasdai. Abraham Halkin, in his masterful critical edition of the *Iggeret*, notes that the sentence in question is clearly present in but one of the eight known manuscripts of the Ibn Tibbon edition[78] and in one of the two known manuscripts of the Nahum ha-Ma'aravi edition, and that the known complete manuscripts of the Ibn Ḥasdai edition, both of which do contain it, are only two in number. Nonetheless, despite the absence of this sentence in the majority of the known Hebrew manuscripts, the fact that it does appear in three different, yet similar, renderings in three different translations indicates, in the opinion of this author, that it did indeed exist in the original Arabic from which they were translated. However, regarding the three complete Arabic manuscripts available to Halkin, he notes that the sentence is absent from two of them—including the one regarded as the most authoritative by both Halkin (p. xxxii) and Sheilat (p. 164)—while the third manuscript which does contain it is characterized by Halkin and Sheilat as a later abridgment.[79] Moreover, both Halkin and Sheilat posit that all three translators worked off copies of the abridged edition, which diminishes the value of all of the Hebrew manuscripts regarding the matter at hand. What emerges is that the authenticity of this sentence suffers from serious doubts.[80]

---

77 On Naḥum ha-Ma'aravi, see Halkin, ibid., p. xxxiii (Heb.), n. 337.

78 Ibid., pp. 38-39. In five of them the sentence is absent and of the three that contain it only one of them was accessible to Halkin, the existence of the other two being known only from the notes of Professor Friedlander.

79 Although Halkin does favor the possibility that the abridgment is the work of Maimonides himself.
The use of the inferior London MS as the basis of the text of both the Halkin and Sheilat editions is, by their own word (p. xxxii and p. 80 respectively), due to its similarity to the Hebrew translations. Kafiḥ, *Igrot ha-Rambam* (Jerusalem: Mossad ha-Rav Kook, 1994) borrowed Halkin's text as the basis of his own (p. 13). Hence, the inclusion of the sentence in question in the text of all the contemporary editions should not be taken as an indication of its pedigree.

80 As stated, the above reflects the research of Halkin in 1952, which remains the most authoritative published work on the text of the *Iggeret Teiman*. A proper analysis of the issue would require professional examination of the many more manuscripts available today. According to its catalogue, the National Library of Israel collection <web.nli.org.il> includes at least 26 microfilms of complete

As for the proper translation of the passage, it too seems difficult. The original Judeo-Arabic reads ולו פי נקטה, the most literal translation of which would seem to be as Ibn Tibbon rendered ואפילו בנקדה (note the phonetic similarity of נקטה to נקדה, both of which mean "a point" or "a dot"). As they were most probably perplexed as to what "dots" are present in the text of the Torah scroll, the other translators interpreted them as the vowel or cantillation signs and took the liberty of translating as such.[81] As neither of these are traditionally marked in Torah scrolls, it seems strange that Maimonides would draw evidence from them, unless one assumes that he was referring to the vowelized codices used for private study or for following the Torah reading. This would only deepen the problem of the transparency of Maimonides' "ruse," as these books had a much higher incidence of errors, and it is difficult to imagine any consumer of the *Iggeret* being unaware that his personal *ḥumash* is frequently at odds with that of his neighbor in the synagogue.[82]

I would, therefore, suggest that the word נקטה here should be understood not as a "dot" but as a "particular item," in the same sense as the word נקודה is used in Hebrew and "point" is used in English. Maimonides is stating that there exist no variations of any of the points, or details, of the *content* of Scripture, and certainly not in the general subjects (ואף כי בענין). This is indeed a true statement which, as described earlier, cogently addresses the challenge Maimonides was confronting and precludes the need to attribute to him disingenuousness.[83]

---

manuscripts of the *Iggeret* (besides many Genizah fragments), 17 of which are accessible on its online portal (as of July 2020). Excluding five of these manuscripts which were used by Halkin and four within which this author could not locate the relevant section, the remaining eight (four Ibn Tibbon, three Naḥum ha-Ma'aravi, and one Ibn Ḥasdai) all contain the relevant sentence. The Vatican Digital Library <digi.vatlib.it> contains one additional Ibn Tibbon MS which includes the sentence, as well.

81 Naḥum: ואפילו בדקדוקה ואפילו בין קמץ חטף לשורוק לא נמצא בה שום חילוף. Ibn Ḥasdai: ואפילו בנקודה ובטעמיה לא נמצא שם שום שינוי. Cohen: not even in the vocalization.

82 See Moshe Goshen-Gottstein, "Biblical Manuscripts in the United States," *Textus* 2 (1962), p. 40: "After handling thousands of these fragments, it becomes obvious that we should not expect these 'private' codices to reflect the exact spelling of a model *receptus* text any more than we would of a biblical quotation in a non-biblical text. In quality these are the same differences we encounter even in Massora and Study codices…, in quantity per unit they outnumber them by far."

83 In private correspondences with this author, R. Yitzhak Sheilat and R. Yaakov Wincelberg (translator of R. Abraham Maimoni's *ha-Maspik le-Ovdei ha-Shem*

The Ninth Principle: The Eternity of the Torah

The third area to which Shapiro applies his theory is the Ninth Principle, which states that the *mitzvot* will never be abrogated. Shapiro (p. 131) contends that while Maimonides certainly believed this to be true, as is evident from his numerous emphatic statements on the matter, he could not have truly held it to be indisputable dogma in light of the "good number of talmudic and midrashic texts [that] do not accept this position." It is therefore reasonable to assume that Maimonides included this idea in his Principles to serve as a bulwark against the Islamic doctrine of supersessionism, i.e., that Mosaic Law lapsed upon the emergence of the teachings of the Koran. This too, is "a 'necessary belief', directed towards the masses and designed to help them deal with ideological assaults from the Islamic world." [84]

Let us examine each of these rabbinic sources. The first is a passage in T.B. *Niddah* (61b), which records an opinion that although the Torah prohibits the wearing of *sha'atnez*, it is permissible to wrap a corpse in shrouds which contain it. R. Joseph then observes that a corollary of this law is the notion that the *mitzvot* will be nullified in "the future."[85] Seemingly, the period referenced here is the post-Resurrection era, with the logic being that since the dead will arise with their clothing intact (as the Sages describe elsewhere), if the prohibition of *sha'atnez* would still be in force, it would be immediately transgressed by the resurrected. Since the dead may indeed be buried in shrouds of *sha'atnez*, it follows that the laws of the Torah—including the prohibition of *sha'atnez*—will have lapsed before the Resurrection occurs.[86] Shapiro suggests that being that elsewhere Maimonides seems to assume that the Resurrection will occur during the Messianic Era—which, in Maimonides' opinion, will not involve any ongoing supernatural changes in the world order—it emerges that, according to R. Joseph, the Torah's laws will expire at some future date within human history.

---

from the Arabic [Feldheim, 2013]) confirmed that this is a plausible rendering of the Arabic original of this passage. R. Sheilat noted that it does not seem to fit with Ibn Tibbon's translation.

84 Notably, unlike the previous two items, Shapiro does not repeat this evidence in his later essay, *Mesorah*.

85 "זאת אומרת מצות בטלות לעתיד לבא".

86 This is indeed the understanding of Tosafot and Ritva. Shapiro, like R. Unterman and many others before and after him, followed the older printed editions of *Ḥiddushei ha-Ritva*, which erroneously attributed Rashba's comments to Ritva. Ritva's actual writings on the end of *Niddah* were printed from manuscript in the Mossad ha-Rav Kook edition. See the introduction to that volume.

However, as noted by Shapiro (p. 122, n. 4), there is an alternative understanding of this passage that was adopted by Rashba and Ran.[87] They took "the future" to refer to the afterlife, with the point being that there is no prohibition on the part of the living to clothe a dead body—which is no longer obligated to observe halakhah—in *sha'atnez* (unlike the similar proscription for adults to do so with unobligated children). As further noted by Shapiro, R. Isser Yehuda Unterman conjectured that Maimonides may have also understood the passage in this manner, which would, of course, obviate any conflict with the Ninth Principle. Indeed, there is considerable evidence to support this reading of Maimonides. Firstly, Maimonides' *Commentary* on the relevant *mishnah* (*Kilayim* 9:4, Kafiḥ vol. 1, p. 133, free translation) unambiguously states as much:[88]

> תכריכי המת, "אכפאן אלמיית", לפי שכשמת האדם נפטר מכל המצות, ואין החיים חייבין להזהר בו בשום לאו או לקיים בו שום מצוה מכל המצות האמורות בתורה כגון הציצית והתפלין וזולתם.
>
> *The shrouds of a corpse* [*aren't subject to the prohibition of* sha'atnez]... For when a person dies he is rendered exempt from all of the commandments and the living aren't responsible to be wary of [his transgression of] any prohibition or to facilitate his fulfillment of any *mitzvah* of the Torah, such as *zizit*, *tefillin*, or the like.

Clearly, Maimonides understood the novelty of this halakhah to be the preclusion of the concern of transgressing the prohibition of *sha'atnez* in the here and now, not in the post-Resurrection era.

More importantly, Maimonides rules in the *Mishneh Torah* that a corpse may be buried in *sha'atnez*, which is predicated on the idea that מצות בטלות לעתיד לבא. Being that Shapiro concedes, as mentioned, that Maimonides' personal opinion was indeed that the Torah's laws are immutable, what we have before us, then, is not merely a problem with the dogmatization of this immutability, as Shapiro presents it. Rather, we face a contradiction within Maimonides' own halakhic system, one which wouldn't be resolved even if we would accept Shapiro's theory that the dogmatic elements of the Ninth Principle don't reflect Maimonides' true opinion. The resolution must be that Maimonides understood R. Joseph's

---

87 This also seems to be the opinion of Meiri and Rivash (Respona 128).

88 As noted by R. Unterman, R. Dovid Metzger in his notes to *Ḥiddushei ha-Rashba, Niddah* (Mossad ha-Rav Kook, ad loc, n. 58), and R. Koreach in his notes to the Makhon ha-Ma'or edition of the *Commentary on the Mishnah* (Jerusalem, 2009), vol. 1, p. 255.

statement according to the aforementioned alternative approach.[89] Thus, according to Maimonides, the passage in *Niddah* does not discuss the lapsing of the *mitzvot* at all.

Shapiro casts doubt on the legitimacy of this approach by suggesting that even the aforementioned *Rishonim* may have disingenuously "advanced this view as an apologetic response to Christian polemicists" who indeed cited this passage as a source that the *mitzvot* were expected to lapse in the Messianic Era. I would counter that strong evidence that this wasn't the case is found in the testimony of Ritva that he had personally challenged his teacher Rashba about this interpretation of his, with Ritva ultimately rejecting it.[90] Clearly, Rashba came across with his student as being earnest in his explanation of the passage.[91]

The second source (p. 123) cited as evidence of rabbinic acknowledgment of eventual changes to the Torah—the future dispensation of the laws of *sheḥita* to allow for the consumption of the Behemoth by the righteous (*Vayikra Rabbah* 13:3)—is rather difficult to understand. Maimonides (*Hilkhot Teshuvah* 8:4) himself explains this promised feast as an allegorical reference to the incorporeal afterlife.[92] Clearly, Maimonides would have interpreted the above details of the feast's preparation in the same vein.

Regarding how Maimonides dealt with other midrashic passages cited by Shapiro, which speak of future abrogation of specific *mitzvot*, such as the holidays or the sacrifices, I would note that we have a precedent of

---

89 Another possibility is that while the *mitzvot* will not lapse at any future time, the experience of death permanently exempts its participants from the obligations of the Torah even after they return to life. Hence, in the post-Resurrection era, those who lived to see it will continue to practice *mitzvot*, while the resurrected will not. This approach flows most naturally from the talmudic source for this law, **במתים חפשי**. See R. Elḥanan Wasserman, *Kovez Shiurim* (Tel Aviv: 1989), vol. 2, ch. 29.

90 וכמה הקשיתי לפניו [...] ועדיין לא הניח דעתי בתשובותיו ואין לנו אלא שיטת הראשונים ז"ל.

91 Saul Lieberman, whose *Sheki'in* Shapiro references regarding this deflection, does not claim that the *Rishonim* were being disingenuous. He only focuses on the polemical discussion surrounding this passage, which is indeed explicit in Rashba's *Ḥiddushei Aggadot*, *Berachot* 12b and *Ḥiddushei ha-Ritva*, *Niddah ad loc.*

92 See R. Abraham Maimoni's elaboration of this view, in response to his father's critics who assumed a literal understanding of this event, *Milḥamot ha-Shem*, ed. Margolies, pp. 61-67. See however Halberstam (ed.), *Kevutzat Mikhtavim* (Bamberg, 1875), p. 94, cited in David Berger, "Judaism and General Culture in Medieval Times," *Judaism's Encounter with Other Cultures* (Jerusalem: Maggid, 2017), p. 119.

Shapiro himself cites this passage of Maimonides, *Mesorah le-Yosef*, p. 366.

how Maimonides viewed *midrashim* that seemingly contradict what he held to be logically or dogmatically correct. This is found in Maimonides' discussion of creation *ex nihilo*. As discussed earlier, in the *Guide* (2:26), Maimonides grapples with a passage in *Pirkei d'Rabbi Eliezer* that seemingly advocates the Platonic stance. As Maimonides considered this view unacceptable and heretical, he confessed that the proper understanding of the passage eluded him and warned the reader not to be led astray by its apparent meaning.[93] This, despite the midrash's authorship by a reputed *tanna*. Clearly, the existence of such passages—which may be allegorical, incorrect, or reflect the opinion of an outlier—wasn't sufficient to change Maimonides' mind when it was made up.[94] Shapiro himself discusses this idea at length in an essay dedicated to cataloging Maimonides' rejection of halakhic statements predicated on astrology, superstition, demonology, and magic.[95] While a distinction can be made between the Sages' application of the Halakhah to their misconceived perceptions of supernatural phenomena on the one hand and the attribution of theological errors to them on the other, I would suggest that it is reasonable to assume that Maimonides would have reacted similarly to the aforementioned *midrashim* that seem to allow for abrogation.

This argument would not appear to apply to the talmudic passages, cited by Shapiro (pp. 123-124), that discuss normative halakhic opinions, such as the view that the commandment to remember the Exodus will expire in the Messianic era (T.B. *Berachot* 11b) or the view that *mamzerim* will then be purified of their marital prohibition (T.B. *Kiddushin* 72b). However, these sources do not imply a challenge to the general immutability of the *mitzvot*, as they are both derived from *derashot* of scriptural verses, which inform the details of all *mitzvot*. Just as the requirement to waive the laws of Shabbat for the sake of *pikuaḥ nefesh* or *milah* does not constitute an abrogation of Shabbat—only a scripturally prescribed limitation of its scope—so too, the *mitzvah* of remembering the Exodus and the prohibition of marriage with a *mamzer* were initially designed to be in

---

93 "ראיתי לר' אליעזר הגדול דברים [...] לא ראיתי כל יותר תמוהים מהם בדברי אף אחד מההולכים בתורת משה רבנו [...] ומי יתן וידעתי מה סובר חכם זה [...] כללו של דבר הם דברים המשבשים דעתו של המלומד הדתי מאד מאד, ולא נתברר לי בו באור מספיק, ולא הזכרתיו לך אלא כדי שלא תטעה בו" (Kafiḥ, pp. 221-222).

94 Shapiro follows Fox's lead in deducing the very opposite conclusion: the very existence of the midrashic passage is evidence that Maimonides could not have been serious about his rejection of the Platonic view (pp. 75-76). This, however, flies in the face of Maimonides' own clear remarks and demands recourse to the esoteric method of Maimonidean interpretation.

95 Shapiro, *Studies*, pp. 95-150.

force only until the advent of the Messianic Era.[96] This is completely unlike the scenario Maimonides precludes in his Principles: the unanticipated and extra-halakhic "divine" repeal of the *mitzvot* through a prophet, such as was claimed by the Church Fathers and the Koran.[97]

In sum, none of the passages marshaled by Shapiro provide persuasive evidence that Maimonides was aware of an authoritative rabbinic opinion which allowed for the future abrogation of specific commandments of the Torah. The argument that Maimonides was being disingenuous by including the Ninth Principle in his dogma, in turn, would seem to have no firm basis upon which to rest.[98]

Conclusion

Dr. Shapiro makes the case that Maimonides engaged in disingenuousness when presenting critical matters of faith to his readership, drawing upon an impressive array of sources to do so. Yet, he presents no direct evidence to that effect. Rather, Shapiro collects a list of problems within Maimonides' writings—in the same manner that scholars have done for centuries—and proposes that their difficulty defies the conventional method of resolution, namely a better understanding of the subject matter, preferring instead to resolve these difficulties with the counterintuitive idea that Maimonides did not actually mean what he wrote in these passages. While such a possibility always exists, I contend that the evidence brought on its behalf would need to be highly compelling to justify its countenance. In this essay, I have touched on every piece of evidence that

---

96 Abarbanel, *Rosh Amanah* (Konigsberg, 1861), p. 16, makes this point regarding the former example. My thanks to R. Yitzhak Grossman for bringing it to my attention.

97 The passage in *Kiddushin* is inconclusive for another reason. It is possible that Maimonides understood it in accordance with the first explanation of Ran (Rif 30a) according to which all agree that identifiable *mamzerim* will maintain their prohibition. The discussion relates only to unidentifiable ones, with the lenient opinion asserting that Elijah will merely refrain from calling them out, despite being aware of their pedigree. Ran in fact prefers this approach precisely because it maintains halakhic invariance in the Messianic Era!

98 Shapiro's (p. 131) excessively subtle reading of the language in *Hil. Teshuvah* seems incomprehensible. If Maimonides leaves the door open for the possible abrogation of the Torah *in the future*, how could the assertion of that abrogation *in the past* be considered heretical? In other words: after the unspecified future point in time when the "admissible" lapsing of the Torah occurs, this repeal will be past history. How, then, can any claim that the Law has already been repealed be heretical—perhaps we have indeed passed its "future" abrogation?

Shapiro cites and have shown virtually every one to be either misunderstood, misrepresented, or to have alternative resolutions or explanations that are at least as plausible as Shapiro's readings. To my mind, the sole item worthy of serious consideration is Maimonides' language in his Eighth Principle—yet, even there, sufficient counterevidence exists to allow for the possibility of infelicitous wording on Maimonides' part.

I therefore submit that the case made by Dr. Shapiro is weak. There is no compelling reason to deny Maimonides the presumption of sincerity accorded every author—particularly to a scholastic and religious giant of Maimonides' caliber, engaged in what he would consider the most sacred duty a Jew can engage in: the transmission of the essence of Judaism to posterity. What should be clear from all this is that those who choose to maintain the traditional perception of Maimonides need not be concerned that the historical record insists otherwise. In this instance, dogma need not call for one's own self-deception. ☙

The Exodus and Historical Truth: A Critique of Ani Maamin by Joshua Berman, and the Late Date Exodus Theory

By: GEULA TWERSKY

In *Ani Maamin: Biblical Criticism, Historical Truth, and the Thirteen Principles of Faith*, Joshua Berman sets out to address many of the intellectual and spiritual challenges facing those committed to both Torah and academic studies. Berman advocates for understanding the Torah within its historical context, cautioning that applying modern notions such as *history*, *fact*, and *fiction* to biblical texts, in whose milieu these terms did not exist, is anachronistic. Berman underscores the "exhortative" nature of biblical narrative texts, which although rooted in reality, are primarily intended to convey moral lessons. This approach informs Berman's methodology for resolving both narrative and legal inconsistencies in the Torah. Berman presents a masterful refutation of biblical source criticism in *Ani Maamin* that reinforces the structural integrity of the Torah. The second half of the book is devoted to tackling challenging theological questions pertaining to Maimonides' 13 Principles of Faith.

It is precisely because Berman is such an eloquent, prolific, and influential spokesperson for the harmonization of Torah and academic studies that it is crucial to note where his approach falls short. For this reason, I present here a critique of his extended discussion pertaining to the Exodus. Berman's approach to the historicity of the biblical Exodus narrative

* My deepest appreciation to my husband, Yitzchak Twersky, whose insightful comments and suggestions helped me immeasurably in preparing this essay. Thanks also to the *Ḥakirah* editors for carefully editing my manuscript, making sure that my argument is presented in the best possible way.

Geula Twersky holds MA degrees in Bible from Bernard Revel Graduate School and from Bar Ilan University. She is the author of *Song of Riddles: Deciphering the Song of Songs* (Gefen, 2018) and *Torah Song: The Theological Role of Torah Poetry* (Kodesh, forthcoming). Her articles on Biblical topics have appeared in *SJOT, JSOT JBQ, Torah u-Madda* and *Tradition*. A collection of her articles on biblical archaeology and Egyptology is forthcoming from *BDD*. An award-winning professional artist, her artwork can be viewed at Geulaart.com.

appears in condensed form in chapters two and three of *Ani Maamin*, and more extensively in earlier academic volumes.[1]

To be clear, this is not a book review. This essay has a dual goal: to offer a critique of Berman's approach to the Torah's account of the Exodus and to present the case for the historicity of the Torah's account of the Exodus based on the evidence. *Ani Maamin* presents itself as a defense of the biblical Exodus narrative, reconciling the narrative with the scientific facts. The compromises offered in this book have therefore been warmly received by many leaders, teachers, and lay learners in the Orthodox Jewish community. Unfortunately, this is based on the misperception that the biblical narrative is irreconcilable with the archeological and historical record. In fact, the record lends rich support, not a challenge, to the biblical narrative, as we will see. It is only the current trends and opinions labeled as scholarly consensus that stand in opposition to the biblical narrative. The approach of *Ani Maamin* is an attempt at aligning the biblical narrative with this body of belief. For one who feels a need for such reconciliation, *Ani Maamin* does an admirable job. But for someone who is concerned exclusively with the light that the historical evidence sheds on the biblical text, it is deleterious. For such individuals, the "threat" that *Ani Maamin* saves them from is illusory, the price paid all too real. The two aspects of this article are, therefore, two sides of one coin. Clarifying the historical evidence and responding to Berman's approach are complementary tasks.

The 13th Century Approach

In step with current trends in scholarship, Berman takes a 13th cent. BCE approach to the Exodus.[2] The biblical chronology, however, places the Exodus in the mid-15th cent. BCE. This is primarily based on 1Kings 6:1 which dates the beginning of the construction of the Temple of Solomon

---

1 Cf. Joshua Berman, *Inconsistency in the Torah: Ancient Literary Convention and the Limits of Source Criticism* (New York: Oxford Univ. Press, 2017), 17–62; idem, "The Kadesh Inscriptions of Ramesses II and the Exodus Sea Account (Exodus 13:17–15:19)," pp. 93–112 in *Did I Not Bring Israel Out of Egypt? Biblical, Archaeological, and Egyptological Perspectives on the Exodus Narratives* (James Hoffmeier et al. ed.; Winona Lake: Eisenbrauns, 2016).

2 Cf. the following volumes which advocate a 13th century Exodus: "*Did I Not Bring Israel Out of Egypt?" Biblical, Archaeological, and Egyptological Perspectives on the Exodus Narratives* (James Hoffmeier, Alan Millard, and Alan Rendsburg eds.; Bulletin for Biblical Research Supplement; Winona Lake: Eisenbrauns, 2016); James Hoffmeier, *Ancient Israel in Sinai: The Evidence for the Authenticity of the Wilderness Tradition* (New York: Oxford Univ. Press, 2005).

to the 480th year from the Exodus (coinciding with Solomon's fourth regnal year, in the mid-10th cent. BCE).[3] The 13th century approach, however, is essentially grounded in the appearance of the topographic name Raamses in Exodus 1:11.[4] Ramesses II was the most celebrated pharaoh of Egypt's 19th Dynasty, ca. the 13th cent. BCE.[5] The name Ramesses was not used as a pharaonic name before the 19th Dynasty and was used intermittently only afterwards. A resolution to this challenge facing the biblical chronology will be suggested after a presentation and evaluation of Berman's approach.

Berman introduces his discussion of the Exodus with the following bold statement:[6] "The case against the historicity of the Exodus is straightforward, and its essence can be stated in five words: a sustained lack of evidence." To be fair, Berman then proceeds to offer a variety of plausible explanations for this apparent lacuna, however, that does not mitigate his assertion that there is no credible documentary and archaeological evidence of the Exodus.[7]

---

3 Cf. Kenneth A. Kitchen, "How We Know When Solomon Ruled," *BARev* 27.4 (2001), 32–37, 58.

4 Naville's 1883 excavation of Tell el-Maskhuta, one of the treasure cities of Ramesses II, and what Naville assumed to be the site of biblical Pithom, served as further basis for the Ramesses II theory. Cf. John Day, *In Search of Pre-Exilic Israel* (London: Bloomsbury, 2005), 29. However, if Ramesses II was the Pharaoh of the Exodus, then Moses would have had to have fled from Ramesses' father, Seti I (Ex. 2:15). Since Pithom and Raamses were built prior to these events (Ex. 1:11), the city of Raamses had to have been built well before the rise of Ramesses II and his storage city at Tell el-Maskhuta. Therefore, the fact that one of the storage cities was named Raamses cannot serve as a basis for identifying the pharaoh of the Exodus with Ramesses II. Gardiner attempted to identify biblical Raamses with Pi-Ramesses. Cf. Alan H. Gardiner, "The Delta Residence of the Ramessides," *JEA* 5 (1918), 127–138, 242–271. Redford rejects this association in part based on the omission of the *pr* prefix meaning house. Cf. Donald Redford, "The Land of Ramesses," pp. 175–177 in *Causing His Name to Live: Studies in Egyptian Epigraphy and History in Memory of William J. Murnane* (Peter Brand and Louise Cooper, eds.; Leiden, Boston: Brill, 2009).

5 Cf. Lawrence T. Geraty, "Exodus Dates and Theories," pp. 55–64 in *Israel's Exodus in Transdisciplinary Perspective: Text, Archaeology, Culture and Geoscience* (Thomas E. Levy et al., eds.; Cham: Springer, 2015); Kenneth Kitchen, *On the Reliability of the Old Testament* (Grand Rapids: Eerdmans, 2003), 256, 309–310.

6 Joshua Berman, *Ani Maamin: Biblical Criticism, Historical Truth, and the Thirteen Principles of Faith* (Jerusalem: Maggid Books, 2020), 44.

7 Cf. the following article which presents new evidence for a 15th cent. Exodus. Geula Twersky, "Redating the Mount Eval Altar: A Re-evaluation of the Evidence," *Bekhol Derakhekha Daehu* 37 (2022), forthcoming.

The expectation of finding something in the wrong location simply because it is easier to look there is commonly referred to as *the streetlight effect.* This phenomenon is dramatized in a joke featuring a man and a police officer standing beneath a streetlamp. The policeman says, "What are you doing?" The man says, "Looking for my lost keys." The police officer asks, "Are you sure you lost them here?" To which the man replies, "No, but the light is better here." It should come as no surprise that looking for tangible evidence of the Exodus in the wrong century is an exercise in futility. In the pages that follow, I will show that whereas the Bible is not a history book per se, it does indeed record historically accurate information that is supported by abundant corroborating evidence. However, it should be understood that the supporting data is only accessible to those who look for it in the right place. Before presenting the case for a 15th century Exodus, we need to first understand the methodological deficiencies in Berman's approach.

Berman's Approach

Berman lays the foundation for his argument on the idea that numbers in the Tanakh are often meant to be understood qualitatively as opposed to quantitatively.[8] He proceeds to suggest that the number 480 cited in 1Kings 6:1 should not be taken literally. Berman claims that this number is problematic as "it is difficult to reconcile this time span with the total number of years that seem to be chronicled in the book of Judges."[9] Indeed, if one were to insist that all the twelve recorded judges operated in strict succession, then there is indeed a surplus of ca. 100 years. It is widely accepted, however, in both Torah sources and secular scholarship, that there was some degree of overlap during the period of the judges. The limited regional sphere of influence of the individual judges would certainly support this assumption. The book of Judges itself appears to suggest that Shamgar and Deborah were contemporaries,[10] and that there was some degree of overlap between Jephthah and Samson, who both operated during the period of Philistine oppression.[11] Furthermore, the Sages did not assume all of the judges to have been strictly consecutive.[12] There is therefore no reason to dogmatically assert that the number 480 recorded in the book of Kings contradicts the chronology of the book of

8 Berman, *Ani Maamin*, 29–33.

9 Ibid. 33.

10 Jud. 3:31; 4:1; 5:6.

11 Jud. 10:7; 14–16.

12 C.F. *Ruth Rabba* 1:1.

Judges. The same cannot be said, however, concerning the 13th century theory, which openly contradicts Jephthah's statement that 300 years had elapsed since the Israelite occupation of Moabite lands, allowing for an impossibly short amount of time for the judges period.[13] Late date Exodus supporters are at a loss to account for the length of the judges period.[14] Kitchen's assertion that Jephthah's statement was a propagandistic bluster nonetheless fails to explain how the entire judges period might be condensed into ca. 150 years.[15]

In attempting to bolster the figurative interpretation of the number 480, Berman cites the theory that the number 480 represents the idea of the passage of twelve generations since the Exodus, with the number 40 standing as a trope for a generation.[16] Berman cites a twelve-generation priestly genealogy from 1Chr. 5:30–36 as proof. However, 1Chr. 6:18–22 lists eighteen generations between the Temple musician Heman who lived in the time of King David, and his Levite ancestor Korah, thereby placing Solomon's Temple in the 19th generation from the Exodus. In an attempt to buttress the twelve-generation theory, Berman cites the Septuagint, which records the number 440 as the Temple's foundational year. Berman suggests that this chronological discrepancy arose because the Septuagint counted eleven generations between the Temple and the Exodus.

To begin with, it is accepted in the scholarship that the Septuagint altered the traditional chronology.[17] Specifically regarding Kings, Gooding showed that the Septuagint tends to pedantically "correct" Masoretic

---

13 Jud. 11:26.

14 Kitchen, *Reliability*, 209.

15 Jephthah ruled for 6 years, approximately a century before the monarchic period, ca. 1100 BCE [cf. Eugene H. Merrill, *Kingdom of Priests: A History of Old Testament Israel* (Ada, MI: Baker Books, 1996), 170]. The following leaders are known to have preceded the 18-year Ammonite oppression and subsequent 6-year rule of Jephthah: Joshua (40 yrs. wandering in the wilderness + ? yrs. conquest), Othniel (40 yrs. + 8 yrs. Aram Naharaim oppression), Ehud (80 yrs.+ 18 yrs. Moabite oppression), Barak and Deborah (40 yrs. + 20 yrs. Canaanite oppression), Gideon (40 yrs. + 7 yrs. Midianite oppression), Abimelech (3 yrs.), Tola (23 yrs.), Yair (22 yrs.). The following events followed the period of Jephthah: Ibzan (7 yrs.), Elon (10 yrs.), Abdon (8 yrs.), Samson (20 yrs. + 40 yrs. Philistine oppression, although those two figures were probably concurrent, as indicated in Jud.16:31), Eli (40 yrs.).

16 Cf. David H. van Daalen, "Number Symbolism," pp. 561–63 in *The Oxford Companion to the Bible* (Bruce M. Metzger and Michael D. Coogen, eds.; New York: Oxford University Press, 1993).

17 Cf. Gerhard Larsson, "The Chronology of the Pentateuch: A Comparison of the MT and LXX," *JBL* 102.3 (1983), 401–409.

chronologies that it perceived to be problematic.[18] Northcote proposed that the schematic nature of the Septuagint's chronological alterations become apparent when we view its overall Temple related records:

First Temple foundation	4277
Temple destruction	4707
Second Temple completion	4777

"It is the 777 aspect of this final dating that seems to have been the main consideration in the LXX [Septuagint] chronographer's reckoning."[19] Whereas I chose to bring the opinion of Northcote to the discussion, a variety of suggestions have been put forth to explain the systematic chronological discrepancies in the Septuagint.[20] Whatever the overriding considerations of the Septuagint chronologer, it certainly was not to allow for eleven generations between the Exodus and Solomon's Temple. This is evidenced by the Septuagint's failure to "correct" the 18-generation genealogy cited above, linking Heman, the Temple musician, to his Levite ancestors.

There is not a hint in the verse in Kings that the number 480 implies the passage of twelve generations. What is clear, however, is that the verse was formulated to convey calendrical precision. Cassuto notes that ascending number order, as in "eighty years and four hundred years" is a biblical device for conveying numerical precision.[21] Furthermore, when the very same verse states "in the fourth year of King Solomon" and "in the month of Ziv, that is the second month" we understand the verse to be authenticating an occasion of great significance. This plethora of calendric detail marks the historic fulfillment of the telos of the Exodus: "You will bring them in and plant them on the mountain of your inheritance, the place, O Lord, you made for your dwelling, the sanctuary, O Lord, your hands established."[22] In like fashion, the completion of the Temple is again reported with abundant calendric detail: "In the eleventh year in the month of Bul, the eighth month, the Temple was finished in

---

18 D. W. Gooding, "Pedantic Timetabling in the 3rd Book of Reigns," *Vetus Testamentum* 15.2 (1965), 153–166.

19 J. Northcote, "The schematic development of Old Testament Chronography: Towards an integrated model," *Journal for the Study of the Old Testament* 29. 1 (2004), 3–36, 18.

20 Cf. Gerhard Larsson, "The Chronology of the Pentateuch: A Comparison of the MT and LXX," *JBL* 102.3 (1983), 401–409.

21 Umberto Cassuto, *The Documentary Hypothesis and the Composition of the Pentateuch* (Jerusalem: Magnes, 1961), 52.

22 Ex. 15:17.

all its details according to its specifications. He had spent seven years building it."[23]

Berman's figurative approach to the number 480 in Kings is in line with his sustained approach to the entire biblical Exodus narrative, in which he chooses to interpret much of the text exhortatively as opposed to literally, thereby obfuscating the plain sense of the text. That is not to say that it is illegitimate to suggest that the Torah speaks in the language of metaphor. It certainly does. It is imperative, however, to first put forth a methodology for when a non-literal interpretation is indeed called for, and when it is not. Whereas Berman explains why the Garden of Eden story and other instances of biblical metaphor ought not be interpreted literally, at no point does he present a clear methodology for interpreting the story of the Exodus as hortatory. [24]

Maimonides, in his discussion on the primacy of creationism over belief in an eternal universe, states "a mere argument in favor of a certain theory is not sufficient reason for rejecting the literal meaning of a biblical text and explaining it figuratively, when the opposite theory can be supported by an equally good argument."[25] Similarly, Saadia Gaon, whose remarks likely served as the model for Maimonides, writes in his introductory remarks to his commentary on the Torah, "It is appropriate to explain the Torah according to the plain sense of the words… except if it contradicts either the senses or rational thinking, or if the plain sense of the words under discussion contradicts another clear verse or a received tradition of the prophets."[26]

It is important to understand the spurious nature of the all too prevalent "scholarly" argument regarding the lack of evidence. The claim is often made that there are no reflections of the Exodus in the historical record. This is the result of the following circle: Whenever something that seems to reflect the events of the Exodus is noted, it is dismissed because it could not reflect the Exodus, as we know that the Exodus did not take place. Some other explanation must be advanced, even if we must attribute it to some fabricated event for which there is no evidence. And what is the basis for the assertion that the Exodus did not take place and therefore cannot be reflected in any given piece of evidence? The "fact" that there is no reflection of it in the historical record! The academic a priori rejection of the possibility of the Exodus having occurred is cloaked in

---

23 1Kings 6:38.

24 Berman, *Ani Maamin*, 39–40.

25 Maimonides, *Guide to the Perplexed*, II:25.

26 Saadia Gaon, *Commentary on the Torah* (trans. Yosef Kapach; Jerusalem: Mosad Harav Kook, 1976), 162 (Heb.).

the guise of the argument that it could not have occurred as there is no evidence for its historicity. Again, it is crucial to understand the distinction between *fact* and *opinion*. The former, and not the latter, must be considered in interpreting the biblical text. This is the essence of the approach of Saadia Gaon and Maimonides.

In his approach to the Exodus material Berman implements a circular methodology. He begins by establishing that the number 480 in Kings is figurative, even though it does not contradict the senses, rational thinking, or another received prophetic tradition. From there Berman goes on to adopt the consensus of current trends in scholarship, which go against the plain sense of the text, and bear no correlation to the facts. Berman's unfortunate assertion that the case for the historicity of the Exodus is plagued by "a sustained lack of evidence," will be shown to go against the historical and archaeological record.[27]

Support for a 15th Century Exodus, and 14th Century Conquest

- ### The Archaeological Record

In this section, archaeological evidence supporting a 14th century conquest will be presented. The discussion begins with a look at the pottery evidence from Israel's highlands. From there the discussion moves to the epigraphic evidence from ancient cultures spanning the Levant, most notably, the Tetragrammaton's appearance at a temple from the Reign of Amenhotep III. Archaeological evidence is then presented from cities in Israel that play a prominent role in the biblical conquest story. The analysis begins in Jericho, which exhibits a plethora of harmonizing features with the biblical text. Evidence of the well-fortified city having suffered a devastating earthquake, and its subsequent wholesale burning together with abundant unplundered stores of post-harvest grain, correlates seamlessly with the biblical narrative. Jericho's centuries-long period of abandonment also correlates well with the biblical account. The discussion then turns to the cities of Bethel, Lachish, Debir, Ai, Hazor and Khirbet el-Ahwat, which has been identified by Adam Zertal as Haroseth Haggoyim.

a. The Pottery

The Israeli archeological record provides rich support for the biblical chronology.[28] Aharoni's surveys of the Upper Galilee yielded pottery evidence that led him to date the beginnings of Israelite infiltration to the

---

27 Berman, *Ani Maamin*, 44.

28 Cf. Bryant Wood, "The Rise and Fall of the 13th Century Exodus Conquest

14th century.[29] Meitlis observes that Mycenaean and Cypriot vessels, considered to be the main chronological anchors for the Late Bronze Age, have been found at central highlands sites assigned to the Iron Age. His examination of the chronology of the Israeli highlands and the concurrence of different pottery types led him to the conclusion that the beginning of the Iron Age, and the Israelite conquest, should be dated to the 14th cent. BCE.[30] Meitlis bases his conclusions on the pottery assemblages of the following highland sites: Mount Eval, Tell en-Nasbeh, Beth Zur, Tel Sasa, Shiloh, and Tel Qiri.[31]

b. Epigraphic Evidence

Whereas the Merenptah stela is commonly referenced in demonstration of Israel's firmly established presence in Canaan by at least 1210 BCE,[32] a column base fragment from the 18th Dynasty housed in the Egyptian Museum in Berlin has posed a challenge to the widely accepted 13th century Exodus theory.[33] Updated deciphering methods have shown the inscription, like the Merenptah stela, to list Israel together with Ashkelon and Canaan, in support of a 15th century Exodus.[34]

Theory," *Journal of the Evangelical Theological Society* 48.3 (2005), 475–489.

29 Yohanan Aharoni, "The Israelite Occupation of Canaan: An Account of the Archaeological Evidence," *Biblical Archaeological Review* 8.3 (1982), 14–23; idem, *The Land of the Bible: A Historical Geography* (trans. and ed. A. F. Rainey; Philadelphia: Westminster Press, 1967).

30 Itzhak Meitlis, "A Re-analysis of the Archaeological Evidence for the Beginning of the Iron Age," p. 105–111 in *Bene Israel: Studies in the Archaeology of Israel and the Levant During the Bronze and Iron Ages, in Honour of Israel Finkelstein* (A. Fantalkin and A. Yasur-Landau, eds.; Leiden: Brill, 2008). These findings are supported by 14C tests of carbonized wood from Strata V and VI at Tel Dan, idem, 109–110.

31 Idem, *Excavating the Bible: New Archaeological Evidence for the Historic Reliability of Scripture* (Jerusalem: Rubin Mass, 2012), 136–150 (Heb.).

32 Michael G. Hasel, "Israel in the Merneptah Stela," *BASOR* 296 (1994), 45–61.

33 Manfred Görg, "Israel in Hieroglyphen," *Biblische Notizen* 106 (2001), 24.

34 Cf. Peter van der Veen, Christopher Theis, Manfred Görg, "Israel in Canaan (long) before Merenptah? A Fresh Look at Berlin Statue Pedestal Relief 21687," *Journal of Ancient Egyptian Interconnections* 2:4 (2010), 1–11. Not all scholars agree with the reading suggested by these scholars due to a slight variation in the spelling from the Merneptah stela. The authors attribute this discrepancy to the earlier orthography of 18th Dynasty spelling. Thomas Römer's objection to Görg's reading in idem, *The Invention of God* (Cambridge: Harvard Univ. Press, 2015), 75, fails to take into account that the hieroglyphic "r" can also sound like an "l", as it does in Chinese. The preference of the "Israel" reading is further indicated by the word's grouping together with Ashkelon and Canaan, as in the Merneptah stela.

Further epigraphic evidence favoring the biblical chronology includes a victory stele erected by Pharaoh Seti in Beth-shean that reports battles fought in the Lower Western Galilee against a tribe bearing what appears to be the Hebrew name Asher,[35] Assyrian records reporting battles fought against a tribe named Yairi (son of Menashe?) on the banks of the Euphrates,[36] and two Late Bronze tablets from the city of Ugarit containing the name "ysril," Israel, within a list of names.[37]

c. The Tetragrammaton's Appearance at a Temple from the Reign of Amenhotep III

The temple of Amun-Ra at Soleb, located in Soleb, Nubia, is dedicated to the 14th cent. 18th Dynasty pharaoh, Amenhotep III.[38] One of the temple's inscribed columns references an ethnic group, *š3sw* (Shasu), associated with the name *yhw3* (Yahweh).[39] In addition to the pillar inscription, a fragmentary wall list from the same temple features a similar inscription.[40] Egyptians used the term *š3sw* to refer to nomadic peoples located in the southern Levant, especially the areas of Sinai, Edom, Moab, Transjordan, and Canaan.[41] Kennedy explains that "Since the word order infers that the construct is being used, the phrase translates as the 'land of

---

35 Sh. Yeivin, *The Israelite Conquest of Canaan* (Istanbul: Nederlands Historisch Archaeologisch Instituut in Nabije Oosten, 1971), 23; Abraham Malamat, Hayim Tadmor, *A History of the Jewish People* (Cambridge: Harvard Univ. Press, 1976), 23.

36 Benjamin Mazar, "Yair, Yairi," *Encyclopedia Biblica*, vol. 3 (Jerusalem: Mossad Bialik, 1965), 415–416 (Heb.).

37 Cyrus Gordon, *Ugaritic Textbook: Grammar, Texts in Transliteration, Cuneiform Selections, Glossary, Indices* (vol. 38 of *Analecta Orientalia*; Rome: Pontificio Instituto, 1998), 1.2. (UT 2069, 00-4.623:3; UT 328, R1-4.50:6).

38 James H. Breasted, "Second Preliminary Report of the Egyptian Expedition," *American Journal of Semitic Languages and Literature* 25 (1908), 1–110, 84.

39 J. Leclant, "Le 'Tétragramme' à l'Époque d'Aménophis III," pp. 215–219 in *Near Eastern Studies dedicated to H. I. H. Prince Takahito Mikasa on the Occasion of His Seventy-Fifth Birthday* (M. Mori et al, eds.; Wiesbaden, 1991); E. Edel, "Die Ortsnamenlisten in den Tempeln von Aksha, Amarah und Soleb im Sudan," *Biblische Notizen* 11 (1980), 63–79, 68.

40 Titus Kennedy, "The Land of the *š3sw* (Nomads) of *yhw3* at Soleb," p. 175–192 in *Dotawo: A Journal of Nubian Studies* 6.1 (2019), 178. https://escholarship.org/uc/item/07x6659z .

41 Thomas Levy, Russel Adams and Adolfo Muniz, "Archaeology and the Shasu Nomads: Recent Excavations in the Jabal Hamrat Fidan, Jordan," pp. 63–89 in *Le David Maskil: A Birthday Tribute for David Noel Freedman* (William Henry Propp and Richard Elliott Friedman, eds; Ann Arbor: Winona Lake: Eisenbrauns, 2004), 63–89, 65–66; David Hopkins, "Pastoralists in Late Bronze Age Palestine: Which Way Did They Go?" *The Biblical Archaeologist* 56. 4 (1993), 200–211, 210.

the nomads of *yhw3*.'"[42] Kennedy further explains that since the inscription does not feature a land determinative, *yhw3* must therefore be understood as a proper name as opposed to a toponym. Furthermore, the lack of the *nṯr* "god" determinative indicates that *yhw3* was not an Egyptian deity. Kennedy concludes, "Since the only ancient people known to have worshipped a deity named *yhw3* (Yahweh) in ancient times were the Hebrews or Israelites, it also logically follows that these particular *š3sw* nomads associated with *yhw3* could be identified with the early Israelites before they became a sedentary population in Canaan, and that the Egyptians had familiarity with this group and this deity during the 18th Dynasty at the end of the 15th century BCE."[43]

d. Jericho

The Jericho excavations have generated numerous correlations with the details of the story recounted in Joshua. John Garstang's excavations at Jericho yielded an array of 18th Dynasty royal scarabs, amulet seals fashioned in the form of the dung beetle and bearing pharaonic throne names from Hatshepsut and Tuthmosis III through Amenhotep III (early 15th cent. – early/mid-14th cent. BCE). [44] Garstang noted the conspicuous absence from this rich collection of any fragments relating to Akhenaton's distinctive rule (early 14th century BCE).[45] He further buttressed his 15th century assessment for the fall of Jericho by citing Jericho's glaring absence from the 14th century BCE Amarna Letters.[46]

Kathleen Kenyon's re-assessment of the data, dating the destruction of Jericho to no later than the mid-16th century BCE, was primarily based on the absence of pottery imported from Cyprus and common to the Late Bronze I period.[47] Bryant Wood's re-examination of both excavation reports led him to the conclusion that whereas Kenyon had correctly dated a collapsed wall that Garstang mistakenly assumed to be Late Bronze, her

---

42 Kennedy, "The Land of the *š3sw* (Nomads)," 184.

43 Ibid., 189.

44 J. Garstang and J. B. E. Garstang, *The Story of Jericho* (London: Hodder & Stoughton, 1940).

45 Piotr Bienkowski argues that the scarabs could have been re-makes or heirlooms. Cf. Piotr Bienkowski, "Jericho Was Destroyed in the Middle Bronze Age, Not the Late Bronze Age," *Biblical Archaeology Review* 16.5 (1990), 45; idem, *Jericho in the Late Bronze Age* (Wiltshire: Aris & Phillips, 1986), 68.

46 J. Garstang and J. B. E. Garstang, *The Story of Jericho*, 2nd ed. (London: Marshall, Morgan & Scott, 1948), 126–127.

47 K. Kenyon, *Digging Up Jericho* (London: Ernest Benn, 1957), 262; idem, *The Bible in Recent Archaeology* (Atlanta: John Knox, 1978), 33–37.

primary argument, which was based on the absence of distinctive period pottery, was fundamentally flawed.[48] Wood points to the abundant imitation bichrome "Cypriot" pottery uncovered by Garstang and referred to by him as "red-ware," as having been overlooked by Kenyon. Wood further argues that given Hatshepsut's detested place in the Egyptian pantheon of Pharaohs, the scarab found by Garstang bearing her inscription could not be a re-issue and should be viewed as authentic, lending credence to the authenticity of the rest of the scarab collection.[49] The combined evidence of the wide assortment of 18th Dynasty scarabs found at Jericho together with its abundant imitation bichrome "Cypriot" pottery support Garstang's original ca. 1400 BCE conquest date.

e. Bethel, Lachish, Debir, Ai and Hazor

Proponents of the 13th cent. Exodus-conquest theory cite Albright's excavations at Bethel, Lachish, Debir and Ai,[50] and Yadin's excavations at Hazor.[51] Re-evaluation of the data, however, by Wood and Ussishkin, has shown that Beitin/ Bethel was destroyed in the early 12th century, likely by the Philistines,[52] and that inscriptions unearthed at Lachish indicate an even later destruction.[53] It has further been demonstrated that Albright's identification of Ai was mistaken, as the proposed site lacks critical topographical features presented by the text.[54] Wood identifies Khirbet el-Maqatir as biblical Ai, based on its Late Bronze occupation/ destruction and its topographical agreement with the narrative specifications of the story told in Joshua. Moshe Kochavi's excavations at Khirbet Rabud have

---

48 Bryant Wood, "Did the Israelites Conquer Jericho? A New Look at the Archaeological Evidence," *Biblical Archaeology Review* 16.2 (1990), 44–59.

49 Bryant Wood, "Dating Jericho's Destruction: Bienkowski Is Wrong on All Counts," *Biblical Archaeology Review* 16.5 (1990), 45, 47–49, 68.

50 Cf. John J. Bimson, *Redating the Exodus and Conquest* (Sheffield, England: Sheffield, 1981), 30–73; William F. Albright, "Ai and Beth-Aven," p. 141–149 in *Excavations and Results at Tell el-Fûl (Gibeah of Saul)* (Benjamin W. Bacon ed.; AASOR 4; New Haven, American Schools of Oriental Research, 1924).

51 William F. Albright, *The Biblical Period from Abraham to Ezra* (New York: Harper & Row, 1963), 27–28.

52 Bryant G. Wood, *Palestinian Pottery of the Late Bronze Age: An Investigation of the Terminal LB IIB Phase* (Ph.D. thesis, University of Toronto, 1985), 353–355, 447–448, 471–472.

53 David Ussishkin, "Lachish," *The Oxford Encyclopedia of Archaeology in the Near East* (1997), 3:317–323, 319.

54 Bryant Wood, "Locating 'Ai: Excavations at Kh. El-Maqatir 1995–2000 and 2009–2014," *In the Highland's Depth: Journal for the Study of Archaeology and History of the Highland's Region* 6 (2016), 17–49.

likewise presented a far more likely candidate for biblical Debir.[55] Regarding Hazor, it remains undetermined if its 13th cent. destruction layer should be attributed to Joshua or to Deborah. Bruce Waltke makes a strong case for an even earlier Late Bronze destruction layer.[56] Adam Zertal's identification of Khirbet el-Ahwat with Haroseth Haggoyim (a single occupation site, which was populated only briefly between the 13th and 12th centuries and which closely resembles unique Late Bronze Age sites in Sardinia) correlates with a contemporary timeframe for the Deborah-Barak battle at Hazor.[57]

- **The Historical Record**

In this section, the period of time spanning the 15th–13th centuries in Egypt is examined. The overriding question is: Given the geopolitical climate, at what point in time is it at all reasonable to consider an Israelite conquest? There were very few periods in the Late Bronze Age during which Canaan was not firmly under Egyptian control.[58] It will be shown that the only window of time that might have reasonably allowed for the conquest of Canaan was sometime between the 18th Dynasty's sharp decline and its ultimate dissolution. The discussion presented here begins with the 15th cent. pharaoh, Thutmose III, the "Napoleon" of Egypt's 18th Dynasty, and concludes with the legendary 13th cent., 19th Dynasty pharaoh, Ramesses II.

During the reigns of the great warrior pharaohs Thutmose III and his son/coregent Amenhotep II, Egypt's 18th Dynasty reached its military, territorial and economic apex.[59] Thutmose III led yearly expeditions to

---

55 Moshe Kochavi, "Khirbet Rabud," *Tel Aviv: Journal of the Institute of Archaeology of Tel Aviv University* 1 (1974), 2–23.

56 Bruce K. Waltke, "Palestinian Artifactual Evidence Supporting the Early Date of the Exodus," *Bibliotheca Sacra* 129 (1972), 33–47.

57 Cf. Adam Zertal, *Sisera's Secret* (Or Yehuda, Israel: Dvir Pub., 2010); Baruch Brandl, "Nine Scarabs, a Scaraboid, a Cylinder Seal and a Bifacial Plaque from el-Ahwat," p. 233–263 in A. Zertal, *El-Ahwat, A Fortified Site of the Early Iron Age near Nahal 'Iron, Israel* (Leiden and Boston: Brill, 2010).

58 Lester Grabbe, "Reflections on the Discussion," p.179–188 in *The Land of Canaan in the Late Bronze Age* (Lester Grabbe, ed.; London: Bloomsbury, 2017).

59 Ann Rosalie David, *Handbook to Life in Ancient Egypt* (Oxford Univ. Press, 1999), 230.

the Levant,[60] and like his grandfather Thutmose I,[61] erected a monumental stela on the bank of the Euphrates River celebrating his victories.[62] Amenhotep II, a revered warrior in his own right as well as a legendary archer, also embarked on northern campaigns, although only early on in his career.[63] Suspicion that the demise of the 18th Dynasty stemmed from events occurring sometime during the early years of Amenhotep II's reign will be elaborated upon below.

Thutmose IV, the successor of Amenhotep II, whose court consisted almost entirely of a bureaucratic as opposed to a military administration,[64] began his reign with the appellation "conqueror of Syria." This is especially ironic considering the fact that there are no records of Thutmose IV conducting any military campaigns![65] Furthermore, neither Thutmose IV, who ruled for only a decade, nor Amenhotep III, who succeeded him, are believed to have conducted any northern expeditions.[66] Despite Amenhotep III's lack of military forays, he seems to have found alternative ways of inflating his stature; he erected more statues of himself throughout Egypt than any other Pharaoh.[67] Whereas Amenhotep III's

---

60 Betsy Bryan, "Antecedents to Amenhotep III," p. 27–62 in *Amenhotep III: Perspectives on His Reign* (David O'Connor, Eric H. Cline, eds.; Ann Arbor: Michigan Univ. Press, 2001), 27.

61 Cf. Colleen Manassa, *The Great Karnak Inscription of Merneptah: Grand Strategy in the 13th Century BC* (Bristol: ISD LLC, 2004), 75.

62 Richard Gabriel, *Thutmose III: A Military Biography of Egypt's Greatest Warrior King* (Lincoln: Potomac Books. 2009).

63 William Stiebing Jr. and Susan Helft, *Ancient Near Eastern History and Culture* (London: Routledge, 2017), 180.

64 Bryan, "Antecedents to Amenhotep III," 61. It is noteworthy that Thutmose IV had probably not always been the crown prince. This suspicion is based on a stele Thutmose IV erected between the paws of the Great Sphinx at Giza, propagandizing his accession. The text of the stele asserts that Thutmose IV ascended the throne following a dream in which the sun god represented by the Sphinx informed him of his future ascendancy contingent on his removing the sand covering its body. Cf. William Stiebing Jr. and Susan Helft, *Ancient Near Eastern History and Culture* (London: Routledge, 2017), 181.

65 Thutmose IV is twice referred to as "conqueror of Syria" on the Stele of Semen (*Smn*) in the Louvre (C 202). Cf. P. Pierret: *Recueil d'inscriptions inédites du Musée Égyptien du Louvre,* II partie (Paris, 1878), 35; R. O. Faulkner, "Egyptian Military Standards," *Journal of Egyptian Archaeology*, 27 (1941), 12–18, 18.

66 Lester L. Grabbe, "Canaan Under the Rule of the Egyptian New Kingdom: From the Hyksos to the Sea Peoples," in idem, *The Land of Canaan*, 90–101, 93.

67 Cf. William Stiebing Jr. and Susan Helft, *Ancient Near Eastern History and Culture* (London: Routledge, 2017), 182.

reliance on foreign diplomatic alliances as opposed to military confrontation has been interpreted by some as a sign of security and prosperity,[68] the Amarna Letters, which document the last years of Amenhotep III through the reign of Tutankhamun, provide ample evidence of what can be best be described as Amenhotep III's and Akhenaton's wholesale neglect of the greater Egyptian empire.[69] These letters report lavish gifts being sent to Egypt's allies and vassals who often brazenly protested that the amount sent was insufficient. Egypt's presence abroad continued to deteriorate during the reign of Akhenaton, the religious reformer.[70]

The death knell of the 18th Dynasty may be detected in the bizarre behavior of the widowed queen (perhaps Nefertiti or possibly Tutankhamun's widow), who for all intents and purposes offered the throne of Egypt to a foreigner and rival, with her request for a marriage alliance with Egypt's erstwhile arch nemesis, Hittite king Suppiliumas.[71] The extinction of the royal line of the 18th Dynasty culminates with the ascension of a succession of army officers.[72]

It was mentioned above that the demise of the 18th Dynasty is suspected to have stemmed from events occurring sometime during the reign of Amenhotep II. This supposition is reinforced by Amenhotep II's uncharacteristic "retirement" from war during the prime of his life (especially in light of his well-documented tendencies to savage violence),[73] following his second campaign (or possibly third) early on in his military career, that took him no further than the Canaanite territories,[74] and from which he returned with what appears to be an astronomical number of

---

68 Trevor Bryce, *Letters of the Great Kings of the Ancient Near East: The Royal Correspondence of the Late Bronze Age* (London: Routledge, 2004), 19.

69 Ibid. 187.

70 Akhenaton's drastic monotheistic-like religious reform and defamation of other gods in other temples are especially interesting considering the events surrounding the Exodus. Cf. Jan Assman, *The Search for God in Ancient Egypt* (Ithaca: Cornell University Press, 2001), 198–221.

71 Carlos Ramirez-Faria, *Concise Encyclopedia of World History* (Delhi; Atlantic Publishers & Dist, 2007), 192. The Hittite groom (Zananza), was summarily assassinated. Cf. Trevor Bryce, *The Kingdom of the Hittites* (Oxford Univ. Press, 1999), 194.

72 Cf. Aidan Dodson, *Amarna Sunset: Nefertiti, Tutankhamun, Ay, Horemheb, and the Egyptian Counter-reformation* (Oxford Univ. Press, 2009).

73 Note especially the sacrifice of the seven Asiatic princes. Cf. James Henry Breasted, *Ancient Records of Egypt: Historical Documents from the Earliest Times to the Persian Conquest, Vol. II: The Eighteenth Dynasty* (William Rainey Harper ed.; Chicago: Univ. of Chicago Press, 1906), 313.

74 Sh. Yeivin, "Amenophis II's Asianic Campaigns," *Journal of the American Research Center in Egypt* 6 (1967), 119–128.

human booty.[75] The unusual timing of the launching of this campaign in the winter season adds to the suspicion that it was undertaken to recoup the loss of slave labor sustained in the Exodus.[76] Shea comments, "While some have questioned the very high number given here, if one looks at the need for slave labor right after the Exodus, the number does not look so high after all."[77] We may add another suspicious event concurrent with Amenhotep II's early retirement from military forays: the dramatic decline in domestic turquoise mining activity at Serabit el-Khadem, in southwest Sinai. Expeditions to the turquoise mines at Serabit el-Khadim were conducted regularly for a period of c. 800 years (spanning the Late Middle and New Kingdoms).[78] These mining expeditions inexplicably seem to have come to a near standstill during the reigns of Amenhotep II and his successor, Thutmose IV.[79] The same circumstances which would explain the lack of military adventure and the attempt at replenishing the depleted slave supply can also account for the paucity of mining activity. A shortage of slave labor would have surely rendered mining impractical.[80] Furthermore, the mysterious desertion of the 18th Dynasty's royal complex and vital port city at Peru-nefer/Avaris, while Amenhotep II still sat on the throne, adds to the suspicion that unprecedented catastrophic events were behind the abandonment of this palatial complex and vital port city.[81]

---

75 Cf. James B. Pritchard, ed., *Ancient Near Eastern Texts Relating to the Old Testament* (Princeton: Princeton Univ. Press, 1969), 239, 246; "The Memphis and Karnak Stelae of Amenhotep II," in *The Context of Scripture: Canonical Compositions, Monumental Inscriptions and Archival Documents from the Biblical World*, vol. 2 (William Hallo and K. Lawson Younger, eds.; James K. Hoffmeier, trans.; Leiden: Brill, 2000), 19–23, 22; Hoffmeier, "The Annals of Thutmose III," ibid, 12.

76 Cf. Pritchard, *ANET*, 246; Claude Vandersleyen, *L'Égypte et la Vallée du Nil*, vol. 2 (Paris: Presses Universitaires de France, 1995), 321.

77 William Shea, "Amenhotep II as Pharaoh of the Exodus," *Bible and Spade* 16:2 (2003), 42–52, 47.

78 William Flinders Petrie, *Researches in Sinai* (New York: E. P. Dutton & Co., 1906).

79 Cf. Alan Gardiner and T. E. Peet, *The Inscriptions of Sinai*, vol. II (Jaroslav Cerny ed.; 45th Memoir of the Egypt Exploration Society; London: Oxford Univ. Press, 1955), 150–169.

80 It is agreed that the miners in Serabit el-Khadem were of Asiatic origin. Cf. Petrie, *Researches in Sinai*; Alan Gardiner, "The Egyptian Origin of the Semitic Alphabet," *Journal of Egyptian Archaeology* 3 (1916), 1–16; Orly Goldwasser, "Canaanites Reading Hieroglyphs: Horus Is Hathor? The Invention of the Alphabet in Sinai," *Ägypten und Levante* 16 (2006), 121–160.

81 Manfred Bietak, "A Thutmosid Palace Precinct at Peru-nefer (Tell El-Dab'a)," p. 223–250 in *Ancient Egyptian and Ancient Near Eastern Palaces: Proceedings of the Conference of Palaces in Ancient Egypt, held in London 12th–14th June 2013, organized by the Austrian Academy of Sciences, the University of Würzburg and the Egypt Exploration*

It is critical to stress here that whereas the unusual events documented to have occurred during the reign of Amenhotep II do not constitute *proof* of an Exodus during the days of Amenhotep II, they do constitute *evidence* that bears looking into. If this evidence can be shown to work in concert with the larger biblical, historical, archaeological, and epigraphic record, then the evidence may cautiously be understood to corroborate the biblical story.[82]

Egypt's waning foreign influence was restored during the 19th Dynasty under Pharaohs Sety and Ramesses II who embarked on campaigns to reinstate the territories lost during the Amarna period.[83] Sety led an expedition to Southern Canaan, and Ramesses II, the renowned military leader, pursued numerous campaigns up the Mediterranean coast, plundering towns in his path.[84] Considering Ramesses II's multiple forays in Canaan, he certainly appears to be, to quote Grabbe, "an unlikely ruler for the exodus!"[85] Even if we assume, based on the Hittite archives, that Ramesses II exaggerated his performance on the battlefield, he nevertheless succeeded in preventing further Hittite incursions into Egyptian territory.[86] Skepticism of Ramesses II having been the pharaoh of the Exodus is reinforced by the tremendous increase in the archaeological record of the remains of 19th Dynasty Egyptian buildings, municipal and military, found within Israel.[87]

Society, vol. I (Manfred Bietak and Silvia Prell, eds.; Austrian Academy of Sciences Press, 2018), 224, 241; idem, "Nomads or mnmn.t-shepherds in the eastern Nile delta in the New Kingdom," p. 123–136 in *"I Will Speak the Riddles of Ancient Times": Archaeological and Historical Studies in Honor of Amihai Mazar on the Occasion of His Sixtieth Birthday, vol. 1* (Amihai Mazar, ed.; Winona Lake: Eisenbrauns, 2006), 123.

82 Cf. Geula Twersky's analysis of the inner political intrigues of the court of Amenhotep II, which provides a broader glimpse at the aftershocks of the Exodus in idem, "'Where Have all the Viziers Gone?' Footprints of the Exodus in the Historical Record," *Bekhol Derakhekha Daehu* 38 (2023), forthcoming.

83 Charlotte Booth, *Horemheb: The Forgotten Pharaoh* (Gloucestershire: Amberley, 2009).

84 Lester L. Grabbe, "Canaan Under the Rule of the Egyptian New Kingdom: From the Hyksos to the Sea Peoples," p. 90–101 in Grabbe, ed., *The Land of Canaan in the Late Bronze Age*.

85 Ibid. 101.

86 Gérard Chaliand, *A Global History of War: From Assyria to the Twenty-First Century* (Berkeley: Univ. of California Press, 2014), 20.

87 Alan Millard, "Ramesses Was Here . . . and Others, Too!" pp. 305–312 in *Ramesside Studies in Honour of K. A. Kitchen* (M. Collier and S. Snape, eds.; Bolton: Rutherford, 2011); the biblical silence on relations between Israel and Egypt, essentially until the reign of Solomon, is explained by Wood to reflect Israel's settlement in the highlands, while Egypt concentrated on preserving its access

• The Geopolitical Climate of the Judges/Amarna Period

In this subsection, we will examine the geopolitical climate and topography of the land of Canaan/Israel during the period of the judges and the Amarna period, respectively. Evidence related to the major players on the world stage at the time, and the general climate of anarchy presented in the Amarna Letters, will be shown to resonate with the biblical chronology, specifically as described in the book of Judges.

a. Cushan Rishathaim and Othniel

The book of Judges opens with the story of Israel's oppression and salvation from Cushan Rishathaim, King of Aram Naharaim, by Othniel, the first of the judges.[88] Aram Naharaim (also the home of Abraham's brother Nahor,[89] and Bil'am ben Be'or)[90] has been identified by many scholars as Mittani, a major Near Eastern power from upper Mesopotamia between the 16th and 14th centuries, and referred to in ancient Egyptian texts as Nahrima/Naharin.[91] Mittani disappears from the world stage shortly after the 13th century when it was defeated by Hatti and Assyria.[92] Hansler

---

to the Canaanite lowland fertile lands and trade routes. Cf. Bryant Wood, "The Biblical Date for the Exodus Is 1446 BC: A Response to James Hoffmeier 2007," *Journal of the Evangelical Theological Society* 50 (2007), 249–258.

88 Jud. 3: 8–11.

89 Gen. 24:10.

90 Deut. 23:5.

91 W. M. Flinders Petrie, *A History of Egypt, vol. II, The XVIIth and XVIIIth Dynasties* (London: Methuen & Co., 1896), 285; Hugo Winckler, "Die Volker Vorderasiens," *Der Alte Orient* 1 (1900), 1–36, 21 ff; Maurice Bloomfield, "On Some Alleged Indo-European Languages in Cuneiform Character," *The American Journal of Philology* 25.1 (1904), 1–14, 7; H. Hänsler, "Der Historische Hintergrund von Richter 3, 8–10," *Biblica* 12.4 (1931), 395–410; idem, "Der Untergang Mitannis im Kampfe um Syrien und Palästina," *Biblica* 12.3 (1931), 271–296; Clyde E. Billington, "Othniel, Cushan-Rishathaim, and the Date of the Exodus," pp. 117–132 in *Beyond the Jordan: Studies in Honor of W. Harold Mare* (Glenn A. Carnagey, Sr., et al., eds.; Eugene: Wipf and Stock, 2005). Cf. A. Malamat, "Cushan Rishathaim and the Decline of the Near East around 1200 B. C.," *Journal of Near Eastern Studies* 13.4 (1954), 231–242. Malamat identifies Cushan Rishathaim with a Syrian ruler named Irsu, who briefly seized the Egyptian throne between the 19th and 20th Dynasties, during the early 12th century. The prophet Samuel is dated to the mid-11th century. Malamat's approach not only disregards the role of Aram Naharaim in the story, but it also reduces the entire period of the Judges, including the reign of Eli, into a mere 150 years!

92 Gernot Wilhelm, "The Kingdom of Mittani in Second-Millenium Upper Mesopotamia," pp.1243–1254 in *Civilization of the Ancient Near East,* vol. 2 (Jack Sasson, ed.; New York: Scribner, 1995).

identifies Cushan Rishathaim with Tusratta, the King of Mitanni, a contemporary of Amenhotep IV, who is mentioned in the Amarna Letters. Hansler notes that the letters *Kaph* and *Thaw* are often transposed in Moabite inscriptions. He assumes the name Rishathaim to be a play on the word "*rasha,*" wicked, and points to further instances of antonomasia in the book of Ruth.

Billington believes the name Rishathaim to be an actual name. He emphasizes that the text does not say that Cushan was an Aramean, but rather a member of a people named Rishathaim. Billington explains that the Rishathaim are one and the same as the "Country of Reshet" from 16th–15th century Egyptian inscriptions, who were located far north of Egypt.[93] He cites Der Manuelian's interpretation of the Karnak Stella (ca. 1450 BCE) in which Amenhotep II appears to equate Naharin with the Mitanni,[94] and explains the "im" ending in Rishathaim to be the Hebrew plural suffix.[95]

Whether we accept Hansler's antonomastic identification of Cushan Rishathaim with Tusratta, or Billington's literal identification of the Mittani king, the fact is that Aram Naharaim ceases to threaten the nascent Israel following the story of Othniel. The sudden disappearance of this foreign menace accords well with the historical data relating to the fall of the Mittani no later than the 13th cent. BCE, which is of course incompatible with the 13th cent. BCE Exodus theory.[96]

---

93 Breasted, *Ancient Records of Egypt*, 135, listing no. 321.

94 P. der Manuelian, *Studies in the Reign of Amenophis II* (Hildesheimer Agyptologische Beitrage 26; Hildesheim, 1987), 67–68.

95 Billington further points to Ugaritic texts dating before 1200 BCE that mention a people called Rishim and a city called Rish, north of Ugarit, in northwest Syria. Cf. Freuke Gondahls, *Die Personennamen Der Texte Aus Ugarit* (Rome: Pontificium Institutem Biblicum, 1967), 178. Billington also suggests that the Rish people are synonymous with the Urshu, an ancient northern Mesopotamia people mentioned in Ebla and Hittite texts. Cf. Harvey Weiss, "Conflict and Conquest Among the Amorite Kingdoms," pp. 186–193, 204–212 in *Ebla to Damascus: Art and Archaeology of Ancient* Syria (Washington, D.C.: Smithsonian, 1985), 191; O. R. Gurney, *The Hittites* (Baltimore: Penguin, 1966), 191.

96 Hittite King Suppiluliumas overthrew the Mitanni in the late 14th cent. but left a small portion of the former empire beyond the Euphrates as a vassal kingdom to serve as a buffer state against Assyria, into which it was eventually absorbed. A diminished Aram Naharaim reappears later as part of a larger Armenian confederation in the days of King David. Cf. Ps. 60:2, 1 Chron. 19:6.

b. The Amarna Letters

The Amarna Letters, which document the last years of Amenhotep III through the reign of Tutankhamun, provide ample evidence of what can be best described as Amenhotep III's and Akhenaton's wholesale neglect of the greater Egyptian empire.[97] The letters reveal the Land of Canaan, while still presumably a province of the Egyptian empire, to be in a state of utter anarchy. Vassal kings sent frantic appeals to the Pharaohs for help against marauding invaders, which went unanswered. The 18th Dynasty's bizarre abandonment of the northern territories documented in the Amarna Letters,[98] despite the threat of the *Apiru* (a term suggested by some to describe the Hebrews,[99] or more broadly understood to include other Semitic tribes as well,[100] or perhaps landless marauders and mercenaries) matches the political climate described in the book of Judges.[101] Whichever definition one prefers, the biblical book that best typifies that state of affairs is the book of Judges.[102] Doak points to Abimelek, Gaal and kinsmen, Jephthah and his band of outlaws, and the landless Danite mob, to be broadly indicative of the book of Judges as "the most sustained literary product in the ancient Near East depicting a world of Habiru-like actors generating political transformation."[103] Meitlis further observes that "The main list of city states from the Amarna Letters almost perfectly matches the names of the cities pointed out by the biblical text as Canaanite cities that survived during the period of the judges."[104] This stands in

---

97 Trevor Bryce, *Letters of the Great Kings of the Ancient Near East: The Royal Correspondence of the Late Bronze Age* (London: Routledge, 2004), 187.

98 Neither Thutmose IV nor Amenhotep III are believed to have conducted any northern expeditions. Cf. Lester L. Grabbe, "Canaan Under the Rule of the Egyptian New Kingdom: From the Hyksos to the Sea Peoples," in idem, *The Land of Canaan*, 90–101, 93.

99 Cf. S. Brooks, "The Habiru/'Apiru and 'Ibrim and the connection with I Samuel," *Bulletin of the Anglo-Israel Archaeological Society* 19–20 (2001–2002), 65–70, 67.

100 Yehuda Elitzur, *Israel and the Bible: Studies in Geography, History and Biblical Thought* (Ramat Gan: Bar Ilan Univ. Press, 1999), 53 (Heb.).

101 The term is also explained more broadly as a social stratum between tribal and urban society, cf. M. B. Rowton, "Dimorphic structure and the problem of 'Apiru-'Ibrim," *Journal of Near Eastern Studies* 35 (1976), 13–20. The term may also connote military mercenaries, cf. Ronald Youngblood, "The Amarna Letters and the Habiru," pp. 133–145 in Carnagey et al., eds., *Beyond the Jordan*, 137.

102 Meitlis, *Excavating the Bible: New Archaeological Evidence for the Historic Reliability of Scripture* (Jerusalem: Rubin Mass, 2012), 167–172 (Heb.).

103 Brian Doak, ""Some Worthless and Reckless Fellows": Landless and Parasocial Leadership in Judges," *The Journal of Hebrew Scriptures* 11.2 (2011), 2–29, 6.

104 Meitlis, *Excavating the Bible*, 170.

stark contrast to the absolute silence in the Amarna record concerning cities known to have been captured by Joshua, such as Jericho, Bethel, Gibeon, Shiloh, Miẓpeh and Debir.[105] Of particular interest is the city of Shechem, regarding which, curiously, no battle is recorded in the Bible, and which the Amarna Letters confirm to have been given over without the use of force.[106] Elitzur further notes the failure of the Amarna Letters, as well as the New Kingdom annals, to mention any cities in the mountain region of Samaria, the center of Canaan.[107] This accords seamlessly with the densely forested early topography of the area, described in Joshua 17.[108]

The 15th cent. Exodus has been shown in this exceedingly brief survey to be supported by extensive epigraphic and archaeological evidence spanning the Levant. Furthermore, the historical record documenting the decline and dissolution of Egypt's 18th Dynasty, the contemporary geopolitical climate of Canaan, and the unique topographic conditions of the land ca. the period of the judges resonate seamlessly with the biblical chronology; hardly a "sustained lack of evidence."

Berman's Numeric Argument

Berman sets out to prove that the numbers documented in the Exodus material, most specifically the figure 600,000 adult males, is not meant to be taken literally, but rather as a reflection of status. Berman bases his revisionist interpretation of the numerical data on the secondary meaning of *elef* as clan or troop.[109]

Berman develops this argument in response to the problem of the absence of any Egyptian record of the Exodus. Berman's initial answer to this question relates to the fact that the Egyptians did not differentiate between Asiatic ethnic groups, nor did they recount their own failures. In an attempt to nonetheless account for this lacuna in the Egyptian record, Berman goes on to offer a numeric argument.[110] Berman suggests that the

---

105 Edward F. Campbell, Jr., "The Amarna Letters and the Amarna Period," *Biblical Archaeologist* 23 (1960),11; Theophile James Meek, *Hebrew Origins* (New York: Harper & Brothers, 1960), 21.

106 Cf. *EA* 289, the letter of Abdi-Heba of Jerusalem, *The Context of Scripture, vol. 3*, 238; Bryant G. Wood, "The Role of Shechem in the Conquest of Canaan," pp. 245–256 in *To Understand the Scriptures: Essays in Honor of William H. Shea* (David Merling, ed.; Berrien Springs, MI: Institute of Archaeology, Andrews U, 1997).

107 Y. Elitzur, *Israel and the Bible*, 340.

108 Yehuda Kiel quotes Yehuda Elitzur in his introduction to the book of Joshua. Cf. Y. Kiel, *Joshua* (Daat Mikra; Jerusalem: Mosad Harav Kook, 1976), 34 (Heb.).

109 Berman, *Ani Maamin*, 50.

110 Ibid. 44 ff.

answer essentially lies in the relatively small number of Israelites involved. In other words (mine): The inconsequential number of Israelites who left Egypt simply did not warrant appearance on the front pages of the Egyptian news cycle. Berman states, "Despite the Torah's apparent declaration that the Israelite men numbered 600,000 when they left Egypt, a wealth of material *from within the Torah itself* (the italics are Berman's) points to a number dramatically and perhaps even exponentially lower." My refutation of Berman's approach to the numbers in the Exodus narrative will follow the summary of his argument.

Berman poses three questions relating to numbers in the Exodus narrative which he then cites as proof that the numbers were "manipulated by the text of the Torah."[111]

- **Questions Relating to the Numbers in the Exodus Narrative**[112]

1 The Two Census Figures:
If the two census figures presented in the Torah (Num. 1 and 26) are meant to be accurate, then why are both totals nearly identical? Furthermore, how may we account for the disparity between the seemingly rounded tribal figures, and the ostensibly precise final total figures?

2. An Unusual Rounding Pattern:
None of the tribal tallies are rounded off to the nearest thousand. Whereas they often seem to be rounded to the nearest hundred, they never present a remainder of 100, 800 or 900, displaying a clear tendency to cluster towards the middle, with most tribes tallying a remainder of either 400 or 500.

3. The Firstborn Males:
The Torah reports in Numbers 3:43 that there was a surprisingly if not impossibly low number of firstborn males (22,273), which poses a serious statistical anomaly for a nation numbering upwards of 2,000,000 people.

Berman's response to these questions is to insist that the census figures do not represent factual figures, but rather "a reflection of status"… "the Torah seems to suggest that the total figure to leave Egypt was not

---

111 Ibid. 51.

112 The first to formulate the numeric argument and approach adopted by Berman was Flinders Petrie. Cf. Idem, *Researches in Sinai*, 209–216.

600,000 men, but much fewer."[113] Berman suggests that the actual number of Israelites involved in the Exodus was more likely to have been "enough people to fill a stadium."[114]

A Response to Berman's Numeric Argument

Berman's argument presupposed two basic assumptions:

1 The numbers of Israelites recorded in the Torah are figurative and not literal.
2 The actual number of Israelites that left Egypt were relatively few; certainly few enough to explain their having been overlooked by the annals of ancient Egypt.

I will begin by addressing the latter assumption. The discussion of Israel's relative size at the time of the Exodus will be followed by an inquiry into the possibility of the census numbers as tropes, and the term *elef* as "clan" or "troop."

• Israel, Relatively Few in Number?

Berman cites a verse in Deuteronomy as proof of Israel's underwhelmingly small size at the time of the Exodus: "The Lord did not set his affection on you and choose you because you were more numerous than other peoples, for you were the fewest of all peoples."[115] This is of course a *relative* statement. In other words, Israel was indeed *smaller* than other nations, but that is not to say "small" in *absolute* terms. Berman adds, "It goes without saying that there is no archaeological evidence that the Land of Israel contained tens of millions of inhabitants at this time (or indeed ever), as would be necessitated by a literal reading of Deuteronomy 7:7 and the figure of 600,000 men of fighting age in the dessert."[116] To begin with, the stated inequality between the two respective populations in no way necessitates a hyperbolic "tens of millions" inhabitants of the land. Furthermore, the archaeological record indeed shows there to have been a *five hundred percent increase* in Early Iron Age settlement activity in the Israeli highlands.[117]

---

113 Ibid. 50–51.

114 Ibid. 51, nt.4.

115 Deut. 7:7.

116 Berman, *Ani Maamin*, 49, nt. 2.

117 Cf. William Dever, *What Did the Biblical Writers Know and When Did They Know It?: What Archeology Can Tell Us About the Reality of Ancient Israel* (Cambridge: Eerdmanns, 2001), 110.

Berman presents further "proof" that the Torah itself depicted Israel as "incapable of populating the land they were destined to enter":[118] "But I will not drive them out in a single year, because the land would become desolate and the wild animals too numerous for you. Little by little I will drive them out before you, until you have increased enough to take possession of the land."[119] A brief look at the preceding verse puts the message of these verses into context: "I will send the hornet, הצרעה, ahead of you to drive the Hivites, Canaanites and Hittites out of your way."[120] At the height of the 18th Dynasty, Egypt held a firm grip on the Canaanite territories, which they referred to as *Retjenu.* Garstang, Jericho's original excavator, offers a highly insightful explanation of the hornet metaphor. The hornet was the Egyptian hieroglyph for itself. Garstang explains that at the end of the 15th cent. the Egyptian northern expeditions came to a sudden halt, paving the way for the Israelite conquest.[121] Garstang's interpretation was accepted, albeit modified by Bodenheimer, who added that the symbol represented "the ruler of Lower Egypt since the first dynasty… spreading fear before the powerful King."[122] Neufeld adds that "The Egyptian king, in his role of King of Lower Egypt (the Delta) was literally 'He-who-belongs-to-the-Bee' or rather 'He-of-the-Bee.' This dates back almost to the beginning of history."[123] In these verses, the Torah may be understood to be framing the Egyptian policy of domination and subjugation in the Canaanite territories prior to Israel's entry as having unwittingly played a providential role in paving the way for Israel's subsequent entry into the land.[124] Even those who interpret the hornet metaphor differently would agree that these verses refer not to the *effects* of the Israelite conquest, but rather to events that gradually *preceded* it. In other words, the land's emptying out over time *prior* to the Israelite conquest prevented the formation of a void and the infiltration of wild animals, thus laying the foundation for an unfettered entry. To sum up, the above cited verses in no way indicate a paucity in Israel's numbers.

---

118 Berman, *Ani Maamin*, 48.

119 Ex. 23:29–30.

120 Ex. 23: 31.

121 John Garstang, *Foundations of Bible History: Joshua, Judges* (London: Constable & Co., 1931), 112ff., 258ff.

122 Friedrich S. Bodenheimer, *Animal and Man in Bible Lands* (Leiden: Brill, 1960), 74.

123 Edward Neufeld, "Insects as Warfare Agents in the Ancient Near East (Ex. 23:28; Deut. 7:20; Josh. 24:12; Isa. 7:18–20)," *Orientalia* 49.1 (1980), 30–57, 40–41.

124 For a rich discussion of the various interpretations of the role of the hornet in these verses cf. idem and Yehuda Feliks, *Nature and Man in the Bible: Chapters in Biblical Ecology* (London, Jerusalem, New York: Soncino, 1981), 32–38.

Contrary to Berman's claim of low population size at the time of the Exodus, time and time again we find the Torah confirming Israel's prodigious size. Egypt's horror at the prospect of Israel's burgeoning population certainly does not reflect a paucity of numbers.[125] Following Israel's escape, Egypt sends 600 chariots and its elite troops to give chase.[126] The absolute largest number of chariots mentioned in the Annals of Thutmose III, "the Napoleon of Ancient Egypt," is the 924 taken at Megiddo, and in all other cases the figures are far lower,[127] giving us a yardstick by which to evaluate the significance of the 600-chariot fleet in the Exodus narrative. Moshe's introductory words in *Devarim*, "You are today as numerous as the stars in the sky," hardly convey low population density.[128] Indeed, Balak, king of Moab, experiences a fit of terror at the prospect of "the approaching horde,"[129] and twice describes Israel to be "covering the face of the land," "כסה את עין הארץ".[130] This unusual expression appears only once more in the Tanakh, to describe the descent of millions of locusts upon Egypt.[131] Later, in the book of Joshua we read that the substantial land allotment of the tribe of Ephraim, which encompassed the entire middle swath of Canaan, was contested by the tribe in Joshua 17, on account of the allotment being *too small.* Even taking into account the forested areas that required clearing, this story depicts an enormous tribal population. The list goes on and on, belying Berman's characterization of the Jewish nation as "a tiny populace."[132]

- **Numbers in the Exodus Narrative**

Our attention now returns to the meaning of the numbers in the Exodus narrative, specifically as they relate to the census material. To recap, how can it be that both census figures are nearly identical? And how is it possible to account for the disparity between the seemingly rounded tribal figures, and the ostensibly precise final total figures? Furthermore, whereas the tribal tallies often seem to be rounded to the nearest hundred, they never present a remainder of 100, 800 or 900, displaying a clear tendency to cluster towards the middle.

125 Ex. 1.

126 Ex. 14:7.

127 Arne Furumark, "The Settlement at Ialysos and Aegean History c. 1550–1400 BC," *Opuscula Archaeologica* 6 (1951), 150–271, 260.

128 Deut. 1:10.

129 Num. 22:4.

130 Num. 22:5, 11.

131 Ex. 10:5.

132 Berman, *Ani Maamin*, 48.

Eli Merzbach, a distinguished mathematician, explains that when the number obtained was in tens (with no units), then it was registered as is and the Torah did not round it. However, when the number obtained was not in complete tens, it was rounded to the nearest hundred. Merzbach explains the logic as follows:[133]

"If you round a number that ends in units, then it is rounded to hundreds (the error being less than a hundredth), but a number that ends in tens is left as is. It should be noted that the simple notion which we understand of rounding numbers to the nearest hundred was totally foreign to science until the end of the Middle Ages…[regarding the Torah] numbers were rounded according to the two rules I mentioned above. If we look at the figures in the Torah, this is patently clear. In each of the two censuses of the Israelites in the wilderness, 11 out of 12 figures are multiples of hundreds, whereas one (in the first census the tribe of Gad, and in the second census the tribe of Reuben) is a multiple of ten. The probability of any number ending in zero but not being a multiple of one hundred is 9/100, therefore if one takes any 12 numbers, the expectancy of such a number appearing is equal to 12 x 9/100 = 1.08. In other words, on the average, out of 12 numbers, one will be a multiple of ten (but not of a hundred). Moreover, if we compute the different probabilities (according to binomial distribution), it turns out that the greatest probability is obtained when exactly one out of twelve numbers has this form. The probability of this equals 12 x (1-9/100)11 x 9/100, and all the other probabilities are smaller. Examining both censuses together also yields the same results: out of 24 figures, the average number of occurrences of the specifically desired form is close to 2, and the maximal probability is obtained when k=2, which is indeed what happened."

Merzbach further explains why the Torah had to write down the total sums of Israelites in both censuses:

"Since all the numbers were rounded, one could have had a situation where the grand total obtained would be far off from the actual number in the census… there is a mathematical theorem stating that as the number of figures being summed increases, the deviations resulting from rounding are more likely to offset one another. Actually that is precisely what happened with the census of the Israelites. All the deviations, both upwards and downwards, counterbalanced so that the sum matched the total census."

---

133 Eli Merzbach, "The Census of the Israelites in the Wilderness," https://www.biu.ac.il/JH/Parasha/eng/bamidbar/mer.html

Regarding the problem of the firstborn males, and the Torah's report of a surprisingly if not impossibly low number of firstborn males (22,273), R. Elchanan Samet cites R. Yochanan in *Bekhorot*,[134] who understood the commandment in Ex. 13:1–2, to sanctify every firstborn, to refer only to those male children born *after* the Exodus from Egypt.[135] This opinion is again suggested (although ultimately rejected) by Nachmanides.[136] Berman's sweeping assertion that classical rabbinic literature did not entertain questions arising from mathematic calculations ("it did not cross their minds that these were the types of questions that one would ask of the text") is without support.[137]

Samet further cites mathematics Prof. Eliyahu Beller, who presents a demographic model confirming the relationship between the 22,273 firstborn of Israel and the 300 firstborn Leviim.[138] His statistical calculations take into account the relevant data from the Torah as well as *Seder Olam Raba*, which assumes Israel's sojourn in Egypt to have lasted for 210 years,[139] as this number most accurately reflects the genealogy of the tribe of Levy.[140] Beller's model, which assumes the average lifespan to have been 50 years, projects approximately 23,000 firstborn male children in the final year, and 395,000 firstborn men in the general population. Regarding the Leviim, Beller's model anticipates the birth of approximately 140 newborn males in the final year and 5,600 first-born males in the general tribal population.

Berman's minimalist interpretation of the demographic material presupposes the term *elef* in the Exodus material to mean "clan" or "troop" as opposed to "thousand." Although this is indeed one of the legitimate interpretations of the term, this understanding is counter-indicated by the Exodus material.[141] The census tax collection of one half-shekel, incumbent upon every adult male, recorded in Exodus 38:25–26, unequivocally

---

134 TB *Bekhorot* 4b.

135 Elchanan Samet, "The Census of the Leviim and the Number of Firstborn," https://www.etzion.org.il/en/census-leviim-and-number-firstborn

136 Nachmanides, Ex. 33:45.

137 Berman, *Ani Maamin*, 52.

138 Eliyahu Beller, "The Problem of the Firstborn," *Higgayon* 2 (1993), 103–117 (Heb.).

139 *Seder Olam Raba* edition Leiner, ch.3.

140 Ex. 6.

141 The inflated military figures recorded in Chronicles, which Berman posits as proof of the inaccuracy, or exhortative nature of numbers in general in the Tanakh, may indeed be best understood as referring to troops, and not thousands. Berman, however, selectively chose to apply this definition solely to the Pentateuchal material and not to the Chronicles material. Cf. Idem, *Ani Maamin*, 29–30.

demonstrates this. The sum collected amounted to 100 talents and 1,775 shekels. A single talent is equivalent here to 3,000 shekels.[142] This brings the amount collected to 301,775 shekels, approximately half of the stated number, 603,550, in Numbers 1:46. Unless one assumes the Bible to have deliberately skewed the data with a non-typological figure, the half-shekel tax data leaves no room for a minimalist interpretation.

The Exodus and the Egyptian Reality

Berman introduces two 13th cent. Ramesside monuments into the discussion, the Kadesh bas-reliefs and the Kadesh Poem. Berman presents the multiple points of contact between these monuments and the Torah's account of the Exodus. Berman contends that the similarities between these monuments and Torah texts indicate interdependence. A presentation of each of these monuments together with Berman's interpretation of their significance will be followed by an analysis of the data in light of relevant 15th century Egyptian material that Berman does not relate to.

- **The Kadesh Bas-Reliefs**

Berman presents the bas-reliefs illustrating Ramesses II's military camp at Kadesh, from the wall of the Great Hall of Abu Simbel and the pylon at the temple at Luxor, pointing out the striking correlations between the layout of the ancient Egyptian military camp and the desert Tabernacle.[143] Berman concludes that this data substantiates the late date approach for the Exodus, ca. the reign of Ramesses II. The fundamental problem with this approach is in its underlying assumption that Ramesses II was necessarily the first pharaoh to adopt this military camp formation. Ramesses II embarked on a campaign to regain Egypt's lost territorial domination, the likes of which it had formerly enjoyed at its apex under Thutmose III. This is clearly demonstrated by his appropriation of the prenomen (the pharaonic throne name) of Thutmose III, Menkhepere, for use on his own royal seals.[144] Military culture, contemporary and ancient, is well

---

[142] The Torah's system of dividing the talent into 3,000 shekels was the same as the Ugaritic system where the talent was also divided into 3,000 shekels. Cf. Carlo Zaccagnini, "Notes on the Weight System at Alalah VII," *Orientalia* 48 (1979), 472–475, 472; J. D. Douglas, Merrill Tenney, *Zondervan Illustrated Bible Dictionary* (Grand Rapids: Zondervan Academic, 2011), 1524.

[143] Cf. Hugo Gressmann, *Mose und seine Zeit* (Gottingen: Vanderhoeck and Ruprecht, 1913), 240–242, who was the first to make this observation.

[144] Cf. H. R. Hall, *Catalogue of Egyptian Scarabs in the British Museum, vol. I: Royal Scarabs* (London: Oxford Univ. Press, 1913), XXXV–XXXVI.

known for being deeply rooted in tradition. It is highly unlikely that Ramesses II was the original architect of the Egyptian military camp formation. Ramesses II is known to have scrupulously followed the military patterns of Thutmose III.[145] Indeed, many scholars presume the military camp formation of Ramesses II to have been modeled on that of his 18th cent. predecessor and namesake, Thutmose III.[146] Hoffmeier and Schulman point out that the annals of Thutmose III provide unique terminology related to his military camp that suggests a similar configuration.[147] To quote Hoffmeier, "The verbal description provided by the annals accords well with the military camp of Ramesses II as portrayed in his temples, suggesting that this had been used in the previous dynasty as well."[148] The evidence suggests the 15th cent. Exodus approach to be equally, if not better aligned with the biblical data.

- **The Kadesh Poem and the Account of the Splitting of the Sea**

Berman devotes ten pages in *Ani Maamin* to exploring literary links between The Song at the Sea (*Az Yashir*) and the Kadesh Poem of Ramesses II. These are but a condensed form of his scholarly article on the topic.[149] In my assessment of the material I will relate to both the book and the article. Berman asserts, "I believe it reasonable to claim that the narrative account of the splitting of the sea (Exodus 14) and the Song at the Sea (Exodus 15) may reflect a deliberate act of cultural appropriation."[150] The following list summarizing the links that Berman proposes will be followed by a refutation of his claim of interdependence.

---

145 Cf. Anthony Spalinger, *Leadership Under Fire: The Pressures of Warfare in Ancient Egypt* (vol. 20 of Études d'égyptologie; Paris: Soleb, 2020), 45.

146 Cf. Richard A. Gabriel, *Thutmose III: A Military Biography of Egypt's Greatest Warrior King* (Washington, D.C.: Potomac Books, 2009), 215 nt. 75; Anthony Spalinger, "The Organization of the Pharaonic Army (Old to New Kingdom)," pp. 393–478 in *Ancient Egyptian Administration* (Juan Carlos Moreno García ed.; Leiden Boston: Brill, 2013), 414.

147 A. R. Schulman, "The N'rn at Kadesh Once Again," *Journal for the Society for the Study of Egyptian Antiquities* 11 (1981), 7–19, 19.

148 Hoffmeier, *Ancient Israel in Sinai*, 206.

149 Berman, "The Kadesh Inscriptions," 93–112.

150 Idem, *Ani Maamin*, 60.

- **Berman's Proposed Correlations Between the Kadesh Poem and the Song at the Sea**

1 Numerous phrases relate to Pharaoh's/God's "strong" or "mighty hand/arm."[151]
2 The protagonist army is on the march, though unprepared for battle, when they find themselves attacked by a large force of chariots.[152]
3 The protagonist army breaks ranks in fear.[153]
4 Pharaoh/God confronts the enemy on his/His own.[154]
5 The protagonist makes an appeal for divine intervention.[155]
6 The enemy himself confirms the potency of the god/God.[156]
7 The enemy perishes in a body of water.[157]
8 There are no survivors.[158]
9 The protagonist offers praise for the mighty salvation.[159]
10 The defeated enemy is described as chaff/straw.[160]
11 The protagonists declare Pharaoh/God to be without peer in battle.[161]
12 Neighboring peoples are intimidated.[162]
13 Blessings are uttered for the eternal rule of Pharaoh/God in their respective palace/Temple.[163]

Berman recognizes that many of these parallels may be commonly found motifs in victory hymns; however, he stresses that a number of them are distinct to "only" these two works and appear largely in common sequence.[164] Berman asserts that the unusual depiction of the enemy as chaff/straw substantiates the assumption of textual interdependence.[165]

---

151 Idem, "The Kadesh Inscriptions," 94, 95.
152 Ibid. 98.
153 Ibid.
154 Ibid.
155 Ibid. 99.
156 Ibid.
157 Ibid. 100.
158 Ibid.
159 Ibid. 101.
160 Ibid. 103.
161 Ibid. 104.
162 Ibid.
163 Ibid.
164 Ibid. 94, 106.
165 Ibid. 107; idem, *Ani Maamin*, 65.

The Gebel Barkal Stela of Thutmose III

The Gebel Barkal Stela of Thutmose III offers an overview of the military accomplishments of Thutmose III, ca. 15th century BCE.[166] This Stela is understood by scholars to have served as a template for the victory stelas of later pharaohs.[167] Our assessment of the merits of Berman's thesis relating to the Kadesh Poem of Ramesses II should therefore include a reflection on the possible relevance of the Gebel Barkal Stela of Thutmose III.

The Kadesh Poem uses a remarkably unusual phrase to describe the strength of Ramesses II: "a rampart of iron."[168] The only earlier Egyptian text to use this phraseology is the stella from Gebel Barkal, in which Thutmose III is thusly described.[169] Hart points out that both texts feature the unusual description of the king's Uraeus as a flaming serpent that overthrows enemies.[170] These unique textual correlations reinforce the need to consider the possible relevance of the Gebel Barkal Stela to the above-cited Kadesh Poem data.

- **Correlations Between the Kadesh Poem and the Gebel Barkal Stela**

1 **The mighty hand/arm of Thutmose III** is described no fewer than 25 times, as in "who captures with his *powerful arm*… the *strong-armed* one who tramples his enemies."[171]

2 **The Egyptians are met along their forward march by enemy chariots** (which are mentioned four times): "they came in order to engage (in battle) with my majesty with a myriad of men, hundreds

---

166 Cf. the rendering of James Hoffmeier in *The Context of Scripture,* vol. II, 14–18.

167 Roberto Gozzoli, "Piye Imitates Thutmose III: Trends in a Nubian Historiographical Text of the Early Phase," p. 204–212 in *Egyptology at the Dawn of the Twenty-first Century: Language, Conservation, Museology, vol. 3 of Egyptology at the Dawn of the Twenty-first Century: Proceedings of the Eighth International Congress of Egyptologists* (Zahi A. Hawass, ed.; Cairo: American Univ. in Cairo Press, 2000).

168 *The Context of Scripture*, vol. II, 37.

169 Ibid. 15. Cf. Carsten Vang, "Israel in the Iron-Smelting Furnace? Towards a New Understanding of the כור הברזל in Deut. 4:20," *HIPHIL Novum* 1(2014), 25–34, 31.

170 George Hart, *The Routledge Dictionary of Egyptian Gods and Goddesses* (East Sussex: Psychology Press, 2005), 161. The only other pharaoh to use this description was Queen Hatshepsut, who was coregent with Thutmose III. Cf. Pritchard, *ANET*, 231.

171 *The Context of Scripture*, vol. II, 14.

of thousands with the headmen of all foreign lands, *standing on their chariots...*"[172]

3 **The Egyptian soldiers fail to rise and defend themselves and their king**, "*without a multitude to back him up.*"[173]

4 **Thutmose III faces the enemy alone, without the assistance of his troops**: "He is a king who *fights alone*, without a multitude to back him up… who slaughters everyone, *by himself alone.*"[174]

5 Whereas there is no *appeal* for salvation, **divine intervention** arrives in the form of an astronomical miracle, "Pay attention… then you will know *the miracle* of [Amun-Re] in the presence of the Two Lands… There were two astronomers (present). *A star approached*, coming to the south of them. The like had not happened before. It shot straight toward them (the enemy)."[175]

6 **The enemy confirms the potency of the pharaoh**, "Give us your breath O our Lord… Never again will we do evil against Menkheperre, may he live forever, our lord in our lifetime since we have seen his awe. It was because of his love that he gave us breath. It was his father [Amun-Re, lord of the thrones of the two lands?] who performed it, *it was indeed not a human hand.*"[176]

7 **Thutmose III chases the enemy across the Euphrates**: "who *crossed the Euphrates* after the one who had attacked him."[177]

8 **There are no survivors**: "numerous armies of Mitanni were overthrown in the space of an hour, *annihilated completely* like those who had not existed… He caused me to smite all foreigners *without there being one to challenge him… not one of them could stand.*"[178] (Admittedly, no one drowns in the water, but neither is there any claim of the enemy drowning in the Poem of Kadesh.)

9 **The protagonist offers praise for the mighty salvation**: "He is Horus, the strong-armed one, an excellent fortress for his armies, a refuge for the people, one who subdues all lands when they invade, one who rescues Egypt on the field of battle, a defender who is not afraid of ravenous ones."[179]

---

172 Ibid. 16.
173 Ibid. 15.
174 Ibid. 14, 15.
175 Ibid. 17.
176 Ibid. 16.
177 Ibid. 15.
178 Ibid. 15, 16, 17.
179 Ibid. 15.

10 To be fair, there is no mention in the Gebel Barkal Stela of chaff/straw, although that is hardly significant. One could just as easily cite one of several common motifs with the Song at the Sea, such as the Gebel Barkal Stela's description of Thutmose III "shattering" the enemy,[180] and the enemy being *dashed to pieces*, "תרעץ אויב",[181] in the Song at the Sea.[182]

11 **The protagonist declares Thutmose III to be without peer in battle**: "He is a king who is valorous like Montu, who captures but *no one captures from his hand*."[183]

12 **Neighboring peoples are filled with dread**: "What the people said [...]. Foreigners [...]your awe. *Your battle-cry reaches to the Horns of the Earth, respect of you makes their hearts quiver*, reaching [...] the people [...] all [Nubians who would transgress your plans."[184]

13 **Thutmose III is installed at his palace amid blessings**: "All of the chieftains of Lebanon [made ?] the royal boats in order that their workers sail south in order to bring all the wonderful things [...] belonging to the [...] land to the *Palace* (life, prosperity, and health)."[185]

Berman rightly points out that the Kadesh Poem contains many elements that are not paralleled in the Song at the Sea, such as the Prayer of Ramesses to his god, and his rebuke of his own troops.[186] It is salient to note that these added elements are not present in the Gebel Barkal Stela of Thutmose III.

Another critical piece of Berman's argument of interdependence between the Song at the Sea and the Kadesh Poem of Ramesses II revolves around the theme of boasting. Berman draws a parallel between Pharaoh's boasts in the Song at the Sea and enemy boasts in the literature of Seti, a 19th Dynasty pharaoh preceding Ramesses II.[187] Berman writes, "The concern with silencing the enemy's boasting is distinctly Egyptian and is not found in any other cognate military literature."[188] That may or may not be the case; however, it is irrelevant to the question at hand. The

---

180 Ibid. 14.

181 Ex. 15:6.

182 Cf. Ludwig Koehler, et al., *The Hebrew and Aramaic Lexicon of the Old Testament*, electronic ed. (Leiden, PA: Brill, 1994–2000), s.v. "רעץ", 1285–1286.

183 *The Context of Scripture*, vol. II, 15.

184 Ibid. 18.

185 Ibid. 17, 18.

186 Berman, *Ani Maamin*, 66.

187 Ibid. 67.

188 Idem, "The Kadesh Inscriptions," 107.

Kadesh Poem does not make any mention whatsoever of enemy boasting. It *is* salient however to note that both the Kadesh Poem and the Gebel Barkal Stela emphasize that the self-aggrandizing of the pharaoh is not boastful. The Kadesh Poem describes Ramesses II, "Going forth bravely, returning after triumphing personally, without speaking *boastfully*,"[189] "You are great in victory in front of your army, in the presence of the entire land, without *boastful* claims."[190] Similarly, the Gebel Barkal Stela quotes Thutmose III, "It is *without exaggeration* and without falsehood that I have said this."[191] This significant correlating feature once again points to the interdependence of these two Egyptian texts.

The correlation between the Gebel Barkal Stela of Thutmose III and the Kadesh Poem of Ramesses II is further supported in the ancient Egyptian story "Thutmose III in Asia." Although composed during the 19th Dynasty, the story presents a fictional version of the battle of Thutmose III at Megiddo. Manassa relates to the insertion of sections of the Kadesh Poem in the tale. "The quotation of part of the Kadesh Battle poem in the story suggests that the author intended to equate the two warrior pharaohs Ramesses II and Thutmose III and their military achievements in the Battle of Kadesh and Battle of Megiddo respectively."[192] This points to a clear 19th Dynasty agenda of linking the military exploits of Ramesses II with those of Thutmose III, and hence to a fundamental interdependence between the Gebel Barkal Stela of Thutmose III and the Kadesh Poem of Ramesses II.

Berman argues that "the large number of highly distinctive motifs that appear in these two works alone" suggests an interdependence between the Kadesh Poem and the Song at the Sea. "No other battle account known to us either from the Tanakh or from the epigraphic remains of the ancient Near East provide even half the number of shared narrative motifs exhibited here."[193] These sweeping assertions are indeed surprising in light of the fact that virtually all of Berman's examples apply equally well, if not better, to the Gebel Barkal Stela of Thutmose III. Furthermore, whereas the Gebel Barkal Stela tells of divine miraculous intercession, the likes of which could easily be compared with Israel's miraculous deliverance in the Song at the Sea, the Kadesh Poem does not.

For the sake of clarity, **I am not claiming interdependence between the Gebel Barkal Stela of Thutmose III and the Song at the**

---

189 *The Context of Scripture*, vol. II, 33.

190 Ibid. 37.

191 Ibid. 16.

192 Colleen Manassa, *Imagining the Past: Historical Fiction in New Kingdom Egypt* (New York: Oxford Univ. Press, 2013), 146.

193 Berman, *Ani Maamin*, 67.

Sea. Rather, Berman's claim that the said parallels are "distinct to only these two works" is simply not supported by the facts. One feeling the need to assume interdependence between the Song at the Sea and an ancient Egyptian text need look no further than the 15th century Gebel Barkal Stela of Thutmose III.

Ramesses

In the beginning of this essay the question was raised regarding the appearance of the topographic name Raamses in Exodus 1:11. In light of the fact that the pharaonic name Ramesses was never used before the 19th Dynasty, the appearance of this topographical name in the Exodus narrative presents a difficulty that cannot be ignored.

It is not uncommon in the Bible to find the editorial updating of names.[194] Two such examples in the Torah are Bethel[195] and Dan.[196] Berman himself, in the second section of *Ani Maamin*, devotes considerable attention to the subject of post-Mosaic addenda to the Torah.[197] Given Berman's rich and comprehensive presentation of this very topic in the same book, it is most surprising that he does not even suggest this as a possible answer.

Bietak has excavated the palatial complex and port at Avaris (Tell el-Dab'a), biblical Raamses.[198] Today, we know that Ramesses built his royal city on the very site that had functioned as the palatial district and port city during the 18th Dynasty, known then as Peru-nefer, until sometime during the reign of Amenhotep II (who reigned after Thutmose III), at which point it was mysteriously abandoned. Bietak's excavations point to the epicenter of Israel's affliction during Egypt's 18th Dynasty as one and the same with what later became the capital city of Ramesses II.

---

194 Kitchen, *Reliability*, 335, 348, 354, 493.

195 Cf. Gen. 12:8; 13:3; 28:19.

196 Cf. Gen. 14:14; Judg. 18:29.

197 For more on this topic see Amnon Bazak, *Until This Day: Fundamental Questions in Bible Teaching* (Tel Aviv: Yediot Ahronot Books and Chemed Books, 2013), 49–80 (Heb.).

198 Manfred Bietak and Irene Forster-Müller, "Ausgrabung eines Palastbezirkes der Tuthmosidenzeit bei 'Ezbet Helmi/Tell el-Dab'a, Vorbericht für Herbst 2004 und Frühjahr 2005," *Ägypten und Levante/ Egypt and the Levant* 15 (2005), 65–100; Manfred Bietak, "The Aftermath of the Hyksos in Avaris," p. 26–32 in *Culture Contacts and the Making of Cultures: Papers in Homage to Itamar Even-Zohar* (Rakefet Sela-Sheffy and Gordon Toury, eds.; Tel Aviv: Tel Aviv University Unit of Culture Research, 2011), 25.

Conclusion

I see no more fitting way to conclude this essay than to quote from Berman's introduction to his analysis of the Exodus material in *Ani Maamin*:[199]

> Excising the Exodus from Judaism would seem to undercut Judaism itself. After all, the biblical rationale for Israel's obligation to God is premised not on His identity as Creator, or on His supreme moral authority, but on the fact that the Israelite slaves in Egypt cried out to Him from their bondage and He saved them. This is the sole driving force behind the opening line of the Ten Commandments: "I am the Lord your God, *Who took you out of Egypt, the house of bondage*."

The Bible is consistently clear about the awesome magnitude of the Exodus.

> Has any god ever tried to take for himself *one nation out of another nation*, by trials, by signs and wonders, by war, by a mighty hand and an outstretched arm, or by great and awesome deeds, like all the things the Lord your God did for you in Egypt before your very eyes? (Deut. 4:34)

Insisting that the Torah inflated the numbers of people who witnessed God's revelation at Sinai runs counter to the sine-qua-non of the Mosaic faith. Even if one were to assume the number 600,000 to be symbolic (which it was shown not to be), it nonetheless clearly represents a mass multitude. The biblical message is unequivocal and consistent. The Exodus was a major national event, both for Egypt and the Jewish people. Reducing Israel's size at the time to "a tiny populace," or "enough people to fill a stadium," too small to merit attention in the historical record, dilutes and warps the text beyond recognition. The Bible is consistently clear on the magnitude and significance of the Exodus and its being the foundation of the Bible and Judaism. Ignoring this for the sake of resolving an imaginary problem not only damages the biblical text and narrative, and undermines Judaism itself; it accomplishes nothing. It is impossible to reconcile the biblical account of a monumental Exodus with a perceived lack of evidence by diluting it to the point where it becomes a non-event. Attempting to "rescue" the Exodus narrative in this way renders it not worth saving. Berman's solution to a nonexistent problem is neither necessitated by the evidence nor does it promote Jewish faith.

---

199 Berman, *Ani Maamin*, 43.

Berman writes in *Ani Maamin* about the *seder* meal at which sit not only a child who knows not how to ask but a father who knows not how to answer. To the father I would say, as Berman rightly notes, that history is for telling and not for proving.[200] The Torah concerned itself with *telling* the story of the Exodus as opposed to *proving* it. *History* may indeed be an anachronistic term when applied to the Torah; however, *truth* and *falsehood* are not. Do we not repeat twice daily? "I am the Lord your God, Who brought you out of Egypt to be your God. I am the Lord your God…*Emet.*"[201]

200 Ibid. 22.

201 Num. 15:41, BT *Berakhot* 14a.

Emotion and Intent in Prayer: *אימה ויראה ופחד*

By: ASHER BENZION BUCHMAN

Praying with Body and Mind

Rambam devotes the fourth chapter of *Hilchos Tefillah* to five things that are mandatory in prayer.[1] The last of these requirements is כוונת הלב, "intent of the heart." Later in the chapter he explains what this means.

> כוונת הלב כיצד: כל תפילה שאינה בכוונה, אינה תפילה; ואם התפלל בלא כוונה, חוזר ומתפלל בכוונה. מצא דעתו משובשת וליבו טרוד--אסור לו להתפלל, עד שתתיישב דעתו. ...טז כיצד היא הכוונה--שיפנה ליבו מכל המחשבות, ויראה עצמו כאילו הוא עומד לפני השכינה; לפיכך צריך לישב מעט קודם התפילה, כדי לכוון את ליבו, ואחר כך יתפלל, בנחת ובתחנונים. ולא יעשה תפילתו כמי שהיה נושא משאוי, משליכו והולך לו; לפיכך צריך לישב מעט אחר התפילה, ואחר כך ייפטר. חסידים הראשונים היו שוהין שעה קודם התפילה, ושעה אחר התפילה, ומאריכין בתפילה שעה. (הל' תפילה ד:טו)
>
> Proper intention: What is implied? Any prayer that is not [recited] with proper intention is not prayer. If one prays without proper intention, he must repeat his prayers with proper intention…What is meant by [proper] intention? One should clear his mind from all thoughts and envision himself as standing before the Divine Presence. Therefore, one must sit a short while before praying in order to focus his attention and then pray in a pleasant and supplicatory fashion. One should not pray as one carrying a burden who throws it off and walks away. Therefore, one must sit a short while after praying, and then withdraw. The pious ones of the previous generations would wait an hour before praying and an hour after praying. They would [also] extend their prayers for an hour.

The core of this description of כוונה—standing before the שכינה (Presence of G-d) with the heart purged of all other thoughts—is very

---

1 חמישה דברים מעכבין את התפילה, אף על פי שהגיע זמנה--טהרת הידיים, וכיסוי הערווה, וטהרת מקום התפילה, ודברים החופזים אותו, וכוונת הלב. ד:א.

Rabbi Asher Benzion Buchman, a *musmakh* of RIETS, is the author of *Encountering the Creator: Divine Providence and Prayer in the Works of Rambam* (Targum, 2004) and *Rambam and Redemption* (Targum, 2005). He is the editor-in-chief of *Ḥakirah.*

general and somewhat obscure. The latter phrases, describing that one should pray slowly and in a beseeching manner, and not as a burden, are apparently intended to clarify the manner of this כוונה. Rambam's son, Rav Avraham, explains[2] that these two phrases constitute one idea—the prayer must be done "without hastening as if it is a chore one wishes to rid oneself of, but with a tone appropriate for fulfilling כוונת הלב: with a soft heart at the time of making the requests, and with fear and trembling when speaking of G-d's greatness, and in the form of gratitude and recognition when proclaiming the thanks."[3] This, indeed, clarifies the meaning of כוונה; however, Rambam did not choose to include these details in his own explanation and we cannot be certain that this is what he meant. Moreover, part of Rav Avraham's definition is found elsewhere in *Hilchos Tefillah* in another context.

The next chapter (chapter five) deals with eight things pertaining to one's physical state that are ideally required (לכתחלה) for prayer, but if lacking do not invalidate the prayer.[4] The third of these requirements is called תקון הגוף, "positioning of the body." Yet, in his description of this feature, Rambam seems to be explaining much more clearly what the proper כוונת הלב of *tefillah* consists of:

> תיקון הגוף כיצד: כשהוא עומד בתפילה, צריך לכוון את רגליו זו בצד זו; ונותן עיניו למטה, כאילו הוא מביט לארץ; ויהיה ליבו פנוי למעלה, כאילו הוא עומד בשמיים; ומניח ידיו על ליבו כפותין, הימנית על השמאלית. ועומד כעבד לפני רבו, באימה ויראה ופחד. ולא יניח ידיו, על חלציו. (ה:ד)
>
> The preparation of one's body: What is implied? When one stands in prayer, he should place his feet together side by side. He should set his eyes downwards as if he is looking at the ground, and his heart upwards as if he is standing in Heaven. His hands should be resting on his heart, with the right hand clasped over the left hand. He should stand like a servant before his master, in fear, awe, and dread. He should not rest his hand on his hips [during the *Amidah*].

First comes the startling description, that though one's eyes are towards the earth, one's heart must be turned upward and thus one must feel as if he is standing in the heaven. However, what follows, though more understandable, seems out of place. "He should stand as a slave

---

2 In his ספר המספיק לעובדי ה', p. 62.

3 He bases this on *Avos* 2:13.

4 שמונה דברים, צריך המתפלל להיזהר בהן ולעשותן; ואם היה דחוק, או נאנס, או שעבר ולא עשה אותן--אינן מעכבין. ואלו הן--עמידה, ונוכח המקדש, ותיקון הגוף, ותיקון המלבוש, ותיקון המקום, והשווית הקול, והכריעה, וההשתחוויה (ה:א).

before a master, באימה ויראה ופחד." Perhaps the "standing as a slave before his master" is a physical description of the pose one should take, but these last words explain the emotion that must accompany prayer. What is this description doing here? Should it not be used as a description of what constitutes the proper כוונה? Rav Avraham had maintained that the aspect of "fear" is appropriate during the opening blessings of the *Amidah*[5] and constitutes part of the description of כוונת הלב. Why in the midst of a description of physical position does Rambam conclude his explanation of what comprises the intellectual act of כוונת הלב?

In the halachah that precedes that of תקון הגוף, we see that at least one physical requirement of this fifth chapter is in fact unquestionably related to an intellectual issue:

> נוכח המקדש כיצד: היה עומד בחוצה לארץ, מחזיר פניו נוכח ארץ ישראל ומתפלל; היה עומד בארץ, מכוון פניו כנגד ירושלים; היה עומד בירושלים, מכוון פניו כנגד המקדש; היה עומד במקדש, מכוון פניו כנגד בית קודש הקודשים. סומה, ומי שאינו יכול לכוון את הרוחות, והמהלך בספינה--יכוון ליבו כנגד השכינה, ויתפלל. (ה:ג)
>
> Facing the Temple: What is implied? A person standing in the Diaspora should face *Eretz Yisrael* and pray. One standing in *Eretz Yisrael* should face Jerusalem. One standing in Jerusalem should face the Temple. One standing in the Temple should face the Holy of Holies. A blind person, one who is unable to determine direction, or one traveling in a boat should direct his heart towards the Divine Presence and pray.

Prayer must be facing *Yerushalayim*, but when one does not know where this is, he should substitute by directing "his heart towards the *Shechinah.*" In other words, while the desired purpose is best actualized by facing the *Beis HaMikdash*, this purpose can also be accomplished בדיעבד (in a non-ideal but valid way) by "directing one's heart to the *Shechinah.*" In fact, it, would seem that all of the eight physical directives in this fifth chapter—

> עמידה, ונוכח המקדש, ותיקון הגוף, ותיקון המלבוש, ותיקון המקום, והשווית הקול, והכריעה, וההשתחוויה
>
> 1) standing; 2) facing the Temple; 3) preparation of his body; 4) proper clothing; 5) proper place; 6) control of his voice; 7) bowing; and 8) prostration.

---

5 He says it should be felt "when speaking of G-d's greatness."

—are intended to bring about the proper state of mind, and thus the halachah states that if the physical act cannot be done, one should nevertheless try to direct oneself to the proper state of mind.[6] Thus, we can explain our out-of-place halachah by viewing all the laws of chapter five as means of focusing and deepening the כוונה that was mandated in chapter four.

Praying With Emotions and Intellect

Still, a closer look at these laws uncovers another factor in the understanding of the structure of Rambam's presentation. Rambam had said in chapter four that one must "see himself as if standing before the *Shechinah*." כוונה is the intellectual knowledge that one is standing in the presence of G-d. The elements defined in chapter five are indeed physical requirements, and although they are certainly meant to create a state of mind, they do not primarily enhance intellectual understanding.[7] Rather, they bring about emotional "understanding." Rambam often refers to a concept he calls שלמות הגוף [8] (Perfection of the Body) and defines it as incorporating physical well-being and the perfecting of one's character and emotional traits. The directing of "the body" detailed in chapter five is intended to direct man's emotions in such a way that he is enabled to pray properly. In chapter four we are told that "יראה עצמו כאלו עומד לפני

---

6 A careful look at all eight requirements will confirm that this is so. We will mention some points here and others later in the text itself. In תקון המלבוש Rambam also lists:

לא יאחוז תפילין בידו או ספר תורה בזרועו, מפני שליבו טרוד בהן; ולא יאחוז מעות וכלים ביד...

Even though the topic is dress, the issue of holding something is that it will interfere with one's כוונה. We all understand the clothes one wears affects one's state of mind. With regard to תקון מקום , Rambam states:

יעמוד במקום נמוך, ויחזיר פניו לכותל. וצריך לפתוח חלונות או פתחים, כנגד ירושלים, כדי להתפלל כנגדן. וקובע מקום לתפילתו, תמיד. ואין מתפללין, בחורבה ואסור לישב בצד העומד בתפילה, או לעבור לפניו--עד שירחיק ממנו ארבע אמות.

One prays facing the wall and away from other people, clearly factors to ensure that one's כוונה is not interrupted. With regard to השווית קול, it is obvious that the purpose is to enhance כוונה.

לא יגביה קולו בתפילתו, ולא יתפלל בליבו--אלא מחתך הדברים בשפתיו, ומשמיע לאוזנו בלחש. ולא ישמיע קולו, אלא אם כן היה חולה; או שאינו יכול לכוון את ליבו, עד שישמיע קולו--הרי זה מותר: ובלבד שלא יהיה בציבור, כדי שלא תיטרף דעתן מקולו.

7 Except in that they create the avoidance of things that interfere with concentration.

8 See *Hakdamah L'Pirush HaMishnah. Moreh HaNevuchim* 3:26, *Shemonah Perakim,* ch. 1.

"השכינה, one "must see himself as standing before the *Shechinah*" and "seeing oneself"[9] means understanding intellectually that this is the case. By contrast, in chapter five Rambam uses a different phrase, יכוון ליבו כנגד השכינה, meaning, "to direct one's being towards the *Shechinah*." The different phraseology represents a different concept. Here it is the emotional essence of man[10] that is being "מכוון". The word מכוון has a dual meaning, "physically straight" and "with one's intention." So too does the word לב,[11] as Rambam explains in the *Moreh*, always refer to the essence and thus can refer to one's intellect or to his emotions.

In chapter four, the prohibition of drinking wine is stated immediately after the requirement of כוונת הלב, for wine confuses the mind:

> שיכור--אל יתפלל, מפני שאין לו כוונה; ואם התפלל, תפילתו תועבה--לפיכך חוזר ומתפלל, כשיתרונן משכרותו. שתוי, אל יתפלל; ואם התפלל, תפילתו תפילה. איזה הוא שיכור, ואיזה הוא שתוי--שיכור, זה שאינו יכול לדבר בפני

---

9 See *Moreh HaNevuchim* 1:4 on "seeing."

10 *Mori V'Rebbe Rav* Yosef Dov Soloveitchik, *zt"l*, speaks at length about the dual roles of emotion and intellect in prayer, in the lectures recorded in *Worship of the Heart.* Some of the concepts mentioned in this essay are explained there and in other works of the Rav in greater depth and precision, as only the Rav can do. The purpose of this essay is not to develop these ideas but to explain the specific deductions that can be made from the exact words Rambam uses in several places. The Rav's teaching permeates the works of all who ever studied with him or his students and certainly apply to all that I write. I will quote little from him here in confirmation for what I say, for my purpose is to deduce all ideas directly from Rambam's words and the explanations I give must stand on their own. I may occasionally note cases where I diverge from something the Rav states, and at other times this may be the case although I do not note it. Differing from the Rav does not necessarily mean differing with his interpretation of Rambam, as he states in his introduction that his explanation of religious experience is his own "coordinated with *halachah*." The Rav at times states that he is diverging from Rambam's position—his own views sometimes being supported by other *rishonim* who disagree with Rambam on particular points. While there is great value in the Rav's analysis of an issue and his understanding of "religious experience," for writers such as myself the only value we bring is in faithfully portraying the meaning of Rambam's words.

11 Note that in the first six qualities the words לב and כוון are always present. The חולה can lie and not stand, but this does not free him from the requirement of לכוון דעתו—the choice of word דעת here implies that Rambam is referring to כוונה of chapter 4. He must tell us that although we forgo the proper כוונת הלב if sick, we may not forgo the obligation of fundamental כוונה של דעת. Note the term in chapter 4 of דעתו משובשת.

> המלך; ושתוי, שיכול לדבר בפני המלך ואינו משתבש. אף על פי כן, הואיל ושתה רביעית יין--לא יתפלל, עד שיסור יינו מעליו. (ד:יז)
>
> A person who is drunk should not pray, because he cannot have proper intention. If he does pray, his prayer is an abomination. Therefore, he must pray again when he is clear of his drunkenness. One who is slightly inebriated should not pray, [but] if he prays, his prayer is prayer. When is a person considered as drunk? When he is unable to speak before a king. [In contrast,] a person who is slightly inebriated is able to speak before a king without becoming confused. Nevertheless, since he drank a *revi'it* of wine, he should not pray until his wine has passed from him.

Drinking, however, also has a second effect of unleashing one's emotions. Not only is the confusion of the mind a problem, but also the unleashing of the emotions, as is most likely the explanation for the rejection of the *avodah* of **נדב ואביהו** according to the Rabbinic opinion that they had drunk wine before entering the *Mikdash*.[12] Nor is prayer to be introduced from the midst of an act of laughter or from anger, just as it is not to be introduced from a complicated period of study.

> וכן אין עומדין להתפלל לא מתוך שחוק, ולא מתוך קלות ראש, ולא מתוך שיחה, ולא מתוך מריבה, ולא מתוך כעס--אלא מתוך דברי תורה. ולא מתוך דין הלכה, אף על פי שהן דברי תורה, כדי שלא יהא ליבו טרוד בהלכה--אלא מתוך דברי תורה שאין בהן עיון, כגון הלכות פסוקות. (ד:יח)
>
> Similarly, one should not stand to pray in the midst of laughter or irreverent behavior, nor in the midst of a conversation, argument or anger, but rather in the midst of words of Torah. [However, one should not stand to pray] in the midst of a judgment or a [difficult] halachic issue, even though these are words of Torah, lest one's mind be distracted by the halachah in question. Rather, [one should pray] in the midst of words of Torah that do not require deep concentration, e.g., laws that have already been accepted.

In chapter four, where Rambam defines the requirement of intellectual **כוונה**, he explains that difficult study which imposes a disruption to the intellect, levity and emotion are all to be avoided for all cloud the intellect.

---

12 The sin and death of Nadav and Avihu is followed by G-d introducing the prohibition of drinking wine before doing *avodah* or issuing a halachic decision and thus one opinion of *Chazal* is that they had drunk wine before their error. See *Kedushas HaLevi,* ibid.

Rambam in chapter four speaks of praying in נחת ותחנונים [13] and not as משא as these are characteristics of one's intellectual state of mind—of concentration. It is in chapter five that Rambam tells us ועומד כעבד לפני רבו, באימה ויראה ופחד. This is a description of an emotional state. In fact, Rambam writes elsewhere that by intellectually contemplating the unfathomable essence of the Creator one is brought to this state of fear:

> וכשמחשב בדברים האלו עצמן, מיד הוא נרתע לאחוריו, ויירא ויפחד (יסדה"ת ב:ב)
>
> When he [continues] to reflect on these same matters, he will immediately recoil in awe and fear.

Thus, the initial כוונה of contemplating the presence of G-d, as defined in chapter four, is meant to initiate the proper emotions for prayer, the types of fear defined in chapter five, and then the process of immersing oneself in this emotion is intended to heighten the כוונה.

Three Types of Fear—but Where Is the Love?

Rambam speaks of three types of fear—אימה, יראה ופחד. The questions we wish to answer in this essay are what exactly are these three elements? How do they differ from each other? Moreover, why is there only a requirement of fear of Heaven, and no need to feel love?[14]

According to one *girsa* in the Talmud (*Berachos* 31a), one is supposed to pray מתוך שמחה של מצוה[15], which we generally associate with אהבה.[16]

Rambam does not have such a *girsa*, but Rashba, though not having this *girsa* either, allows a שליח צבור to display obvious joy in his prayer as long as the joy springs from יראה, and he quotes the verse in *Tehillim* (2), עבדו את ה' ביראה וגילו ברעדה, which is also quoted by Rav Nachman in the discussion of *tefillah* (*Berachos 30b*). In the *Shulchan Aruch* (*OC* 93) the *girsa* calling for שמחה is reflected, with the *Mechaber* writing, based on Rashi

---

13 Thus we say אתה חונן לאדם דעת.

14 Rav Soloveitchik, *zt"l*, in *Worship of the Heart,* sees in שבח והודאה at the beginning and end of the *Amidah* an obvious outpouring of love. Yet the words are missing from Rambam's presentation and it is this that we deal with.

15 The *Ra'ah* says this issue is a מחלוקת תנאים.

16 I am associating *simchah* with *ahavah* which is logical but in fact not *muchrach.* See *Hil. Teshuvah* 8:2 which is one place where it is implied. In any event, the issue is whether emotions conflicting with *yirah* are appropriate.

and Rosh's[17] understanding of the Gemara, that one rises to pray [18] באימה והכנעה but also:

> מתוך שמחה כגון דברי תנחומין של תורה סמוך לגאולת מצרים או סמוך לתהלה לדוד שכתוב בו רצון יראיו יעשה שומר ה' את כל אוהביו... אלא מתוך הלכה פסוקה

The Rama adds [19] that the halachah of מתוך הלכה פסוקה is related to the concept פקודי ה' משמחי לב, and is an application of the rule of introducing prayer with שמחה.[20] Yet here in the heart of *Sefer Ahavah*, "The Book of Love," Rambam tells us that one is to be steeped in יראה, but שמחה and אהבה is nowhere to be found.[21] The two *mitzvos* of אהבה ויראה are crucial to one's עבודת ה', so why is the quality which Rambam says must motivate one's *avodah* (ויעבדו מאהבה (הל' תשובה י missing from עבודה שבלב?[22]

The *Mitzvah* of *Yirah* and Stepping Backward Before the King

Before we look for an answer to our questions, let us look at the *mitzvah* of יראת ה'. We have noted that in *Hilchos Yesodei HaTorah* (2:2), Rambam tells us that one reaches the level of יראה when:

> מיד הוא נרתע לאחוריו, **ויירא ויפחד** ויידע שהוא בריה קטנה שפלה אפלה, עומד בדעת קלה מעוטה לפני תמים דעות.
>
> He will immediately recoil in awe and fear, appreciating how he is a tiny, lowly, and dark creature, standing with his flimsy, limited, wisdom before He Who is of perfect knowledge.

Apparently, an act of fulfillment of this *mitzvah* of יראה is intended to precede prayer. We note, however, that in describing this *mitzvah* the terms

---

17 Also quoted by the *Tur*.

18 This is how the phrase כובד ראש of the Mishnah (*Berachos* 30b) is interpreted by Rashi as the Gemara bases it on עבדו ה' ביראה. The Mishnah may in fact be the source of Rambam's אימה יראה ופחד.

19 Also based on the *Tur*.

20 *Mechaber* also quotes an opinion that interprets the Yerushalmi to say that one can pray after engaging in צרכי צבור, for this too gladdens the heart.

21 Rambam defines the naming of this book in this way אכלול בו המצוות שהן תדירות, שנצטווינו בהם כדי לאהוב את המקום ולזוכרו תמיד--כגון קרית שמע, ותפילה, ותפילין, וברכות.

22 מצות עשה להתפלל בכל יום, שנאמר "ועבדתם את ה' אלוקיכם" (שמות כג,כה): מפי השמועה למדו שעבודה זו--היא תפילה, ונאמר "ולעובדו, בכל לבבכם" (דברים יא,יג); אמרו חכמים, איזו היא עבודה שבלב, זו היא תפילה.

יראה ופחד are used, while for prayer one must approach with yet another quality, אימה. Why the extra requirement and indeed, what does it mean? Is perhaps נרתע לאחוריו the counterpart to אימה? If so, why when we engage in prayer should we not take steps backward, since the ירא is expected to move backwards? The prevailing custom is, in fact, to take three steps forward. How can this be reconciled with prayer in fear?[23]

The difficulty raised by this last question can perhaps be mitigated by the realization that when one steps back from prayer, he is yet engaged in prayer, for the concept of כריעה is one of the eight elements of prayer listed in chapter five:

> וכשגומר התפילה, כורע ופוסע שלוש פסיעות לאחוריו כשהוא כורע; ונותן שלום משמאל עצמו, ואחר כך מימין עצמו, ואחר כך מגביה ראשו מן הכריעה ... ולמה נותן שלום לשמאלו תחילה, מפני ששמאלו הוא ימין שכנגד פניו: כלומר שהוא עומד לפני המלך, נותן שלום לימין המלך ואחר כך לשמאל המלך; וקבעו שייפטר מן התפילה, כמו שיהיו נפטרין מלפני המלך. (ה:י)[24]
>
> Upon completing the *Amidah*, one bows and takes three steps backwards while bowing. He takes leave from his left and afterwards, from his right. Then, he lifts his head up from the bowed position.

Nor is this stepping back the last element of prayer listed in chapter five. The last is השתחויה:

> השתחוויה כיצד: אחר שמגביה ראשו מכריעה חמישית, יושב לארץ, ונופל על פניו ארצה, ומתחנן בכל התחנונים שירצה.
>
> Prostration, what is implied? After one lifts his head from the fifth bow, he sits on the ground, falls with his face towards the earth, and utters all the supplications that he desires.

Actually, the culmination of prayer is at the moment of prostration, that is the final act of prayer, which is only done after one has stepped back from the King. Thus, there is a similarity between the fulfillment of the *mitzvah* of יראה and the act of prayer.

But still, even if we should posit that there is a connection between אימה and נרתע לאחוריו, for which there is really little proof, we still have

---

23 This custom is in fact non-halachic and is apparently based on what we will discuss in the next paragraph—the need to end prayer by stepping backward.

24 See also 2:9. Also see 9:2–4 that the שליח צבור takes three steps back after praying his silent *Amidah* and then remains in this place to pray the communal prayer. Does this perhaps mean that he prays the entire communal prayer as נרתע לאחוריו? The צבור is not allowed to return to their seats until the ש"צ reaches קדושה. Perhaps they too are required to continue with נרתע לאחוריו for this section.

no evidence as to what the individual term "fear" refers. Let us begin our search for an answer to our questions by looking at where else "fear" is mandated in the service of G-d.

Walking in the House of G-d

One who enters the *Azarah* of the *Beis HaMikdash* is commanded to demonstrate a high level of respect.[25] This is part of the *mitzvah* of מורא מקדש:

> וכל הנכנס לעזרה--יהלך בנחת במקום שמותר לו להיכנס לשם, ויראה עצמו שהוא עומד לפני האדון ה' שאמר "והיו עיני ולבי שם, כל הימים" (מלכים א ט,ג; דברי הימים ב ז,טז); ומהלך באימה ויראה ופחד ורעדה, שנאמר "בבית אלוקים, נהלך ברגש" (תהילים נה,טו). (הל' בית הבחירה ז:ה)
>
> Everyone who enters the Temple Courtyard should walk in a dignified manner, in the region where he is permitted to enter. He should conceive of himself as standing before G-d, as [1 Kings 9:3] states: "My eyes and My heart will be there forever." One should walk with awe, fear, and trembling, as [Psalms 55:15] states: "We would walk in the House of the Lord with fervor."

All three terms of fear that were used for תפילה are used for being in the place designated for עבודה.[26]

It would seem that one's walking in the *Azarah* is a form of עבודה itself. The *mitzvah* of עלייה לרגל and ראיית פני הבית is performed with the sacrifice of the עולת ראייה but actually going up to the *Beis HaMikdash* and seeing and being seen is also part of the *mitzvah* (*Hil. Chagigah* 1:1-2, 4[27]). Of course, there are other *mitzvos* associated with coming to the *Beis*

---

25 The language of the Mishnah (*Berachos* 30b) for how one should come to prayer, which Rambam did not choose to use, is מתוך כובד ראש. But with regard to the בית המקדש we are told that one must refrain from the opposite of כובד ראש. (*Hil. Beis HaBechirah* 7:5).

לא יקל אדם את ראשו כנגד שער מזרחי של עזרה, שהוא שער ניקנור--מפני שהוא מכוון כנגד קודש הקודשים.

And, over and above the prohibition of קלות ראש when facing the *Beis HaMikdash*, Rambam uses the opposite term also when explaining what is prohibited in the בית הכנסת: "אין נוהגין בהן קלות ראש" (יא:ו)

26 Plus one more רעדה which we shall discuss.

27 הראייה האמורה בתורה--הוא שייראה פניו בעזרה ביום טוב הראשון של חג, ויביא עימו קרבן עולה.

HaMikdash. The קרבן חגיגה ושלמי שמחה[28] are in fact associated with worshiping via celebration and rejoicing before G-d as so clearly delineated in the verse ושמחתם לפני ה' אלקיכם.[29] Within the *mitzvah* of ראייה, however, the obligation of מורא מקדש necessitates an experience that Rambam refers to as הליכה and he presents it here as a parallel to תפילה which is עומד לפני השכינה, standing before the Holy Presence. In this experience of הליכה, walking, one is to see himself as if he is עומד לפני אדון ה' similar to the language of עומד לפני השכינה which describes prayer. But here the experience is even more intense, for whereas the שכינה refers to G-d's השגחה,[30] here the presence of G-d is more direct and the verse speaks not only of G-d's "eyes," which is His knowledge and His השגחה, but also G-d's "heart," which is His רצון, "will."[31]

Thus, in the מהלך before G-d of the *Beis HaMikdash*, the emotions are the same as in תפילה but over and above them is the added fourth emotion of fear, רעדה. But still we have not discovered the meaning of any of these terms. Let us add this word רעדה to the list and seek the meanings of אימה, יראה, פחד, ורעדה.

Sitting Before the *Shechinah*

Fear before G-d is also mandated of judges sitting in *Beis Din* (*Hilchos Sanhedrin* 3:7):

> כל בית דין של ישראל שהוא הגון, שכינה עימהן; לפיכך צריכין הדיינין לישב באימה ויראה, ועטיפה[32] וכובד ראש. ואסור להקל ראש או לשחוק או לספר בשיחה בטילה בבית דין, אלא בדברי תורה וחכמה.
>
> Whenever a suitable court among the Jewish people sits in judgment, the Divine Presence rests among them. Accordingly, the judges must sit in awe and fear, wrapped in *tallitot*, and conduct themselves with reverence. It is forbidden to act frivolously, to joke, or to speak idle matters in court. Instead, one may speak only words of Torah and wisdom.

The *Shechinah* is present in court and the judges must be aware of it and demonstrate אימה ויראה. What they do is ישיבה, sitting. Thus, we have

---

28 See the first chapter of *Hilchos Chagigah* and *Hilchos Yom Tov* 6:17ff.

29 See the end of *Hilchos Lulav*.

30 See *Moreh* 3:52.

31 See *Moreh* 1:39.

32 We will not deal with the concept of עטיפה here, but it is also a requirement of prayer as תקון מלבוש.

three positions before G-d in which fear is mandated: sitting (for judgment), standing (for prayer), and walking (while in the *Beis HaMikdash*). And a different level of fear is mandated for each position.

Fear and Joy at קבלת התורה

With regard to listening to the reading of the Torah at הקהל, Rambam comments explicitly upon what the emotional experience was meant to be:

> וגרים שאינן מכירין, חייבין להכין ליבם, ולהקשיב אוזנם לשמוע באימה ויראה וגילה[33] ורעדה, כיום שניתנה בו בסיני. אפילו חכמים גדולים שיודעים כל התורה כולה, חייבין לשמוע בכוונה גדולה יתרה. ומי שאינו יכול לשמוע--מכוון ליבו לקריאה זו, שלא קבעה הכתוב אלא לחזק דת האמת; ויראה עצמו כאילו עתה נצטווה בה, ומפי הגבורה שומעה--שהמלך שליח הוא, להשמיע דברי הקל. (סוף הלכות חגיגה)
>
> Converts who do not understand are obligated to concentrate their attention and direct their hearing, listening with reverence and awe, rejoicing while trembling as on the day the Torah was given at Sinai. Even great Sages who know the entire Torah are obligated to listen with exceedingly great concentration. One who is unable to hear should focus his attention on this reading, for Scripture established it solely to strengthen the true faith. He should see himself as if he was just now commanded regarding the Torah and heard it from the Almighty. For the king is an agent to make known the word of G-d.

The receiving of the Torah had the fear of רעדה added to the commonly required אימה ויראה but there is no פחד. More significantly, one of the terms of happiness, גילה, finally comes into play. This experience of הקהל demands the same emotions as Mount Sinai, and while Rashba relates תפילה to the verse in *Tehillim* (2:11), עבדו את ה' ביראה וגילו ברעדה, according to Rambam the verse is related to Revelation but not prayer.[34]

The experience of מתן תורה and הקהל that is modeled after it, comprises a mixture of emotions including joy and trembling. In prayer, where it is man speaking to G-d, not hearing from G-d, the experience is different and there is no גילה.

---

[33] Some *girsaos* read גילה ברעדה and Mechon-Mamre chooses this *girsa* and it does seem more accurate as we will note later.

[34] We should note that Rambam does not mention this fear as a requirement to those who understand the meaning of the words and he tells us merely that all, even the scholars, are obligated לשמוע בכוונה גדולה יתרה—they are to concentrate their intellectual powers on the words and their meaning. It would seem that for those who truly fathom the meaning of what they are hearing, the feelings that are mandated for others will naturally be present.

אֵימָה חֲשֵׁכָה גְדֹלָה, The Fear of the Prophet

Let us now return to our first question. Why does Rambam use four distinct terms for fear, and why does he vary his usage in every case he uses them? The general word יראה would seem to be sufficient to explain that fear with which one must imbue his prayer. Rambam, however, precedes it with the word אימה and then follows it with the word פחד. What do these two words add to my understanding of how one should approach prayer? The word פחד is in fact used in Rambam's definition of the *mitzvah* of יראת ה', "fear of G-d," but אימה is not. אימה is found, however, in every source that we have quoted with regard to an emotional experience before G-d.

In Tanach the word אימה is found rarely, and in the Torah only in four places. With regard to a relationship with G-d it is found only once, at the ברית בין הבתרים (the Covenant Between the Pieces).

> וַיְהִי הַשֶּׁמֶשׁ לָבוֹא, וְתַרְדֵּמָה נָפְלָה עַל-אַבְרָם; וְהִנֵּה אֵימָה חֲשֵׁכָה גְדֹלָה, נֹפֶלֶת עָלָיו. (בראשית טו:יב)
>
> As the sun set, a deep sleep fell upon Avram, and a great dark *eimah* descended upon him.

Rambam uses this verse to explain the experience of prophecy:

> וכולן, כשמתנבאין, אבריהן מזדעזעין וכוח הגוף כושל, ועשתונותיהם מיטרפות ותישאר הדעה פנויה להבין מה שתראה: כמו שנאמר באברהם, "והנה אימה חשיכה גדולה נופלת עליו" (בראשית טו,יב); וכמו שנאמר בדניאל, "והודי נהפך עלי למשחית, ולא עצרתי כוח" (דניאל י,ח). (יסדה"ת ז:ב)
>
> When any of them prophesy, their limbs tremble, their physical powers become weak, they lose control of their senses, and thus, their minds are free to comprehend what they see, as [Genesis 15:12] states concerning Abraham: "and a great, dark dread fell over him." Similarly, Daniel [10:8] states: "My appearance was horribly changed and I retained no strength."

In a later halachah and in *Pirush HaMishnah,* Rambam makes clear that this is an experience of fear as is certainly clear from the verse itself.

> כל הנביאים, יראין ונבהלין ומתמוגגים. כי הנביא כשתבוא אליו הנבואה, ואע"פ שהוא במראה וע"י מלאך, יחלשו כוחותיו ויתקלקל בניינו ויגיע לו מורא גדול מאוד, כמעט שתצא רוחו ממנו. כמו שאמר בדניאל. (פיה"מ חלק יסוד השביעי)
>
> All the prophets are in fear and confusion and dissolution for when prophecy comes to the prophet, even while in a vision and through an angel, his powers weaken and his body crumbles and he attains a high state of fear, almost to the point that his spirit leaves him, as it says with regard to Daniel.

In the fear that is אימה, there is absolute focus on the source of this fear—it is a reflection of sensing the immanence of G-d's Majestic Presence. While the body weakens, the mind is absorbed by the Presence "and the mind remains clear, enabled to understand what it will see." We have heard similar words with regard to the requirement for prayer.

> כיצד היא הכוונה--**שיפנה ליבו מכל המחשבות**, ויראה עצמו כאילו הוא עומד לפני השכינה.

As we explained above, the emotional experiences in chapter five of *Tefillah* have as their purpose the directing of the intellect[35] to כוונה, so of course it is אימה that is the first requirement. As Avraham is our father in prophecy, so too he is our father in prayer. In our relationship with the "G-d of Avraham" we must approach with אימה.

אימה was necessary on Mount Sinai so that the people could receive Revelation and thus those who listen at הקהל must have it as well. It was necessary for judges to clear their mind so they may find the truth. It is a necessity to he who comes to the *Azarah* for he comes לראות וליראות (to see and be seen), and he must imbibe knowledge from this experience.[36]

---

35 אבל המראה, והוא אמרו במראה אליו אתוודע, והוא הנקרא מראה הנבואה, ונקרא גם יד ה' בדניאל, והוא נקרא גם מחזה, הוא מצב מחריד ומפחיד שיארע לנביא בהקיץ, כמו שנתבאר באומרו ואראה את המראה הגדולה הזאת, ולא נשאר בי כוח, והודי נהפך עלי למשחית ולא עצרתי כוח, ואמר ואני הייתי נרדם על פני ופני ארצה, אבל דיבור המלאך עמו והעמידו אותו - כל זה במראה הנבואה ובכגון מצב זה נשבתים גם החושים מפעולתם, ויבוא אותו השפע לכוח ההגיוני, ויושפע ממנו על המדמה, ויגיע לשלמות ויפעל פעולתו. ויש שמתחיל החזון במראה הנבואה, ואחר כך תגדל אותה החרדה וההתפעלות העצומה הנספחת לשלמות פעולת המדמה, ואז יבוא החזון, כמו שנאמר באברהם אשר נאמר בתחילת אותו החזון היה דבר ה' אל אברהם במחזה, וסופו ותרדמה נפלה על אברם וגו' ואחרי כן ויאמר לאברם וגו' (מו"נ ב:מא).

36 The word אימה is also found in halachah with regard to the halachic obligation of giving honor to the king:

כבוד גדול נוהגין במלך, ומשימין לו אימה ויראה בלב כל אדם--שנאמר "שום תשים עליך מלך" (דברים יז,טו), שתהיה אימתו עליך. אין רוכבין על סוסו, ואין יושבין על כיסאו, ואין משתמשין בשרביטו, ולא בכתרו, ולא באחד מכל כלי תשמישו; וכשהוא מת, כולן נשרפין לפניו.

Included in the *mitzvah* to appoint a king is the obligation to accept not only his authority but his "kingship," and this entails not only practices of extreme respect but acquiring a state of mind that includes אימה. *Chazal* single out this word שתהיה אימתו עליך. We address G-d as "King" in our prayer and thus clearly the term that is central to מלכות is appropriate for prayer and indeed it is Avraham who reinstalled G-d as the King of the universe. Nevertheless, it would seem to be totally removed from the emotion that motivates a prophet with which we have identified it.

Yet, Rambam provides a contrast that enables us to see the link.

פחד and the Fear of G-d

Yet, in the very *mitzvah* of יראת ה', "fear of G-d," there is no mention of אימה, but only of יראה ופחד. The reason for this is that the purpose of the *mitzvah* of "fear of G-d" does not include this element of directing our intellects to the service of G-d. Rambam explains quite clearly (*Hil. Teshuvah* 10) that the motivation for the service of G-d must be אהבה, love. The fear of G-d is a goal unto itself. Rambam explains the fulfillment of the *mitzvah* of יראה is when:

> נרתע לאחוריו ויירא ויפחד ויידע שהוא בריה קטנה שפלה אפלה, עומד בדעת קלה מעוטה לפני תמים דעות.
>
> recoil in fear and terror, appreciating how he is a tiny, lowly, and dark creature, standing with his flimsy, limited, wisdom before He Who is of perfect knowledge *(Hil. Yesodei HaTorah* 2:2)

There is a devaluation of man's דעת and a feeling of elevated fear, פחד, perhaps to be translated as terror. It is the quality attributed to our father Yitzchak, פחד יצחק (*Bereishis* 31:42, 53) which was a function of the עקדה.[37] It was with the עקדה that Avraham, whose relationship with G-d epitomizes love,[38] is told כי עתה ידעתי כי ירא אלקים אתה, "for now I know that you fear G-d," for with his desire to sacrifice his son he demonstrated his realization of man's insignificance. He and his son who went together with him, יחדו,[39] with the same understanding, had attained יראה, and the son had gone even higher than the father, acquiring פחד. The word פחד relates to man's realization of his helplessness. And the essence of this realization moves one back from G-d, נרתע לאחוריו, not towards Him.

הציווי שנצטווינו למנות עלינו מלך מישראל שיאחד את כל אמתנו וינהיג את כולנו. והוא אמרו יתעלה: "שום תשים עליך מלך" (שם יז, טו). ... "שום תשים עליך מלך - שתהא אימתו עליך" ושיהיה בלבנו בתכלית הכבוד והגדולה והרוממות שאין למעלה ממנה, עד שתהיה מעלתו אצלנו גדולה ממעלת נביא מבין הנביאים שבדורו. ובפירוש אמרו: "מלך קודם לנביא" (סה"מ).
"A king comes before a prophet." Despite the greatness of a prophet, he himself is not the embodiment of authority but rather an intermediary to the highest of authorities, while the king is himself authority. אימה is the emotion that prepares one to tap into the will of the higher authority and it prepares the prophet to hear and obey G-d. Similarly, our אימה of the king is meant to prepare our minds to hearken to his word and to follow his leadership and his instructions. אימה is the central component of the general *mitzvah* of creating and accepting a government. This initial emotional acceptance is meant to guide the people to a loyalty and respect that is intellectual and rational.

37 See Rashi to *Bereishis* 31:42.

38 See *Sefer HaMitzvos, Aseh* 3, *Hilchos Teshuvah* 10.

39 See Rashi, ibid.

Prayer has both the immanence of אימה and the distancing of פחד, but the *mitzvah* of יראה in its pure state does not include the experience of אימה.

The Three Fears of the *Avos*

Thus, the word אימה is related to the most formative moment in the life of Avraham and the word פחד to the most formative moment in the life of Yitzchak. In the life of the third of the *Avos,* Yaakov, the moment that formed his destiny was that of ויפגע במקום, his encounter with G-d when he fled to the house of Lavan, and at that moment of his epiphany the Torah explains (בראשית כח:יז) ויירא ויאמר מה נורא המקום הזה, "He feared and said how awesome is this place." The vision of Yaakov that guided him throughout his life was an experience of יראה. Yaakov's experience was a different experience than the אימה that sent Avraham on his path to discovery, and different from the פחד that drove Yitzchak from his youth. It is an emotion spurred by the vision he saw in בית קל. It is an emotion born of profound understanding, of the truth, אמת, that is identified with Yaakov[40] and a function of his profound knowledge. Rambam explains that the angels of Yaakov's ladder represent the rules by which the world functions. The awe that springs from contemplating the wonders of Creation, that Rambam identifies with the *mitzvah* of יראה, is in fact the meaning of the word יראה.[41]

Thus Rambam tells us that as we prepare to say ברוך אתה ה'... אלקי אברהם אלקי יצחק ואלקי יעקב we must prepare ourselves by internalizing the qualities that our *Avos* embodied and that drove them on their spiritual quests.

רעדה, Walking to and Trembling in G-d's Presence

He who comes to the *Beis HaMikdash* must come bearing these three qualities of the three *Avos.* However, Rambam requires of him yet one other

40 See *Hilchos Yesodei HaTorah* 2:2 above that *yirah* arises from the understanding and contemplation of G-d's wonders. See *Encountering the Creator* (*parshas Vayeitzei*). Rambam in *Moreh* (2:10) explains that the angels in the vision represent an understanding of the workings of the world
השכלים הנבדלים והם המלאכים, והשני גופי הגלגלים, והשלישי החומר הראשוני כלומר: הגופים תמידי השינוי אשר תחת הגלגל.

41 While Avraham appreciated the incomprehensibility and thus came to אימה, the יראה is associated with a higher level of understanding of the workings of G-d's design.

quality,[42] that of רעדה. This is generally translated as "trembling." The source for demanding these emotions is the verse בבית אלקים נהלך ברגש.[43] Clearly, Rambam, based on the *Mechilta*,[44] translates ברגש to mean "with a slow gait," reflecting the fear in one's soul. The details of the meaning of רגש—the four types of fear—are inferred from the fact that these four qualities of fear, including רעדה, are alluded to in the earlier verses of the chapter[45] and this verse tells us that all these qualities are to be brought when one is מהלך in the *Beis HaMikdash*.

As this הליכה of the Rambam in the *Mikdash* is a form of *avodah* comparable to עמידה that is done during *tefillah*, thus Rambam states:

> וכל הנכנסין להר הבית, נכנסין דרך ימין ומקיפין ויוצאין דרך שמאל ... כל שהשלים עבודה ונסתלק לו, אינו יוצא ואחוריו להיכל; אלא מהלך אחורנית מעט מעט, ומהלך על צידו עד שיצא מן העזרה. וכן אנשי משמר ואנשי מעמד, ולויים מדוכנן--כך הם יוצאין מן המקדש, כמו שפוסע אחר תפילה לאחוריו. כל זה ליראה מן המקדש... וכל הנכנס לעזרה--יהלך בנחת במקום שמותר לו להיכנס לשם, ויראה עצמו שהוא עומד לפני האדון ה' שאמר "והיו עיני ולבי שם, כל הימים" (מלכים א ט,ג; דברי הימים ב ז,טז); ומהלך באימה ויראה ופחד ורעדה, שנאמר "בבית אלוקים, נהלך ברגש". (תהילים נה,טו)
>
> All who enter the Temple Mount should [face] the right side, walk around [in that direction], and leave on the left side… Anyone who has completed his service [in the Temple and desires] to leave, should not [turn around and] leave with his back to the Temple. Rather, he should walk backwards slightly and [then] walk slowly, and [turn] to his side until leaving the Temple Courtyard. Similarly, the members of the priestly watch, the representatives of the Jewish people, and the Levites [when they descend] from their platform, should

---

42 All the four terms of fear are found in the אז ישיר; however, because they are used in a poetic context, the exact meanings of the words are more difficult to discern from there than from anywhere else.

43 The word רגש only exists in this verse (*Tehillim* 55:15) and two other places in *Tehillim*. Interestingly, one of the places is in the second chapter of *Tehillim* where later the phrase וגילו ברעדה is found. Generally, it is translated as "gathered together."

44 The *Mechilta* (*Mechilta d'Rashbi* on *Shemos* 20:23) is the source for Rambam in his understanding of the word רגש. "שכשעולה למזבח לא יהא פסיעה גסה אלא מהלך עקב בצד גודל, אין לי אלא למזבח, לעזרות מנין, ת"ל ולא תעלה במעלות על מזבחי, ונאמר עליו – אין עליו אלא בסמוך לו, וכן או' בבית אלקים נהלך ברגש".

45 In verse 5 ואימות מות נפלו עלי and in 6 יראה ורעד יבא בי, ותכסני פלצות. The word פלצות is certainly akin to פחד. The *girsa* of the old printed version omits פחד and would then match the words explicit in *Tehillim*. However, saying that Rambam refers to taking all these emotions mentioned earlier to the *Mikdash* requires a radically different reading of this chapter from that of the standard commentaries.

> leave the Temple in this manner, similar to one who steps backwards after his prayers. All these [are expressions of] reverence for the Temple… Everyone who enters the Temple Courtyard should walk in a dignified manner, in the region where he is permitted to enter. He should conceive of himself as standing before G-d, as [1 Kings 9:3] states: "My eyes and My heart will be there forever." One should walk with awe, fear, and trembling, as [Psalms 55:15] states: "We would walk in the House of the Lord with fervor."

Walking forward must be done in a specific way, and leaving the *Azarah* must be done as one leaves prayer.[46] Prayer itself is, by definition[47] (*Hil. Tefillah* 1:3, 5:3), נוכח המקדש.[48] Actually entering the *Beis HaMikdash* represents a higher step in *avodah* that is referred to as הליכה. There is not only the *mitzvah* of standing before G-d but the *mitzvah* of עליה לרגל—going up in order לראות וליראות. One who prays, stands in his place. נהלך ברגש requires that we go towards G-d, we commit ourselves to reach a higher level. We do not merely look from afar at G-d's place, but we walk to it and in it.

What does רעדה mean? Rambam had told us that the prophet trembles in his experience איבריהן מזדעזעין וכח הגוף כושל. He proves this both from Avraham's תרדמה of אימה and also from Daniel's והודי נהפך עלי למשחית ולא עצרתי כח which indeed proves that the body weakens. However, where do we see physical trembling? The figure in the vision speaks to Daniel and orders him to stand and the verse continues, ובדברו עמי את הדבר הזה עמדתי מרעיד, "As he spoke with me these words, I stood trembling."

The prophet is a מהלך on a journey to G-d:

> והוא מתקדש **והולך** פורש מדרכי כלל העם ההולכים במחשכי הזמן, **והולך** מזרז עצמו ומלמד נפשו שלא תהיה לו מחשבה כלל באחד מדברים בטילים. (הל' יסדה"ת ז:א)
>
> He will become holy. He will advance and separate himself from the masses who proceed in the darkness of the time. He must continue and diligently train himself not to have any thoughts whatsoever about fruitless things or the vanities and intrigues of the times.

---

46 Rambam's requirement of walking בנחת is disputed by Raavad (ibid.). Rambam's source is the *Mechilta* which Maharik there also misses.

47 From the fact that Rambam mentions it already in the first chapter, it's clear that it is fundamental within the entire concept.

48 This was the prayer of שלמה המלך, that all prayer should go through his house.

And in his journey to the place of G-d he feels the intensity of G-d's presence and even standing is an effort. Just as Daniel struggles to lift his body and trembles, so too he who walks in the *Azarah* trembles. Over and above the feeling of helplessness that is פחד, which controls the mind, the trembling of רעדה is an emotion that overwhelms the body.

Sitting, Standing, Walking, Revelation

As we look back over the requirements of fear in different cases, we find that those engaged in judgment maintain the stance of ישיבה and this requires אימה ויראה. For those engaged in prayer, the stance is described as עמידה and this requires אימה ויראה ופחד. For those experiencing the *Beis HaMikdash*, the stance is הליכה, and for this we need אימה ויראה ופחד ורעדה. In each case, one is in the presence of the שכינה and each level of ascension requires another level of fear of G-d. What is appropriate in one instance is not appropriate in another. For example, after Rambam details the law of הליכה in the *Azarah*, he explains (*Hil. Beis HaBechirah* 7:6) that it is prohibited to sit (ישיבה) in the *Azarah*. So, too, in prayer there is no call for רעדה, and thus should it exist for prayer, we can assume it would be deemed wrong. Thus, while some authorities justify the custom of swaying[49] during prayer as a fulfillment of רעדה,[50] according to Rambam it is inappropriate.[51]

We have also noted that at the moment of mankind's highest ascension before G-d, at Revelation, there is an element of joy added to this fear. *David HaMelech* saw a connection between fear and joy: עבדו את ה' ביראה וגילו ברעדה (תהילים ב:יא). Rambam relates this emotion halachically to הקהל which he tells us is modeled after קבלת התורה. The emotions are "אימה ויראה וגילה ורעדה". The Ran's[52] (*Berachos* 31a) explanation of the verse is that while in general fear and joy are opposites, with regard to the awe of G-d that leads one to His worship, joy is compatible since one knows that he will be rewarded for his *avodah*. Thus, he says, the Torah demands עבדו את ה' ביראה as well as עבדו את ה' בשמחה.

---

49 *Shuckling.*

50 See *Torah Shleimah Yisro* 20:449. The *Mishnah Berurah* (95:7) quotes the *Pri Chadash* saying one should *shuckle* based on כל עצמותי תאמרנה ה'.

51 The רמ"ע מפאנו says it is prohibited. Perhaps in fact the custom began with the belief that this is an enhancement of *pachad*.

52 See *Tosafos* to *Berachos* 30b–31a who does not interpret the *Gemara* to be learning from this verse that fear can lead to joy but rather that days of fear will be transformed to joy by those who commit themselves to יראת שמים

Rambam focuses on the contradictory nature of the two emotions that are demanded in the worship of G-d when he explains the method of performing the commands of אהבה ויראה.

> [ב] והיאך היא הדרך לאהבתו, ויראתו: בשעה שיתבונן האדם במעשיו וברואיו הנפלאים הגדולים, ויראה מהם חכמתו שאין לה ערך ולא קץ--מיד הוא אוהב ומשבח ומפאר ומתאווה תאווה גדולה לידע השם הגדול, כמו שאמר דויד "צמאה נפשי, לאלוקים--לקל חי" (תהילים מב,ג).ב וכשמחשב בדברים האלו עצמן, מיד הוא נרתע לאחוריו, ויירא ויפחד ויידע שהוא בריה קטנה שפלה אפלה, עומד בדעת קלה מעוטה לפני תמים דעות, כמו שאמר דויד "כי אראה שמיך . . . מה אנוש, כי תזכרנו". (תהילים ח,ד-ה).
>
> What is the path [to attain] love and fear of Him? When a person contemplates His wondrous and great deeds and creations and appreciates His infinite wisdom that surpasses all comparison, he will immediately love, praise, and glorify [Him], yearning with tremendous desire to know [G-d's] great name, as David stated: "My soul thirsts for the Lord, for the living G-d" [Psalms 42:3]. When he [continues] to reflect on these same matters, he will immediately recoil in awe and fear, appreciating how he is a tiny, lowly, and dark creature, standing with his flimsy, limited, wisdom before He Who is of perfect knowledge, as David stated: "When I see Your heavens, the work of Your fingers... [I wonder] what is man that You should recall Him" [Psalms 8:4–5].

On the one hand, man is brought to love by his knowledge of G-d's works, but deeper contemplation brings him to awe and fear. Whereas at first he is pulled to draw near, at the end he wishes to flee נרתע לאחוריו. At the end of the process is he found distant? No. Rambam is again merely echoing the words of *David HaMelech*. We must read until the end of the last verse he quotes.

> ד כִּי-אֶרְאֶה שָׁמֶיךָ, מַעֲשֵׂה אֶצְבְּעֹתֶיךָ--יָרֵחַ וְכוֹכָבִים, אֲשֶׁר כּוֹנָנְתָּה.ה מָה-אֱנוֹשׁ כִּי-תִזְכְּרֶנּוּ; וּבֶן-אָדָם, כִּי תִפְקְדֶנּוּ.ו וַתְּחַסְּרֵהוּ מְּעַט, מֵאֱלֹהִים; וְכָבוֹד וְהָדָר תְּעַטְּרֵהוּ.ז תַּמְשִׁילֵהוּ, בְּמַעֲשֵׂי יָדֶיךָ; כֹּל, שַׁתָּה תַחַת-רַגְלָיו....ד' אֲדֹנֵינוּ: מָה-אַדִּיר שִׁמְךָ, בְּכָל-הָאָרֶץ.
>
> When I behold Your heavens, the work of Your fingers, the moon and stars that You set in place, what is man that You have been mindful of him, mortal man that You have taken note of him, that You have made him little less than divine, and adorned him with glory and majesty. You have made him master over your handiwork, laying the world at his feet…O L-rd, our L-rd, how majestic is Your name throughout the earth.

While man realizes his insignificance, he also realizes that G-d has given him a central role in His creation— ותחסרהו מעט מאלקים —empowered to bring praise to the Name of G-d.[53]

The experience of מתן תורה brought the nation to this נרתע לאחוריו "trembling backward" of יראה as the Torah clearly states וירא העם וינעו ויעמדו מרחק (שמות כ:טו),[54] "The nation saw and they trembled and stood from afar." The midrash (*Seder Eliyahu Rabbah,* chap. 24) interprets this as meaning "באותה שעה נזדעזעו **ורעדו ופחדו** חרדה גדולה", "At that moment they shook and trembled and feared with great terror." Moshe's directions to the people at this moment of their flight are confusing and contradictory. אל תיראו כי לבעבור נסות אתכם בא אלקים ובעבור תהיה יראתו על פניכם לבלתי תחטאו. The people are told "not to fear … for this experience is meant to instill fear." Moshe's meaning is that though this experience was meant to instill fear and awe in their nature, it must not prevent them from drawing close.

Although this sentiment expressed by Rambam is similar to the concept explained by the Ran—that these contradictory emotions can coexist—in fact, Rambam never mentions happiness as a result of this process of love and fear. While we must certainly worship out of love, this does not mean that we are always meant to experience happiness in so doing. We will present a different understanding of גלו ברעדה later on to try to understand why the two are compatible according to Rambam.

The Joy of Talmud Torah?

First, let us determine if the mixture of גילה ורעדה at *Har Sinai,* which is not mandated for prayer, is a model instead for the *mitzvah* of *talmud Torah.* Is *talmud Torah* to be viewed as a *mitzvah* that embodies Revelation and thus to be approached with joy?

Those who listen to the reading of the Torah are commanded only in attentive listening without emotional involvement.

> כיון שהתחיל הקורא לקרות בתורה, אסור לספר אפילו בדבר הלכה--אלא הכול שותקין ושומעין, ומשימין ליבן למה שהוא קורא: שנאמר "ואוזני כל העם, אל ספר התורה" (נחמיה ח,ג). (הל' תפלה יב:ט)
>
> Once the reader begins reading the Torah, it is forbidden [for the congregants] to talk, even regarding matters of Torah law. Rather,

---

53 שמע שמועה רעה, מברך ברוך אתה ה' אלוקינו מלך העולם דיין האמת: וחייב אדם לברך על הרעה בטובת נפש, כדרך שמברך על הטובה בשמחה--שנאמר "ואהבת, את ה' אלוקיך . . . ובכל מאודך" (דברים ו,ה), ובכלל אהבה זו היתרה שנצטווינו בה, שאפילו בעת שיצר לו, יודה וישבח בשמחה. (הל' ברכות י:ג)

54 See Rashi and *Targum* that this refers to trembling and going backward.

everyone should listen, remain silent, and pay attention to what is being read, as [Nechemiah 8:3] states: "The ears of all the people were [attentive] to the Torah scroll."

The only halachic demand is that an intellectual effort be made to hear the reading. Only of one listener is more required.

ואין המתרגם נשען לא לעמוד ולא לקורה, אלא עומד ביראה ואימה.
The translator should not lean on a beam or on a pillar. Rather, he should stand with awe and fear.

Once again, we find a dual obligation of fear, but not on the part of listeners nor of the reader, but upon the translator.[55] He is unique, for his is a dual task. He must understand each word and then he must transmit the meaning clearly to the people.[56] The Yerushalmi quoted by R. Manoach explains "that just as it was given with אימה, so must we conduct ourselves with אימה." Those who stood on Mount Sinai received it with this emotion. That generation was not only the receivers of the Torah but they were entrusted with passing it on to further generations. This is the role that the מתרגם embodies. This experience was not only one of יראה but particularly of אימה (as the Yerushalmi states) which we have associated with preparation for Revelation. But unlike הקהל, the reading of the Torah in a בית הכנסת is not a full reenactment of *Har Sinai* even for the מתרגם and certainly not for the public. Rambam does not here repeat the comparison to *Har Sinai* of the Yerushalmi as he does by הקהל, for as it is not a reenactment of Revelation thus there is no גילה. The reading of the Torah is merely a public act of learning Torah (תלמוד תורה).[57]

Rambam extols the virtue of *talmud Torah* in the third chapter of *Hilchos Talmud Torah*. He emphasizes[58] the commitment and self-sacrifice that is necessary in acquiring Torah.

אין דברי תורה מתקיימין במי שמרפה עצמו עליהן, ולא באלו שלומדין מתוך עידון ומתוך אכילה ושתייה--אלא במי שממית עצמו עליהן, ומצער גופו תמיד, ולא ייתן שנת לעיניו, לעפעפיו תנומה.

---

55 The commentaries assume that certainly the reader must have these emotions and probably the listeners as well. There is no evidence of this in Rambam's words. The point of this essay is that every word in *Mishneh Torah* is carefully selected and thus we must pay close attention to exactly what Rambam says.

56 There is no reason to believe as ר' מנוח ורמ"ך that the קורא must also do so.

57 *Moshe Rabbeinu* made a *takkanah* that three days not go by without everyone learning Torah. See *Hil. Tefillah* 12:1.

58 As does the *Baraisa* in *Avos*.

יג אמרו חכמים דרך רמז, "זאת, התורה, אדם, כי ימות באוהל" (במדבר יט,יד)--אין התורה מתקיימת, אלא במי שממית עצמו באוהלי החכמה. וכך אמר שלמה בחכמתו, "התרפית, ביום צרה--צר כוחך" (משלי כד,י); ועוד אמר, "אף חכמתי, עמדה לי" (קוהלת ב,ט)--חכמה שלמדתי באף, עמדה לי. (ג:יב)

The words of Torah will not be permanently acquired by a person who applies himself feebly [to obtain] them, and not by those who study amid pleasure and [an abundance] of food and drink. Rather, one must give up his life for them, constantly straining his body to the point of discomfort, without granting sleep to his eyes or slumber to his eyelids. The Sages alluded to this concept [interpreting Numbers 19:14:]: "This is the Torah, a man should he die in a tent..." [to mean that] the Torah cannot be permanently acquired except by a person who gives up his life in the tents of wisdom. Similarly, Solomon said in his wisdom [Proverbs 24:10]: "If you faint in the day of adversity, your strength is small." He also said [Ecclesiastes 2:9]: "Also, my wisdom remained with me." [This can be interpreted to mean:] The wisdom which I learned in anger, this is what remained with me.

In the *Pirush HaMishnah* (end of *Avos*) he clarifies what this אף refers to: "Therefore they commanded the teacher to place אימה on the students." There must be אימה in learning Torah as there was at *Matan Torah*. Here Rambam echoes the aforementioned Yerushalmi, in explaining that the giving over of Torah must be with אימה. Rambam expands upon this in *Hilchos Talmud Torah,* explaining the relationship between Rebbe and student.

אבל אם ניכר לרב שהן מתרשלין בדברי תורה ומתרפין עליהן, ולפיכך לא הבינו--חייב לרגוז עליהן ולהכלימן בדברים, כדי לחדדן; ובעניין זה אמרו חכמים, זרוק מרה בתלמידים. לפיכך אין ראוי לרב לנהוג קלות ראש בפני התלמידים, ולא לשחוק בפניהם, ולא לאכול ולשתות עימהם--כדי שתהא אימתו עליהן, וילמדו ממנו במהרה... ואין שואלין אלא מיראה.(ד:ה)

If it appears to the teacher that they are not applying themselves to the words of Torah and are lax about them, and, therefore, do not understand, he is obligated to display anger towards them and shame them with his words, to sharpen their powers of concentration. In this context, our Sages said: "Cast fear into the students."

Therefore, it is not fitting for a teacher to act frivolously in the presence of his students. He should not amuse himself in their presence, nor should he eat and drink with them. [These restrictions are intended] so that they fear him and study under him at a fast pace... One does not ask except with fear.

However, Rambam closes Chapter 3 with the following statement:

טו [יג] אף על פי שמצוה ללמוד ביום ובלילה, אין אדם למד רוב חכמתו אלא בלילה; לפיכך מי שרצה לזכות בכתר התורה, ייזהר בכל לילותיו, ולא יאבד אפילו אחת מהן בשינה ואכילה ושתייה ושיחה וכיוצא בהן, אלא בתלמוד תורה ודברי חכמה. אמרו חכמים, אין [59] {גורנה} (רנה) של תורה אלא לילה, שנאמר "קומי רוני בלילה" (איכה ב,יט). וכל העוסק בתורה בלילה, חוט של חסד נמשך עליו ביום, שנאמר "יומם, יצווה ה' חסדו, ובלילה, שירה עמי--תפלה, לא-ל חיי" (תהילים מב,ט). וכל בית שאין דברי תורה נשמעין בו בלילה, אש אוכלתו. .. אמרו חכמים, כל המבטל את התורה מעושר, סופו לבטלה מעוני; וכל המקיים את התורה מעוני, סופו לקיימה מעושר. ועניין זה מפורש הוא בתורה: הרי הוא אומר "תחת, אשר לא עבדת את ה' אלוקיך, בשמחה, ובטוב לבב--מרוב, כול. ועבדת את אויבך" (דברים כח,מז-מח); ואומר "למען ענותך, ולמען נסותך--להיטיבך, באחריתך". (דברים ח,טז).

Even though it is a *mitzvah* to study during the day and at night, it is only at night that a person acquires most of his wisdom. Therefore, a person who desires to merit the crown of Torah should be careful with all his nights, not giving up even one to sleep, eating, drinking, talk, or the like. Rather, [they should be devoted to] the study of Torah and the words of wisdom. Our Sages declared: "The song of Torah can [be heard] only at night, as [Lamentations 2:19] states: 'Arise, sing out at night...'"Whoever occupies himself with Torah study at night will have a strand of [Divine] favor extended over him during the day, as [implied by Psalms 42:9]: "During the day, G-d ordains His kindness and, at night, His song is with me, a prayer to the living G-d."...Our Sages declared: "Whoever neglects Torah study when wealthy will ultimately neglect it amidst poverty. Whoever maintains the Torah in poverty will ultimately maintain it amidst prosperity." This concept is explicitly mentioned in the Torah [Deuteronomy 28:47–48], which states: "Because you did not serve G-d, your Lord, with happiness and good feeling when there was an abundance of everything, you shall serve your enemies," and [Deuteronomy 8:16] states: "so that you shall suffer...so that ultimately He will make you prosper."

At first glance, we may gather from Rambam's statement and particularly from the verses he quotes, that Torah must be learned with רנה and

59 Most *girsaos* have the word גורנה though some have רנה. The *Vayikra Rabbah* and *Shir HaShirim Rabbah* upon which it is based have both *girsaos* as well. Logically the word should be רנה since that is what the verse from *Eichah* supports. If it is in fact גרנה it may very well be גרונה meaning the throat and refer to singing rather than גורנה meaning a storage area, which really is hard to deduce from the verse. In any event, *Chazal* relate learning Torah at night to the verse of רנה.

with שמחה[60], as well as with אימה. However, when carefully examining Rambam's meaning and the context of the verse he quotes, it is clear that the רנה of the quoted verse refers to a cry (see Ibn Ezra in *Eichah*[61]) and the correct *girsa* is גורנה של תורה, the gathering of fully processed Torah.[62] And when Rambam tells us that we are at fault for not having learned Torah with שמחה, he does not mean with the emotion of שמחה, but rather when we were living lives that were imbued with contentment and happiness. The study of Torah itself, however, is pursued only with fear. Indeed, פקודי ה' ישרים משמחי לב and thus it is forbidden to learn Torah on *Tishah B'Av* (*Taanis* 30a), but this is the result of learning Torah, not the emotions with which we approach our study.[63]

Still, as we have noted, Rambam makes no mention of the listeners standing during the reading of the Torah, nor of the יראה ואימה of which the מתורגמן is obligated. As this is a public act of *talmud Torah,* should not those listening and learning have a similar obligation?[64] Rambam writes:

> ובראשונה, היה הרב יושב והתלמידים עומדים; ומקודם חורבן בית שני, נהגו הכול ללמד לתלמידים, והן יושבין.
>
> At first the Rebbe sat and the students stood. Then before the destruction of the Second Temple, all changed to sitting.

The *Gemara* attributes the change from the ideal of standing to sitting, to a "weakness" that came upon the world. Thus, *l'halachah*, standing and the accompanying יראה of the students was abandoned. The Rebbe should teach in such a way as to instill אימה, but the obligation of the students to actually carry themselves with יראה is only active upon asking a question. The ideal is preserved only with the מתורגמן. It is his listening where he is entrusted with repeating that must be done with this [65] יראה ואימה. It is not his reciting of the *Targum* that requires his standing, for a

---

60 In fact Rambam is saying that one must learn when his standard of living is good and he has no worries, not specifically that a state of שמחה should be brought to his studies. Yet, his application of the verse demonstrates that the state of mind caused by שמחה and prosperity is ideal for Torah learning, even while he states that physical suffering and self-denial should be imposed.

61 See also how Rambam uses the word יתרונן in *Hilchos Tefillah* 4:17 quoted above.

62 Alternately גרונה, the "throat of Torah," i.e., its full expression.

63 לולי תורתך שעשועי אז אבדתי בעניי Torah is the source of happiness and salvation, but it lifts dispirited man—he does not approach it with joy.

64 And indeed, some *rishonim* assume so. See ibid.

65 While normally the order is אימה ויראה, in this case Rambam reverses it since יראה pertains to the absorption of what he hears and אימה to help in the creativity of translating.

Rebbe of students does not stand. It is his role as the listener entrusted with repeating that gives him this responsibility. His role is similar to that of Israel at *Har Sinai* who were charged to repeat what they heard to future generations.

Sitting Before the Torah

However, a halachah in *Hilchos Sefer Torah* (10:10–11) presents us with a question. Rambam states:

> כל מי שיישב לפני ספר תורה, יישב בכובד ראש ובאימה ופחד, שהוא העד הנאמן על כל באי העולם, שנאמר "והיה שם בך, לעד" (דברים לא,כו)
>
> Anyone who sits before a Torah scroll should sit with respect, awe, and fear, because [the Torah] is a faithful testimony [of the covenant between G-d and the Jews] for all the inhabitants of the earth, as [Deuteronomy 31:26] states: "And it will be as a testimony for you."

Should not this obligation of honor to the *Sefer Torah* obligate all those who listen to the Torah being read to do so in אימה ויראה? Technically, we can answer this question easily. The Torah is placed on the בימה when it is read; those sitting in the בית הכנסת would not be considered sitting before the *Sefer Torah*.[66] But we must also realize that conceptually the above halachah is not dealing with an act of *talmud Torah* in relation to the *Sefer Torah*, but an act of sitting before the *Sefer Torah*. Rambam states earlier:

> מצוה לייחד לספר תורה מקום, ולכבד אותו המקום, ולהדרו יתר מדי: דברים שבלוחות הברית, הן הן שבכל ספר וספר. לא ירוק אדם כנגד ספר תורה, ולא יגלה ערוותו כנגדו, ולא יפשוט רגליו, ולא יניחנו על ראשו כמשאוי. ולא יחזיר אחוריו לספר תורה, אלא אם כן היה גבוה ממנו עשרה טפחים. (י:י)
>
> It is a *mitzvah* to designate a special place for a Torah scroll and to honor it and glorify it in an extravagant manner. The words of the Ten Commandments are contained in each Torah scroll. A person should not spit before a Torah scroll, reveal his nakedness before it, take off his footwear before it, or carry it on his head like a burden. He should not turn his back to a Torah scroll unless it is ten handbreadths higher than he is.

---

66 See *Hilchos Sefer Torah* 10:10 that if the *Sefer Torah* is 10 *tefachim* higher than oneself one can turn one's back to it.

The קדושה of the *Beis HaMikdash* itself is an emanation from the ארון ולוחות[67] and thus the *Sefer Torah*, comparably to the לוחות, creates a קדושת מקום, "a sanctified place."

Whereas in the *Azarah* it is forbidden to sit, in the presence of the *Sefer Torah* it is permitted. But this sitting in front of the Torah in contemplation is the counterpart to what one does in the *Beis HaMikdash*, i.e., הליכה. As such, it must be with אימה ופחד, although the qualities of יראה ורעדה are not required as is the case in *Mikdash*. We understand that רעדה is the highest level of fear and only pertains to *Mikdash*, and here there is the terror of פחד without reaching the level of רעדה. Why is the intermediary יראה not required? יראה is on the one hand related to the epiphany of Yaakov, and on the other hand the higher level of fear that Avraham graduated from after a lifelong אימה that was part of his process of seeking. Thus, אימה ויראה are a pair. The אימה need not rise to יראה nor the פחד to רעדה.[68] By contrast, the sitting of a דיין, we have noted above, is to be accompanied with אימה ויראה as both forms of fear are related to the intellectual struggles of Avraham and Yaakov.

גלו ברעדה

Thus far, we have seen that the גילה at *Har Sinai* does not translate to the experience of *talmud Torah*. Nor is there גילה in prayer, standing before the *Shechinah* נוכח המקדש. Nor is there גילה in the presence of a *Sefer Torah* or of the *Shechinah,* even in the מקדש itself, before the לוחות. In all these cases, the obligation of יראה precludes joy, and גילה is only present during the act of Revelation. How is this to be understood? Are our most fundamental and constant forms of *avodah* to be done without joy, despite the imperative of עבדו את ה׳ בשמחה?

We know that שמחה is also a requirement for prophecy:

> כל הנביאים--אין מתנבאין בכל עת שירצו, **אלא מכוונין דעתן ויושבין שמחים וטובי לב** ומתבודדין: שאין הנבואה שורה לא מתוך עצבות ולא מתוך עצלות, **אלא מתוך שמחה.** לפיכך בני הנביאים, לפניהם נבל ותוף וחליל וכינור, והם מבקשים הנבואה; וזה הוא שנאמר "והמה מתנבאים" (שמואל א י,ה)--כלומר[69] מהלכין בדרך הנבואה עד שיינבאו, כמו שאתה אומר פלוני מתגדל.

---

67 See, for example, *Eretz HaZvi* of Rav Hershel Schachter, *shlita,* page 91, where this principle is quoted in the name of Rav Soloveitchik and is applied to the מקדש מעט of the בית הכנסת.

68 This arrangement is reminiscent of how Rambam speaks regarding צרעת of שאת and בהרת as אבות with each having respective תולדות and in total four נגעים.

69 Note the word מהלכין —for after the process of הליכה comes גילוי.

All the prophets do not prophesy whenever they desire. Instead, they must concentrate their attention [upon spiritual concepts] and seclude themselves, [waiting] in a happy, joyous mood, because prophecy cannot rest upon a person when he is sad or languid, but only when he is happy. Therefore, the prophets' disciples would always have a harp, drum, flute, and lyre [before them when] they were seeking prophecy. This is what is meant by the expression [1 Samuel 10:5]: "They were prophesying"—i.e., following the path of prophecy until they would actually prophesy—as one might say, "So-and-so aspires to greatness."

Whereas prophecy itself is an experience of fear, the mind is prepared for this via happiness. איבריהן מזדעזעין וכח הגוף כושל. The physical emotional experience that affects the גוף, the body, i.e., the emotions, is one of trembling,[70] for this is how one feels in the presence of G-d. But the emotion that prepares one for G-d's presence is שמחה. Thus, *Har Sinai* is referred to in the Mishnah as the day of the חופה (see Mishnah end of *Taanis*). Rabbah would begin his lesson with a מילתא דבדיחותא (a matter of levity) but the lesson would then proceed with אימה.[71]

Ran has explained גילו ברעדה as joy that is an outgrowth of the awe and comes with the anticipation of encountering G-d:

כשהאדם מתבונן בגדולתו וירא מפניו ישמח ויגל באותו היראה מפני **שבעמצעיתה מתעורר לקים המצוות** ושש ונעלה בקיומה שיודע כי שכרו אתו ופעולתו לפניו.

When a man contemplates His greatness and fears Him, he has happiness and joy from this fear because he knows it is the medium that will spur him to fulfill the *mitzvos* and he rejoices and is elevated with their fulfillment for he knows that his reward is assured and his actions are before G-d.

This explanation to some degree runs counter to Rambam who says that יראה is not to be the motivation for serving G-d. As Ran himself notes, the *gemara* learns something else from this verse—that the joy one feels at any time must always be tempered by the awe that one must feel in the presence of G-d: במקום גילה שם תהא רעדה.[72] גלו ברעדה means that

---

[70] Note that Rambam presented אימה יראה ופחד as תקון הגוף by prayer.

[71] See TB *Shabbos* 30b and Rashi and Meiri (ibid). They say the happiness was necessary for the desired *Hashraas Shechinah,* nevertheless it is but fleeting.

[72] Ran also states that this is the intent of the *gemara*, but notes what he considers the simple meaning of the verse וגילו ברעדה.

the joy of the כלה coming to the חופה is joined by awe at the moment of the marriage ceremony. The joy of the people who had uttered נעשה ונשמע out of *ahavah* and in anticipation of experiencing the *Shechinah,* is joined by such terror at the actual moment of Revelation that there is a need for כפה עליהם הר כגיגית,[73] so that that they would go through with the acceptance of the Torah. Both emotions coexist, but גילה comes first.[74]

Even though the righteous are עובד מאהבה and this is expected of all of us, this does not mean that this love was meant to be translated into joy in our daily *avodah* of *talmud Torah* and *tefillah*. Indeed, there must always be an underlying שמחה in our souls reflecting our knowledge that we are engaged in G-d's service.[75] And we openly celebrate this fact in performing the *mitzvah* of שמחה that Rambam refers to as עבודה גדולה היא,[76] but this obligation exists on the ימים טובים specifically and on individual occasions when it is appropriate.[77] עבודה must be done because of אהבה, but our most constant *mitzvos* are themselves exercises in יראה.

The Rambam explains in the *Moreh*[78] that our loss of prophecy is linked to the sadness of our exile. The *mitzvos* of the Torah were given for times of both גאולה and גלות and those *mitzvos* that must be our constant preoccupation must be structured for גלות. Without שמחה we must still be able to pray and indeed we can, for *tefillah* is an act of אימה יראה ופחד. Today, even our scholars cannot conjure up enough joy in the midst of our גלות to emulate the emotions present at *Har Sinai* to attain prophecy. And even in the past, only in the *Beis HaMikdash,* once in seven years at הקהל, was there an expectation of גלו ברעדה.

---

73 See *Tosafos* in TB *Shabbos.*

74 In describing the performance of the *mitzvos* of אהבה ויראה the אהבה comes first (*Hil. Yesodei HaTorah* 2:2). The *mitzvah* of *Hallel* is Rabbinic according to Rambam and linked to the *mitzvah* of שמחת יו"ט.

75 See Rambam in ninth *perek* of *Hilchos Teshuvah.*

76 End of *Hilchos Lulav*. Also we must note that the *mitzvah* of שמחה on יום טוב is an offshoot of שלמי שמחה showing that עבודה can be rooted in שמחה.

77 See *Hil. Lulav* 8:12–15.

78 הנבואה בזמן הגלות בלי ספק, איזו עצלות או עצבות וזוהי הסיבה העצמית הקרובה לסילוק מהיותו עבד נשלט ומשועבד לכסילים הרשעים, אשר כללו יהיו לאדם באיזה מצב שיהיה יותר אשר רצה והוא ,ובכך יועדנו ,התאוות הבהמיות ואין לאל ידך העדר ההגיון האמיתי וכללות בגויים אין תורה גם נביאיה ואמר מלכה ושריה ,באומרו ישוטטו לבקש את דבר ה' ולא ימצאו והוא גם הסיבה בשיבת הנבואה .כי הכלי כבר בטל ,וזה נכון וסיבתו ברורה ,'לא מצאו חזון מה לנו כפי שהייתה לימות המשיח מהרה יגלה כמו שהובטח (ב:לו).

But if this is so—that daily worship does not contain joy—how are we to attain the prophecy that will lift us out of our גלות, for prophecy must return to Israel before Mashiach comes.[79] Moreover, is it not somewhat paradoxical that the highest type of knowledge, prophecy, emerges from happiness, while in Torah learning, that which we are to devote our life to, we have seen that only the emotion of fear is to be engaged in the process? Indeed, the answer lies in the fact that *talmud Torah* produces within us the שמחה that will eventually elevate our עבודה, but I believe there is still one element that needs to be added.

In the Rambam's explanation of learning at night, we failed to focus on one line:

> וכל העוסק בתורה בלילה, חוט של חסד נמשך עליו ביום, שנאמר "יומם, יצווה ה' חסדו, ובלילה, שירה עמי--תפלה, לא-ל חיי".

This learning in the night is called תפלה and thus an act of יראה. The Mishnah in *Avos* (3:2,8) tells me that the שכינה is present during the learning process, and consequently יראה must be there. But calling it תפלה is of course difficult since *talmud Torah* is listening to G-d, while prayer is speaking to G-d. It is also called שירה. Is this not joyous?

Rambam in the *Moreh*[80] speaks of a man who reaches the highest levels of Torah learning, and his thoughts are on these deepest matters in the quiet of the night, while he lies upon his bed. In the aforementioned Mishnah in *Avos* (3:2) he refers to this idea as well:[81]

> אבל שנים שהיו יושבין ועוסקין בדברי תורה, שכינה עמהם שנ' **אז נדברו יראי ה'** איש אל רעהו ויקשב ה'... ומנין לאחד שיושב ודורש **כאלו קיים את כל התורה** שנ' ישב בדד וידם {כי נטל עליו}.
>
> two who are sitting together and there are words of Torah [spoken] between them, the Divine Presence rests with them, as it is said (Malachi 3:16): "Then those who feared the Lord spoke one with another, and the Lord hearkened and heard." From where [is there proof that] that when there is one person sitting and expounding that it is as if he fulfilled the whole Torah? As it is said (Lamentations 3:28): "He sits alone and is silent."

---

79 *Hil. Melachim* 10:2.

80 *Moreh HaNevuchim* 3:51.

81 Rambam's text differs from our printed texts.

פיה"מ – וידם – הדברים החשיים מן דממה דקה, ומזה פירש התרגום וידום אהרון ושבח אהרון.[82] וראיתו שהוא כמי שנטל על עצמו כל התורה הוא ממה שאמר **"נטל עליו" כאלו קבלת כל התורה עליו בלבד.**

"Being silent"—the words of quiet as in the verse דממה דקה {קול}, based on which the Targum explains "and Aharon was silent" as Aharon praised, and the proof [of the Mishnah] is that the phrase "he took it upon himself" is that he took upon himself the full obligation of the Torah as if קבלת התורה was for him alone.

The יראי השם who learn together in pairs, do so in the presence of G-d. So too a *Rebbe* is to instill אימה in his students. It is possible for individuals to transcend even the environment of Exile and experience גילה along with their יראה. Those who learn alone, those who are unique in their search for truth and despite the deprivations of their toils and despite the hardships of their life, gain such a clarity of vision in their understanding of Torah that they also bring joyous love into the experience and are משבח[83] in the long night of גלות, these are the people who experience קבלת התורה and fulfill גילה ברעדה.[84] These people will return prophecy and revelation to Israel and end our גלות.

82 שמע שמועה רעה, מברך ברוך אתה ה' אלוקינו מלך העולם דיין האמת: וחייב אדם לברך על הרעה בטובת נפש, כדרך שמברך על הטובה בשמחה--שנאמר "ואהבת, את ה' אלוקיך... ובכל מאודך" (דברים ו,ה), ובכלל אהבה זו היתרה שנצטווינו בה, שאפילו בעת שיצר לו, יודה וישבח בשמחה. (הל' ברכות י:ג)

83 See *Sefer HaMitzvos, Aseh* 5, when Rambam tells us that *tefillah* is *avodah shebalev* he also quotes *Chazal* that *talmud Torah* is also *avodah shebalev.* This refers to this ability to praise G-d while listening to His word.

84 צחי רנה וצהלי. בעשרה לשונות נקראת נבואה, גילה, שמחה, עליסה, עליצה, פצחה, רנה, צהלה, חדוה, דיצה (ילקוט שמעוני ישעיה נט).

Untangling the Mystery of Women's Hair Covering in Talmudic Passages

By: ARI STORCH

I. Introduction

Women wearing various styles of headdress are a relatively commonplace sight in many Orthodox Jewish communities. Some wear kerchiefs, others wear wigs and yet others wear different styles of hats. This rich tradition is steeped in the culture of the Jewish people and dates back thousands of years. This article presents an analysis of many of the Talmudic and rabbinic sources that discuss this issue for the purpose of providing background to the vast spectrum of thought that developed throughout the ages.[1]

II. Analysis of Head Covering in Rabbinic Sources

A. Mosaic and Judaic Practices in Talmud *Bavli*

The Mishnah states:

> ואלו יוצאות שלא בכתובה העוברת על דת משה ויהודית... ואיזו היא דת יהודית יוצאה וראשה פרוע...
>
> And these [women] may be divorced without [receiving the compensation afforded to them in their] marriage contracts, one

1 This article is intended only to provide background and should not be relied upon for halachic purposes. Some of the approaches cited are inconsistent with contemporary practice and may not conform to halachic practice. A competent rabbi should be consulted for halachic direction.

Ari Storch received *semichah* from Ner Yisroel and is the rabbi of Congregation Ohr Simcha in Baltimore. He is a real estate attorney who graduated from Georgetown University Law Center.

> who transgresses Mosaic[2] or Judaic[3] practices… And what is Judaic practice? One who goes out with her head uncovered…[4]

The Talmud elucidates:

> ראשה פרוע דאורייתא היא דכתיב (במדבר ה:יח) ופרע ראש האשה ותנא דבי רבי ישמעאל אזהרה לבנות ישראל שלא יצאו בפרוע ראש דאורייתא קלתה שפיר דמי דת יהודית אפילו קלתה נמי אסור אמר רבי יוחנן קלתה אין בה משום פרוע ראש הוי בה רבי זירא היכא אילימא בשוק דת יהודית היא ואלא בחצר אם כן לא הנחת בת לאברהם אבינו שיושבת תחת בעלה אמר אביי ואיתימא רב כהנא מחצר לחצר ודרך מבוי.
>
> [But] her head uncovered is a biblical prohibition as it states (*Bamidbar* 5:18), "And he uncovers the head of the woman," and [the disciples in] R. Yishmael's study hall derive [from this verse] a prohibition for Jewish women to go out with their heads uncovered. Biblically, a *kaltah*[5] is sufficient, but [according to] Judaic practice even a

---

2 Mosaic practice is simply understood as a biblical obligation (*Rashi, Kesubos* 72a s.v. *de'oraisa*). However, *Terumas HaDeshen* maintains *Rambam* saw it only as rabbinic in nature (*Terumas HaDeshen* 242). It is unclear how *Terumas HaDeshen* derives this from *Rambam*'s writings. *Magid Mishneh* and *Maaseh Rokeach* note that *Rambam* categorizes certain rabbinic ordinances within Mosaic practice (*Maggid Mishneh Hilchos Ishus* 24:11; *Maaseh Rokeach Hilchos Ishus* 24:11). However, *Maaseh Rokeach*'s approach, finding Mosaic practice to be biblical but to include rabbinic corollaries, seems a more reasonable assertion than to posit that the entirety of Mosaic practice is only rabbinic (*Maaseh Rokeach Hilchos Ishus* 24:11). Furthermore, *Terumas HaDeshen*'s wording indicates something more pronounced in *Rambam*'s writings insinuating that Mosaic practice is rabbinic, not simply an obscure inference (*Terumas HaDeshen* 242 [stating that *Rambam* believes the uncovering of a woman's head is a rabbinic prohibition as clearly indicated in his writings]).

3 Judaic practice is not a formal prohibition; rather, it is a customary practice of Jewish women to preserve a level of modesty (*Chiddushei Rabbeinu Yonasan MiLuniel Kesubos* 72a; *Tosefos Rid Kesubos* 72a; *see also Mishneh Torah Hilchos Ishus* 24:12 [utilizing language that indicates it is only a customary practice developed by Jewish women to preserve modesty]; *Shulchan Aruch Even HaEzer* 115:4 [utilizing language that indicates it is only a customary practice developed by Jewish women to preserve modesty]; but see *Rashi Kesubos* 72a s.v. *das yehudis* [suggesting it is only a custom, but defining custom as that which is not explicitly written in the Torah]). Nevertheless, the ruling of the Mishnah is to permit a man to divorce his wife without paying her the requisite compensation as mandated by her marriage contract if she deviates from these practices.

4 *Kesubos* 72a.

5 The word *kaltah* is purposely left untranslated at this time because it is the subject of dispute, which will be addressed later in this article.

> *kaltah* [by itself] is prohibited. R. Yochanan states, "[Wearing] a *kaltah* does not constitute [going out] with one's head uncovered." R. Zeira questioned in what setting [this applies]. If it is in the marketplace then [it violates] Judaic practice. Rather, it refers to a courtyard setting. If so, [R. Yochanan] has not left a daughter of the Patriarch Abraham who may remain married [and who would then lose the compensation afforded her under her marriage contract]. Abaye or Rav Kahana states [that it refers to] going from one courtyard to another while passing through a public alleyway.[6]

The simple understanding of the above Talmudic passage, and the explanation embraced by *Tosafos*, recognizes three different locations with varying requirements for women's head coverings: (i) a marketplace, (ii) a public alleyway, and (iii) a courtyard.[7] A woman may enter a marketplace with only a *kaltah* according to Mosaic practice, but Judaic practice mandates that she wear a more comprehensive head covering.[8] Both Mosaic and Judaic practice mandate that a woman at least wear a *kaltah* in a semi-public alleyway.[9] A woman may leave her head uncovered when in a private courtyard.[10] The reason for the differing levels of requirement emanates from the amount of privacy each location affords.[11]

The definition of *kaltah* is a matter of dispute. *Rashi* maintains it is a basket to place one's knitting materials whose underside has a depression allowing it to be placed on one's head.[12] Consequently, according to *Rashi*, Judaic practices compels a woman to wear something more concealing and dignified than a basket when entering the marketplace, but she may wear only a basket when walking through an alleyway. *Rambam*, however, maintains that a *kaltah* is a kerchief that covers one's hair.[13] In the marketplace, a woman must wear an additional shawl to comply with Judaic

---

6 *Kesubos* 72a–72b.

7 *Tosafos Kesubos* 72b s.v. *v'elah.*

8 Ibid.

9 Ibid.

10 Ibid.

11 *See Rashi, Kesubos* 72b s.v. *vederech mavoy* (explaining the leniency for a *kaltah* in an alleyway is because not many people are present).

12 *Rashi, Kesubos* 72b s.v. *kaltah.* This approach is also embraced by *Aruch. Aruch* s.v. *k-l-th.*

13 *Peirush HaMishnayos, Kesubos* 7:4; *Mishneh Torah, Hilchos Ishus* 24:12. There is disagreement whether the kerchief must fully conceal the hair (*Igros Moshe* 1 *Even HaEzer* 58).

practice, but she may wear only a kerchief when in a semi-public alleyway.[14]

B. Mosaic and Judaic Practices in Talmud *Yerushalmi*

When elucidating the aforementioned Mishnah, the *Yerushalmi* does not seem bothered by the Mishnah's classification of being in public with an uncovered head as merely Judaic practice, not Mosaic. The *Yerushalmi* seems either unaware of the *Bavli*'s statement from the disciples of R. Yishmael that biblically mandates head covering, as derived from the shaming of a suspected adulteress, or finds the Mishnah's classification as Judaic practice more authoritative. Alternatively, the recorders of the *Yerushalmi* may have synthesized the two Tannaitic statements, but did not feel it necessary to record that discussion. Notwithstanding whether head covering is Mosaic or Judaic practice, the *Yerushalmi* takes a more stringent approach than the simple reading of *Bavli* when discussing where women must cover their heads. The *Yerushalmi* states:

> וראשה פרוע לחצר אמרו ק"ו למבוי רבי חייה בשם רבי יוחנן היוצאה בקפלטין שלה אין בה משום ראשה פרוע הדא דתימא לחצר אבל למבוי יש בה משום יוצאה וראשה פרוע יש חצר שהוא כמבוי ויש מבוי שהוא כחצר חצר שהרבים בוקעין בתוכה הרי הוא כמבוי ומבוי שאין הרבים בוקעין בתוכו הרי הוא כחצר.
>
> And her head uncovered [is reason for her to lose her compensation in her marriage contract, and applies] in a courtyard. They said that *a fortiori* in an alleyway [her head must be covered]. R. Chiyyah [stated] in the name of R. Yochanan, "One who goes out with [only] her kerchief is not [an issue] of an uncovered head." This is taken to apply in a courtyard, but in an alleyway it is considered [to be the problematic issue of] going out with one's head uncovered. Some courtyards are treated as alleyways and some alleyways are treated as courtyards. A courtyard that the public regularly enters is like an alleyway; an alleyway that the public does not regularly enter is like a courtyard.[15]

---

14 *Mishneh Torah Hilchos Ishus* 24:12. *Perishah* compares the shawl to a *talis* that covers the entire body (*Perishah Even HaEzer* 115:9). A woman is permitted to wear a fully concealing head covering instead of two coverings, even in a marketplace, according to some who express the opinion that the kerchief need not fully conceal. *Igros Moshe* 1 *Even HaEzer* 58.

15 *Yerushalmi Kesubos* 44b.

Unlike the simple understanding of the *Bavli*, the *Yerushalmi* mandates that women must have some head covering even when in a courtyard. Thus, according to the *Yerushalmi*, in a non-public area a kerchief is sufficient, but in a public area a more stringent head covering is required.

C. The Classic Halachists's Approaches

Tur's position regarding what head coverings are sufficient in which locations is disputed by later rabbis. *Tur* defines *kaltah* like *Rambam* and seemingly adheres to the simple understanding of the *Bavli* presented above.[16] *Tur* maintains that a man should divorce his wife, who then loses her right to collect the compensation included in her marriage contract, if she does not wear a kerchief and shawl when in a public forum.[17] However, *Tur* states that he need not divorce her if she walks around with her head uncovered in a private forum.[18] *Beis Yosef* acknowledges that *Tur* takes the *Bavli*'s approach, which *Beis Yosef* presents as the only option, but questions *Tur*'s reluctance to state that a woman may walk around a private courtyard without a head covering.[19] *Beis Yosef* sees hesitation in *Tur*'s choice not to permit such behavior explicitly and instead resorts only to stating that her husband need not divorce her.[20] When codifying the halachah in his *Shulchan Aruch*, *Beis Yosef* chose to place more emphasis on the definition of Judaic practice than simply discuss the subject in the context of divorce.[21] He does not list being without a head covering in a private courtyard as a violation,[22] which may indicate he feels it is permissible.

Rema maintains that Tur believes walking around in a private courtyard is permissible even though he did not explicitly permit it.[23] *Rema* first cites an earlier ruling of *Tur* that Jewish women, whether single or married, are prohibited from going out into the marketplace with their heads uncovered.[24] *Rema* contends that *Tur* intended for readers of his earlier ruling to infer that women are permitted to have their heads uncovered when outside of public areas, such as private courtyards.[25] Nevertheless, *Tur*

---

16 *Tur Even HaEzer* 115.
17 Ibid.
18 Ibid.
19 *Beis Yosef Even HaEzer* 115 s.v. *um"sh vedavka.*
20 Ibid.
21 *Shulchan Aruch Even HaEzer* 115:4.
22 Ibid.
23 *Darkei Moshe Even HaEzer* 115:4.
24 Ibid. (citing *Tur Even HaEzer* 21).
25 Ibid.

wanted the reader to perceive that some impropriety exists when uncovering one's head in private.[26] So, when *Tur* codified the halachah more comprehensively, he did so in the context of divorce and did not explicitly state it is permissible to uncover one's head in a courtyard.[27] *Rema* references the Talmudic story of Kimchis to support his position that it is inappropriate for a woman to uncover her head in private.[28] Seven of Kimchis's sons served as High Priests in the Temple.[29] When asked what good deeds merited her such reward, she responded, "The walls of my home never saw the braids of my hair.[30] Thus, says *Rema*, *Tur* wanted to convey that even when permissible, it is inappropriate for women to uncover their heads.[31] *Taz*, however, maintains *Tur* was simply stating the halachah in accordance with the simple understanding of the *Bavli* and was not advocating for women to take a more stringent approach in a private forum.[32] Hence, according to *Tur*, as understood by Beis Yosef, the *Shulchan Aruch*, *Rema* and *Taz*, a woman must wear a shawl and kerchief when in public, at least a kerchief when in a semi-public area, and may uncover her head when in a private area. However, *Rema* contends that *Tur* maintains it is inappropriate for a woman to have her head uncovered even in the privacy of her own home.

Bach and *Beis Shmuel* disagree with the interpretation of *Tur* by both *Beis Yosef* and *Rema*. Partially based on *Beis Yosef*'s aforementioned question, *Bach* understands both *Rambam* and *Tur* to require a kerchief even in a courtyard. [33] Consequently, a woman would need a kerchief in a courtyard or semi-public alleyway, and an additional shawl when in a marketplace.

---

26 Ibid.

27 Ibid.

28 Ibid.

29 *Yoma* 47a.

30 Ibid, but see *Tosafos Yeshanim Yoma* 47a s.v. *lo ra'u* (maintaining that Kimchis only meant when it was possible to cover her hair); *Beis HaBechirah Yoma* 47a s.v. *shivah* (stating that Kimchis's statement was an exaggerative expression meant to convey extreme modesty).

31 *Darkei Moshe Even HaEzer* 115:4. Based on the *Zohar*, *Magen Avraham* contends that married women should scrupulously cover every strand of hair in all situations (*Magen Avraham* 75:4). For halachic reasons, *Chasam Sofer* requires married women to cover all their hair in every situation (*Chasam Sofer Orach Chaim* 36; but see *Igros Moshe* 1 *Even HaEzer* 58 [countering *Chasam Sofer*'s position and presenting a more lenient approach]).

32 *Turi Zahav Even HaEzer* 115:5.

33 *Bayis Chadash, Even HaEzer* 115 s.v. *um"sh*.

The problem with *Bach*'s approach is the *Bavli*'s retort of, "If so, [R. Yochanan] has not left a daughter of the Patriarch Abraham who may remain married [and who would then lose the compensation afforded her under her marriage contract]."[34] The *Bavli* posited that R. Yochanan held wearing only a *kaltah* in a courtyard does not violate Mosaic or Judaic practice.[35] The retort seemingly rejected that approach under the assumption that women regularly do not wear even a *kaltah* on their heads in courtyards.[36] Hence, this quip seems to undermine the basis of *Bach*'s position that women must wear a *kaltah* even in a courtyard. *Bach* counters this by providing a novel interpretation of this retort.[37] *Bach* suggests that the Talmud assumed a *kaltah* is both necessary and sufficient in a courtyard because that is the common practice.[38] The Talmud assumes that R. Yochanan must have been demanding something more than common practice because he would never have stated something so obvious.[39] However, retorts the Talmud, he could not have demanded something more because then he would have "not left a daughter of the Patriarch Abraham who may remain married [without losing the compensation in her marriage contract]."[40] *Beis Shmuel* champions *Bach*'s approach because it harmonizes the *Bavli* with the *Yerushalmi*, something *Rashi, Tosafos* and the simple understanding of the *Bavli* fail to accomplish.[41]

In summation, the halachists understand that a *kaltah* is a kerchief that covers the head, like *Rambam*, and Judaic practice compels a woman to don an additional shawl when in a more public area. There is a dispute whether a woman requires any head covering when in a private area, like a courtyard, and there are Talmudic passages that seem to laud the praises of one who is diligent to keep her head covered even when not required. However, all seem to maintain that a *kaltah* is sufficient in a semi-public area.

---

34 *Kesubos* 72b.

35 Ibid.

36 Ibid.

37 *Bayis Chadash Even HaEzer* 115 s.v. *um"sh*.

38 Ibid.

39 Ibid.

40 Ibid.; but see *Turi Zahav Even HaEzer* 115:5 (challenging the viability of the answer of his father-in-law, the *Bach*, by stating that phrasing such a question in this fashion is awkward; had the Talmud intended to state what *Bach* purports, it should simply have used its regular rhetorical verbiage, "*peshita*," which means, "it is obvious," and is used in such situations).

41 *Beis Shmuel* 115: 9.

D. Unmarried Women

i. In Talmudic Literature

The Talmudic passages seem somewhat conflicting on the issue of whether unmarried women must cover their heads. None of the passages from *Kesubos* in the *Bavli* or *Yerushalmi* nor the earlier passages from the halachists differentiate between married and unmarried women, which indicates that unmarried women must cover their heads. However, those passages primarily deal with divorce and marriage contracts; the subjects are implicitly married women. Furthermore, the biblical source the *Bavli* uses for the assertion that women must cover their heads refers to a suspected adulteress who is married.[42] Thus, although the simple understanding of these passages insinuates unmarried women must cover their heads, no definitive proof may be ascertained.

The Talmudic passage in Tractate *Nedarim* suggests unmarried women must cover their heads. The Mishnah states that one who vows not to benefit from "black-headed" people is prohibited from benefiting

---

42 *Kesubos* 72a. Similarly, *Sifri* unequivocally states that Jewish women must cover their heads, which indicates that the obligation is for married and unmarried women (*Sifri Naso* 11). After making its statement, *Sifri* utilizes the verse that states that Tamar put ash and her hand on her head after being violated by Amnon as an allusion to this obligation (ibid). Some deduce from this *Sifri* that an unmarried woman who was violated must cover her head because she is no longer a virgin (e.g., *Shevus Yaakov* 103; *Emek HaNetziv Naso* 11 s.v. *shene'emar*; *Torah Temimah Bamidbar* 5:96). This indicates that other unmarried women need not cover their heads. Nonetheless, this does not prove that *Sifri* maintains that unmarried women have no obligation to cover their heads. These deductions may be predicated on an anachronistic assumption that unmarried virgins do not cover their heads. *Sifri* may mandate that all women covered their heads, as indicated by its generally stated rule. The allusion from Tamar may simply be from a verse explicitly demonstrating head covering without any focus on the specifics of Tamar's situation. The authorities who maintain that unmarried women who were violated need not cover their hair are compelled to understand *Sifri* in this fashion. See *Pischei Teshuvah Even HaEzer* 21:2 (citing authorities that maintain that a woman who never married who is not a virgin need not cover her head). *Sifri* seems to acknowledge that it is not using Tamar's case with specificity by emphasizing that Tamar's case is not a proof, only an allusion (*Sifri Naso* 11). Accordingly, Tamar covered her head regularly even before this incident; it became uncovered only because Amnon violated her and threw her out of the room abruptly (2 *Shmuel* 13:17–18). The allusion sees Tamar then utilizing whatever resources she had to restore her head covering. Consequently, *Sifri* is similar to the passages from *Kesubos* in both *Bavli* and *Yerushalmi*, the simple reading indicates all unmarried women must cover their hair, but the subject used as the example casts some doubt on that understanding.

from men, even if they are bald or have aged with white hair, but is permitted to benefit from women and children.[43] The Talmud elucidates that "black-headed" is a reference to people whose dark hair is sometimes revealed, but sometimes covered.[44] The reference is therefore limited to men because women always cover their heads and children keep their heads uncovered.[45] "Black-headed" could apply equally to women if unmarried women did not always cover their heads; rather, it seems unmarried women always covered their heads. However, since most young women attempted to marry no later than age twelve,[46] it is possible that relatively few remained unwed by the age of majority. Thus, even if unmarried women exposed their heads, people might not refer to adult women as black-headed because the overwhelming majority were married and covering their heads. Similar to the passages from *Kesubos* in the *Bavli* and *Yerushalmi* cited earlier, the simple understanding of this passage indicates that unmarried women covered their heads, but no conclusive deduction can be made.

The simple reading of one of Rav's homiletic passages, as cited in *Midrash Rabbah*, supports the assertion that unmarried women covered their heads in earlier times. Rav states that On b. Peles's wife saved him from the tragic end that befell the other members of Korach's rebellion.[47] Rav stipulates that On initially joined Korach's challenge to Moshe's authority; however, when On returned home the evening after challenging Moshe, his wife greeted him with wine and On fell asleep after becoming inebriated.[48] When the rabble-rousers came to gather On, On's wife and daughter sat in their doorway.[49] On's wife proceeded to unravel her hair and the group of rebels departed so as not to be in the presence of an immodestly clad woman.[50] Although the focus of the story is on On's wife, the inclusion of his daughter indicates that she also unraveled her hair. Presumably, the daughter who sat in the doorway lived in On's home, which indicates she was not married. The unmarried daughter's unraveled hair would only be considered immodest if it would have otherwise been covered. Therefore, the simple reading of this passage indi-

---

43 *Nedarim* 30b.
44 Ibid.
45 Ibid.
46 *Rashi Kesubos* 57b s.v. *nosnin lah.*
47 *Bamidbar Rabbah* 18:20.
48 Ibid.
49 Ibid.
50 Ibid.

cates that single women of earlier generations covered their heads. Nevertheless, no definitive proof may be brought from this passage. Although classic interpreters assume the *Midrash Rabbah* includes the daughter in the story,[51] the same story is referenced in several other Talmudic sources with no reference to her.[52] Thus, it is possible the inclusion is nothing more than a scrivener's error. Furthermore, the story never explicitly states that the daughter unraveled her hair or that she was unmarried; if either she did not unravel her hair or was married then there is no proof. Consequently, similar to the simple understandings of the passages cited earlier from *Bavli Kesubos*, *Yerushalmi Kesubos* and *Nedarim*, the simple understanding of this passage inconclusively indicates that unmarried women covered their heads in previous generations.

Tractate *Berachos* contains a passage indicating that both married and unmarried women must cover their heads. In the context of discussing what areas of the body are considered immodest, Rav Sheshes states that a woman's exposed hair qualifies as immodest.[53] Rav Sheshes's statement does not differentiate between married and unmarried women, so it seems that any woman's hair is considered immodest when exposed. Nevertheless, many later authorities seemingly narrow the application of Rav Sheshes's statement to married women,[54] which indicates their belief that

---

51 *Matnos Kehunah, Bamidbar Rabbah* 18:20; *Peirush Maharzu, Bamidbar Rabbah* 18:20.

52 *Sanhedrin* 109b–110a; *Tanchuma, Korach* 10; *Midrash HaGadol, Bamidbar* 16:1.

53 *Berachos* 24a. The biblical source of Rav Sheshes's ruling may reference an unmarried woman. The verse describes a woman's beautiful hair (*Shir HaShirim* 4:1). The simple understanding, *pshat*, identifies this woman as an unmarried virgin (*Ibn Ezra, Shir HaShirim HaPaam HaSheinis* 8:10 s.v. *ani chomah*). *Rashi* maintains that the text describes this woman as covering her hair with a kerchief (*Rashi, Shir HaShirim* 4:1 s.v. *tzamasech*). Consequently, the Talmudic source that women's hair is immodest may refer to an unmarried woman who is naturally seen as covering her head. However, some do not understand the woman to be using a kerchief (*Ibn Ezra, Shir HaShirim HaPaam HaRishonah* 4:1 s.v. *tzamasech*; *Metzudas David Shir HaShirim* 4:1 s.v. *einayich yonim*). Moreover, the homiletical approach, *drush*, sees the text describing a discussion between an estranged married couple pining for the closeness of their initial relationship (*Rashi, Shir HaShirim Hakdamah*; see also *Yoma* 75 [understanding verses that apparently describe the woman's virginity as allegorizing the Jewish nation's fidelity to God in Egypt]). Consequently, some verses in this text describe the currently married woman, but others describe her in her youth. Accordingly, the verse in question may refer to the currently married woman. Hence, the marital status of the subject of the source of Rav Sheshes's ruling is ambiguous.

54 E.g., *Rashba Berachos* s.v. *amar Rav Chisda*; *Rosh, Berachos* 24a; but see *infra* note 94 and accompanying text (presenting an alternative understanding of these sources).

unmarried women did not cover their heads in the Talmudic era. Thus, the simple understanding of this passage supports the assertion that unmarried women covered their heads in the Talmudic era, consistent with the simple understandings of the passages from *Kesubos* in the *Bavli* and *Yerushalmi*, *Nedarim* and *Midrash Rabbah*, but later interpretations seemingly reject that supposition.

The Mishnah in Tractate *Kesubos* may indicate that common practice was for unwed women to uncover their heads, even in public. The Mishnah records that previously unwed brides attended their wedding ceremonies with their heads uncovered.[55] It appears that unwed women may leave their heads uncovered when in public because the Mishnah does not take issue with this normative practice. Although it is possible the Mishnah only meant the bride's head was partially exposed in an appropriate fashion,[56] it is likely that it was exposed in a fashion that would otherwise be considered inappropriate. The Mishnah uses the word *parua* (פרוע),[57] which is the same word used by the Talmud when describing the prohibition to go out with one's head uncovered.[58] So, it would seem that the manner described in the Mishnah is what is prohibited elsewhere in the Talmud. Nevertheless, the Mishnah does not prove that unmarried women were permitted to uncover their heads. *Shevus Yaakov* maintains that the Mishnah's case is a rare exception, which results from the extreme

---

55 *Kesubos* 15b.

56 R. Yochanan understands that the bride would don a ceremonial scarf, which implies that her head may not have been completely uncovered (ibid, at 16b). Mosaic practice may permit incomplete head coverings even in the marketplace; it is Judaic practice that certainly mandates a more concealing head covering (*Id* at 72a–72b). Customary wedding adornments likely conform to customary practice, and Judaic practice is predicated on customary practice (*Rashi, Kesubos* 72a s.v. *das yehudis*; *Mishneh Torah Hilchos Ishus* 24:12; *Chiddushei Rabbeinu Yehonasan MiLuniel, Kesubos* 72a; *Tosafos Rid, Kesubos* 72a; *Shulchan Aruch Even HaEzer* 115:4). So, customary bridal garments that partially expose a bride's head could be consistent with both Mosaic and Judaic practice and be consistent with the normative practice of unmarried women covering their heads. Surchav b. Papa cites Zeiri as disputing R. Yochanan's interpretation that the bride wore a ceremonial scarf (*Kesubos* 16b). But it is unclear if Zeiri's argument with his teacher, R. Yochanan, extends so far as to suggest that the bride's head was completely uncovered. Interestingly, the *Yerushalmi* maintains that those in the Land of Israel embraced Zeiri's opinion, but those in Babylonia followed R. Yochanan's approach (*Yerushalmi Kesubos* 9b). This is somewhat peculiar because R. Yochanan lived in the Land of Israel while Zeiri was Babylonian (*Rashi, Kiddushin* 71b s.v. *nasiv bartai*).

57 *Kesubos* 15b.

58 Ibid, at 72a.

unlikelihood for a bride to have an inappropriate relationship.[59] The bride is accompanied by family and friends, and it would be extraordinarily brazen for her to have an illicit relationship on her wedding day.[60] Alternatively, the exception may result from the underlying reason why brides uncovered their heads. This custom developed as a display of mourning for the loss of the Temple.[61] The assumption may have been that the populace would not view this exposure as lewd because the bride would be seen as disheveled and mourning. Moreover, the need to display mourning in this setting may supersede the imperative for one's head to be covered.[62] It is for similar reasons that the Talmud finds no issue with uncovering a suspected adulteress's head and exposing her chest; both were considered necessary deterrents and were done to shame her while she was in the Temple.[63] Because the bride's uncovered head may be an exception, it cannot be used to prove the rule.

ii. In Classic Halachic Literature

Seemingly contradictory statements regarding whether unmarried women must cover their heads exist in classic halachic literature. Both *Tur* and *Shulchan Aruch* state that both married and unmarried women are prohibited from entering the marketplace with their heads uncovered,[64] which apparently conflicts with their statements permitting one to read *Shema* while facing an unmarried woman's uncovered head.[65] To avoid the apparent contradiction, *Beis Shmuel* reinterprets the passages of *Tur* and *Shulchan Aruch* that require unmarried women to cover their heads by translating their contextual usage of the word *p'nuyah*, typically meaning an unmarried woman, as a widow or divorcée; the word *besulah* better refers to

---

59 *Shevus Yaakov* 103.

60 Ibid.

61 *Yerushalmi Kesubos* 9b; see also *Pnei Moshe, Kesubos* 9b s.v. *yotza'ah* (explaining the *Yerushalmi* to be stating that the uncovering of the head was a sign of mourning); *Ridvaz, Kesubos* 9b (explaining the *Yerushalmi* to be stating that the uncovering of the head was a sign of mourning); but see *Korban HaEidah, Kesubos* 9b s.v. *k'gon eilu* (explaining the *Yerushalmi* in a different fashion).

62 The superseding imperative may not have been a suspension of the underlying obligation; rather, the obligation may not apply in this circumstance. See *infra* note 120 and accompanying text (presenting an approach that the bride's uncovered head does not reflect a suspension of the obligation to cover one's head even if unmarried women were otherwise required to cover their heads).

63 *Sotah* 7a, 8a–8b.

64 *Tur, Even HaEzer* 21; *Shulchan Aruch, Even HaEzer* 21:2.

65 *Tur, Orach Chaim* 75; *Shulchan Aruch, Orach Chaim* 75:2.

unmarried women according to *Beis Shmuel*.[66] Supporting this contention is that *Tur* and *Shulchan Aruch* use the word *besulah* when permitting one to recite *Shema* while facing an unmarried woman's exposed hair.[67] Consequently, only women who currently are or previously were married need to cover their heads.

Magen Avraham differs from *Beis Shmuel* and suggests a novel approach to resolve the apparent contradiction. *Magen Avraham* finds the suggestion that the word *p'nuyah* refers to widows and divorcées untenable.[68] Rather, *Magen Avraham* reinterprets the prohibition to go into the marketplace with an uncovered head to mean that it is prohibited to go into the marketplace with one's hair unbraided, not uncovered.[69] *Magen Avraham* further asserts that the prohibition for an unmarried woman to go into the marketplace with unbraided hair is only rabbinic, but a married woman is required to cover her head based on biblical law.[70] Thus, unmarried women are not required to cover their heads, but they must wear braids when in public.

---

66 *Beis Shmuel, Even HaEzer* 21:5. *Bach* and *Chelkas Mechokek* similarly maintain that *p'nuyah* in this context means an unmarried woman who is not a virgin. *Bayis Chadash, Even HaEzer* 21 s.v. *lo yelchu*; *Chelkas Mechokek* 21:2.

67 *Tur, Orach Chaim* 75; *Shulchan Aruch, Orach Chaim* 75:2.

68 *Magen Avraham* 75:3.

69 Ibid.

70 Ibid. The use of the word *p'nuyah* in one place and *besulah* in another likely results from *Tur* and *Shulchan Aruch* quoting different authors. When discussing *Shema*, they were quoting *Rosh* who uses the term *besulah* (see *Rosh, Berachos* 24a [using *besulah*]). When discussing head coverings, they were quoting *Rambam* who uses the term *p'nuyah* (see *Rambam, Hilchos Isurei Biyah* 21:17 [using *p'nuyah*]). Supporting this assertion is that earlier in that same chapter *Rambam* uses the word *p'nuyah* to refer to single women, whether previously married or not (ibid, at 21:3). There is no conflict from *Rambam*'s clarification in that earlier halachah, "and it is permissible to stare at the face of a *p'nuyah* and determine [if he wishes to marry her], whether she is a virgin or not…" (ibid). It is erroneous to assume *Rambam* provided greater definition of *p'nuyah* in this halachah to distinguish it from the one discussing head covering; this halachah would include virgins and non-virgins and the one about head covering would be limited to non-virgins. Had *Rambam* intended to distinguish in this fashion, he should have more succinctly stated, "and it is permissible to stare at the face of a *p'nuyah* or a virgin to determine [if he wishes to marry her]." Rather, *Rambam*'s broader definition is seemingly included to clarify that *p'nuyah* refers to all types of single women, most likely because in this particular ruling *Rambam* cites a verse from *Iyov* that appears applicable only to virgins (ibid [citing *Iyov* 31:1]; see also *Peirush HaMishnayos, Sanhedrin* 7:4 (presenting the same concept and citing the same verse).

E. Women's Hair and *Ervah*

There is debate whether a woman's hair is a specified *ervah*, a specific area of the body designated as immodest. Rav Sheshes states that a woman's exposed hair qualifies as immodest.[71] *Rashba* and *Rosh* understand that Rav Sheshes is designating hair as an *ervah*, an immodest portion of the body that one may not face while reciting *Shema*.[72] Thus, according to *Rashba* and *Rosh*, a woman's hair is a distinct area of the body, which has a defined halachic status of *ervah*.

Although *Rambam* understands Rav Sheshes as prohibiting one from deriving benefit by staring at a woman's hair, he does not understand that Rav Sheshes specifically designated hair as an *ervah*. Instead, *Rambam* generically prohibits deriving benefit from staring at any portion of a woman's body, including her hair.[73] Similarly, when discussing the rules of *Shema*, *Rambam* does not specifically designate hair as an *ervah*.[74] Therefore, *Kesef Mishneh* maintains that *Rambam* understood that it is permissible to recite *Shema* while facing a woman's exposed head because hair is not a specified *ervah*.[75] Thus, there is debate whether hair is an *ervah*, and this debate has halachic significance.

F. The Impact of Societal Norms

Several authorities limit Rav Sheshes's statement that a woman's hair is immodest in ways that open the possibility that societal norms may impact

---

71 *Berachos* 24a.

72 *Rashba, Berachos* 24a s.v. *amar Rav Chisda*; *Rosh, Berachos* 24a.

73 *Mishneh Torah, Hilchos Issurei Biah* 21:2. There are differing opinions regarding *Rambam*'s position on whether one may read *Shema* while facing a woman who is not his wife who has less than a handbreadth of her body exposed. See *Lechem Mishneh, Hilchos Ishus* 3:16 s.v. *v'im haysah* (stating that *Rambam* prohibits reciting *Shema* if even less than a handbreadth is exposed); *Bayis Chadash, Orach Chaim* 75 s.v. *tefach* (stating that *Rambam* permits reciting *Shema* if it is less than a handbreadth that is exposed).

74 *Mishneh Torah, Hilchos Kriyas Shema* 3:16.

75 *Kesef Mishneh, Hilchos Kriyas Shema* 3:16 s.v. *v'im hayah*; see also *Beis Yosef, Orach Chaim* 75 s.v. *kasav* (asserting the same contention as done in *Kesef Mishneh*). This assumption is predicated on *Kesef Mishneh*'s contention that when *Rambam* restricts reciting *Shema* while facing any exposed area of a woman, it is limited to areas that are typically concealed. Interpreting *Rambam* in a simpler fashion that understands that *Rambam* prohibits reading *Shema* while facing any exposed area of a woman, whether typically concealed or not, compels one to conclude that hair is included in the overall prohibition. The lack of designation as an *ervah* then has no direct halachic significance.

halachic matters pertaining to head covering. Based on the *Raavad*, *Rashba* suggests that hair that normally protrudes from one's covering is not considered immodest for the purposes of recitation of *Shema*.[76] The impropriety of exposed hair results from one having impure thoughts when seeing it; however, pedestrian matters do not stir arousal.[77] Thus, hair that typically protrudes from a covering will not cause one to have impure thoughts.[78] *Rosh* extends this and states that unmarried women's hair is not considered immodest for the purposes of reciting *Shema* because it is regularly uncovered.[79] Both *Tur* and *Shulchan Aruch* follow suit and apply Rav Sheshes's statement to the recitation of *Shema*, but exclude from it hair that is normally exposed and unmarried women's hair.[80] Based on this line of reasoning, Maharam Alashkar extends this concept by stating that women may expose hair that is considered normal to expose by the societal standards of the Jewish community.[81] It is not simply that one may recite *Shema* while facing such exposed hair; rather, it is permissible for women to expose such hair outright. Thus, classic authorities explicitly state that societal norms impact the requirements of women's head coverings for reading *Shema* and later authorities extend this impact to general head covering requirements.

Although the aforementioned discussions of societal impact on halachic requirements may be limited to cases of Judaic practice, there is debate if societal norms can abolish the Mosaic practice requirement to cover one's head. *Aruch HaShulchan* seems to hold that normative behavior cannot displace Mosaic practice because he lambasts the widespread practice of the married women of Lithuania of not covering their heads in public.[82] He refers to the women as licentious and states that their immoral practice of uncovering their heads plagues society.[83] If normative practice displaces Mosaic practice, these women would not be acting im-

---

76 *Rashba, Berachos* 24a s.v. *amar Rav Chisda.*

77 Ibid.

78 Ibid.

79 *Rosh, Berachos* 24a. When discussing *ervah* for the purposes of reciting *Shema*, the *Mordechai* cites *Raavyah* as similarly maintaining that unmarried women's hair is not an *ervah* because it is regularly uncovered (*Mordechai, Berachos* 80 [citing *Sefer Raavyah* 76, which is discussing reciting *Shema*]).

80 *Tur, Orach Chaim* 75; *Shulchan Aruch, Orach Chaim* 75:2.

81 *Teshuvos Maharam Alashkar* 35.

82 *Aruch HaShulchan, Orach Chaim* 75:7.

83 Ibid.

modestly, so the harsh rebuke indicates that *Aruch HaShulchan* did not believe that Mosaic practice could be displaced.[84] It also seems that *Aruch HaShulchan* assumes that Mosaic practice never extended to unmarried women because he directs his rebuke only to married women. In contradistinction, R. Yosef Messas states that once the women in Moroccan communities abandoned the practice of covering their heads en masse, it obviated the need even under Mosaic practice.[85] Mosaic practice derived its ruling from the Torah's requirement for the priest to remove the suspected adulteress's head covering.[86] *Rashi* elucidates that one of the following explanations is the underlying Talmudic reasoning: (i) it must be prohibited to expose her hair if doing so degrades her, or (ii) implicit in the verse is that her head was initially covered in conformance with the standard practices of Jewish women and deviation is prohibited.[87] R. Messas suggests that the first reason only sufficiently shows a prohibition on others to remove her headdress, but does not restrict a woman from degrading herself.[88] The second reason only mandates that a woman must adhere to the societal norms of her community.[89] In biblical times, the societal norm was for women to cover their heads; however, Moroccan women chose to abandon this practice.[90] Thus, R. Messas contends that there is no more need for members of the Moroccan community to cover their heads because the societal norm no longer mandates it.[91]

Contemporary practice may show support for R. Messas's position. Although not customary practice in current Judaism, the simplest resolution to the contradiction between the statements of *Tur* and *Shulchan Aruch* prohibiting unmarried women to uncover their heads and the ones permitting the recitation of *Shema* while facing an unmarried woman whose

---

84 Although *Aruch HaShulchan* rules that married women must retain their head coverings in public even though society has abandoned the practice, he holds that it is not problematic to read *Shema* while facing exposed hair because it is normal to be exposed and does not arouse immoral thoughts (ibid).

85 *Otzar HaMichtavim* vol. 3:1884.

86 *Kesubos* 72a.

87 *Rashi, Kesubos* 72a s.v. *azharah*. *Rashi* comments that the second of these explanations is the primary reason (ibid).

88 *Otzar HaMichtavim* vol. 3:1884; but see *Igros Moshe* 1, *Even HaEzer* 57 (citing *Ritva* and stating that the degradation results from lewd behavior, which is prohibited).

89 *Otzar HaMichtavim* vol. 3:1884.

90 Ibid.

91 Ibid. It is unclear how R. Messas distinguishes between Mosaic and Judaic practice because his approach sees both mandating adherence to societal norms.

hair is uncovered is to take all of these statements literally. *Tur* and *Shulchan Aruch* maintain that unmarried women must cover their heads in public; nevertheless, unmarried women's hair is not considered immodest for the purposes of reciting *Shema* because over time it came to be considered mundane. Unmarried women's hair is thus similar to married women's hair according to *Aruch HaShulchan*'s approach; it is prohibited to be uncovered, but not considered immodest for the purposes of reciting *Shema*.[92] The simple reading of the Talmudic source requiring head covering under Mosaic practice does not distinguish between married and unmarried women, which is consistent with the simple reading of *Tur* and *Shulchan Aruch*.[93] So, it seems that the exclusion of unmarried women from this obligation may result from an anachronistic projection of later halachists. Unlike the earlier authorities who only seem to permit one to recite *Shema* while facing a woman's exposed hair,[94] the Maharam Alashkar, *Beis Shmuel* and *Magen Avraham* even permit unmarried women to uncover their heads.[95] This extension may have arisen from then contemporary practice, likely the result of changed normative practices since the Talmudic era. Consequently, the widespread acceptance of unmarried

---

92 See *Aruch HaShulchan, Orach Chaim* 75:7 (contending that a married woman's hair is prohibited to be exposed in public, but is not immodest for the purposes of reciting *Shema*). In a similar context, R. Yom Tov Lipman Heller suggests that the Sages were concerned that people would frequently fail to recite *Shema* in its proper time if the modesty standards for *Shema* were equated with those of modest dress; therefore, one may recite *Shema* while facing certain otherwise immodest exposures (*Maadanei Yom Tov, Berachos* 3:60, 80).

93 *Kesubos* 72a; *Tur, Even HaEzer* 21; *Shulchan Aruch, Even HaEzer* 21:2.

94 *Rashba, Berachos* 24a s.v. *amar Rav Chisda*; *Rosh Berachos* 24a.

95 See *Teshuvos Maharam Alashkar* 35 (including unmarried women's hair in the list of types of commonly exposed hair, which are permissible to expose); *Beis Shmuel* 21:5 (resolving an apparent contradiction by excluding unmarried women from the requirement to cover their heads); *Magen Avraham* 75:3 (resolving an apparent contradiction by excluding unmarried women from the requirement to cover their heads with material). *Bach* maintains that *Raavyah*, as cited by the *Mordechai*, believed it is permissible for unmarried women to expose their hair (*Bayis Chadash, Even HaEzer* 21 s.v. *lo yelchu*). However, this attribution may result from *Bach*'s conflating the concept of *ervah* for reciting *Shema* and the rules of when it is permitted for a woman to uncover her head. The *Mordechai* only quoted *Raavyah* in the context of reciting *Shema*, not in the context of the prohibition of uncovering one's head (*Mordechai, Berachos* 80 [citing *Sefer Raavyah* 76, which is discussing reciting *Shema*]).

women exposing their heads may unwittingly display support for R. Messas's approach that Mosaic practice may evolve.[96] This line of reasoning then compels one to conclude that *Rashba* and *Rosh* never intended to narrow Rav Sheshes's initial statement; they were stating that the subsequent practice of unmarried women exposing hair caused such hair to be considered mundane for the purposes of *Shema*.[97] Accordingly, the simple understandings of all the Talmudic passages that unmarried women covered their heads in Talmudic times are acknowledged and the Mishnah in *Kesubos* is recognized as the sole exception.[98]

G. Covering vs. Braided

Much of the discussion about women covering their heads results from Tractate *Kesubos*'s interpretation of the verse that requires the priest to shame the suspected adulteress by removing her headdress.[99] However, Tractate *Sotah* states that the priest unravels her braids, which indicates that the focus is on unbraiding.[100] *Sifri* and *Rashi*'s exegesis both adopt Tractate *Sotah*'s understanding, and *Rashi*'s commentary immediately recognizes this as the biblical source that a woman's uncovered hair is undignified, which insinuates that women are only in violation if their hair is exposed to the point that it is uncovered and unbraided.[101] Nevertheless,

---

96 Some great halachists see the prohibition for widows and divorcées to uncover their heads as only Judaic practice (e.g., *Igros Moshe* 1, *Even HaEzer* 57–58.) However, this mindset is predicated either on the answers of *Beis Shmuel* or *Magen Avraham*, or on similarly structured answers (e.g., ibid).

97 *Rosh*'s Talmudic glosses include a comment limiting the application of Rav Sheshes's statement to married women (*Tosafos HaRosh, Berachos* 24a s.v. *saar*). However, it is unclear if the intent is to explain the Talmud or present contemporary halachic practice.

98 This exception may not represent a suspension of the underlying obligation. See *infra* note 120 and accompanying text (presenting an approach that the bride's uncovered head does not reflect a suspension of the obligation to cover one's head even if unmarried women were otherwise required to cover their heads).

99 *Kesubos* 72a.

100 *Sotah* 7a, 8a; *Rashi, Sotah* 7a s.v. *vesoser*; *Rashi, Sotah* 8a s.v. *soser*. The word used for unbraiding is *soser* (סותר), which typically means to demolish (ibid). Interestingly, the Talmud compares braiding one's hair to building even with regard to building restrictions on Shabbos (*Shabbos* 95a). So, it is not surprising that the word to unbraid is demolish. *Rashi* expresses that the purpose of unbraiding the adulteress's hair is to expose it considerably. *Rashi Sotah* 8a s.v. *soser*.

101 *Sifri, Naso* 11; *Rashi, Bamidbar* 5:18 s.v. *u'phara*; see also *Igros Moshe* 1, *Even HaEzer* 58 (similarly asserting that one may only derive from the biblical source that the prohibition is for women to wear their hair in the same manner as the adulteress's hair).

Tractate *Sotah*'s presentation is not regularly used for halachic interpretation with regard to head covering. One notable exception is the approach of *Magen Avraham* who references Tractate *Sotah* when stating that unmarried women must braid their hair in public,[102] but he acknowledges that this is only a rabbinic ordinance; the biblical imperative is to cover the hair and is only applicable to married women.

After noticing Tractate *Sotah*'s approach, a new possibility arises to interpret the original passage in Tractate *Kesubos*. The Talmud understood that a *kaltah* is sufficient in public under Mosaic practice, which was derived from the verse regarding the adulteress; however, Judaic practice mandates more.[103] Starting from *Rashi* and continuing until the present, the classic interpreters understood *kaltah* to be some sort of head covering.[104] However, the Talmudic passages in *Sotah* and *Kesubos* would be more integrated if the word *kaltah* (קלתה) was a scrivener's error and the word was originally either *kilatah* (קלעתה) or *kliatah* (קליעתה), which would mean her braids. It is for similar reasons that *Shevus Yaakov* posited that the word *kaltah* should be translated as a derivative of *kliyah*, meaning braids.[105] If either of the above methods is true, there would be no biblical source that women must cover their hair; biblical law would only mandate braiding.

The question then is why no classic interpreters saw this as a valid option. The similarities in the words and the passage from *Sotah* make it seem likely that the word in *Kesubos* should be *kilatah*. The likely answer is that the passages in *Berachos* and *Nedarim* would conflict with the passage in *Kesubos* if a woman was not obligated to cover her hair in semi-public domains. The passage in *Berachos* states that a woman's exposed hair is immodest.[106] If women only braided their hair in semi-public domains, it would remain exposed. It is unlikely the Talmud would permit a display elsewhere described as immodest. Suggesting the passage in *Berachos* only meant unbraided hair is immodest is unreasonable because it says "hair," without qualification. The passage in *Nedarim* maintains women are not called "black-headed" because they always cover their hair.[107] Black-headed references hair color; if women braided their hair in semi-public

---

102 *Magen Avraham* 75:3.

103 *Kesubos* 72a–72b.

104 E.g., *Rashi, Kesubos* 72b s.v. *kaltah; Mishneh Torah, Hilchos Ishus* 24:12.

105 *Shevus Yaakov* 103. The disadvantage to *Shevus Yaakov*'s method of integrating the passages is that the word *kaltah* is mentioned elsewhere in the Talmud and means a basket in those contexts (e.g., *Gittin* 77a). However, this disadvantage similarly exists for Rambam's position that a *kaltah* is a kerchief.

106 *Berachos* 24a.

107 *Nedarim* 30b.

domains without covering it, their heads would commonly have a black appearance. Thus, to avoid contradictions between Talmudic passages, one must assume that *kaltah* is neither the result of a scrivener's error from *kilatah* nor a derivative of *kliyah*.

H. A Theoretical Approach Based on the Approach of Rav Sherira Gaon and Meiri

i. Rav Sherira Gaon and Meiri

Unlike the more popular approach that assumes the Amoraim focus on elucidating the earlier positions of Tannaim, Rav Sherira Gaon and Meiri suggest that many Amoraic statements that seem to interpret Tannaitic positions really represent dissenting opinions. A very different picture is painted when analyzing the Talmudic passages that discuss women's head covering through this lens. Rav Sherira Gaon writes:

> השתא אתו רבנן אמוראי של התלמוד ומפרשין הני מילי היכא דחזו כדחזא רבי ומגליא להו מילתא דהלכה כאותו היחיד והיכא דלא חזי כדחזא רבי ולא מגליא להו מילתא כההיא דהמביא יום טוב: אמר רב יהודה אמר שמואל אין מביאין עצים אלא מן המוכנין שבקרפף ומקשינן והא אנן תנן מן הקרפף אפילו מן המפוזר תיובתא דשמואל ומפרקינן מתניתין יחידאה היא ואישתכח לה סייעתא מן ברייתא. והיכא דמשכחינן במתניתין מילתא משבשא וצריכא למסמי מינא מדי דאית בה קושיא ולא סליק אמרינן סמי מכאן כך וכך כי הנך דאותו ואת בנו דאמרינן אמר ר' חייא אמר ר' יוחנן פרת חטאת אינה משנה עגלה ערופה אינה משנה אלמא אי קשיא מתניתין ולא סלקא מברייתא ואף מסברא דחינן מתניתין כולה כי ההיא דתנינן בטהרות מסרק של פשתן שנטלו שיניו ואמרינן בהחולץ רבי יוחנן וריש לקיש דאמרי תרוייהו זו אינה משנה ולא עבדינן כוותה ממאי דמסיימי דווקני וכו'. ואי צריכא מתניתין לחסורא מחסרינן לה ואי צריכא לתרוצה מתרצינן לה . . . .
>
> At this point came our Sages, the Amoraim of the Talmud, and explained these things. Where they agree with Rebbe that the halachah follows an individual opinion, they make it known, and where they do not agree, they also make it known. An example is found in [Chapter] *HaMevi*, in Tractate *Yom Tov*: R. Yehudah said that Shmuel said: "One may bring wood only from a stacked pile in an enclosure." And we ask: But have we not learned [in a Mishnah]: "If it is in an enclosure, [one may bring] even from scattered [wood]"? This is a refutation of [the statement of] Shmuel! And we answer: Our Mishnah represents [only] an individual opinion; but support for [Shmuel] can be found in a Baraisa. Where we find in our Mishnah a defective passage and we need to remove it, because it contains a

difficulty which cannot be resolved, we say: Remove from here such-and-such. Examples can be found in [Chapter] *Oso Ve'es Bno*, where we say: R. Chiyya bar Abba said that R. Yochanan said: "The 'red heifer' does not belong in our Mishnah. The 'beheaded calf' does not belong in our Mishnah." Thus [because of a difficulty], we removed [a statement] from the Mishnah and not from the Baraisa. Sometimes, even an entire Mishnah is rejected because of [its inconsistency with] logic. An example is that [Mishnah] which we learn in *Taharos*: A flax comb with missing teeth... And we say in [Chapter] *HaCholetz*: R. Yochanan and Reish Lakish both say [about the above Mishnah in *Taharos*]: 'This is not Mishnah, and we do not follow it in practice. Why? Because painstaking scholars [add the conclusion: "This is the ruling of R. Shimon.]"'[108] If we find it necessary to declare that a Mishnah has words missing, we do so. And if we find it necessary to interpret a [Mishnah,] we do so.[109]

In his *Kovetz Shiurim*, R. Elchanan Wasserman specifically cites this passage of Rav Sherira Gaon to demonstrate that certain great Sages understood that Amoraim sometimes argue with Tannaim.[110] Rav Sherira Gaon's listed methods of how Amoraim argue with Tannaim include techniques such as inserting missing words of an apparently deficient text, which indicates that statements that appear facially as interpretative are sometimes argumentative. Such interpretations are inconsistent with the original Tanna's intent and are actually new positions that disagree with the earlier viewpoints. While some of these approaches present other Tannaitic opinions, others, says Rav Sherira Gaon, posit opposing opinions based on the Amoraim's logical analyses.[111]

R. Elchanan Wasserman presumably deduced that Rav Sherira Gaon understood the Amoraim as arguing with Tannaim from the context in which Rav Sherira Gaon presents the listed methods. Rav Sherira Gaon had been discussing various techniques Rebbe utilized to present opinions he preferred so they would be accepted as halachah.[112] Rav Sherira Gaon's introduction of Amoraic techniques at this juncture seems to be to show how the Amoraim voiced their opinions regarding Rebbe's positions, as

108 The bracketed portion is not cited directly in the Aramaic text, but is part of the Talmudic passage cited by Rav Sherira Gaon.

109 *Iggeres Rav Sherira Gaon* 63–65 (Moznaim ed. 1988).

110 *Kovetz Shiurim Bava Basra* 633. A more contemporary example of one who R. Elchanan Wasserman states professed Amoraim occasionally argue with Tannaim is R. Chaim Soloveitchik (ibid).

111 *Iggeres Rav Sherira Gaon* 64.

112 *Ibid,* at 60–62.

suggested by Rav Sherira Gaon's words, "[a]t this point came our Sages, the Amoraim of the Talmud, and explained these things."[113] The methods that Rebbe used to indicate his position on halachah are the "things" they were explaining. The focus is on whether they agreed or disagreed with Rebbe, as further seen in Rav Sherira Gaon's first example when he states, "Where they agree with Rebbe that the halachah follows an individual opinion, they make it known, and where they do not agree, they also make it known."[114] Rav Sherira Gaon then proceeds to list how Amoraim presented opinions or texts that differ from Rebbe's Mishnah, presumably to indicate where they disagree with Rebbe. Including methods such as amending texts in the list of ways Amoraim signal dissent indicates that Rav Sherira Gaon saw these methods as argumentative, not interpretive.[115]

Meiri's writings support R. Elchanan Wasserman's understanding that Rav Sherira Gaon's approach maintains that certain Amoraic statements that appear to be elucidations of earlier opinions are sometimes dissenting opinions. Meiri writes:

> ועם כל זה נתמעטו הלבבות מרוב הצרות והוצרכו האחרונים לחבר אחריו דרך ביאור והרחבה ולפעמים דרך סתירה ותיקון כשהיו חכמי הדור מסכימים לכך ממה שרואים בו קושיא חזקה כמ״ש במסכת יום טוב אמר שמואל אין מביאים עצים . . . וכן אמרו סמי מכאן כך וכך וכן אמרו פרת חטאת אינה משנה וכן בפרק החולץ על משנת מסרק . . . האמורה בטהרות מסכת כלים רבי יוחנן ור״ל דאמרי תרוייהו אינה משנה וכן תמיד איתמר חיסורי מחסרא וכן לאו תרוצי מתרצת לה תריץ ואימא הכי וכן הרבה כיוצא באלו כמו שנעשה היום אף אנחנו מראשינו וזקנינו הקודמים ועוברים לפנינו ועל ראשינו וכמ״ש דרך כלל מקום הניחו לנו כו׳ כלומר שאין השלמות נמצא בנבראים ואפי׳ במובחרים שבהם עד שלא יהיו אחרונים רשאין לחלוק עמהם בקצת דברים.
>
> And with all this, people's hearts dwindled due to the many difficulties and the latter [Amoraim] needed to author an interpretive and elucidative [text] and sometimes amend and make corrections when

---

113 *Ibid*, at 63.

114 Ibid.

115 Some attribute a similar position to the *Gra*. *Pe'as HaShulchan* maintains that the *Gra* believed all cases of *chisurei mechserah*, suggestions that a text is missing components, are not attempts to recreate a corrupted text, but are amendments of Amoraim who were presenting alternative Tannaitic opinions that disagree with the earlier Sages's positions (*Pe'as HaShulchan Hakdamah* s.v. *v'hayah yodea*). Unlike Rav Sherira Gaon, though, the *Gra* seems to limit the Amoraim's argument to presentations of alternative Tannaitic approaches.

> the Sages of that generation agreed [it was necessary] as a result of a strong question. For example, in Tractate *Yom Tov*, Shmuel says, "One may bring wood… " And similarly, they said, "Remove such and such [passages]." And similarly they stated, "The red heifer is not a Mishnah." And similarly, in Chapter *HaCholetz* on the Mishnah discussing a comb… that is stated in *Taharos* Tractate *Keilim*, R. Yochanan and Reish Lakish both state, "It is not a Mishnah." And similarly, they frequently state, "The text is missing words." And similarly [they state], "Haven't you [already] interpreted [the passage, why don't you] interpret it in this fashion?" And many similar examples [may be found that are] comparable to the contemporary practice that even we engage in, [which is] based on our leaders and elders who have risen and passed before [both] us and our [current] leaders. And as is [commonly] written as a general rule, "[The earlier generations] left for us a path, etc.;" meaning, since perfection is not found among those [people] who were created, even among the choicest of them, to the point that later [generations] are not permitted to disagree with them in a few matters.[116]

Seeing Meiri's words juxtaposed next to the passage of Rav Sherira Gaon makes clear that Meiri was paraphrasing Rav Sherira Gaon's opinion. Meiri makes the exact points of Rav Sherira Gaon in the same order and references the same Talmudic passages in the same order. In other words, Meiri essentially presented a Hebrew translation of Rav Sherira Gaon's Aramaic passage. The last line of Meiri indicates how far he believed Rav Sherira Gaon's position should be taken, "since perfection is not found among those [people] who were created, even among the choicest of them, to the point that later [generations] are not permitted to disagree with them in a few matters."[117] This conclusion emphasizes that scholars may disagree with any earlier generation because nobody, not even the finest, is perfect. This particular paragraph provides examples of how Amoraim elucidated and amended the Tannaitic texts, with examples dating as far back as the first generation of Amoraim. Meiri's conclusion seemingly clarifies that these methods sometimes represent disagreement with those Tannaitic texts. The methods include apparently interpretive methods, which indicates that some apparently interpretive Amoraic statements may be dissenting opinions according to Meiri.

---

116 *Beis HeBechirah, Pesichah LeMaseches Avos* s.v. *v'im kol zeh.*

117 Ibid.

ii. The *Bavli* and *Yerushalmi*

If one assumes that the latter scholars of the Talmud sometimes intended to argue with earlier Sages instead of elucidating their opinions, as described in the works of Rav Sherira Gaon, Meiri and, more recently, R. Elchanan Wasserman, then there may be value in reading each Talmudic statement independently to see if it may represent an additional position on the subject matter even though these additional positions are given no consideration for the purposes of halachic determination.[118] Employing this technique within the context of head coverings compels one to read the Mishnah and the statement of the disciples of R. Yishmael independently. To resolve the apparent contradiction of the Mishnah, which states that women must cover their heads based on Judaic practice, and the statement of the disciples of R. Yishmael that contends head covering is required by Mosaic practice as derived from the biblical case of the suspected adulteress; the Talmud proffers that the Mishnah applies to women who only don the more revealing and less dignified *kaltah*, but the disciples of R. Yishmael's statement applies to women who have no head covering whatsoever.[119] However, neither the Mishnah nor the disciples of R. Yishmael mentioned these specifics. Taken as independent statements, each appears to refer to women who have their heads completely uncovered. Without the need to synthesize these statements, one would therefore assume that the Mishnah disputes the disciples of R. Yishmael's derivation from the biblical case of the adulteress. The Mishnah contends that women who uncover their heads are violating Judaic practice,[120] but

---

118 Although such additional positions are not useful for determining halachah, there may be value in analyzing them. R. Yosef Dov Soloveitchik asserted that studying the approaches of *Beis Shammai* is a biblical component of Torah study even though these approaches have no bearing on halachic decisions. R. Herschel Schachter, *Ginas Egoz* 186 n.3 (2007).

119 *Kesubos* 72a–72b.

120 Therefore, there is no proof regarding whether unmarried women are required to cover their heads even if the Mishnah in *Kesubos* is not an exception and means that previously unwed brides had their heads fully uncovered. The Mishnah maintains that head covering is Judaic practice and based on societal norms. Full exposure of one's head in conformance with customary practice is not a violation of Judaic practice (see *Igros Moshe* 1, *Even HaEzer* 57 [asserting that this leniency may even apply when the customary practice resulted not from a proactively instituted custom, but from people refraining from covering their heads to avoid financial loss]). Since brides customarily expose their heads, the bride's behavior conforms to customary practice. Hence, even if unmarried women regularly covered their hair, the exception at the wedding would not represent a

the disciples of R. Yishmael believe they violate Mosaic practice. The *Yerushalmi*'s omission of the statement of the disciples of R. Yishmael and their biblical analysis indicates that it agrees with the Mishnah; women who uncover their heads only violate Judaic practice.[121]

Similarly, there is no need to assume that different levels of head coverings are required in different locations once the need to synthesize the Mishnah and the statement of the disciples of R. Yishmael is abandoned. The *Bavli* only created those levels to uphold R. Yochanan's statement while distinguishing the settings in which the Mishnah's and the statement of the disciples of R. Yishmael's rules applied.[122] Neither the Mishnah nor the disciples of R. Yishmael set limitations on their respective rulings, so the same head covering should be sufficient in any location.

iii. *Kaltah vs. Kilatah*

R. Yochanan addresses what type of head covering is sufficient because neither the Mishnah nor the disciples of R. Yishmael mention what head covering satisfies Judaic or Mosaic practice. The *Bavli* records a statement of R. Yochanan that a *kaltah* suffices,[123] and the *Yerushalmi* has R. Chiyyah citing R. Yochanan as permitting a kerchief.[124] While it is possible a *kaltah* is a kerchief and these are two recordings of the same statement, it is more likely that a *kaltah* is either a scrivener's error for *kilatah* or *kliatah*, meaning braids, or is a derivative from the same root thereof. Tractate *Sotah* derived from the same verse the disciples of R. Yishmael analyzed that the priest unbraids the suspected adulteress's hair.[125] It therefore seems likely that *kaltah* means braiding, a common hairstyle specifically referenced in the context of the Talmud's source for head covering. This seems

---

suspension of an obligation because the bride would be adhering to custom and Judaic practice only mandates conformance with custom.

121 *Yerushalmi Kesubos* 44b.

122 The *Yerushalmi* does not explicitly reconcile the rulings of the Mishnah and R. Yishmael, but maintains that different settings mandate differing requirements. (*Ibid.*). The *Yerushalmi* does not state why there are different requirements in these settings, so it is possible that these customs resulted from Babylonian influence. The *Yerushalmi* is simply recording common practice. It seems unlikely that the *Yerushalmi* holds head covering is required under Mosaic practice in any setting because it never cites any sources indicating such. Thus, the *Yerushalmi* maintains that head covering is mandated by Judaic practice, but there are varying customary levels, which may have resulted from Babylonian influence.

123 *Kesubos* 72b.

124 *Yerushalmi Kesubos* 44b.

125 *Sotah* 7a, 8a.

especially true if the alternative is understanding *kaltah* as a basket, which does not seem to be commonly found as a head covering in Talmudic passages. As previously mentioned, synthesizing this passage with Rav Sheshes's statement recorded in Tractate *Berachos* that uncovered hair is immodest and with the passage in Tractate *Nedarim* discussing the term "black-headedness" either compelled an early scrivener to change the word *kilatah* or *kliatah* to *kaltah* or forced interpreters to translate *kaltah* as something other than braids."[126] Disregarding the need to synthesize these passages permits one to take the more likely approach that the word was originally *kilatah* or *kliatah* or a derivative of the same root thereof.

R. Yochanan's statement recorded in the *Bavli* suggests that braiding one's hair is a sufficient head covering,[127] and R. Yochanan's statement recorded in the *Yerushalmi* contends that a woman may cover her head with a kerchief.[128] Although these statements contain different information, there is no indication that there is disagreement as to R. Yochanan's position. It is possible that R. Yochanan made both statements and holds that either braiding one's hair or using a kerchief is a sufficient head covering for a woman.

iv. Land of Israel vs. Babylonia

The statements of the Mishnah, the disciples of R. Yishmael and R. Yochanan may all be read under the assumption that braiding one's hair is a sufficient head covering. It is only once the statement of Rav Sheshes and the passage regarding black-headedness were accepted that the Talmud is compelled to embrace the position that a woman must use some material to cover her head. The reason for this apparent change may be a result of changes that occurred during that time period and between the locations where the aforementioned scholars lived.

Talmudic scholars in the Land of Israel lived under Roman rule; whereas, Babylonian Talmudic scholars lived under Persian control. The Mishnah, the disciples of R. Yishmael and R. Yochanan all lived in the Land of Israel, which was the center of Talmudic influence at the time. It was during R. Yochanan's lifetime that Rav, a contemporary of R.

---

126 See *Berachos* 24a (citing Rav Sheshes that a woman's uncovered hair is immodest); *Nedarim* 30b (insinuating that women covered their heads with material). Undoubtedly, the synthesizing of the Mishnah and the statement of the disciples of R. Yishmael, which resulted in a rabbinic mandate for women to cover their heads with material in public domains, also contributed to this understanding.

127 *Kesubos* 72b.

128 *Yerushalmi Kesubos* 44b.

Yochanan, moved from the Land of Israel to Babylonia and Babylonian influence became more pronounced.[129] Roman culture mandated that women of stature would braid, bun, lavishly style or cover their hair before entering the public.[130] Wearing disheveled hair or hair that was not styled or braided was considered undignified, something typical of prostitutes.[131] Conversely, Persian culture had more emphasis on hair covering, especially for dignified women.[132] There is evidence that many Persian women of that era may have covered their heads with garments similar to chadors, which are now common in many Middle Eastern countries.[133]

A new understanding emerges when recognizing that cultural influences that societies use to define dignity and modesty may have impacted the Talmudic statements.[134] The Mishnah, the disciples of R. Yishmael and R. Yochanan presumably felt that either a hair covering or braiding was sufficient to cover one's head because that was considered modest and dignified.[135] However, the Babylonian Rav Sheshes found exposed hair, even if braided, to be immodest. Discussions subsequent to R.

---

129 See *Iggeres Rav Sherira Gaon* 93–96 (Moznaim ed. 1988) (describing the history and development of the Talmud and noting that although initially somewhat hesitant, R. Yochanan acknowledged the prowess of Talmudic scholars in Babylonia); cf. *Bava Kamma* 117b (citing a story in which R. Yochanan acknowledges the prowess of Talmudic scholars in Babylonia in a limited fashion).

130 Victoria Sherrow, *Encyclopedia of Hair: A Cultural History* (Greenwood Publishing Group, 2006), pp. 334–35.

131 Ibid.

132 Sahar Amer, *What Is Veiling?* (University of North Carolina Press, 2014), pp. 5–6; *Encyclopaedia Iranica*, https://iranicaonline.org/articles/cador-a-loose-female-garment-covering-the-body-sometimes-also-the-face (last visited Sept. 11, 2020).

133 *Encyclopaedia Iranica*, https://iranicaonline.org/articles/cador-a-loose-female-garment-covering-the-body-sometimes-also-the-face (last visited Sept. 11, 2020).

134 This is not only true if one embraces the approach of R. Messas that even Mosaic practice may evolve (see *Otzar HaMichtavim* 3:1884 [stating that Mosaic practice evolves]). Even if Mosaic practice cannot evolve, it is likely that Talmudic Sages imposed stricter regulations when the general populace had more stringent standards.

135 It should be stressed that it is clear that even women living under Roman rule sometimes wore head coverings. Sherrow, *supra* note 130, at 334–35. The assertion here is that such covering was not considered obligatory; women had the alternative of braiding their hair. References to women's head coverings can be found in many Tannaitic statements (e.g., *Sotah* 8b; *Kesubos* 64b; *Zavim* 4:1; *Keilim* 24:16; *Tosefta Keilim Bava Basra* 6:5; *Shabbos* 57b).

Yochanan, which were influenced by Babylonian thought, project the Persian influence into the text and mandate covering as a requirement. The synthesizing of the Talmudic statements and Babylonian influence led to the scrivener's error of the word *kaltah* instead of *kliatah* or the inability to translate the word as a derivative of the same root of *kliatah*.[136]

v. Supporting Passages

The passages from Tractate *Sotah* support the supposition that braiding is a sufficient covering. The passages in *Sotah* are Tannaitic statements and focus on the priest unbraiding the suspected adulteress's hair as an act of shaming her.[137] These statements were formulated in the Land of Israel by earlier Talmudic scholars who lived under Roman rule and prior to Babylonian influence.

Rav's homiletic passage about On b. Peles supports the assertion that earlier Talmudic scholars, those living under Roman rule and prior to Babylonian influence, believed that braiding was a sufficient head covering. Rav states that On's wife unbraided her hair to disperse the group of rebels who were coming to collect On to join Korach's rebellion against Moshe because they would not want to remain in the presence of an immodestly clad woman.[138] Rav specifically states that she unbraided her hair,[139] which indicates that it was only braided until that point, not covered. It was only after being unbraided that it was deemed immodest,

---

136 The lack of extant variant texts is not surprising even if there was a scrivener's error considering the synthesizing of texts and subsequent scrivener's error would have occurred in the early Amoraic period and may have been an intentional amendment. If intentionally amended, the Talmud may have chosen to state a *kaltah* is sufficient instead of braids when referencing the biblical minimum, similar to the *Yerushalmi*, because women no longer wore braids in public as a result of Judaic practice and societal norms.

137 *Sotah* 7a, 8a.

138 *Sanhedrin* 109b–110a; *Bamidbar Rabbah* 18:20; *Tanchuma, Korach* 10; *Midrash HaGadol, Bamidbar* 16:1. In a very creative fashion, *Yedei Moshe* suggests that On's wife chose this particular method to save her husband because certain Talmudic passages indicate that one may be rewarded with progeny who serve as High Priest due to modest behavior. *Yedei Moshe, Korach* 18:20 s.v. *chochmos nashim.* Korach's dispute centered on the designation of Aharon as High Priest, so On's wife refused to act in an exceptionally modest fashion to counter any possibility of On's offspring achieving the status of High Priest (ibid). On's wife was trying to persuade him to recuse himself from the fight because there was no longer any possibility of personal gain (ibid).

139 See *supra* note 100 (discussing the term "demolish" and its connection to unbraiding).

which indicates that braiding is sufficient. More than one source records Rav's statement stating that On's wife unbraided her hair,[140] which indicates that the reference to unbraiding is not a scrivener's error or a matter of dispute. Although Rav eventually moved to Babylonia, he studied under R. Yehudah HaNasi, "Rebbe" in the Land of Israel,[141] so Rebbe's influence naturally permeates Rav's understanding of Torah and Talmud. Thus, the Persian influence is lacking when Rav expresses the indecency of a woman's head as being unbraided instead of uncovered.

The passage from Tractate *Nedarim* describing "black-headed" people is not problematic. Although the Talmud interprets the Mishnah to mean that women covered their heads,[142] this is a projection of latter Talmudic scholars living in Babylonia. The Mishnah only states that one who vows not to benefit from "black-headed" people may not benefit from men, regardless of age or whether they have hair.[143] Women are excluded from the term "black-headed" because the Talmud assumes black-headed refers to people who are sometimes black-headed and sometimes are not and women always cover their heads.[144] A plausible alternative is that the term "black-headed" excludes women because they are always black-headed since their hair is always black. Jewish law prohibits men from plucking their white hair because that is considered a practice commonly performed by women.[145] Thus, only men are people who sometimes have black-heads and sometimes do not because women's hair would typically be black; whereas, men's heads are normally black when young, but either bald or white when old.

The Tannaitic passage describing Kimchis's exceptional modesty is not problematic for the assertion that Jewish women in Tannaitic times were not obligated to cover their heads. Kimchis maintained that she merited seven of her children becoming High Priests because the walls of her home never saw her braids,[146] which indicates that her braids were covered. However, the intent of the story is to paint Kimchis in an exceptional light. Kimchis attributes her extraordinary reward for acting in an exceptional manner. The Sages's respond to Kimchis that many others

---

140 *Sanhedrin* 109b–110b; *Bamidbar Rabbah* 18:20; *Tanchuma, Korach* 10; *Midrash HaGadol, Bamidbar* 16:1.

141 *Iggeres Rav Sherira Gaon* 91–94 (Moznaim ed. 1988).

142 *Nedarim* 30b.

143 Ibid.

144 Ibid.

145 *Shabbos* 94b.

146 *Yoma* 47a.

acted accordingly and did not receive similar reward,[147] which indicates that while Kimchis's actions were not unique, they were also not customary practice. *Meiri* explicitly mentions that Kimchis's response was an exaggeration meant to convey extreme modesty,[148] which similarly indicates that her actions were atypical. Because the Talmud specifically uses Kimchis as an exception, nothing in her story can be used to discern the rule.

Tannaitic passages that state that women need to cover their heads are not problematic for the assertion that in the Tannaitic period only braiding was necessary. There are a few Tannaitic statements that use the terminology "cover" when referring to the requirement a woman has regarding her head.[149] These should not be taken to exclude braiding as permissible. Covering is a term used to indicate one's head is covered, not necessarily that the hair is covered. In Roman parlance, it would be acceptable to state that one's braids covered her head. Paul of Tarsus explicitly states that a woman's hair is a covering for her head.[150] Paul finds long hair unacceptable for men because they are to have their heads uncovered, but women should have long hair because they need to cover their heads.[151] While Paul's opinion is not accepted in Jewish thought, his vernacular reflects that of the time and culture. Thus, when Tannaitic texts mandate covering, they may include braiding. In fact, *Sifri*, which is one of the Tannaitic sources that uses the terminology "cover" in the context of women's hair covering, indicates that women had the option of covering or braiding.[152] *Sifri* recognizes the verse that states that Tamar placed ash and her hand on her head after being violated by Amnon as an allusion to the requirement to cover one's head, which indicates an actual cover must be used; but *Sifri* proceeds to discuss how the priest unbraids the suspected adulteress's hair, which indicates braiding is sufficient.[153] Thus, it seems *Sifri* approves of either covering or braiding as a means for women to cover their heads.

The fact that all statements explicitly referring to hair covering emanate only after Babylonian influence became prevalent supports the assertion that braiding was sufficient prior to then. All earlier statements either imply that hair was exposed or are at best ambiguous. Although the lack of passages is not a definitive proof, it lends credence to the overall assertion.

---

147 Ibid.

148 *Beis HaBechirah, Yoma* 47 s.v. *shivah.*

149 E.g., *Sifri, Naso* 11.

150 1 Cor. 11:15.

151 Ibid, 11:4–7.

152 *Sifri, Naso* 11.

153 Ibid.

III. Conclusion

The topic of women's head coverings in Talmudic thought is rich, complex and has been the subject of dispute throughout the ages. Accordingly, many diverse opinions and practices regarding this topic have emerged over the course of Jewish history. Disagreement exists among rabbinic authorities as to whether the primary Talmudic sources, the *Bavli* and *Yerushalmi*, are in agreement regarding the application of this obligation, resulting in varying practices. On one hand, throughout history many pious women covered their heads even when not obligated; conversely, unmarried women do not cover their heads in contemporary times even though some may maintain that this was not always the case. Some opinions maintain that certain hairstyles are obligatory for unmarried women; others have no such requirement. Whether the obligation as a whole may evolve based on the cultural norms of the Jewish community is hotly disputed and, based on some early approaches, it is possible that changes in practice may have taken place even during Talmudic times. It is only by understanding the primary sources as a backdrop that one can understand how these approaches developed over time.

Yom Tov Sheini: Reasons and Relevance

By: STEWART RUBIN

The Halakhic Cost of *Yom Tov Sheini*

Almost half of the thirteen Jewish holidays in which work is abjured are mandated by the rabbinical decree or the custom[1] of *Yom Tov Sheini Shel Galuyot* ("YTSG," second day of holiday in diaspora)—not a direct Torah prohibition. YTSG was originally mandated because there was uncertainty as to the proper day of Yom Tov. That uncertainty has not existed since the calendar became fixed.[2] Nevertheless, the Sages ruled that the observance of YTSG continue. On first impression, the high halakhic *and* economic cost of YTSG appear to tower over the theological benefit. Consider how far *Ḥazal* went to establish *Yom Tov Sheini*:

- The positive command of putting on *tefillin* is abrogated on the last day of each holiday.
- *Kiddush*, *hadlakat neirot*, *Yom Tov Amidah,*[3] and the blessings for *matzah and maror* on Pesaḥ are recited on both days despite the prohibition of reciting a blessing in vain.

---

1 There are several positions on the nature of the obligation to observe YTSG. Rambam, as explained by the *Leḥem Mishneh* (Rav Avraham Khiyya de Boton (c. 1560–c. 1605) says that it is a *minhag* and when *Ḥazal* mandated to observe that *minhag*, it became a rabbinic enactment (*Hilkhot Talmud Torah* 6:14). Rabbeinu Tam said that it is a *minhag*, and there are certain *minhagim* over which blessings are made. (*Tosafot*, *Sukkah* 44b, *d"h Kan*). Rabbeinu Zeraḥiah ben Yitzḥak ha-Levi Gerondi (the Rezah or Baal ha-Maor, 1115–c. 1186) states that it is a great *minhag* that has spread throughout the entire diaspora (*Pesaḥim*, *Dappei ha-Rif* 17a). Rabbeinu Nissim (Ran) (*Sukkah* 22a, *d"h Itmar*) and Ritva (*Rosh ha-Shanah* 18a) maintain that the primary reason is that it is a *takanah* because of *kilkul*. The author of *Sefer ha-Ḥinukh* states that it is because of *minhag*, see *Mitzvah* 301, *d"h Yesh Omrim*. The *Ḥatam Sofer* believes that it is a *minhag* which the nation accepted upon itself as an oath (*Responsa Ḥatam Sofer, Oraḥ Ḥayyim* 145).

2 Established by Hillel II, great-grandson of Rebbi Yehudah ha-Nasi (Rabbeinu ha-Kadosh), and his court in the year 359 CE.

3 *Shabbat* 23a.

Stewart Rubin, a real estate professional, enjoys studying the intersection of anthropology, archaeology, history, philosophy, sociology, and religion. This is his third published *Ḥakirah* article.

- The *She-heḥiyanu* blessing, meant for the first night of the holiday, is recited at the end of *Kiddush* on both nights. One of those blessings is technically not correct.
- *Havdalah* is not recited after the first day of Yom Tov,[4] so that one does not come to disrespect YTSG.
- With few exceptions, there is little difference between the first and second day of Yom Tov.[5]

Background

Originally the new month was proclaimed on the basis of eyewitness testimony before *Beit Din*[6] in Jerusalem. By sanctifying the new month, *Beit Din* also set the day of Pesaḥ and Sukkot[7]. To spread the news, fire signals were lit on a series of mountaintops until the information reached the diaspora.[8] This practice was ended in response to sabotage by those who were antagonistic to the Jewish religion.[9] The fire signal system was then replaced with a messenger system. Wherever the messengers reached, people would celebrate the holiday for one day. Places that were too far for the messengers to reach within ten days, observed two days because of uncertainty (*safek*),[10] since they did not know which day *Beit Din* had sanctified as the beginning of the month and by extension, which day is Yom Tov.

When Jewish communities began to observe Rosh Ḥodesh and the *Yamim Tovim* based on fixed calendrical calculations, the observance of *Yom Tov Sheini* was no longer based on uncertainty. Nevertheless, the Sages from Eretz Yisrael (EY) sent to the Jews of the diaspora that they should continue to keep the custom of their forefathers because of the fear of *kilkul,* meaning that an anti-Jewish government may issue a decree against Torah study that would lead to the loss of the knowledge

---

4 Rashba and *Ḥidushei ha-Meiri, Beitzah* 4b; Ritva, *Sukkah* 47a.

5 Exceptions pertaining to the second day include certain laws associated with *kevurah* and *ḥoleh sh'en bo sakanah*. Another difference would be *milah she-lo bi-zmano* (circumcision that was postponed past the eighth day) on YTSG according to Rambam, Semag, Kol Bo, Shakh, and the Bartenura. Rosh and others don't hold that way.

6 *Rosh ha-Shanah* 21b–25b.

7 It was unknown when the new moon would be witnessed and if a given month would have 29 days or 30 days and which day would be Rosh Ḥodesh.

8 *Rosh ha-Shanah*, chapter 2, mishnah 2–4.

9 Ibid.

10 Rambam, *Sefer Zemanim, Hilkhot Kiddush ha-Ḥodesh* 3:11.

necessary to do the calendrical calculations. That persecution would cause them to make a mistake in designating the correct day of the holidays. This is detailed in *Beitzah* 4b. The Gemara asks:

> **And now that we know the determination of the** first day of the new **month, what is the reason** that **we observe two** Festival **days** in the Diaspora? **Because they sent** a warning **from there,** from Eretz Yisrael: Although now there is a fixed calendar and there is no uncertainty, **be careful to** observe **the custom of your fathers** that **you received,** because **at times the monarchy** will **issue decrees** of persecution restricting Torah study and the fixed calendar may be forgotten. **And** the people will **come to** have their proper observance of the Festivals **be disrupted** again.[11]

A simple understanding of the Talmudic text seems to indicate that the reason to continue observing two days[12] is as a precaution in case *Bnei Yisrael* are unable to calculate when the new month begins, and as a corollary, know when Yom Tov is.[13] Read more broadly, an additional reason may be keeping up a custom or a rabbinic decree that cannot be abrogated even though it is no longer relevant.[14]

---

11 *Beitzah* 4b, Koren translation.

12 Earlier, the Talmud records a dispute between Rav and Rav Asi which appears to center around whether the two days of Yom Tov are one *kedushah* or two separate *kedushos*. (All agree that the two days of Rosh ha-Shanah are one *kedushah*). The halakhah as recorded in *Mishneh Torah* (*Hilkhot Yom Tov* 1:24) is that it is two *kedushos* and the *Shulḥan Arukh* (*OḤ* 513:5) follows Rav with the implication that it is two separate *kedushos*. However, Rabbeinu Eliezer ben Natan of Mainz (Ra'avan, 1090–1170) stated in accordance with the Sages of Mainz that YTSG is not due to uncertainty (after calendar established) but because of *minhag*, adding that both days are now "one holiness" (*Sefer Ra'avan* 419, *Beitzah* 4a and b).

13 This reason is brought down by the *Mishnah Berurah*: "Even though we are expert in calculating the month based on the calculations that are in our hands. Nonetheless, the *Ḥakhamim* were concerned that maybe because of the many persecutions and wanderings from place to place in exile the calculation will be forgotten and they will come to render a short month (*ḥaser*, a month of 29 days) as a full month (*malei*, a month of 30 days), or a full month out of a short month and end up eating *ḥametz* on Pesaḥ. They therefore left it that outside EY they would conduct the calendar as in earlier days (i.e., two days outside EY)" (*Mishnah Berurah*, *OḤ* 495.1).

14 Rambam, *Hilkhot Mamrim* 2:2–3 states that a *beit din*'s *gezeirah* or *takanah* cannot be upended by a subsequent *beit din* unless the second *beit din* is greater in wisdom and numbers. Rambam further states that this applies even if the original reason no longer applies. *Kesef Mishneh* (Rav Yosef Karo) asks why the previously noted

Several questions arise. First, why in the face of great halakhic and economic cost did *Ḥazal* insist on the continuation of YTSG when there was a time when it could have been abrogated?[15] Second, why is there concern for *kilkul* in the diaspora and not in Roman-occupied Eretz Yisrael? Third, from a historical perspective, how often did the Jewish situation deteriorate to the point that they no longer could know the proper day for Pesah or Sukkot? Also, why is this unlikely scenario of *kilkul* or the "*minhag* of our fathers" a sufficient reason to increase the amount of

---

text in *Beitzah* 4b does not simply state that the previous decree of YTSG cannot be eradicated—even if the original reason is no longer true—because there is no *beit din* of greater wisdom and numbers to upend it? Why was it necessary for the Sages of EY to specifically direct the diaspora to continue the practice? *Kesef Mishneh* answers that perhaps the initial *takanah* was predicated on the premise that should they be able to determine based on calendrical considerations, the original decree would no longer apply and accordingly it was necessary for the Sages of EY to message the diaspora that it should continue.

15 See *Kesef Mishneh* on Rambam, *Hilkhot Mamrim* 2:2–3. A further analysis of why at times decrees are upended because the original decree no longer applies is beyond the scope of this paper. However, there are times decrees are rescinded if their original reason is no longer in effect if there is counter-pressure from an abrogated *mitzvah* (in this case that may apply to *tefillin* and proper *berakhot*). Examples of decrees that were changed because their original reason no longer applies include the prohibition of drinking *mayim giluyim* (revealed water), clapping and dancing on Shabbat and Yom Tov, *Kesuvot Bnin Dikhrin*, and *mayim aḥaronim* according to *Tosafot*. *Mayim Giluyim* in a container is forbidden for consumption due to the danger of snake venom getting into the water. However, in the times and lands in which the *Ba'alei Tosafot* lived, snakes were not commonly found in residential areas and so they ruled that this halakhah no longer applies (*Tosafot, Avodah Zarah* 35a, *d"h Khada*; *Tosafot, Beitzah* 6a, *d"h Vi-haidna*; *Tosafot, Yoma* 77b, *d"h Mishum*). That was not the opinion of Rambam who maintained the restriction (*Mishneh Torah, Hilkhot Rotze'aḥ u-Shmirat Nefesh* 11:14). Clapping and dancing on Shabbos and Yom Tov were proscribed because it could lead to fixing musical instruments. However, *Tosafot* say it is permitted now because average people were not experts in the art of fixing musical instruments and don't fix them (see *Beitzah* 30a, *Tosafot, d"h Tinan Ein Mi-Tapḥim*). Rama is lenient like *Tosafot*, see *Shulḥan Arukh, Oraḥ Ḥayyim* 339:3; see also *Arukh ha-Shulḥan, Oraḥ Hayyim* 339.7–9 who is lenient for another reason, and the view of the *Mishnah Berurah* which is somewhat more stringent. Regarding *Kesuvot Bnin Dikhrin*, see *Ketubbot* 52b *Tosafot Rid, d"h Amar* R. *Yoḥanan,* as to why this no longer applied. The view of *Tosafot* regarding *mayim aḥaronim* is that it is no longer customary either because salt from Sedom is not used or because they did not dip their fingers into salt at the end of the meal (*Eruvin* 17b, *Tosafot d"h mayim aḥaronim* and *Ḥullin* 105b, *Tosafot d"h mayim aḥaronim*). Rosh, Tur, and others disagree.

labor-forbidden Jewish holidays by 86 percent? Fourth, why would not the concept of *safek berakhot de-rabbanan le-hakel* (if in doubt regarding the necessity of making a rabbinically mandated blessing, leniency is mandated)[16] apply to not make rabbinically mandated blessings on the second day?

The question of why *Ḥazal* went so far to strengthen and maintain *Yom Tov Sheini* increases by a level of magnitude when considering the holiday of Shavuot. Since Shavuot takes place fifty days from the second day of Pesaḥ, it would have been known when Shavuot was regardless of when Rosh Ḥodesh Sivan took place. Despite that equation, *Ḥazal* wanted uniformity and instituted the second day of Shavuot in order to buttress the other *Yom Tov Sheinis*.[17] (More on the special status of *Yom Tov Sheini* of Shavuot later). *Ḥazal* went even further. They decreed two days Yom Tov for Pesaḥ in places that the messengers who went out in Nisan could reach, but the messengers who went out in Tishrei could not reach.[18] The Sages decreed that two days must be observed in Nisan as a rabbinic decree due to Tishrei, for if they observe Pesaḥ for only one day, they will come to observe Sukkot for one day as well.[19] So, in this scenario the two extra days of Pesaḥ and the extra day of Shavuot are observed to protect the second days of Sukkot and Shemini Atzeret.

The practice is further complicated by the fact that there is no second day for Yom Kippur. If there was truly a concern that the next day may be Yom Kippur, with all its severity and holiness, why would there not be a second day of Yom Kippur? Further, why is there no double counting for *sefirah?* After all, in the *Musaf Amidah* on all days of Sukkot, two days' worth of *korbanot* are mentioned, due to *safek*.

In addition to the halakhic cost, there is the economic cost. Six additional days must be taken off from work. Those who run small businesses lose six days of income. This is especially burdensome in Tishrei as it follows the three days of Rosh ha-Shanah and Yom Kippur. Some find it theologically challenging to observe *Yom Tov Sheini*.

Some Fundamentals

To answer the aforementioned questions and concerns, it is important to note that there are many reasons for rabbinic enactments beyond the primary stated purpose.

---

16 *Shulḥan Arukh, Oraḥ Hayyim* 209:3.

17 Ritva, *Rosh ha-Shanah* 18a, *d"h Al Elul Mipnei Rosh ha-Shanah*.

18 The messengers did not travel on Rosh ha-Shanah or Yom Kippur, and therefore they could travel three days further in Nisan than in Tishrei.

19 *Rosh ha-Shanah* 21a, Rambam, *Hilkhot Kiddush ha-Ḥodesh* 3:12.

King Shlomo stated 1,005 reasons for rabbinic legislations as detailed in *Eruvin* 21b.

> Rav Hamnuna said: What is the meaning of that which is written: "And he spoke three thousand proverbs, and his poems were a thousand and five" (1 Kings 5:12)? This teaches that Solomon pronounced three thousand proverbs for each and every word of the Torah, and one thousand and five reasons for each and every word of the Scribes.[20]

This concept is noted by Rav Hai Gaon (939–1038)[21] who maintains that the real reason or "secret" behind many of the enactments of the *Neviim* is often not known. Rav Eliyahu of Vilna (Vilna Gaon or HaGra, 1720-1797) states that there are many reasons for a rabbinic enactment aside from the primary stated one.[22] Accordingly, it follows that YTSG has a much larger and wider meaning beyond its primary stated purpose.

The Origins of *Yom Tov Sheini*

To expound on the concept of Rav Hamnuna and to more comprehensively understand the deep reasons behind *Yom Tov Sheini*, one must explore its earliest origins. Rav Hai Gaon noted that Rav Saadiah Gaon (882/892–942) stated:

> There is no doubt that initially Hashem commanded his servant Moshe and he told Israel that in the land it will be one day and outside of the land two days. And so it was always, just as Hashem said to Moshe that in the land it will be one day and outside of the land two days. And our master, Rav Saadiah Gaon, said in his responsa to the men of Kabas that it is a decree from the days of the early *Neviim* and so the early *Neviim* led Israel from the beginning of the exile that they observe *Yamim Tovim* outside of Israel two days and Yom Kippur one day.[23]

Rav Hai Gaon continues and states that,

---

20 *Eruvin* 21b, Koren translation.

21 *Otzar ha-Geonim, Masekhet Yom Tov,* 3-9, referencing *daf* 4b.

22 As quoted by R. Meir Simḥah ha-Kohen of Dvinsk in *Meshekh Ḥokhmah*, Volume *Shemot*, p. 76, Rabbi Y. Copperman, Jerusalem College for Women 1974.

23 *Otzar ha-Geonim, Masekhet Yom Tov,* 3-9, referencing *daf* 4b.

> His own view is that *Yom Tov Sheini* outside of Eretz Yisrael began in the days of the *Neviim,*[24] and perhaps even in the days of Yehoshua bin Nun.

He further explains the wording of the Talmud *Beitzah* 4b "**be careful to** observe **the custom of your fathers** that **you received**." Why not just state that "because **at times the monarchy** (an anti-Jewish government) will **issue decrees** of persecution restricting Torah study and the fixed calendar may be forgotten"? Rav Hai Gaon maintains that it is a decree (*gezeirah*) from the days of the first *Neviim* and so the *Neviim* led Israel. Interestingly, in the Gemara it does not say who made this *gezeirah* because the *Neviim* commanded Israel to do it and that is what Yeḥezkel did and what Daniel did and not only that, but Hashem commanded them to do it.[25]

Rav Hai Gaon added that since it was the *Neviim* who decreed this and the exact reason for their decree is not known, it is also not known for certain that the reason for the decree doesn't apply anymore. In any event, the decree cannot be abrogated without a *beit din* that is greater in number and in wisdom (than the *beit din* of the *Neviim*). So, in addition to the Gra maintaining that there are many reasons for these rabbinic decrees and Rav Hai Gaon stating that the reason the *Neviim* made this decree is not known, perhaps one can speculate that there were reasons beyond *safek* and *kilkul.*

Accordingly, the Talmud warns that you should "be careful to keep the customs of your forefathers," as the custom of keeping two days of Yom Tov in the diaspora is not just about satisfying a doubt, but about adhering to an enactment instituted by the *Neviim.* The key takeaway is that there may be a reason for observing *Yom Tov Sheini* other than *kilkul* or *safek.* We can conclude from the words of Rav Saadiah Gaon and Rav Hai Gaon that there was a very early dictum mandating two days of Yom Tov for those outside Eretz Yisrael.

Eretz Yisrael or Ten-Day Journey

Rav Yekhiel Mikhel Tukachinsky (1874–1955) maintains that the words of the Geonim resonate and he used it to explain the view of Rabbeinu Yom Tov ben Avraham Asevilli (Ritva, c. 1260–1320), that YTSG is predicated on whether the area is inside or outside the borders of EY and not based on whether or not it is a ten-day journey from *Beit Din.*

---

24 Rav Hai Gaon's view was that Rav Saadiah Gaon only said this in response to criticism from those who were not followers of the Rabbis and YTSG was instituted due to uncertainty and the practice dates to the time of the *Neviim.*

25 *Otzar ha-Geonim, Masekhet Yom Tov,* 3–9, referencing *daf* 4b.

The YTSG nomenclature would imply that it applies in EY and not outside of it. But if the reason is because of *safek,* then any place outside of a ten-day journey from Jerusalem would be subject to it even in EY. Conversely, a place outside EY within a ten-day journey of Jerusalem would have one day. In fact, that is the view of Rambam.[26] Rambam maintains that only places within a ten-day journey of Jerusalem, which could have been reached by the messengers and which were actually inhabited during that time, may observe one day of Yom Tov. Communities farther than a ten-day journey from Jerusalem, or new communities which did not exist in the time of the Talmud, must observe two days.

Ritva[27] disagrees and explains that when the Rabbis established the obligation to observe *Yom Tov Sheini,* they decided that since most of the communities in the diaspora generally observed two days, outside of Israel, all communities should observe two days. Similarly, since most communities within the Land of Israel observed one day, all communities within Israel should observe one day.

Rav Yekhiel Mikhel Tukachinsky, quoting Ritva, maintains that YTSG never applied inside EY. He believes the words of the Geonim shown to him by Chief Rabbi Ben-Tzion Meir Ḥai Uziel (1880–1953) reinforce the point and that "the decree (for YTSG) was in place from the days of the *Neviim.*"[28] He further notes that initially he was hesitant to accept the Geonic documents that were discovered in a *genizah* and thought that they may even conflict with the Talmud, and also because they were not mentioned by the *poskim.* But after studying the newly found documents he realized they were authentic, and that they give a clear perspective on the whole concept of YTSG.[29]

The View of Netziv

Rav Naftali Tzvi Yehudah Berlin, the Netziv (1817–1893), agrees with and expounds upon Rav Saadiah Gaon's view. Netziv interprets the verse in *Vayikra* 22:31, which is presented before the laws of the *Yamim Tovim* and which on the surface seems very general and even superfluous. Netziv interprets the verse "And you should observe my commands and do them I am Hashem your G-d" as referring to taking special care to make sure the *Yamim Tovim* are in the proper time. He sees this as a mandate for two days Yom Tov from the Torah. Netziv believes that,

---

26 *Mishneh Torah, Hilkhot Kiddush ha-Ḥodesh* 5:4 and 11–12.

27 Ritva, *Rosh ha-Shanah* 18a, *Sukkah* 43a.

28 Rav Yekhiel Michel Tukachinsky, *Sefer Eretz Yisrael,* p, 40.

29 Ibid.

> this is what Rav Hai Gaon referred to when he said that "concerning *Yom Tov Sheini Shel Galuyot* that the *Neviim* commanded Israel to do it and that is what Yeḥezkel and Daniel did. And Rav Hai Gaon concluded with this language: and maybe from the days of Yehoshua bin Nun all those who left and stayed outside of the Land of Israel conducted themselves that way. And all this is certainly hinted to in the Torah because based on the depth of the law we should not have to be concerned if Adar near Nisan (even Adar II) was 30 or Elul because most of the time they are *ḥaser*. And know that there is no *safek* because we do not do *safeka d-yoma* by *sefirat ha-omer* even though it is also from the Torah outside of the Land of Israel according to the *shittah* of the Rif[30] and Rambam, and because of the (possible) denigration of the Yom Tov of Atzeret [Shavuot][31] they did not establish it. And similarly in the month of Tishrei we do not do it by Yom Kippur because it is not possible to observe two days. But we establish it based on most years that it is 29 days (*ḥaser*). In any event, with the actual holidays they acted as though there was doubt (*noheg safek*) because of added watchfulness. And this is the word of the *Shiltot* "and make a fence around the Torah" and in this was included this warning here.[32]

Netziv concludes that the above verse: "And you should observe my commands and do them I am Hashem your G-d" teaches us that *Bnei Yisrael* should be careful with the times of Yom Tov and observe two days to make sure outside EY the date of Tom Tov is correct. Netziv wrote that the instruction to protect Yom Tov by creating YTSG is mandated by the Torah.

---

30 Rabbeinu Yitzḥak ben Yaakov Alfasi ha-Cohen (1013–1103).

31 The Ba'al ha-Maor states that first there is no need to be stringent when it comes to *sefirah* since in his view it is not that paramount because it is only a remembrance for what was done in the time of the *Beit ha-Mikdash*. He then goes on to state that if each day was counted twice, it would lead to a count on the first day of Shavuot and that would lead to a denigration of the first day of Shavuot which is from the Torah or *di-oraita* (see *Ba'al ha-Maor*, *Pesaḥim* in *Dappei ha-Rif* 28a). Rav Avraham Dov-Ber Kahana Shapiro (1870–1943) maintains that the reason to not double count *sefirah* is that counting must be definitive and cannot be in doubt (see *Dvar Avraham*, Vol. 1, *Siman* 34).

32 *Harḥev Davar*, *Vayikra* 22:31.

No Second Day of Yom Kippur and What It Reveals

Why are two days of Yom Kippur not observed? If there is truly a concern that the next day may be Yom Kippur with all its elevated severity, holiness, and prominence above other holidays, why would there not be a second day of Yom Kippur? The Talmud (*Rosh ha-Shanah* 21a) states that in fact Rava observed two days Yom Kippur.[33] However, the majority opinion is not to do so. Observance of a second day of Yom Kippur is considered a danger (JT *Ḥalah* 2b). Likewise, Rav Naḥman considers a second day of fasting to be life threatening (later in *Rosh ha-Shanah* 21a). Ritva[34] explains that two days of Yom Kippur are not observed especially after the establishment of the fixed calendar, as this would constitute an enactment that the majority of the community could not fulfill. *Arukh ha-Shulḥan* (*Oraḥ Ḥayyim* 624:8) enumerates three reasons why two days of Yom Kippur are not observed: 1) We are now expert with calendrical calculations; 2) From the time of Ezra, Elul was never found to be full (*m-uber*, 30 days)[35]; and 3) It is a danger (see JT *Ḥalah* first chapter [2b]).

Based on the fact that since the days of Ezra there was never really a *safek* regarding the dates of Tishrei holidays, why is there YTSG for Sukkot and Shemini Atzeret?

Second Day Shavuot and What It Reveals

As noted earlier, even though there is no chance the proper day of Shavuot would not be known, *Ḥazal* instituted a second day to not differentiate between holidays[36] as explained by the Ritva and Rambam.[37]

Rav Menaḥem Azariah da Fano (Rema mi-Pano, 1548–1620),[38] points out that the Torah was given specifically in the diaspora and on the 51st day of the *omer*[39] and specifically on the day that Moshe Rabbeinu added, and that it hints to *Yom Tov Sheini Shel Galuyot*.[40] As Hashem Himself agreed to celebrate this day He revealed that He was giving power to the

---

33 According to Rabbeinu Ḥananel (965–1055), Rava observed it as a stringency.

34 Ritva, *Rosh ha-Shanah* 18a, *d"h Al Elul Mipnei Rosh ha-Shanah*.

35 It is always 29 days, so the proper day for Yom Kippur is known.

36 Ritva, *Rosh ha-Shanah* 18a.

37 *Mishneh Torah, Hilkhot Kiddush ha-Ḥodesh* 3:12.

38 Rema mi-Pano was a student of Rav Moshe Cordovero (Ramak, 1522–1570).

39 I.e., on *Yom Tov Sheini*.

40 Rema mi-Pano, *Ma'amar Ḥikur ha-Din*, Vol. 2, Chap. 15, quoted by *Magen Avraham, Oraḥ Ḥayyim* 494. See also Responsa of *Ḥasam Sofer, Oraḥ Ḥayyim* 145.

Ḥakhamim to sanctify a weekday. The words of Rema Mi-Pano appear to state that YTSG is from the Torah or at least hinted to in the Torah.

Rav Yosef Dov Soloveitchik (Beit ha-Levi, 1820–1892) offers a profound and very interesting take on the second day Shavuot stemming from the acts of Moshe Rabbeinu.[41]

> And this can solve the question of the Magen Avraham[42] how we can say that Shavuot is the time of the giving of the Torah for we conclude that on the seventh of the month the Torah was given... and that Moshe Rabbeinu added a day on his own for he expounded that today is like tomorrow as it says in *Masekhet Shabbat*[43] and Hashem agreed with him as the *Shekhinah* did not descend until the morrow. And we find this is the gift that the Torah was given and like it was expounded (*darshened*) it was... that the Torah was given on the sixth and accepted on the seventh...[44]

He goes on to say the sixth day for the Written Torah and the seventh day for the Oral Torah. That the Torah was given as a gift on the sixth day of Sivan and was accepted on the seventh day of Sivan and this explains what is meant by *Matan Torateinu* (the giving of our Torah) and not *Matan Torah. Torateinu* means our Torah, the Oral Law and the *derashot* (expounding on the Torah) is called in the name of Israel (i.e., is actualized by Bnei Yisrael).

What an amazing Oral Torah statement. Moshe Rabbeinu added the seventh day—an additional day—representing the Oral Torah and it would lead to believing that YTSG of Shavuot is on a higher level than the other *Yom Tov Sheinis*. In fact, Ḥatam Sofer maintains that the second day of Shavuot should be treated more stringently than other second days of Yom Tov (except Rosh ha-Shanah[45]). For the other holidays, the second day of Yom Tov was established based on a doubt, but the second day of Shavuot was established as a certainty.[46]

---

41 *Shabbat* 87a.

42 *Magen Avraham, Oraḥ Ḥayyim* 494.

43 *Shabbat* 87a.

44 *Beit ha-Levi* on the Torah, *Parashat Yitro, d"h Ha-Kol Modim.*

45 For the fundamental reason behind two days Rosh ha-Shanah, see *Beitzah* 5b.

46 As noted earlier, it was always known which day would be Shavuot by counting from Pesaḥ.

Mystical Reasons: Two Days Needed to Absorb Holiday Holiness Outside Eretz Yisrael

The concept that there are other reasons for rabbinic enactments aside from the stated ones is noted by Rav Hamnuna in *Eruvin* 21b and was postulated by Rav Hai Gaon and the Vilna Gaon. In addition, the concept that not all the reasons for rabbinic enactments are known dovetails with mystical reasons cited by *Tzemaḥ Tzedek* in name of Ramak and also by Ḥakham Yosef Ḥayyim (the Ben Ish Ḥai, 1835–1909). In the world of mysticism and Kabbalah, there are references to the importance of Eretz Yisrael and why YTSG is required outside of it. Rav Moshe Cordovero (Ramak, 1522–1570) is quoted by *Tzemaḥ Tzedek* (Rav Menachem Mendel Schneersohn, the third Lubavitcher Rebbe, 1789–1866), in explaining that since holiness is more revealed in Eretz Yisrael, the *Yamim Tovim* can be revealed and received there in one day. However, those in the diaspora require two days to absorb the spirituality of Yom Tov.

In a similar vein, Ben Ish Ḥai, in *Ben Yehoyada* on Talmud, states that,

> By way of the holiness of EY there is strength to complete the *tikkun* on one day which is not the case outside EY where there are two days Yom Tov. We find that the concept (*inyan*) of *tikkun* of the *tefillot* and the *mitzvot* of EY are double and therefore also for the *inyan* of acquiring the Torah they are double because one of us (in Eretz Yisrael) is more like two of them (outside of Eretz Yisrael) (this refers to greatness in Torah learning that is expanded by virtue of the holiness of the land that enhances spiritual connection and ability). And we learn this from Rav Yirmiyah … and we find that a *Ḥakham* outside of EY if he ascends to EY he will become wiser and ascend in wisdom four-fold compared to what he was outside EY. And he believes that there is a *remez* from *Devarim* 3:25.[47]

Perhaps one can point to these mystical reasons to explain why there are two days Sukkot and Pesaḥ, but only one day Yom Kippur outside EY. The spiritual power of Yom Kippur allows all to absorb the import of the holiday in one day even outside EY.

Meshekh Ḥokhmah

Rav Meir Simḥah of Dvinsk (1843-1926) in *Meshekh Ḥokhmah* (*Parashat Bo* 12:1) details yet another reason for the observance of YTSG.

---

47 *Ben Yehoyada, Ketubot* 75a, Senlake edition, 2019, based on *Ben Yehoyada,* Jerusalem, 1897.

> With this, we derive a wondrous explanation of the statement of the Gemara, "Be careful with the *minhag* of your forefathers; [ignoring it] may cause damage." For there is a difficulty. Areas outside EY and areas within EY should have the same ruling. The reasoning should apply to EY as well [A decree imposed by a wicked kingdom could lead to *kilkula*]! We must therefore say that [outside EY] they already practiced [a second day Yom Tov]. It is thus as if the reason behind the decree never ceased. It is not applicable here to say that a greater *beit din*—in knowledge and size—is needed. This does not appear to be the main reason. Rather, we have a tradition from Rabbeinu ha-Gra that even when *Ḥazal* explained their reasoning, they nevertheless left hidden in the recesses of their hearts, thousands of reasons, great and many…

He goes on to mention that there will be a time period in the future when there is a Beit Din in EY that has the ability to sanctify the new month by sight while there are *Bnei Yisroel* living in the diaspora. He brings proof from Rambam's *Perush ha-Mishnah* in the beginning of *Masekhet Sanhedrin and JT Ma'aser Sheini*, chapter *Kerem Rivai* (chapter 5, halakha 2). He then continues

> If so, there will be a *beit din* in the Land of Israel, and we will be obligated to sanctify the new lunar month based on sight. If the moon is not visible on the thirtieth day, even if according to our calculation it would be proper to establish the new month on that day, nevertheless that month would need to be *m-uber*, lengthened by a day. They will then be forced in the diaspora to make two days [Yom Tov]. Therefore, they decreed that it is applicable now too. This is similar to what R. Yoḥanan ben Zakai (first century) decreed to forbid *Yom Hanef, gezeirah,* perhaps *yibaneh Beit ha-Mikdash.*[48] This is the proper reason to observe in our time, a second day Yom Tov in the diaspora…

The Possibility of *Kilkul* was Very Real to *Ḥazal*

It is not hard to understand why *Ḥazal* told Jews of the diaspora to observe a second day because of *kilkul*. The possibility of *kilkul* was very real to *Ḥazal*. The Hadrianic persecutions which criminalized teaching of Torah, circumcision, rabbinical ordination and Sabbath observance were not that far in the past. In addition, before the Maccabean revolt, the Seleucid King Antiochus IV Epiphanes decreed against the Jews observing three *mitzvot*: Rosh Ḥodesh, Shabbat and circumcision (*Megillat Antiyokhus*

48 See Mishnah Tractate *Rosh Ha-Shanah,* chapter 4, mishnah 3.

7:11). The aforementioned persecution took place in Eretz Yisrael. Perhaps one can speculate that, in addition to a very real concern for *kilkul*, *Ḥazal* were also sending a message about the religious prominence of Eretz Yisrael. Conceivably that can be an additional reason why, despite a history of persecution and the possibility of *kilkul*, YTSG was not established in Roman-occupied EY.[49]

Berakhot Bestow Gravitas on YTSG

The concept of *safek berakhot rabbanan le-hakel*, that when there is uncertainty regarding rabbinically mandated blessings[50] one is to be lenient (i.e., not recite the blessings), would seem to apply and mandate that holiday-related *berakhot* on YTSG not be recited. Nevertheless, they are. *Ḥazal* can mandate *berakhot* for *mitzvot di-rabbanan* and even on *minhagim*. A full suite of *berakhot* was mandated for YTSG to lend gravitas to the day. *Ḥazal* were concerned lest the second day be disrespected.[51]

Teleological and Practical Benefits of *Yom Tov Sheini* in Modern Times

Teleology[52] explain things by the purpose they serve rather than their causes. This can apply to certain religious observances and for common secular customs and legal and economic practices. In the spirit of Rav Hamnuna, the Geonim, the Gra, and *Meshekh Ḥokhmah*, that there are many reasons for rabbinic decrees, perhaps one can postulate that there is also a teleological reason for YTSG. Even though the original reason was *safek* and then it became because of *kilkul*, perhaps another reason, especially applicable in the 21st century, is the need to have an added day of connection to Hashem, to family, to community, without the distractions of the contemporary world. Two days can be dedicated to Torah learning, prayer, family and friends with no iPhone, e-mail, Facebook, Twitter or work distractions.

---

49 Ritva on *Rosh ha-Shanah* 18a maintains that the reason is that there was already an existing decree, so it was maintained for that reason. In EY with no existing decree, it was not started ab initio.

50 The only Torah-mandated *berakhot* are grace after meals and possibly *birkhat ha-Torah*.

51 See *Shabbat* 23a and Ritva, *Sukkah* 47a.

52 This is to differentiate from describing YTSG as stemming from hysteresis or the dependence of the state of a system on its history alone. Hysteresis can be found in physics, chemistry, engineering, biology, and economics.

Conclusion

There are sources and reasons for the observance of YTSG beyond *safek* and *kilkul.* Rav Saadiah Gaon's view that it was commanded to Moshe Rabbeinu and as detailed by Netziv that it is a mandate from the Torah to ensure the proper date for Yom Tov is fascinating. Rav Hai Gaon's view is that YTSG is an early decree of the *Neviim.* Rema mi-Pano's observation that the Torah was given outside of EY and on the 51st day of the *omer* (on YTSG) and specifically on the day that Moshe Rabbeinu added, is a compelling reference to the Oral Law in general, and YTSG in particular. Similarly, the Beit ha-Levi's explanation of *Matan Torateinu,* that the Torah was given as a gift on the sixth day of Sivan and was accepted on the seventh day of Sivan, the second day of Shavuot, a day that Moshe Rabbeinu added on his own, and that it refers to the Oral Law, is profound. The Har Sinai/ Matan Torah/ Shavuot connection to YTSG resonates as an amazing Oral Law intimation. Mystical/Kabbalistic reasons include that two days are needed to absorb the holiday holiness outside Eretz Yisrael as elucidated by Ramak, Tzemaḥ Tzedek, and the Ben Yehoyada. *Meshekh Ḥokhmah*'s reason is that there will be a need to sanctify the new month by sight during a future time period when there is a Beit Din that has the halakhic ability to do so and those residing outside EY will need to observe two days. The notion that YTSG is a reminder of the religious prominence of EY is a theme that can be extracted from some of the rabbinic YTSG literature. It is also important to highlight the teleological and practical benefits of *Yom Tov Sheini* in the modern world. YTSG offers a connection to Hashem, to family, to community—without the prevailing distractions. Two days can be dedicated to Torah learning, prayer, family, and friends with no technological interferences.

Let Him Bray: The Stormy Correspondence Between Samuel David Luzzatto and Elia Benamozegh

By: DANIEL A. KLEIN

> *True reciprocal tolerance is that which knows how to love and esteem others, while preserving intact the belief in one's own doctrines. Indeed, true fraternal love is not given when one does not loudly proclaim that which one believes to be true. The first right of our fellow beings is to hear the truth from us.*[1]
>
> *Why can't we be friends? Why can't we be friends?*[2]

Nineteenth-century Italy produced two outstanding Jewish religious figures: Samuel David Luzzatto ("Shadal," 1800-1865) and Rabbi Elia Benamozegh (1823-1900). Both were staunch defenders of Jewish tradition, but just as one was from the east (Trieste) and the other from the west (Livorno), it can be said that never the twain did meet. In particular, they took polar opposite positions with regard to the value of the mystical teachings of the Kabbalah. And when they proclaimed their truths to each other in a remarkable exchange of letters, sparks flew.

For some reason, the story of the Shadal-Benamozegh rivalry has not received the attention it deserves, at least outside Italy. Not a word about it appears in Morris B. Margolies's otherwise comprehensive biography

---

1 Elia Benamozegh, *Storia degli Esseni* (Florence: 1865), p. IV.

2 Papa Dee Allen et al., "Why Can't We Be Friends?" From the album of the same name by War (1975).

Daniel A. Klein, an attorney and legal writer, is a graduate of Yeshiva University and New York University School of Law. Translating from the original Hebrew and Italian, he has published English versions of Shadal's interpretations of Genesis (1998, revised 2nd ed. 2019), Exodus (2015), and Leviticus (2021). His articles on Shadal's writings and on aspects of Jewish law—some of them translations from Italian, others the fruit of his own research—have appeared in *Ḥakirah*, *Jewish Bible Quarterly*, and *La Rassegna Mensile di Israel*, and online in *Lehrhaus* and the website of the Jewish Community of Rome.

of Shadal,[3] for example, and their correspondence has not been thoroughly discussed or presented in English until now.[4] A closer look at their exchanges is rewarding, not only for their elegant and acerbic literary style, but also for the windows that they open to the writers' principles and personalities, and for their treatment of key issues that remain relevant to Jewish thought today.

Background

Shadal's great-granduncle, Moses Ḥayyim Luzzatto (Ramḥal, 1707-1747), was an eminent Kabbalist, and Shadal's father Hezekiah (1761-1824), though a carpenter by trade, was also a Kabbalah devotee. At the age of 13, however, Samuel David Luzzatto broke from this family tradition. While reading the collection of Talmudic legends in *Ein Ya'akov*, Shadal noticed indications that although a system of chanting the Bible existed in Talmudic times, the text was not yet marked then with written vowels (*nekudot*) or accents (*te'amim*). This discovery, Shadal later related, became an *idea madre* for him, an idea that gave birth to many others, first and foremost the idea that the Zohar, which frequently mentioned the written *nekudot* and *te'amim*, could not have been written by the authors of the Mishnah and Talmud, as it claimed to be. And if this Kabbalistic masterwork was a forgery, he reasoned, then the Kabbalah as a whole could not stand.[5]

In 1826, Shadal wrote *Vikkuaḥ al Ḥokhmat ha-Kabbalah*, presented in the form of a series of dialogues between two scholars who first meet at a late-night Hoshana Rabbah study session. One scholar defends the antiquity and validity of the Zohar's doctrines, but the other scholar (clearly Shadal's alter ego) offers challenging arguments to the contrary, including the following:

- Although there was indeed a form of secret mysticism during the Talmudic period, it came to be forgotten and had no connection to the Zohar.

---

3 Morris B. Margolies, *Samuel David Luzzatto: Traditionalist Scholar* (New York: Ktav, 1979).

4 A few translated excerpts from some of their letters do appear in Alessandro Guetta, "The Last Debate on Kabbalah in Italian Judaism," in Barbara Garvin, Bernard Cooperman, eds., *The Jews in Italy: Memory and Identity* (University Press of Maryland, 2000), pp. 256-275.

5 Samuel David Luzzatto, *Autobiografia di S. D. Luzzatto* (Padua: 1878), pp. 56, 57.

- The concept of *Sefirot* (Divine emanations) did exist in that earlier period, but it was then understood as having no more than a mathematical significance, as opposed to the much more crucial metaphysical role later given to the *Sefirot* by the Kabbalah.
- The written system of *nekudot* and *te'amim*, introduced by post-Talmudic authorities as a practical means of preserving the proper reading of the received biblical texts, had no mystical significance and could not have been a proper basis for the interpretations that the Zohar purported to derive from it.
- The very fact that the Zohar referred to this post-Talmudic system was proof that the Zohar itself had to be an even later work.
- Kabbalistic mysticism posed a threat to the survival of the true Jewish faith.

Concerned that publicizing these views might undermine the simple faith of the pious, Shadal withheld the *Vikkuaḥ* from publication until 1852. This is one reason why Elia Benamozegh offered no response to it in 1826. The other reason is that in 1826, Benamozegh was only three years old.

Born in Livorno (sometimes known as Leghorn in English) to a family that had emigrated from Fez, Morocco, Benamozegh was precocious and largely self-taught, like Shadal, but unlike his fellow autodidact, he remained attached to the Kabbalism of his youth after a period of doubt (as he noted in a letter to Shadal in August 1863). Benamozegh's first book (*Emek Mafgi'a*, Livorno, 1845) was a refutation of Leone Modena's anti-Kabbalistic work, *Ari Nohem* (written in 1639 but first printed only in 1840). Benamozegh went on to serve as a rabbi and professor of theology at the Collegio Rabbinico of Livorno—a rival institution of the Collegio Rabbinico of Padua, where Shadal taught—and to author several important works, including a Torah commentary, a history of the Essenes, and the posthumously edited *Israël et l'Humanité* (Paris, 1914), discussing universal religion and the roles of and relationships between Judaism, Christianity, and Islam.

Calm Before the Storm

The first preserved communication that we have from Benamozegh to Shadal, written in November 1857, expresses effusive praise for a letter by Shadal that had appeared in the Hebrew-language periodical *Ha-Maggid*. Shadal's letter had argued that although Moses Mendelssohn, who remained faithful to the Torah and Jewish observance, had gained the respect of the non-Jewish public, those who came after him and had cast aside their faith could not now complain that German intellectuals were attacking the Jews. "They do not understand that they [the intellectuals] are writing ill not about the Jews, but about the hypocrites who call themselves Jews, but who are neither Jews nor Christians but disciples of Spinoza" (*Ha-Maggid*, Oct. 9, 1857, pp. 165-166). Benamozegh could not have agreed more. "You were magnificent in that letter," he wrote. "Nestor was no less mighty in weaponry for being mature in judgment and wise in counsel."[6]

In an 1859 letter to a Livornese rabbi, Shadal floated the idea of starting a new Italian Jewish periodical that would be "sincerely *Yehudi*" and would break with the *oltremontani*, those nontraditional Jews who lived "over the mountains," i.e., in Germany. At the same time, Shadal reserved the right to dispute amicably in this periodical with the "mysticists." He suggested Livorno as the place of publication and said that it would be up to the "young people" to take up the idea or let it drop.[7] Naturally, Benamozegh learned of this proposal and reacted enthusiastically to the prospect of collaborating with Shadal. Noting that the proposed journal would have many adversaries, he said, "Therefore, cannons of large caliber will be needed, and your name is already a promise of a brave battalion" (Benamozegh, *Lettere*, p. 19). However, Benamozegh wanted to make it clear that in his own participation in the project, he would express support for the "revealed theology" of the Kabbalah (*Lettere*, p. 16).

Perhaps it was at least in part because of this consideration that Shadal apparently lost interest in the plan by the end of the year, and it never did come to fruition. A letter from Shadal to Benamozegh dated November 3, 1859, closed as follows: "To believe that the Zohar predates Dante is to willfully close one's eyes. Believe me that the Zohar was born with Dante, and that I am your *affezionatissimo* S. D. L." (*Epistolario*, p. 950). In other words, Shadal was insisting that the Zohar, like Italy's greatest poet, was a product of the thirteenth century C.E. These words foreshadow the storm that was brewing between the "most affectionate" Shadal and his younger colleague.

6 Elia Benamozegh, *Lettere dirette a S. D. Luzzatto da Elia Benamozegh* (Livorno: 1890), p. 3. Nestor was a proverbially wise elder statesman in Greek mythology.

7 Letter to Israel Costa, included in the collection of Shadal's letters in Italian, French, and Latin, *Epistolario italiano francese latino* (Padua: 1890), p. 938.

The Clouds Gather

In 1852, Shadal had at last published his *Vikkuaḥ*,[8] having been persuaded that "the evils of the Kabbala's mystic cult outweighed its benefits as a bulwark of piety" (Margolies, *Samuel David Luzzatto*, p. 49). Notwithstanding his profound respect for Shadal, Benamozegh felt compelled to respond. The result finally appeared ten years later: *Ta'am le-Shad* (Livorno, 1862). This book's title was derived from a phrase in Num. 11:8 describing the taste of manna, *ke-ta'am leshad ha-shemen* ("the flavor of soft oiled dough," as per Shadal's translation), but in a play on words, it could be understood as "reasoning in response to S. D." Weighing in at 223 pages, considerably longer than its target, *Ta'am le-Shad* was formatted, like the *Vikkuaḥ*, as a dialogue between two scholars. The gist of Benamozegh's argument is that (1) the Zohar can be shown to be in perfect agreement with the Talmud; (2) the Kabbalah is of ancient origin, notwithstanding the silence of pre-medieval authorities on the subject; and (3) the Kabbalah is a necessary and fundamental doctrine of Judaism. Although Benamozegh promptly sent a copy of his book to Shadal, the latter decided not to respond.

Meanwhile, a debate broke out within the Italian Jewish community as to whether or how to pay the expenses of fundraising emissaries (*Missioni* in Italian) who came to Italy from the land of Israel. Benamozegh wrote a pamphlet, "Le Missioni di Terra Santa" (Livorno, 1863), contending that their activities deserved the continued support of Italian Jewry. Among other things, Benamozegh maintained that such emissaries served as an important line of communication between the Semitic people and the "Japhetic" people of Europe, in keeping with the biblical ideal of Japheth dwelling in the tents of Shem (Gen. 9:27). Then Benamozegh waded into more dangerous waters. He noted that some, including "Professor Luzzatto," had unwisely sought to dig an abyss between the Japhetic Greece and the Semitic Palestine. Such people, he remarked, were "more Orthodox than the Masters of Orthodoxy," i.e., the ancient Rabbis, who spoke of Greek civilization with "sympathy and respect" ("Le Missioni," p. 20).[9]

---

8 Samuel David Luzzatto, *Vikkuaḥ al Ḥokhmat ha-Kabbalah*. Gorizia: 1852. A new edition, edited by Yonatan Bassi, was published in Jerusalem by Carmel in 2013.

9 It is true that Shadal often expressed the view that there was a fundamental difference between Judaism, with its emphasis on compassion and justice, and "Atticism," with its emphasis on the intellect and the self (see, for example, his 1863 article "Atticisme et Judaïsme," *Otzar Neḥmad* 4, pp. 131-132). As for Benamozegh's treatment of the Japheth-Shem relationship, Shadal would have

Again, Shadal made no public response to this provocation, but he gave vent to his feelings in a letter to an unidentified third party.[10] Expressing his preference to refrain from attacking Benamozegh in the open, Shadal said, *Penso lasciarlo ragliare*—"I intend to let him bray."

Unfortunately, word of this pungent remark made its way to Benamozegh's attention. And this is when the storm broke.

Some Words of Explanation

Before proceeding to the correspondence itself, a few preliminary observations are in order. First, even though both Shadal and Benamozegh were fluent Hebrew writers, all of the letters they wrote to each other in the crucial years 1863 and 1864 are in their native Italian,[11] which is undoubtedly the reason why these exchanges have remained relatively unknown to most of the Jewish world. Hence, I thought it would be interesting and instructive to translate these letters into English.

Shadal's letters to Benamozegh are collected in the 1890 *Epistolario italiano francese latino*, while Benamozegh's letters to Shadal appear in the separate volume *Lettere dirette a S. D. Luzzatto da Elia Benamozegh*, also published in 1890. Yoseph Colombo (1897-1975), a Livorno-born rabbi, was the first to splice excerpts of these letters together to form a continuous narrative, which originally appeared in "Il dibattito tra Luzzatto e Benamozegh intorno alla Kabbalà," *La Rassegna Mensile di Israel*, vol. 8, no. 10/12, February-April 1934, pp. 471-497. Colombo published a slightly revised version of this article 32 years later in the same Italian Jewish journal, as part of a symposium marking the hundredth anniversary of Shadal's passing: "La Polemica col Benamozegh," *La Rassegna Mensile di Israel*, vol. 32, no. 9/10, September-October 1966, pp. 179-204. More recently and more briefly, the subject was revisited by one of the leading Italian Jewish scholars of the twenty-first century, Rabbi Gianfranco Di Segni, in an article called "Le polemiche fra rabbini non sono certo una novità" ("Polemics

---

viewed it as based on a mistranslation. His own rendering of Gen. 9:27 was, "May God extend the borders of Japheth, and may He [i.e., God, not Japheth] reside in the tents of Shem...."

10 It has been suggested that this third party may have been Rabbi Israel Costa of Livorno, who was acquainted with both Shadal and Benamozegh, and to whom Shadal had written in 1859 with his proposal for a new Jewish periodical (Yoseph Colombo, "La Polemica col Benamozegh," *La Rassegna Mensile di Israel*, vol. 32, no. 9/10 (Rome: 1966), p. 189).

11 *Iggerot Shadal*, the collection of Luzzatto's Hebrew letters (Przemysl and Cracow, 1882-1894) does include one earlier letter from Shadal to Benamozegh in Hebrew (Nov. 6, 1859, p. 1363), but it deals with an unrelated subject.

between rabbis are certainly nothing new"), which appeared on the website *Kolòt* <http://www.kolot.it/2010/09/16/le-polemiche-fra-rabbini-non-sono-certo-una-novita/>.

In preparing the present article, I made use of all of the above resources. Neither Colombo nor Di Segni nor I present all the letters in their entirety; some editing was called for to omit some extraneous matter and to focus on the most essential arguments (note that Benamozegh's full letter of Sept. 21, 1863, alone runs to 30 printed pages). Where I wanted to insert more of Shadal's writing than Colombo or Di Segni had included, I went back to the *Epistolario* to retrieve the desired material, and in order to expand my coverage of Benamozegh's writing, I collected it from the *Lettere* volume.[12,13]

As the reader will note, the exchanges of these two giants of Italian Jewry are couched in the high, florid literary style of their century, laced with flashes of wit and sarcasm, and oscillating between blunt invective and protestations of respect and friendship. The effect, it might be said, is almost operatic—a Verdi or a Meyerbeer could have set these words to stirring music.

One repeatedly used term in these letters calls for comment: *Mosaismo materiale*. This term, which I have translated literally as "material Mosaism," is hard to define because each writer seems to give it his own spin. Shadal uses it to refer to the simple, "non-mystical" type of Judaism that he reveres, and he alleges that Benamozegh finds it "absurd." Benamozegh, in turn, expresses his full support for *Mosaismo materiale* in the sense of Judaism as traditionally practiced, but he argues that it needs to be complemented and supported by the teachings of the Kabbalah.

And now, let the debate begin.

---

12 The entirety of Benamozegh's letter of Sept. 12, 1863 (*Lettere*, pp. 57-74) can also be accessed via another resource: Benamozegh, Elia "Scritti sparsi," *La Rassegna Mensile di Israel*, vol. 21, no. 7. Rome: 1955, pp. 262-272.

13 While hunting (with ultimate success) for an online version of this rare book, I devised a temporary workaround with the help of one of my friends in high library places. So, I express my thanks to Nachum Zitter, Director of the Reference Department of the National Library of Israel, for providing me with scanned copies of some of the key Benamozegh pages.

Benamozegh to Shadal, Aug. 16, 1863 (*Lettere*, pp. 49-51)

Most esteemed Sir and friend,

...I want to give you now a proof of the great account in which I hold your opinion, and at the same time the honesty of my conduct. It would displease me greatly—disposed as each of us are, I have no doubt, to love and respect the adversary as a man of honor and a friend—if misunderstandings arose that could poison the relations between us that I always wish to keep cordial. Through information that I have reason to believe beyond any suspicion, I know for certain... that you, having had occasion to express yourself in writing concerning my polemic, availed yourself of this precise phrase: *lasciatelo ragliare* ("let him bray").

Samuel D. Luzzatto holds himself in such noble regard, he is so free of mean-spirited passions, he has such fame that none can obscure, that he could not possibly have used such indecencies, for which reason I could surely vouch that you are not their author. It is no less true, however, that they circulate in your name and perhaps have been put into the service of passions or schemes that are quite other than noble. This cannot and will not be. Your name cannot serve as an instrument of denigration, nor do I deserve to be repaid, against your will, with such coin for the respect that I have invariably shown and will show for you. I therefore believe that I have looked after your dignity by giving notice of this matter and submitting a demand upon your honesty for an explicit declaration that would paralyze the effects of a denigration that cloaks itself in your most reputable name....

I will leave off for today, requesting you to answer me and to keep in mind, when you wish to pay me some disagreeable compliment, to at least treat me as a *behemah tehorah* [a kosher animal].

Whether as a shade or as a real man, I will never cease to address myself to you as

Most devoted and affectionate always,
Elia Benamozegh

Shadal to Benamozegh, Aug. __ [no precise date given]**, 1863** (*Epistolario*, pp. 1027-1028)

Most esteemed friend,

I received some time ago the *Ta'am le-Shad*, and I did not write you so as not to enter into useless disputes. I was asked if I intended to respond, and I said no. And so it is. The little life and strength that are left to me[14] I wish to employ in endeavoring to leave to posterity a little more truth and a little less error, and not in fruitless controversies. Let anyone combat me who so desires; let anyone mistreat me at his pleasure; I will not waste my time in defending myself; I would be deflected from my mission, which is to discover new things. As long as there exists one verse in the Holy Scriptures that is not understood exactly, I must not think of defending my writings. Truth and time will defend them.

Besides, I cannot believe that you think you have refuted me. I do not believe that you are blinded. And if you believe it useful to defend mysticism, I will not oppose that.

Recently I saw your pamphlet about the Missionaries, and there I observed a page with libelous insinuations hurled needlessly against me, as if I were a hypocrite.[15] In this case I should have responded. But God made me strong, and I said and wrote in a confidential letter, *Penso lasciarlo ragliare*, never thinking that these words of mine could come to be used as weapons against you.[16] Nor did I intend to attribute to you the nature of the braying quadruped, an animal that has always been held in higher esteem by me than is commonly the case.

"S. D. L.," as you say in your letter, "holds himself in a noble regard, is free of mean-spirited passions, and has such fame that none can obscure"; therefore, upon seeing himself publicly treated as intolerant for lack of orthodoxy, he lets others bray.

The choice of word might have been less indecent if I had said *latrare* ("bark"). Crusca[17] would have offered me examples of barkers that are not dogs, but it gives me no example of brayers that are not donkeys. Still, braying seems to me less odious, less offensive than

---

14 Shadal was 63 and in failing health when he wrote this letter, and in fact he had only two more years to live. A few months previously, he had written to one of his students, "I am exhausted by old age and by melancholy.... Nevertheless, I persevere in my work. I do not wish to lose a solitary day, for who knows how few are the days left me? I must consolidate my work and get it published" (*Epistolario*, p. 1017, quoted in Margolies, *Samuel David Luzzatto*, p. 54).

15 Evidently this is a reference to Benamozegh's comment, in "Le Missioni di Terra Santa," that those including Luzzatto who sought to dig an abyss between Greece and Palestine were "more Orthodox than the Masters of Orthodoxy."

16 In fairness to Shadal, the phrase *Penso lasciarlo ragliare* ("I intend to let him bray"), worded as a private remark, is not the same as the phrase that Benamozegh accused him of using: *lasciatelo ragliare* ("let him bray," in the second person plural imperative, that is, as if Shadal were directly addressing the public at large).

17 This is a reference to the *Vocabolario degli Accademici della Crusca*, the first dictionary of the Italian language (first edition 1612). Shadal may have consulted the fourth edition (1729-1738). The publisher was the Accademia della Crusca, the world's oldest language academy, founded in Florence in 1583 and dedicated to separating the linguistic "wheat" from the corrupt *crusca*, or "bran."

barking. In any case, you do not need me to declare to you that you have never been a donkey in my eyes; rather, I have used the verb *ragliare* by way of simile, just as Crusca has *latrare* as a simile.

And in so doing, it was not you who was the offended party, but the poor donkey. For the donkey's brayings are always sincere, that is, they are the expression of genuine feelings or sensations, such as hunger, love, or the like. To the contrary, the words that were published by you against me in the aforementioned pamphlet express falsities and calumnies, not only against me, but equally against all the ancient masters who expressed an affinity for Greek culture, converting them all into so many apostates, similar to that Elisha [ben Abuyah] of whom it was said that "Greek tunes never ceased from his mouth" [*Ḥagigah* 15b]....

Live in happiness and believe me to be always a friend of the truth, and a friend of all men, but without hope or fear of them.

Your most devoted S. D. L.

Benamozegh to Shadal, Aug. 24, 1863 (*Lettere*, pp. 52-56)

Most esteemed friend,

If I were to act only out of self-love, I should not respond to your letter. Not only is the offense affirmed, but it is reaffirmed and pursued... But underneath your anger, which I believe to be undeserved, I still see the virtues and the selflessness that do you honor, and that is what makes me answer you. The fact that you prefer not to respond to the *Ta'am le-Shad*, not even privately... spares me the displeasure of finding myself once again in opposition to you. It is another thing, however, when you say, "Let anyone mistreat me who so desires." In my refutation, have I perhaps forgotten any of the requisite forms of respect? This I think you cannot say. With regard to believing or not believing that I have refuted you, allow me to say to you that it is not up to me or you to judge, but with this difference: you may sincerely believe that I have not refuted you, while I could not, as you say, believe that I have not refuted you without being a charlatan or a writer in bad faith. I appeal to your good sense. Is it something to be envied nowadays, the defense of certain abandoned principles? Is mystical theology so in vogue that one may be tempted to take up its defense, if a conviction that surpasses all other considerations did not obligate one to do so?... I make allowances for you because you do not know my life, my studies, my past; nor do you know how, after having loved the Kabbalistic books as a young man, I too began to speak ill of them seeing that everyone was doing so, and how it was only further reflections that brought me to believe that Mosaism without that theology was absolutely without basis... In sum, it would be inconceivable that I—having had such a wide scope for lashing out in the Kabbalistic polemic in *Ta'am le-Shad*—would have shown myself respectful in one whole volume but irreverent in four incidental words. That cannot be and is not the case.

Let us not speak of the minute disquisition concerning *latrare, ragliare,* etc. ... this is a type of comparative philology that I have never enjoyed and that I wish you would not enter into. Such weapons do not suit you.... Keep in mind as well that Elisha was not an apostate merely because he was familiar with Greek literature. Three quarters of the ancient and modern sages would be deemed so as well; it was for the reason that you know and that I need not tell you, the author of the *Vikkuaḥ*. As for "Greek tunes," if I am not mistaken, it was you yourself who interpreted this in the sense of erotic poetry or something of that sort. Am I wrong?...

I would like you to see in this letter a proof of my desire to be your friend, no more or less. If you justly speak of not fearing or hoping for anything from anyone, tell me now, why would I, your adversary, show you affection if I did not love you, especially for your studious self-sacrifice? What do I hope for or fear from you? But I would be a liar my whole life if I kept silent whenever I thought you spoke incorrectly....

Say to me something better than "most devoted,"
and believe me to be your most affectionate

Elia Benamozegh

Shadal to Benamozegh, Sept. 8, 1863 (*Epistolario*, pp. 1029-1030)

Most esteemed Sir,

...Your reflections have brought you to believe that Mosaism without that theology is absolutely lacking in basis. Now see whether we can be friends. I have dedicated my life and my entire being to the defense of simple Mosaism, which is and always was understood by all of antiquity, while you aim for nothing less than making it appear absurd and vain. Christianity sought to do the same. But Christianity has produced good outside the Synagogue. To the contrary, the new Kabbalists, new but worse Christians, tend to attack the Synagogue without benefiting any other people. You, in order to be consistent, will take the field with all those accusations that Christianity typically makes against material Mosaism. What does Christianity typically produce, when preached to the Jews? Vacillation in faith in some, faith in Christianity in none. Today Kabbalistic mysticism, preached in your sense, would have the same result.

Is this not a frightful abyss that you are digging between you and me? Are we not two opposite poles? Nevertheless, I do not wish to go to battle against you, for the age is too materialistic to allow the forces of mysticism to gain power against Mosaism, while you yourself, I hope, would never wish to imitate the Christians and make yourself an open adversary of the pure and straightforward material, civil, and political Mosaism. And if you would ever do such a thing, the institutions of Moses would still, even in our times, have valiant apologists, and the very consonance of your objections with those so often repeated by the followers of the Nazarene would be sufficient to render them innocuous to our coreligionists.

Besides, can you believe that you have refuted me?

You yourself say that your work is not finished. Have you said a word against the most evident proofs of the non-antiquity of the Zohar?...

Without wishing to call you a charlatan or a writer in bad faith, I can believe you to be convinced that you have created a pious work defending to the best of your ability a doctrine that you can believe to be salutary and necessary for the correction of the current materialism.

...I am not disgusted with you, nor am I ever disgusted with a person for personal motives. But the principle professed by you, the absurdity of material Mosaism (which I adore and for which I sacrifice myself), does not permit me to declare you (without hypocrisy) a friend....

Polemics with Christianity have never stirred my blood. If someone came to attack me, I would respond, "The swords still exist; they have not yet been turned into plowshares." So no one has come. "But be a good Christian," [I say,] "and let everyone be faithful to their native beliefs." It was in this sense that I often spoke with Monsignor Nardi, when he was a professor here, and we lived for many years in good harmony.[18]

---

18 Monsignor Francesco Nardi (1808-1877) was a Professor of Canon Law at the University of Padua. An obituary described him as "one of the most indefatigable, earnest, and even violent defenders of the cause of the Pope," but it went on to observe that "no difference in political opinions, even the most diametrically opposite, ever interfered with the affection and esteem for those whom he had once reckoned among his old friends" (*Proceedings of the Royal Geographic Society*, London, 1877, pp. 426-427). In an 1839 monograph on the history of embroidery, Nardi acknowledges Shadal's assistance in furnishing biblical references and calls him "an ornament of our city" (*Sull' origine dell' arte del ricamo*, Padua, 1839, p. 19). In 1847, he and Shadal served together on a commission to decipher a supposedly ancient bronze tablet that had been discovered in Sicily (*Epistolario*, pp. 514-515). In an 1850 letter to Nardi (*Epistolario*, p. 585), Shadal takes issue with a point that Nardi made in a book about the "truth of the Catholic religion" (see note 26 below). But seven years later, another letter from Shadal to Nardi opens with the salutation *Chiarissimo professore, amico carissimo* ("Most distinguished professor, dearest friend"), followed by a discussion of Genesis ch. 14 and certain Hebrew and Arabic Dead Sea-related place names (*Epistolario*,

Live in happiness for many, many years, and always believe me to be

Your most devoted
S. D. L.
faithful to the plain truths
unmixed with fables;
friend of peace
even with the mysticists,
even with the Christians.[19]

Benamozegh to Shadal, Sept. 12, 1863 (*Lettere*, pp. 57-74)

Most esteemed Sir and Friend,

...If I am to judge from certain phrases in your letter... it would seem that I am nothing less than a Christianizer, who wishes to deviate from that which all of antiquity understood as the Mosaic faith. But what is this antiquity for which you reserve a privilege? Is it the Mosaic antiquity? And would you call the Mosaic antiquity simple?... But you know very well that simplicity is not a legitimate mark of a true religion, for the truth by its nature is complex, organic, harmonic, nor is Mosaism a simple thing in this sense of simplicity. Material Mosaism, as you call it—does it seem simple to you?... The religious laws, ceremonies, rituals that regulate the relationship between humankind and God and which provide the primary criteria for correctly judging the nature of a religion—do they seem simple to you?... That immense, multiform body of practices and rites, however it may be explained, can it exist together with that meager Deism that wants to attach itself to the majestic Jewish organism, like the head of a dwarf to the body of a giant? Can you deny that even in the Talmudic tradition there is an esoteric knowledge? S. D. L. is too much a person of good faith to try to deny it.... You will say that those mysteries did exist, to be sure, but that they disappeared and were taken over by false ones. But is there anything more unlikely than this? In such a short time? With hardly any interruption or vacancy of position, given that the last of the Amoraim were not far distant from the Geonim?... Then you cannot allege that traditional antiquity consisted of simple Mosaism. Where is this antiquity, then? In R. Hai Gaon, who was a Kabbalist, in Raavad [R. Abraham ben David], in R. Eliezer the teacher of Ramban, in Ramban [Naḥmanides], in Rashba [R.

---

pp. 916-917). Shadal closes this letter with *di Lei devotissimo amico* ("your most devoted friend").

19 In Italian, the last two lines share a rhythm and rhyme: *anche coi misticisti/ anche coi gesucristi.*

Solomon ben Abraham ibn Adret], in [R. Moses] Cordovero, in [R. Joseph] Caro, in Abrabanel, in Rashbatz [R. Simeon ben Zemaḥ Duran], not to speak of a thousand other pureblooded Kabbalists? Will you say that these, too, are Mysticists and Christians? You may say it and think it. As for me, I consider those named—let it not displease you—more authoritative masters of that which is Mosaism than any others, no matter how much learning and fame they may have in the world....

Who are the new Christians who aim to destroy the Synagogue? Who is it who is proclaiming the abolition of the Law as Jesus or his followers did? Certainly not the new Kabbalists, who, to the contrary, are closing off the way to any innovation... and elevating [religious] practice from a mere externality, from an insipid ceremonial... to a necessity of the highest order, to a cosmic, eternal, universal need... If by "Mosaism" you mean only the written law, this type of Mosaism will never suffice to satisfy the religious sentiment, if there is not united with it the dual tradition, that is, the practical (Mishnah-Talmud) and the speculative (Kabbalah). Indeed, the Kabbalah renders Christian propaganda useless and powerless, because it fills the immense void left by material Mosaism.

...Who ever thought or maintained that the Zohar did not contain interpolations, even large and copious ones? Did I not clearly say so in the *Ta'am le-Shad*? Are there not, according to the Talmud, interpolations even in the Pentateuch (*Shemonah Pesukim*),[20] and in the Talmud, the Mishnah, and the Midrashim are there not continuous and well-known interpolations? But why do you want to have two systems of weights and measures concerning the one and the other? And then—and then—if the truth were not impeding me, do you know that I would be capable of conceding to you that the Zohar is false from top to bottom, while nevertheless requiring you to agree that the Kabbalah is ancient? What does the Zohar have to do with the Kabbalah, the bibliographical question with the critical and theological question?... Yes, sir: there are interpolations in the Zohar; what of it? And if you insist—*ve-im takniteni*—I would add, yes sir, the Zohar is false; so what? The Kabbalah existed before it among the Amoraim, Geonim, Rabbanim, and it will exist after it.

At all costs, you do not want to declare yourself a friend to me. And why? Because [you say] I assert the absurdity of material Mosaism. Do you mean to say "practical"? Then guard yourself from believing that I call it absurd, because you would be libeling me. It is precisely because I do not call it absurd that I attribute to it a spirit, its own contemporaneous twin theory, which is the Kabbalah. There once was a

---

20 That is, the final eight verses of the Torah, relating the death of Moses. According to a Tannaitic opinion cited in *Bava Batra* 15a, Joshua wrote these verses.

mysticism that despised practice, and that was the mysticism of the Kabbalist Jesus, who abolished the law—and that of Shabbetai Zevi, another Kabbalist Jesus, who declared himself superior to it, as you know—but this is not mine. Mine is that of Naḥmanides, of those who entered the *Pardes* (except for Elisha),[21] of R. Hai Gaon, the Rashba, the Rashbatz, R. Caro, R. Cordovero, the Ari [R. Isaac Luria], and all that beautiful school of thought that raised up the value of practice. And on the day that I come to imitate the Kabbalist Jesus or Shabbetai Zevi and violate the material Mosaism that I adore as you do and in which I take delight in fulfilling the practical *mitzvot*, I will say as I said fifteen years ago in my first sermon, *tivash yadi ve-ein yemini kahoh tikh'heh*[22].... Perhaps you are dubious about me, seeing that I have neglected the defense of the Written Torah and the Oral Torah, strictly speaking, and have taken a fancy to the Kabbalah, but the reason is clear:

1. Because in my opinion, the Kabbalah contains the principles, the theory of the Written Torah and the Oral Torah, and once the principles are defended, the consequences are validated.

2. Because it is the more mistreated one, and I have a secret inclination toward causes that are unfortunate but true. You may even call me, if you will, an advocate of lost causes. That is my character, enough said. I consider the Kabbalah to be a *met mitzvah she-ein lo koverim* [i.e., an unattended dead body with no one to bury it], whose care takes precedence over all other obligations.

I tell you this because I have been looked upon with similar doubts by others, and to all of them I have replied the same.

Why, then, do you not want to call me a friend? We both believe in God, in the Mosaic revelation; may I say, also in the tradition? For the love of Heaven, do not tell me no. Then what difference remains between us? That you do not believe that the Kabbalah is part of Mosaism, and that I believe it. We are both of good faith, but let us guard ourselves against being intolerant; excuse the term and do not take any offense. Would you not feel capable of being a friend to a Christian, to a Deist, to a Karaite, as long as they were of good faith? I myself feel capable of doing so, and I have had and still have several such friends, whom I have instinctively considered adversaries before getting to

---

21 "The Rabbis taught: Four entered the *Pardes* ['the orchard,' i.e., Heaven]. They were Ben Azzai, Ben Zoma, Aḥer [Elisha ben Abuyah], and Rabbi Akiva... Ben Azzai gazed [at the Divine Presence] and died... Ben Zoma gazed and was harmed [he lost his sanity]... Aḥer cut down the plantings [he became a heretic]. Rabbi Akiva came out safely" (*Ḥagigah* 14b).

22 "May my arm be withered and my right eye utterly darkened"—a paraphrase of Zechariah 11:17.

know them, and afterwards I have valued and loved. If Naḥmanides were alive, would you not throw yourself into his arms, and would you not kiss his hand? Would you tell him, too, that he is not your friend? Let us imagine, then, what you would say to the Rambam [Maimonides], who Aristotelizes Mosaism—and it is he who in fact partly disfigures its fair face. I stop my ears so as not to hear it. Ah, but the holy Naḥmanides did not act this way; great Kabbalist (and Christian?) that he was, he took up against everyone the defense of—who? Of one who, like you, stood at the opposite pole of Kabbalism—of the Rambam. Although old and dying, he went wandering from city to city to save the Rambam from infamy and his books from the flames. And the Christian Benamozegh, he swears to God that he would know how to do as much for S. D. L. if another Philippson tried to stain his reputation,[23] and if the Orthodox defamed him for faults that he does not have. And he would do so more worthily and meritoriously than the crowd of admirers who swear upon his every word and who know how to say nothing but amen. I would add yehei shemeih rabba mevorakh to all (and it is a great deal) that you have well said....

It would be wrong, then, for you to refuse to declare yourself my friend.... I would not care so much if it were a millionaire [who was so refusing], but you, whose abnegation and sincerity I admire, I must care about; and that same ingenuous declaration of not wanting to be my friend—in an age in which *affezionatissimi* and *sviceratissimi* [i.e., insincere declarations of "most affectionate" and "passionately yours"] rain down like roof tiles on one's head—makes me love you all the more. I am like those women who fall ever more deeply in love with one who makes a show of not loving or caring for them. What can one do? Everyone has his own tastes....

Polemics with Christianity do not please you. It is certainly more convenient not to conduct them. But they are necessary for the fate of future humanity. How unfortunate for us if our predecessors in the world had fled from polemics! We would still be at the level of fetishism. You say, "*If* someone came to attack me, I would respond," etc. But when the arena is open and there is publishing and printing, the attack and the defense must be permanent. When there was no printing,

---

23 Ludwig Philippson (1811-1889) was a Reform Jewish journalist and scholar in Germany, founder and editor of the *Allgemeine Zeitung des Judentums*. Benamozegh may be referring to an article in this journal (vol. 21, no. 48, Nov. 23, 1857, pp. 657-659) in which Philippson subjected Shadal to a lengthy and savage attack, saying among other things, "The ridiculous vanity and self-worship of this great Italian *Havdolos-Fabrikant* is known to everyone." Philippson's colorful Hebrew-German epithet, literally "manufacturer of distinctions," has been understood as "philological hairsplitter" (Margolies, *Samuel David Luzzatto*, p. 53).

or when it existed but with the counterweight of the Inquisition, I understand that the Jews would have had to wait for the knock on the doors of the synagogue and be pulled by their pigtails before responding. But today! Certainly tact, moderation, and prudence are necessary, but one must do battle. Otherwise Judaism will be taken away; it is not enough to say that it is divine and therefore immortal, because we are not speaking of Judaism per se; rather, we are speaking of Judaism in the hearts and minds of the people, and that can go away. Truth and virtue, too, are divine and immortal; is that a reason why one should not exert all one's efforts to make people better and more fully educated? Without a doubt this is not the way to live peacefully in the world; rather, it is an obligation that must be fulfilled.

One thing, I cannot deny, has surprised me. Can you really say, "Be a good Christian and let everyone be faithful to their native beliefs"? It must be one of two things: either you said this in order to flee from bother and disturbance—and I can sympathize, but this is not a system to build oneself as a rule—or you said it in good faith, and in that case it is religious indifferentism,[24] for it is as if to say that if all the religions cannot be equally good and true, it follows that they are all equally false. Moreover, would it not be a grave sin to speak this way to a tritheist, a Christian, if it is not for the sake of fleeing from danger? *Ve-lifnei ivver lo titten mikhshol* ["Do not place a stumbling block before the blind"—Lev. 19:14]. What I ask of you is not to live with me in good harmony as you lived with Monsignor Nardi. Let my "nard" send forth to you a different scent: *nirdi natan reiḥo*[25]–not to live with me in that sort of peace in which you are disposed to live with Christians; good politics, no doubt, but not what I would want you to employ with me.[26]

---

24 The term "indifferentism" is used in Catholic teaching to refer to the mistaken belief that no one religion or philosophy is superior to another.

25 "My nard sent forth its fragrance"—Song of Songs 1:12. Nard (*nerd* in Hebrew) is a flowering plant of the honeysuckle family that yields spikenard, a perfume oil.

26 As noted above, however (see footnote 18), Shadal did not shy away from asserting religious disagreement with Nardi on at least one occasion. In a note on p. 239 of Nardi's book *Verità della religione naturale e cristiana cattolica* ("The Truth of the Natural and Christian Catholic Religion," Padua, 1840), Nardi had said that "the idea that God could suffer and die would be opposed to reason, but not that a Person uniting in himself, to be sure in an incomprehensible manner, the divine nature with the human could, like a man, be born, suffer, die, and rise again." In a letter to Nardi dated June 25, 1850 (*Epistolario*, p. 585), Shadal expressed the view that one's "eternal health" cannot depend on "the acceptance of incomprehensible dogmas. God can indeed demand of us the sacrifice of our passions, but never that of our sound reason.... This, reduced to the most basic terms, is the Jewish-Christian question. In a word, a Jew does not find the Note

...I believe that we can still come to an understanding, that we can each make reciprocal concessions, and on the day in which we present ourselves to the world united together, and by dint of good will and love of the truth we combine together the *Vikkuaḥ* and the *Ta'am le-Shad*, then I believe I will hear in the distance a different braying from the one that you heard in my pamphlet—the braying of the donkey of the King Messiah.

...Tomorrow you will hear the shofar and I will hear it. What will that sound say to you? Your material Mosaism, what will it say to you? Surely nothing other than one of the charming but puerile reasons that have been given outside of the Kabbalah, and to hear it with devotion, to give importance to the *teki'ah, shevarim, teru'ah*, will require of you an extraordinary effort of faith. For me, as you know, the matter is quite different. Every note has its importance, just as every atom of material is a mystery, just as every physical object has its place and value in Creation. For me, the Torah is the prototype of the world, it is the world in the mind of God, it is the true incarnate word of the *mitzvot ha-ma'asiyyot.* What does it seem to you? Am I or am I not a devoted friend of material Mosaism? But with a slight difference from you.

And when I hear the shofar tomorrow, I too will say, "Let S. D. L. live many, many happy years; God spare him further suffering so that his mind may be kept serene and strong in the cultivation of sacred literature, and so that if one day he, too, decides to be a Christian like Rabbi Akiva and Naḥmanides, he will be able to direct his potent scholarship to the triumph of the Truth." I too say, "Live many years," but I do not add the restricted complimentary close of "most devoted"; rather, I say, with a love that I pray to God is the same for me as I feel for you, O good and brave Luzzatto, at this moment,

Most lovingly yours,

Elia Benamozegh

Shadal to Benamozegh, Sept. 18, 1863 (*Epistolario*, pp. 1032-1036)

Most esteemed friend,

...I will tell you that the trills of the shofar were (as I believe) commanded by God to put into public notice (at a time when no calendars were printed) the beginning of the year, just as on the tenth day of the year, with the same shofar, the arrival of the Jubilee year was brought into universal awareness. If today such sounds have lost their [original] purpose, they still preserve (as do so many ceremonies) the immense

---

on p. 239 convincing." It is significant that Shadal refused to accept "incomprehensible" ideas from Christianity and Kabbalism alike.

value of reminding us of our ancient political existence, and they revive in us the feeling of nationality, which—without so many small but repeated reminders—perhaps might have become extinct among us, as it did among all the other ancient nations. Those trills excite in me clear ideas, profound sensations, the most edifying reflections. The miracle of our existence animates me, it encourages me to endure in the struggle against Spinoza,[27] against all the supposedly enlightened ones, and to risk everything, whatever may occur, in defense of a cause that has been victorious until now and that will certainly remain victorious.

To me, that horn is the drum of nationality, of the existence of a people that was once a nation and that today lives only in God, and that will cease to exist only when it ceases to believe in God.

I now take in hand the *Mishnat Ḥasidim* of the unfortunate Ricchi,[28] and I search therein for the mysterious value of those trills, and I understand nothing of it. But I suppose that others do understand it, and I equally suppose (for the moment) that there is a real and true interaction between the two worlds, and that true and quite real are all the celestial and more than celestial effects of those trills. Then I ask myself, those who groundlessly call Mosaism "literal," with its precepts that have no motivation other than being *gezerat ha-melekh* ("the King's decree"), do they have anything better? Granted all their mysterious motives for the Mosaic precepts, have they taken one step forward, do they have some more advanced theory than the one which we all know—that is, that "God has commanded that which He desired"?

Fools! They do not know that the ultimate reason for all things is the Divine good pleasure,[29] and that on earth and in Heaven, everything that has happened could have happened in a completely different manner, if the Creator had been otherwise pleased. If our trills electrify and put in motion the most exalted worlds, that happens only through

---

27 Benedict (Baruch) Spinoza was Shadal's particular *bête noire*. See, for example, his commentary to Exod. 15:3: "According to Spinoza, everything that exists in the world is of necessity, and not at all a matter of will; but according to the Jews (from Abraham until today), nothing exists of necessity, and everything is a product of God's will. The faith of Spinoza and the faith of the Hebrews are as distant from each other as east and west, and the opposition of one to the other is total."

28 Immanuel Hai Ricchi (1688-1743) was an Italian rabbi and Kabbalist who was killed by robbers (hence Shadal's description of him as "unfortunate"). *Mishnat Ḥasidim* (Amsterdam, 1727), considered his most important book, is an intricate Kabbalistic work that contains a subdivision devoted to *kavvanot*, or mystical meditations.

29 Italian *beneplacito*. Its French equivalent, *bon plaisir*, appears in a phrase once used by monarchs when signing a law: *Car tel est notre bon plaisir* ("For such is our good pleasure").

the Divine good pleasure; any reason beyond this one does not exist, and cannot exist. And so no matter how many mysteries may be invented, nothing will ever go beyond the *gezerat ha-melekh.*

Besides, the notion that one's execution of the Divine precepts must be accompanied by sublime meditations [*kavvanot*] is never stated in the Law, and the ancient Rabbis disputed as to whether the precepts can be fulfilled only if they are carried out with *kavvanah*. Such *kavvanah* is not that of the mysticists, but is the simple consciousness of executing a Divine precept. And if not even such consciousness was believed to be necessary by some of the great Sages, who would dare to deny the epithet of "Orthodox" to one who cannot agree that the material execution of the Divine precepts is nothing if it is unaccompanied by mysterious *kavvanot*?

Metaphysical delusions are certainly ancient. But our Masters knew of their futility and evil consequences, and they lamented, "Anyone who speculates about four things [it would have been better if he had not come into the world: what is above, what is below, what was before, and what will be after]."[30] Thus they did not profess any doctrine that purported to scrutinize the incomprehensible. They were not so foolish as to ask why the world was created when it was, and not before or after that time, only to respond (see *Etz Ḥayyim, Heikhal* 1, Gate 1, Branch 2)[31] that the present lower world could have existed only after the creation of all the other worlds above it, which came into existence one after the other—without realizing that the Creator, Who was in existence an eternity ago, could have begun His work some millions of centuries previously or subsequently, as He wished, and that the moment in which our world's existence became possible could have been brought forward or backward by some millions of centuries without any why or wherefore, for the eternal and unique Being has no one on whom to depend, and there can be no other why or wherefore than His own good pleasure.

---

30 The citation is from Mishnah *Ḥagigah* 2:1. The *Tiferet Yisrael* commentary explains this statement as a warning against speculation as to what is beyond space and time, since such matters are beyond human understanding, and seeking such knowledge will lead to error and heresy.

31 *Etz Ḥayyim* (1573) is a Kabbalistic work based on a compilation of the teachings of R. Isaac Luria by R. Ḥayyim Vital (1542-1620). "Anyone who enters the complex world of the *Etz Ḥayyim*... will quickly realize that these are texts which have little regard for Scripture and are not founded on what we may call normative rabbinic and/or the early theosophic Kabbalistic tradition." (Magid, Shaul. "From Theosophy to Midrash: Lurianic Exegesis and the Garden of Eden," *AJS Review*, Vol. 22, No. 1. New York: 1997, p. 38).

Most wisely, our Masters gave the label of "one who has no consideration for the honor of his Maker" to such metaphysicians [Mishnah *Ḥagigah* 2:1], who pose absurd questions and resolve them with answers that are even more absurd. Such questions and such answers were not handed down by them to us, because they declared themselves openly opposed to such impertinences. These cannot be traced back to the Mosaic revelation, because they are absurd, and if they could be traced back to that source, they would have been respected by the ancient Masters.

These ancient Sages of ours, who did not permit the Oral Law to be written down—would they ever have dreamed of entrusting to paper, or allowing others to write down, the arcane doctrines that they confided only to their most experienced disciples? Is it possible that Simeon bar Yoḥai could actually have given the order, "Rabbi Abba will write [the secrets of the Torah]"?[32]

If fanaticism allows itself to see here and there in the Zohar a few egregious outliers[33] and to admit to the presence of a few interpolations, the dispassionate observer finds that the book contains not even half a page that could possibly belong to those personages to whom it is attributed.

And if, then, a Kabbalist wanted to renounce the Zohar and keep the Kabbalah, he could absolutely not do so, for his inspired men—Isaac Luria, Joseph Caro, and whoever else there may be—all accepted the Zohar as a work of the Masters whose names it bears, and so they would all be false prophets.

Would that Kabbalist want to renounce even Luria and go back to Naḥmanides? We will talk then.

I cannot examine your lengthy book, which I read with great effort only once. It will suffice for me to let you know that my aversion to Kabbalah does not stem from incredulity or heterodoxy, but is a profound religious sentiment. It will suffice for me to let you know that it would be quite easy for me to rebut the *Ta'am le-Shad*, and that I do not do so in order to avoid wasting time, since mysticism itself is too contrary to the spirit of the age, with its partisans becoming scarcer every day.

If you defend mysticism, I will let you do it; if you speak ill of me, I will let you do it. Can you call for more friendship than this?

You want to be my friend, but at the same time you would like to see me converted. And I evade missionaries. Friend or not, you know

---

32 This is a reference to the *Idra Zuta*, a portion of the Zohar (*Ha'azinu*) describing a gathering of Rabbi Simeon bar Yoḥai's students on the day of his death, at which time it is said that he told Rabbi Abba to write down the secret Torah teachings that he had not previously revealed to them.

33 Italian *farfalloni*, literally "butterflies" and idiomatically "philanderers."

me as an honest man, ready to be of service to you sincerely, more than many professed friends.

I will add, to avoid any misunderstanding, that by "simple and material Mosaism" I mean, for example, sounding the shofar, or hearing it sounded, without engaging in mystical *kavvanot* [meditations], but with the sole *kavvanah* [intention] of fulfilling a Divine precept, which is holy for us for the simple reason that it was imposed upon us by God, and which had its social purposes in the Israelite republic, but which for us, in our dispersion, is a religious ceremony that sanctifies us and brings us closer to God (see *Lezioni di Teologia morale,* §§ 21, 29).[34]

One who defends the *kavvanot* defends doctrines of which not a trace is found in the Mishnah or Talmud; and one who, in so doing, considers himself Orthodox is a fanatic, which can be tolerated. But one who dares to declare heterodox someone who does not think of such things as he does—he is impertinent and insults without any shade of reason our entire antiquity, which never knew anything of *kavvanot,* and in which great and venerable Masters denied even that precepts can be fulfilled only with *kavvanah.*

Having now re-read your letter, I find that I must respond to the objections that you make to my remark, "Be a good Christian."

This is not politics, and it is not indifferentism. I am convinced that Christianity is not a polytheism. Christianity professes one single God, and its first followers suffered martyrdom for not worshipping "the gods."

The mysteries with which it defaces pure monotheism are errors, but it does not thereby cease to be a monotheism. It is a calumny, an iniquity, to declare a person to be a polytheist or a tritheist if that person sincerely wants to be and believes himself to be a monotheist.

Convinced that the world does not have to become Jewish and will not, at some time, have to become circumcised, I want the Christian to live as a good Christian and be faithful to the evangelical morality, and not—in renouncing Christ—to renounce Moses, renounce God, and worship Spinoza.[35]

---

34 This book ("Lessons in Moral Theology"), published by Shadal in Padua, 1862, states in § 21 that the laws relating to the service of God serve the purpose of keeping the idea of God and Providence in our minds, as a means of keeping us honest and virtuous. In § 29, Shadal emphasizes that the ceremonial laws never lose this beneficial effect and thus continue to merit observance, even though many of them were originally intended to distance the Israelites from idolatry.

35 It would seem that later in life, Benamozegh's attitude toward Christianity underwent a change. Consider the following passage from an English translation of *Israël et l'Humanité*, a work edited by Aimé Pallière from Benamozegh's notes after his death: "And now we turn to the followers of the two great messianisms, Christian and Moslem. It is to Christians in particular that we wish to address a

Of God there is very little that we can comprehend, and I am quite tolerant, and you might say indifferent—or, if you like, an indifferentist—regarding theoretical errors when it comes to metaphysics. I would never have condemned or scorned our ancient anthropomorphists, nor would I have condemned Maimonides for his spiritualism; nor do I despise the Kabbalists for their beliefs, but they are my enemies when they insult non-mystical Mosaism, when they vilify the *peshat de-oraita*, the plain meaning of the Torah.

You see that our opinions are more than slightly in discord, and that we will never be able to come to agreement. But if in any case you want me as a friend, I will be one, as I am with so many others, always telling you the truth without a veil and without reticence.

...The Zohar says that Hoshana Rabbah is the *siyuma de-dina* ('the conclusion of judgment'), and yet you would make Shemini Atzeret analogous to Yom Kippur, that is, the Day of Judgment. Is this not making a mockery of the Zohar and your readers?[36] And by putting this argument at the front of your book, is this not as if it said:

Lasciate ogni speranza, voi ch'entrate,
Di trovar qui sode ragioni e belle;
Ma sofismi e menzogne imbelletate,
E falso giorno e notte senza stelle—?[37]

---

frank and respectful word, and God knows that it is with fear in our heart lest our advances be taken for hypocrisy. No! No impartial and reasonable man can fail to recognize and appreciate, as is appropriate, the exalted worth of these two great religions, more especially of Christianity. There is no Jew worthy of the name who does not rejoice in the great transformation wrought by them in a world formerly defiled…As for ourself, we have never had the experience of hearing the Psalms of David on the lips of a priest without feeling such sensations. The reading of certain passages of the Gospels has never left us unresponsive. The simplicity, grandeur, infinite tenderness, which these pages breathe out overwhelms us to the depths of our soul…." (Luria, Maxwell, trans. and ed. *Israel and Humanity*. New York: Paulist Press, 1995, pp. 50–51.)

36 Here Shadal is criticizing the opening section of *Ta'am le-Shad*, in which Benamozegh notes that the two protagonists of Shadal's *Vikkuaḥ* conducted their debate on the night of Hoshana Rabbah. This serves as a point of departure for an extended discussion between Benamozegh's own two protagonists (pp. 2-21) as to the Kabbalistic significance of Hoshana Rabbah and the holiday that immediately follows it, Shemini Atzeret.

37 Here Shadal has borrowed a famous line from Canto III of Dante's *Inferno* and added three more of his own devising. These lines may be translated as follows: "All hope abandon, ye who enter here/ Of finding here firm and fair reasonings/ But only sophisms and painted fallacies/ And false day, and night without stars."

...Live happily and believe me to be
Your sincere friend,
S. D. L.

P.S. You make mention of those who "entered the *Pardes*," as if they were Kabbalists. R. Hai [Gaon] had it by tradition that by means of certain preparations, they came to see the heavenly hosts. Thus, neither they nor he were Kabbalists in the modern sense, but they were all anthropomorphists, professing a material mysticism which is that of the *Shiur Komah*[38] and the *Pirkei Heikhalot*,[39] a doctrine that has fallen into discredit and practically into oblivion after the war waged by Maimonides against every form of *hagshamah* [i.e., belief in the corporeality of God].

The author of the *Kuzari* [Judah ha-Levi] contributed some words and ideas to the Zohar (see Munk, *Gebirol*, p. 277),[40] but he did not know the Kabbalah strictly speaking, for in the *Sefirot* he saw only abstract numerical ideas, never real substances, worlds, emanations, or what have you, like those of the Kabbalists, to which prayers are addressed. Steinschneider (*Mazkir*, p. 59)[41] gives you credit for attempting to show elements of the Kabbalah in the *Kuzari*, and then he adds, "It remains to be asked, however, how much of the *Kuzari* entered into the Kabbalah of the thirteenth century."

Benamozegh to Shadal, Sept. 21, 1863 (*Lettere*, pp. 75-105)

Most esteemed friend,

...You believe that the trills of the shofar were commanded by God to put into public notice, when no calendars were printed, the beginning of the year. Permit a few questions that my meager intellect suggests:

---

38 A Midrashic work purporting to describe the measurements of God's bodily parts. Maimonides claimed that it was a heretical Byzantine-era forgery.

39 Otherwise known as *Heikhalot Rabbati*, a work of uncertain date and authorship, in which Rabbi Ishmael relates how he, with a company of colleagues, learned the secrets of ascending to see "the King in His beauty."

40 That is, Munk, Salomon. *Mélanges de philosophie Juive et Arabe.* Paris: 1857-1859, pp. 277-278. There, Munk asserts that the concept of Israel as the heart of all the nations was adopted by the Zohar from the *Kuzari*. Shadal refers to the book as "Gebirol" because its first part contains excerpts from Solomon ibn Gabirol's *Mekor Ḥayyim* (*Fons Vitae*).

41 Steinschneider, Moritz, ed. *Ha-Mazkir* (*Hebräische Bibliographie*), vol. 5. Berlin: 1862. Founded in 1858, *Ha-Mazkir* was a bibliographical journal of Judaica that enumerated each year's literary publications. Shadal (who is listed as a contributor to the volume in question) is referring to a notice describing Benamozegh's *Ta'am le-Shad.*

1. Was it really necessary for God to reveal Himself in order to unveil this fine idea? Does it not seem to you that it would have been better for the Divine mind to have revealed some kind of signal that was unknown then and only put into practice afterward, since such a thing would have better verified the intervention of the Supreme Intellect?
2. How would the shofar have been more effective than a simple public announcement?
3. Why would practices such as this one have to be observed today, since, as you say, their purpose has ceased? Is it reasonable for people to be chained to inane practices, and—notwithstanding the bright light of civilization and a plethora of more befitting means—be petrified in antiquated and obsolete ways that can have nothing more than a simply archeological value?
4. If they are practiced today for no other reason than to remind us of our political existence, I ask: (1) What is the purpose, then, of all those rules, prescriptions, minute details that regulate the form, time, mode, and instrumentation of those sounds? (2) Are you not afraid that a rabbi who has been indoctrinated in these principles of yours, and who does not believe it precisely necessary to perpetuate the remembrance of bygone times, this empty ceremonial, might put a stop to these practices, among the most incomprehensible and alien of our customs, or at least suppress with a coup d'état all the *dinim* of the shofar and substitute some instrument, some sound, some form in its place?[42] (3) Furthermore, are you not afraid that some Italian or German reformer or deformer, starting out from your own premises, might say, "Better than this horn-blaring, a fine and unctuous sermon speaks to the heart and mind," thus lending authorization to the German Reform, which, it is well to remember, has been motivated by none other than this precise principle, that is—as you say—that this and so many other ceremonies have only a commemorative purpose? (4) And if this is true, what idea do you have of a wise God Who knows no better than to order this amorphous means of proclamation and then—with the progress of the times and human erudition in civil life—not only

---

42 In fact, at one time, many Reform congregations dispensed with the shofar, perceiving it as "primitive sounding, raucous, informal, antiquated, and therefore inherently inappropriate to their religious aesthetics;... many American Reform congregations simply substituted a modern trumpet... while still others relied altogether on the organ's trumpet stop." (Levin, Neil W., liner notes to Herman Berlinski's *Shofar Service* (1999 recording), Milken Archive of Jewish Music, <https://www.milkenarchive.org/music/volumes/view/masterworks-of-prayer/work/shofar-service/>.)

fails to sanction new and more fitting ideas by means of another revelation, but wishes His people to continue living in the temple of a semi-barbaric life of forty centuries ago, and Who permits and indeed wants them to say, "Blessed be You, O Eternal, Who commanded us to hear the sound of the shofar"?...

5. I cannot discern that connection that you see between the sound of the shofar and our nationality. Does national life consist of perpetuating antiquated customs? A nation that has no current life and is reduced to feeding upon memories shows itself to be a nation no longer.
6. Furthermore, our nationality is a noble and sacred thing, no doubt, but nobler and holier is our religion; indeed, the former is no more significant than other nationalities if it does not serve as a means of perpetuating and augmenting the latter. To reduce the revealed precepts to mere national preservatives is to make them lose three quarters of their value; it is to reduce God to the rank of a Lycurgus or a Romulus[43]; it is to fuse religion, which can never die, with our nationality, which can; it is to expose religious truth to all those changes and vicissitudes and perils to which nationality is exposed; it is to say to the Jew, "If you no longer care to live a separate national existence, you no longer have any reason to be observant"; it is to make eternity into a satellite of the present time.
7. Given the above, it cannot be understood why you so strongly condemn Spinoza, the enlightened ones, etc. For Spinoza thought precisely as you do with regard to the ceremonies and their origin and significance—only more logically and coherently than you, he made them human works, for truly there is no need for God to inconvenience Himself to do what you and I would have known to do. Spinoza and the enlightened ones have nothing against our nationality, but they are against our religion; and it is not an effective means of combating rationalism, pantheism, and illuminism to say to their advocates, "God's precepts are nothing but national commemorative institutions and are simply ceremonial."...

As for your declaration, "Fools! They do not know that the ultimate reason for all things is the Divine good pleasure": "Of course," say these fools, but they add, "Such good pleasure is not without great wherefores"; in other words, God's intelligence cannot be separated from His will, and one would truly be a fool if one were to make the

[43] In other words, a flesh-and-blood legislator. Lycurgus (fl. 820 BCE?) was the quasi-legendary lawgiver of Sparta, and Romulus was the legendary founder and first king of Rome.

Divine will into an idea similar to the bon plaisir of the French despots....

What you mean by "metaphysical delusions" I truly cannot say. Metaphysics is one of the primary needs of the human mind, and every time the mind reflects on things that are not physical bodies, that is metaphysics, like it or not. Woe to humanity if it could not occupy itself with metaphysical matters, but only with physical bodies and the relationships among them! Is this the material Judaism that you adore, that is, religious skepticism and obscurantism? You are frank with me; allow me to be so with you....

If, when reading the *Ta'am le-Shad*, all hope is abandoned at the entrance, as you say, then when reading the *Vikkuah*, it is abandoned at the exit....

I have been reading these days, in the *Maggid*, your long and sensible reflections on Mendelssohn and his disciples.[44] You investigate with great sorrow how it was that from such a religious man was derived a school of skeptics, rationalists, and worse; and there passes in review an infinite number of causes that seem not to fully satisfy you, nor, truth be told, can they be satisfying. The true reason was too close to you for you to see it. Remember what I said to you in the pages above, that when it is established as a premise that in Mosaism there is nothing but *peshat*, when one denies absolute reasons for the precepts, independent of times or places, the consequences sooner or later are inevitable. This is what Mendelssohn did, and even if he did so with not quite as much solemnity as you do, certainly his inclinations with respect to sod [that is, esotericism] were not dissimilar to yours. See, now, the consequences. Those political, geographical, social, and moral motives that the *pashtanim* assign to the precepts do not stand up to analysis, to criticism, to human needs, interests, or passions. If one wants to preserve the *mitzvot*, they must be put on a higher plane in which these influences cannot make themselves heard, and this is the plane of the absolute. Otherwise, Mendelssohn and Luzzatto, by sentiment, habit, personal persuasion, and pious and generous heart, will be pious, observant models of moral and religious virtue, but not being able to transmit these felicitous inclinations to those who succeed them, they will sooner or later have disciples who will draw out the consequences of their premises, who will say, "If the purpose of the Sabbath is only rest and a reminder of the creation, would it not be all the same to celebrate it a day later? Must we encounter thousands of sacrifices of interests, separate ourselves from the majority, cut ourselves off from the universal for a difference that amounts to nothing? If one eats matzah for no other reason than the memory of the blessed unleavened dough,

44 See *Ha-Maggid*, Sept. 17, 1863, p. 293; Sept. 24, p. 301.

can we not remember it equally well with a good sermon, without submitting our teeth and stomach to torture for seven days? And above all, are they not ridiculous, those many minute precautions with which that bread is prepared?" I challenge a reasoning mind to stop the mouth of these terrible logicians and nevertheless to stay with the *peshat* exclusively.

The example of Mendelssohn seems to be made especially for you. If you do not pay heed in time, my prediction will be in vain, and you will be the Mendelssohn of our age in Italy and the rest of Europe. This is what you will be in delayed effect, just as you already are now in scholarship, fame, and inclinations. You who love Judaism, who I believe would give his life's blood for it—why would you want to leave within your mind this fatal germ that will bring forth its bitter fruits, perhaps when neither you nor I are in this world any longer to weep for it and remedy it? Do you want to see the advance signs now? Observe on whose side are the reformist aspirations, on your side or mine—that is to say, on the side of those who deny the Kabbalah like you, or of those who continue to accept it, relatively few to be sure (as you rejoice to say, with a joy that makes me shudder), but those who still remain. I would like to serve you in the manner of the squire of Xerxes, who said to him every morning when he awoke, "Sire, remember the Greeks." And I would like to whisper in your ear, "Remember Mendelssohn!"

I know how sterile this polemic of letters would be with anyone else, and I would not waste my time with one who was not capable of everything for the love of the true and the good. But I am writing to Luzzatto, to the man who... [could] make himself a hundred times greater than he is, becoming—as I said many years ago in *L'Univers Israélite*—after Moses, Ezra, and Hillel, the fourth restorer of our religion....

See that I speak to you with my heart on my lips and without reticence. I believe that in so doing, I will merit your friendship all the more....

This letter, which was begun before Yom Kippur, I finish today as Shemini Atzeret has gone. Show yourself more solicitous than I am, and honor me more promptly with your response.

Always most devotedly and affectionately yours,

Benamozegh

Benamozegh to Shadal, Feb. 24, 1864 (*Lettere*, pp. 108-110)

Most esteemed friend,

At this time I do not doubt that you have received the *Vayikra*,[45] the sending of which was delayed by a day. You will find your interpretations cited in many places, sometimes disputed, other times approved and endorsed, always, I believe, with respect, and I regret it wherever I have not shown enough.[46] Here, too, you will find much that can be restated about the Kabbalah, which is our Helen—and as for which one of us is Menelaus and which one is Paris, I will leave the choice to you.[47] Only please, let there not break out between us a ten-year war, of which new Homers would have to sing after us: "*Cantami, o Diva, del pelide Achille le ire funeste/ che infiniti addusse lutti agli Achei.*"[48] I hope at least that you do me the justice of agreeing that my opinions are reasoned and serious. Why do you not write me more often? Writing itself can be a form of study, and if you do not care to continue our Kabbalistic polemic, is there any lack of subjects on which we can exchange our ideas? I do not know how much delight you might derive from it, but I do know that I would enjoy it infinitely, since here one lives, or at least I live, in a nearly perfect solitude, and except for the company of my books, my children, and my new students, I will tell you that now I see few people and visit no one. What is more, I live in a villa and I am

---

45 That is, the Leviticus volume of *Torat Hashem*, Benamozegh's edition of the Pentateuch, including his commentary *Em la-Mikra* (Livorno, 1863).

46 Benamozegh's first comment, on Lev. 1:2, would certainly have aroused Shadal's ire. He cites Shadal's opinion, in *Ha-Mishtadel*, that the idea of offering sacrifices to God originated not from a divine command, but from human impulses, and that the Torah—whose purpose was not to teach the people wisdom and knowledge, but to guide them on the paths of righteousness—did not abolish this custom. However, Benamozegh asserts not only that this opinion was mistaken, but that Shadal failed to perceive that he was following in the path of one whom he rightly despised, namely Spinoza, and that the same approach had been taken by the Christians and the leaders of the Reform movement.

47 As recounted in Homer's *Iliad*, the beautiful Helen of Troy was the wife of Menelaus, king of Sparta, and was abducted by Paris, son of the king of Troy. This act was one of the immediate causes of the ten-year Trojan War. Benamozegh gives her name in the Italian form, "Elena." There is probably no way to know for certain whether Benamozegh was aware of it, but Elena (Leah in Hebrew) was in fact the name of Shadal's wife! In any case, Benamozegh's attempt at humor here may have fallen flat.

48 "Sing, goddess, the anger of Peleus' son Achilles/ and its devastation, which put pains thousandfold upon the Achaians." These are the opening lines of the *Iliad* (trans. Richmond Lattimore, 1951). Benamozegh quotes the Italian version by Vincenzo Monti (1810).

a *villano* ["peasant"] all year. It can be said of me that I am a field mouse, and that if you accept me as a table-mate at the banquet of learning and friendship, the "feast of the Leviathan," I can also be one who is *oleh al shulḥan melakhim*.[49]

...[Teaching my new students] is a labor that is taking ever greater proportions. God give me strength, and may He give it to you, our Italian Nestor, as He would to anyone who strives for goodness and truth.

I repeat then: write me and let us reason together by letter as we would do verbally if we saw each other in person.... But what need is there to keep in mind what divides us? Let us concentrate on what unites us and, in our discussions, let us seek to eliminate any remaining division. And I am, without any reservation, as always, your most affectionate and devoted friend,

Benamozegh

Benamozegh to Shadal, March 18, 1864 (*Lettere*, pp. 111-112)

Most esteemed friend,

You so tight-fisted with letters and I so extravagant! This shows how much you are worth, and how little I am. Are you perhaps less than content with the somewhat free way that I treat your opinions in *Em la-Mikra*? I do not believe that I have ever fallen short of the respect due to you, but when one is as honest and of good faith as you are, one must understand that others who are equally convinced to the contrary may sometimes put slightly too much energy into defending their opinions. I have no need to praise you, but the esteem that I have for your learning and above all for your scholarly honesty makes me wish for you to care for me as much as I love you. Reading yesterday your response to Pineles in *Ha-Maggid*,[50] I said, "Poor me! Must I, too, have aroused your anger?" For if I am not mistaken, on one occasion I

---

49 This is a jocular reference to a statement in *Avodah Zarah* 68b that a field mouse (as opposed to a city mouse) is considered a delicacy and is *oleh al shulḥan shel melakhim* ("is served at the table of kings").

50 Hirsch Mendel Pineles (1805-1870) was a Galician scholar. In the March 9, 1864 edition of *Ha-Maggid* [p. 77], Shadal defends his view, which Pineles had criticized, that an unintentional manslayer who leaves a city of refuge may be killed only by a particular blood-avenger (*go'el ha-dam*) and not by any member of the public at large. Shadal says, "If the words of the scholar Pineles had merely wounded my honor, I would have kept silent (as I have kept silent a number of times and have not responded to those who asserted empty claims against me, so as not to waste my time), but those words inflict a not inconsiderable injury upon the honor of our Torah, so how can I keep silent?" Note that Shadal's statement echoes the wording of his letter to Benamozegh of August 1863.

> wrote in *Em la-Mikra*, "In *Ha-Mishtadel*, the Scriptures have been distorted"; I said "In *Ha-Mishtadel*" [the title of your work, instead of referring to you by name], to be sure, to avoid defaming your name, but otherwise the signs of my esteem and the affection that I bear for you are not lacking. I would like to tell you here about my opinion of your response to Pineles, but I am avoiding a discussion for fear of writing 20-page letters and, what is worse, not receiving a reply....
>
> One word about your response to Pineles. You oppose this writer, and rightly so, when he says that the Torah could suppress the instinct for revenge only up to a certain point. But oh, most honest Luzzatto! Do you not do the same? For what is that power left to—or that obligation imposed upon—the *go'el ha-dam*, whether one person or a hundred, to shed the blood of the unintentional manslayer if not (under the system of pure *peshat*) a concession to the concepts and customs of the times? Can you maintain that a well-ordered society could tolerate similar abuses? Therefore it seems to me that between you and Pineles there is only a difference of degree. He makes the greater concession, you the lesser, but the system is entirely...

[Editor's note: Unfortunately, this is all we have of Benamozegh's last letter. In his introduction to the *Lettere* volume, p. 4, Benamozegh apologizes for the truncation, and he explains that the original letter, which Shadal's sons had returned to him, had been misplaced, and that the only available copy was incomplete.]

Conclusion

To paraphrase T. S. Eliot, this is the way the correspondence ends, not with a bang but a whimper. Not only is the last part of Benamozegh's final letter missing, but Shadal has already left off writing well beforehand. It is not that Shadal stopped reaching out to colleagues toward the end of his life; to the contrary, both the *Epistolario* and *Iggerot Shadal* contain letters written as late as the month of his death, September 1865. It is also not the case that he was avoiding all controversy; one of his later letters (written in French on Oct. 27, 1864) was to a Christian acquaintance, the Swiss pastor and proto-Zionist Abram-François Pétavel, urging him to concentrate his efforts on promoting peace, reconciliation, and charity without attempting to change anyone's religious convictions (*Epistolario*, pp. 1052-1053). However, one might hazard a guess that Shadal simply concluded that he had nothing more to say to Benamozegh, or that he had had enough of his younger rival's blend of harsh criticisms and fawning praise.

To put things in historic perspective, it was just at the height of the Shadal-Benamozegh polemic in September 1863 that the Battle of Chickamauga was being fought in Georgia. Unlike that horrific battle, the polemic involved no bloodshed, and yet the two conflicts can be seen as comparable in some respects. The polemic involved a "civil war" of sorts between two contrasting strains of Italian Judaism. Benamozegh saw himself as fighting for a "lost cause," the same term that came to be embraced (*lehavdil*) by the defeated American South. But most significantly, both conflicts centered on issues that can be said to remain incompletely resolved to this day.

True, Benamozegh's gloomy characterization of his cause seems to have been premature. He would have been pleasantly surprised (and Shadal would have been baffled) to learn that mysticism in general and Kabbalah in particular are currently enjoying both academic respect and broad popularity. Nevertheless, the debate continues with regard to the following questions that the Shadal-Benamozegh letters raise:

- What is the true origin and nature of the Zohar?
- If the Zohar is not all that it is claimed to be, is it still an important mystical work? If not, can the Kabbalah stand without it?
- Can Orthodox Judaism survive without Kabbalah, or without some form of mysticism? Or, to the contrary, is it harmed more than helped by it?
- Do we perform mitzvot (1) because of the unseen cosmic effects that such performance engenders on a higher plane, (2) to commemorate events in Jewish history, (3) to reinforce our feelings of peoplehood, (4) for social and moral benefits, (5) simply because God told us to, or (6) more than one of the above?
- What is our proper relationship with followers of other religions, and in particular with Christians?
- Is Jewish national sentiment a key component of Judaism? Is the fusion of religion and nationality a dangerous thing?
- If one no longer cares to live a separate Jewish national existence, does one still have any reason to be observant?
- Can Jews who passionately espouse different *hashkafot*, even within the Orthodox community, learn to agree to disagree? Co-exist? Love each other?

Some of these questions may have to remain without definitive answers until Elijah comes. But when he does, and on the day that we hear at last the *Mashiaḥ*'s humble mount approaching, we will all be able to smile and say, "Let him bray." ☙

The Origin and Evolution of "Mesoret ha-Shas"[1]

By: ELI GENAUER

The *Mesoret ha-Shas* is an indispensable tool for studying Talmud. When readers look at the text of the Talmud and see an asterisk, their eyes immediately move to the inner margins to see what the *Mesoret ha-Shas* has to say.[2] The cross-referencing of sources, a basic tool to assist in learning, was not always available to those "swimming in the sea of the Talmud." The first examples of such aids were in a rudimentary state and using them was quite challenging. The *Mesoret ha-Shas* most often refers the reader to other places in Talmudic literature where the same subject is discussed. These references serve to broaden the reader's knowledge base and oftentimes help him to better understand the *sugya*. At times the *Mesoret ha-Shas* corrects the text, and there is even one instance where it provides a diagram to illustrate the words of the Talmud (*Shabbat* 60b). We will use Talmud *Shabbat* 60b and *Eruvin* 2a to show some changes that evolved in this important resource. We will also investigate who "wrote" the *Mesoret ha-Shas* and the genesis of how it was received.

---

1 I would like to thank Marvin Heller for his comments on this article and for his ongoing support of my research.

2 *Mesoret ha-Shas* is one of three citation tools found in the standard editions of the Talmud. The other two, *Ein Mishpat* and *Torah Or*, compiled by R. Yehoshua Boaz are not within the purview of this article. Regarding the relationship between *Ein Mishpat* and another citation device, *Ner Mitzvah*, see Marvin J. Heller, *Printing the Talmud* (New York: Im Hasefer, 1992), 188-89. R. Shlomo ben Eliezer's *Avodat ha-Levi*, first published in Constantinople in 1515, is likely the basis of *Ein Mishpat*. The bibliographer Ben Jacob is incorrect when he states that R. Shlomo intended to publish a larger work on the topic, titled *Ein Mishpat*. See Isaac Ben Jacob, *Otzar ha-Sefarim* (Vilna: Romm Press, 1880), 428, entry 26. R. Shlomo ben Eliezer does not mention any such work in his author's addendum to *Avodat ha-Levi*. Instead, *Ein Mishpat* was a later work based upon *Avodat ha-Levi* but not written by the same person.

Eli Genauer is a collector of antique *sefarim* with a special emphasis on early printed editions of the Talmud. He has written extensively on this topic with articles appearing on the *Seforim Blog, Lehrhaus, Giluy Milta, Safranim* and *Tablet Magazine*. This is his third article published in *Ḥakirah*. Eli serves as the treasurer of the Samis Foundation based in his native Seattle, Washington.

Was R. Boaz the Author of *Mesoret ha-Shas*?

The Vilna Shas (*Masekhet Berakhot*, Vilna, 1880) notes on its title page that *Mesoret ha-Shas* was organized and composed by R. Yehoshua Boaz, the author of the *Shiltei Ha-Giborim* commentary on the *Rif*.

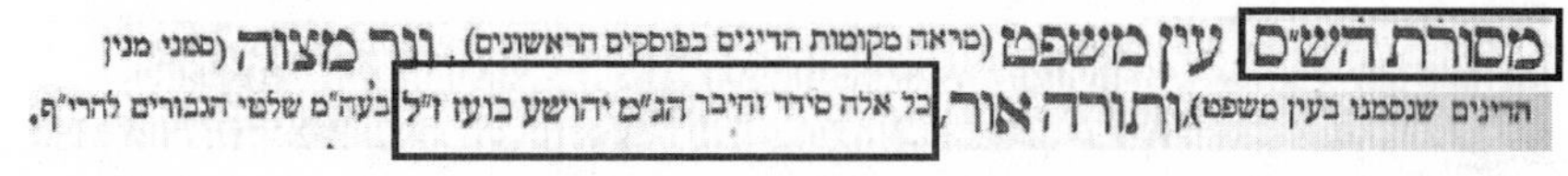
מסורת הש"ס עין משפט (מראה מקומות הדינים בפוסקים הראשונים) . ונר מצוה (סמני מנין
הדינים שנסמנו בעין משפט) ,ותורה אור, כל אלה סידר וחיבר הג"ם יהושע בועז ז"ל בעה"מ שלטי הגבורים להרי"ף.

A contemporary expert in the history of the printing of the Talmud, Marvin Heller, writes that Yehoshua Boaz ben Simon Barukh was "responsible for the innovations introduced into this edition (that of Giustiniani [1546-51]) that have been reprinted in all subsequent Talmud editions." This included three indices placed on each *amud*; "the third reference, *Mesoret ha-Talmud* (now called *Mesoret ha-Shas*) references comparable passages elsewhere in the Talmud and is located along the inner border of the page."[3] Thus, according to Heller, R. Boaz authored the *Mesoret ha-Shas* which was originally titled *Mesoret ha-Talmud.*

Likewise, a nineteenth-century expert on the history of the printing of the Talmud, Rav Raphael Nathan Nata Rabbinovicz, seems to indicate in his *Maamar 'al hadpasat ha-Talmud* that R. Boaz is the author of *Mesoret ha-Talmud.*[4] There he lists all the improvements in the Giustiniani edition of the Talmud:

---

3 See Marvin J. Heller, *Printing the Talmud: A History of the Earliest Printed Editions of the Talmud* (Brooklyn, NY, 1992), pp. 188, 190. It is possible that Heller means the innovation was placing this reference tool on the side of the page, not that he was the original author, but it is not clear.
In a conversation with Marvin Heller, he encouraged me to write an article which highlighted the origins of *Mesoret ha-Shas,* as he feels that many are unaware of the fact, as discussed below, that the identification of parallel statements in the Talmud predated the inclusion of *Mesoret ha-Shas* in the Giustiniani edition of the Talmud.

4 Raphael Nathan Nata Rabbinovicz, *Maamar 'al hadpasat ha-Talmud with Additions*, ed. A.M. Habermann (Jerusalem: Mossad ha-Rav Kook, 2006), 48. The *Maamar*, as it is colloquially known, was first printed in 1868 by the author in his *Dikdukei Sofrim* at the end of *Masekhet Berakhot*, and was revised by the author and printed in *Dikdukei Sofrim* at the end *of Masechet Megillah* in 1877. It was reissued as a work on its own in 1953 by Mossad ha-Rav Kook with additions by A.M. Habermann and again by Mossad ha-Rav Kook in 2006.
Rabbinovicz later indicates that R. Boaz did not author *Mesoret ha-Talmud* but does not explain the earlier statement. See *Maamar*, 50.

ובמהדורה זו של התלמוד ניתוסף על דפוס בומבירגי מראה מקום לפסוקים המובאים בגמרא עם מקומם בתנ"ך, **ומסורת התלמוד**, ומראה מקום בתוספות כל מקום שמביאין התוספות גמרא ממקום אחר, ועין משפט והוא מראה מקום בפוסקים, ונר מצוה והוא מניין הדינים המובאים בעין משפט, **חיברם כולם הגאון מו"ה יהושע בעז מברוך**, בעל המחבר ספר שלטי הגבורים על הרי"ף.

And in this edition of the Talmud are added—in addition to those of the Bomberg Edition—citations for Biblical verses that appear in the Talmudic text along with their sources in Tanakh; and ***Mesoret ha-Talmud***, and sources for Tosafot wherever Tosafot quotes a Talmudic passage from another area; and *Ein Mishpat*, which is the collection of citations to *Poskim*; and *Ner Mitzvah* which is an accounting of laws that appear in *Ein Mishpat*. **All these were written by ha-Gaon Yehoshua Boaz Mi-Barukh**, the author of *Shiltei Ha-Giborim* on the *Rif*."

The words "חיברם כולם" seem to indicate that Rav Yehoshua Boaz (Mi-Barukh) was the original author. But was R. Boaz the author of *Mesoret ha-Talmud* and why is the title different than the present day *Mesoret ha-Shas*? In reality, R. Boaz authored neither *Mesoret ha-Talmud* nor a book titled *Mesoret ha-Shas*.

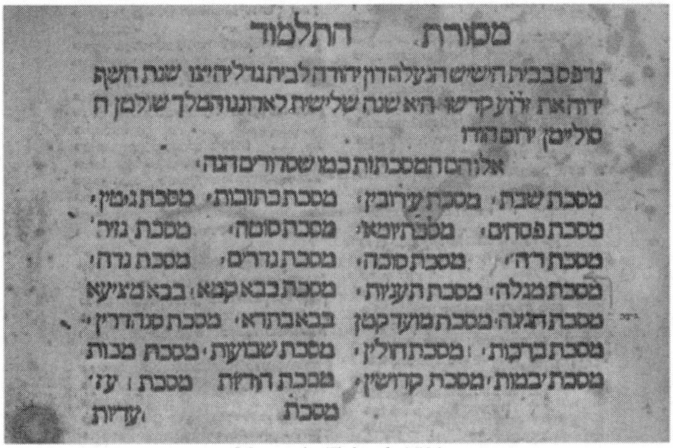
מסורת התלמוד
נדפס בבית השר הנעלה דון יהודה לבית גדליה יצו שנת השף
יזהאת ז'ר'ו'ע' קדשו היא שנה שלישית לאדוננו המלך שולטן ח
סולימן ירום הודו
אלו הם המסכתות כמו שסדורים הנה׃
מסכת שבת׃ מסכת עירובין׃ מסכת כתובות׃ מסכת גיטין׃
מסכת פסחים׃ מסכת יומא׃ מסכת סוטה׃ מסכת נזיר׃
מסכת ר"ה׃ מסכת סוכה׃ מסכת נדרים׃ מסכת נדה׃
מסכת מגלה׃ מסכת תענית׃ מסכת בבא קמא׃ בבא מציעא
מסכת חגיגה׃ מסכת מועד קטן בבא בתרא׃ מסכת סנהדרין׃
מסכת ברכות׃ מסכת חולין׃ מסכת שבועות׃ מסכת מכות
מסכת יבמות׃ מסכת קדושין׃ מסכת הוריות מסכת ע"ז׃
מסכת עדיות׃

Mesoret ha-Talmud, 1523

There is agreement that the first edition of the work *Mesoret ha-Talmud* was printed in 1523.[5] The printing year is calculated using the word ז'ר'ו'ע'

5 The Bibliography of the Hebrew Book lists it as follows

(5)383 (1523).[6] It was printed by Yehudah Gedaliah in Salonika but the work itself was anonymous. Like the *Mesoret ha-Shas,* the *Mesoret ha-Talmud* collects and identifies parallel passages in Talmud Bavli for twenty-nine *masekhtot.* But it is slightly different than *Mesoret ha-Shas*; the *Mesoret ha-Talmud* only provides citations to the chapter and not the page of the Talmudic text. According to Rabbinovicz and Heller, the anonymous author of *Mesoret ha-Talmud* is actually R. Boaz. Yet that appears to be impossible. R. Boaz wrote a commentary, *Shiltei ha-Giborim,* on R. Alfasi's Talmudic commentary. In the introduction to *Shiltei ha-Giborim,* first published in Sabionetta in 1554,[7] Rav Yehoshua Boaz writes that he has been working on his "*Melekhet Shamayim*" from the age of 23 until 36, his then age.[8] That would put his date of birth at approximately 1518. He therefore could not have authored a book printed in 1523.

Let us examine the title page of the edition of the Talmud wherein R. Boaz's commentaries first appeared, the Giustiniani edition. Giustiniani was the second publisher to print a complete edition of the Talmud. Daniel Bomberg published his first edition between 1519/1520 and 1523. Bomberg eventually published three complete editions of the Talmud.[9] Giustiniani's edition was published in Venice between 1546 and 1551. R. Boaz was one of the editors of this edition, which also included indices. The title page reads:

> This heavenly work includes new additions not previously contained in prior editions; the citations of the *Mesoret ha-Talmud*; citations of

---

http://uli.nli.org.il/F/MAJ44XQRAFNDCEJC1RUKY8BNDUE8CXK3SPLRKQM5QHMUDIVHBF-44798?func=full-set-set&set_number=007042&set_entry=000144&format=999

מסורת התלמוד .
... מסכת שבת ... עירובין ... פסחים ... יומא ... ר"ה [ראש-השנה] ... סוכה ... מגלה ... תעניות ... חגיגה ... מועד קטן ... ברכות ... חולין ... קדושין ... יבמות ... כתובות ... גיטין ... סוטה ... נזיר ... נדרים ... נדה ... בבא קמא ... בבא מציעא ... בבא בתרא ... סנהדרין ... שבועות ... מכות ... הוריות ... ע"ז [עבודה זרה] ... עדיות.

[שאלוניקי]. דפוס יהודה לבית גדליה [רפ"ג.] 1523

6 A note indicates that it was printed in the third year of the reign of סוליימן. This would have been 1523, as Suleiman the Magnificent was sultan of the Ottoman Empire from 1520 to 1566.

7 http://uli.nli.org.il/F/MAJ44XQRAFNDCEJC1RUKY8BNDUE8CXK3SPLRKQM5QHMUDIVHBF-39402?func=full-set-set&set_number=006968&set_entry=000012&format=999

8 He died in 1555. For biographical information see R. Shlomo Gottesman, "*Kuntres 'Elef ha-Magen,'* Rebi Yehoshua Boaz Mi-Barukh and his Torah," *Yeshurun* 20, 75-82.

9 For the history of the Bomberg editions, see Heller, *Printing of the Talmud*, 135-82.

Tosafot, citations of the *Poskim*, citations of the laws of the Talmud that appear in Rambam, R"M of Coucy, R. Yaakov the author of the *Turim*, each one corresponding to a unique letter and is titled *Ein Mishpat*. The work *Ḥoker Din* that is based upon all the laws found in the Talmud, with the corresponding tractate, chapter, law, and page number, using the system that appears in *Yad ha-Ḥazakah*, and citations to the laws in the Talmud, and is titled *Ner Mitzvah*. All of these additions were done by one of the students, whose name is our master and teacher R. Yehoshua Boaz ha-Mevorakh the son of the rabbi, Shimon Barukh, for the public good, and he [R. Yehoshua] and his descendants should be remembered for good.

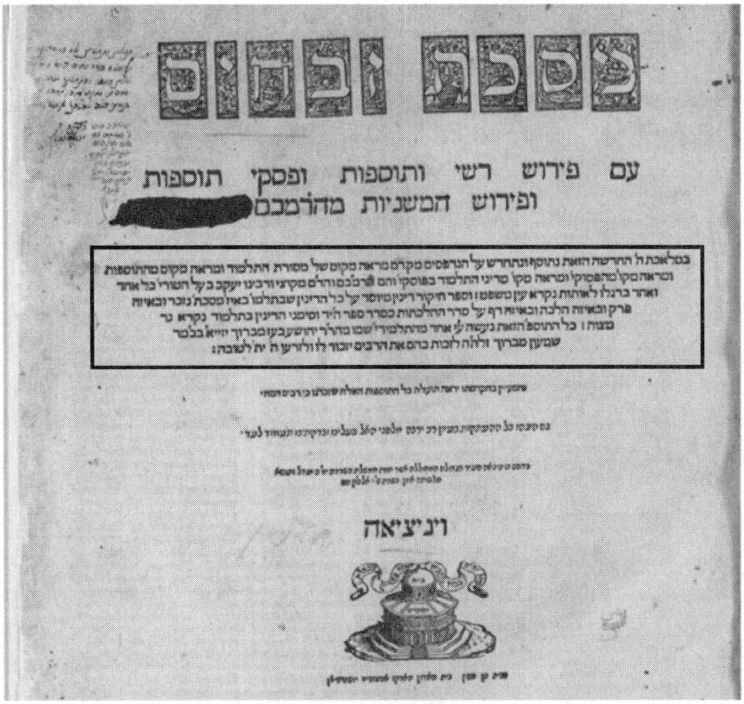

מסכת זבחים

עם פירוש רשי ותוספות ופסקי תוספות

ופירוש המשניות מהרמבם [redacted]

ויניציאה

Tractate Zevaḥim, Giustiniani, Venice
From the National Library of Israel

A careful reading of the title page makes clear that the citations "of the *Mesoret ha-Talmud*," a stand-alone work, was included, and that R. Boaz only took credit for two works, *Ein Mishpat* and *Ner Mitzvah*.[10] Although not mentioned on the title page, there is a significant change to the citations that appear in *Mesoret ha-Talmud;* it now identifies the specific page

10 The history of the printing of the *Ein Mishpat* and *Ner Mitzvah*, in addition to *Torah Or*, is beyond the scope of this article.

but not the chapter. Of course, when the *Mesoret ha-Talmud* was originally published there was no complete edition of the Talmud, let alone standard pagination. The standard pagination only appeared in the Bomberg edition which was then incorporated into the Giustiniani edition. But the identification of those parallel passages, arguably the bulk of the work, was completed by the author of the *Mesoret ha-Talmud.*[11] Thus, it is not surprising that R. Boaz did not take credit for those citations and did not retitle the original work.

The fact that R. Boaz only modified and incorporated *Mesoret ha-Talmud* into the Giustiniani edition did not stop later printers from mistakenly attributing it to R. Boaz. The first publisher to do so was Moshe Dias in his edition of *Avodah Zarah*, published in Amsterdam in 1712. All of R. Boaz's works are in bold, and for the first time, *Mesoret ha-Talmud*[12] appears amongst R. Boaz's works, *Ein Mishpat* and *Ner Mitzvah.* This, despite the fact that Dias copied the title page from an earlier Amsterdam edition—which only bolds *Ein Mishpat* and not *Mesoret ha-Talmud.*

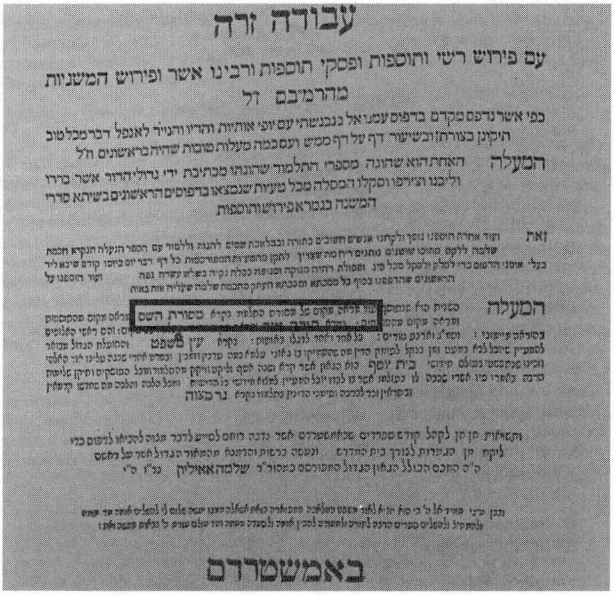
עבודה זרה
עם פירוש רשי ותוספות ופסקי תוספות ורבינו אשר ופירוש המשניות
מהרמבם זל
כפי אשר נדפס מקדם בדפוס עמנואל בנבנשתי עם יפי אותיות והדיו והנייר לא נפל דבר מכל טוב
תיקון בצורתו ובשיעור דף על דף ממש ועם כמה מעלות טובות שהיה בראשונים ז״ל
המעלה האחת הוא שהוגה מספרי התלמוד שהוגהו מכתיבת ידי גדולי הדור אשר ברור
וליבנו וצירפו וסקלו המסלה מכל טעיות שנמצאו בדפוסים הראשונים בשיטא סדרי
המשנה בגמרא פירוש ותוספות
באמשטרדם

Tractate Avodah Zarah, Moshe Dias, Amsterdam, 1712

[11] R. Boaz also added citations for tractates that do not appear in *Mesoret ha-Talmud—Bezah* and *Zera'im.*

[12] Dias refers to the work as *Mesoret ha-Shas* and not *Mesoret ha-Talmud,* a point we discuss below.

From then on, in most editions of the Talmud the *Mesoret ha-Talmud/Shas* was attributed to R. Boaz. For example, in the *Orphans of Solomon Proops* edition of the Talmud from the mid-1700s, the lengthy paragraph describing all of the changes incorporated in the Giustiniani edition is omitted and instead an abridged version simply groups all the titles together: "with the citations in Rashi and Tosafot, and ***Torah Or***, and ***Ner Mitzvah***, and ***Mesoret ha-Shas***, and ***Ein Mishpat***…"

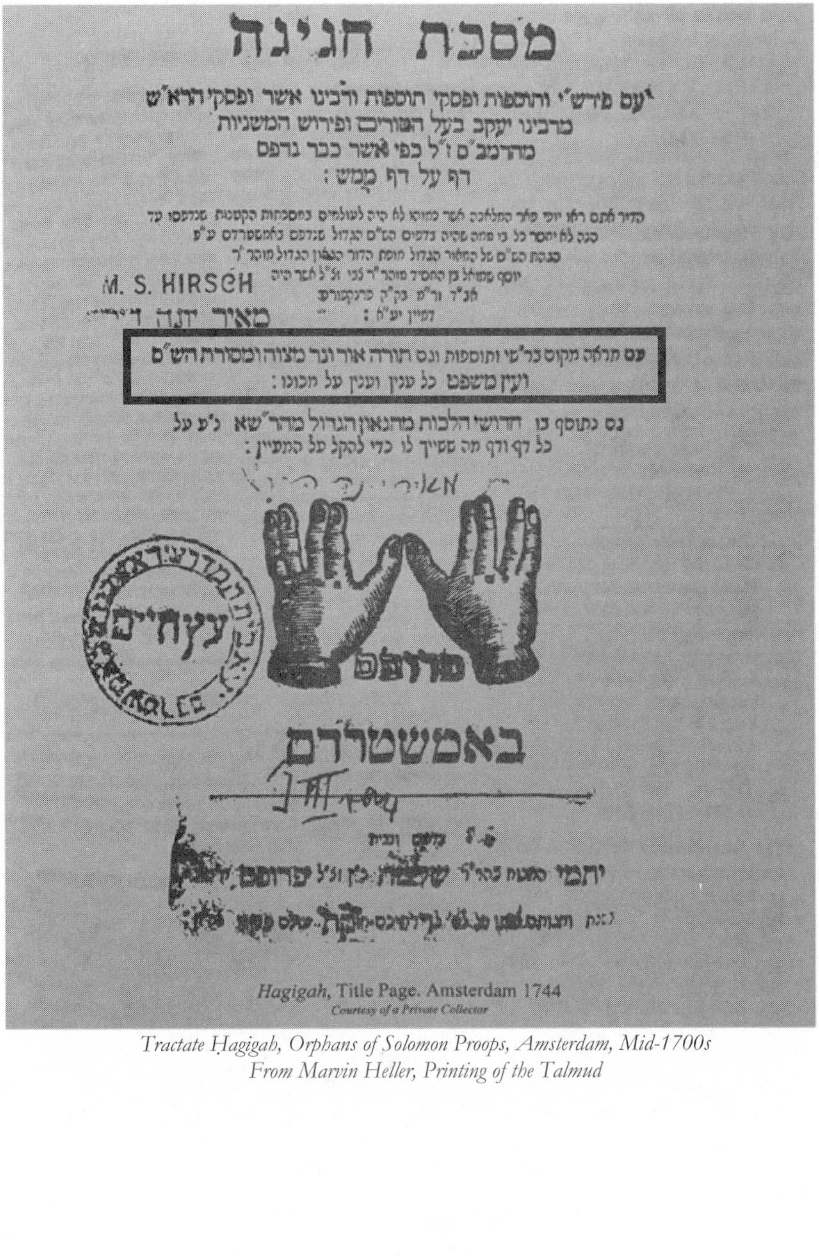

Tractate Ḥagigah, Orphans of Solomon Proops, Amsterdam, Mid-1700s
From Marvin Heller, Printing of the Talmud

Now that we have established that R. Boaz was not the author of *Mesoret ha-Talmud*, nor did he take credit for the work, we have to examine how and when the title changed to *Mesoret ha-Shas*. One might (erroneously) argue that although R. Boaz never authored *Mesoret ha-Talmud,* nevertheless he was the author of a new work, *Mesoret ha-Shas*. As discussed above, however, the original title page that Boaz printed makes no mention of *Mesoret ha-Shas*. Nor was there any other work with that title published during R. Boaz's lifetime. Instead, *Mesoret ha-Talmud* and *Mesoret ha-Shas* are the same book.

In 1553, Pope Julius III banned the printing of the Talmud, which resulted in the burning of thousands of copies of the Talmud (including most copies of the Giustiniani edition). In 1564, the Council of Trent reversed that decision and permitted the publication of the Talmud—but with numerous restrictions and modifications. In particular, the Council found the very word "Talmud" offensive to Christian religious sensibilities. So, an alternative vocabulary was employed; Talmud was now "Gemara" or "Shas." The Church also imposed severe restrictions on passages that relate to non-Jews. Thus, when the Talmud was finally reprinted in Basel beginning in 1578, the entire tractate *Avodah Zarah* was omitted. Additionally, in the volumes that were printed, all references to Talmud were revised to one of the acceptable terms. This included the title page. The Basel edition used the Giustiniani edition and R. Boaz's additions, reprinted the same title page language, but with a slight modification to one of the book's titles. The *Mesoret ha-Talmud* is now the *Mesoret ha-Shas*.

שאו שערים ראשיכם

בבא קמא

עם פירוש רשי ותוספות ופסקי תוספות ורבינו אשר

ופירוש המשניות מהר'מבם ז'ל

Tractate Bava Kamma, Basel, ca. 1578
From Marvin Heller, Printing of the Talmud

Thus, there is no book titled *Mesoret ha-Shas*; that title is simply the result of Church censorship, and certainly not a work by R. Boaz.

A clear summary of this history, including the history of *Mesoret ha-Talmud* and specifically what R. Boaz added, appears in the *Oz Vehadar* edition of the Talmud (2006) which writes,

> "מסורת התלמוד" נדפס מקודם כספר בשאלוניקי שנת רפ"ג ע"י דון יהודה גדליה. אבל הוא נחבר טרם שהיה התלמוד בדפוס, והוא מציין המסורת על פי הפרקים, ורבי יהושע בעז הוא שהוסיף את דפי הדפוס בנוסף על הפרק.

R. Boaz's Modifications of *Mesoret ha-Talmud*

Let us now examine some of the ways that R. Boaz diverged from *Mesoret ha-Talmud*.[13]

If we look at *Shabbat* 60b, we find that the *sugya* of "אין בין יום טוב לשבת אלא אוכל נפש בלבד", is cross referenced as follows:

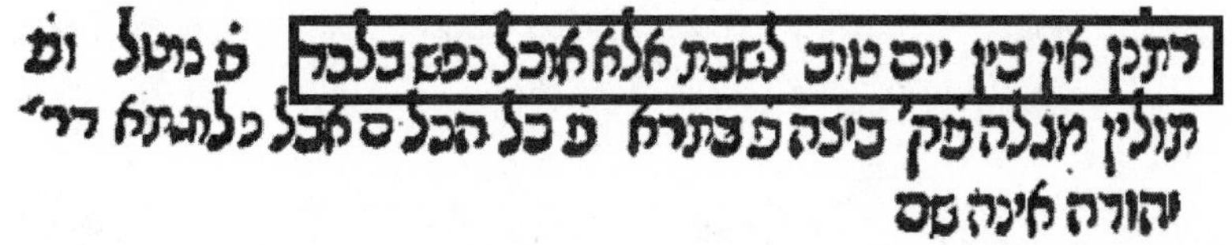
דתנן אין בין יום טוב לשבת אלא אוכל נפש בלבד פ' נוטל ופ'
תולין מגלה פק' ביצה פ' בתרא פ' כל הכלים אבל פלוגתא דר'
יהודה אינה שם

> פ' נוטל, ופ' תולין, מגילה פק' (פרק קמא), ביצה פ' בתרא פ' כל הכלים, אבל פלוגתא דרבי יהודה אינה שם.

Since the original *Mesoret ha-Talmud* was not based on the Venice, Bomberg edition (1520-1523) which had just appeared, it does not contain the page numbers, leaving it to the reader to flip through a *perek* until he found the reference.

1. First we are told to look in *Masekhet Shabbat* in *perek Notel* (17th *perek* ("כל הכלים נוטלין") where we find the referenced source in our *Gemarot* on 124a. This source does not include the *Tanna* Rabbi Yehudah's opinion that מכשירי אוכל נפש are also permitted on Yom Tov.
2. Second, we are told to look at *perek Tolin* (20th *perek*), where we find the referenced source on *daf* 137b. This source does include Rabbi Yehudah's dissenting opinion.

---

13 *Mesoret ha-Talmud* was first printed as a stand-alone book in Salonika in [5]283 (1523) by Don Yehudah Gedaliah. It was printed before the printed editions of the Talmud, and the citations are only given with the corresponding chapter. R. Yehoshua Boaz was the one who added the page numbers to the chapter citations.

3. Third, we are told to look at *Megillah "Perek Kamma."* Here we find the main recording of this *halakhah*, as a *Mishnah* on 7b. It is followed by Rabbi Yehudah's opinion which is stated in the following passage of the Talmud.
4. Finally, we are told to look in the last *perek* of *Bezah* called "כל הכלים". It turns out that there are two references in this *perek: Bezah* 28a, which includes Rabbi Yehudah's opinion, and 36b, where it is stated without Rabbi Yehudah's dissenting opinion. Most likely, it is to this source, *Bezah* 36b, to which *Mesoret ha-Talmud* refers when it states "אבל פלוגתא דרבי יהודה אינה שם".

The next iteration of the *Mesoret ha-Talmud* we will examine is in the Basel 1581 edition of *Masekhet Shabbat* 60b. By then, the name had been changed to *Mesoret ha-Shas,*[14] and it had been positioned on the side of the page and modified by Rabbi Yehoshua Boaz. Only three references are listed, but possibly it is because only those include the *Mishnah* followed by Rabbi Yehudah's opinion. Nevertheless, the fact remains that Rav Yehoshua Boaz edited out three references that were included in the original source.[15]

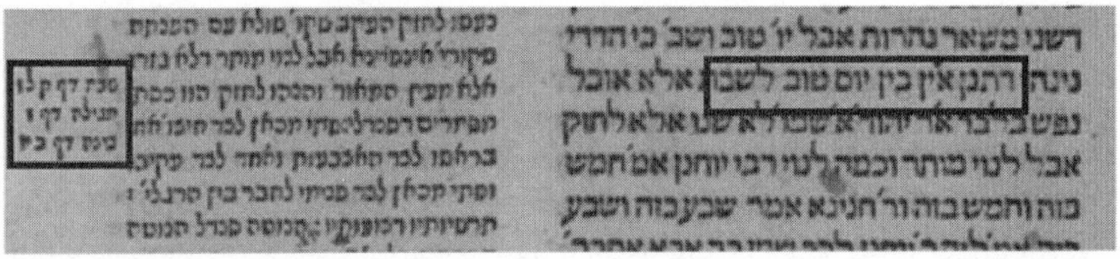

Finally, we have the *Vilna Shas* of 1881 which goes back to listing all six sources in Talmud Bavli (even those which do not include Rabbi Yehudah's opinion) as was done in 1523 by *Mesoret ha-Talmud.*[16] It seems as if this was important to those who wanted to improve this reference tool.

---

14 Heller, p. 243: "substituted in place of 'Talmud,' [were] 'Gemara' . . . 'Shas' [six orders] of Mishna."

15 https://books.google.co.il/books?hl=iw&id=X8BSAAAAcAAJ&q=%D7%91%D7%A1%D7%99%D7%9C%D7%99%D7%90%D7%94#v=onepage&q=%D7%91%D7%A1%D7%99%D7%9C%D7%99%D7%90%D7%94&f=false

16 By then, *Mesoret ha-Shas* had been expanded upon by Rav Yosef Shmuel of Cracow and Rav Yeshayah Pick. *Mavo L'Shas* Vilna, J. Weinfeld (Jerusalem, 1994), p. 4.

כי הדדי נינהו *דתנן אין בין י"ט לשבת אלא
אוכל נפש בלבד א"ר יהודה אמר שמואל
לא שנו אלא לחוק אבל לנוי מותר וכמה לנוי
ר' יוחנן אמר חמש בזה וחמש בזה ור' חנינא

לגזירה שגזרו מחמת מאורע הי
להם לגזור אלא מעין המאורע
דשאני משאר נסרוס · ברוחב א
בעומק : אלא לחוק · שמסמרותי
נעשו לחוק הענק שקורין שול"א עם

לקמן קכד: קלו:
מגילה ז: ביצה
כח. לו:
[תוספ' דמגילי
פ"א]

It also includes the page number and a reference to the *Tosefta Megillah, Perek Aleph*, although it leaves out that it is *Halakhah* 8.

Another example of a change from the original *"Mesoret ha-Talmud"* to the newer effort by Rav Yehoshua Boaz can be found on *Eruvin* 2a.

The entry in the original *Mesoret ha-Talmud* appears as follows:

פרקא קמא

הכשר מבוי בית שמאי אומרים
בלחי פרק כל כתבי

הכשר מבוי בית שמאי אומרים
בלחי, פרק כל כתבי

There is no text at the beginning of *Eruvin* which begins with the words הכשר מבוי. Apparently, *Mesoret ha-Talmud* is referring to the fact that the first *Mishnah* in *Eruvin* speaks about fixing an alleyway so that it is permitted to carry within it, but leaves out information about how it is done. *Mesoret ha-Talmud* then tells us that the source for how to do this can be found later in *Masekhet Shabbat* 117a where it states,

דתנן הכשר מבוי ב"ש אומרים לחי וקורה וב"ה אומרים או לחי או קורה

In editing the Giustiniani edition, Rav Yehoshua Boaz understandably chose to eliminate this reference, although important, because it was not focused on words found on the page.

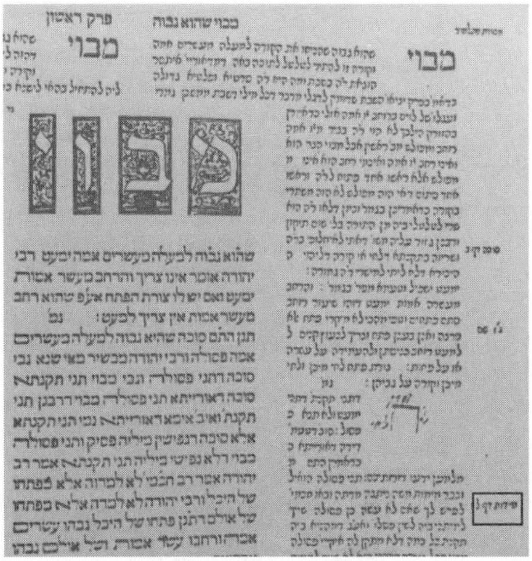
מבוי

Tractate Eruvin, Giustiniani,
Scan courtesy of Jewish Theological Seminary

Another interesting occurrence on the same page is towards the bottom of the picture where *"Mesoret ha-Talmud"* indicates to look at *Masekhet Middot daf* 36. This refers to the text that says "דתנן פתחו של היכל גבוה עשרים אמה".

Since *Masekhet Middot* is only *Mishnayot*, it is somewhat puzzling to be referred to as מידות דף ל"ו. Apparently, Rav Yehoshua Boaz was following the pagination of the Giustiniani Shas which was patterned after the Bomberg editions of Venice which printed the *Mishnayot* of *Masekhet Middot* after *Masekhtot Meilah*, *Kinim* and *Tamid*. The *Mishnah* of "פתחו של היכל" was printed on *daf* 36b of that edition.

Mesoret ha-Talmud indicates that the *Mishnah* is found in "מידות פ׳ד", (without indicating it is *Mishnah* 1.)

It continued to be listed as מידות דף ל"ו for many hundreds of years, but by the time it was listed in the Vilna edition, it reverted to the type of listing in the *Mesoret ha-Talmud* of 1523 and is rendered "מידות פ׳ד,מ׳א" (פרק ד׳,משנה א׳).

Finally, we can see the issues a reader faced when looking at the original *Mesoret ha-Talmud* printed in 1523. On the same *daf*, *Eruvin 2a* it gives us the following *Mareh Mekomot*,

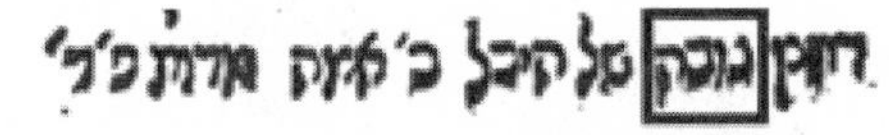

דתנן **גובהו** של היכל כ׳ אמה

The correct text in the *Mishnah* is,

פתחו של היכל **גובהו** כ׳ אמה

Another *"ta'ut defus"* looks like this,

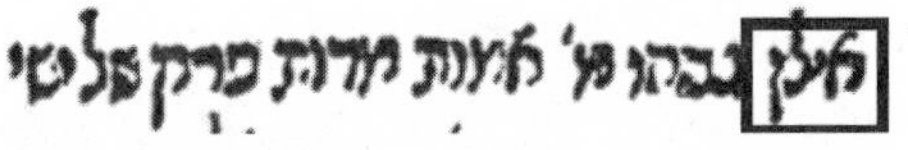

אילן גבהו מ׳ אמות מדות פרק שלישי

The correct text in *Middot* 3:7 (which deals with the measurements of the *Beit HaMikdash*) is

אולם גבהו מ׳ אמות

Although *Mesoret ha-Shas* has undergone major changes since its inception, it was always a helpful tool to those who studied the Talmud. It should be appreciated for its revolutionary nature at that time. ☙

The Mystery of the Medical Training of the Many Isaac Wallichs: Amsterdam (1675), Leiden (1675), Padua (1683), Halle (1703)

By: EDWARD ISAAC REICHMAN

The Wallich family is a prominent dynastic Jewish family dating back to the Middle Ages, comprised of rabbis, businessman, laymen and physicians. There were at least seven consecutive generations of Wallich physicians, with one Wallich physician treating Louis XV, King of France. A number of the physicians were also rabbis, community leaders and authors of rabbinic works.[1]

In the late seventeenth and early eighteenth centuries, in the span of twenty-eight years, we find the name Isaac Wallich appearing in the archival records of no less than four different medical institutions: Amsterdam (1675), Leiden (1675), Padua (1683) and Halle (1703) (heretofore referred to as Isaac Amsterdam, Isaac Leiden, Isaac Padua, and Isaac Halle). To this day, there remains ambiguity as to the identity of these names, one of which, Isaac Amsterdam, is added to the list here for the first time. While some historians have innocently confused or

---

1 On the history of the Wallich family, see H. Schultze, "*Geschichte der Familie Wallich*," *Monatsschrift für Geschichte und Wissenschaft des Judentums*, Vol. 49 (1905), Issue 1, pp. 57-77; Vol. 49 (1905), Issue 2, pp. 183-192; Vol. 49 (1905), Issue 3, pp. 272-285; Vol. 49 (1905), Issue 4, pp. 450-458; Vol. 49 (1905), Issue 5, pp. 571-580. This classic work has been updated recently. See Jona Schellekens, "The Wallich List from Worms," *Aschkenas* 25:1 (2015), 181-204; idem, "Use of Rare First Names in the Search for Ancestors: Example of the Physician David Wallich in Trier," *Avotaynu* XXXVI, Number 4 (Winter 2020), 21-24.

Edward Isaac Reichman is a Professor of Emergency Medicine at the Albert Einstein College of Medicine, where he practices Clinical Emergency Medicine and teaches Jewish medical ethics. He received his rabbinic ordination from the Rabbi Isaac Elchanan Theological Seminary of Yeshiva University and writes and lectures internationally in the field of Jewish medical ethics. His research is devoted to the interface of medical history and Jewish law.

conflated them,[2] others have debated the total number of distinct Isaac Wallichs, suggesting some may have attended multiple institutions.[3] Here we present new evidence and previously unpublished archival material clarifying for the first time the definitive unique identities and medical education of the different Isaac Wallichs. This discovery takes on greater significance when placed in the context of Jewish medical history.

Isaac Amsterdam and Isaac Leiden or Isaac Leiden-Amsterdam

It is remarkable that the name Isaac Wallich appears on two separate dissertations in 1675 from two different institutions in the Netherlands.

---

2 For example, Asher Salah, in his invaluable biographical dictionary, *La République des Lettres: Rabbins, Ecrivains et Médicins Juifs en Italie au XVIII Siècle* (Brill: Leiden, 2007), has an entry for Yitzhaq Wallich (667, n. 1035). While the basic biographical information is for Isaac Padua, the list of Wallich's works mentions those of Isaac Halle.

3 M. Freudenthal, *Aus der Heimat Mendelsohns* (Berlin, 1900), 132-133; idem, "*Notiz*," *Zeitschrift fur Hebräische Bibliographie* 14:4 (September- October, 1910), 158-159; R. Yaakov Shmuel Spiegel, "The Physician R. Yitzhak Isaac Wallich from Dessau and His Manuscript Responsum" (Hebrew) *Yerushateinu* 4 (5770), 63-84; Kenneth Collins, "Jewish Medical Students and Graduates at the Universities of Padua and Leiden: 1617-1740," *Rambam Maimonides Medical Journal* 4:1 (January, 2013), 1-8. Freudenthal confuses Isaac Leiden with Isaac Halle. Collins suggests that perhaps Isaac Leiden later attended Padua in 1683 to enhance his qualifications. There is precedent for this. Dennj Solera suggests that Rodrigo Lopez, the famous Jewish physician of Queen Elizabeth, whose name appears in the Padua graduation rolls for July 1559, attended Padua after his graduation from Coimbra in 1540 to enhance his qualifications (personal communication, September, 2020). His article is forthcoming.

Dissertation of Isaac Wallich (Athenaeum Illustre, Amsterdam 1675):[4]

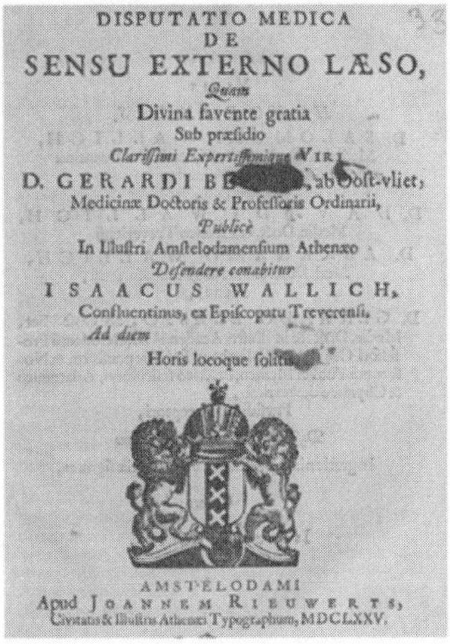

DISPUTATIO MEDICA
DE
SENSU EXTERNO LÆSO,
Quam
Divina favente gratia
Sub præsidio
Clarissimi Expertissimique VIRI,
D. GERARDI B[illegible], ab Oost-vliet,
Medicinæ Doctoris & Professoris Ordinarii,
Publicè
In Illustri Amstelodamensium Athenæo
Defendere conabitur
ISAACUS WALLICH,
Confluentinus, ex Episcopatu Treverensi,
Ad diem
Horis locoque solitis.
AMSTELODAMI
Apud JOANNEM RIEUWERTS,
Civitatis & Illustris Athenæi Typographum, MDCLXXV.

Dissertation of Isaac Wallich (Leiden 1675):[5]

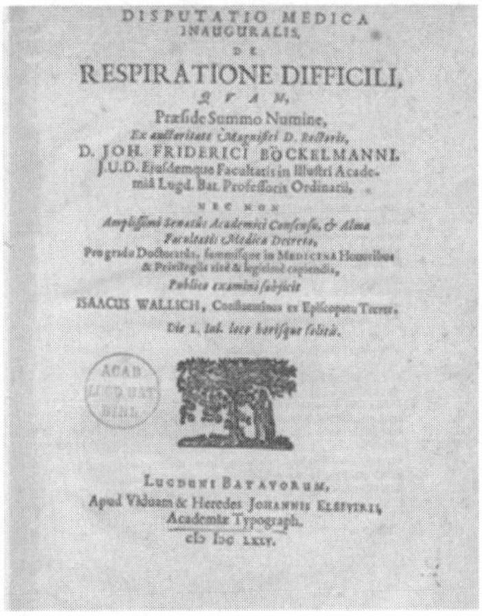

DISPUTATIO MEDICA
INAUGURALIS,
DE
RESPIRATIONE DIFFICILI,
QUAM,
Præside Summo Numine,
Ex auctoritate Magnifici D. Rectoris,
D. JOH. FRIDERICI BOCKELMANNI
J.U.D. Ejusdemque Facultatis in Illustri Academiâ Lugd. Bat. Professoris Ordinarii,
NEC NON
Amplissimi Senatus Academici Consensu, & Almæ Facultatis Medicæ Decreto,
Pro gradu Doctoratûs, summisque in MEDICINA Honoribus & Privilegiis ritè & legitimè capiendis,
Publico examini subjicit
ISAACUS WALLICH, Confluentinus ex Episcopatu Trever.
Die 1. Jul. loco horisque solitis.
LUGDUNI BATAVORUM,
Apud Viduam & Heredes JOHANNIS ELSEVIRII,
Academiæ Typograph.
CIↃ IↃC LXXV.

4 The dissertation is housed at the Wellcome Library in London and is available online, https://wellcomecollection.org/works/ccayfpfy/items?canvas=2&langCode=lat.

5 The dissertation is housed in the University of Leiden, Special Collections (KL) 236 B 7: 28 and only recently became available online. It is called a disputation, as the student defended a thesis before university faculty members, with roles occasionally delegated for additional disputants. There is a matriculation record for "Isaacus Wallich Confluentinus. 20, M" on August 21, 1674 in the Leiden University archives. See *Album Studiosorum Lugduno Batavae* (Martinus Nijhof: Den Haag, 1875), column 590.

For both dissertations, the student is identified in the identical fashion, "*Confluentinus ex Episcopatu Trever,*" from the city of Koblenz and the region of Trever in Germany. While scholars have noted the graduation of an Isaac Wallich from Leiden,[6] to my knowledge, no Jewish scholar has ever noted the existence of an Isaac Wallich who attended or graduated from the Athenaeum Illustre, the precursor of the University of Amsterdam, in 1675. Could there have been two Isaac Wallichs from Koblenz who graduated the same year?

While it may appear that these are two graduation dissertations, this is not the case. The Athenaeum Illustre was not granting medical degrees at this time and only attained status as a full university at a later date.[7] To complete one's medical degree, it would have been required to attend a formal university, like Leiden. Typically, the degree would culminate with the student defending a thesis. The Leiden dissertation is entitled "*Disputatio Medica Inauguralis.*" "*Dissertatio Inauguralis*" or "*Disputatio Inauguralis*" refer to the inaugural or formal graduation dissertation or thesis defense. Isaac's dissertation from Amsterdam does not contain the word "inauguralis." The thesis defense of Isaac Wallich in Amsterdam appears to have been a dry run for his formal degree from Leiden. Defending theses like this one was apparently quite common in Amsterdam and was obviously taken quite seriously given the formality of the publication.

This clearly establishes that Isaac Amsterdam and Isaac Leiden are one and the same person (heretofore Isaac Leiden-Amsterdam, Leiden being the primary place of training). Yet, we have not learned about the family origins of this Isaac. We begin to grow his family tree from the dedication page of the Amsterdam dissertation.[8]

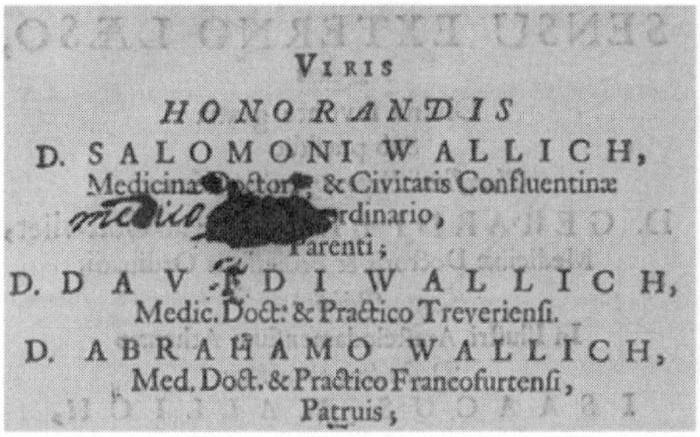
VIRIS
HONORANDIS
D. SALOMONI WALLICH,
Medicinæ ... & Civitatis Confluentinæ
... rdinario,
Parenti;
D. DAVIDI WALLICH,
Medic. Doct: & Practico Treverienſi.
D. ABRAHAMO WALLICH,
Med. Doct. & Practico Francofurtenſi,
Patruis;

6 See Spiegel, *op. cit.*

7 I thank Professor Paul Dijstelberge of the University of Amsterdam for this information.

8 The Leiden dissertation has no dedication page or mention of family.

Isaac Leiden-Amsterdam mentions his father Salomon (Shlomo), as well as two paternal uncles ("*patruis*"), David from Trever[9] and Abraham from Frankfurt,[10] all of whom were physicians.

We can further expand the family tree by viewing two additional medical dissertations from the Netherlands.

Dissertation of Simon Wallich (Leiden 1678):[11]

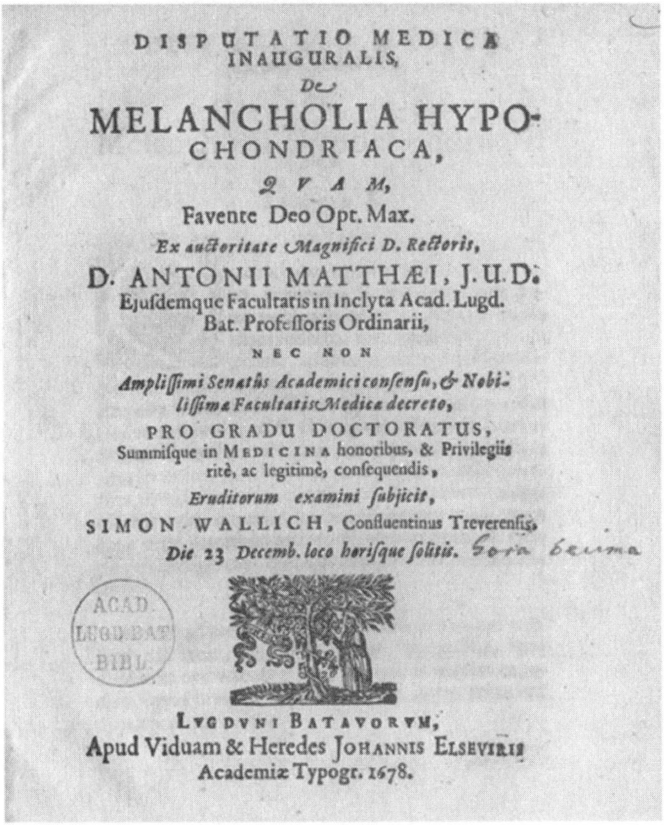

DISPUTATIO MEDICA
INAUGURALIS,
De
MELANCHOLIA HYPO-
CHONDRIACA,
QUAM,
Favente Deo Opt. Max.
Ex auctoritate Magnifici D. Rectoris,
D. ANTONII MATTHÆI, J.U.D.
Ejusdemque Facultatis in Inclyta Acad. Lugd.
Bat. Professoris Ordinarii,
NEC NON
Amplissimi Senatûs Academici consensu, & Nobi-
lissimæ Facultatis Medicæ decreto,
PRO GRADU DOCTORATUS,
Summisque in MEDICINA honoribus, & Privilegiis
ritè, ac legitimè, consequendis,
Eruditorum examini subjicit,
SIMON WALLICH, Confluentinus Treverensis.
Die 23 Decemb. loco horisque solitis.

LUGDUNI BATAVORUM,
Apud Viduam & Heredes JOHANNIS ELSEVIRII
Academiæ Typogr. 1678.

---

9 David was also known as Tevle. On David, see Jona Schellekens, "Use of Rare First Names in the Search for Ancestors: Example of the Physician David Wallich in Trier," *Avotaynu* XXXVI, Number 4 (Winter 2020), 21-24.

10 On Abraham Wallich, graduate of the University of Padua in 1655, see below.

11 There is a matriculation record in Leiden for "Simon Wallich Treveirensis 21, M" on May 12, 1678 in the Leiden University archives. See *Album Studiosorum Lugduno Batavae* (Martinus Nijhof: Den Haag, 1875), column 622.

Dissertation of Menaḥem Manlin Wallich (Utrecht 1685):[12]

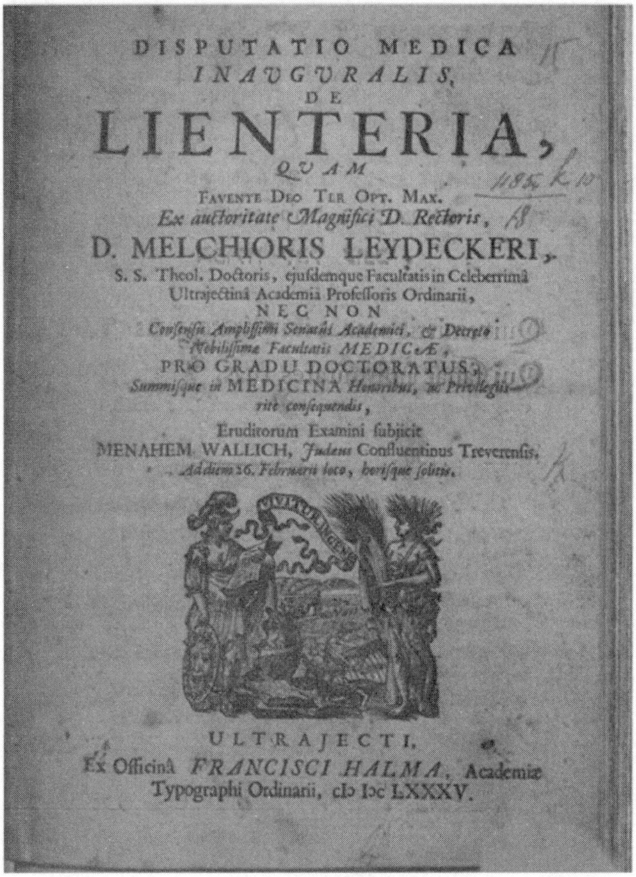

DISPUTATIO MEDICA
INAVGVRALIS,
DE
LIENTERIA,
QVAM
FAVENTE DEO TER OPT. MAX.
Ex auctoritate Magnifici D. Rectoris,
D. MELCHIORIS LEYDECKERI,
S. S. Theol. Doctoris, ejusdemque Facultatis in Celeberrimâ
Ultrajectinâ Academiâ Professoris Ordinarii,
NEC NON
Consensu Amplissimi Senatus Academici, & Decreto
Nobilissimae Facultatis MEDICÆ,
PRO GRADU DOCTORATUS,
Summisque in MEDICINA *Honoribus, ac Privilegiis*
rite consequendis,
Eruditorum Examini subjicit
MENAHEM WALLICH, *Judaeus* Confluentinus Treverensis.
Ad diem 26. Februarii loco, horisque solitis.

ULTRAJECTI,
Ex Officinâ *FRANCISCI HALMA,* Academiae
Typographi Ordinarii, clɔ Iɔc LXXXV.

The cover pages shed light, albeit limited, on the relationship of these graduates to Isaac. Both Simon and Menaḥem are referred to as "*confluentinus treverensis*," thus Isaac, Simon and Menaḥem are all from the same family.

It is in the body of Menaḥem's dissertation, however, that we find clues as to the exact nature of their relationship. At the end of Menaḥem's dissertation there are two congratulatory letters, one by Isaac Wallich in Latin, and one by Simon Wallich in Hebrew and Latin.

---

12 There is a matriculation record in Utrecht for "Menaḥem Wallich Confluentinus" in 1684. See *Album Studiosorum Academiae Rheno-Traiectinae* (J. L. Beijers and J. van Boekhoven: Utrecht, 1886), column 80.

Congratulatory letter of Isaac Wallich to the graduate Menaḥem Wallich:

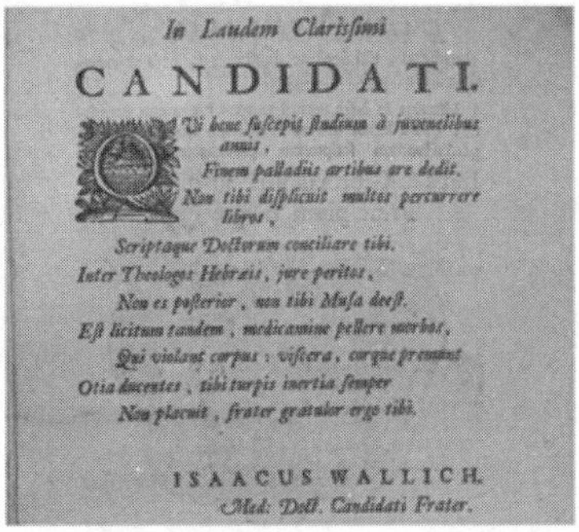

In Laudem Clarissimi

CANDIDATI.

Ut bene suscepis studium à juvenelibus annis,
Finem palladiis artibus ore dedit.
Non tibi displicuit multos percurrere libros,
Scriptaque Doctorum conciliare tibi.
Inter Theologos Hebræis, jure peritos,
Non es posterior, non tibi Musa deest.
Est licitum tandem, medicamine pellere morbos,
Qui violant corpus: viscera, corque premunt
Otia ducentes, tibi turpis inertia semper
Non placuit, frater gratulor ergo tibi.

ISAACUS WALLICH.
Med: Doct. Candidati Frater.

Congratulatory letter of Simon Wallich to the graduate Menaḥem Wallich:

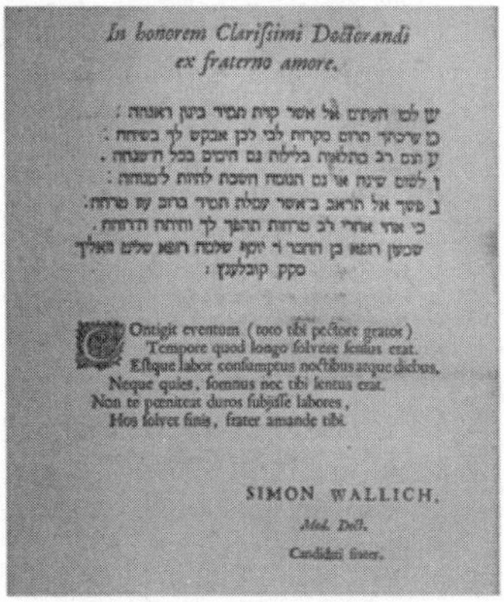

In honorem Clarissimi Doctorandi
ex fraterno amore.

[illegible]
כן שיכתך הרום מקרות לבי לכן אבקש לך בשוחה :
עד תם רב בתלונה בלילה גם חסם בכל תשנתה .
לשום שנה או גם תנומה חשבת לזוות לנצחה :
נ פחד אל תראב באשר עמלת תמיד ברב עם טרחה :
כי אחי אחרי לב מרוות תהפך לך וזוהת הרוחה .
שמעון רופא בן החבר ר׳ יוסף שלמה רופא שלום מאלך
סקק קובלענץ :

Contigit eventum (toto tibi pectore grator)
Tempore quod longo solvere sensus erat.
Estque labor consumptus noctibus atque diebus,
Neque quies, somnus nec tibi lentus erat.
Non te pœniteat duros subjisse labores,
Hos solvet finis, frater amande tibi.

SIMON WALLICH.
Med. Doct.
Candidati frater.

Both Isaac and Simon identify themselves as "*candidati frater*," brother of the graduate. Furthermore, Simon identifies himself as the son of *Yosef Shlomo Rofei* Wallich, and as a resident of Koblenz. Thus, we learn from these dissertations that there were three Wallich brothers, Yosef Shlomo, David and Abraham, all of whom were physicians. Isaac Leiden-Amsterdam was the son of Yosef Shlomo, and had two brothers, Simon and Menaḥem, who were also physicians.[13]

---

13 Schultze, *op. cit.*, 283, in his discussion of the Koblenz line of the Wallich family mentions that Simon is the son of Yosef Shlomo but does not mention Simon's other brothers. I have found no records of Yosef Shlomo Wallich in the university archives of the medical schools of Italy, Germany or the Netherlands. He was likely a non-university-trained physician, which was far more common during this time.

Isaac Halle[14]

Isaac Halle attended the University of Halle in the first years of the eighteenth century. His matriculation record from 1703 is below, where he is identified as "*confluentinus*":[15]

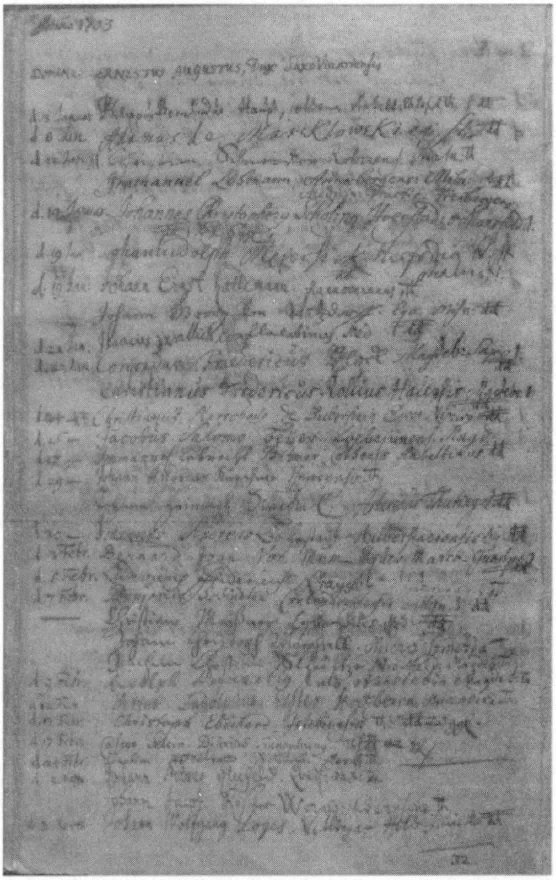

[14] For a comprehensive biography of Isaac Halle, see Spiegel, *op. cit.*

[15] Universitätsarchiv Halle vor. Jedoch konnte ich in dem Matrikelband UAHW, Rep. 46, Nr.1. The archivist at Halle was not able to locate either the dissertation or further records for Isaac Halle.

Isaac Halle is perhaps most famous for his remarkable letter exchange with a fellow medical student, Shmuel Shimon of the University of Frankfurt on Oder.[16] Shimon and Isaac Halle were both lone Jewish students at their respective medical schools in Germany in 1702, and Shimon wrote Isaac Halle describing his difficult situation, beseeching Isaac Halle to consider transferring to Frankfurt on Oder so they could learn Torah and medicine together. Isaac Halle responded that in contrast to Shimon, he was quite content with his situation. Isaac Halle reports that he developed a special relationship with Professor Hoffman, one of the most prominent medical educators of the day, and among other special privileges, was granted the right to carry a sword in public, not generally allowed for Jews. He graciously declines Shimon's offer and extends a reciprocal one. Isaac Halle signed the letter as follows:[17]

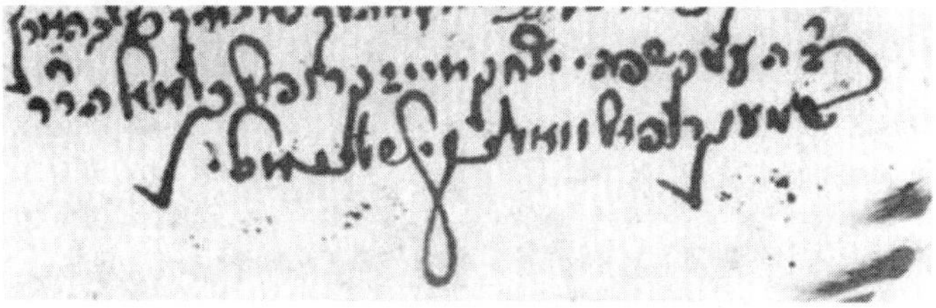

Isaac Halle identifies himself as the son of Shimon (Simon) Rofei (the physician). The only known Shimon Wallich physician[18] is the one who graduated Leiden in 1678. He is clearly Isaac Halle's father.

Isaac Halle was a student of the *Shev Yaakov*, from whom he received rabbinic ordination.[19] Both Isaac Halle and his father, Simon, are

---

16 This exchange was first published and transcribed by A Freimann, "Briefwechsel eines Studenten der Medizin in Frankfurt a. d. Oder mit dem in Halle Medizin studierenden Isak Wallich im Jahre 1702," Zeitschrift für Hebräische Bibliographie 14:4 (July-August, 1910), 117-123. For discussion of the letters, see Shmuel Feiner, *The Jewish Enlightenment* (Philadelphia: University of Pennsylvania Press, 2011), 21-23.

17 See http://beta.nli.org.il/en/manuscripts/NNL_ALEPH003922973/NLI#$FL40949517 (accessed February 24, 2021). The letters are found on pp. 205-209 of the manuscript.

18 See Spiegel, *op. cit.*, note 3, for further evidence supporting Simon as Isaac Halle's father.

19 On the *semikhah* of Wallich, see Yosef Onah, "Two Certificates of the Author of Shev Yaakov," (Hebrew) *HaMa'ayan* 14:4 (*Tammuz*, 5734), 46-48.

mentioned in the published responsa, *Shev Yaakov*.[20] Isaac Halle was a prolific author, and a number of his manuscripts are extant. Among his other works, he expanded upon the work of his uncle, Menaḥem. A manuscript collection of Wallich's halakhic and aggadic writings, as well as assorted letters, entitled *Pi Shnayim*, were recently sold at auction.[21]

In Isaac Halle's letters to his brother Menaḥem, they speak of an uncle also named Menaḥem, who authored a commentary on the *Beraita* of *Melekhet HaMishkan*.[22] This is Menaḥem, Simon's brother, who graduated Utrecht in 1685.

Isaac Halle was therefore the son of Simon (graduate of Leiden), and grandson of Yosef Shlomo Rofei (Salomon) Wallich. He was the nephew of Isaac Leiden-Amsterdam, who graduated from Leiden in 1675.

Isaac Padua

Isaac Padua was one of three Jewish medical graduates from the university of Padua in the year 1683. One, Tuviya Cohen, the author of *Ma'ase Tvviya*, has received disproportionate attention in the Jewish historical literature.[23] The second, Gabriel Felix, is known primarily for his rela-

---

20 Spiegel, *op. cit.*, notes the mention of Isaac in the responsa of his Rebbe, R. Poppers, *Shev Yaakov*. He neglects to mention that *Shev Yaakov* refers multiple times to a physician named Shimon, whom he holds in high regard, and is identified as a member of "our community" (i.e., Koblenz). See nos. 36, 40, 41. Zimmels identifies him as Shimon Wallich in his *Magicians, Theologians and Doctors* (Goldston and Sons: London, 1952), 28.

21 Kedem Auction House (Auction 48, Lot #28, 2018). Wallich also authored a separate commentary on *Pirkei Avot* titled *Ateret Avot*. The manuscript is housed at the University of Frankfurt am Main library.

22 Spiegel, *op. cit.*, note 4.

23 See the forthcoming book, Kenneth Collins and Samuel Kottek, eds., *Ma'ase Tuviya (Venice, 1708): Tuviya Cohen on Medicine and Science* (Jerusalem: Muriel and Philip Berman Medical Library of the Hebrew University of Jerusalem, in press). See also A. Levinson, "A Medical Cyclopedist of the Seventeenth Century," *Bulletin of the Society of Medical History* (January 1917): 27-44; D. A. Friedman, *Tuviya Ha-Rofe* (Palestine Jewish Medical Association, 1940); M.J. Mahler, *A Precursor of the Jewish Enlightenment: Dr. Tobias Cohen and his Ma'ase Tuviya* (unpublished thesis for ordination, Hebrew Union College, 1978); N. Allan, "Illustrations from the Wellcome Institute Library: A Jewish Physician in the Seventeenth Century," *Medical History* 28 (1984): 324-8; D. Ruderman, "On the Diffusion of Scientific Knowledge within the Jewish Community: The Medical Textbook of Tobias Cohen," in *Jewish Though and Scientific Discovery in Early Modern Europe* (Yale University Press, 1995), 229-55; S.G. Massry, et. al., "Jew-

tionship with Tuviya.[24] Isaac Padua is the least known of the three. Below is part of Isaac Padua's original University of Padua Archives graduation record:[25]

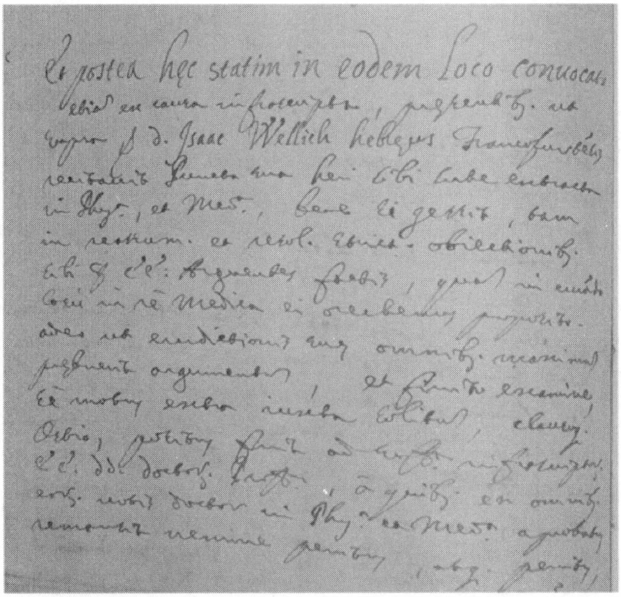

Et postea hec statim in eodem Loco conuocat...

Kaufmann published a transcription of the entire graduation record of Isaac Padua, along with the records of Gabriel Felix and Tuviya HaRofe.[26] In Isaac Padua's archival record there is only one identifier, Francofurtentis (from Frankfurt). It unfortunately does not mention his father's name, as the archival record often does. Schultze, a biographer of the Wallich family, delineates different lines of the family, including the Metz-Frankfurt line and the Koblenz line. Isaac Leiden-Amsterdam

ish Medicine and the University of Padua: Contribution of the Padua Graduate Toviah Cohen to Nephrology," *American Journal of Nephrology* 19:2 (1999): 213-21; E. Lepicard, "An Alternative to the Cosmic and Mechanic Metaphors for the Human Body? The House Illustration in *Ma'ase Tuviya* (1708)," *Medical History* 52 (2008): 93-105. See also *Koroth* 20 (2009-2010), in which five articles are devoted to Tobias Cohen and his *Ma'ase Tuviya.*

24 See E. Reichman, "Some Notes on the Renaissance Physician Gabriel Felix: His Grammar Tree and His Family Tree," Koroth 25 (2019-2020), 339-353.

25 CO.V. 284, c. 36 r. I thank Filippo Valle for his research assistance and for obtaining the photograph.

26 D. Kaufmann, "Trois Docteurs de Padoue: Tobias Moschides, Gabriel Selig b. Mose, Isak Wallich," Revue des Etudes Juives 18 (1889), 293-298.

and Isaac Halle were from the Koblenz line, while Isaac Padua is from the Frankfurt family line of Wallichs. Schultze identifies Isaac Padua as the son of Abraham Wallich, the uncle of Isaac Leiden-Amsterdam,[27] making Isaac Padua and Isaac Leiden-Amsterdam first cousins.

Abraham Wallich graduated from the University of Padua in 1655. In the Padua archive Abraham is identified as *ebrei Gallo*, a French Jew, as he derived from the Metz Wallich line. In the long and distinguished line of physicians in the Wallich family tree, the majority were not university trained. Abraham was not the first Wallich physician, however, to graduate Padua. He was preceded by Eliezer Wallich of the Worms Wallich line, who graduated in 1626.[28] Upon Abraham's graduation from Padua, he applied for a position in Frankfurt. Below is Abraham's application to the Frankfurt council for his position as community physician.[29]

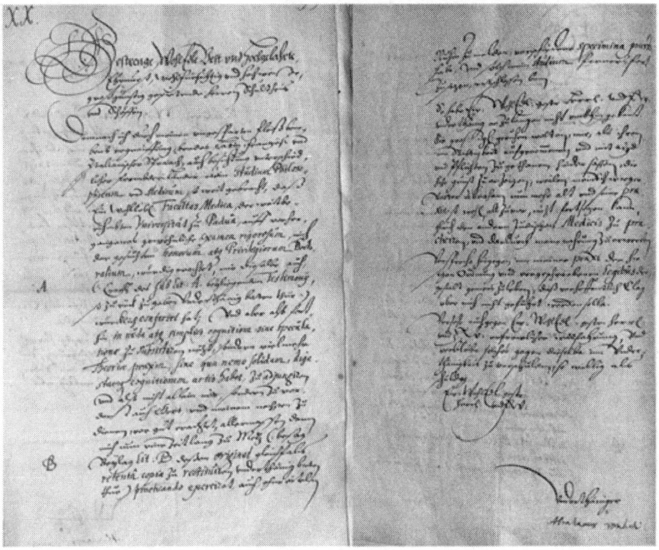

27 Schultze, 282. Kaufmann also offers this identification.

28 Abdelkader Modena and Edgardo Morpurgo, Medici E Chirurghi Ebrei Dottorati E Licenziati Nell'Università Di Padova dal 1617 al 1816 (Bologna, 1967), 11. See Schellekens, op. cit., who notes an earlier family member who graduated from the University of Padua around 1590.

29 Stadt Frankfurt am Main, Institut für Stadtgeschichte, Medicinalia, Akten, Nr. 250 (fol. 51-53v).

It includes a notarized copy of his medical diploma from Padua, the first and last pages of which are below.[30]

In this copy, as opposed to the archival copy held in the University of Padua, Abraham is identified specifically as being from Metz, and the word "*ebrei*" (Jew) is omitted.

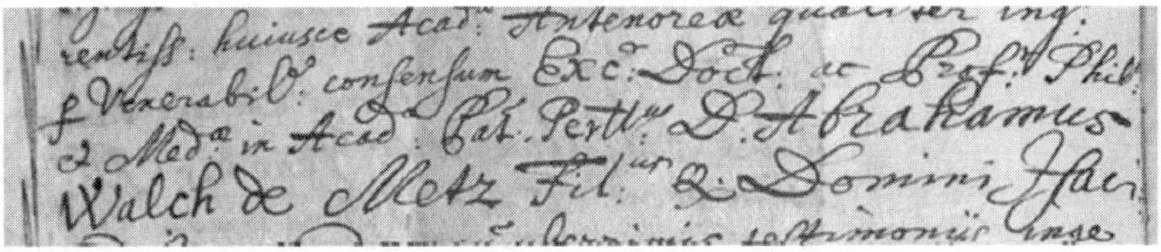

30 Among the witnesses to Abraham's diploma we find Rabbi Moshe Catalano, poet and son of Abraham Catalano, author of *Olam Hafukh* on the 1631 Padua plague, Rabbi Benedetto (Baruch) Luzzato, and Shabtai Astruch, a University of Padua medical graduate from 1643. Moshe Catalano wrote a poem in honor of Astruc's medical graduation (JTS Ms. 9027 V5:1). Luzzatto wrote a poem in honor of Binyamin Forli's graduation which was translated into Hebrew (NLI 990034442450205171).

Perhaps he requested of the copyist to amend this specifically for his application to the Jewish community, who would have been familiar with the Wallichs of Metz, and for whom the word "*ebrei*" would have been superfluous.

Abraham assumed the position in Frankfurt in 1657 and established a line of the Wallich family there. Abraham had five sons, Yehuda (Leone) Loeb, Isaac, Naftali Hirsch, Meir and Salomon. He is known for his medical work, *Dimyon Refuot: Harmonia Wallichia Medica*, published posthumously by his son Loeb.[31]

Neither Schultze nor Kaufmann were able to benefit from the work of Modena and Morpurgo, who gathered all the graduation records of the Jewish medical graduates from Padua from 1617-1816.[32] Abraham's graduation from 1655 is listed there, as are three subsequent Wallich graduates, all identified as being from Frankfurt. These graduates correspond to three of the five sons of Abraham- Isaac (1683), Leone (Loeb) (1692), and Naftali Hirsch (1692).[33] Thus, Isaac Padua is the son of Abraham, and from the Metz-Frankfurt line of the Wallich family.

From Three Isaacs to a Thousand Isaacs

We have succeeded in identifying and "reuniting" the Isaacs of the Wallich family. Isaac Leiden and Isaac Amsterdam are one and the same. Isaac Leiden-Amsterdam and his nephew, Isaac Halle, are from the Koblenz line of Wallichs. Isaac Padua is the first cousin of Isaac Leiden-Amsterdam and stems from the Frankfurt Wallichs. We can only conjecture if these Isaacs ever intersected during their lifetimes, and as to the stories of their respective training and practice that they might have shared. Yet, beyond the particular story of this one family, there is a larger narrative of which these three Isaacs are a part. Isaac is prototypical Jewish name. There have been hundreds, if not thousands, of "Isaacs," "Abrahams," and "Jacobs" who have trained to become physicians over the centuries. Theirs is a tale of rejections, discriminations, ghettos, translations, apprenticeships, Torah learning when possible, occasional conversions, executions, service of popes, kings and queens,

---

31 On Abraham Wallich and his work, see, Samuel Kottek, "The German-Jewish Physician Leib Walakh," (Hebrew) *Koroth* 7:3-4 (December, 1976), 154-168; Nimrod Zinger, *Ba'alei haShem viha-Rofei* (Haifa University, 2017), 242-251.

32 Modena and Morpurgo, *op. cit.*

33 Modena and Morpurgo, *op. cit.*, nos. 97, 117 and 118. Leone and Naftali are clearly identified as the children of Abraham in the Padua archives, where they are called figlio dell'Ecc.mo dr. Abramo.

all bound together with superhuman determination and persistence. The road traveled to becoming a physician is an integral part of Jewish history and a window into the interface of the Jews with the secular world across the ages.

The University of Padua, where one of our Isaacs graduated, was the first university to officially accept Jewish medical students. Here Jews could freely study academic medicine for the first time.[34] Prior to Padua, Jews were barred from formal medical education, and largely trained through apprenticeship. For centuries, Padua was the main address for any Jewish medical student wishing to pursue a formal university education. To be sure, Jewish students attended other universities, such as Sienna, Rome, Ferrara and others, but this was the exception.[35] It was only around 1650 that the University of Leiden in the Netherlands accepted its first Jew,[36] followed by other Netherland universities such as Utrecht. It was not until the early eighteenth century that universities in Germany[37] and other European countries followed suit.

Isaac Padua's father Abraham and his ancestor Eliezer attended Padua, the only option at the time for a Jew desiring university medical training. Isaac Padua, along with his brothers, followed in the footsteps of his father and attended the University of Padua, with its long history of tolerance and acceptance of the Jewish student.

Isaac Leiden-Amsterdam was from a different branch of the family. His father did not attend university. By the time he was ready for medical school, there were new options. Isaac Leiden-Amsterdam represents the first generation to transition away from Padua into the Netherlands. His brothers, Simon and Menaḥem, followed his lead.

By the beginning of the eighteenth century, when Isaac Halle decided to become a physician, a number of schools in Germany began to open their doors to the Jews. Isaac Halle would pioneer the next fron-

---

34 On the Jews and the University of Padua, see, for example, E. Reichman, "The Valmadonna Trust Broadside Collection and a Virtual Reunion of the Jewish Medical Students of Padua," *Verapo Yerapei: Journal of Torah and Medicine of the Albert Einstein College of Medicine Synagogue* 7 (2017), 55-76.

35 With the exception of Padua, special Papal permission was required for Jewish students to attend university. See, for example, the story of Judah Gonzago, in Harry Friedenwald, *The Jews and Medicine* (Johns Hopkins Press: Baltimore, 1944), 229-231.

36 For discussion on the transition of Jewish students from Padua to Leiden, see Collins, *op. cit.*

37 Tuviya Cohen and Gabriel Felix were the first Jews to attend the University of Frankfurt on the Main in 1678, but transferred to Padua shortly thereafter.

tier. He was one of the very first (if not the first) Jewish students to attend the University of Halle in Germany. In just a few decades, a number of other schools in Germany would open their gates to Jews,[38] though Halle would become the premier destination for Jewish medical students in the eighteenth century.[39] Thus, these three Dr. Isaac Wallichs, whose training spanned some three decades, represent the transition from the towering dominance of the University of Padua and its virtual monopoly over formal Jewish medical education, to the birth and ascendency of Jewish medical training in the Netherlands, followed by Germany and beyond. This transition from Padua to the Netherlands to Germany is also reflected in the medical training of the members of another Jewish family. Benjamin Levi Buxbaum graduated Padua (1669),[40] his sons Libman and Gutman graduated Leiden (1697), and his grand-

[38] On the Jews in German medical schools, see Adolf Kober, "*Rheinische Judendoktoren, Vornehmlich des 17 und 18 Jahrhunderts," Festschrift zum 75 Jährigen Bestehen des Jüdisch-Theologischen Seminars Fraenckelscher Stiftung,* Volume II, (Breslau: Verlag M. & H. Marcus, 1929), 173-236; Monika Richarz, *Der Eintritt der Juden in die akademischen Berufe: Judische Studenten Und Akademiker in Deutschland 1678-1848* (Schriftenreihe Wissenschaftlicher Abhandlungen Des Leo Baeck: Tubingen, 1974); M. Komorowski, *Bio-bibliographisches Verzeichnis jüdischer Doktoren im 17. und 18. Jahrhundert* (K. G. Saur Verlag: Munchen, 1991); John Efron, *Medicine and the German Jews* (Yale University Press: New Haven), 2001.

[39] Wolfram Kaiser and Arina Volker, *Judaica Medica des 18 und des Fruhen 19 Jahrhunderts in den Bestanden des Halleschen Universitatsarchivs (Wissenschaftliche Beitrage der Martin Luther Universitat* Halle-Wittenberg: Halle, 1979).

[40] Below is a copy of a poem written in honor of his graduation from the University of Padua in 1669:

I thank Laura Roumani for this reference. The original is housed in the Kaufmann Collection in the Hungarian Academy of Sciences Library in Budapest.

children, Baehr Liebmann and Anschel Gutmann, graduated from Geissen (1729).[41]

After Isaac Halle there would be a rapid proliferation of medical schools accepting Jewish students across the world. While this diminished the prominence of any one specific institution, the explosion of opportunity for the Jewish medical student was unprecedented. The ubiquity of the Jewish student in medical schools, in disproportionately high numbers, ultimately led to quotas, but this hurdle was also eventually overcome.

The tradition of prominent Wallich physicians continued into the modern era with Dr. Moshe Wallach, who trained in Germany, and later came to Jerusalem, where he founded and served as longtime director of Shaare Zedek Hospital.

Today there are hundreds of medical schools across the world that accept and promote Jewish students. We have never enjoyed the equality and options in the field of medicine as we do presently. It is through the lens of the three Isaacs that we gain a glimpse into the path of the Jewish medical student from the past to the present. They collectively trained at the cusp of a transition point in Jewish medical education, with each representing a unique student experience. The three Isaacs would scarcely recognize the medical training of today, neither for its treatment of the patient, nor for its treatment of the Jewish student.[42]

Edward Isaac Reichman (AKA Isaac Einstein[43])

---

41 See Wolfgang Treue, "Lebensbedingungen Judischer Arzte in Frankfurt am Main wahrend des Spatmittelalters und der Fruhen Neuzeit," *Medizin, Geschichte und Gesellschaft* 17 (1998), 9-55, esp. 49 and 52; Komorowski, *op. cit.*, 38, 41, 42.

42 For a discussion of the challenges faced by Jewish medical students throughout history, see E. Reichman, "From Maimonides the Physician to the Physician at Maimonides Medical Center: The Training of the Jewish Medical Student throughout the Ages," *Verapo Yerape: The Journal of Torah and Medicine of the Albert Einstein College of Medicine* 3(2011), 1-25.

43 Isaac Einstein = Isaac of Albert Einstein College of Medicine.

Appendix:

Archival Record of Wallichs who attended the University of Padua.[44]

Lazarus Walch (*Wallich*) f. ex.mii ***
Vormatiensis, Wormiensis hebreus
26.11.1626, in philosophia et medicina (AGAPd, 274, ff. 206r-v)
25.11.1626, praesentatio et puncta (274, f. 206)

03.01.1655, Abram Wallich, Gallus hebreus, (n. 57, Modena-Morurgo p. 23, C. III; padre di Jehudà e Hirsch)

Isaac Wallich, *Wellich*
Francofurtensis hebraeus
25.06.1683, in philosophia et medicina (AGAPd, 284, ff. 36r-37r)
23.06.1683, praesentatio (284, f. 35v); 24.06, puncta (284, ff. 35v-36r)

Leo Wallichius, *Wallich*, f. exc.mi Abrahami doctoris
Francofurtensis, hebreus, frater Hirtii
24.01.1692, in philosophia et medicina (AGAPd, 285, ff. 39v-40v)
20.01.1692, praesentatio (285, f. 38r); 23.01, puncta (285, f. 39v)

Hirtius, *Hircius*, *Hirsch,* Wallichius f. exc.miAbrahami doctoris
Francofurtensis hebreus, frater Leonis
24.01.1692, in philosophia et medicina (AGAPd, 285, ff. 39v-40v)
20.01.1692, praesentatio; privilegium suum phil. praesentavit datum Salisburgi die 7 mensis septembris 1690 (285, f. 38r); 23.01, puncta (285, f. 39v)

---

[44] Courtesy of Dr. Dennj Solera, who has compiled a soon-to-be-published comprehensive database of the University of Padua graduates.

What Does It Mean to Be a Jewish Hospital in America Today?

By: JASON WEINER

In addition to exploring crucial Jewish values, it is also essential to study history, to appreciate how core elements of social and personal responsibility have been incorporated into Jewish communal life in response to changing social needs and circumstances.[1] This communal history is both instructive and inspiring. It helps explain how we got to where we are today, as well as the context of our current situation. The lessons of the past are especially important, since history tends to repeat itself, as the story of Jewish hospitals in America illustrates. This article thus provides a detailed overview of the history of Jewish hospitals in America, followed by my suggestions as to what Jewish hospitals could mean to the Jewish community and our society at large going forward.

As far as we know, amongst the first Jews to arrive in North America was a group of twenty-three refugees from Brazil who made their way to New Amsterdam (New York City) in 1654. They were not welcomed warmly, as Peter Stuyvesant, the Dutch director general of the colony, initially tried to block their entry. He only relented and permitted them to enter on the condition that the Jews would pledge to ensure that the poor among them not become a burden on the community by agreeing to take responsibility for supporting them.[2] The Jewish community internalized this expectation and worked hard to avoid stirring public resentment. This "sacred promise" to the larger society to care for their own became known as "the Stuyvesant Pledge."[3] As the American Jewish community slowly

---

1 On the importance of studying history in the field of bioethics, see R. Baker, "How Should Students Learn about Contemporary Implications of Health Professionals' Role in the Holocaust?" *AMA Journal of Ethics* 23(1) (2021): 31–36.

2 E. Halperin, "The Rise and Fall of the American Jewish Hospital," *Academic Medicine* 87(5) (May 2012): 611.

3 R. Katz, "Paging Dr. Shylock! Jewish Hospitals and the Prudent Reinvestment of Jewish Philanthropy," in D. Smith (ed.), *Religious Giving* (Indiana University Press, 2010), 165.

Rabbi Dr. Jason Weiner, BCC, is the Senior Rabbi and Director of Spiritual Care at Cedars-Sinai Medical Center and the Rabbi of Knesset Israel Synagogue of Beverlywood.

grew, they created their own voluntary social support, educational, health and welfare systems to try not to be a societal burden, similar to what they had previously done in other countries, which eventually led to founding Jewish hospitals in the mid-nineteenth century.[4]

First Wave

Jewish hospitals in the United States were founded in three waves. The first wave began in 1850 as a shortage of hospital beds developed across the United States,[5] primarily as a result of urban epidemics, such as cholera and yellow fever outbreaks.[6] The founders of these first Jewish hospitals expressed feelings of shame when they were unable to take care of their own.[7] They framed their goal not only as an attempt to avoid becoming a burden, but primarily as a positive mission of obligation and responsibility to live up to Jewish values of "*tzedakah*" (charity/righteousness) and "*bikur cholim*" (visiting the sick).[8] The founders of these hospitals thus spoke with a strong sense of purpose to be of assistance to the sick and the poor.[9]

However, there was also a negative impetus for founding these hospitals. As a minority group, Jews tried not to complain publicly, but in internal publications and discussions another motive became apparent. At that time, anti-Semitism was increasing,[10] and there was also very widespread missionizing of sick Jews in American hospitals, often including forced reading of Christian scriptures to them, as well as deathbed conversions and baptisms.[11] The most desperately ill Jews were the most vulnerable. Jewish hospitals were thus needed for protection and to provide

4 J. Sarna, *American Judaism: A History* (Yale, 2004), 222.

5 D.E. Bridge, *The Rise and Development of the Jewish Hospital in America* (Rabbinical Thesis, Hebrew Union College, 1985), 25.

6 Kraut, *Covenant of Care*, 3–4; Bridge, *The Rise and Development of the Jewish Hospital in America*, 18.

7 Ibid., 2.

8 Ibid., 22–24; L. Levin, *Cedars-Sinai: The One-Hundred Year History of Cedars-Sinai Medical Center* (Cedars-Sinai Medical Center, 2002), intro.

9 Kraut, *Covenant of Care*, 24.

10 Katz, "Paging Dr. Shylock!" 166. For example, after the Civil War, in 1862, Ulysses S. Grant expelled all Jewish residents from their homes in the areas under his control.

11 Kraut, *Covenant of Care*, 3; Bridge, *The Rise and Development of the Jewish Hospital in America*, 25–28. Another example is from the laying of the cornerstone ceremony in 1866 for Baltimore's "Asylum for Israelites." Dr. J. Cohen stated, "Many of us know the instances in which poor co-religionists, stricken down

culturally sensitive care, with access to kosher food, a rabbi, and a range of religious services,[12] where nobody would ever be turned away due to an inability to pay.[13]

Although there was initially some debate over whether or not these hospitals should be exclusively for Jews,[14] the consensus quickly became that Jews should not treat others the way they had been treated by being exclusive, and that perhaps by welcoming all people, they would reduce anti-Semitism and create goodwill for the Jewish community.[15] Furthermore, there was a recognition that Jewish law requires Jews to "sustain the poor who are not Jewish along with poor Jews, and visit the sick who are not Jewish along with sick Jews, and one buries the dead who are not Jewish along with dead Jews, because these are the ways of peace."[16]

---

upon the bed of illness in the hands of strangers, have been greatly annoyed and their last moments embittered by the obtrusion of sentiments, in the vain attempt to draw them away from the God of their fathers. It was the occurrence of a case of this kind which a few years ago warmed us up to the necessity of making provisions to protect ourselves" (ibid., 26).

12 Halperin, "The Rise and Fall of the American Jewish Hospital," 611. Additional essential religious services included *mezuzos*, avoidance of autopsies unless it would save a life, a separate room for *bris milah*, availability of a rabbi, services on the various holidays, and in some cases, daily prayers and kosher food. See also Bridge, *The Rise and Development of the Jewish Hospital in America*, 32, 57, 59, 61. Interestingly, some Jewish hospitals, such as Mount Sinai in New York, had a synagogue before they had an operating room, which shows their priorities at the time (Aufses & Niss, *This House of Noble Deeds* [New York University Press, 2002], 4). Similar issues arose in Europe around the same time, and these services were so important to many Jews, and the ill treatment they received at non-Jewish hospitals was so bad, that some European Jews reported preferring to be poorly cared for in a Jewish hospital over going to municipal hospitals (J. Vanderhoek, "A Tale of Two Nineteenth-Century Dutch Jewish Hospitals," *Rambam Maimonides Medical Journal* 11(4) (2020): 6).

13 Levin, *Cedars-Sinai*, 14.

14 Levin, *Cedars-Sinai*, 4; Kraut, *Covenant of Care*, 24. Some rabbis opposed opening Jewish hospitals, and there were frequent debates, many of which stalled the opening of these hospitals, about religious perspective, ritual practice, location, if the hospital should be "sectarian" (only for Jews) or "nonsectarian" (open for all). See also Bridge, *The Rise and Development of the Jewish Hospital in America*, 64.

15 Katz, "Paging Dr. Shylock!" 166–67.

16 *Gittin* 61a.

From the earliest days of Jewish hospitals in America, Jews were thus very proud that all people in need were equally welcomed by them.[17] For example, at the opening ceremony for the Jewish Hospital in Denver in 1889, it was announced that its goal was to "rear a Temple unbounded by any creed. As pain knows no creed, so is this building the prototype of the grand idea of Judaism, which casts aside no stranger no matter of what race or blood."[18] In New York it was declared that "Beth Israel, like Abraham's tent, will be open to sufferers without distinction as to race or creed."[19] There are numerous examples of this type of inclusive sentiment at Jewish hospitals at that time.[20]

Second Wave

From the late 1880s until the 1920s, over two million Eastern European Jews immigrated to the United States, and during that period, the number of Jewish hospitals in America increased five-fold.[21] These immigrants tended to be poor, religiously observant,[22] and frequently resented by many Americans at the time, thus exacerbating much of the impetus for Jewish hospitals during the first wave.[23] Furthermore, the disproportionately high volume of Jewish tuberculosis patients at this time triggered a nationwide effort to create Jewish hospitals and relief societies to care for Jewish patients.[24]

---

17 Bridge, *The Rise and Development of the Jewish Hospital in America*, 37, 65. Many Jewish hospitals boasted of having equal numbers of Jewish and non-Jewish patients. See also Levin, *Cedars-Sinai*, 58.

18 Bridge, *The Rise and Development of the Jewish Hospital in America*, 38.

19 Kraut, *Covenant of Care*, 27.

20 Similarly, at the dedication in 1908 for a new facility for Newark's Beth Israel, the community rabbi proclaimed that "while this hospital shall be mainly supported by Jews, it will open its doors just as wide as they can swing to receive the non-Jew who may desire to enter and his religious sentiments shall be carefully safeguarded" (Kraut, *Covenant of Care*, 33). Similarly, in 1866, Philadelphia's Jewish community opened a nonsectarian hospital that proclaimed right on its entrance, "The Hospital was erected by the voluntary contributions of the Israelites of Philadelphia, and is dedicated to the relief of the sick and wounded without regard to creed, color or nationality" (Katz, "Paging Dr. Shylock!" 167).

21 Kraut, *Covenant of Care*, 64–66. From 1919 to 1922, the number of Jewish hospitals more than doubled.

22 Bridge, *The Rise and Development of the Jewish Hospital in America*, 32–35, 57.

23 Kraut, *Covenant of Care*, 4, 21; Bridge, *The Rise and Development of the Jewish Hospital in America*, 20.

24 Ibid., 23.

Despite the Jewish community's effort to care for their own sick, many Jews had to seek care outside their community, where they were again subjected not only to cultural insensitivity, but also to severe mistreatment and sometimes even physical assaults.[25] American physicians began labeling Jewish patients as being "subhuman," "dirty," "nervous," "difficult," and even created specific phrases and diagnoses for them, such as "Hebraic Debility," and "Jew-Neurasthenia."[26] Needless to say, Jewish patients did not receive proper medical care at most hospitals and needed to be sheltered from the consequences of this type of prejudice. Of course, most Jewish physicians would have the necessary language skills and cultural sensitivity to mitigate some of these concerns, but then another problem developed that exacerbated the need for Jewish hospitals.

Whereas in the nineteenth century most physicians apprenticed with private physicians in home-based practices, in the twentieth century this training transitioned to medical schools and hospitals.[27] However, for the first half of the twentieth century, anti-Semitic policies restricted Jewish medical school graduates access to internship and residency programs, and Jews were denied staff privileges in hospitals, while the few who had access were subject to harassment and verbal abuse.[28] In the 1920s, many American hospitals would not accept any Jews on their medical staff and if Jewish physicians wanted to find a hospital to accept their patients, they could usually only do so by making a referral via a non-Jewish colleague.[29] If they could get their patients admitted at all, Jewish doctors found that they often had to wait weeks longer than non-Jewish doctors.[30] In some cases, a hospital's medical staff even went on strike and made physical threats, to prevent Jewish doctors from being hired and to force them to be fired or resign.[31] Jews also faced difficulty in the area of medical school education. For example, in 1927 many medical schools had restricted personnel policies, such that of the thousand Jewish physicians in New York

---

25 E. Halperin, "'This is a Christian institution and we will tolerate no Jews here': The Brooklyn Medical Interns Hazings," *American Journal of Medical Sciences* 356(6) (2018): 505–17.

26 Kraut, *Covenant of Care*, 5; Katz, "Paging Dr. Shylock!" 170.

27 Bridge, *The Rise and Development of the Jewish Hospital in America*, 29.

28 Halperin, "The Rise and Fall of the American Jewish Hospital," 611.

29 Kraut, *Covenant of Care*, 120.

30 Ibid., 117.

31 E. Halperin, "'We do not want him because he is a Jew': The Montreal Interns' Strike of 1934," *Annals of Internal Medicine* 174 (2021): 852-857.

City at that time, not one of them held a full-fledged professorship in any medical school that was part of a university.[32]

On top of that, and perhaps most significantly for the history of Jewish hospitals in America, medical schools used many methods of determining if an applicant was Jewish, in which case they were often denied admission. Quotas were put into place on the number of Jews that medical schools would accept, so for example, between 1920 and 1940, when these quotas took effect, Jewish enrollment at Columbia's College of Physicians fell from 47% to 6%.[33] Similarly, Cornell Medical School's percentage of Jewish students dropped from 40% to 5% during that time.[34] Those Jews who did manage to graduate from medical school at that time were often denied residencies in non-Jewish hospitals and were refused hospital privileges after graduation.[35]

The need for Jewish physicians to have the ability to freely train, practice medicine, and care for their patients in hospitals became the primary impetus for the development of many of the Jewish clinics and hospitals between approximately 1912 and 1936.[36] These hospitals faced many obstacles, as they often had a hard time finding anyone to sell them land for a Jewish hospital,[37] and national accrediting boards frequently did not approve or allow graduate residencies at Jewish hospitals, even though these institutions met the accreditation standards.[38] Despite these challenges, the Jewish community rallied around this cause, as communal Jewish federations allocated approximately 25% of their local grants to Jewish hospitals.[39] Jewish hospitals were often the Jewish community's most impressive and identifiable philanthropy in each city,[40] and because even Jewish philanthropy was not accepted by the broader society at this time, Jewish hospitals were one of the few ways that individual Jews could give to humanity.[41]

---

32 Kraut, *Covenant of Care*, 119.

33 Ibid., 118.

34 Ibid.

35 Ibid., 117.

36 Bridge, *The Rise and Development of the Jewish Hospital in America*, 30–31; Kraut, *Covenant of Care*, 24, 117.

37 Kraut, *Covenant of Care*, 72.

38 Ibid., 124–25.

39 Katz, "Paging Dr. Shylock!" 172.

40 Ibid., 162.

41 Interview with Jonathan Schreiber, Vice President of Community Engagement at Cedars-Sinai, January 2021.

Third Wave and Beyond

There was also a brief third wave of development of Jewish hospitals during the 1940s and '50s, spurred by the Hospital Survey and Construction Act of 1946 (also known as the Hill-Burton Act), which created thousands of new hospital beds, primarily in suburban areas.[42] This legislation had a significant impact on the older Jewish hospitals, which were mostly located in urban areas, and enabled many of them to relocate, merge, or create new hospitals. Quotas limiting Jews came to an end in the 1960s, thanks to a combination of societal attitudes and government policies.[43] These hospitals remained welcoming places for Jews to seek care and employment, and they made sure to publicize the fact that patients and staff of all backgrounds remained equally welcomed in them.[44] Even as demographics changed and many historically Jewish hospitals were gradually made up primarily of people who were not Jewish, these institutions continued to articulate the same sense of purpose to care for all people who were suffering in their communities.[45]

The need for Jewish hospitals gradually declined. Jews were allowed to seek care and employment at any hospital,[46] and many non-Jewish hospitals even opened kosher kitchens or created access to Jewish religious needs.[47] The Medicare and Medicaid plans that were developed in the 1960s made hospitals less dependent on private philanthropy, and by 1981 Jewish federations allocated only 2.3% of their funding to healthcare and hospitals[48] (a number which has continued to shrink since then[49]). Furthermore, the attitude toward anti-Semitism gradually shifted from combating it via philanthropy to fighting it head-on, through organizations such as the Anti-Defamation League.[50] The hospital industry also became

---

42 Kraut, *Covenant of Care*, 140–41; Halperin, "The Rise and Fall of the American Jewish Hospital," 611.

43 E. Halperin, "Why Did the United States Medical School Admissions Quota for Jews End?" *American Journal of Medical Sciences* 358(5) (2019): 317–25.

44 Kraut, *Covenant of Care*, 174.

45 Ibid., 187.

46 Halperin, "The Rise and Fall of the American Jewish Hospital," 612. Ironically, the reduction of anti-Semitism in the medical profession adversely affected some Jewish hospitals as Jewish doctors and researchers gained more options (Aufses & Niss, *This House of Noble Deeds*, 13).

47 Katz, "Paging Dr. Shylock!" 172.

48 Ibid., 173.

49 Interview with Jonathan Schreiber, Vice President of Community Engagement at Cedars-Sinai, January 2021.

50 Katz, "Paging Dr. Shylock!" 173.

much more competitive at this time, and financial pressures forced many smaller community hospitals to merge with larger systems or close.[51]

Throughout American history, there have been approximately 113 Jewish hospitals in a total of twenty-four American cities, but as of 2012, twenty-four of them had merged with other Jewish hospitals, thirty-five closed, and twenty-four were purchased by or merged with non-Jewish hospitals, leaving just twenty-two remaining independent.[52] As of 2021, estimates are that there are only about ten left, and possibly as few as five, depending on how one defines a "Jewish hospital."[53]

What Has It Meant to Be a Jewish Hospital?

Christian hospitals in America are typically built on a strong church base, with articles of incorporation that guarantee the sponsoring church or organization will maintain a formal role in its governance, and often including precise ethical and religious directives of operation.[54] Jewish hospitals in America, on the other hand, have no such structure or official association. How exactly to define what it has meant to be a "Jewish hospital" has been the subject of much debate, and the difference between a Jewish hospital and a hospital for Jews is not always clear. At earlier periods in American history, some suggested that to be considered a Jewish hospital it would have to have had some of the following attributes:[55]

1. Founded primarily by members of the Jewish community;
2. Built primarily for members of the Jewish community;
3. Funded primarily by members of the Jewish community;
4. A Jewish name;
5. Governed primarily by members of the Jewish community;

---

51 Halperin, "The Rise and Fall of the American Jewish Hospital," 612.

52 Ibid.

53 Ibid., and personal correspondence with Dr. Halperin in January 2021. A current list of American Jewish hospitals can be found at this link (though many of these hospitals no longer identify as being Jewish): https://www.kosherdelight.com/HospitalsUSA.shtml.
As of 2016, 18.5% of hospitals in the United States were religiously affiliated. Between 2001 and 2016 the number of nonprofit religious hospitals decreased by 38.3%, but during this time the number of acute care hospitals that were Catholic owned or affiliated grew by 22%, even though the overall number of acute care hospitals decreased by 6% (M Guiahi, P.E. Helbin, S.B. Teal, D. Stulberg, J. Sheeder, "Patient Views on Religious Institutional Health Care," *JAMA* 2(12) (2019)).

54 Bridge, *The Rise and Development of the Jewish Hospital in America*, 9, 52–53, 175; Halperin, "The Rise and Fall of the American Jewish Hospital," 612.

55 Bridge, *The Rise and Development of the Jewish Hospital in America*, 2 and 51–52.

6. Staffed by an especially high percentage of Jews;
7. Viewed as "Jewish" by the Jewish community;
8. Adheres to Jewish religious or ritual practice to a greater degree than other religions or ritual practices;
9. A place in which Jewish patients feel comfortable (likely including cultural sensitivity, not displaying symbols from other faith traditions, and in-language care).

What Does It Mean to Be a Jewish Hospital in America Today?

The obvious question that arises is if there is any need for Jewish hospitals in America today. There is a certain integrity or sacred trust to the founders of these hospitals to maintain the institutions that they founded and built, but are they still needed for any uniquely Jewish reasons? Anti-Semitism is still a concern in the Jewish community, and it remains important to promote goodwill and maintain an infrastructure in case of a severe resurgence of anti-Semitism in society or within the medical establishment.[56] People often also praise the sense of community, comradery, and tradition at Jewish hospitals. I believe, however, that what makes them unique is far deeper. I suggest that the survival of some proudly Jewish hospitals in America today is crucial to maintaining essential areas of focus in the tapestry of our healthcare system. The rich and impressive history of Jewish hospitals in America serves as a powerful reminder and incentive for these hospitals to maintain fidelity to certain profound ideals, which will hopefully serve as role models for others:

1. Inclusivity

Jewish hospitals, by their very existence and hopefully by their example, teach the importance of inclusivity and welcoming the stranger.

The Hebrew Bible uses the story of the Jewish people's slavery in Egypt as national moral education intended to transform their perspective of humanity and morality.[57] Right after the exodus narrative, the Torah gives numerous commands to remind the people to learn these lessons, not just as knowledge, but as shared memory of their own experience.[58] The Torah, in multiple places,[59] is very clear about the obligation to love

56 Katz, "Paging Dr. Shylock!" 176.

57 J. Sacks, *Not in God's Name* (Schocken Books, 2015), 183–84.

58 Ibid.

59 Depending on how one counts the commandments, the Torah warns against wronging a stranger either 36 or 46 times, more than any other commandment

the stranger. For example, it commands, "Do not wrong or oppress the stranger for you yourselves were once strangers in the land of Egypt" (Ex. 22:21), and, "Do not oppress the stranger, for you know what it feels like to be a stranger, for you yourselves were once strangers in the land of Egypt" (Ex. 23:29).[60]

So, too, remembering the difficult history that led to the creation of Jewish hospitals in America should continue to sensitize and inspire contemporary Jewish hospitals to embody these crucial lessons. Having lived and suffered as strangers at many points of Jewish history, Jews are obligated by the Torah to become people who are dedicated to caring for strangers.[61] Jewish hospitals were necessary in America because they were a place for people who otherwise were excluded, alienated, isolated, or unwelcome in the broader society to feel safe and at home. Remembering what it was like for Jews to be victims, a Jewish hospital must therefore be a place where all people feel comfortable and welcome, not with the intention of encouraging them to become Jewish, but simply as an act of solidarity and identification with the stranger.

It is therefore no coincidence that in 1906, the Jewish Kaspare Cohn Hospital in Los Angeles hired the first female physician to practice in Los Angeles, Sarah Vasen, MD, who went on to become the hospital's superintendent.[62] That hospital later changed its name to Cedars of Lebanon and, along with many other American Jewish hospitals, became a safe haven for Jewish physicians who were driven out of Germany during the Nazi era.[63] Another important example of the enduring values of Jewish hospitals relates to their involvement in the civil rights movement. For example, in 1951, Louisville Jewish Hospital hired Jesse Bell, MD, the first African-American doctor to practice at a non-African-American hospital in that region.[64]

(*Bava Metzia* 59b).

60 See also Leviticus 19:34.

61 Sacks, *Not in God's Name*, 188. Rabbi Sacks goes so far as to argue that, "Judaism is the voice of the other throughout history. The whole of Judaism is about making space for the other…" (J. Sacks, *Future Tense* [Schocken, 2009], 83).

62 https://en.wikipedia.org/wiki/Sarah_Vasen.

63 Levin, *Cedars-Sinai*, 63.

64 Jewish Kentucky Oral History Project, "Interview with Morris Weiss, August 1, 2016," https://kentuckyoralhistory.org/ark:/16417/xt7crj48sc8k; H. Thimson, "Louisville Jewish Hospital's 'Tikkun Olam': A Case Example of Continuity for American Jewish Hospitals" (2019), https://uknowledge.uky.edu/cgi/viewcontent.cgi?article=1002&context=libraries_undergraduate_scholarship.

This is an example of particularity leading to universalism. Ironically, in this case, if fidelity to a people's own history and identity is maintained, they can be motivated to be more inclusive and welcoming to others. It is less of a challenge to love one's neighbor, who is part of the same community, than it is to love the stranger, whom some people might regard with fear or animosity.[65] Jewish hospitals are a profound reminder that not only is "love your neighbor as yourself" a foundation of Jewish medical ethics, but so is the crucial commitment to "love the stranger."

2. Faith Friendly, Not Faith Enforced

Jewish hospitals serve as unique models of faith-based institutions, because unlike those under the auspices of some other faiths, Jewish hospitals do not impose any specific religious directives of practice. A Jewish hospital should indeed be a place that is faith friendly and a place where faith is facilitated, but not a place where it is enforced. A lesson that Jewish communities have learned over the course of Jewish history is that not only have Jews frequently had other religions imposed on them (as mentioned above), and not only is religious coercion usually ineffective at promoting religion[66] and risks anti-religious backlash,[67] but, perhaps counterintuitively, it is bad for religion. As Rabbi Jonathan Sacks taught, religion only truly acquires influence when it relinquishes power and instead becomes the voice of the voiceless, and the conscience of the community.[68] Religion can thrive without exerting power,[69] and many rabbinic thinkers posit that religious acts only have true value when they are done free of any coercion.[70] Religion is at its best, taught Rabbi Sacks, when it relies on the strength of example, and at its worst, when it seeks to impose truth by force.[71] The phrase "religious coercion" is thus an oxymoron. One

---

65 Sacks, *Not in God's Name*, 181.

66 Rabbi J. Soloveitchik, *Community and Covenant* (Ktav, 2005), 211.

67 K. Nueman, "Religious Zionism and the State" (Hebrew) in Y. Stern, et al., *When Judaism Meets the State* (Tel Aviv: Yediot Ahronot, 2015), 330-333. See also R. Schwartz, "The Political Theology of Rabbi Nachum Eliezer Rabinovitch," *The Torah u-Madda Journal* 18 (2021): 19.

68 Sacks, *Not in God's Name*, 222.

69 Ibid., 236.

70 Schwartz, "The Political Theology of Rabbi Nachum Eliezer Rabinovitch," 10-11. R. Rabinovitch bases his argument primarily on Maimonides in the *Guide to the Perplexed*.

71 Sacks, *Not in God's Name*, 234. See also extensive discussion in A. Ravitzky, "Is a Halakhic State Possible? The Paradox of Jewish Theocracy," *Israel Affairs* 11(1) (2005): 137–64.

cannot impose truth or spirituality by force,[72] as the Talmud rules, "Coerced agreement is not consent."[73]

This is why some leading rabbinic thinkers have argued that according to Jewish law governments should always limit their authority to the civil realm and never involve themselves in religious matters.[74] Indeed, some suggest that it was the American separation of church and state that created the reality that religion has no power, but enormous influence,[75] and this can also be true for Jewish hospitals.

At the same time, however, steps are often taken in Jewish hospitals to ensure that religion can indeed be fully practiced by those who *choose* to do so. One example of this is the development of "reasonable accommodation" policies to facilitate religious patients' abilities to receive treatment in accordance with their own values and to provide a practical and compassionate way to resolve conflicts.[76] Such policies are important ways in which the faith-based practices or beliefs of religious patients can be enabled without being forced on all patients in a given institution. While such accommodations are beneficial to many populations, they may prove to be especially important to the rapidly growing Orthodox Jewish community,[77] and could revive a very relevant need for Jewish hospitals where

---

72 Ibid., 225. Rabbi Sacks expands elsewhere that "Faith, coerced, is not faith. Worship, forced, is not true worship." (J. Sacks, *Covenant & Conversation: Exodus* [Maggid Books, 2010], 197). Rabbi Sacks elaborates on this topic elsewhere, citing numerous rabbinic sources, arguing that: 1. Although there is an obligation to reprove wrongdoing, it does not apply when it is certain that reproof will not be heeded; 2. Nowadays rabbinic authorities rule that coercive punishments would be seen as unwarranted and would therefore not improve but worsen the religious environment, and that reduction of the power of coercion prepares the world for the Heavenly Kingdom as society gradually moves towards uncoerced acceptance of Jewish law; 3. Education is Judaism's classic alternative to coercion, and is the best way to internalize religion (J. Sacks, *One People?* [Littman Library of Jewish Civilization in association with Liverpool University Press,1993], 218-9).

73 *Shabbos* 88a and *Avodah Zarah* 2b, cited by Sacks, *Not in God's Name*, 230.

74 Schwartz, "The Political Theology of Rabbi Nachum Eliezer Rabinovitch," 12, 17, 24-5.

75 J. Sacks, *Morality* (Basic Books, 2020), 254–55.

76 L.S. Johnson, "The case for reasonable accommodation of conscientious objections to declarations of brain death," *Journal of Bioethical Inquiry* 13(1) (2016), 105–15; E. Gabbay, J.J. Fins, "Go in Peace: Brain Death, Reasonable Accommodation and Jewish Mourning Rituals," *Journal of Religion and Health* 58 (2019):1672–86.

77 https://forward.com/news/402663/orthodox-will-dominate-american-jewry-in-coming-decades-as-population/.

they can obtain religiously/culturally congruent care.

The fact that Jewish hospitals accommodate religious needs but don't dictate them can also be helpful when it comes to procedures that other faith-based hospitals prohibit, such as abortions, but which Judaism sometimes allows and in certain situations may even require. Since all legal, standard of practice procedures are permitted at Jewish hospitals, one who wants to fully observe one's religion is able to do so if one chooses to, which is often not the case when one religious tradition dictates the range of permitted medical practices for all of its staff and patients.

3. Values

Examining the history and mission of Jewish hospitals in America also reminds us that there remain certain values that are widely recognized, but always in need of encouragement and deeper focus:[78]

a. *Research and education*: Jewish hospitals' roots in providing institutions where Jewish medical students can train is a reminder of the centrality of education and rigorous research in Judaism.[79] Early on in their history, American Jewish hospitals developed a reputation for being very innovative, thanks in part to the emphasis on education in the Jewish community.[80] At a time when many faith-based institutions place limits on the types of research they permit, such as some forms of stem-cell research, Jewish hospitals ensure robust access to potentially lifesaving innovation. Education is a core Jewish value[81] that ensures high-quality medicine, and promotes human dignity and resilience in challenging times. It is thus central to the practice of modern medicine.

b. *Care for body and soul*: American Jewish hospitals have tended to place great importance on certain inconspicuous but meaningful symbols, such as *mezuzos*.[82] These powerful religious and cultural symbols in places of science and medicine can serve as reminders that a hospital is not just a place where physical ailments are treated, but also a source of holistic care, which goes much deeper. As the traditional Jewish prayer for healing, the "*mi sheberach*," declares, we pray for both "a healing of the soul

---

78 Ibid.; Halperin, "The Rise and Fall of the American Jewish Hospital," 613.

79 See discussion in Katz, "Paging Dr. Shylock!" 175.

80 Kraut, *Covenant of Care*, 54.

81 Sacks, *Covenant & Conversation: Exodus*, 79, 138. Rabbi Sacks argues, based on *Bava Basra* 21a, that Jews developed the world's first system of public, universal compulsory education, over two thousand years ago because Judaism regards studying as the highest religious value.

82 Halperin, "The Rise and Fall of the American Jewish Hospital," 611.

and a healing of the body." Traditional symbols and respect for faith can help humanize and give deeper meaning to healthcare.

c. *Responsibility to care for the sick and the poor.* The history of striving not to be a burden, but rather to focus on the duty to care for the sick and poor of one's community is a reminder that healthcare is about taking on responsibility. Throughout history, Jewish communities have cared for those in need instead of relying on others to do it for them. Jewish hospitals remind us to continue this vital tradition.

Of course, these values sometimes come into conflict with each other and aren't always simple to apply. A difficult, but very practical example of implementing the history and mission of being a Jewish hospital arose during the Covid 19 pandemic. As vaccination mandates were enacted, the only exemptions allowed were for either medical or religious accommodations. Each institution took a different approach to how strict they would be in allowing religious accommodations. For a Jewish hospital, this presents a significant dilemma because on the one hand, inclusivity and embracing the right of all individuals to freely practice their own religion are core aspects of a Jewish hospital's identity and mission. On the other hand, care for the vulnerable, sophisticated practice of the art of healing, and engagement in the science of research and advanced medicine are also central tenets. This requires attempting to sensitively balance the desire to respect everyone's ability to live in accordance with their own sincerely held beliefs with promoting the protection that vaccination offers, as well as the communal responsibility and accountability that vaccination engenders. That said, one side often must be chosen, and I believe that for a Jewish hospital the duty to protect vulnerable patients supersedes the need to accommodate every single sincerely held belief.

Conclusion

Many of the values discussed in this article are not exclusively Jewish, and several of them can be found to some extent at many hospitals today. Many religions and indeed those with no religion strive for many similar ideals and commitments. This history may indeed have implications for other faith-based hospitals and perhaps even the entire healthcare system. My argument is simply that utilizing some teachings of the Jewish tradition and studying its rich recent history can serve as an anchor and inspiration to help clarify many of these values and ensure that they are substantial and firmly rooted. Without this foundation, it would be less certain that these values become embodied with the same sense of urgency and dedication, and transmitted to the next generation. It is therefore essential to remember the past, so that we can build a better world. ☙

L-Ḥayyim

By: ZVI RON

There is a popular custom to raise a glass of an alcoholic beverage and say *L-Ḥayyim* at various special occasions. In this article, we will trace the origin and development of this practice.

Early Sources

Using a version of the form *L-Ḥayyim* as a blessing is already found in 1 Samuel 25:6, as part of the greeting David sent to Nabal, *L-ḥai* (לחי).[1] Although commentators have different explanations as to the exact meaning of this salutation, the common theme is that of a blessed life for Nabal and his family.[2] However, there is no biblical example of this blessing being connected with drinking wine.

Saying *L-Ḥayyim* in the context of drinking wine is found in *Tanḥuma* (*Pekudei* 2). There we are told how the Sanhedrin cross-examined witnesses. "At the time they examined the witnesses concerning a sin an individual had committed the Sanhedrin and all the Israelites would go out into the public square. They brought there the individual who had been charged with the offense which required stoning or one of the four death penalties that were imposed by the *beit din*. Two or three of the most distinguished leaders of the community would come forth and would ques-

1 In the verse it is not clear if the greeting phrase is just *L-ḥai* or a phrase *ko l-ḥai* (כה לחי), as the section reads: "And David sent ten young men, and David said unto the young men: 'Get you up to Carmel, and go to Nabal, and greet him in my name; and thus ye shall say (כה): To life (לחי)! Peace be both unto thee, and peace be to thy house, and peace be unto all that thou hast" (1 Samuel 25:5–6). The term כה may be the introduction to the greeting, as in this JPS English translation, or part of the greeting itself.

2 See Yehuda Kiel, *Da'at Mikra, Shmuel* vol. 1 (Jerusalem: Mossad HaRav Kook, 1981), p. 252.

Zvi Ron received *semikhah* from the Israeli Rabbanut and his PhD in Jewish Theology from Spertus University. He is an educator living in Neve Daniel, Israel, and the author of *Sefer Katan V-Gadol* (Rossi Publications, 2006) about the big and small letters in Tanakh, and *Sefer HaIkkar Ḥaser* (Mossad HaRav Kook, 2017) about the variable spellings of words in Tanakh.

tion the witness. After they returned from the cross-examination, a member of the Sanhedrin would say to them: '*savri maranan* (gentlemen, what do you think).' They would announce whether he was to live (לחיים) or to die. If he were to be sentenced to stoning, they would bring a pleasant-tasting but potent wine, and give it to him to drink so that he would not suffer pain from the stoning." Later on, this midrash describes a practice to say *L-Ḥayyim* at *Kiddush* and *Havdalah*. "Similarly, when the representative of the community held the *Kiddush* or *Havdalah* cup in his hand he would say: '*savri maranan*,' and the congregation would respond: '*L-Ḥayyim*'; that is to say, 'May this cup be for the living.'"

This is the earliest explanation for the custom, to say *L-Ḥayyim* to distinguish this cup from the cup associated with death. It is the standard explanation brought in the classic works that explain Jewish customs such as *Sefer Ta'amei ha-Minhagim u-Mekorei ha-Dinim*,[3] *Otzar Kol Minhagei Yeshurun*[4] and *Otzar Dinim u-Minhagim*.[5]

In *Tanḥuma* it is the assembled congregation who says *L-Ḥayyim* rather than the person drinking. The idea that the person drinking says *L-Ḥayyim* is found in TB *Shabbat* 67b in a discussion of what things may be considered unlawful due to being categorized as superstitions ("the ways of the Amorite"). There we find: "(One who says while drinking:) 'Wine and life to the mouth of the Sages,' this does not fall into the category of the ways of the Amorite. There was an incident with Rabbi Akiva who made a banquet for his son, and over each and every cup he brought he said: 'Wine and life to the mouth of the Sages (חמרא וחיי לפום רבנן), life and wine to the mouth of the Sages and to the mouth of their students.'"[6] The Jerusalem Talmud (*Berakhot* 6:8) records another version of what R. Akiva did in a discussion of the special blessing of *ha-tov v-ha-meitiv* on wine.[7] "There was an incident with Rabbi Akiva who made a banquet for Shimon his son, and over each and every barrel that was opened he would bless and say: 'Good wine to the life of the Sages (חמרא טבא לחיי רבנן) and their students.'" Another version is found in *Tosefta Shabbat* 8:3, "There was an incident with Rabbi Akiva who made a banquet for his son, and over each

3 Avraham Sperling, *Sefer Ta'amei ha-Minhagim u-Mekorei ha-Dinim* (Jerusalem: Shai Lamora, 1999), p. 137.

4 A. Hershovitz, *Otzar Kol Minhagei Yeshurun* (St. Louis, MO, 1918), *siman* 28:1, p. 66.

5 J.D. Eisenstein, *Otzar Dinim u-Minhagim* (New York, 1917), p. 192.

6 Regarding the transposing of life and wine in this blessing, see Maharsha and *Iyun Ya'akov* here. Many interpretations are found in the literature regarding this switch.

7 On the differences between the two Rabbi Akiva stories, see *Yefeh Einayim* to *Shabbat* 67b.

and every barrel that was opened he would say 'Wine to the life of the Sages (חמרא לחיי רבננא) and the life of their students.'"

Tanḥuma talks about *L-Ḥayyim* as a response to *savri*, which is the prevalent Sephardic custom of having *L-Ḥayyim* as a response said by those hearing the blessing over wine, rather than something said by those drinking themselves. However, the R. Akiva stories do not mention *savri* and so indicate that *L-Ḥayyim* functions as an independent blessing said by the person pouring or drinking the wine, similar to the prevalent Ashkenazic custom.[8]

No explicit reason is given in the Talmud for R. Akiva's blessing. R. Ḥayyim David Azulay (Ḥida, 1724–1806) gives two explanations.[9] His primary explanation, that he considers the simple meaning, is based on *Tanḥuma* (*Pekudei* 2) that due to the connection between wine and the death penalty noted there, when someone is making *Kiddush* or *Havdalah* on wine, people say *L-Ḥayyim*, and so too at the occasion of R. Akiva's banquet.[10]

These are the earliest examples in Jewish literature of saying a version of *L-Ḥayyim* over wine. R. Shmuel Avigdor Tosfa'a (1806–1866) in his *Minḥat Bikkurim* on the *Tosefta* explicitly states that what R. Akiva did was just like the current practice to say "To your life (לחייכון)" when drinking wine.

Dangerous Wine

Among the *rishonim* we find other reasons to say *L-Ḥayyim*, beyond the idea of distinguishing the wine from the wine drunk by a person sentenced to death. These are all based on the idea that there is danger inherent in drinking wine, thus necessitating saying *L-Ḥayyim* to offset potential harm.

Sefer ha-Pardes brings that R. Yitzḥak b. Yehudah (11th century), one of Rashi's teachers, explained that the reason people say *savri* before *Kiddush* is "since wine brought a curse to the world in the time of Noah, who got drunk from it and a curse went forth on Canaan" the person about to drink announces "understand (*savru*) that I am planning to drink something that brought a curse to the world." When the people respond *L-Ḥayyim*, they are saying "the drinking should be for you for life and not

8 See Menachem Mendel Landa, *Siddur Tzluta d-Avraham*, vol. 1 (Tel-Aviv: Grafika, 1958), p. 455.

9 Ḥayyim David Azulay, *Petaḥ Einayim* (Livorno, 1790), 43a.

10 He also gives a second reason that it may be that R. Akiva was referring specifically to TB *Nedarim* 49a where we find that rabbis are weak and sickly and he was saying that they should drink wine for their health.

for any harm."[11] This explanation is also brought by R. Eliezer b. Yoel (Ra'aviah, c.1140–1220).[12]

The commentary of the *Ba'alei ha-Tosafot* to Lev. 10:9 states that it is customary that when someone is saying a blessing over wine in public and says *savri maranan*, the congregation responds *L-Ḥayyim* because Adam got drunk on the wine from his marriage blessings (ברכת נישואין) and therefore sinned and was cursed with mortality. *Tosafot* then references what R. Akiva did at his son's banquet, implying that it is for the same reason. Abudraham gives this explanation as well, based on the idea that the forbidden fruit which brought death to the world was grapes (TB *Berakhot* 40a, *Bereishit Rabbah* 15:17).[13] This same idea appears in *Tikkunei Zohar* (*tikkun* 24), where it is written that one must say *savri maranan* and the others answer *l-ḥaye* (לחיי) "in order to be connected to the Tree of Life and not the Tree of Death."[14]

Tosafot brings many other negative associations of wine, ending with the teaching in TB *Sanhedrin* 70a based on Proverbs 31:6, "Give strong drink to him that is ready to perish, and wine to the bitter in soul," that wine was created to comfort mourners. TB *Ketubbot* 8b reports the multi-

---

11 Chaim Ehrenreich, ed., *Sefer ha-Pardes* (Budapest, 1924), pp. 186–187. Also brought in *Shibbolei ha-Leket, seder Berakhot, siman* 140. Note that halachic reasons are brought in both works for saying *savri* as well, before R. Yitzḥak's explanation. See also *Tosafot Berakhot* 43a *hoil.* For an overview of halakhic and other reasons, see Aron Maged, *Beit Aharon* vol. 13 (New York: Balshon, 1978), *siman* 90, pp. 605–607; Yehuda Ben David, *Shevet m-Yehudah* (Jerusalem: 2018), vol. 1, *siman* 42, note 181, pp. 366–367. The Noah explanation is brought in *Baḥ*, *Oraḥ Ḥayyim* 174:9 in the name of R. Menaḥem of Mirzburg (Mahari Metz, often misquoted as Mahari Mintz, 14th century, see *Ḥiddushei u-Biurei Maharshal* to *Tur*, *Oraḥ Ḥayyim* 192).

12 David Devilsky, ed., *Sefer Ra'aviah* vol. 2 (Bnei Brak, 2005), *Pesaḥim*, *siman* 511. He also mentions in *Berakhot, siman* 120 that *L-Ḥayyim* is said because wine "brings a curse to the world," but he does not specify there what the curse is.

13 Shlomo Wertheimer, ed., *Abudraham ha-Shalem* (Jerusalem, 1963), p. 151.

14 Although some sources indicate that the forbidden fruit itself was grapes and that Ḥavah crushed it into wine for Adam (*Bereishit Rabbah* 19:5), from the language of *Tosafot* here it appears that they are not following that approach, as they state that Adam got drunk and then sinned, so the drinking itself was not the sin of eating the forbidden fruit. See also TB *Sanhedrin* 70b, *Bamidbar Rabbah* 10:4. However, *Tikkunei Zohar* explicitly states that this explanation is connected to the idea that grapes were the forbidden fruit. Sperling, *Sefer Ta'amei ha-Minhagim u-Mekorei ha-Dinim*, p. 137 note *alef* understands that *Tosafot* here is following that approach as well.

ple cups of wine that were drunk at the home of the mourner as a component of comforting. Based on that, *L-Ḥayyim* expresses the desire not to drink in the context of mourning, but rather in that of life.[15]

The four major negative associations of wine, the wine drunk by those about to receive capital punishment (*Tanḥuma*), the sin of Adam (*Tosafot*), the curse of Noah (*Sefer ha-Pardes*)[16] and the association with mourning are the standard explanations[17] brought for saying *L-Ḥayyim* in most discussions of this topic.[18]

There are various customs regarding whether more words are added to the *L-Ḥayyim* statement, such as לחיים טובים ולשלום,[19] and whether a handshake is involved as well.[20] The custom of the Bulgarian rabbi, R.

---

15 See *Baḥ*, *Oraḥ Ḥayyim* 174:9 who brings this idea in the name of Maharshal. It is found in *Ḥiddushei u-Biurei Maharshal* to *Tur*, *Oraḥ Ḥayyim* 182. It is also found in the *Etz Yosef* commentary to *Tanḥuma* by Ḥanokh Zundel ben Joseph (d. 1867).

16 These three are mentioned by Aaron b. Yaakov ha-Cohen, *Orḥot Ḥayyim* (Jerusalem, 1956), p. 73, *hilkhot birkat ha-mazon* 20.

17 For more mystical and *gematria*-based explanations, see R. Ḥayyim Palagi, *Kaf ha-Ḥayyim*, *Oraḥ Ḥayyim* 167:108.

18 It is because of this that the Munkacs Rebbe, R. Chaim Elazar Spira (1868–1937) brings in the name of his father, R. Zvi Hirsch Spira, that it is inappropriate to say *L-Ḥayyim* at the Shabbat daytime *Kiddush*, as it implies that protection from harm is needed, whereas fulfilling a *mitzvah* that needs wine itself provides protection. Since people do not customarily say *L-Ḥayyim* at the Friday night *Kiddush* and only in the daytime, it implies that the daytime *Kiddush* is less of a *mitzvah*. He notes that although R. Akiva said *L-Ḥayyim* over wine at a *mitzvah* meal, since there is no particular *mitzvah* to drink wine at such a meal, saying *L-Ḥayyim* for protection was warranted, but it should not be said at *Kiddush* where the *mitzvah* is to use wine. He understands *Tikkunei Zohar* as only referring to wine drunk not in the context of *Kiddush*, although that entire *tikkun* is in fact talking about *Kiddush*. He goes on to say that "there is no greater degradation of the daytime *Kiddush*" than "yelling to each other *arf, arf* (הב, הב), *L-Ḥayyim*, *L-Ḥayyim*, like in a bar." Chaim Elazar Spira, *Nimukei Oraḥ Ḥayyim* (Brooklyn, New York: Emes Publishing Institute, 2004), pp. 195–196, *siman* 289, note 2. Still, *Tanḥuma* did explicitly talk about *Kiddush* and *Havdalah* when discussing saying *savri* and *L-Ḥayyim*, and this is the normative practice.

19 See Yissachar Tamar, *Alei Tamar*, *Yerushalmi, Zera'im* vol. 1 (Givatayim, Israel: Atir, 1979), *Berakhot* 6:8, 229–230; Gavriel Zinner, *Nitei Gavriel, Hilkhot Nesuin* vol. 2 (Jerusalem: Shemesh, 1998), 80:24, p. 147; Simḥa Rabinowitz, *Piskei Teshuvot* (Jerusalem, 2002) volume 2, 174:15, 518–519.

20 Zinner, *Nitei Gavriel, Hilchot Nesuin* vol. 2, 80:23, p. 147. The handshake is an ancient and well-known "symbol of amity." Raymond Firth, *Symbols: Public and Private* (London: Allen & Unwin, 1973), p. 137.

Astruc b. David ibn Sangi (1570–1643),[21] reported by his student R. Ḥayyim Benvenisti (1603–1673) in his book *Shayarei Knesset ha-Gedolah*, was to say בשמחתכם ("in your happiness") instead of *L-Ḥayyim*.[22] Thus, we see an idea to simply add a positive statement to counter the negative associations of wine, and it does not have to be *L-Ḥayyim* or even a variation of the word "*ḥayyim*" per se.

L-Ḥayyim on Liquor

In all of these sources the reason for *L-Ḥayyim* is wine specific. Because of that, it is not customary for people to say *savri* over other alcoholic drinks, which as we saw was considered the first part that would generate the *L-Ḥayyim* response.[23] Still, nowadays it is common to say *L-Ḥayyim* over liquor as well. In Ḥassidic literature, explanations for this can be found revolving around *gematria* and word play.[24]

Many sources add that beyond the specific incidents with Adam and Noah, the more general reason for saying *L-Ḥayyim* is "since wine causes drunkenness and much harm occurs due to drunkenness… he says *savri maranan* that this cup should be for life and not cause matters of death."[25] R. Sinai Sapir in his *Olat Ḥodesh* writes that R. Akiva's blessing became the source to say *L-Ḥayyim* not only when drinking wine, but any drink that is considered the "wine of the land" (חמר מדינה).[26] Similarly, *Otzar Kol Minhagei Yeshurun* explains that nowadays liquor functions in place of wine

21 On this figure, see Matt Goldish, *Jewish Questions: Responsa on Sephardic Life in the Early Modern Period* (Princeton, NJ: Princeton University Press, 2008), p. lxi; Moshe Amar, *Sefer She'eilot u-Teshuvot R. Astruc b. David ibn Sangi* (Ramat Gan: Bar Ilan University Press, 1982).

22 *Shayarei Knesset ha-Gedolah, Oraḥ Ḥayyim* 174:2.

23 See *Baḥ*, *Oraḥ Ḥayyim* 174:9 who brings a quote from R. Menachem of Mirzburg (Mahari Metz, 14th century) that *savri* is not said over beer, and presumably not *L-Ḥayyim* either, as he connects the two. See also *Ateret Zekeinim* on *Oraḥ Ḥayyim* 190:1, who says that there are reasons not to say *savri* on anything other than wine, but only gives the reason of R. Menachem of Mirzburg that wine caused a curse in the time of Noah. See also Elazar Giman, *Sifran shel Tzaddikim* (Lublin: 1928), 1:8, p. 9, where it is reported that the Baal Shem Tov said not to say *L-Ḥayyim* over beer, but no explicit reason is given.

24 Sperling, *Sefer Ta'amei ha-Minhagim u-Mekorei ha-Dinim*, p. 496.

25 *Shayarei Knesset ha-Gedolah, Oraḥ Ḥayyim, Beit Yosef* 167:4. Similarly in *Shibbolei ha-Leket, seder Berakhot, siman* 140 and *Tanya Rabbati, siman* 24.

26 Sinai Sapir, *Olat Ḥodesh* (Warsaw, 1847), Iyar, *drush* 2, p. 199.

so we say *L-Ḥayyim* on liquor as well.[27] This seems to be the simple explanation of the custom; it started with wine and spread to other alcoholic drinks. We saw that wine was associated with certain negative outcomes, and these concerns apply equally to liquor, if not more so, so *L-Ḥayyim* would be appropriate for liquor as well.

Poison

The earliest versions of *Tanḥuma* add a few words when discussing the practice to say *L-Ḥayyim* at *Kiddush* and *Havdalah*.[28] "Similarly, when the representative of the community held the *Kiddush* or *Havdalah* cup in his hand and he was scared of poison that there may be in the cup (והוא ירא מסם המות שלא יהא בכוס), he would say: *savri maranan* and the congregation would respond: *L-Ḥayyim*..."[29] In some current editions of *Tanḥuma* these words are either left out entirely or included in parentheses or brackets.[30]

Why would anyone be scared that their *Kiddush* cup was poisoned? There are a number of ways to understand this unusual concern.

It is possible to understand that the reference is not to actual poison, but to the "pleasant-tasting but potent wine" given to those about to be stoned so that their pain is lessened.[31] Although in *Tanḥuma* no substance is added to the wine to make it potent, we do find the idea of adding an ingredient to the wine in TB *Sanhedrin* 43a. There we find the statement of Rav Ḥisda, "The court gives one who is being led out to be killed a grain of frankincense in a cup of wine in order to confuse his mind, as it is stated: "Give strong drink to him that is ready to perish, and wine to

27 A. Hershovitz, *Otzar Kol Minhagei Yeshurun* (St. Louis, MO, 1918), *siman* 28:1, p. 65.

28 Constantinople 1522, Venice 1545 (the Bomberg edition), Mantua 1563, Prague 1613. This is the version of *Midrash Tanḥuma* also known as *Tanḥuma C* or the "printed *Tanḥuma,*" as distinct from the Buber *Tanḥuma*. This *Tanḥuma* is understood to date from the Geonic period. See Anat Raizel, *Introduction to the Midrashic Literature* (Alon Shvut, Israel: Tevunot-Michlelet Herzog, 2011), pp. 234–237.

29 This is the version quoted by Ḥida in his discussion of the topic. Ḥayyim David Azulay, *Petaḥ Einayim* (Livorno, 1790), 43a.

30 These words do not appear in Samuel Berman, *Midrash Tanhuma-Yelammedenu: An English Translation of Genesis and Exodus* (Hoboken, New Jersey: KTAV, 1996), as he translated based on the Vienna 1863 edition, see p. x, note 2.

31 Avraham Orenstein, *Encyclopedia l-Taarei Kavod b-Yisrael* vol. 3 (Tel Aviv: Netzaḥ, 1963), p. 1662. This would also be indicated by the fact that the *Kiddush* section in *Tanḥuma* opens with the word וכן (and similarly), indicating a connection to the previous passage about the cup given to the person about to be put to death. See Shmuel Pesach Bagamilsky, "B-Inyan Amirat Savri Maranan," *Kovetz Hearot ha-Temimim v-Anshei Shlomeinu* (Morristown, New Jersey), vol. 3 (1988), p. 17.

the bitter in soul" (Proverbs 31:6)."[32] It is possible to understand that the term "poison" in *Tanḥuma*, literally "drug of death"(סם המות), is referring to the potent wine or the frankincense given to the person sentenced to death. This basic approach is brought by R. Zedekiah ben Abraham Anav (1210–c. 1280) in his *Shibbolei ha-Leket* in the name of his brother, R. Binyamin, who heard it from his teacher, R. Yitzḥak.[33]

Not only was the cup a cup of death, the frankincense added to it was dangerous on its own, a fact known in the ancient world. The 1st century Greek physician Pedanius Dioscorides describes frankincense as "a good medicine, but if drunk by a healthy person brings on madness and, if too much is taken, produces fatal results."[34] Thus, it would not be strange for frankincense to be termed a "drug of death." Still, it would be an unusual thing for a person to actually be worried about, particularly considering that no trial took place and whatever the case capital punishment was extremely rare (Mishnah, *Makkot* 1:10).

Another approach is to understand the poisoned cup in a more metaphoric sense as something denoting harm and suffering. Maharal in his comments to the R. Akiva episode in TB *Shabbat* 67b gives numerous examples of verses in Tanakh where a cup of wine is used metaphorically to refer to destruction or calamity. Most explicitly, Psalms 60:5 uses the terminology of drinking "bitter/poisoned wine" (יין תרעלה) to describe being subjected to hardships. In this understanding, there is no actual poison in the cup, but more of a general concern that there may be a tragic outcome of the drinking, figuratively termed a cup poisoned with the drug of death.[35] This would make the statement in *Tanḥuma* in line with the approach we saw of the *rishonim*, that *L-Ḥayyim* comes to offset the dangers associated with wine, here symbolically termed poison.

Toasts in the Ancient World

Drinking to good health is a practice found in many cultures around the world. A popular explanation for this is that this was originally done in order to "assure guests that the wine they were about to consume was not

---

32 Regarding the psychoactive properties of frankincense, see Arieh Moussaieff, et al., "Incensole acetate, an incense component, elicits psychoactivity by activating TRPV3 channels in the brain," FASEB Journal, 2008 Aug; 22(8): 3024–3034.

33 *Shibbolei ha-Leket, seder Berakhot siman* 140.

34 John M. Riddle, *Dioscorides on Pharmacy and Medicine* (Austin, Texas: University of Texas Press, 1985), p. 66.

35 S. Z. Ehrenreich, ed., *Iggeret ha-Tiyul* (Jerusalem, 1957), p. 97.

poisoned."[36] However, historians have not found evidence of this assertion.[37]

Drinking, and drinking to health in particular, is attested to as a major component in the ancient Greek *symposium*, a banquet that took place after the meal.[38] The *symposium* had an elaborate introductory procedure which included numerous cups of wine dedicated to pagan gods.[39] First of these was the *metaniptris*, a cup of undiluted wine "offered to perform a libation to a Good Daemon (most probably an apotropaic name for the dangerous aspect of Dionysus, god of wine)." There was also a cup to honor Hygieia, the goddess of health. Later there was "a triple libation of mixed wine honoring Zeus the Olympian (or another Olympian god), some hero or heroes, and finally Zeus the Savior." This was followed later by "a choral song most often addressed to Apollo in his capacity as a healer or savior of mortals."[40] These basic practices were adopted by the Romans as well,[41] and were found in many cultures in the ancient world.[42]

Note that all of these introductory rites "have something in common, namely an apotropaic character, as if insuring the diners against the dangers inherent in the symposium. This menace is usually understood pragmatically as resulting from the subsequent excessive consumption of wine—the kingdom of Dionysus is a dangerous realm indeed, in which the help of Hygieia becomes truly indispensable."[43] The final cup to Zeus the Savior had the particular intention to serve as "as a token of gratitude for the safe outcome of the feast and perhaps had the added connotation

---

36 Charles Panati, *Extraordinary Origins of Everyday Things* (New York: Harper and Row, 1987), p. 91.

37 Micah Issitt, Carlyn Main, *Hidden Religion: The Greatest Mysteries and Symbols of the World's Religious Beliefs* (Santa Barbara, California: ABC-CLIO, 2014), p. 7.

38 Fiona Hobden, *The Symposion in Ancient Greek Society and Thought* (Cambridge: Cambridge University Press, 2013), 105–107.

39 For examples of these dedication toasts, see S. Douglas Olson, trans., Athenaeus, *The Learned Banqueters* (Cambridge, Massachusetts: Harvard University Press, Loeb Classical Library, 2009), Book 11, p. 367.

40 Marek Wecowski, *The Rise of the Greek Aristocratic Banquet* (Oxford: Oxford University Press, 2014), pp. 38–39.

41 Everett Ferguson, *Backgrounds of Early Christianity* (Grand Rapids, Michigan: William B. Eerdman's Publishing Company, 2003), p. 106.

42 For example, the Norse custom where "a toast was first drunk to Odin for victory, then toasts to Njord and Frey for bountiful harvest and peace." Kimberley Christine Patton, *Religion of the Gods: Ritual, Paradox, and Reflexivity* (Oxford: Oxford University Press, 2009), p. 222.

43 Wecowski, *Rise of the Greek Aristocratic Banquet*, p. 39.

of averting danger in the future."[44] Beyond this, there was a pagan concern that the gods would be angered by the joy and happiness expressed by the mortals at the banquet, and so must be placated.[45] These ancient toasts were intended as "a dedication to a superior power whose benevolent aid the banqueters desired."[46]

We can now better understand why TB *Shabbat* 67b must specifically state that "(One who says while drinking:) 'Wine and life to the mouth of the Sages,' this does not fall into the category of the ways of the Amorite." There the Talmud previously notes that "One who says: 'My fortune be fortunate [*gad gaddi*] and be not weary by day or by night,' contains an element of the ways of the Amorite. Rabbi Yehudah says: *gad* is nothing other than a term of idolatry, as it is stated: "And you that forsake the Lord, that forget My holy mountain, that prepare a table for Gad, and that offer mingled wine in full measure unto Meni" (Isaiah 65:11)." Similarly, saying 'Let my barrels be strengthened [*donu danei*],' that contains an element of the ways of the Amorite. Rabbi Yehudah says: *dan* is nothing other than a term of idol worship, as it is stated: "They that swear by the sin of Samaria and say: As your god Dan lives" (Amos 8:14)." Rashi explains that in both instances R. Yehudah explains that these incantations go beyond the "ways of the Amorite" and are actually real idolatry, as the terms *gad* and *dan* here are the names of pagan gods. In the other view, these words in the incantation do not refer to the names of pagan gods. In any event, we see that there was a fine line between superstitious incantations and actual idolatry.

In the context of this discussion, being that in the ancient world it was customary to drink to the pagan god of wine and goddess of health to insure that no harm would come from wine, it was important for the Talmud to explicitly state that wishing someone health or life while drinking wine and not referring to any pagan god or superstitious, apotropaic practice is considered appropriate.

We now have an additional insight to the halachic discussion regarding whether it is appropriate for the one drinking to say *L-Ḥayyim* before the blessing is said or only after drinking a bit after the blessing, since it may be considered inappropriate to wish people *L-Ḥayyim* before thanking God for the wine.[47] Being that among pagans the toast was actually

---

44 Delight Tolles, *The Banquet-Libations of the Greeks* (Ann Arbor, Michigan: Edwards Brothers, 1943), p. 96.

45 Wecowski, *Rise of the Greek Aristocratic Banquet*, p. 40.

46 Tolles, *Banquet-Libations of the Greeks*, p. 78.

47 See *Eliyah Rabbah, Oraḥ Ḥayyim* 174:17; *Pri Megadim, Mishbetzot Zahav, Oraḥ Ḥayyim* 174:11. Also J.D. Eisenstein, *Otzar Dinim u-Minhagim* (New York, 1917), p. 192.

an aspect of worship through libation, its function was similar to the *berakhah* Jews recite. Placing the *L-Ḥayyim* after the blessing and after some wine was drunk would further distance it from the ancient Greek and Roman practice.

The Jewish Toast

We have seen from numerous early sources that Jews were concerned about potential negative outcomes from drinking wine. R. Shmuel Eidels (Maharsha, 1555–1631) explicitly states that the purpose of R. Akiva's blessing was that the Sages "will not come to be in danger (שלא יבואו לידי סכנה)" from the drinking of wine. A similar idea is found in *Matteh Moshe* (1591), by R. Moshe ben Avraham of Przemyśl. He writes that by saying *savri* the one saying the blessing is telling all assembled to be part of one group, and when they say *L-Ḥayyim* they are declaring their intention that the drinking of wine should not have destructive results. It was important first to establish that they are all part of the group because "the merit of the many is great" and helps protect from any negative outcome from the wine drinking.[48]

This also explains Rashi's comment to the R. Akiva story that his declaration of *L-Ḥayyim* is not considered superstitious because it is "just a blessing" (ברכה בעלמא). In other words, it has no particular apotropaic intent. Although the *L-Ḥayyim* was said in order for the wine not to have a destructive effect, this was accomplished not in a supernatural or superstitious manner. R. Isaiah Horowitz (1558–1630) in his *Shnei Luḥot ha-Brit* similarly explains that R. Akiva made the *L-Ḥayyim* statement to remind the Sages that their intention drinking wine should be for the words of Torah that would thereby come from their mouths, and not for other more mundane purposes.[49]

While both ancient Greeks and Jews recognized the danger inherent in drinking wine, the Greeks reached out to pagan gods for protection, while Jews, exemplified by the practice of R. Akiva, protected themselves by reminding those present that the wine should only be used for positive purposes, without need of or recourse to supernatural protection.

---

48 Moshe ben Avraham of Przemyśl, *Matteh Moshe* (Frankfurt, 1719), *Amud ha-Avodah* part 2, *siman* 349.

49 *Shnei Luḥot ha-Brit, Shaar ha-Otiot, Kedushat ha-Akhilah, Emek Berakhah* 3:10.

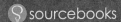

EXCLUSIVE SPECIAL OFFER!
RABBI JONATHAN SACKS
RABBI TZVI HERSH WEINREB
& OTHERS
THE MAGERMAN EDITION
THE NEW KOREN TANAKH
THE ONE-VOLUME EDITIONS OF THE CLASSIC KOREN HEBREW TEXT AND FONT WITH A NEW ENGLISH TRANSLATION
NEW FEATURE! Listing of Torah & haftara readings for Ashkenazi, Sepharadi, British & Yemenite customs
NEW FEATURE! Transliterated names bring readers closer to the original Hebrew
NEW FEATURE! Concise notes to clarify the text
NEW FEATURE! Traditional & conventional markings for chapter & verses
Get 10% off your entire order at www.korenpub.com with code HAKIRAH
Super opaque & strong cream-colored paper for clarity & durability
Thumb tab index to help find your reference quickly
New charts, diagrams, illustrations & maps in full color
KOREN PUBLISHERS JERUSALEM
Order NOW from www.korenpub.com or visit your local Jewish bookstore!

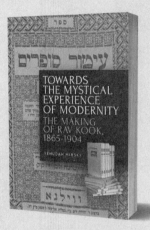

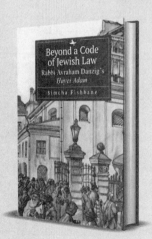

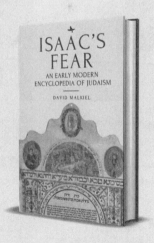

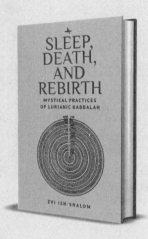

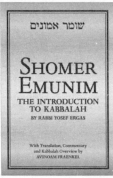

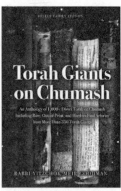

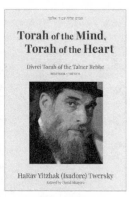

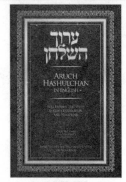

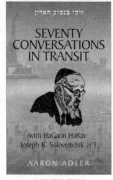

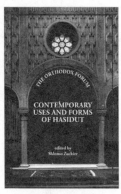

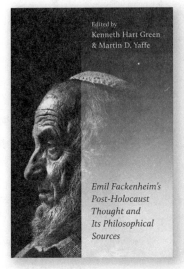

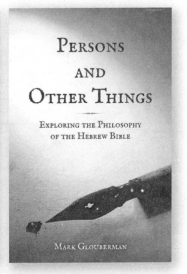

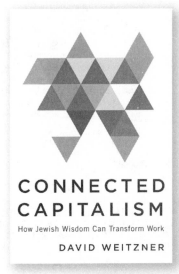

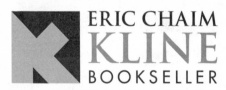

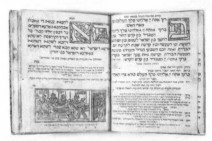

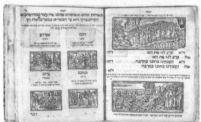

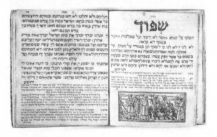

Experience the best.
Check out the best selling books of 2021 from Koren Publishers and Maggid Books!
LAYERS
SHIRA LANKIN SHEPS
YAEL ZIEGLER
LAMENTATIONS
THE SNAKE AT THE MOUTH OF THE CAVE
MOSHE SOKOL
THE KOREN TANAKH OF THE LAND OF ISRAEL
SAMUEL • שמואל
THE KOREN TANAKH OF THE LAND OF ISRAEL
EXODUS • שמות
RABBI JONATHAN SACKS
STUDIES IN SPIRITUALITY
PASSOVER HAGGADAH GRAPHIC NOVEL
SHALOM RAV
THE STEINSALTZ TANYA
Get 10%
off your entire order
at www.korenpub.com
with code HAKIRAH
KOREN PUBLISHERS JERUSALEM
מגיד
MAGGID
www.korenpub.com

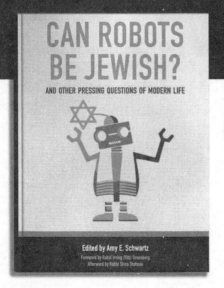

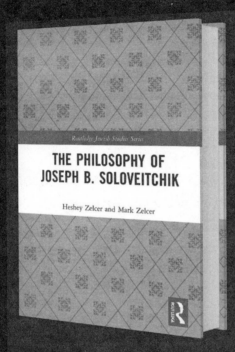

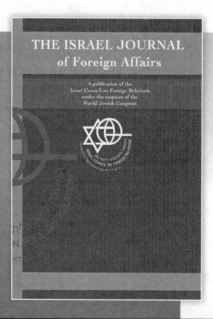

העומד למות אם יכול לצוות לשאריו לא להתאבל עליו

מאמר של הרב משה צוריאל

שאלה עקרונית היא אם העומד למות, ומעוניין להקל על חייהם של שאריו, אם יוכל לוותר על אבלותם עליו. כרוך בזה שיהיה להם קושי לא לעבוד ולהתפרנס משך שבעה ימים, לא להתרחץ, לא להתגלח, לא להחליף בגדים [גם בימי הקיץ החמים] משך שלושים יום וגם לא להשתתף במסיבות של שמחה, חתונות וגם טכסי ברית מילה, משך שנה שלימה.

בשולחן ערוך (יו"ד סי' שמד סעיף י) כתב המחבר "מי שציוה שלא יספדוהו, שומעין לו". והוסיף על כך הרמ"א (בשם מהרי"ו) "אבל אם ציוה שלא לנהוג עליו ז' [ימי אבלות] וגזירת שלושים, אין שומעין לו". [ואפשר כיון שלא הזכיר י"ב חודש, יסכים רמ"א שבזה כן שומעים לו?]

בגליון השו"ע כתב "פתחי תשובה" (ס"ק ב) "עיין בספר 'עיון יעקב' שחיבר הגאון 'שבות יעקב' במסכת סנהדרין דף מו (ע"ב) שחולק על מהרי"ו ועל רמ"א ודעתו דהוא הדין אבלות שבעה וקריעה שומעין לו, אחרי שהוא גם כן לכבוד המתים, דמהאי טעמא המאבד עצמו לדעת אין מתאבלין עליו [והרמב"ם בהלכות אבלות סוף פרק א כתב כך גם על הפורשים מדרכי ציבור, כלומר הרשעים המוחלטים, שאין מתאבלים עליהם. הרי מכאן דעתו שאבלות היא כבוד המת בלבד, ולא כבוד המשפחה]. וכתב 'עיון יעקב' שעשה כן הלכה למעשה" עכ"ל.

והנה כן דעת הגאון ר' דוד אופנהיים בספרו "נשאל דוד" (ח"א עמ' קכא סי' כא). ומפרש שהרמב"ן בענין זה ביטל דעתו מפני פסק הרמב"ם, בענין מאבד עצמו לדעת, כי ב"תורת האדם" מביא דעת הרמב"ם בסוף דבריו.

גם ר' עקיבא איגר, בגליונו שם בשו"ע סבור כי לדעת הרמב"ם המת יכול למחול. ולענין אם ימחול גם על אבלות יום הראשון שהיא מדאורייתא, נשאר ר' עקיבא איגר בצריך עיון.

כיון שלכל הדיעות אבלות שבעה (פרט ליום הראשון), וכן שלושים, וכן י"ב חודש, הם מדרבנן, אפשר להקל בספקות במחלוקת שבין גדולי הפוסקים. ובמיוחד בדיני אבלות, שֶׁכְּלָלוּ כלל בגמרא "הלכה כמאן דמיקל באבלות" (מועד קטן יט, ב). וקבע החיד"א (שו"ת חיים שאל, ח"ב סי' כג) כי הכרעה זו שייכת גם במחלוקת שבין הפוסקים המאוחרים.

לכן הרוצה להקל על שאריו, מותר לו.

---

* After R. Avi Grossman sent the above printed *halakhic* analysis on whether a parent can waive requirements of a*velut* to R. Moshe Zuriel for his review, R. Zuriel responded by disagreeing with R. Grossman's conclusion. R. Zuriel's opinion is being printed here with R. Zuriel's consent.

ואפילו אם נניח שיש לאב למחול על כבודו, היינו שהבן כן פטור מלשרת את אביו, עדיין אין בידי האב לפטור את הבן מן הדברים הנאסרים עליו, ובגלל שבאמת מצוות האבלות הן לאווים ולא עשים, אין האב יכול לפטור את הבן מלהתאבל.

לסיכום, נלע״ד שההיתר המובא בש״ך ליו״ד שד״מ המבוסס על התשובות הנ״ל קשה לקבל, במיוחד לשיטת הרמב״ם. ויש לבן לשמור כל הי״ב חודש דאבלות על אביו אפילו נמחלו לו. וכוונתי להעמיד דברי חז״ל המחייבים י״ב חדשי אבלות על כל אדם שנפטרו הוריו.

פירוש, שכבוד הוא המצוה לשרת את אביו, הנקרא בלע״ז סרבִּיס. וכן מרגלא בפי הרצ״ש. וכשאמרו ״שמכבדו אחרי מותו״ לאוו דווקא נאמר בכבוד = שירות כי זה בלתי אפשרי בהיותו בקבר, אלא כבוד וגם מורא משמע כאן, שבדרך כלל חז״ל כִּוְנו לכבוד וגם מורא באמרם ״כבוד אב ואם״ מן הסתם, וכן לישנא דעמא, וכלומר ״איך הוא ממשיך לקיים מצוות אלו אחרי פטירת האב והאם?״ והתשובה היא:

> היה אומר דבר שמועה מפיו לא יאמר כך אמר אבא אלא כך אמר אבא מרי הריני כפרת משכבו והני מילי תוך שנים עשר חדש מכאן ואילך אומר זכרונו לברכה לחיי העולם הבא.

וזה נחשב כחלק ממצות מורא, כמו שמובא בפוסקים ש״לא יקרא לו בשמו״, הבא מאמרם ז״ל ״תנו רבנן חכם משנה שם אביו ושם רבו״ והוא באמת בגדר מורא ולא כבוד. ולכן, אם נניח שהאב יכול למחול על כבודו אפילו לאחר מותו, שכבר כתבנו שלא נראה לנו, אבל מכל מקום אם נניח, אינו יכול למחול על מוראו, בחייו קל וחומר לאחר מותו, ואפילו אם מוראו אחר מותו גם נקרא ״כבודו״ בחוסר דיוק. ונראה שכל עניין האבלות היא יותר קרובה למורא מכבוד, ולכן אין מוראו נמחל אחר מותו, והאבלות אינה נמחלת כי היא חלק מהמורא.

ואם תאמר, שמא כשאמרו שהאב מוחל על כבודו כבודו מחול גם כבודו גם מוראו במשמע כסתם לישנא דנקטנו לעיל, יש לומר שלא ייתכן שחז״ל יכוונו להתיר לבן, אפילו ברשות אביו, לשבת במקומו או לסתור דבריו או לקוראו בשמו, היינו להתיר איסורים, אלא כמו שראינו מדברי הפוסקים לעיל, כוונתם להקל על הבן בשירות האב, בקיום העֲשין, או למחול לו שלא ייענש.

וראיה לדבר בהשוואת כבוד ומורא אב ואם בכבוד ומורא חכמים. מאי מחילה אצל רבו? הלכות תלמוד תורה פרק ה:

> כשם שאדם מצווה בכבוד אביו וביראתו, כך הוא חייב בכבוד רבו ויראתו ורבו יתר מאביו. שאביו, הביאו לחיי העולם הזה ורבו שלימדו חכמה, הביאו לחיי העולם הבא וכו׳. הרב המובהק שרצה למחול על כבודו בכל הדברים האלו או באחד מהן לכל תלמידיו או לאחד מהן הרשות בידו. ואף על פי שמחל חייב התלמיד להדרו ואפילו בשעה שמחל.

משמע מדבריו ש"מחילת הרב על כבודו" מועילה גם לענין מחילת כבודו גם לענין מחילת מוראו, אבל גם משמע שמחילתו היא כמו שפירשו הרדב״ז וסייעתו את מחילת האב, שכמו שהאב פוטר את הבן מהעונש המגיע לו על זה שלא כבדו כראוי, אבל איננו פוטרו מחיוביו או מתיר לו שום איסור הנכלל במצות מורא אביו, גם הרב רק פוטר את התלמיד מהעונש, אבל אינו פוטרו מחיוביו או מתיר לו שום איסור. וכן משמע מיו״ד רמ״ב ובפוסקים.

המאבד עצמו לדעת אין מתעסקין עמו לכל דבר ולא מתאבלין עליו ולא מספידין אותו. אבל עומדין עליו בשורה ואומרין עליו ברכת אבלים וכל דבר שהוא כבוד לחיים. ואיזה הוא המאבד עצמו לדעת? לא שעלה לראש הגג ונפל ומת אלא האומר הריני עולה לראש הגג וראה אותו שעלה מיד דרך כעס או שהיה מצר ונפל ומת, הרי זה בחזקת שאִבד עצמו לדעת.

והשבות יעקב הניח שכל מצוה אצל המתים, הלא המה ההתעסקות, הקריעה, החליצה, ההספד, העמידה בשורה, וברכת האבלים, צריכה להיות או מפני כבוד המת או מפני כבוד החיים, ואם האבלות איננה מכבוד החיים אז בהכרח היא משום כבוד המת, ודבר תמוה הוא, חדא דלרמב״ם האבלות היא גזרת הכתוב כמו שיוצא מדבריו, ומי אמר שהאבלות בהכרח צריכה להיות או מזה או מזה?! ותרי, דדיוקו לא מדוייק, דכבר הראה לנו הרמב״ם שהדין שאין מתאבלים על המתאבד איננו משום שאין לכבדו, אלא משום שהוא נחשב רשע, וכמו שכתב בהלכות רוצח ושמירת הנפש (ב:ב-ג):

אבל השוכר הורג להרוג את חברו או ששלח עבדיו והרגוהו או שכפת חברו והניחו לפני הארי וכיוצא בו והרגתו החיה וכן ההורג את עצמו, כל אחד מאלו שופך דמים הוא, ועוון הריגה בידו וחייב מיתה לשמים, ואין בהן מיתת בית דין. ומניין שכן הוא הדין? שהרי הוא אומר שופך דם האדם באדם דמו יִשָּׁפֵך, זה ההורג בעצמו שלא על ידי שליח. ואך את דמכם לנפשותיכם אדרוש, זה ההורג עצמו. מיד כל חיה אדרשנו, זה המוסר חברו לפני חיה לטורפו. מיד האדם מיד איש אחיו אדרוש את נפש האדם, זה השוכר אחרים להרוג את חברו. ובפירוש נאמר בשלשתן לשון דרישה, הרי דינם מסור לשמים.

וזה משמע גם מהרמב״ם דלעיל בהלכות אבל, שהזכיר דיני קבורה והספד ואבלות וכו׳ של שאר רשעים מיד לפני דין המתאבד:

כל הפורשין מדרכי ציבור, והם האנשים שפרקו עול המצוות מעל צוארן ואינן נכללין בכלל ישראל בעשיית המצוות וכבוד המועדות וישיבת בתי כנסיות ובתי מדרשות, אלא הרי הן כך בני חורין לעצמן כשאר האומות, וכן המינים והמשומדים והמוסרין, כל אלו אין מתאבלין עליהן. אלא אחיהם ושאר קרוביהם לובשין לבנים ומתעטפים לבנים ואוכלים ושותים ושמחים שאבדו שונאיו של הקדוש ברוך הוא ועליהם הכתוב אומר הלוא משנאיך ה' אשנא.

ואוסיף שחז״ל חילקו בין כבוד ומורא שם בקידושין:

איזהו מורא ואיזהו כבוד? מורא לא עומד במקומו ולא יושב במקומו ולא סותר את דבריו ולא מכריעו.

פירוש, מורא הוא איך שהוא מתייחס אליו בצורה של נימוס יתר, הנקרא בלע״ז רספק״ט,

כבוד, מאכיל ומשקה מלביש ומכסה מכניס ומוציא.

לא נפתרה, אבל כתב רבנו חננאל שקיימא לן שמצוה זו מדרבנן היא, היינו שאין עלינו למצוא טעמא ולדרשו, וכן פסק הרמב״ם בריש פרק י״ב:

ההספד כבוד המת הוא לפיכך כופין את היורשין ליתן שכר המקוננים והמקוננות וסופדין אותו. ואם צוה אל תספדוהו אין סופדין אותו. אבל אם צוה שלא יקָבר אין שומעין לו שהקבורה מצוה שנאמר כי קבֹר תקברנו.

ואם היתה שאלה כזאת לגבי אבלות, ״יקרא דשכבי או יקרא דחיי?״ הראשונים גם היו עונים לנו ״לית דִין ולית דָא אלא תפקידתא דאורייתא (או תקנתא דחכימאי) כמו הקבורה.״ ואל לנו להציע טעם או סיבת האבלות שנהיה בטוחים בו עד שנבוא לומר שיש לבטְלָהּ במקרים מסוימים. נמצא שלפי הרמב״ם, אין דרך לנפטר לפטור אחרים מהחיובים לקוברו, להטמא לו, ולהתאבל עליו, כי כולם מצוות שאינן ניתנות למחילה. ויש לומר שכן גם שיטת עוד ראשונים. וזה ראיה ברורה נגד טענת המהרי״ו.

ונלע״ד שאם האב היה יכול לפטור את בנו מאבלות י״ב חודש כל הדורות, היינו מוצאים היתר עצום זה עוד לפני תקופת האחרונים. איך נפטרים מחיוב דאורייתא או דרבנן בלי רשות מפורשת?

ובאמת, אם האב יכול למחול על כבודו המיוחד לו, והוא מועיל לתקופת האבלות העודפת על שאר אבלות שלושים, למה באמת כל אחד לא ימחול על כבודו הפרטי, ויאמר לקרוביו ״לית לכון לאתאבולי על ההוא גברא?״ ואם תאמר, אכן חז״ל חייבונו להתאבל על קרובינו לפחות כדין, אבל על ההורים הי״ב חודש אינו מן החיוב, לא ראינו זכר להבחנה זו. וזה לשון בעל השבות יעקב המובא בספרי הרע״י:

שכשם שהאומר אל תספידוני שומעים לו, כמו שכתבו כל הפוסקים, ומשום דהספדא הוי יקרא דשכבי, לפ״ז נראה שהוא הדין לענין אבלות שבעה וקריעה שהן לכבוד המתים, ששומעים לו, דהא מה״ט המאבד עצמו לדעת אין מתאבלים עליו ואין קורעים עליו, שהם לכבוד המתים, אבל עומדים עליו בשורה ואומרים עליו ברכת אבלים שהוא כבוד החיים, כמו שכתבו הרמב״ם והשו״ע.

ודייקו במסכת שמחות (ב:א) בדין המאבד עצמו לדעת, הנקרא בלשון העם ״המתאבד״:

המאבד עצמו לדעת אין מתעסקין עמו בכל דבר. רבי ישמעאל אומר קורין עליו "הוי נטלה הוי נטלה". אמר לו רבי עקיבא הנח לו בסתמו. אל תכבדהו ואל תקללהו. אין קורעין עליו ואין חולצין עליו ולא מספידין עליו. אבל עומדין עליו בשורה ואומרין עליו ברכת אבלים מפני שהוא כבוד חיים. כללו של דבר, כל שהוא כבוד של חיים מתעסקין בו. כל שאין כבוד של חיים אין הרבים מתעסקין עמו לכל דבר.

וכן לשון הרמב״ם (הלכות אבל א:ט):

> ההספד כבוד המת הוא, לפיכך כופין את היורשין ליתן שכר המקוננים והמקוננות וסופדין אותו. ואם צוה אל תספדוהו, אין סופדין אותו. אבל אם צוה שלא יִקָבר אין שומעין לו, שהקבורה מצוה, שנאמר כי קבור תקברנו. כל המתעצל בהספדו של חכם, אינו מאריך ימים. וכל המתעצל בהספד אדם כשר ראוי לקוברו בחייו, וכל המוריד דמעות על אדם כשר הרי שכרו על כך שמור אצל הקדוש ברוך הוא.

ומעשים בכל יום שמהדרין אחר המספידים המוכשרים לכך אפילו אינם קרובים ועדיפים הם על הקרובים והיורשים אם הקרובים והיורשים כבדי פה וכד׳. רק שהיורשים ישלמו אם יש טרחא בדבר.

ועוד, יש ריבוי סוגי כבוד, לדוגמא כבוד הבריות. האם המבקש שיזלזלו בגופו בדרך הלווייתו, כגון שמצַוֶּה שיוליכו את גופו ערום כדי לביישו, הנשמע לו?!

אצל הרמב״ם לפחות, אבלות, הן אבלות ז׳ הן אבלות ל׳ הן אבלות י״ב, כולן מצוַת הכתוב המוארכת ע״י תקנת חז״ל, ומניין שהיא צריכה להיות או יקרא דשכבי או יקרא דחיי?

> מצות עשה להתאבל על הקרובים, שנאמר ואכלתי חטאת היום, הייטב בעיני ה׳. ואין אבלות מן התורה אלא ביום ראשון בלבד שהוא יום המיתה ויום הקבורה, אבל שאר השבעה אינן דין תורה אף על פי שנאמר בתורה [אצל יוסף] ויעש לאביו אבל שבעת ימים. נִתנה תורה ונתחדשה הלכה. ומשה רבנו תקן להם לישראל שבעת ימי אבלות ושבעת ימי המשתה. (רמב"ם הלכות אבל א:א)
>
> מדברי סופרים שיהיה האָבל נוהג במקצת דברי אבלות כל שלושים יום. ומניין סמכו לשלושים יום? שהרי הוא אומר ובכתה את אביה ואת אמה ירח ימים, מכלל שהאָבל מצטער כל שלושים יום. (רמב"ם הלכות אבל ו:א)

ואם הדבר שנוי במחלוקת, כי יש אומרים שכל אבלות מדרבנן, מכל מקום לא ראינו שהיא משום יקרא דשכבי או יקרא דחיי, אלא מצוה בפני עצמה. וכמו ההטמאות לקרובים בפרק ב׳ דהלכות אבלות, שהיא מצוה המחייבת את הכהנים, אפילו יש אחרים שיכולים לטפל בקבורת המתים:

> כמה חמורה מצות אבל, שהרי הכהן נדחית לו הטומאה מפני קרוביו כדי שיתעסק עמהן ויתאבל עליהן שנאמר כי אם לשארו הקרוב אליו לאמו ולאביו וכו׳ לה יִטַּמא. מצות עשה שאם לא רצה להִטמא מטמאין אותו בעל כרחו.

ולעניין דברי הרמב״ם למעלה, בסנהדרין מ״ו ע״ב השאלה

> איבעיא להו קבורה משום בזיונא הוא או משום כפרה הוא, למאי נפקא מינה? דאמר לא בעינא דליקברוה לההוא גברא. אי אמרת משום בזיונא הוא, לא כל כמיניה. ואי אמרת משום כפרה הוא, הא אמר לא בעינא כפרה.

הבא." אבל לא שנו ככה. כי ענייני האבלות של י"ב חודש, כמו גידול השיער וההמנעות משמחה מריעות, אינם משום כבוד אב ואם.

וצע"ג בהגדרתו מחילת כבוד אב ואם (או מחילת כבוד הרב). איתא בקידושין ל"ב ע"א:

> ר' יצחק בר שילא א"ר מתנה אמר רב חסדא האב שמחל על כבודו כבודו מחול הרב שמחל על כבודו אין כבודו מחול ורב יוסף אמר אפי' הרב שמחל על כבודו כבודו מחול.

ולעיל איתא:

> ת"ש שאלו את ר"א עד היכן כיבוד אב ואם אמר להם כדי שיטול ארנקי ויזרקנו לים בפניו ואינו מכלימו ואי אמרת משל אב מאי נפקא לי' מיניה בראוי ליורשו וכי הא דרבה בר רב הונא דרב הונא קרע שיראי באנפי רבה בריה אמר איזול איחזי אי רתח אי לא רתח ודלמא רתח וקעבר אלפני עִור לא תתן מכשול? דמחיל ליה ליקריה.

ועל סמך זה הביא הרעק"א ליו"ד רמ:יט תשובת הרדב"ז דהא דכבודו מחול היינו לענין דאין הבן נענש אם אינו מכבדו, אבל אם מכבדו עושה מצות כבוד, ובפתחי תשובה שם גם הביא כלשון הרדב"ז וסיים אבל "מ"מ אכתי מצוה איכא." אבל לא שהאב יכול לפטור את בנו מן החיוב לכבדו.

ובשו"ע שם הביא מן הרמב"ם בממרים ו':

> אף על פי שבכך נצטווינו, אסור לאדם להכביד עֻלּו על בניו ולדקדק בכבודו עמהם, שלא יביאם לידי מכשול, אלא ימחול ויתעלם (נוסח הב"י: ויעלים עיניו מהם) שהאב שמחל על כבודו, כבודו מחול. והמכה [ל]בנו גדול מנדין אותו שהרי הוא עובר על ולפני עִור לא תתן מכשול.

והגר"א ציין כבאר הגולה שדין זה נלמד מהמימרא דלעיל, שהאב שמחל על כבודו כבודו מחול.

נמצינו למדים שעקרי הפוסקים נקטו שמחילת האב היא שאין לו להכביד עול המצוה על בנו כדי לא להכשילו, או שבדיעבד בנו לא ייענש, אבל מ"מ הבן חייב במעשי הכבוד והמורא.

ובקשר לזה שאמר אל תספידוני, כבודו הפרטי שלו כמו ממונו ואינו אותו הכבוד שחייבים לו בניו. והראיה לדבר כמו שכתבנו לעיל, שהאחריות (הכספית) על ההספד מוטלת בראשון על היורשים אבל עצם המצוה מחייב את כולם, וכן כתב הרמב"ם (הלכות אבל יב:א):

ולעצם הטענה, נקדים דברינו בהבחנות הלכתיות בין הספד וקבורה מצד אחד, ואבלות מצד שני. פשוט שההספד והקבורה אינם חובות הגוף כמו אבלות, שהיא חבילת איסורים שהאבל מקיים בגופו. הספד וקבורה הם אחריותם של היורשים ולאו דווקא של האבלים, היינו הקרובים. ונפקא מינה להלכה: ישנם יורשים שאינם מתאבלים, וישנם מתאבלים שאינם יורשים. וישנם קרובי משפחה שאינם לא יורשים ולא מתאבלים. לדוגמא, לנפטר יש בנים וגם נכדים ונכדים מבנו המת, וגם לו אשה, הורים, ואחים. כל קרוביו מתאבלים עליו, למרות שרק בניו הזכרים ונכדיו מבנו המת יורשיו, והנכדים מבנו המת יורשים ולא מתאבלים. ודודיו ובני דודיו לא יורשים ולא מתאבלים. אצל הספד וקבורה, החיובים מוטלים על כלל ישראל, אפילו על הלא-קרובים והלא-יורשים, והרבה פעמים החיוב מוטל על בית הדין. במיוחד כשאין לנפטר קרובים או יורשים הנמצאים בשעת הפטירה, ורק ידעו או יגיעו אצל מקומו של הנפטר שבועות ספורים אח״כ. וההוה אמינה שם בסנהדרין היה רק לגבי הספד וקבורה ולא לגבי אבלות, כי אותם מקיימים ממש בגופו של המת והם בעיקר שייכים אליו למרות שהוא כבר מת, רק שעל היורשים להוציא ממונם עבור הוצאות אלו אם אפשר, ואילו אבלות היא מצוה מוטלת רק על הקרובים ולא על אחרים, חובה כלפי שמים, ואינה קשורה לחיוב המוטל על כלל הצבור והיורש בפרט להספיד ולקבור את המת. ובעוונותינו ראינו בשנתיים האחרונות כמה מתים שנקברו והוספדו על ידי שכנים וחברים, ואילו קרוביהם התאבלו עליהם בערים אחרות בגלל גזרות ההתרחקות של הממשלות.

וצע״ג מנא לן די״ב החודש היתרים על אבלות ל׳ של שאר קרובים הם משום כבוד אב ואם. דווקא מלשון הרמב״ם (ראה למטה) נראה שכן הוא תקנת חז״ל, ולא קשור לכבודם או מוראם של האב והאם. ועוד כבר כתבו חז״ל בקידושין במה מכבדם ובמה מקיים מצות המורא להם, וכולם בחייהם, ולשאלה במה מכבדם בתר חייהון, איתא (ל״א ע״ב):

> ת"ר מכבדו בחייו ומכבדו במותו. בחייו כיצד? הנשמע בדבר אביו למקום לא יאמר שלחוני בשביל עצמי מהרוני בשביל עצמי פטרוני בשביל עצמי אלא כולהו בשביל אבא. במותו כיצד? היה אומר דבר שמועה מפיו לא יאמר כך אמר אבא אלא כך אמר אבא מרי הריני כפרת משכבו והני מילי תוך שנים עשר חדש מכאן ואילך אומר זכרונו לברכה לחיי העולם הבא.

והמשיכו שם "ת"ר איזהו מורא ואיזהו כיבוד? מורא לא עומד במקומו וכו׳" וכן מובאות כל ההלכות אלו בפוסקים. ולא ראינו שהאבלות של י״ב חודש היא משום כבוד או מורא אב ואם. והיה להם ז״ל ללמדנו "במותו כיצד? היה אומר דבר שמועה מפיו לא יאמר כך אמר אבא אלא כך אמר אבא מרי הריני כפרת משכבו. ומגדל שערו עד שישלח פרע, או עד שיגערו בו חבריו, ואין אחרים שואלין בשלומו, ולא יכנס לשמחת מריעות. והני מילי תוך שנים עשר חדש. מכאן ואילך מותרים לו, ואומר זכרונו לברכה לחיי העולם

האם האב יכול לפטור את שאריו מאבלות?

מאת: אב"י גרוסמן

האם האב יכול לפטור את הבן מאבלות י״ב חודש?

> יו״ד שד״מ ס׳ י׳:
> מי שצוה שלא יספידוהו שומעין לו.

זוהי מסקנת הגמרא בסנהדרין מ״ו.

> הגה: אבל אם צוה שלא לנהוג עליו ז׳ וגזרת שלשים אין שומעים לו.

וזה מתשובת המהרי״ו. והוסיף שם הש״ך מאותה התשובה:

> אבל אם צוה האב ואם שלא לנהוג בהם י״ב חודש כיון דאינו שייך בשאר מתים אלא בכבוד אב ואם מצוה לקיים דבריהם.

ויש לעיין בתשובה המקורית, שמא יש על מה להתווכח, כי קשה לנו להתיר לבן לא לנהוג אבלות י״ב חודש על אביו ואמו. ולפני שנדון בעקרי הטענות, אביא אותה איך שהיא מופיעה בספר דרכי משה והועתק משו״ת מהרי״ו (סי׳ יז):

> אשה שצותה בנותיה שלא לישא הסרבל על ראשם כדרך האבלים הדעת מכרעת דהבנות יקיימו מה שצותה מידי דהוי אמי שצוה שלא יספדוהו וה"נ לאחר ל' יום עד י"ב חדש יקרא דשכבי הוא ושומעין לה אבל תוך ל' כיון דאשאר מתים נמי מתאבלים עליהם ואסמכינהו אקראי לא נתברר לי אי יקרא דחיי או דשכבא הוא דהא ודאי אבילות גופה אינה יכולה למחול דא"כ בטלתה דין אבילות.

ואציין שהרמ״א עצמו הכיר את תשובת המהרי״ו בשלמותה, ורק הביא בשולחן ערוך את מסקנת המהרי״ו המחמירה שאין לאב למחול על אבלות ז׳ ושלושים, ולא את הקולא, היינו מחילת י״ב חודש, וכח דהתירא עדיף, ולכן משמע שהרמ״א לא קבל היתר זה, כי אילו היה מקבלו, היה מביאו.

---

* This article is a response to Rabbi Shlomo Brody's "May Parents Waive the Requirements of Avelut?," *Ḥakirah* (vol. 29, 2021). See R. Grossman's introduction in the *Letters Section.*

הרב אב״י גרוסמן הוא חבר כולל ציון נריה בכוכב יעקב, מלמד, חוקר וסופר עצמאי, ומחבר ״הגדת הפסח״, ההגדה הראשונה עם הנוסח וכל ההסברים לסדר שבמרכזו קרבן הפסח. <avrahambenyehuda.wordpress.com>

לקרוא את כל ספר במדבר לפחות עד קרבן היום למפטיר. ויש לצרף לזה שט"ו תשרי חל השנה ה'תש"ף בשבת, ובזה פשיטא דאפשר להשלים אז הפרשיות שבוטלו, ואף אם אין דין יו"ט כשבת ליכא בזה שום פסידא או חשש כלל להאריך עליות.

ומי שביטל פרשיות מסוף ספר שמות צ"ע אם יש לו תקנה להחוששים הנ"ל כיוון דליכא שבת חול המועד סוכות השנה, ושמא מותר לקוראם בצום גדליה דתענית צבור הוא וכדאיתא במגילה ל: בצפרא כנופיא. ועוד י"ל נהי דאין שבת חול המועד אבל קריאת המועדות בכי תשא עדיין מעניינא דיומא היא ומותר להוסיף ממנה לפני קריאת פרשת המועדות דתורת כהנים, שכן מצינו בהושענא רבא שבחו"ל קוראים קודם וביום החמישי שאינו מעניין היום וכן אצל אחינו בני ספרד שמקדימים וקוראים מפסוק והיה היום הזה לזכרון כשחג הפסח חל בשבת אף שהוא קודם הפרשה העיקרית לפי דינא דגמרא, והבוחר יבחר ובחרת בחיים.

(ויש לעיין עוד לדעת המגן אברהם או"ח תרפ"ה דאפשר לצאת ידי חובת זכירת מעשה עמלק בקריאת התורה בפורים, שמא גם כן אפשר לצאת ידי חובת פרשת פרה מדאורייתא בקריאת פרשת מטות במעשה טהרת הצבא, וצע"ג.)

וה' יוציאנו מאפלה זו לאורה ויסיר כל מגפה וכל מחלה וכל מיני פורעניות מעלינו השתא בעגלא ובזמן קריב.

(וכן עשינו מעשה כשהותר לנו להאריך פורתא בתפילותינו לקרוא כמה וכמה פרשיות שבוטלו בכל שבת ושבת עד שבע"ה נשלים את עץ חיינו היא תורת יוצרנו בחגי תשרי כנהוג, ויהי רצון מלפני בורא העולם ורופא כל בשר שכשם שזכינו לקרוא את כל חומשי התורה בציבור השנה כן נזכה לשמור את כל דברי תלמוד תורתך הכלולים בהם באהבה ובשלום לאורך ימים ושנים בהשקט ובטחה, ויקוים בנו מקרא שכתוב וכל המחלה אשר שמתי במצרים לא אשים עליך כי אני ה' רפאך. ברוך שומע תפלת עמו ישראל ברחמים.)

במסכת סופרים במנחה של יו"ט, ויש ששבשו הגירסא, ואין לסמוך עליהם כלל שלא הכירו המנהג ההוא כדאיתא בביאור הגר"א ועוד, ופשוט, ואכמ"ל.)

ויש לעיין אם החסרון בקריאת ימי חול היינו פגם בעצם הקריאה, שהקריאה אינה קריאת התורה העיקרי שאפשר להשלים בו פרשיות, או פגם בחיוב השומעים, שבכל מקרה יקראוהו בשבת ואין צריך לחזור אחריו מקודם. ונ"מ לעניין דילוג בעליה הראשונה בשבת שאכן כבר קראו אותו פסוק בציבור אך בקריאה שהיא טפלה (עיין במאמר מרדכי או"ח קלז, ובשערי אפרים ח:נט, ובשו"ת יוסף אומץ יב:ו, ובאות אמת כ"ח, ועוד).

והנה נשאל התרומת הדשן (כד) על מנהג בני אושטרייך שקראו כל הקהל יחד עם החזן פרשיות שירת הים ועשרת הדברות, בין בשבתות השנה בין במועדים. בעל התה"ד מיישב המנהג על סמך הדין שכל הקהל יכולים לקרות שמו"ת עם החזן, ואכמ"ל, אך בפירוש התייחס לדין דילוג פסוקים וז"ל:

> אבל אין ליישב המנהג דמשום דבלאו הנך פרשיות קורין שבעה בתורה, שהן חובת היום, ואותם שקורין מהנך פרשיות קורין לו גם כן ג' פסוקים קודם שיגיע לפרשה זו, ובהא נפקינן אפילו אי לא הוה קרינן הנך פרשיות כלל; דהא ליתא, דבהגה"ה במיימון כתב שאם קרא ודילג פסוק אחד, אם הוא במנחה בשבת או בשני וחמישי אין צריך לחזור אם קוראין י' פסוקים בלא הדילוג, אבל בשבת אם דילג פסוק אחד חוזר וקורא אותו אפילו לאחר שהפטיר והתפלל מוסף. הא קמן דאפילו פסוק אחד מעכב בשבת, כל שכן פרשה כולה.
>
> ואף על פי שיישבתי המנהג, מכל מקום נכון למי שמדקדק במעשיו שיעמוד אצל השליח צבור ויקרא עמו אותן פרשיות מספר תורה. ואם אינו יודע לקרות, ישמע קריאת ש"צ. אך בשביעי של פסח וביום ראשון דשבועות אין קפידא כל כך, הואיל וקראו כבר הפרשיות בשבתות שלהן, והוי כמו מנחה דשבת ובשני וחמישי וק"ל.

הנה משמע שלדעתו יו"ט דינו בעצם כשבת שקריאתה היא עצם תקנת מרע"ה וכל הצבור בנמצא והקריאה עיקר ולא טפל וכו' ואין לישב מנהג אושטרייך בהכשרת דילוג פסוקים ביו"ט ככלל. אלא שבמקרה אנו קוראים פרשת בשלח קודם חג הפסח ופרשת יתרו קודם חג השבועות ולפיכך אין צורך לקרוא עתה כל פסוק שוב כדי להשלים את התורה. אבל בנידון דידן שלא קראו הפרשיות בשעתן חזר הדין לעיקרו ושוב שוה יו"ט לשבת.

ויש להוסיף ראיה ברורה שאין להשיב עליה שבכל שנה ושנה קוראים סדר וזאת הברכה ביו"ט אפילו כשלא חל בשבת ואעפ"כ חשבינן ליה להשלמת קריאות השנה, דוק ותשכח.

ולפיכך צבור שרוצה להחמיר בעניין העליות מחשש ברכה לבטלה בנידון דידן שרוב הפרשיות החסרות הם מתורת כהנים ומחומש הפקודים, עליהם לקרוא את כל ספר ויקרא ביום ראשון דסוכות, עם רוב הספר בעליה הראשונה וסוף הספר בעליה האחרונה, וכן

הבית יוסף (או"ח קלז) רק הביא דברי ההג"מ ולא השגיח בדעת האו"ז וכן פסק בשו"ע (שם סעיף ג) וכן פסקו כל האחרונים (מלבד בשו"ת יפה נוף או"ח סימן כא לאחד מקדמוני אחרוני אשכנז הרב יצחק מזיא אשר הסיק כן מדעתו, ותימה), ובלבוש נתן טעם בזה וז"ל ואע"פ שבאופן זה תהיה הקריאה שלא כסדר לית לן בה שאין סדר לכל פרשיות התורה שהתורה מגילה מגילה ניתנה ואין מוקדם ומאוחר בתורה עכ"ל.

וכעין זה מצינו לקרות שלא כסדרן במקום הצורך בימי הפסח שקורין כסימן משך תורא וכו' כדאיתא במגילה לא: ופירש הר"ן שם בשם הראב"ד שהיה ראוי לקרות כולם כסדרן אלא שדוחין פרשת בשלח ליום ז' שבו עברו בים ביבשה ומקדימים פרשת שור וכשב ליום הנף עצמו (וע"ע בפרישה או"ח סימן ת"ץ).

אך כל זה באותה שבת שדילגו הפסוק וסתמו האחרונים ולא פרשו מה הדין אם רק נודע הדילוג למחרת השבת, אך קשה לחלק בין דילגו פסוק אחד לדילגו רוב הפרשה או אפילו כולה, שדינו כבר מבואר לעיל, והנה אפילו המהר"ם לא העלה על הדעת שיש לפטור את הצבור מקריאת פרשת פקודי מחמת קריאת רוב הפרשה, דלא אמרינן רובו ככולו שדברי תורה דברים חשובים הם ולא בטלים ואדרבא פשיטא שכל פסוק ופסוק וכל אות ואות קדושים הם ואפילו עטרות ודיבן חוזרים עליהם. וכן דייק במגן אברהם ובביאור הלכה סימן קלה.

ולפי זה הקהלות שלא הותרו להן מיד לקרוא את הפרשיות שבוטלו עליהם לקוראם מיד כשיותר להם, ויקראם בעליה נפרדה לכל חומש כדאיתא בתוספתא מגילה כדלעיל בשו"ת בצל החכמה, ונראה פשוט שלכתחילה יקראם קודם פרשת אותו שבוע שכל מה שאפשר לקרות כסדרן עבדינן, כנלע"ד.

שבתי וראיתי תחת השמש איזה פוסקים שליט"א שחוששים מפני עליות נוספות האלה מחשש ברכה לבטלה, שמא אין הדין כרוב הפוסקים כדעת האור זרוע דלעיל, ושמא הדין הוא שעליות נוספות בשבת חייבים להיקרא ולהיקרה אחר קריאת הסדר הרגיל, ושמא הדין הוא שאסור להוסיף לקרוא בשבת שלא מפרשת השבוע, ועוד שדין דילוג פסוקים משבת לשבת אינו מפורש בכל הפוסקים כדלעיל. ואף שחששות אלו רחוקות הם בעיני ודרך הרבים סלולה לפנינו שכן היא דעת רוב האחרונים ושכן עשו מעשה הרבה מהגדולים ולא ניטה מהם ימין ושמאול, מ"מ יש לעיין אם יש דרך אחרת לקרוא את הפרשיות שלא כסדרן בלי להכנס לשום ספקות כלל ועיקר.

בקצרה, דבר זה הוא אפשרי אך ורק בהוספת פסוקים לקריאות חובה בתוך אותו החומש עצמו, ולכן עלינו לבדוק באיזה ימים בשנה יקראו עוד מחומש זה או אחר וממילא עלינו לדון בהשלמת הפרשיות בימים טובים. דהנה אף דנראה פשוט ממסכת סופרים דלעיל וכן ממחלוקת ר"מ ור"י במגילה ל: שקריאות ימי חול אינן עולות לסדר השנתי ושאין לנו להשלים הפרשיות בימי חול, יש לעיין טובא בדין ימים טובים שנקראו אותם מקראי קודש וקריאת התורה בהם גם מתקנת מרע"ה כדאיתא בשלהי מגילה, אך מאידך מפסיקים בהם מסדר הקריאות של שבתות השנה. (ורבו האחרונים המפלפלים במה שכתב

וכל זה לכתחילה וכשהשנים כתיקונם, אך בנידון דידן האם יש מקום להשלים הקריאות אפילו שלא כסדרן? לדעת רוב הפוסקים דלעיל שחייבים היינו לקרוא כל מה שחיסרנו, נידוננו דומה לקורא שדילג בטעות תיבה או פסוק דמה לי פסוק אחד מה לי אלף פסוקים (ושמא לזה כיון הרמ"א בהפניתו לסימן רפ"ב שמא לסעיף ז' ודו"ק). ועיין במסכת סופרים יא:ו שמחלק בין שחרית של שבת לחול וכן במנחה וז"ל

> ואם קרא ודלג על פסוק ולא קראו אם קרא עשרה מן הפסוק המדולג ביניהם אינו חוזר ואם בתוך עשרה הוא יחזור ויקרא עשר כראוי על שטתן שאין מדלג זו בחול ובמנחה בשבת ובמנחה של יום טוב, אבל בשבת אם שכח ועבר על פסוק ואחר כך נודע לו חוזר וקורא אפילו לאחר שהפטיר בנביא והתפלל מוסף מפסיק מיד וקורא

הנה מדין זה רואים שאפילו אם דילגו איזה צבור את כל הפרשיות שביטלו עדיין חייבים לחזור ולקוראן אפילו אחרי התפילות. אך יש לעיין אם כשחוזרים לקרוא את הפסוקים המדולגים האם חייבים לקרוא משם והלאה כסדרן או שיש לקוראם לבדם בסירוגין למפרע, וכבר דנו בזה הראשונים ז"ל, דהאור זרוע שלנו דלעיל כתב שם וז"ל ואין לומר שאין לקרות משום טורח צבור דהא אמרינן במסכת סופרים שאפילו בעבור פסוק א' חוזר וקורא כל הפרשה כדפרישית לעיל (סימן מד) עכ"ל ומוכח דלדעתו אין לקרוא למפרע וחייבים לקרוא את הכל כולל מה שכבר דלגו אליו וקראו.

אך בהגהות מיימוניות (תפילה י"ב) הביא עוד פסקא ממסכת סופרים כא:ז וזה לשונה:

> מדלגין בנביא ואין מדלגין בתורה שאפי' אם דלג פסוק אחד ולא קראו והחזיר את התורה ואומר קדיש חוזר ופותח ומברך וקורא הוא ושנים אחרים

ופירש בהג"מ קורא הפסוק המדולג עם שני פסוקים אחרים הסמוכים לו כדי שהקריאה לא תפחות מג' פסוקים. ובזה מוכח שמותר בדיעבד לקרוא את הפסוקים המדולגים למפרע שלא כסדרן ויש לחשוש לטירחא דציבורא דלא כמרן האור זרוע. ושמא הראב"ש באור זרוע לא היה לו גירסא זו במסכת סופרים או שמא פירשו פירוש אחר דהיינו קורא הוא העולה ושני קוראים אחרים את שאר הפרשה כדי לא להוציא ספר תורה בלי לקרות בו לפחות תלתא גברי, ודו"ק.

וכן איתא בתוספות רי"ד (מהד"ת מגילה יז.) שהא דתנן הקורא את המגילה למפרע לא יצא היינו דווקא במגילה ולא בתורה, שכן שם הקורא את המגילה על פה לא יצא מה שאין כן בתורה שהכהן גדול קורא בעל פה לעת הצורך. וכן משמע בתוספתא (ברכות ב:ג, מגילה ב:א) שהקורא למפרע לא יצא היינו בק"ש ובמגילה ובהלל ובתפילה ולא נקט קרה"ת. ובפרי חדש (או"ח קמד:א) הביא ראיה לזה מקריאת המלך בחג (סוטה ז:ח) שהיה קורא פרשת כי תכלה וחוזר וקורא פרשת המלך למפרע, אף שיש לחלק. (ועיין עוד במגילה ל. ובטורי אבן שם ודו"ק.)

האמור שם הוא כל צבור של עשרה אנשים, או לכל קהילה שלמה, או שמא רק למדינה שלמה או עדה שלמה.

ועיין בעולת תמיד (רפב) שדין השלמת פרשיות כשבוטלו נוהג רק כשבוטלו בכל העיר ולא רק במנין אחד (ותלה עצמו בדוחק על מעשה של המהר"ם מינץ שסיימו הקריאה בבית כנסת אחד בעיר, עיין א"ר), וכן סברא הוא שקרה"ת היא חובת הציבור במובן הקהילתי ולא במובן של סתם אסיפה של עשרה בני אדם. הנוסעים מחו"ל לארץ אינם מהווים צבור קהילתי אף אם יארע שיתפללו בחדר אחד ולכן אין להם חובת קריאה במיוחד, ודלא כבנידון דידן שכל בני העיר מוסגרים ומוחלטים ובודדים ועל הקהילה לדאוג להשלים הקריאות.

ואיברא יש להעיר דבמעשה קלוניא עצמה כתוב במפורש שאחד קיבל ועיכב תפילה וקרה"ת ומפורסם מנהג קבילה שנהגו בימיהם לעכב החזן מלהתחיל (עיין בחתם סופר או"ח פא ועוד) ונקרא בלשונם ביטול התמיד, ודחוק לפרש שהתפללו בצבור בקלוניא בשבת ההיא בלי ש"ץ בעת הקבילה (והמנהג לקבול קודם יוצר כדאיתא באו"ח נד:ג), וממילא קשיא להשערי אפרים דצע"ג אם חובת הקריאה יחול על האנשים בלי שיקבעו עצמם כציבור.

והנה נראה בהיות אחרי המגפה בשובינו לבתי תפילתנו בשלום כי"ר צמאים לדבר ה' ושואבים מים בששון ממעיני הישועה, על כל רב ביתו לשקול אם קריאת כל הפרשיות היא אפשרי בנידון דידיה, ושמא רק במנין מצומצם מוקדם המיוחד לכך כדי להוציא את חובת הציבור ככלל, ואם לאו רחמנא פטריה דתליא באשלי רברבי ואחד המרבה ואחד הממעיט ובלבד שיכוון אדם את דעתו לשמים.

בברכת ולא יתן המשחית לבוא אל בתיכם לנגף

הוספה

במה אקדם ה' אכף לאלקי מרום אחרי זה כמה חדשים שהמגפה בינינו ורבים חללים קדושים הפילה, יהי זכרם ברוך לה"ה, ונפשנו קצה בהאריך הימים ובכל זאת אנו לי-ה ועינינו לי-ה מצפים לישועה אע"פ שתתמהמה. ועתה בעת כנוס היהודים להתפלל ולזעוק לפני אבינו שבשמים רבו החששות לפקוח נפש במנינים צפופים וארוכים ובכן ברוב רובם של קהילותנו לא הותרו לקרוא את כל הפרשיות שביטלו, והנה נידוננו לפנינו אם עדיין יש אפשרות להשלים הקריאות שלא כסדרן, וזה עתה החלי בעזרת רופא כל חולי.

הנה מסתימת כל הפוסקים דלעיל דפסקו כמהר"ם ודעימיה שצבור שבטלו ב' פרשיות אין להם תקנה משמע שאכן אין לנו תקנה, וה' ירחם על עמו החפצים בדבריו והחיים בהם, דפשיטא דאסור להכנס אפילו לספק סכנה כדי לקרוא בתורה בצבור. וכן בין למנהג מדינחאי בין למנהג מערבאי בין לכל מנהג ומנהג שהובא לעיל, פשיטא שתקנת חכמים היא לקרוא בתורה כסדרה כדאיתא במשנה מגילה ג:ד ורק מפסיקים לחגים (ולדעת ר' אמי שם גם לר"ח וד' פרשיות וכן נראה שהיה מנהג מערבאי ואכמ"ל).

(וכמדומני שכן המנהג כיום במדינת פלורידא כשסוגרים בתי כנסת בעת סערות וסופות.) ופרט דין זה שכיח הוא וכנראה המנהג ידוע מדורי דורות דלא כמרן השערי אפרים.

שאלה דומה ידועה לנו מסוגית הנוסעים מחו"ל לא"י אחרי פסח שחל להיות בשבת. שאלה זו נפוצה ומלובנת ולא אכנס בה לעומקה כעת, אך לרוב מנין ובנין מהפוסקים אין חיוב מעיקר הדין לבן חו"ל הזה לארגן מנין של בני חו"ל כדי לקרוא שתי פרשיות שחובת הקריאה היא על הציבור וכל מי שמשתתף בציבורי א"י מקיימים תקנתם בקריאת מנהג בני א"י. אך בכל זאת אין איסור בדבר ורבים הם המהדרין לשמוע קריאות הפרשיות במנין מיוחד בשבת כזו. ושמא שם נמצא מנהג ליתלות בו להקל דלא כהאו"ז?

אכן נידון זה אינו דומה לראיה שהרי מי שבא למקום חדש יוצא במנהגים שלהם ולא מטריחין יחיד לאסוף מנין כדי לקיים בעצמו מנהג קריאת כל התורה בשנה. אבל בנידונינו בהכרח המנין ההוא כבר ייאסף בעצמו ושמא אי אפשר לפטור מנין שכבר נאסף מחובת כל בני המנין במנהג החשוב ההוא. אין פה לא מנהג ארצי שונה (כגון מנהג בני א"י שקראו סדר נשא בז' סיון) ולא מנהג פרטי שונה כדי להישען עליו, אא"כ נפסוק דיש קבע לפרשיות כהמהר"ם מינץ דלעיל דיש פרשה שהוא חובת היום במובן חיוני ומהותי אפילו למי שעוד לא שמע הפרשה הקודמת. (וכנראה יש חובת היום המשתנה לפי המקום, ודו"ק.)

בניסוח הבריסקאי יש ממה נפשך: אם קריאת התורה היא חובת היחיד, הרי כל היחידים חייבים לקרות כל הפרשיות שבוטלו, ואם היא חובת הציבור, הרי כל בני הציבור וכל הציבורים באזור כולם עומדים עדיין במקום שפסקו בפרשה הראשונה שבוטלה ומשם חיובם הציבורי כמו לפעמים שכל בני א"י קוראים פרשה שונה מבני חו"ל כפי מנהג הציבור הרחב שם (ועליהם לקרוא הרבה פרשיות ביחד מיד רק כדי לחזור לסדר המוכר לא בגלל שממש חייבים עכשיו בכולם, ואם ירצו לקוראם שנים שנים לכל שבוע עד שמחת תורה, באופן עקרוני הרשות בידם לדעה זו, כמפורש בשלחן הטהור שם וכן בשער קריאת התורה שם. העיקר הוא שכל קהילה יבחר סדר פרשיות כדי שיגמור אותם בכל שנה וכמו דכתב הרא"ש בחזה התנופה וכמו דהנהיג ר"ת בצרפת סדר חדש וכדלעיל).

ולכן בנידון דידן שכל הצבור הרחב לא שמעו הפרשיות שבוטלו, לדעת האור זרוע ודעימיה דאין קבע לפרשיות עדיין יש לקרוא כולם ולדעת המהר"ם מינץ ודעימיה דיש קבע לפרשיות אפשר דאין צורך לקרוא אלא האחרון, ובדיוק כדלעיל.

יש לזכור שדין השו"ע דלעיל שמקום שמפסיקים בשבת שם קוראים לשבת הבא הוא ההלכה היחידה בקריאת התורה בשבתות שנודע לנו מימי התנאים במשנה ובתוספתא ומובאה בש"ס להלכה. מסתבר שראו בדרישה זו לקרוא כסדרן באותו צבור את עצם תקנת משה או לפחות דינא דגמרא מדרבנן. הלכה זו לא תלויה בשום מנהג, בין מנהג לסיים התורה בשנה אחת או בשלש שנים, ואפילו בלעדה מעיקר הדין יש לקרוא שבעה עולים לפחות ג' פסוקים לכל אחד ואחד כסדרן משבת לשבת באותו צבור. ואם צבור שלם לא קרא ברור שצריכים להתחיל ממקום שפסקו. מה שנותר לנו הוא לברר אם הציבור

המהר"ם מינץ, אך עם כל זה נראה שאפשר לסמוך עליהם בעת זו אם יקראו פרשיות רבות שבוטלו בתורת ספק הוספה, ובפרט שסברת האור זרוע ודעימיה שרירא ובריראה.

עד כאן ראינו שציבור שביטלו באונס קרה"ת בהרבה שבתות אפשר וראוי לקרוא כל הפרשיות שביטלו בשבת הבא, כסדרן, עם שבעה קרואים לכל אחד ואחד כדי שלא לכבד סדר אחד מחברו וכדי להחמיר שפרשת השבוע ההיא תיקרא בשבעה קרואים כדין לבדה בלי הוספות, וכדי להנצל מחיבור שני חומשים בקורא אחד. ואם בציר מהם גברי ידאגו שלא לקרוא לאחד בשני חומשים ולקרות כמה שאפשר בפרשת השבוע האחרון. ומכל מקום לצבור הטרוד מקשיי המגפה והכוונה, בוודאי יש מקום גדול להקל עליהם מלחייבם בכך משורת הדין. וטוב מעט בכוונה מהרבות בלא כוונה.

מכל מקום, כל זה לעניין מעשה קלוניא, ושמא מעשה קרוניא שונה ממנו? נידון דידן האידנא היא שאין ציבור כלל בבתי כנסיות בשבתות ולא רק מבטלים קריאת התורה אלא גם תפילות הציבור בכלל, כידוע מפני פיקוח נפש. שמא בכלל בנידון דידן אין צורך כלל להשלים הפרשיות שבוטלו עבור הציבור מפני שלא היה ולא נברא ציבור שביטלם? במילים אחרות, כל ציבור שהצטבר לאורך כל שבועות המגפה הזאת אכן קראו הפרשיות, ושמא פסק הראב"ש בקלוניא היה רק כשיש ציבור שהתפללו יחד ומשום אונס פתאומי נפרדו ולא הספיקו לקרות התורה כבמעשה של מהר"ם מינץ. להם חל חיוב לקרוא בשבתות אלו ולהם צריכים להשלים הקריאות. (סברא זו נאה לדעה שקריאת הפרשה שבוטלה הוא מדיו תשלומין.)

כן פסק להדיא השערי אפרים (ז:לט להגרא"ז מרגוליות שחיבר אותו בהיותו רב בברודא ה'תק"פ) ובספר החיים (סימן קלה, להגר"ש קלוגר, שגם חיבר אותו בהיותו רב בברודא ה'תקפ"ה), אך מדברי המהר"י וויל, והנודע ביהודה (עיין בספר לשון חכמים (ג:) להר"ר ברוך יהודה הלוי ברנדס מתלמידיו בפראג שכתב וז"ל ושמעתי שכן הורה גבר בגוברין אמ"ו הרב הגאון אמיתי אב"ד ור"מ מהר"י לנדא זצ"ל שבטלו קריאת שבת אחת ע"י אונס תגבורת המים שהי' פה בשנת תקמ"ד לפ"ק ופסק לקרות אותה שביטלו מקודם אבל לא שמעתי טעמו עכ"ל ואונס תגבורת המים הוא המבול הגדול של 1784 שידוע שקרה בין 27 ל29 לפברואר למניינם, שביניהם ו' אדר ה'תקנד שהיה ראוי לקרות בו פרשת תרומה), והזכור לאברהם, והר' יהודה מילר זצ"ל, והלקט יושר שעשו מעשה בדבר מפני חרם הגלחים או מבול מים או שודדים בעיר או מלחמה בעיר, נראה פשוט שגם לא התפללו בצבור באותה שבת ואעפ"כ קראו לשבת הבאה. וכן בשבות יעקב ג:ו, וחיים שאל (א:עא:ה), ומקור ישראל (שו"ת סימן קה) וברכות מים (שעשו מעשים בשכונות שונות בירושלים באותה שבת אחרי השלג), והפדה את אברהם (מערכת ק אות יט), והלל אומר (ב"שבת השחורה" ה'תש"ו וקראו פרשת קרח בשבוע הבאה עם פרשת חוקת) וירך יעקב מפורש שמנין שבוטל משלים הפרשה שבוטלה, ולא רק שביטלו הקריאה. ומסתימת שאר הראשונים כן מסתברא לענ"ד, דהיה להם לפרש, וכן נקטו כל הני רבותא מסתימתם. וכן פסק בשו"ת תשורת ש"י סימן תנט (במעשה ונסגר בית הכנסת מחמת גשמים) וכן בשו"ת מתת ידי סימן יד (במעשה ונסגר בית הכנסת בפרשת יתרו ה'תשכ"א מחמת ריבוי שלג).

ימים במדבר ולא ימצאו מים, אך לא קיימנו המנהג המקובל והמשובח לסיים את כל התורה בכל שנה. ועיין היטב בדברי האור זרוע שמשבח ומפאר את חשיבות קריאת כל התורה בפני העם ולהזהיר בפניהם חקים ומשפטים ואעפ"כ מסיים שלקרות מה שביטלו הוא וז"ל מצוה מן המובחר עכ"ל. ובפרט בימינו שרוב לימוד היהודים בשיעורים ובספרים נדפסים וכדומה, וקריאת התורה ברבים אינה מוקד תלמוד תורה דרבים כבעבר, ובפרט בימיהם שנהגו במתורגמן, אלא שעדיין יש לה חשיבות כטכס כבודי צבורי וכזכר למעמד הר סיני ועוד. ועם כל זה, וברוב חשיבות מנהג וותיק וחביב זה, אפשר שיש לוותר עליו בשעות הדחוקות והצרות האלה ובטורח רב עד מאד לקרוא כל כך הרבה פרשיות בשעה חדא, ובפרט בימינו שקשה הכוונה לרבים עד מאד וד"ל. ואע"פ שהאור זרוע בפירוש פסק במקום טירחא דציבורא, שאני טירדא דשתי פרשיות משל הרבה פרשיות שאיכה ישאו טורחם הרב עד כדי חשש כבוד הבריות, וראה בשו"ת זרע אמת (ג:יד שהתיר ליישוב שלא היה להם בעל קריאה עד פרשת מקץ שלא להשלים מהטעם הנ"ל). (ויש לשקול בכובד ראש אם אנשים שמוכנים לסבול כל כך הרבה טירחות לעת עתה לכמה דברי חול לא יהיו מסוגלים להפריש פעם אחת כמה שעות לכבוד תורתינו שלא תהא קלה בעיניהם, וד"ל.) והעירני אחד מידידי שליט"א שמא י"ל שבאשר סיום כל התורה בכל שנה הוי מנהג שמא במקום ביטול הציבור לא נהגו בכך (ואפילו להאו"ז י"ל דבמקום ביטול התמיד בכל כך הרבה שבתות לא נהגו בכך).

מאידך גיסא, אם נחמיר לקרוא כל הפרשיות שבוטלו בשובינו לבתי תפילתנו בשלום בב"א, הרי ברור שלדעת האור זרוע ודעימיה יקוים בנו תקנת קריאת התורה ומנהג לסיים כל התורה בכל שנה ונזכה להזהיר העם בכל משפטי וחקי התורה הקדושה. אך לדעת מהר"ם מינץ ודעימיה מה תהא עלינו? באופן יותר כללי, נוכל לשאול מה נפסיד בהוספת קריאות בתורה מעל ומעבר למקובל לאותו זמן? ידוע מנהג רבים לקרוא בתורה אפילו מה שקרא אחר אף שאינו מוציא אף אחד ידי חובתו, ובפרט בשמחת תורה מקילין בזה (כדאיתא או"ח רפ"ב) ובוודאי שאפשר להקל בזה בשעות הדחוקות והצרות האלה. אך כל זה בפסוקים שהם מעצמם חלק מקריאת היום. האם מותר להוסיף ולקרוא מפרשיות אחרות אפילו כשאינו מוציא אף אחד ידי שום חובה (כבנידון דידן לדעת המהר"ם ודעימיה)?

כנראה שאכן סומכים על דעות כאלו בשמחת תורה בקריאת חתן בראשית ואולי גם בקריאת וזאת הברכה בערב, קריאות שאין להם שורש וענף בגמרא. אכן בעבר גם היו מנהגים שונים בקריאת פרשיות אחרות כגון פרשת ואברהם זקן לחתן (עיין ערוך ערך חתן) או קריאה בשעת הנעילה או בתפילת המנחה דיו"ט. וכנראה סומכים על הסברא שכל קריאה בספר תורה בפני עשרה היא חלות מצוה ומברכים עליה (עיין באחרונים דיון מפורסם) אף שאינו ברור שעולה למנין הקרואים. נראה קצת שדיעה זו היא מבוססת על הסברא שאין קבע לפרשיות ובכל יום ראוי לקרוא כל התורה כולה, שאותה חלק עליה

למעשה מובא בתוספת מעשה רב (אות לד) שהגר"א עצמו כשיצא מבית האסורים צוה לקרוא לפניו את כל הפרשיות מארבעת השבתות שחיסר, וממילא אין לנו למצוא חידושים לדינא ממה שדימה דין זה לתשלומין בביאורו.

בספר מגן אברהם הביא דעת המהר"ם מינץ שלא לקרוא יתר על שתי פרשיות ולא בשני חומשים, אך מביא גם הגהות מנהגים (טירנא, שבת שחרית מא) שכתב שלא נראין דבריו בעיניו.

ואכן נחקלו האחרונים בזה שהכנסת הגדולה (רפב) והעולת תמיד (שם) והעטרת זקנים (קלה), והדגול מרבבה (שם), והחכמת שלמה (שם, בעניין פרשת פנחס), והסולת בלולה (קלה:א), והשלחן עצי שטים (ו:ה אלא שאין למחות בידי המשלימים כל הפרשיות), והשערי אפרים (ז:י מעיקר הדין אבל מרשה להחמיר לקרוא יותר, וכן איתא בשער קריאת התורה ב:ז לרב דוב בער קאראסיק) והמשאת משה (או"ח ב:א), והברכת הבית (מד:יב) ועוד הסכימו לדעת המהר"ם מינץ.

אך באליה רבה וזוטא, וזכור לאברהם (או"ח ס ושכן עשה מעשה לקרות קרח חקת ובלק ביחד בשנת ה'תקנ"ג מפני השודדים הארורים הקירגאליס), ובגדי ישע, ושתילי זיתים, ושו"ת זכרון יהונתן (או"ח סימן ב' ושכן עשה מעשה לקרוא ג' סדרים בשבת אחת), והחיד"א (יוסף אומץ יב:ז, לדוד אמת ט:ב ושם בשם המטה יהודה), ופרי חדש (קמד:א) ומהר"ם שיק (או"ח שלה ושכן עשה מעשה רבו הגאון רנ"א) והגר"א (כדלעיל שעשה מעשה לקרוא הרבה פרשיות בצאתו מבית האסורים) ובית דוד (שלונקי, או"ח קו) ותלמידו הדבר משה (ב:א ושכן עשה מעשה דלא כמהר"ם לקרוא פקודי עם ויקרא על סמך הבית דוד ושאין חשש ברכה לבטלה בכל קריאה בציבור, ומובאים דבריו להלכה בעיקרי הד"ט ובאמת ליעקב) ונוהג כצאן יוסף (ויקהל-פקודי א, ושהסכים לחמיו ר' יהודה מילר זצ"ל שעשה מעשה בר"ח אייר ה'תס"ב שבאו הצרפתים בראשית מלחמת הירושה הספרדית לעירו קליווא ולפיכך קראו בשבת הבאה תזריע מצורע אחרי וקדושים כולם יחד) וברכות מים (סימן קלה בדיונו אחרי השלג הגדול בירושלים תובב"א בט"ו בשבט ה'תקמ"ז אשר בעקבותיו קראו בשבוע הבא בשלח עם יתרו) ובשלחן הטהור (קלה:ג) ובצל החכמה (א:ז) והלל אומר (סימן פ) ויירך יעקב (סימן טו-טז שעשה מעשה לקרות מטות ומסעי עם פרשת דברים בשנת התר"ץ) ובני ציון (ליכטמן, קלה:ג שכן משמע באו"ז עצמו) וקריאה הקדושה (ב:טו:ה, וע"ע שם ב:י:יג) ועוד, כולם הסכימו דלא כמהר"ם מינץ שיש לקרוא כל הפרשיות שבוטלו או אפילו בין ספר לספר. וכן נוטה בשו"ת ממעמקים (ד:א בעניין עובדי הכפייה בגטו קובנה).

ובמשנה ברורה הביא כל הדעות ולא הכריע, ושמא דעתו נוטה קצת כדברי כלם לחומרא, ואיננו ברור כל צרכו. ובערוך השלחן נקט בפשיטות כהא"ר דלא כהמ"א.

ובדין זה של ביטול הרבה שבתות שאינו שכיח כלל ואין אנו יכולין לנפוק ולחזי מאי עמא דבר, יש לעיין כיצד להסתלק מן הספק ובאיזה רמת חיוב מדובר. מצד אחד, אם נחמיר שלא לקרוא פרשיות יתרות בשובינו לבתי תפילתנו בשלום בב"א, הרי תקנת משה קריאת התורה בשבת בבוקר בז' קרואים קיימנו לכתחילה ולמהדרין כדי שלא ילכו שלשת

והנה מה ששיבח המנהג לחבר סדרים מחוברים בקורא אחד, כך מובא בספר תיקון יששכר בשם הגאונים ז"ל, ואכן כן המנהג פשוט בארצות המערביות, אך דא עקא שאחינו בני תימן נוהגים עד היום הזה להתחיל סדרא בתרא בקורא חדש שלא כמנהגנו. וכן עיין בלבוש סימן רפב שאם מוסיפים על הקרואים במחוברים יש לקרוא ד' בסדרא קמא ועוד ד' בסדרא בתרא כדי שיהיו שווים, ומשמע שאין דין חיבור במיוחד (והחולקים שם חולקים שלא מן השם). ולפלאי פלאים שמנהג חיבור זה או מנהג ברכת חזק ונתחזק יגרום לביטול קריאת חובה לציבור.

איברא דיש מן הראשונים דפליגי על עיקר דינו של האור זרוע מחשש קלקול הסימנים ליו"ט, עיין בשו"ת מהרי"ל חדשות סימן קמב, ויש דפסקו כהאו"ז בצנעא אבל לא ברבים מחשש להיות מן המתמיהים, עיין לקט יושר נד:ב, אך אין חששות אלו מובאים להלכה וכדלהלן בשו"ע (אך עיין במהריק"ש או"ח קלה ובשבות יעקב ג:ו ודו"ק).

עד כאן בדברי הראשונים ז"ל אשר מפיהם אנו חיים ומימיהם אנו שותים.

דין זה מובא לאור על ידי הרמ"א בדרכי משה ומשם למפתו וז"ל השו"ע או"ח קל"ה:ב

> מקום שמפסיקין בשבת שמפסיקים בשבת בשחרית שם קורין במנחה ובשני ובחמישי ובשבת הבאה:
>
> הגה: אם בטלו שבת אחת קריאת הפרשה בצבור לשבת הבאה קורין אותה פרשה עם פרשה השייכה לאותה שבת (אור זרוע) (ועיין לקמן סימן רפ"ב):

יש לציין, מה שהפנה לקמן סימן רפ"ב שם מדובר בדיני הוספת קוראים בשבת ונראה כוונתו שהוספת הפרשה שבוטלה נעשית על ידי הוספת ז' קרואים ולא כדרך המחוברים, וזה דלא כהמהר"ם מינץ וגם משמע קצת דלא כהאור זרוע עצמו שכתב וז"ל יקראו שתי פרשיות כאחת עכ"ל ודימה בהדיא למנהג המחוברים הרגיל. אכן קשה לברר אם הפניה זו היא מדברי הרמ"א עצמו או ממדפיס כל שהוא, ולאו מר בריה דרב אשי חתים עליה.

ומכאן לדברי האחרונים. ראש וראשון בהם, דברי הגאון החסיד הרב אליהו מווילנא, שחידש בביאורו שפסק הרמ"א הוא מדין תשלומין כעין תפילה. סברא זו העלינו בתחילה, ויש בה השלכות להבנת סדר קריאת התורה כחלק מתפילה בציבור, ושמעתי בשם הגרי"ד זצ"ל שמי ששמע קריאת התורה עם ציבור שונה מהציבור איתם התפלל לא קיים מצוותו כהוגן. אך בכל זה חברא דחברא לית ליה למרן הגר"א בראשונים בזה שלא דיברו בלשון תשלומין כלל, אפילו המהר"ם מינץ שגם כן לא איפשר קריאת פרשיות הרבה, מיגו דלטובתו היה ראוי להעלות סברא זו על שולחנו. וישמע חכם ויוסף לקח, ונקבל שכר על הדרישה. לסברא זו כנראה קוראים רק קריאת השבת שעברה ואפילו היו מחוברים ואפילו בספר אחר ורק אם לא בוטל במזיד, הכל כדין תפילת תשלומין (כן דייק בבאור הלכה ובשער הציון או"ח קלה, אך בספר מרפא לנפש (א:מא:ג) פקפק בדיוק זה מאד). מיהו,

כלומר מאחר דסיימו הפרק או המסכת השמר לך פן תשכח את הדברים כו', חזור בהן שלא תשכח, או כמו שנהגו לומר לחזן ישר כחך, כלומר גמרת מצוותך, יהי רצון שתזכה לומר יתר מצוות, וה"נ פי' סיימת החומש יישר כחך, א"כ הקהל קוראים בקול רם שנסיים החומש, לכן אין סברא ונכון לקרא עוד לאותו גברא תוך החומ' השני, וכן מסתברא שלא לקרות מחומש לחומש בשבת אח', ותו לא מידי. עושה שלום במרומיו כו'

הנה רואים שמהר"ם מינץ מדייק היטב בדברי האגודה (שאינם מפורשים באור זרוע) שכתב שקוראים שתי פרשיות, ושהוא קורא לפרשת השבוע חיובא דיומא, ואפילו שמחברים שתי פרשיות זה חיובא דיומא. אמת שכל הסברות האלו ראויות הן לעלות על שולחן מלכים מאן מלכי רבנן וברוך המקום שזיכנו ללמדם, אך ברור שהם לא עולים בקנה אחד עם שיטת הראב"ש המובאת באור זרוע וכנראה אורחא דמילתא נקט בעל האגודה וכמעשה שהיה בקלוניא. (ולפלא ראה בשו"ת זכרון יהונתן או"ח סימן ב להגאב"ד דביאלוסטוק שהקפיד בחריפות יתירה וכתב וז"ל והמהר"ם מינץ לא ראה גוף דברי האו"ז כי הספר הזה לא נתפשט בימיו רק מה שהובא ממנו בקצרה בספר האגודה, אבל אלו היה רואה עיקר דברי האו"ז כמו שהוא לפנינו בודאי היה חוזר בו, ומזה תראה שאין להורות מתוך הקיצורים כי גם רבותינו גדולי האחרונים ז"ל שגו בזה עכ"ל ועיין בשו"ע חו"מ כה:ב ודו"ק.)

לסברת האור זרוע שאין קבע לפרשיות אזי אין מוסג של ב' או ג' פרשיות. יש רק מה שקוראים היום ויהיה כמה ארוך שיהיה. למהר"ם יש קבע לפרשיות וגם יש עניין לחבר פרשיות כדי לסיים כל התורה בכל שנה, אלא שלא ניתן לנו כלים לאפשר את זה אלא חילוק פרשה אחת לשנים או חיבור שתי פרשיות כאחת. ולפיכך במקום שיצטרך לחבר שלש פרשיות יחד, אי אפשר לקרוא כולם ואונס רחמנא פטריה דאין תקנה לחצאים דממה נפשך לא השלמנו התורה. (מיהו כנראה שאם קהל ביטל שתי שבתות שהיו צריכים לקרוא בהן פרשה אחת המחולקת לשתים, כגון משפטים ואם כסף כדלעיל, נראה שאפילו לדעת מהר"ם אפשר לקרוא כל פרשת משפטים עם פרשת תרומה במחוברים כשחוזרים לביה"כ, וזה דלא כהאומר דין תשלומין לקמן.)

ועוד החמיר המהר"ם מינץ ואסר לקרוא בשבת אחד משני ספרים משום מנהג לחבר פרשיות מחוברים על ידי קורא אחד ושלא מצינו בשום דוכתא שקורא אחד יקרא משני חומשים. ואם קבלה היא נקבל, ואם סברא היא יש להשיב, שהרי הכהן הגדול קרא בספר תורת כהנים ומחומש הפקודים באותה קריאה עם אותן ברכות כדאיתא ביומא ע', ואף שלא קרא בקרבנות היום מתוך הספר עצמו, זהו משום טירחא דציבורא וכבוד התורה שלא לגוללה ברבים. וכן ביומא שם הטעם שמוציאים עוד ספר תורה למפטיר בחגים הוא כדי שלא לגלול בציבור, ולא מפני שעוברים מחומש לחומש אחר. וכן איתא בתוספתא מגילה פרק ג שאם שינה ושייר בסוף ספר רק כדי שיקראו ששה קורא אותן ששה ועוד שבעה בחומש אחר, ומפורש דבמקום צורך אפשר לקרוא בשני חומשים בשבת אחת.

ומאי דיהיב השואל טעמים למילת', כיון דלאו באותו ס"ת נקרא, לכך נראה כאילו ס"ת ראשונה פגומה, זהו' נתינת טעם לפגם ומבלי לב ועיון. הא ע"כ אינה פגמיה, דאל"כ אינו רשאי לקרות בה ויקרא בשבת הבא [...]

והנה אמינא אפי' אם לא סיימו הספר בב"ה של צומריש, ולא יצאו ידי קריאתה דיומ' באות' שבת, מ"מ אין שייך לקרות בשבת הבא ג' סדרו', ויקהל ופקודי עם ויקר'. כי דין זה לא מצינו כ"א בסא"ז ומייתי לה באגודה פ' הקורא וז"ל בא"ז אם בטלו בשב' התמיד ולא קראו הפרש', אז יקראו בשבת הבאה שני פרשיות עכ"ל. הנה לא כתוב רק אם ביטל השבת אחד התמיד, אז יקראו בשבת הבאה שני סדרות, אבל לא כתב אם ביטול ג' או ד' שבתו' יקראו כל אות' סדרות בשבת א', וכן מסתברא דאל"כ אין לדבר סוף. מעתה שק"ק מה שייך לעשות חצי תקנת', רק אמר דווקא שבת אחת, לימא שתי שבתות או ג' דמ"ש שבת אחת משני'. לכן נ"ל דווקא שני סדרו' יקראו יחד אם יתבטל קריאות' שבת, כיון דבלאו הכי מצינו לפעמים שקורין ב' סדרות בשבת אחת, בשנת פשוטו' דהרבה סדרות מחוברות, אבל אם נתבטל ב' שבתות אין קורין בשבת הבא ג' סדרות, דלא מצינו שום דוכתי שקורין ג' סדרות בחד שבת, א"כ הכי עובדא דידן אם באת לקרא מה שלא נקרא בשבת שעבר, היה צריך לקרות ג' סדרות ויקהל ופקודי עם ויקרא, וזה לא מצינו, ואין בזה שום דיעה ולא תקנה לקרות בשבת הבא ג' סדרות. וכן משמע לשונו וז"ל יקראו בשבת הבאה ב' פרשיות עכ"ל, וקשה ה(ו)א לפעמים נמצאו ג' פרשיות כשהיו שתי סדרות דבוקות בשבת שעבר, והכי ה"ל לומ' יקראו בשבת הבא כל סדרות שראוי לקרא בשבת שעבר עם סדרה של שבת וכה"ג, דזה הוי משמע בין שיהיה בשב' שעבר חד סידרה בין יהיו ב' סדרות, אע"כ לכך קאמ' דוקא ב' פ' ולא כשיהיה ג' סדרות, כגון דלא היו דבוקות בשבת זה, אבל היו דבוקות בשבת שעבר אין לו תשלום. מ"ת א"כ מ"מ הכא עובדא דידן דנקר' פקודי לחודיה עם ויקרא, זא"ק כיון דויקהל ופקודי היו דבוקים באותן שבת שעבר, והוי כמו חד סידרה לאותו שבת והוי שניהם חיובה דיומא, לכן אין סברא כלל לחלקם ולקרות בשבת הבא חצי חיובה דיומא שעבר (הוי) הוי חצי תשלום והוי כמאן דליתא.

ועוד יש גריעותה הכא, כיון דפקודי הוי סיום הספר, אין סברא בשבת אחד לקרות מספר לספר, דזה לא מצינו בשום דוכתה, ובפרט למנהגינו דאנן נהגינן כשיש ב' סדרות דבוקות אז חד גברא קרי סוף סידרה ראשונה ותחילת סידרה שנייה יחד, ויפה מנהג' כדי שלא להפסיק בין סידרה לסידרה כדי שיהא נרא' כאלו הוא חד סידרה, א"כ כי קורין הכא פקודי עם ויקרא אז היה צריך לקרות לחד גברא סוף פקודי ותחילת ויקרא, [אין] זה מן הנכון לקרות מתרי חומשי לגבר' חד לחברם יחד, כי תיקון סופרי' להפרידם בארבע שיטי' שיש חלק בין חומש לחומש כדאיתא במסכת סופרים. וכן אנו נהגינו דלאחר סיום הספר עונים הקהל בקול רם חזק, וטעמא של אותו מנהג, כמו שכתב אחר כל פרק או אחר סיום המסכת הדרין עלך,

בערפורט היו הקהל בחרם של הגלחו' בשבת פרשת נשא שלא קראו הסדר' ובשבת פרשת בהעלותך ציויתי לקרות נשא ובהעלותך וכן יש בידי תשובה איך שאירע מעשה בקולוניא שבטל אחד את התמיד בשבת פרשת אמור ובשבת פרשת בהר הורה רבי אליעזר בר שמשון לקרות אמור ובהר והאריך בראיות והתשובה בא"ז בהלכות שבת:

פסק זה הובא בקצרה בספר האגודה, שהוא היה ספר נפוץ ביותר מספר אור זרוע בימי הראשונים, והובאו דבריו הרבה בספרי ההלכה ובבית יוסף. וזה לשונו הטהורה בשלימותה

בספר אור זרוע אם בטלו בשבת התמיד ולא קראו הפרשה יקראו הפרשה בשבת הבאה שתי פרשיות

וכדרכו בקודש מביא פסקים בלי טעמים ובירורים. סיכום זה ביסס לפסק אחר של מהר"ם מינץ (שו"ת סימן פה) בנידון אחר אשר קרה בימיו שכמה מחברי הבית כנסת לא סיימו את סדר פקודי בשבת ויקהל-פקודי מחוברים. מהר"ם מינץ שילל יישום פסק האגודה בנידונו מכמה טעמים [חלקם לא שייכים לעניננו וע"כ דילגתים] וז"ל

מה ששאלת, על מעשה שאירע ק"ק ווירמש, בשב' פרש' החדש שהיא ויקהל ופקודי מחוברים לקרות יחד, ונקראו ששה גברי כדינא, וכשהחזן קורא השביעי להשלים הספר נפל תגרא בין שני גברא, עד שהס"ת מונח' בטיל', ונמשך זה כנגד ב' שעות שלא יכלו להשוותן איזה מהן לקרות לשביעי לסיום הספר, עד שהלכו כמעט כל הקהל חוץ לב"ה, ולקחו עמהם ס"ת מתוך ארון הקדש והלכו לב"ה של בחורים, שקורין צומ"רש, ושם קראו שביעי והשלימו הסידרא כתיקונים, ולא נשאר בב"ה של עיר, רק ד' או ה' אנשים אותם בעלי מחלוקת וצירופה. ועתה אתם מחולקים איך לקרות בשבת אח"כ, בשבת של ויקרא, יש מכם שדעתם נוטה לקרות לשבת שבא פ' ויקהל ופקודי עם ויקרא, ויהיב טעמא למלתא כיון שלא נשלם הסדר בשבת שעבר באותו ב"ה ובאותו ס"ת, כי אם בס"ת אחרת, ונ' כאלו ס"ת ראשונה פגומה, וכן לא חשיב השלמה מה שקראו בב"ה הבחורים, כיון דלא קראו כל ס"ת בחד ב"ה, לכן צריך לקרות בשבת הבא ויקהל ופקודי עם ויקרא. ועוד, השהייה בין ששי לשביעי הוי יותר מכדי לגמור את כולה, ואע"ג דפסק גבי מגילה, אפי' אם שהה כדי לגמור את כולה יצא מ"מ אפשר גבי קריאת התורה חמור טפי ולא יצא, והשהיי' היה בכפליי' ויותר בכדי לגמור את כולה, כי ההפסק היה כנגד ב' שעות. כך דעת השואל. ויש דעתו נוטה דדיי בזה שהשלימו קריאותו בב"ה של בחורים, לכן א"צ לקרא ולחזור ויקהל ופקודי עם ויקרא בשבת הבא, עכ"ל השאילה.

נ"ל דאין לקרות בשבת הבא ויקהל ופקודי, רק מתחיל סדרה דשבוע דהוא ויקרא. מכמה טעמים, חדא מה שהשלימו הסדרה ושהו יותר מכדי לגמור את כולה, בזה אין נפקות' ויצאו ידי קריאה [...]

וחוקים ואין לך לומר כיון שעבר זמן קריאתה הלכה לה אותה פרשה לפי כי **אין קבע בפרשיות** לקרות פרשה זו בשבת זו וזו בשבת זו אלא כי כן נסדרו הפרשיות וראיה לדבר שאם יארע יום [טוב] בשב' ודוחין הפרשה של אותה שבת מפני פרשה של יו"ט הלא מיד בשבת הסמוכה ליו"ט חוזר למקום שפסק ולא אמרינן הואיל ונדחית תדחה. ותו דאפי' תימא **יש קבע בשבתות** בקריאת הפרשיות אפ"ה אין לנו לבטל ולדחות אותה הפרשה שלא נקראת בשבתה אלא לשבת הבאה חוזרין וקורין אותה דתניא בפ' החליל בראשון מהו אומר הבו לה' בני אלים וגו' בשני מהו אומר ולרשע אמר וגו' בשלישי מהו אומר כו' אם חלה שבת להיות באחד מהם ימוטו ידחו פי' אם חלה שבת להיות באחד מהם ודחו שיר המועד מפני שיר של שבת ימוטו ידחה [שהוא] שיר האחרון מפני כי באחד בשבת יאמרו שיר שהיה ראוי לומר אתמול בשבת. ולא יאמרו שיר של אחר השבת [עד יום ב'] נמצא האחרון דחוי אלמא דאין מדלגין סדר השיר וכ"ש סדר הפרשיות שהיא תורת יוצרנו חקים ומשפטים שאין לדלג. וא"ת אי מהתם דון מינה ומינה דמה התם שיר האחרון נדחה אף כאן הפרשה אחרונה תדחה. לא היא דגבי שיר היינו טעמא דכיון דקי"ל דאין מדלגין סדר השיר הא ודאי [א"א] בע"א אבל הכא בסדר הפרשיות התורה כי להשלים התורה אנו באים בכל שנה ואם יותר לנו הפרשה בין מחמת שנה פשוטה בין מחמת יו"ט שחל להיות בשבת ודחה אותה סדר פרשיות בין מחמת כל דבר שלא נקרא אותה פרשה הראוי לקרותה יקראנה בשבת אחר ולא ידלגנה אלא יקראו שתי פרשיות כאחת ויתקנו בזה את אשר חסרו שאם ידלגו הרי חסרו קריאתה על מגן. ואין לומר שאין לקרות משום טורח צבור דהא אמרי' במס' סופרים שאפי' בעבור פסוק אחד חוזר וקורא כל הפרשה כדפרישית לעיל ולא חיישינן משום טורח צבור וכ"ש לכל הפרשה שאין לחוש לטורח צבור כאשר אנו עושים ברוב פרשיות שאנו קורין שתים ביחד כשהם מרובים על שבתות השנים וכך הוא מצוה מן המובחר.

ברור אפוא שסברת ראב"ש היה שאין קבע לפרשיות ולמה יבטל האחד מפני חברו. מוטב שיבטל מנהג המחוברים הנוהג באותו מקום ולא יבטל סדר אחד מהשמיע את העם חקיו ומצוותיו. ועוד הוסיף שנידוננו דומה ליו"ט שחל להיות בשבת שפשוט וברור שאף שלא קוראים סדר השבוע ביו"ט מתחילים ממקום שפסק בשבוע הבא ולא מדלגים פרשה שלמה חקים ומשפטים מתורת יוצרינו. ואף אם תמצי לומר שיש קבע לפרשיות, יש גם קבע לשירים במקדש ואעפ"כ נדחו ליום הבא ולא בוטלו בכדי לשמור על הסדר. ובפירוש חיָב לקרוא הכל אע"פ שיש טירחא דציבורא. (ויש להעיר שכלל השלמת הפרשיות בכל שנה ושנה עם תקנת מרע"ה אך צע"ג ממנהג מערבא המוזכר בתלמוד בבלי ונראה פשוט שהפריז על המידה בכוונה ולא דק.)

תשובה זו מוזכר ומושם למעשה ע"י מהר"י ווייל (סימן סו):

וחלקו במקומו פרשת תרומה בפסוק ואת המשכן או פרשת תצוה בפסוק וזה הדבר. ועיין גם בספר העיבור (לר' אברהם בן חייא הנשיא ב:י) שיש שחלקו במקומו פרשת וירא ושיש מקומות המחברים פרשת שלח עם פרשת קרח בשנים שבהן אנו מחברים פרשת חקת עם פרשת בלק (ובאבודרהם בסדר הפרשיות איתא לחבר שלח עם קרח ברוב השנים במקום לחבר מטות עם מסעי). ובתיקון יששכר (במאמר שנת הכז) העיד על מקום שמחלק פרשת מקץ לשנים בפסוק אם כנים אתם, ועל מקום שמסיים פרשת וארא לפני מכת ברד ולא לאחריה (ונמצא הסדר הבא שמו פרשת השכם שאכן ידוע מכמה כת"י עתיקים ואכמ"ל). ובמאירי העיד גם על מקומות אחדים שחלקו תרומה תצוה וכי תשא בכל שנה מעוברת כדי לשמור אף על סימן פקדו ופסחו לקרוא סדר צו בשבת הגדול בכל שנה, וכן העיד על הנוהגים לחבר בהר עם בחקתי במקום חקת עם בלק בשנה מעוברת שחל שבועות בשבת. ובהשלמה למחזור וויטרי הביא לוח למנהג שמחלק תצוה כי תשא ויקהל (בפסוק ויעש בצלאל) ופקודי כדי לשמור על פקדו ופסחו, וגם שהעדיף לחלק תצוה במקום אפילו לחלק ויקהל מפקודי, והעיד על רבינו תם ששינה מנהג צרפת מדעתו שלא לחלקם ואפילו במעוברת כדי לאפשר למטות ומסעי אי פעם להיפרד. ועד היום הזה יש מאחינו בני תימן החוצים פרשת חקת בפסוק ויסעו מקדש, חציו עם סדר קרח וחציו עם סדר בלק, במקום לחברו כלו עם סדר בלק כמנהגינו בשנים ההן, וגם יש מהם שעושים זאת בכל שנה אשר למנהגינו מחברים מטות עם מסעי. ובבית דינו של שלמה (או"ח יב, עיין שם באריכות) העיד על המנהג בחלב לחבר פרשת קרח עם פרשת חקת ברוב השנים, וכן נוהגים עד היום הזה כמה קהילות יוצאי חלב. וגם בימינו כשחג הפסח מתחיל בשבת או חג העצרת ביום הששי יש מנהגים שונים בין בני א"י ובני חו"ל וקשה להעניק לפרשה אחת דין של חובת היום עצמו. נראה אפוא מכל הני מנהגים שונים שאין קבע לפרשיות וכל צבור ידאג לסיים את כולן בשנה אחת לפי מנהגי אבותיו ומקומו.

וכן משמע מהרמב"ם שהביא תקנת משה והלכות קריאת התורה בפרק י"ב מהלכות תפילה ואח"כ הביא בפרק י"ג מנהגי הפרשיות. וכן מפורש בשו"ת חזה התנופה (קיצור תשובות הרא"ש המלוקט ע"י ר' משה תלמידו, המובאים כמה פעמים להלכה בבית יוסף, נדפס לראשונה מכת"י ע"י החיד"א בגליון ספרו חיים שאל ח"ב) וז"ל סימן נד:

> חילוק הסדרים וחיבוריהם הוא כדי שתעלה קריאת כל התורה בשנה אחת ולכן כל חכם בעירו או בארצו חיבר והפריד הסדרים כפי הסדר שראה שהוא הנאות ואין הסדור ההוא הלכה קבועה רק מנהג ואינו חובה

ואכן כן כתב האור זרוע (ב:מה) ראש וראשון בדיון הזה וז"ל:

> מעשה היה בקלוניא באחד שקבל בשבת הראוי לקרות פרשת אמור אל הכהנים ועיכב תפלה וקריאת תורה כל היום וכשהגיע [שבת] הבאה צוה ה"ר אליעזר בר' שמעון זצ"ל להתחיל בפרשת אמור אל הכהנים ולקרותה וגם בהר סיני הראויה להקראות באותה שבת ושלא לדלג פ"א מן התורה לפי כי מימות משה רבינו נתקן לקרות התורה בפרשיותיה ולהשלימה בכל שנה ושנה כדי להשמיעה לעם מצות

אין קבע לפרשיות

מאת: אדם אריאל

ויהי בימי מגיפת הקורונא בעת סגור שערי בית תפילתנו וייבטל התמיד יום יום ולא יצא איש מפתח ביתו עד תום המשחית מעלינו ומארצינו, רבו הצמאים לדבר ה' אשר מעל ומעבר לשלשת ימים הלכו בלי מים, ושאלו ודרשו מה תקנתם בפרשיות התורה שבוטלו. ושלא יהא התורה משתומם ודורש אין לה, באתי אני הקטן לדרוש ולדון בסוגיא מורכבת וסתומה להעמיד הדין על בוריו ולהחזיר כבוד לתורה.

הנה, מעט כתבו בזה הראשונים. שאלתנו הובאה בראשונה בספר אור זרוע, והובאה משם בקיצור נמרץ על ידי מהר"י ווייל ובספר האגודה, ומשם נדונה בתשובת מהר"ם מינץ, ונראה כל אחד ממקורות חשובים אלו בעתו, אבל ראשית נפרט השאלה המרכזית בסוגיא.

אם נבוא לקרוא פרשיות שנתבטלו בשבוע הבא, זה יקרה מאחד משני טעמים. או שיש פה דין של תשלומין בזמן החיוב הבא כדוגמת תפילה, או שאין זמן קבוע לכל פרשה ואם לא קראו בשבת אחת יקראו לשבת הבאה ממקום שפסקו, ואם ירצו לסיים את כל הפרשיות עם ציבורים אחרים אזי ידאגו לחבר פרשיות יחד כדי לסיים בזמן הרגיל.

אחרון אחרון חביב. מסתבר מאוד שאין זמן קבוע לכל פרשה, שהרי ידוע דבמערבא סיימו התורה בג' שנים ואין פוצה פה ומצפצף. ואף שמנהגינו לסיימה בכל שנה ושנה, הנה רבו בזה המנהגים איזה פרשיות לחבר ולהפריד בשנים פשוטות ומעוברות. ומפורש בגמרא מגילה ל. שהיה מנהג שאירע פרשת שקלים בשבוע בו קוראים כי תשא עצמה, וזה לא יחול כן לעולם למנהגינו. וידוע מנהג פרובנס להפריד סדר משפטים לחצאין, המשתקף בספר החינוך בפרשת אם כסף. מנהג זה שמר על הסימן סגרו ופסחו לקרוא סדר מצורע בשבת הגדול בשנה מעוברת המתחילה ביום חמישי. ועיין בספר המחכים (סדר הפטרות) שהעיד על מקומות שמחלקים פרשת פקודי בפסוק ותכל במקום לחלק פרשת משפטים. ועיין בארחות חיים (הלכות קרה"ת סג) שהעיד על כמה כרכים גדולים שמחלקים סדר כי תשא במקום משפטים, כמה מהם בפסוק ויפן משה וכמה מהם לקמן בפסוק ראה אתה. וגם עיין בקרית ספר להמאירי (א:ה:א) על מקומות שלא רצו להפסיק באמצע מעשה העגל

* ולאלה ייקראו בברכות התורה על עוזרם את תורתי: מו"ר הרב דניאל צבי למש' פלדמן אשר אסף את העם באורו ובסעדו ומו"ח הרב שלמה זלמן הלוי אשר נתן להם מים ואין מים אלא תורה, ואז אשיר על ידידי היקר הרב שאול שליט"א אשר דיקדק אחר כל קוץ וקוץ בדבריי להעמידם על תילם. ויהי רצון שלא תצא תקלה מתחת ידי.

אדם אריאל מתגורר בניו יארק ובנותיה.